# Ford
# Granada
# Owners
# Workshop
# Manual

## Matthew Minter

**Models covered**
All Ford Granada models, including Scorpio
1.8, 2.0, 2.4, 2.8 and 2.9 litre petrol engines

*Does not cover 4x4 or Diesel engine models*

ABCDE
FGHI

*(1245–8S2)*

**Haynes Publishing Group**
Sparkford  Nr Yeovil
Somerset  BA22 7JJ  England

**Haynes Publications, Inc**
861 Lawrence Drive
Newbury Park
California  91320  USA

## Acknowledgements

Thanks are due to the Champion Sparking Plug Company Limited who supplied the illustrations showing spark plug conditions, to Holt Lloyd Limited who supplied the illustrations showing bodywork repair, and to Duckhams Oils who provided lubrication data. Certain other illustrations are the copyright of Ford Motor Company Limited and are used with their permission. Thanks are also due to Sykes-Pickavant Limited, who provided some of the workshop tools, and all those people at Sparkford who helped in the production of this Manual.

A book in the **Haynes Owners Workshop Manual Series**

Printed by J. H. Haynes & Co. Ltd, Sparkford, Nr Yeovil, Somerset BA22 7JJ, England

ISBN 1 85010 440 9

**British Library Cataloguing in Publication Data**
Minter, Matthew, *1952–*
    Ford Granada '85 to '88 owners workshop manual.
    1. Cars. Maintenance & repair – Amateurs' manuals
    I. Title    II. Series
    629.28'722
    ISBN 1-85010-440-9

Whilst every care is taken to ensure that the information in this manual is correct, no liability can be accepted by the authors or publishers for loss, damage or injury caused by any errors in, or omissions from, the information given.

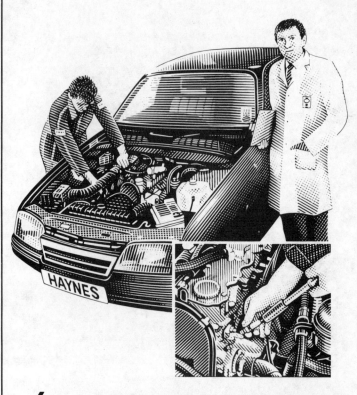

# Contents

Ford Granada GL

Ford Granada Ghia

# About this manual

## Its aim

The aim of this manual is to help you get the best value from your vehicle. It can do so in several ways. It can help you decide what work must be done (even should you choose to get it done by a garage), provide information on routine maintenance and servicing, and give a logical course of action and diagnosis when random faults occur. However, it is hoped that you will use the manual by tackling the work yourself. On simpler jobs it may even be quicker than booking the car into a garage and going there twice, to leave and collect it. Perhaps most important, a lot of money can be saved by avoiding the costs a garage must charge to cover its labour and overheads.

The manual has drawings and descriptions to show the function of the various components so that their layout can be understood. Then the tasks are described and photographed in a step-by-step sequence so that even a novice can do the work.

## Its arrangement

The manual is divided into thirteen Chapters, each covering a logical sub-division of the vehicle. The Chapters are each divided into Sections, numbered with single figures, eg 5; and the Sections into paragraphs (or sub-sections), with decimal numbers following on from the Section they are in, eg 5.1, 5.2, 5.3 etc.

It is freely illustrated, especially in those parts where there is a detailed sequence of operations to be carried out. There are two forms of illustration: figures and photographs. The figures are numbered in sequence with decimal numbers, according to their position in the Chapter – eg Fig. 6.4 is the fourth drawing/illustration in Chapter 6. Photographs carry the same number (either individually or in related groups) as the Section or sub-section to which they relate.

There is an alphabetical index at the back of the manual as well as a contents list at the front. Each Chapter is also preceded by its own individual contents list.

References to the 'left' or 'right' of the vehicle are in the sense of a person in the driver's seat facing forwards.

Unless otherwise stated, nuts and bolts are removed by turning anti-clockwise, and tightened by turning clockwise.

Vehicle manufacturers continually make changes to specifications and recommendations, and these, when notified, are incorporated into our manuals at the earliest opportunity.

**Whilst every care is taken to ensure that the information in this manual is correct, no liability can be accepted by the authors or publishers for loss, damage or injury caused by any errors in, or omissions from, the information given.**

# Introduction to the Ford Granada

The latest vehicles to carry the name Granada bear little visual resemblance to their predecessors, although some mechanical components have been carried over. Only one body style – a 5-door 'notchback' – is available. Petrol engines offered are 1.8 and 2.0 litre 4-cylinder ohc and 2.4, 2.8 and 2.9 litre pushrod V6; all are well-tried units which benefit from the latest engine management systems. The 1.8 litre engine has a twin choke carburettor, the V6 engines have fuel-injection and the 2.0 litre is available in both carburettor and fuel-injection forms.

A 5-speed manual gearbox or a 4-speed automatic transmission is fitted. Drive is to the rear wheels via a conventional differential unit and open tubular driveshafts. A viscous-coupled limited slip differential is available as an optional extra. There is also a four-wheel drive version, but this is not covered in this manual.

Disc brakes are fitted all round, with Ford's new anti-lock braking system (ABS) standard on all models. ABS ensures that maximum braking effect is available under all road conditions, even in the hands of unskilled drivers. Suspension is fully independent.

Interior fittings and trim are of the high standard expected in vehicles of this class. Trim levels range from the relatively basic L, through GL and Ghia to the lavishly equipped Scorpio. Refinements such as electrically-operated windows, control door locking and air conditioning are standard on the Scorpio.

Mechanically the vehicles are very easy to work on in most areas, and thought has obviously been given to the quick replacement of commonly required items such as the exhaust system. Routine maintenance requirements are minimal, a full service being necessary only every 12 000 miles or annually, with an oil change and a brief check at half this interval.

# General dimensions, weights and capacities

*For information applicable to later models, see Supplement at end of manual*

## Dimensions

| | |
|---|---|
| Overall length | 4.669 m (15 ft 3.8 in) |
| Width: | |
|    Including mirrors | 1.963 m (6 ft 5.3 in) |
|    Excluding mirrors | 1.766 m (5 ft 9.5 in) |
| Overall height | 1.426 to 1.450 m (4 ft 8.1 in to 4 ft 9.1 in) |
| Wheelbase | 2.761 m (9 ft 0.7 in) |
| Track: | |
|    Front | 1.477 m (4 ft 10.2 in) |
|    Rear | 1.492 m (4 ft 10.7 in) |

## Weights

| | |
|---|---|
| Kerb weight (nominal): | |
|    1.8 litre | 1225 kg (2701 lb) |
|    2.0 litre carburettor | 1255 kg (2767 lb) |
|    2.0 litre fuel-injection | 1265 kg (2789 lb) |
|    2.8 litre: | |
|       GL and Ghia | 1340 kg (2955 lb) |
|       Scorpio | 1390 kg (3065 lb) |
| Gross vehicle weight | Refer to VIN plate |
| Roof rack maximum load | 75 kg (165 lb) |
| Maximum trailer weight*: | |
|    1.8 litre | 1475 kg (3252 lb) |
|    2.0 litre carburettor, manual | 1525 kg (3363 lb) |
|    2.0 litre carburettor, automatic | 1750 kg (3859 lb) |
|    2.0 litre fuel-injection | 1750 kg (3859 lb) |
|    2.8 litre, manual and limited slip differential | 1625 kg (3583 lb) |
|    2.8 litre, manual | 1750 kg (3859 lb) |
|    2.8 litre, automatic | 1825 kg (4024 lb) |
| Trailer nose weight (all models) | 75 kg (165 lb) max |

*Subject to current legislation. Weight given allow re-starting on a gradient of 12% at sea level; vehicle laden with two occupants only*

## Capacities (approx)

| | |
|---|---|
| Engine oil (drain and refill, including filter): | |
|    ohc | 3.75 litres (6.6 pints) |
|    V6 | 4.25 litres (7.5 pints) |
| Coolant: | |
|    ohc | 8.0 litres (14.1 pints) |
|    V6 | 8.5 litres (15.0 pints) |
| Fuel tank | 70 litres (15.4 gallons) |
| Manual gearbox oil | 1.25 litres (2.2 pints) |
| Automatic transmission fluid (from dry) | 8.5 litres (15.0 pints) |
| Final drive oil: | |
|    7 inch crownwheel | 0.9 litres (1.6 pints) |
|    7.5 inch crownwheel | 1.3 litres (2.3 pints) |
| Power steering system: | |
|    ohc | 0.65 litres (1.1 pints) |
|    V6 | 0.75 litres (1.3 pints) |

# Jacking, towing and wheel changing

## Jacking

Use the jack supplied with the vehicle only for wheel changing during roadside emergencies (photos). Chock the wheel diagonally opposite the one being removed.

When raising the vehicle for repair or maintenance, preferably use a trolley or hydraulic jack with a wooden block as an insulator to prevent damage to the underbody. Place the jack under a structural member at the points indicated, never raise the vehicle by jacking up under the engine sump or transmission casing. If both front or both rear wheels are to be raised, jack up one side first and securely support it on an axle stand before raising the other side.

To avoid repetition, the procedures for raising the vehicle in order to carry out work under it is not included before each relevant operation described in this manual.

It is to be preferred and is certainly recommended that the vehicle is positioned over an inspection pit or raised on a lift. When such equipment is not available, use ramps or jack up the vehicle as previously described, but always supplement the lifting device with axle stands.

## Towing

Towing eyes are provided at both front and rear of the vehicle (photos). The rear towing eye should be used only for emergency towing of another vehicle; for trailer towing a properly fitted towing bracket is required.

Vehicles with automatic transmission must not be towed further than 30 miles (50 km) or faster than 30 mph (50 km/h). If these conditions cannot be met, or if transmission damage has already occurred, the propeller shaft must be removed or the vehicle towed with its rear wheels off the ground.

When being towed, insert the ignition key and turn it to position 11. This will unlock the steering, allow the lights and direction indicators to be used and activate the braking system.

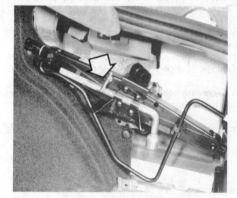

Location of vehicle jack and wheelbrace. Slacken screw (arrowed) to release jack

Vehicle jack head engaged in jacking point

Vehicle jack in use

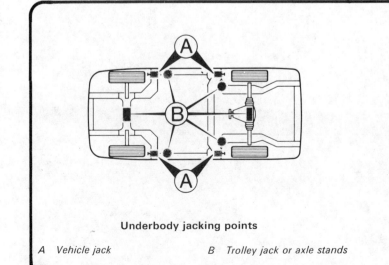

Underbody jacking points

A   Vehicle jack          B   Trolley jack or axle stands

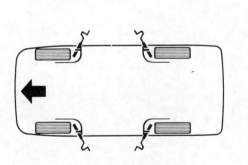

Swivel vehicle jack as shown for each position. Arrow points to front of vehicle

Front towing eye

Rear towing eye

## Wheel changing

Park on a firm flat surface if possible. Apply the handbrake and engage reverse gear or 'P'. Chock the wheel diagonally opposite the one being removed.

Remove the wheel trim, when applicable, for access to the wheel nuts. Prise the trim off if necessary using the plastic-tipped end of the wheelbrace. Use the other end of the wheelbrace to slacken each wheel nut by half a turn.

If the car is fairly new, the wheels and tyres will have been balanced on the vehicle during production. To maintain this relationship, mark the position of the wheel relative to the hub. (This is not necessary if the tyre is to be removed for repair or renewal, since the balance will inevitably be altered.)

Jack up the vehicle until the wheel is clear of the ground. Remove the wheel nuts and lift the wheel off the studs. Transfer the wheel centre cap on alloy wheels, then fit the new wheel onto the studs and secure it with the nuts. Tighten the nuts until they are snug, but do not tighten them fully yet.

Lower the vehicle and remove the jack. Carry out the final tightening of the wheel nuts in criss-cross sequence. The use of a torque wrench is strongly recommended, especially when light alloy wheels are fitted. See Chapter 10 Specifications for the recommended tightening torque.

Refit the wheel trim, when applicable, and stow the tools. if a new wheel has been brought into service, have it balanced on the vehicle if necessary.

# Buying spare parts and vehicle identification numbers

## Buying spare parts

Spare parts are available from many sources, for example: Ford garages, other garages and accessory shops, and motor factors. Our advice regarding spare parts sources is as follows:

*Officially appointed Ford garages* – This is the best source for parts which are peculiar to your car and are not generally available (eg complete cylinder heads, internal gearbox components, badges, interior trim etc). It is also the only place at which you should buy parts if your vehicle is still under warranty – non-Ford components may invalidate the warranty. To be sure of obtaining the correct parts it will always be necessary to give the storeman your car's vehicle identification number, and if possible, to take the 'old' part along for positive identification. Remember that some parts are available on a factory exchange scheme – any parts returned should always be clean! It obviously makes good sense to go straight to the specialists on your car for this type of part for they are best equipped to supply you.

*Other garages and accessory shops* – These are oftenvery good places to buy materials and components needed for the maintenance of your car (eg oil filters, spark plugs, bulbs, drivebelts, oils and greases, touch-up paint, filler paste, etc). They also sell general accessories, usually have convenient opening hours, charge lower prices and can often be found not far from home.

*Motor factors* – Good factors will stock all of the more important components which wear out relatively quickly (eg clutch components, pistons, valves, exhaust systems, brake cylinders/pipes/hoses/seals and pads etc). Motor factors will often provide new or reconditioned components on a part exchange basis – this can save a considerable amount of money.

## Vehicle identification numbers

When ordering spare parts, always give as much information as possible. Quote the car model, year of manufacture, body and engine numbers as appropriate.

The vehicle identification number (VIN) plate is mounted on the right-hand side of the body front panel, and may be seen once the bonnet is open (photo). Besides the VIN it also carries information on vehicle equipment and permissible loads. The VIN is also stamped into the floor panel to the right of the driver'sseat; an inspection cover is provided (photo).

The engine number is stamped on the cylinder block. On ohc engines it is on the right-hand side, near the alternator (photo); on V6 engines it is on the left-hand side, above the fuel pump blanking plate.

Other identification numbers or codes are stamped on major items such as the gearbox, final drive housing, distributor etc. These numbers are unlikely to be needed by the home mechanic.

**Typical VIN plate**

**VIN is repeated next to driver's seat**

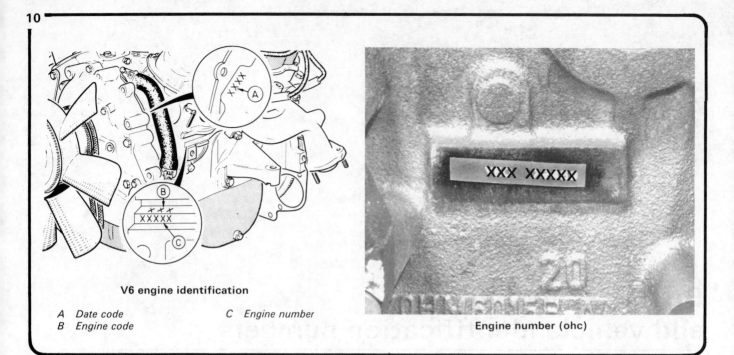

**V6 engine identification**

A  Date code        C  Engine number
B  Engine code

**Engine number (ohc)**

# General repair procedures

Whenever servicing, repair or overhaul work is carried out on the car or its components, it is necessary to observe the following procedures and instructions. This will assist in carrying out the operation efficiently and to a professional standard of workmanship.

## Preparation

Read through the relevant Section(s) of the manual before starting work, to make sure that the necessary tools and spare parts are to hand. If it is not possible to tell in advance what spare parts will be required, check the availability and cost of the appropriate parts so that time is not wasted dismantling an item for which no spares are available, or which would be cheaper to exchange than to repair.

## Joint mating faces and gaskets

Where a gasket is used between the mating faces of two components, ensure that it is renewed on reassembly, and fit it dry unless otherwise stated in the repair procedure. Make sure that the mating faces are clean and dry with all traces of old gasket removed. When cleaning a joint face, use a tool which is not likely to score or damage the face, and remove any burrs or nicks with an oilstone or fine file.

Make sure that tapped holes are cleaned with a pipe cleaner, and keep them free of jointing compound if this is being used unless specifically instructed otherwise.

Ensure that all orifices, channels or pipes are clear and blow through them, preferably using compressed air.

## Oil seals

Whenever an oil seal is removed from its working location, either individually or as part of an assembly, it should be renewed.

The very fine sealing lip of the seal is easily damaged and will not seal if the surface it contacts is not completely clean and free from scratches, nicks or grooves. If the original sealing surface of the component cannot be restored, the component should be renewed.

Protect the lips of the seal from any surface which may damage them in the course of fitting. Use tape or a conical sleeve where possible. Lubricate the seal lips with oil before fitting and, on dual lipped seals, fill the space between the lips with grease.

Unless otherwise stated, oil seals must be fitted with their sealing lips toward the lubricant to be sealed.

Use a tubular drift or block of wood of the appropriate size to install the seal and, if the seal housing is shouldered, drive the seal down to the shoulder. If the seal housing is unshouldered, the seal should be fitted with its face flush with the housing top face.

## Screw threads and fastenings

Always ensure that a blind tapped hole is completely free from oil, grease, water or other fluid before installing the bolt or stud. Failure to do this could cause the housing to crack due to the hydraulic action of the bolt or stud as it is screwed in.

When tightening a castellated nut to accept a split pin, tighten the nut to the specified torque, where applicable, and then tighten further to the next split pin hole. Never slacken the nut to align a split pin hole unless stated in the repair procedure.

When checking or retightening a nut or bolt to a specified torque setting, slacken the nut or bolt by a quarter of a turn, and then retighten to the specified setting.

## Locknuts, locktabs and washers

Any fastening which will rotate against a component or housing in the course of tightening should always have a washer between it and the relevant component or housing.

Spring or split washers should always be renewed when they are used to lock a critical component such as a big-end bearing retaining nut or bolt.

Locktabs which are folded over to retain a nut or bolt should always be renewed.

Self-locking nuts can be re-used in non-critical areas, providing resistance can be felt when the locking portion passes over the bolt or stud thread.

Split pins must always be replaced with new ones of the correct size for the hole.

## Special tools

Some repair procedures in this manual entail the use of special tools such as a press, two or three-legged pullers, spring compressors etc. Wherever possible, suitable readily available alternatives to the manufacturer's special tools are described, and are shown in use. In some instances, where no alternative is possible, it has been necessary to resort to the use of a manufacturer's tool and this has been done for reasons of safety as well as the efficient completion of the repair operation. Unless you are highly skilled and have a thorough understanding of the procedure described, never attempt to bypass the use of any special tool when the procedure described specifies its use. Not only is there a very great risk of personal injury, but expensive damage could be caused to the components involved.

# Tools and working facilities

## Introduction

A selection of good tools is a fundamental requirement for anyone contemplating the maintenance and repair of a motor vehicle. For the owner who does not possess any, their purchase will prove a considerable expense, offsetting some of the savings made by doing-it-yourself. However, provided that the tools purchased meet the relevant national safety standards and are of good quality, they will last for many years and prove an extremely worthwhile investment.

To help the average owner to decide which tools are needed to carry out the various tasks detailed in this manual, we have compiled three lists of tools under the following headings: *Maintenance and minor repair, Repair and overhaul,* and *Special.* The newcomer to practical mechanics should start off with the *Maintenance and minor repair* tool kit and confine himself to the simpler jobs around the vehicle. Then, as his confidence and experience grow, he can undertake more difficult tasks, buying extra tools as, and when, they are needed. In this way, a *Maintenance and minor repair* tool kit can be built-up into a *Repair and overhaul* tool kit over a considerable period of time without any major cash outlays. The experienced do-it-yourselfer will have a tool kit good enough for most repair and overhaul procedures and will add tools from the *Special* category when he feels the expense is justified by the amount of use to which these tools will be put.

It is obviously not possible to cover the subject of tools fully here. For those who wish to learn more about tools and their use there is a book entitled *How to Choose and Use Car Tools* available from the publishers of this manual.

## Maintenance and minor repair tool kit

The tools given in this list should be considered as a minimum requirement if routine maintenance, servicing and minor repair operations are to be undertaken. We recommend the purchase of combination spanners (ring one end, open-ended the other); although more expensive than open-ended ones, they do give the advantages of both types of spanner.

*Combination spanners - 8 to 19 mm*
*Adjustable spanner - 9 inch*
*Gearbox and final drive filler/level plug keys*
*Spark plug spanner (with rubber insert)*
*Spark plug gap adjustment tool*
*Set of feeler gauges*
*Brake bleed nipple spanner*
*Screwdriver - 4 in long x $^1/4$ in dia (flat blade)*
*Screwdriver - 4 in long x $^1/4$ in dia (cross blade)*
*Combination pliers - 6 inch*
*Hacksaw (junior)*
*Tyre pump*
*Tyre pressure gauge*
*Oil can*
*Fine emery cloth (1 sheet)*
*Wire brush (small)*
*Funnel (medium size)*

## Repair and overhaul tool kit

These tools are virtually essential for anyone undertaking any major repairs to a motor vehicle, and are additional to those given in the *Maintenance and minor repair* list. Included in this list is a comprehensive set of sockets. Although these are expensive they will be found invaluable as they are so versatile - particularly if various drives are included in the set. We recommend the ½ in square-drive type, as this can be used with most proprietary torque wrenches. If you cannot afford a socket set, even bought piecemeal, then inexpensive tubular box spanners are a useful alternative.

The tools in this list will occasionally need to be supplemented by tools from the *Special* list.

*Sockets (or box spanners) to cover range in previous list\**
*Reversible ratchet drive (for use with sockets)*
*Extension piece, 10 inch (for use with sockets)*
*Universal joint (for use with sockets)*
*Torque wrench (for use with sockets)*
*Set of 12-spline keys (to fit Ford splined head bolts)*
*Set of 'Torx' keys*
*'Mole' wrench - 8 inch*
*Ball pein hammer*
*Soft-faced hammer, plastic or rubber*
*Screwdriver - 6 in long x $^5/16$ in dia (flat blade)*
*Screwdriver - 2 in long x $^5/16$ in square (flat blade)*
*Screwdriver - 1$^1/2$ in long x $^1/4$ in dia (cross blade)*
*Screwdriver - 3 in long x $^1/8$ in dia (electricians)*
*Pliers - electricians side cutters*
*Pliers - needle nosed*
*Pliers - circlip (internal and external)*
*Cold chisel - $^1/2$ inch*
*Scriber*
*Scraper*
*Centre punch*
*Pin punch*
*Hacksaw*
*Valve grinding tool*
*Steel rule/straight-edge*
*Allen keys*
*Selection of files*
*Wire brush (large)*
*Axle-stands*
*Jack (strong trolley or hydraulic type)*
*Light with extension lead*

*\*Some Imperial size nuts and bolts may be found on air conditioning and automatic transmission components*

## Special tools

The tools in this list are those which are not used regularly, are expensive to buy, or which need to be used in accordance with their manufacturers' instructions. Unless relatively difficult mechanical jobs are undertaken frequently, it will not be economic to buy many of these tools. Where this is the case, you could consider clubbing together with friends (or joining a motorists' club) to make a joint purchase, or borrowing the tools against a deposit from a local garage or tool hire specialist.

The following list contains only those tools and instruments freely available to the public, and not those special tools produced by the vehicle manufacturer specifically for its dealer network. You will find occasional references to these manufacturers' special tools in the text of this manual. Generally, an alternative method of doing the job without the vehicle manufacturers' special tool is given. However, sometimes, there is no alternative to using them. Where this is the case and the relevant tool cannot be bought or borrowed, you will have to entrust the work to a franchised garage.

*Valve spring compressor*
*Piston ring compressor*
*Balljoint separator*
*Universal hub/bearing puller*
*Impact screwdriver*
*Micrometer and/or vernier gauge*
*Dial gauge*
*Stroboscopic timing light*
*Tachometer*
*Universal electrical multi-meter*
*Cylinder compression gauge*
*Lifting tackle*
*Trolley jack*

## Buying tools

For practically all tools, a tool factor is the best source since he will have a very comprehensive range compared with the average garage or accessory shop. Having said that, accessory shops often offer excellent quality tools at discount prices, so it pays to shop around.

There are plenty of good tools around at reasonable prices, but always aim to purchase items which meet the relevant national safety standards. If in doubt, ask the proprietor or manager of the shop for advice before making a purchase.

## Care and maintenance of tools

Having purchased a reasonable tool kit, it is necessary to keep the tools in a clean serviceable condition. After use, always wipe off any dirt, grease and metal particles using a clean, dry cloth, before putting the tools away. Never leave them lying around after they have been used. A simple tool rack on the garage or workshop wall, for items such as screwdrivers and pliers is a good idea. Store all normal wrenches and sockets in a metal box. Any measuring instruments, gauges, meters, etc, must be carefully stored where they cannot be damaged or become rusty.

Take a little care when tools are used. Hammer heads inevitably become marked and screwdrivers lose the keen edge on their blades from time to time. A little timely attention with emery cloth or a file will soon restore items like this to a good serviceable finish.

## Working facilities

Not to be forgotten when discussing tools, is the workshop itself. If anything more than routine maintenance is to be carried out, some form of suitable working area becomes essential.

It is appreciated that many an owner mechanic is forced by circumstances to remove an engine or similar item, without the benefit of a garage or workshop. Having done this, any repairs should always be done under the cover of a roof.

Wherever possible, any dismantling should be done on a clean, flat workbench or table at a suitable working height.

Any workbench needs a vice: one with a jaw opening of 4 in (100 mm) is suitable for most jobs. As mentioned previously, some clean dry storage space is also required for tools, as well as for lubricants, cleaning fluids, touch-up paints and so on, which become necessary.

Another item which may be required, and which has a much more general usage, is an electric drill with a chuck capacity of at least 5/16 in (8 mm). This, together with a good range of twist drills, is virtually essential for fitting accessories such as mirrors and reversing lights.

Last, but not least, always keep a supply of old newspapers and clean, lint-free rags available, and try to keep any working area as clean as possible.

*Spanner jaw gap comparison table*

| Jaw gap (in) | Spanner size |
| --- | --- |
| 0.250 | 1/4 in AF |
| 0.276 | 7 mm |
| 0.313 | 5/16 in AF |
| 0.315 | 8 mm |
| 0.344 | 11/32 in AF; 1/8 in Whitworth |
| 0.354 | 9 mm |
| 0.375 | 3/8 in AF |
| 0.394 | 10 mm |
| 0.433 | 11 mm |
| 0.438 | 7/16 in AF |
| 0.445 | 3/16 in Whitworth; 1/4 in BSF |
| 0.472 | 12 mm |
| 0.500 | 1/2 in AF |
| 0.512 | 13 mm |
| 0.525 | 1/4 in Whitworth; 5/16 in BSF |
| 0.551 | 14 mm |
| 0.563 | 9/16 in AF |
| 0.591 | 15 mm |
| 0.600 | 5/16 in Whitworth; 3/8 in BSF |
| 0.625 | 5/8 in AF |
| 0.630 | 16 mm |
| 0.669 | 17 mm |
| 0.686 | 11/16 in AF |
| 0.709 | 18 mm |
| 0.710 | 3/8 in Whitworth; 7/16 in BSF |
| 0.748 | 19 mm |
| 0.750 | 3/4 in AF |
| 0.813 | 13/16 in AF |
| 0.820 | 7/16 in Whitworth; 1/2 in BSF |
| 0.866 | 22 mm |
| 0.875 | 7/8 in AF |
| 0.920 | 1/2 in Whitworth; 9/16 in BSF |
| 0.938 | 15/16 in AF |
| 0.945 | 24 mm |
| 1.000 | 1 in AF |
| 1.010 | 9/16 in Whitworth; 5/8 in BSF |
| 1.024 | 26 mm |
| 1.063 | 11/16 in AF; 27 mm |
| 1.100 | 5/8 in Whitworth; 11/16 in BSF |
| 1.125 | 11/8 in AF |
| 1.181 | 30 mm |
| 1.200 | 11/16 in Whitworth; 3/4 in BSF |
| 1.250 | 11/4 in AF |
| 1.260 | 32 mm |
| 1.300 | 3/4 in Whitworth; 7/8 in BSF |
| 1.313 | 15/16 in AF |
| 1.390 | 13/16 in Whitworth; 15/16 in BSF |
| 1.417 | 36 mm |
| 1.438 | 17/16 in AF |
| 1.480 | 7/8 in Whitworth; 1 in BSF |
| 1.500 | 11/2 in AF |
| 1.575 | 40 mm; 15/16 in Whitworth |
| 1.614 | 41 mm |
| 1.625 | 15/8 in AF |
| 1.670 | 1 in Whitworth; 11/8 in BSF |
| 1.688 | 111/16 in AF |
| 1.811 | 46 mm |
| 1.813 | 113/16 in AF |
| 1.860 | 11/8 in Whitworth; 11/4 in BSF |
| 1.875 | 17/8 in AF |
| 1.969 | 50 mm |
| 2.000 | 2 in AF |
| 2.050 | 11/4 in Whitworth; 13/8 in BSF |
| 2.165 | 55 mm |
| 2.362 | 60 mm |

# Safety first!

Professional motor mechanics are trained in safe working procedures. However enthusiastic you may be about getting on with the job in hand, do take the time to ensure that your safety is not put at risk. A moment's lack of attention can result in an accident, as can failure to observe certain elementary precautions.

There will always be new ways of having accidents, and the following points do not pretend to be a comprehensive list of all dangers; they are intended rather to make you aware of the risks and to encourage a safety-conscious approach to all work you carry out on your vehicle.

## Essential DOs and DON'Ts

**DON'T** rely on a single jack when working underneath the vehicle. Always use reliable additional means of support, such as axle stands, securely placed under a part of the vehicle that you know will not give way.

**DON'T** attempt to loosen or tighten high-torque nuts (e.g. wheel hub nuts) while the vehicle is on a jack; it may be pulled off.

**DON'T** start the engine without first ascertaining that the transmission is in neutral (or 'Park' where applicable) and the parking brake applied.

**DON'T** suddenly remove the filler cap from a hot cooling system – cover it with a cloth and release the pressure gradually first, or you may get scalded by escaping coolant.

**DON'T** attempt to drain oil until you are sure it has cooled sufficiently to avoid scalding you.

**DON'T** grasp any part of the engine, exhaust or catalytic converter without first ascertaining that it is sufficiently cool to avoid burning you.

**DON'T** allow brake fluid or antifreeze to contact vehicle paintwork.

**DON'T** syphon toxic liquids such as fuel, brake fluid or antifreeze by mouth, or allow them to remain on your skin.

**DON'T** inhale dust – it may be injurious to health (see *Asbestos* below).

**DON'T** allow any spilt oil or grease to remain on the floor – wipe it up straight away, before someone slips on it.

**DON'T** use ill-fitting spanners or other tools which may slip and cause injury.

**DON'T** attempt to lift a heavy component which may be beyond your capability – get assistance.

**DON'T** rush to finish a job, or take unverified short cuts.

**DON'T** allow children or animals in or around an unattended vehicle.

**DO** wear eye protection when using power tools such as drill, sander, bench grinder etc, and when working under the vehicle.

**DO** use a barrier cream on your hands prior to undertaking dirty jobs – it will protect your skin from infection as well as making the dirt easier to remove afterwards; but make sure your hands aren't left slippery. Note that long-term contact with used engine oil can be a health hazard.

**DO** keep loose clothing (cuffs, tie etc) and long hair well out of the way of moving mechanical parts.

**DO** remove rings, wristwatch etc, before working on the vehicle – especially the electrical system.

**DO** ensure that any lifting tackle used has a safe working load rating adequate for the job.

**DO** keep your work area tidy – it is only too easy to fall over articles left lying around.

**DO** get someone to check periodically that all is well, when working alone on the vehicle.

**DO** carry out work in a logical sequence and check that everything is correctly assembled and tightened afterwards.

**DO** remember that your vehicle's safety affects that of yourself and others. If in doubt on any point, get specialist advice.

**IF,** in spite of following these precautions, you are unfortunate enough to injure yourself, seek medical attention as soon as possible.

## Asbestos

Certain friction, insulating, sealing, and other products – such as brake linings, brake bands, clutch linings, torque converters, gaskets, etc – contain asbestos. *Extreme care must be taken to avoid inhalation of dust from such products since it is hazardous to health.* If in doubt, assume that they *do* contain asbestos.

## Fire

Remember at all times that petrol (gasoline) is highly flammable. Never smoke, or have any kind of naked flame around, when working on the vehicle. But the risk does not end there – a spark caused by an electrical short-circuit, by two metal surfaces contacting each other, by careless use of tools, or even by static electricity built up in your body under certain conditions, can ignite petrol vapour, which in a confined space is highly explosive.

Always disconnect the battery earth (ground) terminal before working on any part of the fuel or electrical system, and never risk spilling fuel on to a hot engine or exhaust.

It is recommended that a fire extinguisher of a type suitable for fuel and electrical fires is kept handy in the garage or workplace at all times. Never try to extinguish a fuel or electrical fire with water.

**Note:** *Any reference to a 'torch' appearing in this manual should always be taken to mean a hand-held battery-operated electric lamp or flashlight. It does NOT mean a welding/gas torch or blowlamp.*

## Fumes

Certain fumes are highly toxic and can quickly cause unconsciousness and even death if inhaled to any extent. Petrol (gasoline) vapour comes into this category, as do the vapours from certain solvents such as trichloroethylene. Any draining or pouring of such volatile fluids should be done in a well ventilated area.

When using cleaning fluids and solvents, read the instructions carefully. Never use materials from unmarked containers – they may give off poisonous vapours.

Never run the engine of a motor vehicle in an enclosed space such as a garage. Exhaust fumes contain carbon monoxide which is extremely poisonous; if you need to run the engine, always do so in the open air or at least have the rear of the vehicle outside the workplace.

If you are fortunate enough to have the use of an inspection pit, never drain or pour petrol, and never run the engine, while the vehicle is standing over it; the fumes, being heavier than air, will concentrate in the pit with possibly lethal results.

## The battery

Never cause a spark, or allow a naked light, near the vehicle's battery. It will normally be giving off a certain amount of hydrogen gas, which is highly explosive.

Always disconnect the battery earth (ground) terminal before working on the fuel or electrical systems.

If possible, loosen the filler plugs or cover when charging the battery from an external source. Do not charge at an excessive rate or the battery may burst.

Take care when topping up and when carrying the battery. The acid electrolyte, even when diluted, is very corrosive and should not be allowed to contact the eyes or skin.

If you ever need to prepare electrolyte yourself, always add the acid slowly to the water, and never the other way round. Protect against splashes by wearing rubber gloves and goggles.

When jump starting a car using a booster battery, for negative earth (ground) vehicles, connect the jump leads in the following sequence: First connect one jump lead between the positive ( + ) terminals of the two batteries. Then connect the other jump lead first to the negative (–) terminal of the booster battery, and then to a good earthing (ground) point on the vehicle to be started, at least 18 in (45 cm) from the battery if possible. Ensure that hands and jump leads are clear of any moving parts, and that the two vehicles do not touch. Disconnect the leads in the reverse order.

## Mains electricity and electrical equipment

When using an electric power tool, inspection light etc, always ensure that the appliance is correctly connected to its plug and that, where necessary, it is properly earthed (grounded). Do not use such appliances in damp conditions and, again, beware of creating a spark or applying excessive heat in the vicinity of fuel or fuel vapour. Also ensure that the appliances meet the relevant national safety standards.

## Ignition HT voltage

A severe electric shock can result from touching certain parts of the ignition system, such as the HT leads, when the engine is running or being cranked, particularly if components are damp or the insulation is defective. Where an electronic ignition system is fitted, the HT voltage is much higher and could prove fatal.

# Routine maintenance

The maintenance schedules below are basically those recommended by the manufacturer. Servicing intervals are determined by mileage or time elapsed – this is because fluids and systems deteriorate with age as well as with use. Follow the time intervals if the appropriate mileage is not covered within the specified period.

Vehicles operating under adverse conditions may need more frequent maintenance. 'Adverse conditions' include climatic extremes, full-time towing or taxi work, driving on unmade roads, and a high proportion of short journeys.

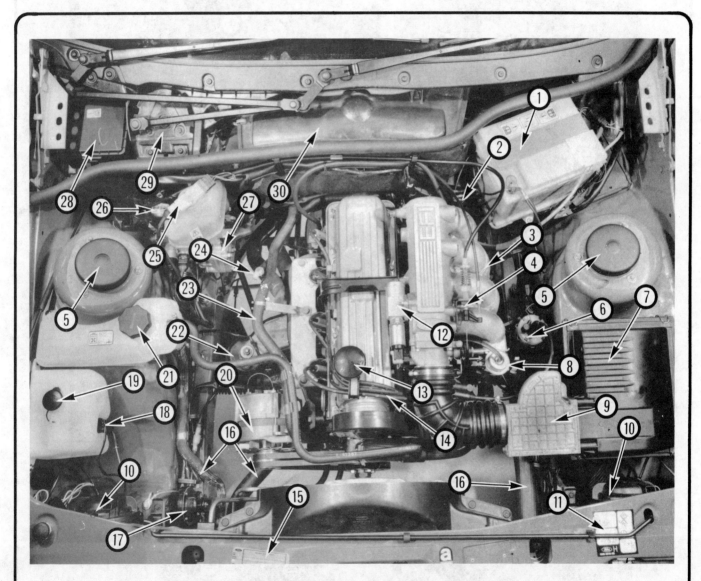

**Under-bonnet view of a 2.0 litre Granada with fuel-injection**

| | | | |
|---|---|---|---|
| 1 Battery | 9 Vane airflow meter | 18 Windscreen washer pump | 25 Brake fluid reservoir cap |
| 2 Engine oil dipstick | 10 Headlight covers | 19 Windscreen washer reservoir | 26 Brake hydraulic unit |
| 3 Inlet manifold | 11 Tune-up label | 20 Alternator | accumulator |
| 4 Throttle/kickdown cable | 12 Idle speed control valve | 21 Coolant expansion tank cap | 27 Brake hydraulic unit valve |
| bracket | 13 Oil filler cap | 22 Engine mounting | block |
| 5 Suspension turrets | 14 Spark plug leads | 23 Heater hose | 28 Main fuse/relay box |
| 6 Ignition coil | 15 VIN plate | 24 Automatic transmission fluid | 29 Wiper motor (behind cover) |
| 7 Air cleaner cover | 16 Radiator hoses | dipstick | 30 Heater blower cover |
| 8 Fuel pressure regulator | 17 Horn | | |

**Under-bonnet view of a 2.8 litre Granada with automatic transmission**

1  Battery
2  Suspension turrets
3  Air cleaner cover
4  Vane airflow meters
5  Headlight covers
6  Tune-up label
7  Auxiliary driving light covers
8  Crankcase ventilation hoses
9  Throttle linkage cover
10  Throttle cable and kickdown switch
11  Plenum chamber
12  Idle speed control valve
13  Radiator top hose
14  Oil filler cap
15  Power steering fluid reservoir
16  Horn
17  Washer fluid level switch
18  Windscreen washer pump
19  Windscreen washer reservoir
20  Coolant level switch
21  Coolant expansion tank cap
22  Engine mounting
23  Heater hose
24  Brake hydraulic unit valve block
25  Brake fluid reservoir cap
26  Brake hydraulic unit accumulator
27  Main fuse/relay box
28  Wiper motor (behind cover)
29  Heater blower cover
30  Fuel pressure regulator
31  Distributor screening lid
32  Engine oil dipstick
33  Automatic transmission fluid dipstick

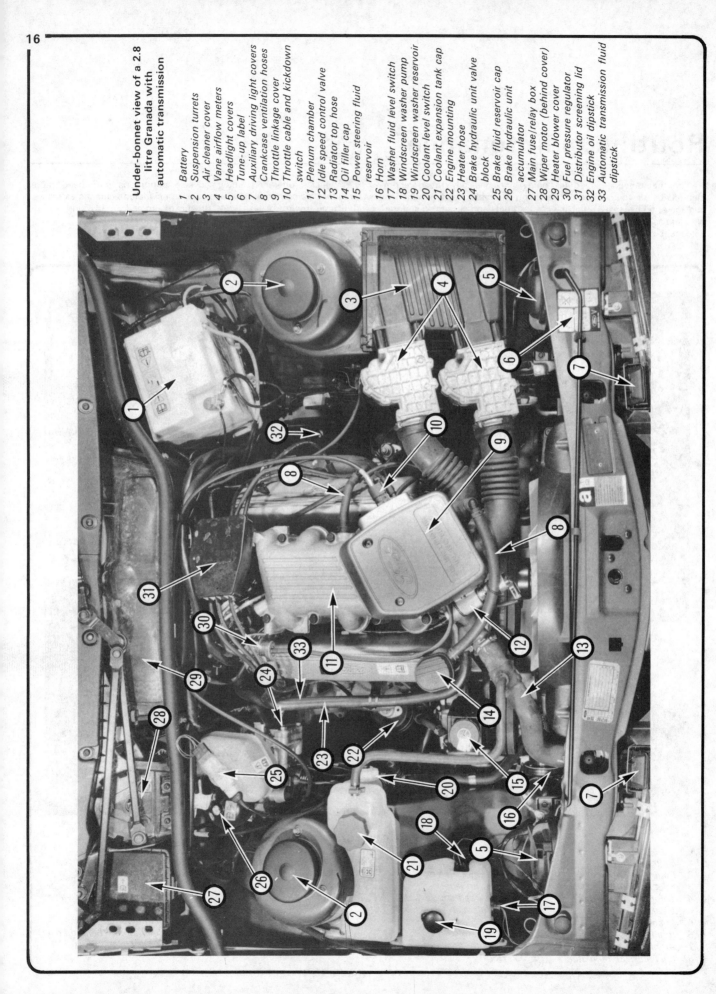

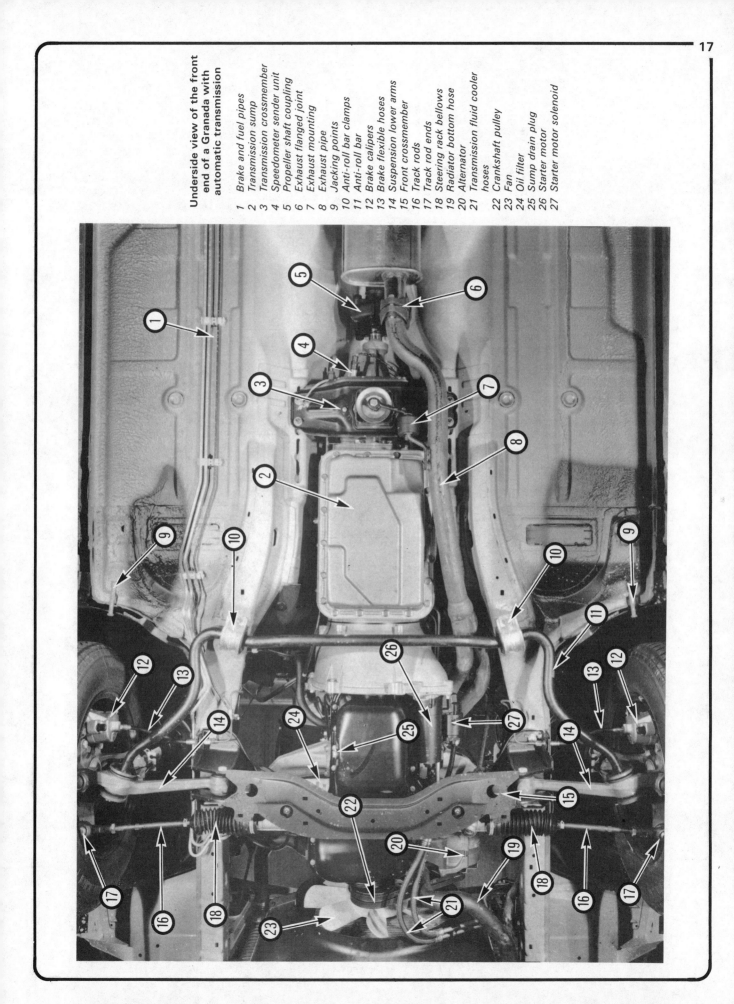

**Underside view of the front end of a Granada with automatic transmission**

1 Brake and fuel pipes
2 Transmission sump
3 Transmission crossmember
4 Speedometer sender unit
5 Propeller shaft coupling
6 Exhaust flanged joint
7 Exhaust mounting
8 Exhaust pipe
9 Jacking points
10 Anti-roll bar clamps
11 Anti-roll bar
12 Brake calipers
13 Brake flexible hoses
14 Suspension lower arms
15 Front crossmember
16 Track rods
17 Track rod ends
18 Steering rack bellows
19 Radiator bottom hose
20 Alternator
21 Transmission fluid cooler hoses
22 Crankshaft pulley
23 Fan
24 Oil filter
25 Sump drain plug
26 Starter motor
27 Starter motor solenoid

18

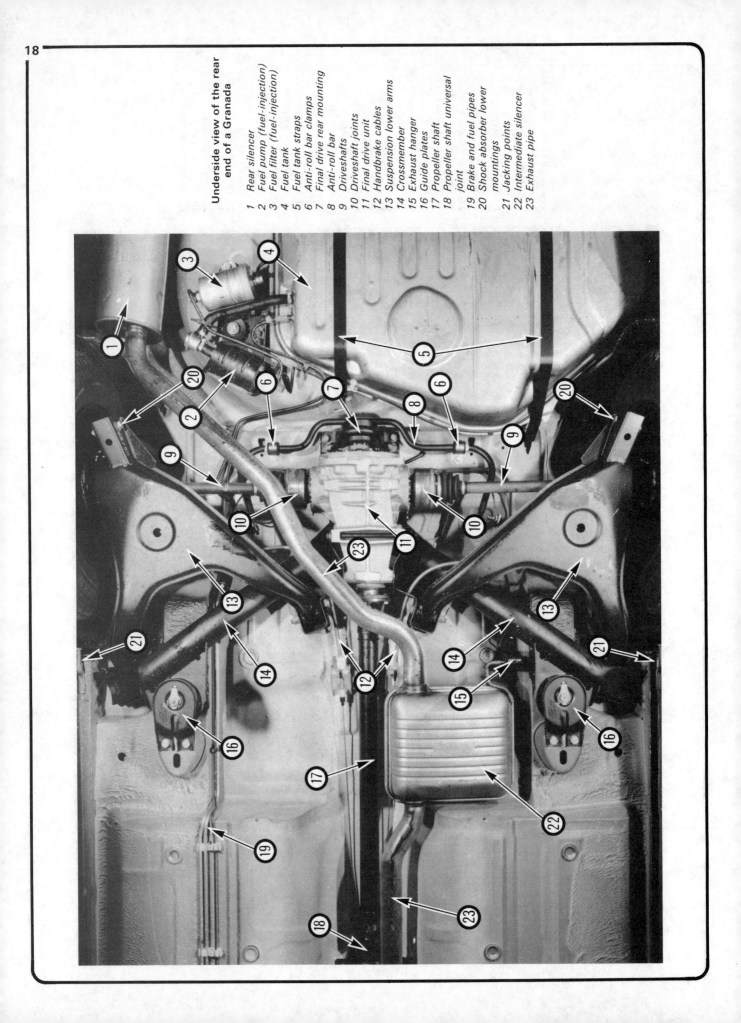

**Underside view of the rear end of a Granada**

1  Rear silencer
2  Fuel pump (fuel-injection)
3  Fuel filter (fuel-injection)
4  Fuel tank
5  Fuel tank straps
6  Anti-roll bar clamps
7  Final drive rear mounting
8  Anti-roll bar
9  Driveshafts
10  Driveshaft joints
11  Final drive unit
12  Handbrake cables
13  Suspension lower arms
14  Crossmember
15  Exhaust hanger
16  Guide plates
17  Propeller shaft
18  Propeller shaft universal joint
19  Brake and fuel pipes
20  Shock absorber lower mountings
21  Jacking points
22  Intermediate silencer
23  Exhaust pipe

**Every 250 miles (400 km), weekly, or before a long journey**

Check engine oil level (Chapter 1, Section 2)
Check brake fluid level (Chapter 9, Section 2)
Check coolant level (Chapter 2, Section 2)
Top up screen washer reservoir, adding screen wash such as Turtle Wax High Tech Screen Wash
Check tyre pressure and inspect tyres (Chapter 10, Section 40)
Check operation of lights, direction indicators, horn etc.

**Every 6000 miles (10 000 km) or six months, whichever comes first**

Renew engine oil and filter (Chapter 1, Sections 2 and 21)
Check brake pads for wear (front and rear) (Chapter 9, Section 8 and 9)
Inspect tyres thoroughly (Chapter 10, Section 40)
Check tightness of wheel nuts
Check idle speed (1.8 litre only) (Chapter 3, Section 16)
Check idle mixture (not fuel-injection models) – at just 6000 miles only (Chapter 3, Section 16 or 21)
Clean oil filler cap
Inspect engine bay and underside of vehicle for fluid leaks or other signs of damage
Check function and condition of seat belts
Check operation of brake fluid level warning indicator
Check condition and security of exhaust system (Chapter 3, Section 34)

**Every 12 000 miles (20 000 km) or 12 months, whichever comes first**

In addition to the work in the previous schedule:

Check operation of latches, check straps and locks; lubricate if necessary
Check condition and tension of auxiliary drivebelt(s); adjust or renew as necessary (Chapter 2, Section 13)
Check tightness of battery terminals, clean and neutralise corrosion if necessary (Chapter 12, Section 3)
Check engine valve clearances (Chapter 1, Section 51 or 93)
Check tightness of inlet manifold bolts (V6 only) (Chapter 3, Section 32)
Renew spark plugs (Chapter 4, Section 3)
Clean air conditioning condenser fins (when applicable) (Chapter 11, Section 56)
Check air conditioning refrigerant charge (when applicable) (Chapter 11, Section 56)

Check manual gearbox oil level (Chapter 6, Section 2)
Check final drive oil level (Chapter 8, Section 2)
Lubricate automatic transmission selector/kickdown linkage
Check security and condition of steering and suspension components, gaiters and boots (Chapter 10, Section 2)
Check condition and security of driveshaft joints (Chapter 8, Section 2)
Inspect underbody and panels for corrosion or other damage
Inspect brake pipes and hoses (Chapter 9, Section 22)
Clean idle speed control linkage at throttle (when applicable) (Chapter 4, Section 11)
Road test and check operation of ABS
Check automatic transmission fluid level (engine hot) (Chapter 6, Section 11)
Check engine for satisfactory hot starting
Check that automatic choke is fully off with engine hot (not fuel-injection models)
Check power steering fluid level (when applicable) (Chapter 10, Section 3)

**Every 24 000 miles (40 000 km) or two years, whichever comes first**

In addition to the work specified in the previous schedules:

Renew air cleaner element (Chapter 3, Section 5)
Clean and inspect distributer cap, rotor arm, HT leads and coil tower (Chapter 4, Section 4)
Adjust automatic transmission brake bands (Chapter 6, Section 13)
Renew fuel filter (fuel-injection models only) (Chapter 3, Section 9)
Renew crankcase ventilation vent valve (carburettor models) (Chapter 1, Section 25)

**Every 36 000 miles (60 000 km) or three years, whichever comes first**

Renew brake hydraulic system seals and hoses if necessary (Chapter 9, Section 11, 13, 21 and 22)
Renew brake hydraulic fluid (Chapter 9, Section 4)
Renew camshaft drivebelt on ohc models – recommended as a precautionary measure (Chapter 1, Sections 14 and 46)

**Every two years, regardless of mileage**

Renew coolant (Chapter 2, Sections 3 to 6)

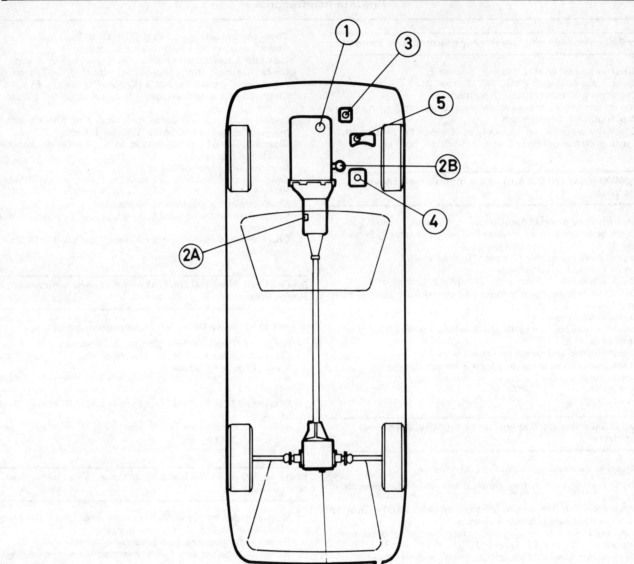

H.12641

# Recommended lubricants and fluids

| Component or system | Lubricant type or specification |
| --- | --- |
| 1 Engine | Multigrade engine oil, viscosity range 10W-30 to 20W-50, to API SF/CC |
| 2A Manual gearbox | Semi-synthetic gear oil to Ford spec. ESD M2C175-A (80 EP) |
| 2B Automatic transmission | ATF to Ford spec. SQM-2C9010-A (TQ Dexron II) |
| 3 Power-assisted steering | ATF (as above) |
| 4 Brake hydraulic system | Hydraulic fluid to Ford spec. SAM-6C9103-A |
| 5 Cooling system | Soft water/antifreeze to Ford spec. SSM-97B9103-A |
| 6 Final drive (normal or limited slip differential) | Gear oil SAE 90EP to API GL5 |

**Note:** *The above are general recommendations for a temperate climate. Lubrication requirements may vary in extreme temperatures or under severe conditions of use. If in doubt consult a Ford dealer, or the operator's handbook supplied with the vehicle.*

# Conversion factors

## Length (distance)

| | | | | |
|---|---|---|---|---|
| Inches (in) | X 25.4 | = Millimetres (mm) | X 0.0394 | = Inches (in) |
| Feet (ft) | X 0.305 | = Metres (m) | X 3.281 | = Feet (ft) |
| Miles | X 1.609 | = Kilometres (km) | X 0.621 | = Miles |

## Volume (capacity)

| | | | | |
|---|---|---|---|---|
| Cubic inches (cu in; in³) | X 16.387 | = Cubic centimetres (cc; cm³) | X 0.061 | = Cubic inches (cu in; in³) |
| Imperial pints (Imp pt) | X 0.568 | = Litres (l) | X 1.76 | = Imperial pints (Imp pt) |
| Imperial quarts (Imp qt) | X 1.137 | = Litres (l) | X 0.88 | = Imperial quarts (Imp qt) |
| Imperial quarts (Imp qt) | X 1.201 | = US quarts (US qt) | X 0.833 | = Imperial quarts (Imp qt) |
| US quarts (US qt) | X 0.946 | = Litres (l) | X 1.057 | = US quarts (US qt) |
| Imperial gallons (Imp gal) | X 4.546 | = Litres (l) | X 0.22 | = Imperial gallons (Imp gal) |
| Imperial gallons (Imp gal) | X 1.201 | = US gallons (US gal) | X 0.833 | = Imperial gallons (Imp gal) |
| US gallons (US gal) | X 3.785 | = Litres (l) | X 0.264 | = US gallons (US gal) |

## Mass (weight)

| | | | | |
|---|---|---|---|---|
| Ounces (oz) | X 28.35 | = Grams (g) | X 0.035 | = Ounces (oz) |
| Pounds (lb) | X 0.454 | = Kilograms (kg) | X 2.205 | = Pounds (lb) |

## Force

| | | | | |
|---|---|---|---|---|
| Ounces-force (ozf; oz) | X 0.278 | = Newtons (N) | X 3.6 | = Ounces-force (ozf; oz) |
| Pounds-force (lbf; lb) | X 4.448 | = Newtons (N) | X 0.225 | = Pounds-force (lbf; lb) |
| Newtons (N) | X 0.1 | = Kilograms-force (kgf; kg) | X 9.81 | = Newtons (N) |

## Pressure

| | | | | |
|---|---|---|---|---|
| Pounds-force per square inch (psi; lbf/in²; lb/in²) | X 0.070 | = Kilograms-force per square centimetre (kgf/cm²; kg/cm²) | X 14.223 | = Pounds-force per square inch (psi; lbf/in²; lb/in²) |
| Pounds-force per square inch (psi; lbf/in²; lb/in²) | X 0.068 | = Atmospheres (atm) | X 14.696 | = Pounds-force per square inch (psi; lbf/in²; lb/in²) |
| Pounds-force per square inch (psi; lbf/in²; lb/in²) | X 0.069 | = Bars | X 14.5 | = Pounds-force per square inch (psi; lbf/in²; lb/in²) |
| Pounds-force per square inch (psi; lbf/in²; lb/in²) | X 6.895 | = Kilopascals (kPa) | X 0.145 | = Pounds-force per square inch (psi; lbf/in²; lb/in²) |
| Kilopascals (kPa) | X 0.01 | = Kilograms-force per square centimetre (kgf/cm²; kg/cm²) | X 98.1 | = Kilopascals (kPa) |
| Millibar (mbar) | X 100 | = Pascals (Pa) | X 0.01 | = Millibar (mbar) |
| Millibar (mbar) | X 0.0145 | = Pounds-force per square inch (psi; lbf/in²; lb/in²) | X 68.947 | = Millibar (mbar) |
| Millibar (mbar) | X 0.75 | = Millimetres of mercury (mmHg) | X 1.333 | = Millibar (mbar) |
| Millibar (mbar) | X 0.401 | = Inches of water (inH₂O) | X 2.491 | = Millibar (mbar) |
| Millimetres of mercury (mmHg) | X 0.535 | = Inches of water (inH₂O) | X 1.868 | = Millimetres of mercury (mmHg) |
| Inches of water (inH₂O) | X 0.036 | = Pounds-force per square inch (psi; lbf/in²; lb/in²) | X 27.68 | = Inches of water (inH₂O) |

## Torque (moment of force)

| | | | | |
|---|---|---|---|---|
| Pounds-force inches (lbf in; lb in) | X 1.152 | = Kilograms-force centimetre (kgf cm; kg cm) | X 0.868 | = Pounds-force inches (lbf in; lb in) |
| Pounds-force inches (lbf in; lb in) | X 0.113 | = Newton metres (Nm) | X 8.85 | = Pounds-force inches (lbf in; lb in) |
| Pounds-force inches (lbf in; lb in) | X 0.083 | = Pounds-force feet (lbf ft; lb ft) | X 12 | = Pounds-force inches (lbf in; lb in) |
| Pounds-force feet (lbf ft; lb ft) | X 0.138 | = Kilograms-force metres (kgf m; kg m) | X 7.233 | = Pounds-force feet (lbf ft; lb ft) |
| Pounds-force feet (lbf ft; lb ft) | X 1.356 | = Newton metres (Nm) | X 0.738 | = Pounds-force feet (lbf ft; lb ft) |
| Newton metres (Nm) | X 0.102 | = Kilograms-force metres (kgf m; kg m) | X 9.804 | = Newton metres (Nm) |

## Power

| | | | | |
|---|---|---|---|---|
| Horsepower (hp) | X 745.7 | = Watts (W) | X 0.0013 | = Horsepower (hp) |

## Velocity (speed)

| | | | | |
|---|---|---|---|---|
| Miles per hour (miles/hr; mph) | X 1.609 | = Kilometres per hour (km/hr; kph) | X 0.621 | = Miles per hour (miles/hr; mph) |

## Fuel consumption*

| | | | | |
|---|---|---|---|---|
| Miles per gallon, Imperial (mpg) | X 0.354 | = Kilometres per litre (km/l) | X 2.825 | = Miles per gallon, Imperial (mpg) |
| Miles per gallon, US (mpg) | X 0.425 | = Kilometres per litre (km/l) | X 2.352 | = Miles per gallon, US (mpg) |

## Temperature

Degrees Fahrenheit = (°C x 1.8) + 32

Degrees Celsius (Degrees Centigrade; °C) = (°F - 32) x 0.56

*It is common practice to convert from miles per gallon (mpg) to litres/100 kilometres (l/100km), where mpg (Imperial) x l/100 km = 282 and mpg (US) x l/100 km = 235

# Fault diagnosis

## Introduction

The vehicle owner who does his or her own maintenance according to the recommended schedules should not have to use this section of the manual very often. Modern component reliability is such that, provided those items subject to wear or deterioration are inspected or renewed at the specified intervals, sudden failure is comparatively rare. Faults do not usually just happen as a result of sudden failure, but develop over a period of time. Major mechanical failures in particular are usually preceded by characteristic symptoms over hundreds or even thousands of miles. Those components which do occasionally fail without warning are often small and easily carried in the vehicle.

With any fault finding, the first step is to decide where to begin investigations. Sometimes this is obvious, but on other occasions a little detective work will be necessary. The owner who makes half a dozen haphazard adjustments or replacements may be successful in curing a fault (or its symptoms), but he will be none the wiser if the fault recurs and he may well have spent more time and money than was necessary. A calm and logical approach will be found to be more satisfactory in the long run. Always take into account any warning signs or abnormalities that may have been noticed in the period preceding the fault – power loss, high or low gauge readings, unusual noises or smells, etc – and remember that failure of components such as fuses or spark plugs may only be pointers to some underlying fault.

The pages which follow here are intended to help in cases of failure to start or breakdown on the road. There is also a Fault Diagnosis Section at the end of each Chapter which should be consulted if the preliminary checks prove unfruitful. Whatever the fault, certain basic principles apply. These are as follows:

**Verify the fault.** This is simply a matter of being sure that you know what the symptoms are before starting work. This is particularly important if you are investigating a fault for someone else who may not have described it very accurately.

**Don't overlook the obvious.** For example, if the vehicle won't start, is there petrol in the tank? (Don't take anyone else's word on this particular point, and don't trust the fuel gauge either!) If an electrical fault is indicated, look for loose or broken wires before digging out the test gear.

**Cure the disease, not the symptom.** Substituting a flat battery with a fully charged one will get you off the hard shoulder, but if the underlying cause is not attended to, the new battery will go the same way. Similarly, changing oil-fouled spark plugs for a new set will get you moving again, but remember that the reason for the fouling (if it wasn't simply an incorrect grade of plug) will have to be established and corrected.

**Don't take anything for granted.** Particularly, don't forget that a 'new' component may itself be defective (especially if it's been rattling round in the boot for months), and don't leave components out of a fault diagnosis sequence just because they are new or recently fitted. When you do finally diagnose a difficult fault, you'll probably realise that all the evidence was there from the start.

## Electrical faults

Electrical faults can be more puzzling than straightforward mechanical failures, but they are no less susceptible to logical analysis if the basic principles of operation are understood. Vehicle electrical wiring exists in extremely unfavourable conditions – heat, vibration and chemical attack – and the first things to look for are loose or corroded connections and broken or chafed wires, especially where the wires pass through holes in the bodywork or are subject to vibration.

All metal-bodied vehicles in current production have one pole of the battery 'earthed', ie connected to the vehicle bodywork, and in nearly all modern vehicles it is the negative (–) terminal. The various electrical components – motors, bulb holders etc – are also connected to earth, either by means of a lead or directly by their mountings. Electric current flows through the component and then back to the battery via the bodywork. If the component mounting is loose or corroded, or if a good path back to the battery is not available, the circuit will be incomplete and malfunction will result. The engine and/or gearbox are also earthed by means of flexible metal straps to the body or subframe; if these straps are loose or missing, starter motor, generator and ignition trouble may result.

Assuming the earth return to be satisfactory, electrical faults will be due either to component malfunction or to defects in the current supply. Individual components are dealt with in Chapter 12. If supply wires are broken or cracked internally this results in an open-circuit, and the easiest way to check for this is to bypass the suspect wire temporarily with a length of wire having a crocodile clip or suitable connector at each end. Alternatively, a 12V test lamp can be used to verify the presence of supply voltage at various points along the wire and the break can be thus isolated.

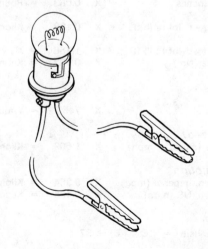

**A simple test lamp is useful for tracing electrical faults**

Carrying a few spares can save you a long walk!

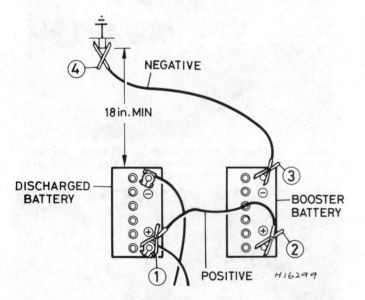

**Jump start lead connections for negative earth – connect leads in order shown**

If a bare portion of a live wire touches the bodywork or other earthed metal part, the electricity will take the low-resistance path thus formed back to the battery: this is known as a short-circuit. Hopefully a short-circuit will blow a fuse, but otherwise it may cause burning of the insulation (and possibly further short-circuits) or even a fire. This is why it is inadvisable to bypass persistently blowing fuses with silver foil or wire.

*Spares and tool kit*

Most vehicles are supplied only with sufficient tools for wheel changing; the *Maintenance and minor repair* tool kit detailed in *Tools*

*and working facilities,* with the addition of a hammer, is probably sufficient for those repairs that most motorists would consider attempting at the roadside. In addition a few items which can be fitted without too much trouble in the event of a breakdown should be carried. Experience and available space will modify the list below, but the following may save having to call on professional assistance:

*Spark plugs, clean and correctly gapped*
*HT lead and plug cap – long enough to reach the plug furthest from the distributor*
*Distributor rotor*
*Drivebelt(s) – emergency type may suffice*
*Spare fuses*
*Set of principal light bulbs*
*Tin of radiator sealer and hose bandage*
*Exhaust bandage*
*Roll of insulating tape*
*Length of soft iron wire*
*Length of electrical flex*
*Torch or inspection lamp (can double as test lamp)*
*Battery jump leads*
*Tow-rope*
*Ignition water dispersant aerosol*
*Litre of engine oil*
*Sealed can of hydraulic fluid*
*Worm drive clips*

If spare fuel is carried, a can designed for the purpose should be used to minimise risks of leakage and collision damage. A first aid kit and a warning triangle, whilst not at present compulsory in the UK, are obviously sensible items to carry in addition to the above.

When touring abroad it may be advisable to carry additional spares which, even if you cannot fit them yourself, could save having to wait while parts are obtained. The items below may be worth considering:

*Clutch and throttle cables*
*Cylinder head gasket*
*Alternator brushes*
*Tyre valve core*

One of the motoring organisations will be able to advise on availability of fuel etc in foreign countries.

## Engine will not start

### Engine fails to turn when starter operated

Flat battery (recharge, use jump leads, or push start)
Battery terminals loose or corroded
Battery earth to body defective
Engine earth strap loose or broken
Starter motor (or solenoid) wiring loose or broken
Automatic transmission selector in wrong position, or inhibitor switch faulty
Ignition/starter switch faulty
Major mechanical failure (seizure)
Starter or solenoid internal fault (see Chapter 12)

### Starter motor turns engine slowly

Partially discharged battery (recharge, use jump leads, or push start)
Battery terminals loose or corroded
Battery earth to body defective
Engine earth strap loose
Starter motor (or solenoid) wiring loose
Starter motor internal fault (see Chapter 12)

### Starter motor spins without turning engine

Flywheel gear teeth damaged or worn
Starter motor mounting bolts loose

### Engine turns normally but fails to start

Damp or dirty HT leads and distributor cap (crank engine and check for spark) (photo) – try moisture dispersant such as Holts Wet Start.
Incorrect starting procedure (see operator's handbook)
No fuel in tank (check for delivery on carburettor models) (photo)
Fouled or incorrectly gapped spark plugs (remove, clean and regap)
Other ignition system fault (see Chapter 4)
Other fuel system fault (see Chapter 3)
Poor compression (see Chapter 1)
Major mechanical failure (eg camshaft drive)

### Engine fires but will not run

Air leaks at carburettor or inlet manifold
Fuel starvation (see Chapter 3)
Ignition fault (see Chapter 4)

## Engine cuts out and will not restart

### Engine cuts out suddenly – ignition fault

Loose or disconnected LT wires
Wet HT leads or distributor cap (after traversing water splash)
Coil failure (check for spark)
Other ignition fault (see Chapter 4)

### Engine misfires before cutting out – fuel fault

Fuel tank empty
Fuel pump defective or filter blocked (check for delivery)
Fuel tank filler vent blocked (suction will be evident on releasing cap)
Carburettor needle valve sticking
Carburettor jets blocked (fuel contaminated)
Other fuel system fault (see Chapter 3)

### Engine cuts out – other causes

Serious overheating
Major mechanical failure (eg camshaft drive)

## Engine overheats

### Ignition (no-charge) warning light illuminated

Slack or broken drivebelt – retension or renew (Chapter 2)

### Ignition warning light not illuminated

Coolant loss due to internal or external leakage (see Chapter 2)
Thermostat defective
Low oil level
Brakes binding
Radiator clogged externally or internally
Engine waterways clogged
Ignition timing incorrect or automatic advance malfunctioning
Mixture too weak

Note: *Do not add cold water to an overheated engine or damage may result*

## Low engine oil pressure

### Gauge reads low or warning light illuminated with engine running

Oil level low or incorrect grade
Defective gauge or sender unit
Wire to sender unit earthed

**Using a spare spark plug to check for HT spark – do not remove plugs from engine otherwise fuel/air mixture may ignite causing fire**

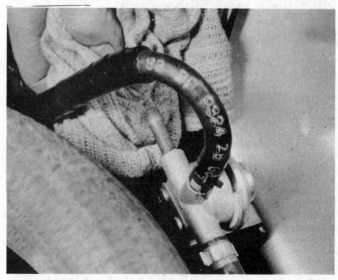

**Checking for fuel delivery at the vapour separator/pressure regulator. Do not try this on fuel-injection models as the fuel pressure is much higher**

Engine overheating
Oil filter clogged or bypass valve defective
Oil pressure relief valve defective
Oil pick-up strainer clogged
Oil pump worn or mountings loose
Worn main or big-end bearings

**Note:** *Low oil pressure in a high-mileage engine at tickover is not necessarily a cause for concern. Sudden pressure loss at speed is far more significant. In any event, check the gauge or warning light sender before condemning the engine.*

_____

**Engine noises**

_____

### Pre-ignition (pinking) on acceleration

Incorrect grade of fuel
Ignition timing incorrect
Distributor faulty or worn
Worn or maladjusted carburettor
Excessive carbon build-up in engine

### Whistling or wheezing noises

Leaking vacuum hose
Leaking carburettor or manifold gasket
Blowing head gasket

### Tapping or rattling

Incorrect valve clearances
Worn valve gear
Worn timing gears or belt
Broken piston ring (ticking noise)

### Knocking or thumping

Unintentional mechanical contact (eg fan blades)
Worn drivebelt
Peripheral component fault (generator, water pump etc)
Worn big-end bearings (regular heavy knocking, perhaps less under load)
Worn main bearings (rumbling and knocking, perhaps worsening under load)
Piston slap (most noticeable when cold)

# Chapter 1 Engine

*For modifications, and information applicable to later models, see Supplement at end of manual*

## Contents

**Specifications**

*In-line ohc engine*

## General

|  | 1.8 HC E | 2.0 HC | 2.0 HC EFi |
|---|---|---|---|
| Manufacturer's code | REC | NEL | NRA |
| Bore | 76.20 mm (3.394 in) | 90.82 mm (3.576 in) | 90.82 mm (3.576 in) |
| Stroke | 86.95 mm (3.030 in) | 76.95 mm (3.030 in) | 76,95 mm (3.030 in) |
| Cubic capacity | 1796 cc (109.6 cu in) | 1993 cc (121.6 cu in) | 1993 cc (121.6 cu in) |
| Compression ratio | 9.5:1 | 9.2:1 | 9.2:1 |
| Compression pressure at cranking speed | 11 to 13 bar (160 to 189 lbf/in²) | 11 to 13 bar (160 to 189 lbf/in²) | 11 to 13 bar (160 to 189 lbf/in²) |
| Maximum power (DIN, kW @ rpm) | 66 @ 5400 | 77 @ 5200 | 85 @ 5500 |
| Maximum torque (DIN, Nm @ rpm) | 140 @ 3500 | 157 @ 4000 | 160 @ 4000 |

## Lubrication system

| | |
|---|---|
| Oil type | See *'Recommended Lubricants and fluids'* |
| Oil capacity (drain and refill, including filter) | 3.75 litres (6.6 pints) approx |
| Oil pressure (SAE 10W/30 oil at 80°C/176°F): | |
| At 750 rpm | 2.1 bar (31 lbf/in²) |
| At 2000 rpm | 2.5 bar (36 lbf/in²) |
| Oil pressure relief valve opening pressure | 4.0 to 4.7 bar (58 to 68 lbf/in²) |
| Oil pressure warning light switch setting | 0.3 to 0.5 bar (4 to 7 lbf/in²) |
| Oil filter | Champion C102 |

## Oil pump

| | |
|---|---|
| Type | Bi-rotor |
| Drive | From auxiliary shaft |
| Operating clearances: | |
| Outer rotor-to-housing | 0.153 to 0.304 mm (0.0060 to 0.0120 in) |
| Inner-to-outer rotor | 0.050 to 0.200 mm (0.0020 to 0.0079 in) |
| Rotor endfloat | 0.039 to 0.104 mm (0.0015 to 0.0041 in) |

## Cylinder block

|  | 1.8 (REC) | 2.0 (NEL and NRA) |
|---|---|---|
| Cast identification mark | 18S | 20S |
| Bore diameter: | | |
| Standard grade 1 | 86.180 to 86.190 mm (3.3929 to. 3.3933 in) | 90.800 to 90.810 mm (3.5748 to 3.5752 in) |
| Standard grade 2 | 86.190 to 86.200 mm (3.3933 to 3.3937 in) | 90.810 to 90.820 mm (3.5752 to 3.5756 in) |
| Standard grade 3 | 86.200 to 86.210 mm (3.3937 to 3.3941 in) | 90.820 to 90.830 mm (3.5756 to 3.5760 in) |
| Standard grade 4 | 86.210 to 86.220 mm (3.3941 to 3.3945 in) | 90.830 to 90.840 mm (3.5760 to 3.5764 in) |
| Oversize grade 5 | 86.690 to 86.700 mm (3.4130 to 3.4134 in) | 91.310 to 91.320 mm (3.5949 to 3.5953 in) |
| Oversize grade B | 86.700 to 86.710 mm (3.4134 to 3.4138 in) | 91.320 to 91.330 mm (3.5953 to 3.5957 in) |
| Oversize grade C | 86.710 to 86.720 mm (3.4138 to 3.4142 in) | 91.330 to 91.340 mm (3.5957 to 3.5961 in) |
| Standard service grade | Not stated | 90.830 to 90.840 mm (3.5760 to 3.5764 in) |
| Oversize 0.5 | Not stated | 91.330 to 91.340 mm (3.5957 to 3.9561 in) |
| Oversize 1.0 | Not stated | 91.830 to 91.840 mm (3.6153 to 3.6157 in) |

## Crankshaft

| | |
|---|---|
| Number of main bearings | 5 |
| Main bearing journal diameter: | |
| Standard | 56.970 to 56.990 mm (2.2429 to 2.2437 in) |
| Undersize 0.25 | 56.720 to 56.740 mm (2.2331 to 2.2339 in) |
| Undersize 0.50 | 56.470 to 56.490 mm (2.2232 to 2.2240 in) |
| Undersize 0.75 | 56.220 to 56.240 mm (2.2134 5o 2.2142 in) |
| Undersize 1.00 | 55.970 to 55.990 mm (2.2035 to 2.2043 in) |
| Main bearing running clearance | 0.010 to 0.064 mm (0.0004 to 0.0025 in) |
| Big-end bearing journal diameter: | |
| Standard | 51.980 to 52.000 mm (2.0464 to 2.0472 in) |
| Undersize 0.25 | 51.730 to 51.750 mm (2.0366 to 2.0374 in) |
| Undersize 0.50 | 51.480 to 51.500 mm (2.0268 to 2.0276 in) |
| Undersize 0.75 | 51.230 to 51.250 mm (2.0169 to 2.0177 in) |
| Undersize 1.00 | 50.980 to 51.000 mm (2.0071 to 2.0079 in) |
| Big-end bearing running clearance | 0.006 to 0.060 mm (0.0002 to 0.0024 in) |

Thrust washer thickness:
    Standard ................................................................. 2.30 to 2.35 mm (0.0906 to 0.0925 in)
    Oversize ................................................................. 2.50 to 2.55 mm (0.0984 to 0.1004 in)
Crankshaft endfloat ....................................................... 0.08 to 0.28 mm (0.0032 to 0.0110 in)

## Connecting rods
Big-end parent bore diameter ....................................... 55.000 to 55.020 mm (2.1654 to 2.1661 in)
Small-end bush internal diameter ................................. 23.964 to 23.976 mm (0.9435 to 0.9439 in)

## Pistons
Diameter:

| | 1.8 (REC) | 2.0 (NEL and NRA) |
|---|---|---|
| Standard grade 1 | 86.145 to 86.155 mm (3.3915 to 3.3919 in) | 90.765 to 90.775 mm (3.5734 to 3.5738 in) |
| Standard grade 2 | 86.155 to 86.165 mm (3.3919 to 3.3923 in) | 90.775 to 90.785 mm (3.5738 to 3.5742 in) |
| Standard grade 3 | 86.165 to 86.175 mm (3.3923 to 3.3927 in) | 90.785 to 90.795 mm (3.5742 to 3.5746 in) |
| Standard grade 4 | 86.175 to 86.185 mm (3.3927 to 3.3931 in) | 90.795 to 90.805 mm (3.5746 to 3.5750 in) |
| Service standard | 86.170 to 86.195 mm (3.3925 to 3.3935 in) | 90.790 to 90.815 mm (3.5744 to 3.5754 in) |
| Oversize 0.5 | 86.670 to 86.695 mm (3.4122 to 3.4132 in) | 91.290 to 91.315 mm (3.5941 to 3.5951 in) |
| Oversize 1.0 | 87.170 to 87.195 mm (3.4319 to 3.4329 in) | 91.790 to 91.815 mm (3.6138 to 3.6148 in) |
| Clearance in bore | 0.015 to 0.050 mm (0.0006 to 0.0020 in) | 0.015 to 0.050 mm (0.0006 to 0.0020 in) |
| Piston ring end gaps: | | |
| Top and centre | 0.3 to 0.5 mm (0.012 to 0.020 in) | 0.4 to 0.6 mm (0.016 to 0.24 in) |
| Bottom | 0.4 to 1.4 mm (0.016 to 0.055 in) | 0.4 to 1.4 mm (0.016 to 0.055 in) |

## Gudgeon pins
Length ............................................................................. 68.0 to 68.8 mm (2.6772 to 2.7087 in)
Diameter:
    Red ........................................................................... 23.994 to 23.997 mm (0.9446 to 0.9448 in)
    Blue .......................................................................... 23.997 to 24.000 mm (0.9448 to 0.9449 in)
    Yellow ....................................................................... 24.000 to 24.003 mm (0.9449 to 0.9450 in)
Clearance in piston ....................................................... 0.008 to 0.014 mm (0.0003 to 0.0006 in)
Interference in connecting rod ...................................... 0.018 to 0.039 mm (0.0007 to 0.0015 in)

## Cylinder head
Identification mark:
    1.8 (REC) ................................................................. 85
    2.0 (NEL and NRA) .................................................. 0
Valve seat angle ........................................................... 44° 30' to 45° 00'
Valve seat width ........................................................... 1.5 to 2.0 mm (0.059 to 0.079 in)
Valve guide bore:
    Standard ................................................................... 8.063 to 8.088 mm (0.3174 to 0.3184 in)
    Oversize 0.2 ............................................................. 8.263 to 8.288 mm (0.3253 to 0.3263 in)
    Oversize 0.4 ............................................................. 8.463 to 8.488 mm (0.3332 to 0.3342 in)
Camshaft bearing parent bores:
    Front ......................................................................... 45.072 to 45.102 mm (1.7745 to 1.7757 in)
    Centre ....................................................................... 47.692 to 47.722 mm (1.8776 to 1.8788 in)
    Rear .......................................................................... 48.072 to 48.102 mm (1.8926 to 1.8938 in)

## Auxiliary shaft
Endfloat .......................................................................... 0.050 to 0.204 mm (0.0020 to 0.0080 in)

## Camshaft
Drive ............................................................................... Toothed belt
Thrust plate thickness ................................................... 3.98 to 4.01 mm (0.1567 to 0.1579 in)
Endfloat .......................................................................... 0.104 to 0.204 mm (0.0041 to 0.0080 in)
Cam lift ........................................................................... 6.3323 mm (0.2493 in)
Cam length ..................................................................... 36.26 to 36.60 mm (1.4276 to 1.4409 in)
Valve timing:
    Inlet opens ............................................................... 24° BTDC
    Inlet closes .............................................................. 64° ABDC
    Exhaust opens ......................................................... 70° BBDC
    Exhaust closes ........................................................ 18° ATDC

Bearing journal diameter:
    Front ............................................................ 41.987 to 42.013 mm (1.6530 to 1.6541 in)
    Centre ......................................................... 44.607 to 44.633 mm (1.7562 to 1.7572 in)
    Rear ............................................................ 44.987 to 45.013 mm (1.7711 to 1.7722 in)
Bearing bush internal diameter:
    Front ............................................................ 42.035 to 42.055 mm (1.6549 to 1.6557 in)
    Centre ......................................................... 44.655 to 44.675 mm (1.7581 to 1.7589 in)
    Rear ............................................................ 45.035 to 45.055 mm (1.7730 to 1.7738 in)

## Valve clearances (cold)
Inlet ................................................................ 0.20 ± 0.03 mm (0.008 ± 0.001 in)
Exhaust ........................................................... 0.25 ± 0.03 mm (0.010 ± 0.001 in)

## Inlet valves
Length:
    1.8 (REC) ..................................................... 111.75 to 112.75 mm (4.3996 to 4.4390 in)
    2.0 (NEL and NRA) ........................................ 110.65 to 111.65 mm (4.3563 to 4.3957 in)
Head diameter ................................................. 41.80 to 42.20 mm (1.6457 to 1.6614 in)
Stem diameter:
    Standard ...................................................... 8.025 to 8.043 mm (0.3159 to 0.3167 in)
    Oversizes ..................................................... +0.2, 0.4, 0.6 and 0.8 mm (0.008, 0.016, 0.024 and 0.032 in)
Stem-to-guide clearance ................................... 0.020 to 0.063 mm (0.0008 to 0.0025 in)

## Exhaust valves
Length:
    1.8 (REC) ..................................................... 111.15 to 112.15 mm (4.3760 to 4.4154 in)
    2.0 (NEL) ..................................................... 110.05 to 111.05 mm (4.3327 to 4.3720 in)
    2.0 (NRA) ..................................................... 110.75 to 111.75 mm (4.3602 to 4.3996 in)
Head diameter:
    1.8 (REL) ..................................................... 34.00 to 34.40 mm (1.3386 to 1.3543 in)
    2.0 (NEL and NRA) ........................................ 35.80 to 36.20 mm (1.4095 to 1.4252 in)
Stem diameter:
    Standard ...................................................... 7.999 to 8.017 mm (0.3149 to 0.3156 in)
Oversizes ........................................................ +0.2, 0.4, 0.6 and 0.8 mm (0.008, 0.016, 0.024 and 0.032 in)
Stem-to-guide clearance ................................... 0.046 to 0.089 mm (0.0018 to 0.0035 in)

## Valve springs
Free length ...................................................... 47.0 mm (1.85 in)
Inside diameter ................................................ 23.45 to 23.95 mm (0.9232 to 0.9429 in)
Wire diameter .................................................. 3.87 to 3.93 mm (0.1524 to 0.1547 in)
Number of turns ............................................... 4.7

## Torque wrench settings (in-line ohc engine)

| | Nm | lbf ft |
|---|---|---|
| Main bearing cap bolts | 88 to 102 | 65 to 75 |
| Big-end bearing cap nuts | 40 to 47 | 30 to 35 |
| Crankshaft pulley bolt: | | |
|    1.8 (REC) and 2.0 (NEL) | 110 to 115 | 81 to 85 |
|    2.0 (NRA) | 115 to 130 | 85 to 96 |
| Camshaft sprocket bolt | 45 to 50 | 33 to 37 |
| Auxiliary shaft sprocket bolt | 45 to 50 | 33 to 37 |
| Flywheel bolts | 64 to 70 | 47 to 52 |
| Oil pump-to-cylinder block bolts | 17 to 21 | 13 to 16 |
| Oil pump cover bolts | 9 to 13 | 7 to 10 |
| Sump bolts (see text): | | |
|    Stage 1 | 1 to 2 | 0.7 to 1.5 |
|    Stage 2 | 6 to 8 | 4 to 6 |
|    Stage 3 (after 20 minutes running) | 8 to 10 | 6 to 7 |
| Sump drain plug | 21 to 28 | 16 to 21 |
| Oil pressure switch | 12 to 15 | 9 to 11 |
| Valve adjustment ball-pins | 50 to 55 | 37 to 41 |
| Cylinder head bolts (see text): | | |
|    Stage 1 | 35 to 40 | 26 to 30 |
|    Stage 2 | 70 to 75 | 52 to 55 |
|    Stage 3 (after 5 minutes) | Tighten 90° further | Tighten 90° further |
| Rocker cover bolts (see text): | | |
|    Bolts 1 to 6 – Stage 1 | 6 to 8 | 4 to 6 |
|    Bolts 7 and 8 – Stage 2 | 2 to 3 | 1.5 to 2 |
|    Bolts 9 and 10 – Stage 3 | 6 to 8 | 4 to 6 |
|    Bolts 7 and 8 – Stage 4 | 6 to 8 | 4 to 6 |

## Torque wrench settings (continued)

| | Nm | lbf ft |
|---|---|---|
| Front cover bolts | 13 to 17 | 10 to 13 |
| Timing belt tensioner bolts | 20 to 25 | 15 to 18 |
| Oil pump pick-up pipe: | | |
|     To pump | 11 to 14 | 8 to 10 |
|     To block | 17 to 21 | 13 to 16 |
| Engine mounting to crossmember | 41 to 51 | 30 to 38 |

*V6 ohv engine*

## General

| | |
|---|---|
| Manufacturer's code | PRE |
| Bore | 93.0 mm (3.66 in) |
| Stroke | 68.5 mm (2.70 in) |
| Cubic capacity | 2792 cc (170 cu in) |
| Compression ratio | 9.2:1 |
| Compression pressure at cranking speed | 11.5 to 12.5 bar (167 to 181 lbf/in²) |
| Maximum power (DIN, kW @ rpm) | 110 @ 5800 |
| Maximum torque (DIN, Nm @ rpm) | 216 @ 3000 |

## Lubrication system

| | |
|---|---|
| Oil type | See 'Recommended lubricants and fluids' |
| Oil capacity (drain and refill, including filter) | 4.25 litres (7.5 pints) approx |
| Oil pressure (SAE 10W/30 oil at 80°C/176°F): | |
|     At 750 rpm | 1.0 bar (15 lbf/in²) |
|     At 2000 rpm | 2.5 bar (36 lbf/in²) |
| Oil pressure relief valve opening pressure | 4.0 to 4.7 bar (58 to 68 lbf/in²) |
| Oil pressure warning light switch setting | 0.3 to 0.5 bar (4 to 7 lbf/in²) |
| Oil filter | Champion C102 |

## Oil pump

| | |
|---|---|
| Type | Bi-rotor |
| Drive | From camshaft |
| Operating clearances: | |
|     Outer rotor-to-housing | 0.15 to 0.30 mm (0.006 to 0.012 in) |
|     Inner-to-outer rotor | 0.05 to 0.20 mm (0.002 to 0.008 in) |
|     Rotor endfloat | 0.03 to 0.10 mm (0.001 to 0.004 in) |

## Cylinder block

| | |
|---|---|
| Cast identification mark | E |
| Bore diameter: | |
|     Standard grade 1 | 93.010 to 93.020 mm (3.6618 to 3.6622 in) |
|     Standard grade 2 | 93.020 to 93.030 mm (3.6622 to 3.6626 in) |
|     Standard grade 3 | 93.030 to 93.040 mm (3.6626 to 3.6630 in) |
|     Standard grade 4 | 93.040 to 93.050 mm (3.6630 to 3.6634 in) |
|     Oversize grade A | 93.520 to 93.530 mm (3.6819 to 3.6823 in) |
|     Oversize grade B | 93.530 to 93.540 mm (3.6823 to 3.6827 in) |
|     Oversize grade C | 93.540 to 93.550 mm (3.6827 to 3.6831 in) |
|     Standard service grade | 93.040 to 93.050 mm (3.6630 to 3.6634 in) |
|     Oversize 0.5 | 93.540 to 93.550 mm (3.6827 to 3.6831 in) |
|     Oversize 1.0 | 94.040 to 94.050 mm (3.7024 to 3.7028 in) |
| Main bearing parent bore: | |
|     Standard | 60.620 to 60.640 mm (2.3866 to 2.3874 in) |
|     Oversize | 61.000 to 61.020 mm (2.4016 to 2.4024 in) |
| Camshaft bearing bore (without bushes): | |
|     Front | 47.025 to 47.060 mm (1.8514 to 1.8528 in) |
|     Front centre | 46.645 to 46.680 mm (1.8364 to 1.8378 in) |
|     Rear centre | 46.265 to 46.300 mm (1.8215 to 1.8228 in) |
|     Rear | 45.885 to 45.920 mm (1.8065 to 1.8079 in) |

## Crankshaft

| | |
|---|---|
| Number of main bearings | 4 |
| Main bearing journal diameter (standard) | 56.980 to 57.000 mm (2.2433 to 2.2441 in) |
| Main bearing running clearance | 0.008 to 0.062 mm (0.0003 to 0.0024 in) |
| No. 3 (thrust) bearing shoulder width (standard) | 26.390 to 26.440 mm (1.0390 to 1.0409 in) |
| No. 3 (thrust) flanged bearing shell width (standard) | 26.240 to 26.290 mm (1.0331 to 1.0350 in) |
| Crankshaft endfloat | 0.08 to 0.20 mm (0.0032 to 0.0079 in) |
| Big-end bearing journal diameter (standard) | 53.980 to 54.000 mm (2.1252 to 2.1260 in) |
| Big-end bearing running clearance | 0.006 to 0.064 mm (0.0002 to 0.0025 in) |

## Pistons

Diameter:
| | |
|---|---|
| Standard grade 1 ........................................................ | 92.972 to 92.982 mm (3.6603 to 3.6607 in) |
| Standard grade 2 ........................................................ | 92.982 to 92.992 mm (3.6607 to 3.6611 in) |
| Standard grade 3 ........................................................ | 92.992 to 93.002 mm (3.6611 to 3.6615 in) |
| Standard grade 4 ........................................................ | 93.002 to 93.012 mm (3.6615 to 3.6619 in) |
| Service standard ........................................................ | 93.000 to 93.020 mm (3.6614 to 3.6622 in) |
| Oversize 0.5 ........................................................ | 93.500 to 93.520 mm (3.6811 to 3.6819 in) |
| Oversize 1.0 ........................................................ | 94.000 to 94.020 mm (3.7008 to 3.7016 in) |
| Clearance in bore ........................................................ | 0.020 to 0.050 mm (0.0008 to 0.0020 in) |

Piston ring end gaps:
| | |
|---|---|
| Top and centre ........................................................ | 0.38 to 0.58 mm (0.015 to 0.023 in) |
| Bottom ........................................................ | 0.40 to 1.40 mm (0.016 to 0.055 in) |

## Gudgeon pins

Diameter:
| | |
|---|---|
| Red ........................................................ | 23.994 to 23.997 mm (0.9446 to 0.9448 in) |
| Blue ........................................................ | 23.997 to 24.000 mm (0.9448 to 0.9449 in) |
| Clearance in piston ........................................................ | 0.008 to 0.014 mm (0.0003 to 0.0006 in) |
| Interference in connecting rod ........................................................ | 0.018 to 0.042 mm (0.0007 to 0.0017 in) |

## Connecting rods

| | |
|---|---|
| Big-end parent bore diameter ........................................................ | 56.820 to 56.840 mm (2.2370 to 2.2378 in) |
| Small-end bush internal diameter ........................................................ | 23.958 to 23.976 mm (0.9432 to 0.9439 in) |

## Cylinder heads

| | |
|---|---|
| Cast identification mark ........................................................ | EN |
| Valve seat angle ........................................................ | 44° 30' to 45° 00' |
| Valve seat width ........................................................ | 1.61 to 2.33 mm (0.0634 to 0.0917 in) |

Valve guide bore:
| | |
|---|---|
| Standard ........................................................ | 8.063 to 8.088 mm (0.3174 to 0.3184 in) |
| Oversizes ........................................................ | +0.2, 0.4, 0.6 and 0.8 mm (0.008, 0.016, 0.024 and 0.032 in) |

## Camshaft

| | |
|---|---|
| Drive ........................................................ | Gear |
| Gear backlash ........................................................ | 0.17 to 0.27 mm (0.007 to 0.011 in) |

Valve timing:
| | |
|---|---|
| Inlet opens ........................................................ | 26° 30' BTDC |
| Inlet closes ........................................................ | 69° 30' ABDC |
| Exhaust opens ........................................................ | 75° 30' BBDC |
| Exhaust closes ........................................................ | 22° 30' ATDC |

Cam lift:
| | |
|---|---|
| Inlet ........................................................ | 6.7 mm (0.264 in) |
| Exhaust ........................................................ | 6.6 mm (0.260 in) |

Cam length:
| | |
|---|---|
| Inlet ........................................................ | 35.995 to 36.165 mm (1.417 to 1.424 in) |
| Exhaust ........................................................ | 35.895 to 36.065 mm (1.413 to 1.420 in) |

Thrust plate thickness:
| | |
|---|---|
| Red ........................................................ | 3.960 to 3.985 mm (0.1559 to 0.1569 in) |
| Blue ........................................................ | 3.986 to 4.011 mm (0.1569 to 0.1579 in) |

Spacer thickness:
| | |
|---|---|
| Red ........................................................ | 4.075 to 4.100 mm (0.1604 to 0.1614 in) |
| Blue ........................................................ | 4.101 to 4.125 mm (0.1615 to 0.1624 in) |
| Camshaft endfloat ........................................................ | 0.02 to 0.10 mm (0.0008 to 0.0039 in) |

Bearing journal diameter:
| | |
|---|---|
| Front ........................................................ | 43.903 to 43.923 mm (1.7285 to 1.7292 in) |
| Front centre ........................................................ | 43.522 to 43.542 mm (1.7135 to 1.7142 in) |
| Rear centre ........................................................ | 43.141 to 43.161 mm (1.6985 to 1.6992 in) |
| Rear ........................................................ | 42.760 to 42.780 mm (1.6835 to 1.6843 in) |

Bearing bush internal diameter:
| | |
|---|---|
| Front ........................................................ | 43.948 to 43.968 mm (1.7302 to 1.7310 in) |
| Front centre ........................................................ | 43.567 to 43.587 mm (1.7152 to 1.7160 in) |
| Rear centre ........................................................ | 43.186 to 43.206 mm (1.7002 to 1.7010 in) |
| Rear ........................................................ | 42.805 to 42.825 mm (1.6852 to 1.6860 in) |

## Valve clearances (cold)

| | |
|---|---|
| Inlet ........................................................ | 0.35 mm (0.014 in) |
| Exhaust ........................................................ | 0.40 mm (0.016 in) |

## Inlet valves

| | |
|---|---|
| Head diameter ............................................................................ | 41.85 to 42.24 mm (1.6476 to 1.6630 in) |
| Length ...................................................................................... | 105.25 to 106.95 mm (4.1437 to 4.2106 in) |
| Stem diameter: | |
|    Standard ............................................................................ | 8.025 to 8.043 mm (0.3159 to 0.3167 in) |
|    Oversizes .......................................................................... | +0.2, 0.4, 0.6 and 0.8 mm (0.008, 0.016, 0.024 and 0.032 in) |
| Stem-to-guide clearance .......................................................... | 0.020 to 0.063 mm (0.0008 to 0.0025 in) |
| Valve stem oil seal type .......................................................... | Rubber, one size |

## Exhaust valves

| | |
|---|---|
| Head diameter ............................................................................ | 35.83 to 36.21 mm (1.4106 to 1.4256 in) |
| Length ...................................................................................... | 105.20 to 106.20 mm (4.1417 to 4.1811 in) |
| Stem diameter: | |
|    Standard ............................................................................ | 7.999 to 8.017 mm (0.3149 to 0.3156 in) |
|    Oversizes .......................................................................... | +0.2, 0.4, 0.6 and 0.8 mm (0.008, 0.016, 0.024 and 0.032 in) |
| Stem-to-guide clearance .......................................................... | 0.046 to 0.089 mm (0.0018 to 0.0035 in) |
| Valve stem oil seal: | |
|    Type ................................................................................ | Nylon, selective sizes |
|    Identification: | |
|       Standard size ............................................................ | White |
|       +0.2 ........................................................................ | Red |
|       +0.4 ........................................................................ | Blue |
|       +0.6 ........................................................................ | Green |
|       +0.8 ........................................................................ | Black |

## Torque wrench settings (V6 ohv engine)

| | Nm | lbf ft |
|---|---|---|
| Main bearing cap bolts ............................................................ | 90 to 104 | 66 to 77 |
| Big-end cap nuts ...................................................................... | 26 to 33 | 19 to 24 |
| Crankshaft pulley/damper central bolt .................................... | 115 to 130 | 85 to 96 |
| Camshaft gear bolt .................................................................. | 42 to 50 | 31 to 37 |
| Camshaft thrust plate bolts .................................................... | 17 to 21 | 13 to 16 |
| Timing cover to cylinder block ................................................ | 17 to 21 | 13 to 16 |
| Timing cover to intermediate plate ........................................ | 13 to 17 | 10 to 13 |
| Intermediate plate to cylinder block ...................................... | 17 to 21 | 13 to 16 |
| Oil pump to cylinder block ...................................................... | 14 to 17 | 10 to 13 |
| Oil pump cover bolts ................................................................ | 9 to 13 | 7 to 10 |
| Rocker shaft securing bolts .................................................... | 62 to 70 | 46 to 52 |
| Sump bolts: | | |
|    Stage 1 ............................................................................ | 4 to 7 | 3 to 5 |
|    Stage 2 ............................................................................ | 7 to 10 | 5 to 7 |
| Sump drain plug ...................................................................... | 21 to 28 | 16 to 21 |
| Oil pressure switch .................................................................. | 12 to 15 | 9 to 11 |
| Oil cooler threaded sleeve ...................................................... | 20 to 40 | 15 to 30 |
| Cylinder head – hexagon bolts: | | |
|    Stage 1 ............................................................................ | 40 to 45 | 30 to 33 |
|    Stage 2 ............................................................................ | 55 to 70 | 41 to 52 |
|    Stage 3 (after 10 to 20 minutes) .................................... | 95 to 115 | 70 to 85 |
|    Stage 4 (after warm-up) .................................................. | 95 to 115 | 70 to 85 |
| Cylinder head – Torx bolts: | | |
|    Stage 1 ............................................................................ | 35 to 40 | 26 to 30 |
|    Stage 2 ............................................................................ | 70 to 75 | 52 to 55 |
|    Stage 3 (after 5 minutes) ................................................ | Tighten 90° further | Tighten 90° further |
| Rocker cover bolts .................................................................... | 6 to 8 | 4 to 6 |
| Fuel pump blanking plate ........................................................ | 16 to 18 | 12 to 13 |
| Flywheel bolts .......................................................................... | 64 to 70 | 47 to 52 |
| Bellhousing-to-engine bolts .................................................... | 27 to 30 | 20 to 22 |

# PART A IN-LINE OHC ENGINE

## 1   General description

The engine is of four-cylinder, in-line overhead camshaft type. It is mounted longitudinally at the front of the car. Three versions are available: 1.8 litre carburettor, 2.0 litre carburettor and 2.0 litre fuel-injection.

The crankshaft incorporates five main bearings. Thrust washers are fitted to the centre main bearing in order to control crankshaft endfloat.

The camshaft is driven by a toothed belt and operates the slightly angled valve via cam followers which pivot on ball pins.

The auxiliary shaft, which is also driven by the toothed belt, drives the distributor, oil pump and on some models the fuel pump.

The cylinder head is of crossflow design with the inlet manifold mounted on the left-hand side and the exhaust manifold mounted on the right-hand side.

Lubrication is by means of a bi-rotor pump which draws oil through a strainer located inside the sump, and forces it through a full-flow filter into the engine oil galleries where it is distributed to the crankshaft, camshaft and auxiliary shaft. The big-end bearings are supplied with oil via internal drillings in the crankshaft. The undersides of the pistons are supplied with oil from drillings in the big-ends. The distributor shaft is intermittently supplied with oil from the drilled auxiliary shaft. The camshaft and cam followers are supplied with oil via a drilled spray tube from the centre camshaft bearing.

A semi-closed crankcase ventilation system is employed whereby piston blow-by gases are drawn into the inlet manifold via an oil separator and on carburettor models a control valve.

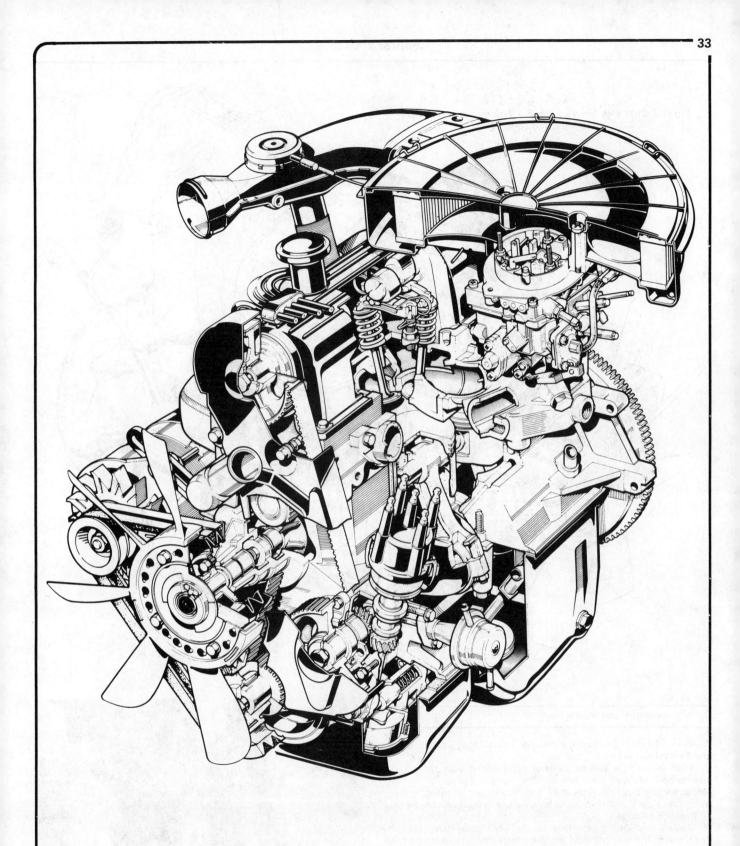

Fig. 1.1 Cutaway view of the 1.8 litre ohc engine with Pierburg carburettor (Sec 1)

**Fig. 1.2 Cutaway view of the 2.0 litre ohc engine with
fuel-injection (Sec 1)**

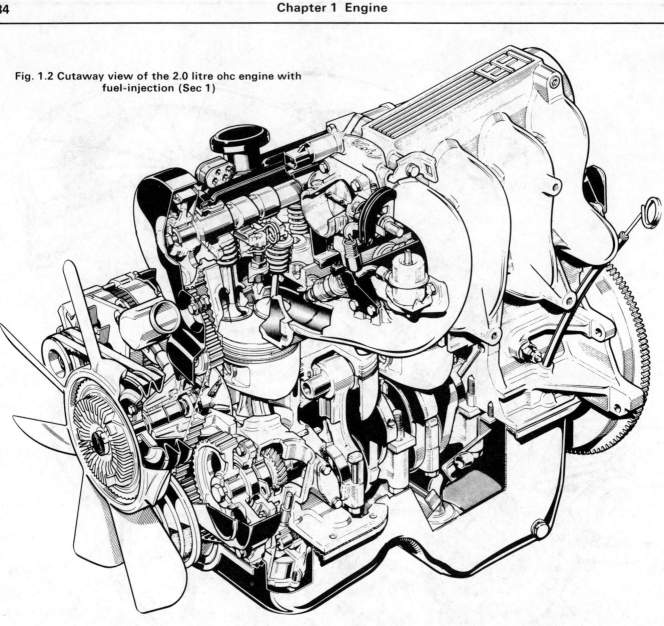

## 2  Maintenance and inspection

1   Every 250 miles (400 km), weekly, or before a long journey, check
the oil level as follows.
2   With the vehicle parked on level ground, and with the engine
having been stopped for a few minutes, open and prop the bonnet.
Withdraw the dipstick, wipe it on a clean rag and re-insert it fully.
Withdraw it again and read the oil level relative to the marks on the end
of the stick (photos).
3   The oil level should be in between the 'MAX' and 'MIN' marks on
the dipstick. If it is at or below the 'MIN' mark, top up (via the oil filler
cap) without delay. The quantity of oil required to raise the lever from
'MIN' to 'MAX' on the dipstick is approximately 1 litre. Do not overfill
(photo).
4   The rate of oil consumption depends on leaks and on the quantity
of oil burnt. External leakage should be obvious. Oil which is burnt may
enter the combustion chambers through the valve guides or past the
piston rings; excessive blow-by past the rings can also force oil out via
the crankcase ventilation system. Driving conditions also affect oil
consumption.
5   Every 6000 miles (10 000 km) or six months, whichever comes
first, drain the engine oil immediately after a run. Park the vehicle on

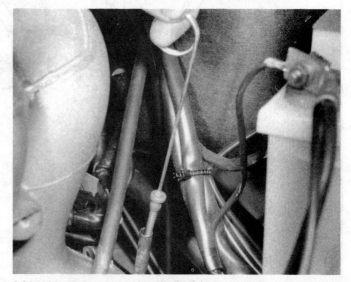

2.2A Withdrawing the engine oil dipstick

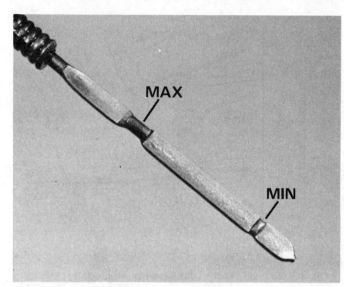

2.2B Dipstick markings

2.3 Topping-up the engine oil

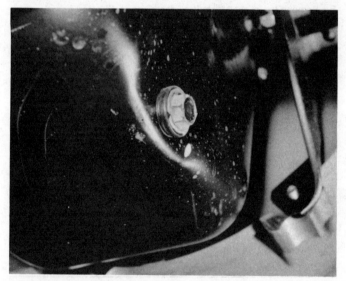

2.5 Sump drain plug

## 3  Major operations possible with the engine in the vehicle

The following operations can be carried out without removing the engine, although the work may be easier and quicker with the engine removed:

(a) Removal and refitting of the cylinder head
(b) Removal and refitting of the camshaft (after removing the cylinder head)
(c) Removal and refitting of the timing belt and sprockets
(d) Removal and refitting of the sump and oil pump
(e) Removal and refitting of the pistons, connecting rods and big-end bearings
(f) Renewal of the engine mountings
(g) Renewal of the crankshaft oil seals
(h) Removal and refitting of the auxiliary shaft
(j) Removal and refitting of the flywheel

## 4  Major operations requiring engine removal

The engine must be removed from the vehicle for the following operations:

(a) Renewal of the crankshaft main bearings
(b) Removal and refitting of the crankshaft

## 5  Methods of engine removal

The engine may be lifted out either on its own or together with the gearbox. Unless work is also necessary on the gearbox it is recommended that the engine is removed on its own. Where automatic transmission is fitted the engine should be removed on its own owing to the additional weight.

If the engine and gearbox are removed together, they will have to be tilted at a very steep angle; make sure that the range of the lifting tackle is adequate.

## 6  Engine – removal alone

1   Disconnect the battery negative lead.
2   Remove the bonnet (Chapter 11, Section 6).
3   On carburettor models, remove the air cleaner (Chapter 3, Section 5) On fuel-injection models, remove the air cleaner cover, vane airflow meter and air inlet trunking (Chapter 3, Section 29).

level ground, position a drain pan of adequate capacity under the sump and remove the drain plug (photo). Allow the oil to drain for at least 15 minutes.
6   Clean the drain plug washer and its seat. Refit and tighten the drain plug, then fill the engine with the correct quantity and grade of oil.
7   Before running the engine, renew the oil filter as described in Section 21. When the engine is next started, there may be a delay in the extinguishing of the oil pressure warning light while the new filter fills with oil. Run the engine and check for leaks from the filter and drain plug, then stop the engine and check the oil level.
8   Every 12 000 miles (20 000 km) or twelve months, whichever comes first, check the valve clearances as described in Section 51 and adjust if necessary.
9   Regularly inspect the engine for leaks of oil, fuel or coolant, and rectify as necessary.
10  For maintenance of the crankcase ventilation system, see Section 25.
11  Although not specified by the manufacturers, consideration should be given to renewing the timing belt as a precautionary measure every 36 000 miles or so. If the belt breaks or slips in service, piston and valve damage will result.

4   If a splash guard is fitted, remove it.
5   Release the securing clips and bolts and remove the upper half of the fan shroud. On carburettor models remove the lower half of the shroud too.
6   Drain the cooling system as described in Chapter 2.
7   Disconnect the radiator top and bottom hoses from the thermostat housing and water pump. Disconnect the top hose spur from the expansion tank and unclip it.
8   Disconnect the heater hoses from the water pump and from the inlet manifold or automatic choke housing. Unclip the hoses.
9   On models with power steering, remove the steering pump, see Chapter 10, Section 15.
10  Disconnect the vacuum pipe(s) from the inlet manifold, labelling them if there is any possibility of confusion.
11  Disconnect the following wiring, as applicable:

   (a)  Alternator
   (b)  Temperature gauge sender
   (c)  Engine management temperature sensor
   (d)  Distributor
   (e)  Oil pressure switch
   (f)  Automatic choke and thermo-switch
   (g)  Carburettor stepper motor
   (h)  Fuel-injection system sub-harness
   (j)  Inlet manifold heater

12  Disconnect the HT lead from the ignition coil.
13  If an oil level sensor is fitted, remove it.
14  Unbolt the throttle cable bracket, disconnect the inner cable and move the cable and bracket aside. Also disconnect the downshift cable on automatic transmission models.
15  On carburettor models, disconnect the fuel lines from the fuel pump (mechanised type) and from the carburettor. **Be prepared for fuel spillage.**
16  On fuel-injection models, disconnect the fuel supply union from the injector rail, and the fuel return pipe from the fuel pressure regulator. **Be prepared for fuel spillage, and for some spray if the supply side is still under pressure.**
17  Unbolt the exhaust downpipe from the manifold.
18  On models with air conditioning, unbolt the compressor and move it aside without straining the flexible hoses.
19  Remove the starter motor (Chapter 12, Section 11).
20  Although not specified by the manufacturers, the author advises that either the radiator or the cooling fan be removed, to reduce the risk of damage. Refer to Chapter 2.
21  Attach the lifting tackle to the two lifting eyes on the engine, so that when suspended the engine will be roughly horizontal. Take the weight of the engine.
22  Remove the single nut on each side which secures each engine bearer to its mounting.
23  Working under the vehicle, remove the bracing strap which connects the engine and transmission. Unbolt the adaptor plate from the bottom of the transmission bellhousing.
24  On automatic transmission models, unbolt the torque converter from the driveplate, see Chapter 6, Section 12.
25  Remove the engine-to-bellhousing bolts. Note the location of the battery earth strap.
26  Support the transmission, preferably with a trolley jack.
27  Check that nothing has been overlooked, then raise the engine and draw it forwards clear of the transmission input shaft. Do not allow the weight of the engine to hang on the shaft, and do not lift the transmission by it.
28  On automatic transmission models, make sure that the torque converter stays engaged with the oil pump in the transmission as the engine is withdrawn.
29  Lift the engine out of the engine bay and take it to the bench.

## 7   Engine – removal with manual gearbox

1   Engine removal with automatic transmission is not recommended – see Section 5.
2   Proceed as in the previous Section, paragraphs 1 to 18.
3   Disconnect the wiring from the starter motor, and release the battery earth cable from its bellhousing bolt.
4   Remove the radiator as described in Chapter 2.

Fig. 1.3 Oil level sensor (not fitted to all models) (Sec 6)

5   Remove the propeller shaft as described in Chapter 7.
6   Disconnect and unclip the reversing light switch and speedometer sender unit wiring.
7   Disconnect the clutch cable as described in Chapter 5.
8   Unbolt the anti-roll bar mounting brackets and lower the anti-roll bar as far as possible.
9   From inside the vehicle remove the gear lever, see Chapter 6, Section 3.
10  Drain the engine oil.
11  Unhook the exhaust system from its mounting on the gearbox crossmember. Either support the system or remove it completely.
12  Support the gearbox, preferably with a trolley jack, then unbolt and remove the gearbox crossmember. Note the earth strap (if fitted) under one of the crossmember bolts.
13  Attach lifting tackle to the two lifting eyes on the engine so that when suspended it will be at an angle of approximately 45°.
14  Take the weight of the engine and remove the two engine bearer-to-mounting nuts.
15  Lift the engine/transmission unit, at the same time lowering the trolley jack. Draw the unit forwards and lift it out of the engine bay.
16  Temporarily refit the anti-roll bar if the vehicle is to be moved.

## 8   Engine – separation from gearbox

1   With the engine and gearbox on the bench, remove the starter motor.
2   Remove the bolt from the engine adaptor plate.
3   Remove the bracing strap and the remaining engine-to-bellhousing bolts.
4   With the aid of an assistant draw the gearbox off the engine. Do not allow the weight of the gearbox to hang on the input shaft.

## 9   Engine dismantling – general

1   It is best to mount the engine on a dismantling stand, but if this is not available, stand the engine on a strong bench at a comfortable working height. Failing this, it will have to be stripped down on the floor.
2   Cleanliness is most important, and if the engine is dirty, it should be cleaned with paraffin while keeping it in an upright position.
3   Avoid working with the engine directly on a concrete floor, as grit presents a real source of trouble.
4   As parts are removed, clean them in a paraffin bath. However, do not immerse parts with internal oilways in paraffin as it is difficult to remove, usually requiring a high pressure hose. Clean oilways with nylon pipe cleaners.

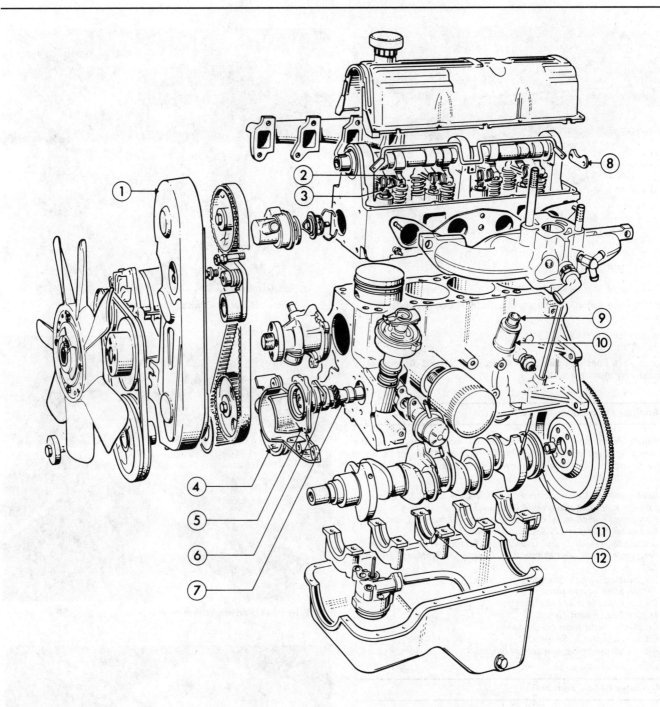

**Fig. 1.4 Exploded view of the ohc engine (Sec 9)**

| | | |
|---|---|---|
| 1 Timing cover | 4 Crankshaft front oil seal | 6 Thrust plate | 10 Oil separator |
| 2 Cam follower | housing | 7 Auxiliary shaft | 11 Crankshaft rear oil seal |
| 3 Retaining spring clip | 5 Auxiliary shaft front cover | 8 Thrust plate | 12 Thrust washer |
| | | 9 Vent valve | |

5   It is advisable to have suitable containers to hold small items according to their use, as this will help when reassembling the engine and also prevent possible losses.

6   Always obtain complete sets of gaskets when the engine is being dismantled, but retain the old gaskets with a view of using them as a pattern to make a replacement if a new one is not available.

7   When possible, refit nuts, bolts and washers in their location after being removed, as this helps protect the threads and will also be helpful when reassembling the engine.

8   Retain unserviceable components in order to compare them with the new parts supplied.

9   A 'Torx' key, size T55, will be needed for dealing with the cylinder head bolts. A 12-spline key (to fit bolt size M8) will be needed for the oil pump bolts. Other 'Torx' and 12-spline bolts may be encountered; sets of the keys required to deal with them are available from most motor accessory shops and tool factors.

10   Another tool which is useful, though by no means essential, is a valve spring compressor of the type which hooks under the camshaft

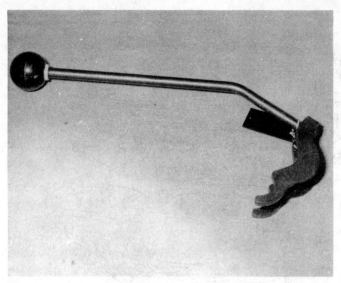

9.10 This valve spring compressor is used by hooking it under the camshaft

10.1A Engine oil pressure switch (arrowed)

(photo). As a Ford tool this bears the number 21-005-A; proprietary versions may also be available.

## 10 Ancillary components – removal

1 Before dismantling the engine into its main components, the following ancillary components can be removed. The actual items removed, and the sequence of removal, will depend on the work to be done:

> Inlet manifold and associated items (Chapter 3, Section 32)
> Exhaust manifold (Chapter 3, Section 33)
> Fuel pump (mechanical type) and pushrod (Chapter 3, Section 7)
> Alternator (Chapter 12, Section 8)
> Distributor, HT leads and spark plugs (Chapter 4, Sections 3 to 5)
> Fan, water pump and thermostat (Chapter 2, Sections 9, 11 and 12)
> Oil pressure switch (photo)
> Temperature gauge sender
> Oil filter (Section 21) and dipstick
> Engine bearer arms (photo)
> Crankcase ventilation components
> Clutch (Chapter 5, Section 5)
> Alternator mounting bracket (photo)

10.1B Removing an engine bearer arm

## 11 Cylinder head – removal

If the engine is still in the vehicle, carry out the following preliminary operations:

(a) Disconnect the battery negative lead
(b) Drain the cooling system (Chapter 2, Section 3)
(c) Remove the inlet and exhaust manifolds (Chapter 3, Sections 32 and 33)
(d) Disconnect the radiator top hose from the thermostat housing, and the spur from the expansion tank
(e) Disconnect the wiring from the temperature gauge sender
(f) Remove the distributor cap, HT leads and spark plugs (Chapter 4, Sections 3 and 4)

1 Unscrew the bolts and withdraw the timing cover (photo). Note the location of the cover in the special bolt.
2 Using a socket on the crankshaft pulley bolt, turn the engine clockwise until the TDC (top dead centre) notch on the pulley is aligned with the pointer on the crankshaft front oil seal housing, and the pointer on the camshaft sprocket is aligned with the indentation on

10.1C Removing the alternator bracket

11.1 Removing the timing cover

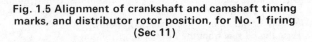

the cylinder head (photo). Note the position of the distributor rotor arm, and mark its contact end in relation to the rim of the distributor body.

3   Slacken the timing belt tensioner bolts. Pivot the tensioner to release the load on the belt and slip the belt off the camshaft sprocket. Do not kink the belt, or get oil or grease on it.

4   Remove the ten bolts which secure the rocker cover, noting the location of the different shapes of reinforcing plates (photos). Remove the cover and gasket.

5   Using the 'Torx' key (Section 9), slacken the cylinder head bolts half a turn at a time in the reverse of the tightening sequence (Fig. 1.16).

6   With the bolts removed, lift the cylinder head from the block (photo). If it is stuck, tap it with a wooden or plastic mallet to free it. **Do not** lever between the head and block, or the mating surfaces may be damaged. **Do not** crank the engine to free the head, as the pistons may contact the valves.

7   Place the cylinder head on a couple of wooden blocks so that the protruding valves are not damaged.

Fig. 1.5 Alignment of crankshaft and camshaft timing marks, and distributor rotor position, for No. 1 firing (Sec 11)

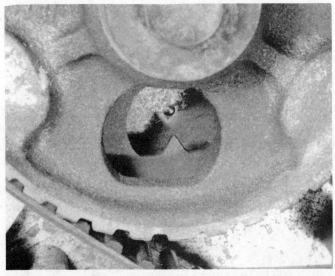

11.2 Camshaft sprocket pointer aligned with the indentation on the cylinder head

11.4A Rocker cover bolts and reinforcing plates – sprocket end

11.4B Rocker cover bolts and reinforcing plates – flywheel end

11.6 Removing the cylinder head

## 12 Camshaft – removal

1   Remove the cylinder head as described in the previous Section.
2   Hold the camshaft with a spanner on the lug behind the sixth cam. Unscrew and remove the camshaft sprocket bolt (photo).
3   Remove the camshaft sprocket using a puller if necessary. Remove the backplate (photos).
4   Unscrew the bolts and remove the camshaft oil supply tube (photos).
5   Note how the cam follower retaining spring clips are fitted, then unhook them from the cam followers (photo).
6   If the special tool 21-005-A is available, compress the valve springs in turn and remove the cam followers, keeping them identified for location. Alternatively loosen the locknuts and back off the ball-pins until the cam followers can be removed (photo).
7   Unscrew the bolts and remove the camshaft thrust plate (photos).
8   Carefully withdraw the camshaft from the rear of the cylinder head, taking care not to damage the bearings (photo).
9   Prise the oil seal from the front bearing (photo).

12.2 Removing the camshaft sprocket bolt

12.3A Removing the camshaft sprocket

12.3B Removing the camshaft sprocket backplate

12.4A Undoing the camshaft oil supply tube centre bolt

12.4B Removing the camshaft oil supply tube

12.5 Cam followers and spring clips

12.6 Removing the cam followers

12.7A Unscrewing the camshaft thrust plate bolts

12.7B Removing the camshaft thrust plate

12.8 Removing the camshaft

12.9 Prising out the camshaft bearing oil seal

## 13 Cylinder head – dismantling

1   Remove the camshaft as described in the previous Section. (If tool 21-005-A is available, leave the camshaft in place until the valves have been removed).

2   Using a valve spring compressor, compress each valve spring in turn until the split collets can be removed. Release the compressor and remove the cap and spring, keeping them identified for location (photos). If the caps are difficult to release do not continue to tighten the compressor, but gently tap the top of the tool with a hammer. Always make sure that the compressor is held firmly over the cap.

3   Remove each valve from the cylinder head, keeping them identified for location (photo).

4   Prise the valve stem oil seals from the tops of the valve guides (photo).

5   If necessary unscrew the cam follower ball-pins from the cylinder head, keeping them identified for location.

6   If necessary unscrew the bolts and remove the timing belt tensioner.

13.2A Compressing a valve spring

13.2B Removing a valve spring and cap

13.3 Removing a valve

13.4 Removing a valve stem oil seal

14.3 Timing belt tensioner bolts (arrowed)

7   Remove the thermostat housing and thermostat, referring if necessary to Chapter 2.
8   Remove the temperature gauge sender unit.
9   Remove the manifold studs if wished by locking two nuts onto each stud in turn and unscrewing it.

## 14  Timing belt and sprockets – removal

If the engine is still in the vehicle, carry out the following preliminary operations:

(a) *Disconnect the battery negative lead*
(b) *Remove the radiator (Chapter 2, Section 7) and disconnect the hose from the thermostat housing*
(c) *Remove the accessory drivebelt(s) (Chapter 2, Section 13)*

1   Unscrew the bolts and withdraw the timing cover. Note the location of the cover in the special bolt.
2   Using a socket on the crankshaft pulley bolt, turn the engine clockwise until the TDC (top dead centre) notch on the pulley is aligned with the pointer on the crankshaft front oil seal housing, and the pointer on the camshaft sprocket is aligned with the indentation on the cylinder head. Note the position of the distributor rotor arm. Mark the contact end of the rotor in relation to the rim of the distributor body.
4   Mark the running direction of the belt if it is to be re-used, then slip it off the camshaft sprocket.
5   Slacken the crankshaft pulley bolt. Prevent the crankshaft from turning by engaging 5th gear (manual gearbox), or by removing the starter motor and jamming the ring gear teeth. Alternatively, if the pulley has peripheral bolt holes, screw in a couple of bolts and use a lever between them to jam it. Do not allow the crankshaft to turn very far, or piston/valve contact may occur.
6   Remove the bolt and washer and withdraw the pulley. If the pulley will not come off easily, refit the bolt part way and use a puller (photo). A puller will almost certainly be required on fuel-injection models.
7   Remove the guide washer from in front of the crankshaft sprocket, then remove the timing belt (photo). Do not kink it or get oil on it if it is to be re-used.
8   Remove the crankshaft sprocket using a puller if necessary (photo).
9   Unscrew the auxiliary shaft sprocket bolt while holding the sprocket stationary with a screwdriver inserted through one of the holes.
10  Remove the auxiliary shaft sprocket using a puller if necessary (photo).

14.6 Using a puller to remove the crankshaft pulley

14.7 Remove the guide washer from in front of the crankshaft sprocket

14.8 Removing the crankshaft sprocket

14.10 Removing the auxiliary shaft sprocket

11 Unscrew the camshaft sprocket bolt while holding the sprocket stationary with a screwdriver engaged in one of the grooves. Alternatively remove the rocker cover and use a spanner on the camshaft lug.
12 Remove the camshaft sprocket using a puller if necessary, then remove the backplate. Note that the oil seal can be removed using a special removal tool or by using self-tapping screws and a pair of grips.

## 15 Auxiliary shaft – removal

1   Remove the timing belt and the auxiliary shaft sprocket (only), as described in the previous Section.
2   Remove the distributor (Chapter 4, Section 5).
3   Remove the fuel pump and pushrod (Chapter 3, Section 7 – not applicable to models with an electric pump).
4   Unscrew the bolts and remove the auxiliary shaft front cover (photos).
5   Unscrew the cross-head screws using an impact screwdriver if

15.4A Auxiliary shaft front cover (engine inverted)

15.4B Removing the auxiliary shaft front cover

15.5A Auxiliary shaft thrust plate screws (arrowed)

15.5B Removing the auxiliary shaft thrust plate

15.5C Removing the auxiliary shaft

necessary, remove the thrust plate and withdraw the auxiliary shaft from the block (photos).
6   Cut the front cover gasket along the top of the crankshaft front oil seal housing and scrape off the gasket.

## 16  Flywheel/driveplate and adaptor plate – removal

If the engine is still in the vehicle, remove the clutch (Chapter 5, Section 5) or the automatic transmission (Chapter 6, Section 12).
1   Prevent the flywheel or driveplate rotating by jamming the ring gear teeth, or by bolting a strap to it – see Section 41.
2   Remove the securing bolts and withdraw the flywheel or driveplate. *Do not drop it, it is heavy.*
3   The engine adaptor plate (backplate) may now be withdrawn from the dowels if required (photo).

## 17  Sump – removal

If the engine is out of the vehicle, start at paragraph 10. If possible, remove the sump without inverting the engine, so that any sludge in the bottom of the sump stays there.
1   Disconnect the battery negative lead.
2   Raise and support the front of the vehicle.
3   Remove the splash guard, if fitted, and drain the engine oil.

4   Remove the starter motor (Chapter 12, Section 11).
5   Remove the two nuts which secure the engine bearers to the engine mountings.
6   Release the steering shaft universal joint strap bolt to allow for subsequent movement.
7   Free the brake hydraulic pipes from the clips on the front crossmember.
8   Support the engine, either with conventional lifting tackle or with a bar positioned across the engine bay and resting on two wooden blocks drilled to fit securely on the suspension turrets. Make sure the support arrangements are satisfactory, as you will be working underneath the suspended engine.
9   Take the weight of the engine. Place a jack under the front crossmember, remove the crossmember mounting bolts and carefully lower the jack. Only lower the crossmember far enough to permit removal of the sump.
10  Remove the 23 bolts which retain the sump (photo).
11  Remove the sump from the cylinder block (photo). If it is stuck, hit it with a soft-faced mallet, or prise it sideways (**not** between the mating faces) with a large screwdriver or bar.
12  Recover the gaskets and sealing strips.

## 18  Crankshaft front oil seal – renewal

1   Remove the timing belt and the crankshaft sprocket (only) as described in Section 14.

16.3 Removing the engine adaptor plate (backplate)

17.10 Removing a sump retaining bolt

17.11 Removing the sump

2   If an oil seal removal tool is available, the oil seal can be removed at this stage. It may also be possible to remove the oil seal by drilling the outer face and using self-tapping screws and a pair of grips.

3   If the oil seal cannot be removed as described in paragraph 2, remove the sump as described in Section 17. Also remove the auxiliary shaft sprocket (Section 14). Unbolt the oil seal housing and auxiliary shaft front cover and remove the gasket. The oil seal can then be driven out from the inside (photos).

4   Clean the oil seal seating, then drive in a new seal using metal tubing or a suitable socket (photo). Make sure that the sealing lip faces into the engine, and lightly oil the lip.

5   If applicable fit the oil seal housing and auxiliary shaft front cover to the block together with a new gasket and tighten the bolts. Make sure that the bottom face of the housing is aligned with the bottom face of the block (photos). Fit the sump as described in Section 40.

6   Refit the timing belt and sprockets as described in Section 46.

### 19 Crankshaft rear oil seal – renewal

1   Remove the flywheel or driveplate and the engine adaptor plate (backplate) as described in Section 16.

18.3A Removing the crankshaft front oil seal housing

18.3B Driving the oil seal out of the housing

18.4 Using a socket and a hammer to seat the new seal

18.5A Oil seal housing and auxiliary shaft cover gasket in position

18.5B Checking the alignment of the front oil seal housing

19.2 Crankshaft rear oil seal location

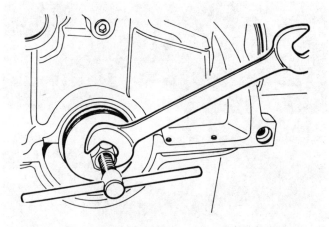

**Fig. 1.6 Using an oil seal removal tool to extract the crankshaft rear oil seal (Sec 19)**

2    Using a special removal tool extract the oil seal. However it may be possible to remove the oil seal by drilling the outer face and using self-tapping screws and a pair of grips (photo).

3    Clean the oil seal seating, then drive in a new seal using a suitable metal tube. Make sure that the sealing lip faces into the engine, and lightly oil the lip.

4    Refit the adaptor plate and the flywheel/driveplate as described in Section 41.

## 20  Oil pump – removal

1    Remove the sump as described in Section 17.

2    Unscrew the bolt securing the pick-up tube and strainer to the block (photo).

3    Using a special splined key, (see Section 9), unscrew the bolts and withdraw the oil pump and strainer (photo).

4    Withdraw the hexagon shaped driveshaft which engages the bottom of the distributor, noting which way round it is fitted (photo).

20.2 Unbolting the oil pump pick-up strainer from the block

20.3 Removing the splined bolts which secure the oil pump

20.4 Removing the oil pump driveshaft

21.1 Oil filter location (manifold and distributor removed)

21.4 Fitting an oil filter

## 21 Oil filter – renewal

1   The oil filter should be renewed at every oil change. It is located on
the left-hand side of the cylinder block, in front of the engine bearer
(photo). Access is probably easiest from below.
2   Place a drain pan under the filter and remove the filter, using a
chain or strap wrench to slacken it and then unscrewing it by hand. If a
suitable wrench is not available, drive a large screwdriver through the
filter and use that as a lever to unscrew it. Be prepared for oil spillage.
3   Wipe clean the filter mounting face on the block.
4   Smear a little oil or grease onto the sealing ring of the new filter.
Screw the filter onto the threaded tube and tighten it by hand only
(photo). If there are no specific instructions with the filter, tighten it
until the sealing ring contacts the block, then tighten a further
three-quarters of a turn.
5   Check for leaks when the engine is next run.

## 22 Pistons and connecting rods – removal

1   Remove the sump as described in Section 17, and the cylinder
head as described in Section 11.
2   Check the big-end caps for identification marks and if necessary
use a centre-punch to identify the caps and connecting rods (photo).
3   Turn the crankshaft so that No 1 crankpin is at its lowest point, then
unscrew the nuts and tap off the cap. Keep the bearing shells in the cap
and connecting rod.
4   Using the handle of a hammer, push the piston and connecting rod
up the bore and withdraw from the top of the cylinder block. Loosely
refit the cap to the connecting rod (photo).
5   Repeat the procedure in paragraphs 3 and 4 on the No 4 piston and
connecting rod, then turn the crankshaft through half a turn and repeat
the procedure on Nos 2 and 3 pistons and connecting rods.

## 23 Crankshaft and main bearings – removal

1   With the engine removed from the vehicle, remove the pistons and
connecting rods as described in the previous Section. (In fact it is not
necessary to push the pistons out of the bores if no work is to be done
on them.)
2   Remove the timing belt and crankshaft sprocket (Section 14), and
the flywheel or driveplate (Section 16). Also remove the auxiliary shaft
sprocket.
3   Unbolt the crankshaft front oil seal housing and auxiliary shaft front
cover and remove the gasket.

22.2 Big-end cap and connecting rod identification numbers

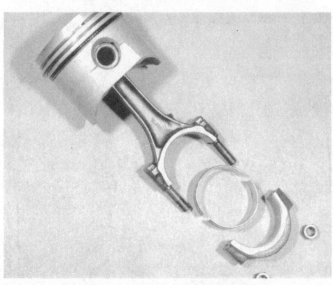

22.4 Piston, connecting rod, cap and bearing shells

23.5 Main bearing cap identification marks. The arrow points to the front of the engine

23.6 Checking crankshaft endfloat

4   Remove the oil pump and strainer as described in Section 20.
5   Check the main bearing caps for identification marks and if necessary use a centre-punch to identify them (photo).
6   Before removing the crankshaft check that the endfloat is within the specified limits by inserting a feeler blade between the centre crankshaft web and the thrust washers (photo). This will indicate whether new thrust washers are required or not.

7   Unscrew the bolts and tap off the main bearing caps complete with bearing shells (photos). If the thrust washers are to be re-used identify them for location.
8   Lift the crankshaft from the crankcase and remove the rear oil seal. Remove the remaining thrust washers (photos).
9   Extract the bearing shells keeping them identified for location (photo).

23.7A Removing the centre main bearing cap

23.7B Removing the rear main bearing cap

23.8A Removing the crankshaft

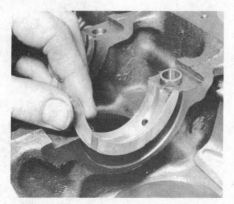

23.8B Removing a thrust washer from the centre main bearing

23.9 Removing the centre main bearing shell

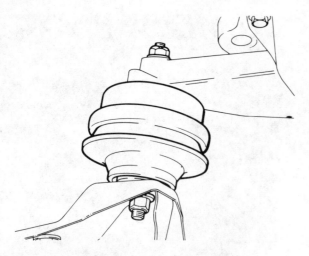

**Fig. 1.7 An engine mounting (Sec 24)**

## 24 Engine mountings – renewal

1   Unscrew the two nuts which secure the engine bearers to the tops of the mountings. Recover the washers.
2   Raise and support the front of the vehicle. Remove the two nuts which secure the mountings to the front crossmember. Recover the washers.
3   Raise the engine with a hoist or a suitable protected jack until the mountings are free, then remove them.
4   Fit the new mountings and lower the engine onto them.
5   Fit the nuts and washers and tighten the nuts.
6   Lower the vehicle.

## 25 Crankcase ventilation system – description and maintenance

### Carburettor models
1   The crankcase ventilation system consists of the special oil filter cap, containing a steel wool filter, and an oil separator and vent valve on the left-hand side of the engine. This is connected by hose to the inlet manifold. The system operates according to the vacuum in the inlet manifold. Air is drawn through the filler cap, through the crankcase, and then together with piston blow-by gasses through the oil separator and vent valve to the inlet manifold. The blow-by gases are then drawn into the engine together with the fuel/air mixture.
2   Every 6000 miles (10 000 km) clean the oil filler cap with paraffin.
3   Regularly inspect the hose for blockage or damage; clean or renew as necessary. A blocked hose can cause a build-up of crankcase pressure, which in turn can cause oil leaks.
4   Every 24 000 miles (40 000 km) renew the vent valve by pulling it from the oil separator and loosening the hose clip (photos). Fit the new valve, tighten the clip, and insert it into the oil separator grommet.

### Fuel-injection models
5   The system is closed, consisting of an oil separator on the left-hand side of the engine and a hose connecting it to the inlet air trunking. Because the trunking is not subject to manifold vacuum, no vent valve is needed.
6   Check the condition of the hose occasionally (paragraph 3).

## 26 Examination and renovation – general

With the engine completely stripped, clean all the components and examine them for wear. Each part should be checked, and where necessary renewed or renovated as described in the following Sections. Renew main and big end shell bearings as a matter of course, unless you know that they have had little wear and are in perfect condition.

If in doubt as to whether to renew a component which is still just serviceable, consider the time and effort which will be incurred should it fail at an early date. Obviously the age and expected life of the vehicle must influence the standards applied.

Gaskets, oil seals and O-rings must all be renewed as a matter of routine. Flywheel and cylinder head bolts must be renewed because of the high stresses to which they are subjected.

Take the opportunity to renew the engine core plugs while they are easily accessible. Knock out the old plugs with a hammer and chisel or punch. Clean the plug seats, smear the new plugs with sealant and tap them squarely into position.

## 27 Oil pump – examination and renovation

1   Unscrew the bolts and remove the oil pump cover (photo).
2   Using feeler gauges check that the rotor clearances are within the limits given in Specifications (photos). If not, unbolt the pick-up tube

25.4A Pulling the vent valve from the oil separator

25.4B Vent valve attached to crankcase ventilation hose

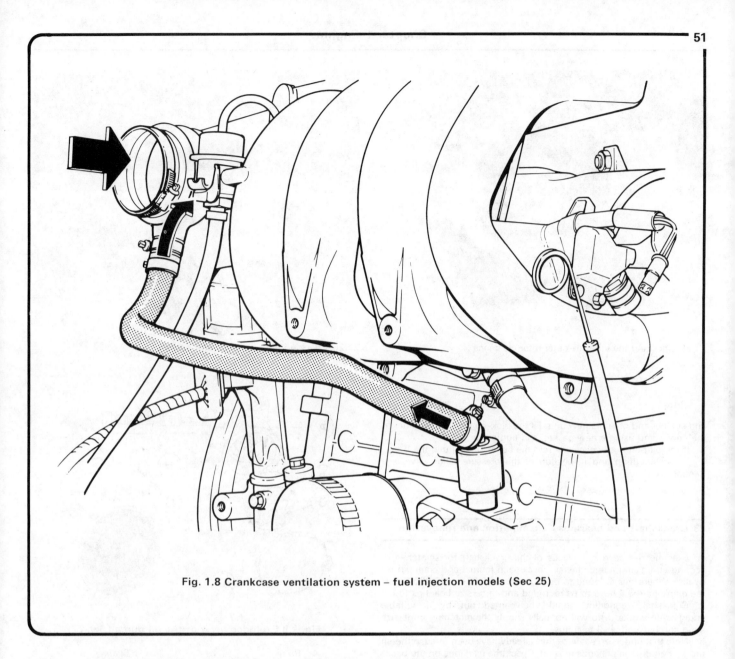

Fig. 1.8 Crankcase ventilation system – fuel injection models (Sec 25)

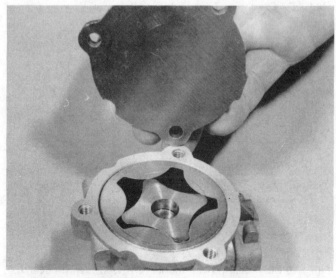

27.1 Removing the oil pump cover

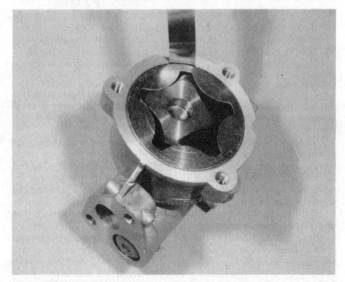

27.2A Checking the outer rotor-to-housing clearance

27.2B Checking the inner-to-outer rotor clearance

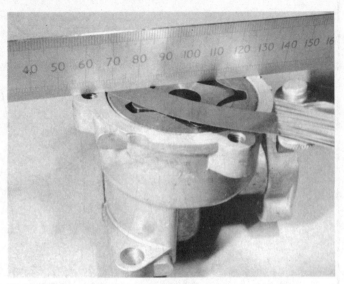

27.2C Checking the oil pump rotor endfloat

and strainer and obtain a new unit. Fit the pick-up tube and strainer to the new pump using a new gasket, and tighten the bolts.
3   If the oil pump is serviceable refit the cover and tighten the bolts.
4   For dismantling and inspection of the pressure relief valve, see Section 81.

## 28  Crankshaft and bearings – examination and renovation

1   Examine the bearing surfaces of the crankshaft for scratches or scoring and, using a micrometer, check each journal and crankpin for ovality. Where this is found to be in excess of 0.001 in (0.0254 mm) the crankshaft will have to be reground and undersize bearings fitted.
2   Crankshaft regrinding should be carried out by a suitable engineering works, who will normally supply the matching undersize main and big-end shell bearings.
3   Note that undersize bearings may already have been fitted, either in production or by a previous repairer. Check the markings on the backs of the old bearing shells, and if in doubt take them along when buying new ones. Production undersizes are also indicated by paint marks as follows:

   *White line on main bearing cap – parent bore 0.40 mm oversize*
   *Green line on crankshaft front counterweight – main bearing journals 0.25 mm undersize*
   *Green spot on counterweight – big-end bearing journals 0.25 mm undersize*

4   If the crankshaft endfloat is more than the maximum specified amount, new thrust washers should be fitted to the centre main bearings. These are usually supplied together with the main and big-end bearings on a reground crankshaft.
5   An accurate method of determining bearing wear is by the use of Plastigage. The crankshaft is located in the main bearings (and big-end bearings if necessary) and the Plastigage filament located across the journal which must be dry. The cap is then fitted and the bolts/nuts tightened to the specified torque. On removal of the cap the width of the filaments is checked against a scale which shows the bearing running clearance. This clearance is then compared with that given in the Specifications (photos).
6   If the spigot bearing in the rear of the crankshaft requires renewal extract it with a suitable puller. Alternatively fill it with heavy grease and use a close fitting metal dowel driven into the centre of the bearing. Drive the new bearing into the crankshaft with a soft metal drift.

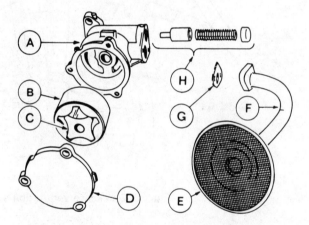

### Fig. 1.9 Exploded view of the oil pump (Sec 27)

A  Body
B  Outer rotor
C  Inner rotor
D  Cover
E  Strainer
F  Pick-up tube
G  Gasket
H  Relief valve

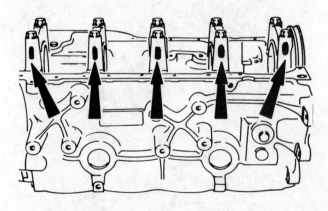

### Fig. 1.10 Main bearing cap marks (arrowed) denote oversize parent bore (Sec 28)

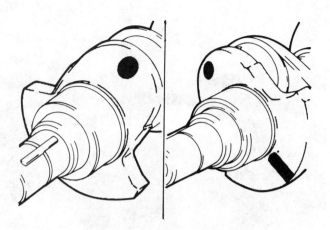

**Fig. 1.11 Undersize crankshaft bearings are indicated by a spot and/or line on the front counterweight (Sec 28)**

28.5A Flattened Plastigage filament (arrowed)

28.5B Checking the width of the filament against the scale on the packet

### 29 Cylinder block and bores – examination and renovation

1   The cylinder bores must be examined for taper, ovality, scoring and scratches. Start by examining the top of the bores; if these are worn, a slight ridge will be found which marks the top of the piston ring travel. If the wear is excessive, the engine will have had a high oil consumption rate accompanied by blue smoke from the exhaust.
2   If available, use an inside dial gauge to measure the bore diameter just below the ridge and compare it with the diameter at the bottom of the bore, which is not subject to wear. If the difference is more than 0.006 in (0.152 mm), the cylinders will normally require reboring with new oversize pistons fitted.
3   Proprietary oil control rings can be obtained for fitting to the existing pistons if it is felt that the degree of wear does not justify a rebore. However, any improvement brought about by such rings may be short-lived.
4   If new pistons or piston rings are to be fitted to old bores, deglaze the bores with abrasive paper or a 'glaze buster'' tool. The object is to produce a light cross-hatch pattern to assist the new rings to bed in.
5   If there is a ridge at the top of the bore and new piston rings are being fitted, either the top piston ring must be stepped ('ridge dodger' pattern) or the ridge must be removed with a ridge reamer. If the ridge is left, the piston ring may hit it and break.
6   Thoroughly examine the crankcase and cylinder block for cracks and damage and use a piece of wire to probe all oilways and waterways to ensure they are unobstructed.

### 30 Pistons and connecting rods – examination and renovation

1   Examine the pistons for ovality, scoring and scratches. Check the connecting rods for wear and damage. The connecting rods carry a letter indicating their weight class; all the rods fitted to one engine must be of the same class.
2   The gudgeon pins are an interference fit in the connecting rods, and if new pistons are to be fitted to the existing connecting rods the work should be carried out by a Ford garage who will have the necessary tooling. Note that the oil splash hole on the connecting rod must be located on the right-hand side of the piston (the arrow on the piston crown faces forwards).
3   If new rings are to be fitted to the existing pistons, expand the old rings over the top of the pistons. The use of two or three old feeler blades will be helpful in preventing the rings dropping into empty grooves. Note that the oil control ring is in three sections.
4   Before fitting the new rings to the pistons, insert them into the cylinder bore and use a feeler gauge to check that the end gaps are within the speciied limits (photos).
5   Clean out the piston ring grooves using a piece of old piston ring as a scraper. be careful not to scratch the aluminium surface of the pistons. Protect your fingers – piston ring edges are sharp. Also probe the groove oil return holes.

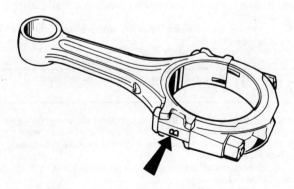

**Fig. 1.12 Weight class mark (arrowed) on connecting rod (Sec 30)**

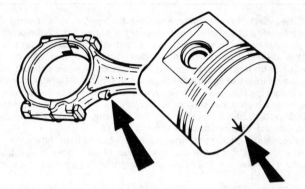

Fig. 1.13 Correct relationship of piston crown arrow and connecting rod oil splash hole (arrows) (Sec 30)

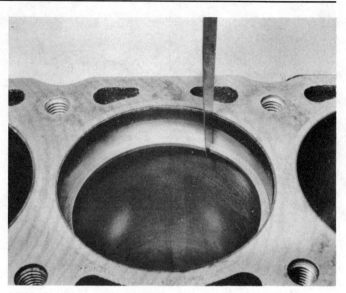

30.4A Checking a piston ring gap at the top of the cylinder

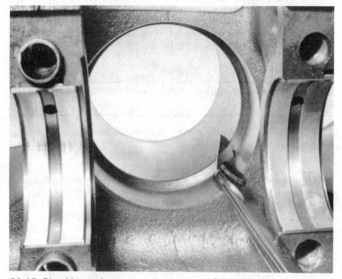

30.4B Checking a ring gap at the bottom of the cylinder

6   Fit the oil control ring sections with the spreader ends abutted opposite the front of the piston. The side ring gaps should be 25 mm (1.0 in) either side of the spreader gap. Fit the tapered lower compression ring with the 'TOP' mark towards the top of the piston and the gap 150° from the spreader gap, then fit the upper compression ring with the gap 150° on the other side of the spreader gap. Note that the compression rings are coated with a molybdenum skin which must not be damaged.
7   Note that the compression rings are made of cast iron, and will snap if expanded too far.

## 31 Camshaft and cam followers – examination and renovation

1   Examine the surface of the camshaft journals and lobes and the cam followers for wear. If excessive, considerable noise would have been noticed from the top of the engine and a new camshaft and followers must be fitted.
2   Check the camshaft bearings for wear and if necessary have them renewed by a Ford garage.
3   Check the camshaft lubrication tube for obstructions and make sure that the jet holes are clear. Obstruction of the holes can be due to sludge build-up which occurs when regular oil changes have been neglected.

## 32 Auxiliary shaft – examination and renovation

1   Examine the auxiliary shaft for wear and damage and renew it if necessary.
2   If the auxiliary shaft endfloat is outside the limits given in the Specifications fit a new thrust plate. If this does not bring the endfloat within limits, renew the shaft.

## 33 Timing belt – examination and renovation

Whenever the timing belt is removed it is worthwhile renewing it especially if it has covered a high mileage. This is more important on the 2.0 litre engine where stripped teeth on the timing belt can cause the pistons to foul the valves.

## 34 Flywheel ring gear – examination and renovation

1   If the ring gear is badly worn or has missing teeth it should be renewed. The old ring can be removed from the flywheel by cutting a notch between two teeth with a hacksaw and then splitting it with a cold chisel. Wear eye protection when doing this.
2   To fit a new ring gear requires heating the ring to 400°F (204°C). This can be done by polishing four equal spaces sections of the gear, laying it on a suitable heat resistant surface (such as fire bricks) and heating it evenly with a blow lamp or torch until the polished areas turn a light yellow tinge. Do not overheat or the hard wearing properties will be lost. The gear has a chamfered inner edge which should go against the shoulder when put on the flywheel. When hot enough place the gear in position quickly, tapping it home if necessary and let it cool naturally without quenching in any way.

## 35 Cylinder head – decarbonising, valve grinding and renovation

1   This operation will normally only be required at comparatively high mileages. However, if persistent pinking occurs and performance has deteriorated even though the engine adjustments are correct, decarbonising and valve grinding may be required.
2   With the cylinder head removed, use a scraper to remove the carbon from the combustion chambers and ports. Remove all traces of gasket from the cylinder head surface, then wash it thoroughly with paraffin.

3   Use a straight-edge and feeler blade to check that the cylinder head surface is not distorted. If it is, it must be resurfaced by a suitably equipped engineering works.

4   If the engine is still in the car, clean the piston crowns and cylinder bore upper edges, but make sure that no carbon drops between the pistons and bores. To do this, locate two of the pistons at the top of their bores and seal off the remaining bores with paper and masking tape. Press a little grease between the two pistons and their bores to collect any carbon dust; this can be wiped away when the piston is lowered. To prevent carbon build-up, polish the piston crown with metal polish, but remove all traces of the polish afterwards.

5   Examine the heads of the valves for pitting and burning, especially the exhaust valve heads. Renew any valve which is badly burnt. Examine the valve seats at the same time. If the pitting is very slight, it can be removed by grinding the valve heads and seats together with coarse, then fine, grinding paste.

6   Where excessive pitting has occurred, the valve seats must be recut or renewed by a suitably equipped engineering works.

7   Valve grinding is carried out as follows. Place the cylinder head upside down on a bench on blocks of wood.

8   Smear a trace of coarse carborundum paste on the seat face and press a suction grinding tool onto the valve head. With a semi-rotary action, grind the valve head to its seat, lifting the valve occasionally to redistribute the grinding paste. When a dull matt even surface is produced on both the valve seat and the valve, wipe off the paste and repeat the process with fine carborundum paste as before. A light spring placed under the valve head will greatly ease this operation. When a smooth unbroken ring of light grey matt finish is produced on both the valve and seat, the grinding operation is complete.

9   Scrape away all carbon from the valve head and stem, and clean away all traces of grinding compound. Clean the valves and seats with a paraffin soaked rag, then wipe with a clean rag.

10   If the guides are worn they will need reboring for oversize valves or for fitting guide inserts. The valve seats will also need recutting to ensure they are concentric with the stems. This work should be given to your Ford dealer or local engineering works.

11   If the valve springs have been in use for 20 000 miles (32 000 km) or more, renew them. Always renew the valve stem oil seals when the valves are removed.

## 36 Engine reassembly – general

1   To ensure maximum life with minimum trouble from a rebuilt engine, not only must everything be correctly assembled, but it must also be spotlessly clean. All oilways must be clear, and locking washers and spring washers must be fitted where indicated. Oil all bearings and other working surfaces thoroughly with engine oil during assembly.

2   Before assembly begins, renew any bolts or studs with damaged threads.

3   Gather together a torque wrench, oil can, clean rag, and a set of engine gaskets and oil seals, together with a new oil filter (photo).

4   If they have been removed, new cylinder head bolts and flywheel bolts will also be required.

## 37 Crankshaft and main bearings – refitting

1   Wipe the bearing shell locations in the crankcase with a soft, non-fluffy rag.

2   Wipe the crankshaft journals with a soft, non-fluffy rag.

3   Fit the five upper half main bearing shells to their locations in the crankcase. If the old shells are being re-used, make sure they are refitted to their old locations.

4   Identify each main bearing cap and place in order. The number is cast onto the cap and on intermediate caps an arrow is also marked which should point towards front of engine.

5   Wipe the cap bearing shell location with a soft non-fluffy rag.

6   Fit the bearing half shell onto each main bearing cap.

7   Apply a little grease to each side of the centre main bearing so as to retain the thrust washer.

8   Fit the upper halves of the thrust washers into their grooves either side of the main bearing. The slots must face outwards.

9   Lubricate the crankshaft journals and the upper and lower main bearing shells with engine oil (photo) and locate the rear oil seal (with lip lubricated) on the rear of the crankshaft.

10   Carefully lower the crankshaft into the crankcase.

11   Lubricate the crankshaft main bearing journals again and then fit No 1 bearing cap. Fit the two securing bolts but do not tighten yet.

12   Make sure that the mating faces are clean, then apply sealant (Loctite 518 or equivalent) to the areas on the rear main bearing cap shown in Fig. 1.14.

13   Fit the rear main bearing cap. Fit the two securing bolts, but as before do not tighten yet.

14   Apply a little grease to either side of the centre main bearing cap so as to retain the thrust washers. Fit the thrust washers with the tag located in the groove and the slots facing outwards (photo).

15   Fit the centre main bearing cap and the two securing bolts, then refit the intermediate main bearing caps. Make sure that the arrows point towards the front of the engine.

16   Lightly tighten all main cap securing bolts and then fully tighten in a progressive manner to the specified torque wrench setting.

17   Check that the crankshaft rotates freely. Some stiffness is to be expected with new components, but there must be no tight spots or binding.

18   Check that the crankshaft endfloat is within the specified limits by

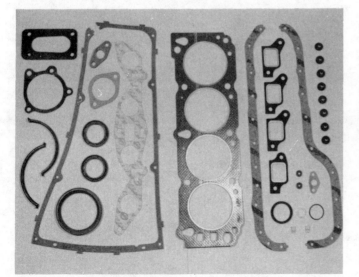

36.3 A complete engine gasket set

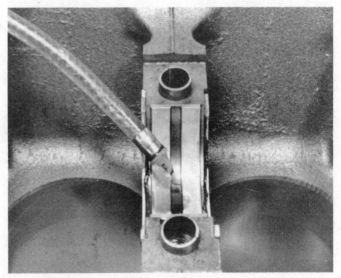

37.9 Lubricating a main bearing shell

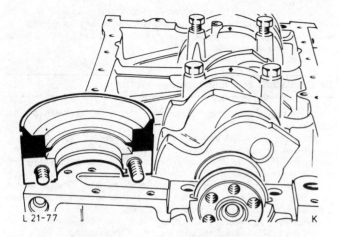

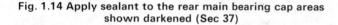

**Fig. 1.14 Apply sealant to the rear main bearing cap areas shown darkened (Sec 37)**

37.14 Fitting a thrust washer to the centre main bearing cap

inserting a feeler blade between the centre crankshaft web and the thrust washers.

19  Make sure that the rear oil seal is fully located onto its seating. Coat the rear main bearing cap wedges with sealing compound, then press them into position with the rounded red face towards the cap (photo).

20  Refit the oil pump and strainer as described in Section 39.

21  Refit the crankshaft front oil seal housing, and auxiliary shaft front cover, if applicable, together with a new gasket and tighten the bolts. Make sure that the bottom face of the housing is aligned with the bottom face of the block.

22  Refit the flywheel or driveplate (Section 41) and the pistons and connecting rods (Section 38).

23  Refit the timing belt and sprockets (Section 46).

## 38 Pistons and connecting rods – refitting

1  Clean the backs of the bearing shells and the recesses in the connecting rods and big-end caps.

2  Press the bearing shells into the connecting rods and caps in their correct positions and oil them liberally. Note that the lugs must be adjacent to each other (photos).

3  Lubricate the cylinder bores with engine oil (photo).

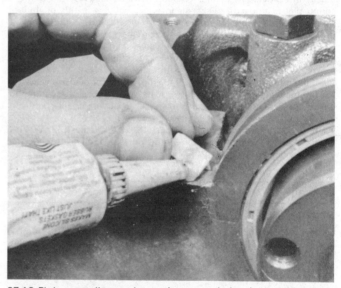

37.19 Fitting a sealing wedge to the rear main bearing cap

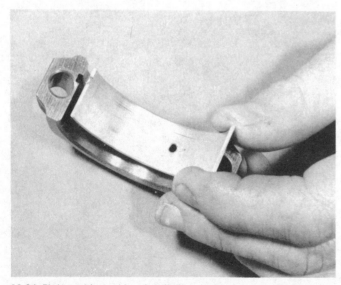

38.2A Fitting a big-end bearing shell to its cap

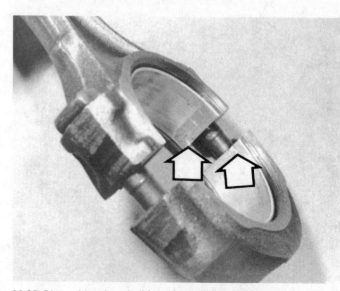

38.2B Big-end bearing shell lugs (arrowed) are adjacent

38.3 Lubricating a cylinder bore

38.4A Fitting a piston ring compressor

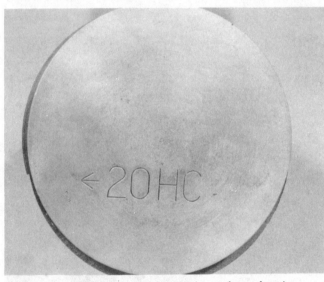

38.4B Piston crown markings – arrow points to front of engine

38.5A Lubricating a crankpin

38.5B Tightening a big-end bearing cap nut

4   Fit a ring compressor to No 1 piston, then insert the piston and connecting rod into No 1 cylinder. With No 1 crankpin at its lowest point, drive the piston carefully into the cylinder with the wooden handle of a hammer, and at the same time guide the connecting rod onto the crankpin. Make sure that the arrow on the piston crown is facing the front of the engine (photos).

5   Oil the crankpin, then fit the big-end bearing cap in its previously noted position. Oil the big-end bearing cap nuts, fit the nuts and tighten them to the specified torque (photos).

6   Check that the crankshaft turns freely.

7   Repeat the procedure given in paragraphs 4 to 6 inclusive on the remaining pistons.

8   Refit the cylinder head as described in Section 45 and the sump as described in Section 40.

### 39  Oil pump – refitting

1   Insert the oil pump driveshaft into the block in its previously noted position.

2   Prime the pump by injecting oil into it and turning it by hand (photo).

39.2 Priming the oil pump

3  Fit the pump, insert the bolts and tighten them to the specified torque with the splined key.
4  Insert the pick-up tube securing bolt and tighten it.
5  Where applicable refit the crankshaft front oil seal housing together with a new gasket and tighten the bolts. Make sure that the bottom face of the housing is aligned with the bottom face of the block.
6  Refit the sump as described in Section 40.

## 40 Sump – refitting

1  Apply sealing compound to the corners of the front and rear rubber sealing strap locations, then press the strips into the grooves of the rear main bearing cap and crankshaft front oil seal housing (photos).
2  Apply a little sealing compound to the bottom face of the cylinder block, then fit the sump gaskets in position and locate the end tabs beneath the rubber sealing strips (photo).
3  Locate the sump on the gaskets and insert the bolts loosely.
4  Tighten the bolts to the specified torques in the two stages given in the Specifications. Refer to Fig. 1.15 and tighten to the first stage in circular sequence starting at point 'A', then tighten to the second stage starting at point 'B'. Tighten to the third stage after the engine has been running for twenty minutes.
5  If the engine is in the vehicle, reverse the steps taken to gain access to the sump (Section 17).

40.1A Applying sealing compound to a rubber strip location

40.1B Fitting the rubber strip into its groove

40.2 Locate the gasket tabs beneath the sealing strips

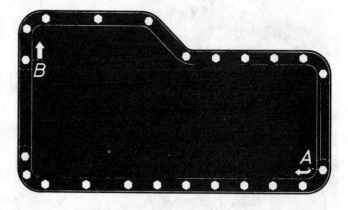

Fig. 1.15 Sump bolt tightening sequence. For A and B see text (Sec 40)

## 41 Flywheel/driveplate and adaptor plate – refitting

1   If it was removed, refit the adaptor plate (backplate) over the dowels on the rear of the block.
2   Wipe the mating faces, then locate the flywheel/driveplate on the rear of the crankshaft (photo).
3   Coat the threads of the bolts with a liquid locking agent then insert them (photo). Note that the manufacturers recommend using new bolts.
4   Using a piece of angle iron, hold the flywheel/driveplate stationary, then tighten the bolts evenly to the specified torque in diagonal sequence (photos).
5   If the engine is in the car, refit the automatic transmission as described in Chapter 6 or the clutch as described in Chapter 5.

## 42 Auxiliary shaft – refitting

1   Oil the auxiliary shaft journals, then insert the shaft into the cylinder block.
2   Locate the thrust plate in the shaft groove, then insert the crosshead screws and tighten them with an impact screwdriver.
3   Support the front cover on blocks of wood and drive out the old oil

41.2 The flywheel located on the crankshaft

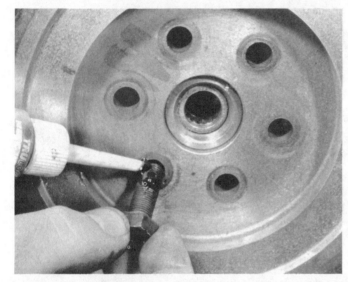

41.3 Applying thread locking agent to a flywheel bolt

41.4A Method of holding the flywheel when tightening the bolts

41.4B Tightening a flywheel bolt

42.3A Driving out the auxiliary shaft cover oil seal

42.3B Fitting a new oil seal in the auxiliary shaft cover

43.3 Cam follower ball-pins and spring clips fitted

seal. Drive in the new seal using a suitable metal tube or socket
(photos). Make sure that the sealing lip faces toward the engine.
Smear a little oil on the lip.
4   If applicable cut the unwanted top half of a new gasket and locate
it on the cylinder block, then fit the front cover and tighten the bolts.
5   Refit the fuel pump and operating rod (when applicable) as
described in Chapter 3.
6   Refit the distributor as described in Chapter 4.
7   Refit the auxiliary shaft sprocket and timing belt as described in
Section 46.

## 43 Cylinder head – reassembly

1   Refit the thermostat and housing, referring to Chapter 2 if
necessary.
2   Refit the timing belt tensioner if it was removed, but do not tighten
the bolts yet.
3   If applicable, screw the cam follower ball-pins in their correct
locations (photo).
4   Oil the valve stems and insert the valves in their correct guides.
5   Wrap some adhesive tape over the collet groove of each valve, then
oil the oil seals and slide them over the valve onto the guides. Use a
suitable metal tube if necessary to press them onto the guides. Remove
the adhesive tape.
6   Working on each valve in turn, fit the valve spring and cap, then
compress the spring with the compressor and insert the split collets. A
dab of grease on the collets will keep them in position on the valve
stem. Release the compressor and remove it. Tap the end of the valve
stem with a non-metallic mallet to settle the collets. If tool 21-005-A is
being used, first locate the camshaft in its bearings.
7   Refit the camshaft as described in Section 44.

## 44 Camshaft – refitting

1   Drive the new oil seal into the camshaft front bearing location on
the cylinder head using a suitable metal tube or socket (photo). Smear
the lip with engine oil.
2   Lubricate the bearings with hypoid SAE 80/90 oil, then carefully
insert the camshaft (photo).
3   Locate the thrust plate in the camshaft groove, then insert and
tighten the bolts.
4   Using feeler gauges check that the endfloat is as given in the
Specifications.
5   Lubricate the ball-pins with hypoid SAE 80/90 oil, then fit the cam

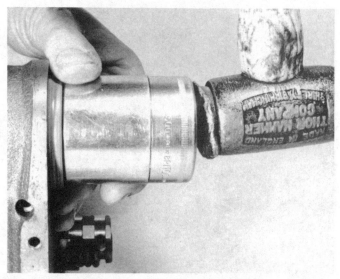

44.1 Fitting the camshaft front bearing oil seal

44.2 Lubricating a camshaft bearing

44.7 Fitting the camshaft sprocket backplate

45.3 Fitting a new cylinder head gasket

followers in their correct locations and retain with the spring clips. It will be necessary to rotate the camshaft during this operation.

6  Fit the oil supply tube and tighten the bolts.

7  Fit the camshaft sprocket backplate and sprocket. Insert and tighten the bolt while holding the camshaft stationary with a spanner on the lug (photo).

8  Refit the cylinder head as described in Section 45.

## 45 Cylinder head – refitting

1  Adjust the valve clearances as described in Section 51. This work is easier to carry out on the bench rather than in the car.

2  Turn the engine so that No 1 piston is approximately 2 cm (0.8 in) before top dead centre. This precaution will prevent any damage to open valves.

3  Make sure that the faces of the cylinder block and cylinder head are perfectly clean, then locate the new gasket on the block making sure that all the internal holes are aligned (photo). *Do not use jointing compound.*

4  Turn the camshaft so that the TDC pointer is aligned with the indentation on the front of the cylinder head.

5  Lower the cylinder head onto the gasket. The help of an assistant will ensure that the gasket is not dislodged. Alternatively, make a couple of guide studs by sawing the heads off two old cylinder head bolts; remove the studs when the head is in position.

6  Lightly oil the heads and threads of the new cylinder head bolts and insert them into their holes.

7  Using the 'Torx' key, tighten the bolts progressively to the Stage 1 specified torque, following the sequence given in Fig. 1.16.

8  In the same sequence tighten the bolts to the Stage 2 specified torque.

9  Wait five minutes, then tighten the bolts through the angle specified for Stage 3, still following the same sequence. (If the engine is on the bench, it may be preferable to leave this final stage until after refitting the engine, when the problem of holding it still will not arise.)

10  Refit the rocker cover, using a new gasket. make sure that the dovetail sections of the gasket engage correctly (photo).

11  Fit the rocker cover bolts and reinforcing plates. Tighten the bolts as follows, referring to the Specifications and to Fig. 1.17:

    *Stage 1 – Bolts 1 to 6*
    *Stage 2 – Bolts 7 and 8*
    *Stage 3 – Bolts 9 and 10*
    *Stage 4 – Bolts 7 and 8 (again)*

12  No further tightening of the cylinder head bolts is required.

13  Refit and tension the timing belt as described in the next Section.

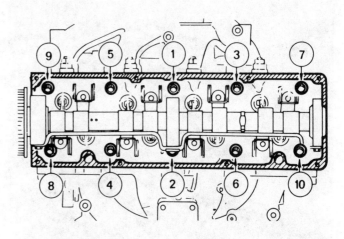

**Fig. 1.16 Cylinder head bolt tightening sequence (Sec 45)**

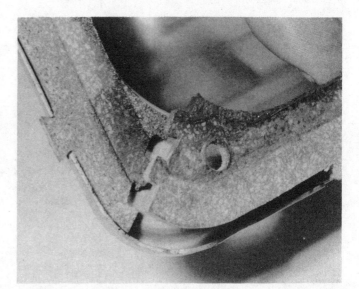

45.10 Dovetail section of rocker cover gasket

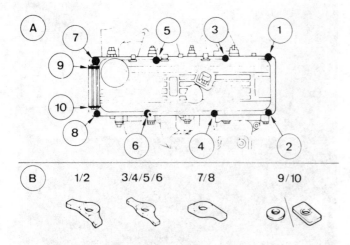

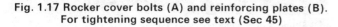

Fig. 1.17 Rocker cover bolts (A) and reinforcing plates (B).
For tightening sequence see text (Sec 45)

## 46  Timing belt and sprockets – refitting

1   Fit the camshaft sprocket backplate and sprocket. Insert the bolt, hold the camshaft or sprocket and tighten the bolt to the specified torque (photo).

2   Fit the auxiliary shaft sprocket with the ribs towards the engine. Fit the sprocket bolt and tighten it to the specified torque, counterholding the sprocket with a bar through one of the holes.

3   Fit the crankshaft sprocket, chamfered side inwards.

4   Fit the timing belt over the camshaft sprocket, but do not engage it with the other sprockets yet (photo). Be careful not to kink the belt. If the old belt is being refitted, observe the previously noted running direction.

5   Refit the guide washer and the crankshaft pulley. Fit the bolt and washer and tighten just enough to seat the pulley, being careful not to turn the crankshaft (photos).

6   Make sure that the TDC pointer on the camshaft sprocket backplate is still aligned with the indentation on the cylinder head.

7   Turn the crankshaft by the shortest route to align the TDC notch in the pulley with the pointer on the oil seal housing.

8   If the distributor is fitted, turn the auxiliary shaft sprocket so that the rotor arm points to the No. 1 HT segment position.

9   Fit the timing belt over the sprockets and round the tensioner.

46.1 Tightening the camshaft sprocket bolt

46.4 Fitting the timing belt over the crankshaft sprocket

46.5A Refitting the crankshaft pulley

46.5B Crankshaft pulley bolt and washer

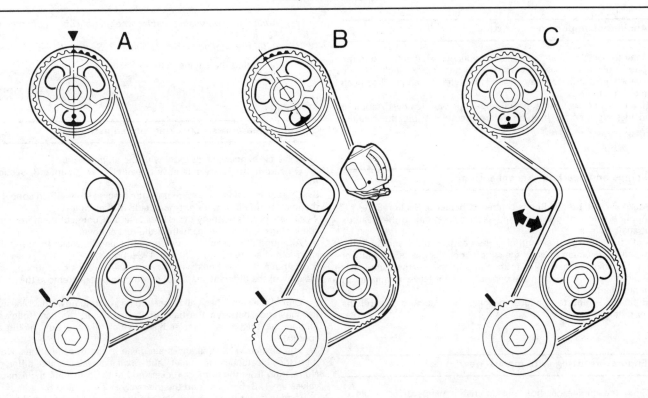

**Fig. 1.18 Timing belt tension checking sequence (Sec 46)**

A   No. 1 at TDC                    B   60° BTDC for checking           C   Return to TDC for adjustment

Move the tensioner to tension the belt roughly and nip up the tensioner bolts.

10 Turn the crankshaft through two full turns clockwise, then 60° anti-clockwise (so it is now at 60° BTDC)

11 The belt tension should now ideally be checked by applying Ford tension gauge 21-113 to the longest run. Desired gauge readings are:

Used belt – 4 to 5
New belt – 10 to 11

12 If the tension gauge is not available, a rough guide is that belt tension is correct when the belt can be twisted 90° in the middle of the longest run with the fingers (photo).

13 If adjustment of belt tension is necessary, turn the crankshaft

clockwise to bring No. 1 cylinder to TDC, then slacken the tensioner bolts and move the tensioner to increase or decrease belt tension. Tighten the tensioner bolts.

14 Turn the crankshaft 90° clockwise past TDC, then anti-clockwise back to the 60° BTDC position. Check the belt tension again.

15 Repeat the above procedure until the belt tension is correct.

16 Tighten the tensioner bolts and the crankshaft pulley bolt to the specified torques (photo).

17 Refit the timing belt cover and tighten its bolts.

18 If the engine is in the vehicle, reverse the preliminary steps given in Section 14.

19 Check the ignition timing when the engine is next run (Chapter 4, Section 6).

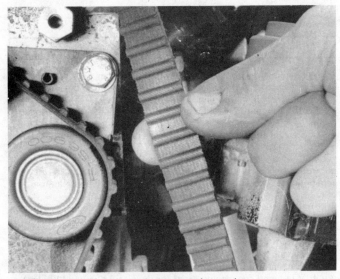

46.12 Twisting the timing belt to assess its tension

46.16 Holding the crankshaft pulley with two bolts and a lever while tightening the central bolt

## 47 Ancillary components – refitting

1   Refer to Section 10 and refit the components listed, referring to the Chapter indicated when necessary. Delicate items such as the alternator and distributor may be left until after the engine has been refitted, if preferred.
2   If the crankcase ventilation oil separator was removed, apply a liquid locking agent to its tube before pressing it into the cylinder block.

## 48 Engine and gearbox – reconnection

1   Make sure that the clutch is centred (Chapter 5, Section 8).
2   Apply a smear of grease or anti-seize compound to the gearbox input shaft splines.
3   With the aid of an assistant, offer the gearbox to the engine. If the input shaft is reluctant to enter the clutch, rock the gearbox slightly or turn the crankshaft back and forth. Support the gearbox until it is engaged with the dowels on the engine – do not leave it hanging on the input shaft.
4   Refit the engine-to-bellhousing bolts, the bracing strap and the starter motor.

## 49 Engine – refitting with manual gearbox

1   Sling the engine/gearbox unit so that it hangs at an angle of approximately 45°.
2   Lower the unit into the engine bay, at the same time moving it towards the rear of the vehicle. Have an assistant watch as the unit is lowered to check that no pipes, wires etc are fouled or trapped.
3   Raise the gearbox as the engine is lowered until the unit takes up its correct position. Secure the engine bearers to the mountings and refit the gearbox crossmember.
4   The remainder of refitting is a reversal of the removal procedure. Refer to Section 7. Also refer to Section 50, paragraph 9.
5   Before starting the engine, refer to Section 52.

## 50 Engine – refitting alone

1   On manual gearbox models, check that the clutch is centred correctly (Chapter 5, Section 8). Apply a smear of grease of anti-seize compound to the gearbox input shaft.
2   On automatic transmission models, check that the torque converter is fully engaged with the transmission oil pump (Chapter 6, Section 12).
3   Sling the engine so that it is roughly horizontal. Lift it and position it over the engine bay.
4   Lower the engine into place. Have an assistant watch as the unit is lowered to check that no pipes, wires etc are fouled or trapped.
5   Guide the engine onto the transmission, raising or lowering the transmission slightly if necessary. Do not place any weight on the transmission input shaft. With manual gearbox models, rock the engine gently from side to side to encourage the input shaft to enter the clutch.
6   When the engine and transmission are fully engaged, refit the engine-to-bellhousing bolts. Do not overlook the earth strap.
7   Lower the engine so that the engine bearers engage with the mountings. Fit the mounting nuts and remove the lifting tackle.
8   On automatic transmission models, bolt the torque converter to the driveplate (Chapter 6, Section 12).
9   The remainder of refitting is a reversal of the removal procedure. Note the following additional points:

(a) Refill the engine with oil
(b) Check the transmission oil level if necessary
(c) Adjust the tension of the accessory drivebelts (Chapter 2, Section 13)
(d) Adjust the throttle cable (Chapter 3, Section 13)

(e) Adjust the downshift cable when applicable (Chapter 6, Section 15)
(f) Refill the cooling system (Chapter 2, Section 5)

10   Before starting the engine, refer to Section 52.

## 51 Valve clearances – checking and adjustment

1   Valve clearances are checked with the engine cold.
2   On carburettor models, remove the air cleaner (Chapter 3, Section 5).
3   On fuel-injection models, remove the bracing strap which connects the inlet manifold to the right-hand side of the engine.
4   On all models, identify the HT leads and disconnect them from the spark plugs. Unclip the leads from the rocker cover.
5   Although not essential, it will make the engine easier to turn if the spark plugs are removed (Chapter 4, Section 3).
6   Remove the ten bolts which secure the rocker cover, noting the location of the different shapes of reinforcing plates. Remove the cover and gasket.
7   One of the cam lobes will be seen to be pointing upwards. Measure the clearance between the base of this cam and the cam follower, finding the thickness of feeler blade which gives a firm sliding fit (photo).
8   The desired valve clearances are given in the Specifications. Note that the clearances for inlet and exhaust valves are different. Numbering from the front (sprocket) end of the camshaft, the exhaust valves are 1, 3, 5 and 7, and the inlet valves 2, 4, 6 and 8.
9   If adjustment is necessary, slacken the ball-pin locknut and screw the ball-pin up or down until the clearance is correct. Hold the ball-pin stationary and tighten the locknut (photo). Recheck the clearance after tightening the locknut in case the ball-pin is moved.
10   Turn the engine to bring another cam lobe to the vertical position and repeat the above procedure. Carry on until all eight valves have been checked.
11   Access to some of the ball-pins is made difficult by the carburettor or fuel-injection inlet manifold. To avoid having to remove the offending components, double cranked spanners or cutaway socket spanners can be used (photo).
12   When adjustment is complete, refit the rocker cover using a new gasket. Make sure that the dovetail sections of the gasket fit together correctly.
13   Fit the rocker cover bolts and reinforcing plates. Tighten the bolts as described in Section 45, paragraph 11.
14   Refit the other disturbed components.
15   Run the engine and check that there are no oil leaks from the rocker cover.

## 52 Initial start-up after overhaul or major repair

1   Make a final check to ensure that everything has been reconnected to the engine and that no rags or tools have been left in the engine bay.
2   Check that oil and coolant levels are correct.
3   Start the engine. This may take a little longer than usual as fuel is pumped up to the engine.
4   Check that the oil pressure light goes out when the engine starts.
5   Run the engine at a fast tickover and check for leaks of oil, fuel and coolant. Also check power steering and transmission fluid cooler unions, when applicable. Some smoke and odd smells may be experienced as assembly lubricant burns off the exhaust manifold and other components.
6   Bring the engine to operating temperature. Check the ignition timing (Chapter 4, Section 6), then adjust the idle speed (if applicable) and mixture as described in Chapter 3.
7   Stop the engine and allow it to cool, then re-check the oil and coolant levels.
8   If new bearings, pistons etc have been fitted, the engine should be run in at reduced speeds and loads for the first 500 miles (800 km) or so. It is beneficial to change the engine oil and filter after this mileage.

51.7 Measuring a valve clearance

51.9 Adjusting a valve clearance

51.11 Cutaway socket spanner can be used on inaccessible ball-pin nuts

## 53 Fault diagnosis – engine

| Symptom | Reason(s) |
|---------|-----------|
| Engine fails to start | Discharged battery |
| | Loose battery connection |
| | Loose or broken ignition leads |
| | Moisture on spark plugs, distributor cap or HT leads |
| | Incorrect spark plug gap |
| | Cracked distributor cap or rotor |
| | Dirt or water in fuel |
| | Empty fuel tank |
| | Faulty fuel pump |
| | Faulty starter motor |
| | Low cylinder compression* |
| | Engine management system fault |
| | Fuel pump inertia switch tripped (electric pump) |
| Engine idles erratically | Inlet manifold air leak |
| | Leaking cylinder head gasket |
| | Worn camshaft lobes |
| | Incorrect valve clearances |
| | Loose crankcase ventilation hoses |
| | Incorrect idle adjustment |
| | Uneven cylinder compressions* |
| | Incorrect ignition timing |
| | Carburettor stepper motor plunger dirty (2.0 litre only) |
| | Engine management system fault |
| Engine misfires | Incorrect spark plug gap |
| | Faulty coil or electronic ignition |
| | Dirt or water in fuel |
| | Idle adjustment incorrect |
| | Leaking cylinder head gasket |
| | Distributor cap cracked |
| | Incorrect valve clearances |
| | Uneven cylinder compressions* |
| | Moisture on spark plugs, distributor cap or HT leads |
| Engine stalls | Idle adjustment incorrect |
| | Inlet manifold air leak |
| | Ignition timing incorrect |
| | Crankcase ventilation system air leak |
| Excessive oil consumption | Worn pistons and cylinder bores |
| | Valve guides and valve stem seals worn |
| | Oil leaking from gasket or oil seal |

*For details of compression testing see Section 97*

## PART B V6 OHV ENGINE

### 54 General description

The V6 engine fitted to the Granada is only available in 2.8 litre fuel-injected form. Mechanically the design of the engine is well-established, and it is improved by the latest fuel, ignition and engine management systems.

The combined crankcase and cylinder block is made of cast iron, and houses the pistons, crankshaft and camshaft. The sump is attached to the bottom of the crankcase and the cylinder heads to the top.

The cylinder heads are of the crossflow design, the inlet manifold being located between them and the exhaust manifolds being on the outboard sides. The overhead valves are operated by tappets, pushrods and rockers from the centrally located camshaft. Camshaft drive is by gears.

The crankshaft runs in four main bearings. Endfloat is controlled by thrust flanges on the No.3 bearing shells. The connecting rods are selected so that all are in the same weight class.

Aluminium alloy pistons are used. The gudgeon pins are an interference fit in their connecting rods.

The lubrication system is of the usual wet sump, pressure fed type, with a full flow disposable canister oil filter. The oil pump is driven by a shaft which engages in the bottom of the distributor drivegear.

### 55 Maintenance and inspection

1   Check the engine oil level every 250 miles (400 km), weekly, or before a long run. See Section 2 for the procedure. On the V6 engine the oil filter cap is on the front of the right-hand rocker cover (photo).
2   Renew the engine oil every 6000 miles (10 000 km) or six months, whichever comes first. Again, the procedure is described in Section 2.

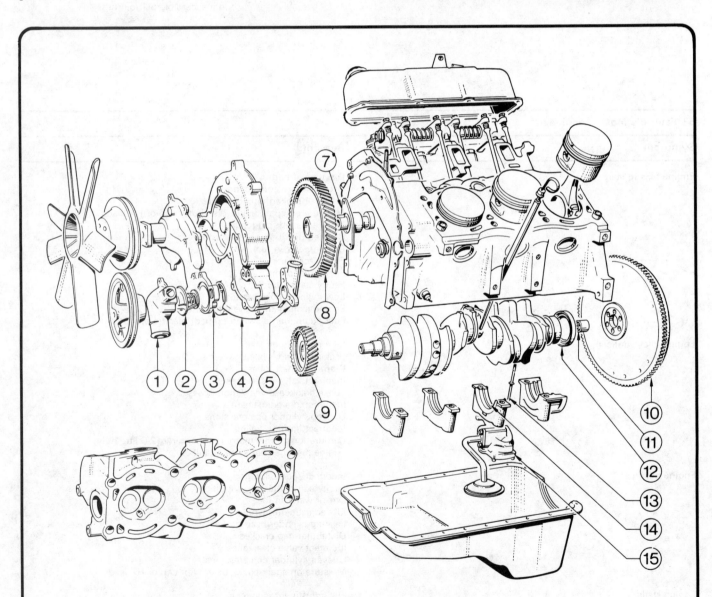

**Fig. 1.19 Exploded view of V6 engine (Sec 54)**

| | | | |
|---|---|---|---|
| 1   Water inlet connection | 5   By-pass hose flange | 10  Flywheel | 13  Oil pump drive shaft |
| 2   Thermostat | 7   Camshaft thrust plate | 11  Crankshaft pilot bearing | 14  Main bearing |
| 3   Water pump | 8   Camshaft gear | 12  Oil seal | 15  Oil pump |
| 4   Timing cover | 9   Crankshaft gear | | |

55.1 Removing the oil filler cap

55.3 Oil filter seen from below

3   At the same intervals renew the oil filter as described in Section 21. On the V6 engine the oil filter is located on the right-hand side of the cylinder block (photo).
4   Every 12 000 miles (20 000 km) check the valve clearance as described in Section 93 and adjust if necessary.
5   For maintenance of the crankcase ventilation system, see Section 83.
6   Regularly inspect the engine for leaks of oil, fuel or coolant, and rectify as necessary.

## 56 Major operations possible with the engine in the vehicle

The following operations can be carried out without removing the engine, although some work will be easier and quicker with the engine removed:

   (a)  *Removal and refitting of the cylinder heads*
   (b)  *Removal and refitting of the sump and oil pump*
   (c)  *Removal and refitting of the timing gears*
   (d)  *Removal and refitting of the pistons, connecting rods and big-end bearings*
   (e)  *Renewal of the engine mountings*
   (f)  *Removal and refitting of the flywheel*
   (g)  *Renewal of the crankshaft front and rear oil seals*
   (h)  *Removal and refitting of the camshaft (after removal of the cylinder heads, tappets and timing gears)*

## 57 Major operations requiring engine removal

The engine must be removed for the following operations:

   (a)  *Renewal of the crankshaft main bearings*
   (b)  *Removal and refitting of the crankshaft*

## 58 Methods of engine removal

The engine is removed from above, without the transmission. Removal with the transmission is not recommended because of the weight and unweildiness of the combined units.

## 59 Engine – removal

1   Disconnect the battery negative lead.
2   Remove the bonnet (Chapter 11, Section 6).

3   Remove the throttle valve cover, which is retained by three screws.
4   Remove the air cleaner cover, valve airflow meters and air inlet trunking (Chapter 3, Section 29). Also remove the oil filler cap, which is connected to the trunking by a crankcase ventilation hose.
5   Release the securing clips and bolts and remove the upper half of the fan shroud.
6   Drain the cooling system and remove the radiator as described in Chapter 2.
7   Disconnect the heater hoses from the heater matrix and from the coolant outlet. Unclip the hoses.
8   Remove the fan and viscous clutch (Chapter 2, Section 11).
9   Disconnect the following wiring:

   (a)  *Alternator*
   (b)  *Temperature gauge sender*
   (c)  *Engine management temperature sensor*
   (d)  *Oil pressure switch*
   (e)  *Idle speed control valve*
   (f)  *Throttle position sensor*
   (g)  *Injector nut-harness*
   (h)  *Distributor multi-plug*
   (j)  *Distributor-to-coil HT lead*

10 Disconnect the throttle cable (Chapter 3, Section 13). When applicable, also disconnect the downshaft cable or switch.
11 Disconnect the fuel supply and return lines. **Be prepared for fuel spillage, and for some spray if the system is still under pressure.**
12 Remove the steering pump and air conditioning compressor drivebelts (as applicable). Unbolt the steering pump and compressor, move them aside within the limits of their flexible hoses and support them by wiring them to adjacent components.
13 Remove the distributor cap and rotor.
14 Remove the starter motor (Chapter 12, Section 11).
15 Drain the engine oil. Unscrew the oil filter with a strap or chain wrench and remove it; be prepared for oil spillage.
16 On manual gearbox models, disconnect the clutch cable from the release lever (Chapter 5, Section 4).
17 Unbolt the exhaust pipes from the manifolds.
18 On automatic transmission models, unbolt the torque converter from the driveplate, see Chapter 6, Section 12.
19 Attach lifting tackle to the engine. If no lifting eyes are fitted, pass ropes or chains round the exhaust manifolds.
20 Take the weight of the engine, then remove the single nut on each side which holds engine bearer to its mountings.
21 From under the vehicle unbolt the engine adaptor plate from the bellhousing.
22 Remove the engine-to-bellhousing bolts. Also disconnect or unclip the battery negative lead, the starter motor lead and the heat shield.

23 Support the transmission, preferably with a trolley jack.
24 Check that nothing has been overlooked, then raise the engine and draw it forwards clear of the transmission input shaft. Do not allow the weight of the engine to hang on the shaft, and do not lift the transmission by it.
25 With automatic transmission, make sure that the torque coverter stays engaged with the oil pump in the transmission as the engine is withdrawn.
26 Lift the engine out of the engine bay and take it to the bench.

## 60 Engine dismantling – general

1  Refer to Section 9, paragraphs 1 to 8.
2  Cylinder head bolts on the V6 engine may be conventional (hexagon-headed) or 'Torx' type. The appropriate 'Torx' key will be needed to deal with the latter.

## 61 Ancillary components – removal

1  Before dismantling the engine into its main components, the following ancillaries can be removed. The actual items removed, and the sequence of removal, will depend on the work to be done:

 *Distributor and bracket (Chapter 4, Section 5)*
 *Spark plugs (Chapter 4, Section 3)*
 *Inlet manifold and associated items (Chapter 3, Section 32)*
 *Exhaust manifolds (Chapter 3, Section 33)*
 *Clutch (Chapter 5, Section 5)*
 *Alternator and bracket (Chapter 12, Section 8)*
 *Oil pressure switch (photo)*
 *Temperature gauge sender*
 *Engine bearer arms*
 *Dipstick*

2  If an oil cooler is fitted between the oil filter and the block, remove it by disconnecting the coolant hoses and unscrewing the central sleeve. The cooler and seal can now be removed. If the threaded bush is removed from the block (it may come out with the sleeve) it must be renewed.

## 62 Cylinder heads – removal

   The procedure is described for the engine in the vehicle. With the engine removed, the preliminary steps can be ignored.
1  Disconnect the battery negative lead.
2  Remove the inlet manifold and associated components (Chapter 3, Section 32).
3  Unbolt the power steering pump, remove the drivebelts and move the pump aside. Support it by wiring it to adjacent components.
4  Remove the alternator and its bracket (Chapter 12, Section 8).
5  Remove the three bolts which secure each rocker shaft. Remove the shafts and pushrods, keeping them in order so that they can be refitted in the same locations.
6  Unbolt the exhaust pipes from the manifolds.
7  Remove the spark plugs.
8  Slacken the cylinder head bolts half a turn at a time, following the reverse sequence to that used when tightening (Fig. 1.31) Remove the bolts.
9  Remove the cylinder heads (photo). If they are stuck, try to rock them free, or tap them with a soft-faced hammer. **Do not** hit them directly with a metal hammer, and **do not** lever in between the joint faces.
10  Recover the head gaskets.

## 63 Sump – removal

   Proceed as described in Section 17, but note that there are 24 bolts retaining the sump, not 23.

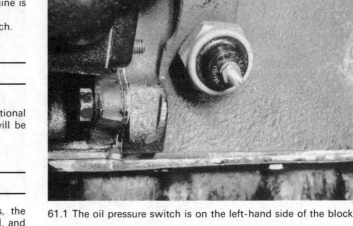
61.1 The oil pressure switch is on the left-hand side of the block

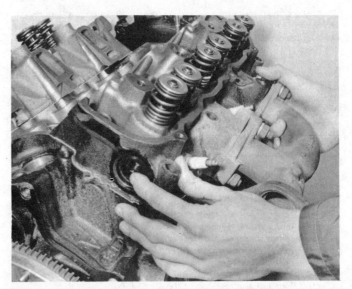
62.9 Removing the right-hand cylinder head

## 64 Timing cover and gears – removal

   The procedure is described for the engine in the vehicle. With the engine removed, the preliminary steps can be ignored
1  Disconnect the battery negative lead.
2  Drain the engine oil.
3  Drain the coolant and remove the radiator (Chapter 2, Sections 3 and 7).
4  Remove the auxilliary drivebelts (Chapter 2, Section 13).
5  Remove the fan and viscous clutch (Chapter 2, Section 11).
6  Jam the crankshaft, either by engaging 5th gear and applying the handbrake, or by removing the starter motor and having an assistant jam a screwdriver in the starter ring gear teeth. Unbolt the crankshaft pulley. When the pulley is secured to a vibration damper, also remove the damper central bolt.
7  Remove the pulley or damper, using a puller if necessary.
8  Disconnect the coolant hoses from the front of the engine, including the water pump bypass hose.
9  Disconnect the heater connecting pipe from the timing cover and unbolt the two clips which secure the pipe to the cover of the cylinder block.

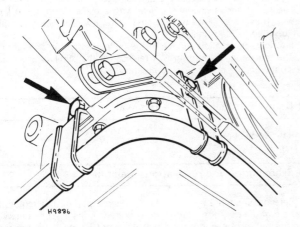

**Fig. 1.20 Heater connecting pipe clip bolts (arrowed) (Sec 64)**

64.13 Camshaft and crankshaft gear marks in alignment (engine inverted). Disregard the other mark on the crankshaft gear

10 If not already done, remove the starter motor (Chapter 12, Section 11).

11 Remove the sump (Sections 17 and 63).

12 Remove the nine securing bolts and remove the timing cover complete with water pump and thermostat.

13 Turn the crankshaft to bring the marks on the timing gears into alignment as shown (photo). *Note that there are two marks on the crankshaft gear – do not get them confused.*

14 Remove the bolt which secures the camshaft gear. It should now be possible to remove the camshaft gear by hand.

15 Draw off the crankshaft gear using a puller. Recover the Woodruff keys if they are loose.

16 Clean the old gasket off the timing cover and the cylinder block. Remove the oil seal from the timing cover.

## 65 Flywheel/driveplate and adaptor plate – removal

Refer to Section 16.

## 66 Oil pump – removal

1 Remove the sump (Sections 17 and 63).

2 Remove the two securing bolts and remove the oil pump complete with pick-up and strainer.

3 Recover the oil pump driveshaft, noting which way round it is fitted.

4 Recover the oil pump-to-block gasket.

## 67 Pistons and connecting rods – removal

1 Remove the cylinder heads (Section 62), the sump (Sections 17 and 63) and the oil pump (Section 66).

2 Check that the big-end bearing caps and connecting rods have identification marks. This is to ensure that the correct caps are fitted to the correct connecting rods and at reassembly are fitted in their correct cylinder bores. Note that the pistons have an arrow (or notch) marked on the crown to indicate the forward facing side.

3 Remove the big-end nuts and place to one side in the order in which they are removed.

4 Pull off the big-end caps, taking care to keep them in the right order and the correct way round. Also ensure that the shell bearings are kept with their respective connecting rods unless they are being renewed. If the big-end caps are difficult to remove they can be tapped lightly with a soft faced hammer.

5 To remove the shell bearings, press the bearing on the side opposite

the groove in both the connecting rod and the cap, and the bearing will slide out.

6 Withdraw the pistons and connecting rods upwards out of the cylinder bores.

## 68 Camshaft and intermediate plate – removal

1 Remove the cylinder heads and pushrods (Section 62).

2 Remove the tappets from their bores, using a pencil magnet or by inserting a piece of bent brass wire through the lubrication holes.

3 Remove the timing cover and the camshaft gear (Section 64).

4 Remove the two bolts which secure the camshaft thrust plate. Withdraw the camshaft, thrust plate and spacer ring.

5 The intermediate plate may now be removed after removing the retaining bolts. Note the oil seals on the timing cover locating dowels, which must also be removed.

**Fig. 1.21 Using a piece of wire to remove the tappets (Sec 68)**

## 69 Crankshaft and main bearings – removal

1 The engine must be removed from the vehicle for this task.

2 Remove the flywheel/driveplate, timing cover and crankshaft gear, and the pistons and connecting rods, as described in the preceding

Sections. (If no work is to be done on the pistons, they need not actually be pushed out of their bores.)

3   Make sure that the main bearing caps carry identification marks, then remove the bolts and lift off the caps. Tap the caps with a soft-faced mallet if necessary to free them. Keep the bearing shells with their caps if they are to be re-used (photo).

4   Note that the rear main bearing cap also retains the crankshaft rear oil seal, and that the shells for No. 3 main bearing have thrust flanges to control crankshaft endfloat.

5   Lift out the crankshaft. *Do not drop it, it is heavy.*

6   Recover the upper half main bearing shells from their seats in the crankcase, again keeping them in order if they are to be re-used.

7   Remove the old oil seal from the rear of the crankshaft.

## 70  Engine mountings – renewal

Refer to Section 24.

## 71  Crankshaft front oil seal – renewal

1   Disconnect the battery negative lead.

2   Remove the crankshaft pulley (and damper, when fitted) as described in Section 64, paragraphs 3 to 7.

69.3 A main bearing shell and cap

74.1 Rocker shaft roll pin (arrowed)

3   Extract the old oil seal by levering it out with a hooked tool.

4   Clean out the seal seat in the timing cover. Lubricate the new seal and fit it, lips inwards. Seat the seal with a piece of tube or a large socket. (If available, Ford tool 21-063 and a non-damper type pulley may be used to seat the seal.)

5   Lubricate the sealing surface of the pulley or damper and refit it.

6   The remainder of refitting is a reversal of the removal procedure. Check the engine oil level on completion.

## 72  Crankshaft rear oil seal – renewal

Refer to Section 19.

## 73  Examination and renovation – general

Refer to Section 26. New cylinder head bolts are not required if they are of the hexagon head type. 'Torx' type bolts must be renewed. The two types of cylinder head bolt must not be mixed on the same engine.

## 74  Rocker shaft – dismantling, examination and reassembly

1   Tap out the roll pin from one end of the rocker shaft and remove the spring washer (photo).

2   Slide the rocker arms, rocker supports and springs off the rocker shaft. Keep them in the correct order so that they can be reassembled in the same position. If a rocker support sticks it can be removed by tapping it with a soft-faced hammer.

3   Examine the rocker shaft and rocker arms for wear. If the rocker arm surface that contacts the valve stem is considerably worn, renew the rocker arm. If it is worn slightly step-shaped it may be cleaned up with a fine oil stone.

4   Oil the parts and reassemble them on their shafts in the original order. With both rocker shafts fitted the oil holes must face downwards to the cylinder heads. This position is indicated by a notch on one end face of the rocker shaft (Fig. 1.23).

## 75  Tappets and pushrods – examination

1   Inspect the tappets for scuffing, surface wear or other damage. Renew them if necessary. It is good practice to renew the tappets if a new camshaft is being fitted.

2   Check the pushrods for bending by rolling them on a flat surface. Straighten or renew as necessary. Also check the pushrod ends for wear or damage.

## 76  Camshaft and bearings – examination and renovation

1   If there is excessive wear in the camshaft bearings they will have to be renewed. As the fitting of new bearings requires special tools this should be left to your local Ford dealer.

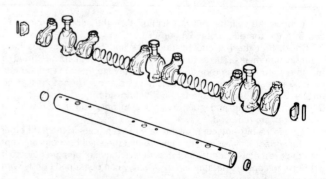

Fig. 1.22 Rocker shaft and associated components (Sec 74)

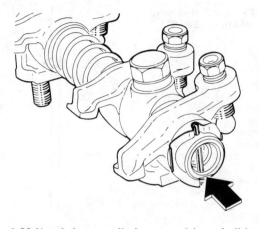

**Fig. 1.23 Notch (arrowed) shows position of oil holes
(Sec 74)**

77.2A Compressing a valve spring to expose the collets

2  The camshaft may show signs of wear on the bearing journals or
cam lobes. The main decision to take is what degree of wear
necessitates renewing the camshaft, which is expensive. Scoring or
damage to the bearing journals cannot be removed by regrinding;
renewal of the camshaft is the only solution.
3  The cam lobes may show signs of ridging or pitting on the high
points. If ridging is slight then it may be possible to remove it with a
fine oil stone or emery cloth. The cam lobes, however, are surface
hardened and once the hard skin is penetrated wear will be very rapid.
4  Excessive endfloat of the camshaft may be remedied by fitting a
thicker spacer and/or thrust plate – see Specifications.
5  Excessive backlash in the camshaft drive gears (timing gears),
which will have been noticed before dismantling by virtue of the
characteristic growling noise, can only be remedied by renewing the
gears.

## 77 Cylinder heads – overhaul

1  Clean the dirt and oil off the cylinder heads. Remove the carbon
deposits from the combustion chambers and valve heads with a
scraper or rotary wire brush.
2  Remove the valves by compressing the valve springs with a
suitable valve spring compressor and lifting out the collets. Release the
valve spring compressor and remove the valve spring retainer, spring
and valve (photos). Mark each valve so that they can be fitted in the
same location. **Note:** *When removing and refitting the valve spring
take care not to damage the valve stem when pressing down the valve
spring retainer to remove or refit the collets. If the stem gets damaged
the sealing will be ineffective and result in excessive oil consumption
and wear of the valve guides.*
3  Remove the valve stem oil seals from the valve guides and discard
them.
4  With the valves removed clean out the carbon from the ports.
5  Examine the heads of the valves and the valve seats for pitting and
burning. If the pitting on valve and seat is slight it can be removed by
grinding the valves and seats together with coarse, and then fine, valve
grinding paste. This process is described in detail in Section 35, along
with the decarbonisation of the pistons.
6  Severe pitting or burning of the valves probably means that they
must be renewed. Badly burnt valve seats can be recut, or inserts can
be fitted, by a Ford dealer or other specialist.
7  Check the valve guides for wear by inserting the valve into its guide
until the valve stem is flush with the end of the guide, then checking
the play at the valve head. Movement in excess of 0.6 mm (0.024 in)
means that the clearance between guide and stem is excessive.
8  Valve guide wear is dealt with by reaming the guides to a known
oversize and fitting new valves with oversize stems. Again, this is a
dealer or specialist task.
9  Inspect the valve springs, if possible comparing their free length
with new springs. Renew the springs anyway if they have been in use
for 20 000 miles (32 000 km) or more.
10  Use a straight-edge and feeler blades to check that the cylinder

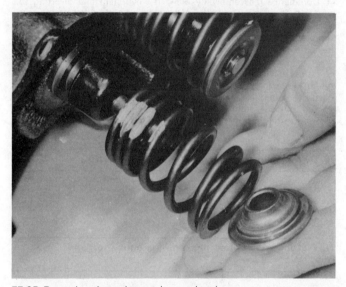

77.2B Removing the spring retainer and spring

77.2C Removing an inlet valve

**Fig. 1.24 Checking valve guide wear using a valve and a dial test indicator (Sec 77)**

head mating faces are not distorted. If they are, have the heads resurfaced by an engineering works.

11  Commence reassembly by oiling a valve stem and inserting the valve into its guide. Cover the collet grooves with adhesive tape and press the new valve stem oil seal down the stem, using a suitable tube to press the seals home. Note that the inlet valve seals are rubber and the exhaust seals nylon; oversize exhaust valve seals must be used when valves with oversize stems are fitted. Remove the adhesive tape.

12  Fit the valve spring and spring retainer. Compress the spring and fit the collets, using a dab of grease to hold them in position. Carefully release the compressor.

13  Tap the valve stem smartly with a mallet to seat the components.

14  Repeat the process on the remaining valves.

## 78  Cylinder bores – examination and renovation

Refer to Section 29. The main bearing caps should be fitted, and their bolts tightened to the specified torque, when making bore measurements.

## 79  Pistons and connecting rods – examination and renovation

Refer to Section 30.

## 80  Crankshaft and bearings – examination

1  Refer to Section 28 for the examination procedure. Note that regrinding of this crankshaft is not permitted, so if significant journal wear is present, a new crankshaft (and new bearing shells) must be fitted.

2  As with the ohc engine, oversize main bearing parent bores may be encountered. These are marked with paint stripes on the bearing caps, corresponding paint marks on the bearing shells and identification codes on the backs of the bearing shells.

## 81  Oil pump – dismantling, examination and reassembly

1  If oil pump wear is suspected, check the cost and availability of new parts and the cost of a new pump. Examine the pump as described in this Section and then decide whether renewal or repair is the best course of action.

2  Remove the pick-up pipe and strainer.

3  Note the position of the oil pump cover relative to the body, then remove the bolts and spring washers. Lift off the cover.

4  Mark the rotor faces so that they can be refitted the same way round, then remove them from the body.

**Fig. 1.25 Exploded view of the oil pump (Sec 81)**

1  *Body*
2  *Bolt*
3  *Bolts*
4  *Lockwasher*
5  *Driveshaft*
6  *Toothed washer*
7  *Rotor set*
8  *Pressure relief valve plunger*
9  *Pressure relief valve spring*
10  *Pressure relief valve plug*
11  *Cover*
12  *Pick-up pipe and strainer*

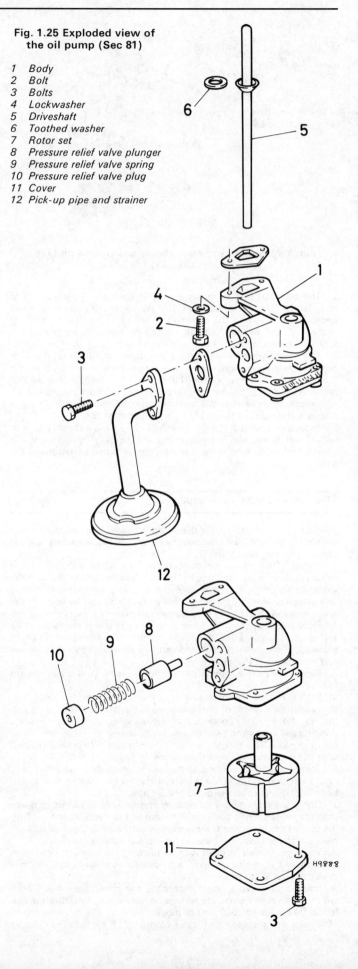

5    Remove the pressure relief valve plug by piercing it with a punch and levering it out. Withdraw the spring and plunger.

6    Thoroughly clean all parts in petrol or paraffin and wipe dry using a non-fluffy rag. The necessary clearances may now be checked using a machined straight-edge (a good steel rule) and a set of feeler gauges. The critical clearances are between the lobes of the centre rotor and convex faces of the outer rotor; between the rotor and pump body; and between both rotors and the end cover plate (endfloat). The desired clearances are given in the Specifications.

7    Endfloat may be measured by refitting the rotors, placing the straight-edge across the bottom of the pump and measuring the clearance between the two rotors and the straight-edge.

8    New rotors are only available as a pair. If the rotor-to-body clearance is excessive, a complete new pump should be fitted.

9    Commence reassembly by lubricating the relief valve plunger. Fit the plunger and spring.

10    Fit a new relief valve plug, flat side outwards and seat it with a drift. until it is flush with the pick-up pipe mating face.

11    Lubricate the rotors and fit them, observing the marks made when dismantling if applicable.

12    Fit the cover and secure it with the bolts and spring washers. Tighten the bolts to the specified torque.

13    Fit the pick-up pipe and strainer, using a new gasket.

14    Temporarily insert the driveshaft into the pump and make sure that the rotors turn freely.

15    A new or overhauled pump must be primed before fitting – see Section 88.

## 82 Flywheel ring gear – examination and renovation

Refer to Section 34.

## 83 Crankcase ventilation system – description and maintenence

1    The crankcase ventilation system is very simple. One hose joins the rear air inlet trunking to the oil filler cap, and another hose joins the left-hand rocker cover to the plemin chamber. Filtered (and metered) air passes through the oil filler cap into the engine, and is extracted, along with any other fumes, via the second hose.

2    Maintenence consists of cleaning the oil filler cap with paraffin every 6000 miles (10 000 km), and regularly inspecting the hose for deterioration or blockage. Clean or renew as necessary.

3    Renew the oil filler cap if oil is discharged from it when the engine is running.

## 84 Engine reassembly – general

Refer to Secton 36, but disregard the reference to new cylinder head bolts when these are of the conventional (hexagon-headed) type. Only 'Torx' type bolts need to be renewed.

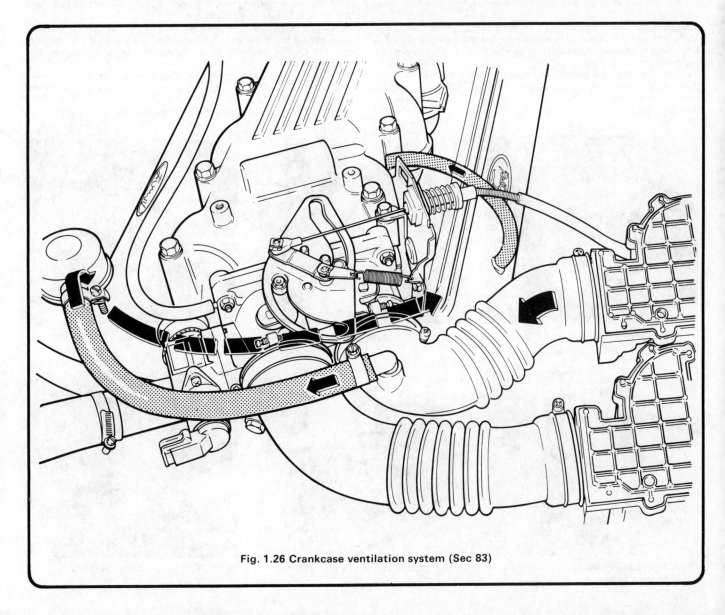

**Fig. 1.26 Crankcase ventilation system (Sec 83)**

## 85 Crankshaft and main bearings – refitting

1  Wipe the bearing shell locations in the crankcase with a clean rag and fit the main bearing upper half shells in position (photo).
2  Clean the main bearing shell locations and fit the half shells in the caps. If the old bearings are being refitted (although this is false economy unless they are practically new) make sure they are fitted in their original positions.
3  Fit the flanged shells to No. 3 bearing.
4  Lubricate the shells and the main bearing journals with engine oil.
5  Lubricate a new rear oil seal and fit it to the end of the crankshaft, lips facing inwards.
6  Carefully place the crankshaft in position (photo).
7  Make sure that the surfaces are clean, then apply a film of sealant (Ford No. A-70SX-19554-BA, or equivalent) to the mating faces of the crankcase and the rear main bearing cap.
8  Fit the bearing caps, with the arrows on the caps pointing to the front of the engine (photo).
9  Insert the main bearing cap bolts. The bolts for bearing caps No. 2 and 3 have rounded heads, and are 14 mm (0.55 in) longer than those for caps 1 and 4.
10  Tighten the main bearing cap bolts progressively to the specified torque (photo).
11  Make sure that the crankshaft is free to rotate. Some stiffness is to be expected with new components, but there should be no tight spots or binding.
12  Press the crankshaft rear oil seal firmly against the rear main bearing.
13  Check the crankshaft endfloat, levering the crankshaft back and forth and inserting feeler blades between the crankshaft and No. 3 main bearing (photo). Excessive endfloat can only be due to wear of the crankshaft or bearing shell flanges.
14  Coat the rear main bearing cap sealing wedges with sealant and press into position with a blunt screwdriver (Fig. 1.27). The rounded end of each wedge carries a red paint mark, which must face the bearing cap.

Fig. 1.27 Fitting the rear main bearing cap sealing wedges (Sec 85)

## 86 Camshaft and intermediate plate – refitting

1  Slide the spacer ring onto the camshaft, chamfered side first. Refit the Woodruff key if it was removed.
2  Lubricate the camshaft bearings, the camshaft and thrust plate.
3  Carefully insert the camshaft from the front and fit the thrust plate and self-locking securing bolts. Tighten the bolts to the specified torque (photos).
4  Fit the timing cover dowels and O-ring seals onto the crankcase. The chamfered end of the dowels must face outwards towards the timing cover (photo).
5  Ensure the mating faces of the crankcase and front intermediate

85.1 Rear main bearing shell in the crankcase

85.6 Placing the crankshaft in position

85.8A Fitting the rear main bearing cap

85.8B Main bearing cap markings – arrow points to front of engine

85.10 Tightening a main bearing cap bolt

85.13 Checking crankshaft endfloat

86.3A Fitting the camshaft into the cylinder block

86.3B Fitting the camshaft thrust plate

86.3C Camshaft thrust plate secured

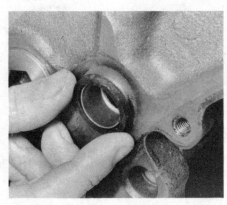

86.4 Timing cover dowel and seal

86.6 Intermediate plate in position – centre bolts arrowed

plate are clean and then apply sealing compound to both faces. Position the gasket on the crankcase and then fit the intermediate plate.

6  Fit the two centre bolts finger-tight, then fit another two bolts temporarily for locating purposes. Tighten the centre securing bolts, then remove the temporarily fitted locating bolts (photo).

7  If the engine is in the vehicle, reverse the steps taken to gain access to the camshaft.

## 87 Pistons and connecting rods – refitting

1  Wipe clean the bearing seats in the connecting rod and cap, and clean the backs of the bearing shells. Fit the shells to each rod and cap with the locating torques engaged in the corresponding cut-outs (photo).

2  If the old bearings are nearly new and are being refitted, then ensure they are refitted in their correct locations on the correct rods.

3  The pistons, complete with connecting rods, are fitted to their bores from the top of the block.

4  Locate the piston ring gaps in the following manner:

*Top: 150° from one side of the oil control ring helical expander gap*
*Centre: 150° from the opposite side of the oil control ring helical expander gap*
*Bottom: oil control ring helical expander: opposite the marked piston front side*
*Oil control ring, intermediate rings: 25 mm (1 in) each side of the helical expander gap*

5  Lubricate the piston and rings well with engine oil.

6  Fit a universal ring compressor and prepare to insert the first piston into the bore. Make sure it is the correct piston-connecting rod assembly for that particular bore, that the connecting rod is the correct

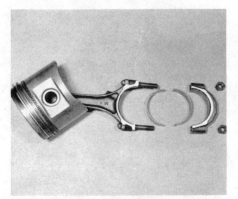

87.1 Piston, connecting rod and shells ready for assembly

87.6A Piston with ring compressor fitted

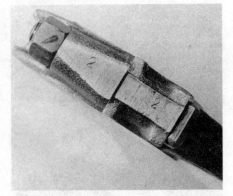

87.6B Connecting rod and cap carry cylinder numbers

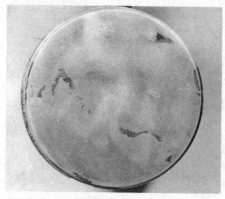

87.6C Arrow on piston crown points to front of engine

87.8 Tapping a piston into the bore

87.10 Fitting a connecting rod cap

way round and that the front of the piston (marked with an arrow or a notch) is to the front of the engine (photos).

7   Again lubricate the piston the piston skirt and insert the connecting rod and piston assembly into the cylinder bore up to the bottom of the piston ring compressor.

8   Gently but firmly tap the piston through the piston ring compressor and into the cylinder bore, using the shaft of a hammer (photo).

9   Generously lubricate the crankpin journals with engine oil and turn the crankshaft so that the crankpin is in the most advantageous position for the connecting rods to be drawn onto it.

10  Lubricate the bearing shell in the connecting rod cap. Fit the cap to the connecting rod (photo).

11  Lubricate the threads and contact faces of the big-end cap nuts. Fit the nuts and tighten them to the specified torque.

12  Check the crankshaft for freedom of rotation.

13  Repeat the operations for the other five pistons.

14  Refit the oil pump, the sump and the cylinder heads (Sections 88, 91 and 92).

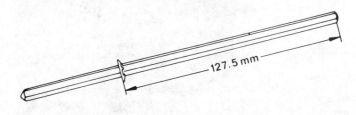

Fig. 1.28 Oil pump driveshaft washer location (Sec 88)

### 89  Flywheel/driveplate and adaptor plate – refitting

Refer to Section 41.

### 90  Timing cover and gears – refitting

1   Lubricate a new oil seal and fit it to the timing cover (photo).

2   If the Woodruff keys were removed from the camshaft and crankshaft, refit them.

3   Refit the crankshaft gear, if removed, using a length of tube to drive it home.

4   Position the camshaft and crankshaft so that their keyways are facing each other. Slide the camshaft gear onto the camshaft, rotating the shafts slightly if necessary so that the marks on the two gears are aligned (photo). Remember that there are two marks on the crankshaft gear.

5   Fit the camshaft gear retaining bolt and washer. Tighten the bolt to the specified torque (photos).

### 88  Oil pump – refitting

1   Make sure that the oil pump and crankcase mating faces are clean.

2   Check that the washer on the oil pump driveshaft is located as shown in Fig. 1.28.

3   If a new or overhauled pump is being fitted, prime it by injecting oil into it and turning it by hand.

4   Insert the oil pump driveshaft into the block with the pointed end towards the distributor (photo).

5   Fit the assembled oil pump, using a new gasket. Insert the two pump-to-block bolts and tighten them to the specified torque (photos).

6   Refit the sump (Section 91).

88.4 Fitting the oil pump driveshaft

88.5A Fitting the oil pump

88.5B Oil pump in position

90.1 Timing cover oil seal

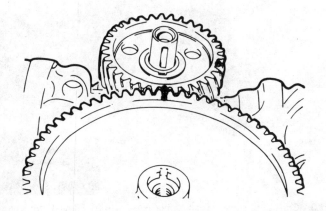

Fig. 1.29 Crankshaft and camshaft gears correctly aligned (Sec 90)

6   Apply sealant to the mating faces of the timing cover and the intermediate plate.
7   Position a new gasket on the intermediate plate and fit the timing cover to the cylinder block (photos).
8   Fit the timing cover bolts, but do not tighten them yet.
9   Oil the sealing face of the crankshaft pulley or damper. Fit the pulley/damper and the central bolt and washer, applying sealant to the inboard face of the washer (photo). Draw the pulley/damper into place by tightening the bolt; this will centralise the timing cover.

10 Tighten the timing cover bolts evenly to the specified torque.
11 Jam the crankshaft and tighten the pulley/damper central bolt to the specified torque.
12 Refit the sump (Section 91).
13 If the water pump was removed from the timing cover, refit it using a new gasket.
14 If the engine is still in the vehicle, reverse the steps taken to gain access.

## 91  Sump – refitting

1   Clean the mating faces of the crankcase and sump. Ensure that the grooves in the seal carriers are clean.

90.4 Fitting the camshaft gear

90.5A Camshaft gear washer and bolt

90.5B Tightening the camshaft gear bolt

90.7A Timing cover gasket in position

90.7B Fitting the timing cover

90.9 Fitting the crankshaft pulley

91.3A Cut-out in sump gasket rubber seal

91.3B Slide the sump gasket tab into the cut-out

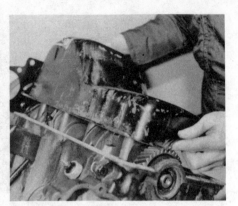

91.4 Fitting the sump

2   Fit the rubber seals in the grooves of the seal carriers.
3   Apply sealing compound on the crankcase and slide the tabs of the gasket under the cut-outs in the rubber seals (photos).
4   Ensure that the gasket hole lines up with the holes in the gasket crankcase and fit the sump. Take care not to dislodge the gasket (photo).
5   Fit the 24 securing bolts. Tighten them in sequence to the Stage 1 specified torque starting at point 'A' (Fig. 1.30), then to the Stage 2 torque starting at point 'B'.
6   Fit the sump drain plug, using a new washer, and tighten it to the specified torque.
7   If the engine is in the vehicle, reverse the steps taken to gain access.

## 92 Cylinder heads – refitting

1   Lubricate the valve tappets with clean engine oil and insert them in the cylinder block. Ensure they are fitted in their original locations (photo).
2   Ensure that the mating faces of the cylinder block and the cylinder heads are clean.
3   Position the new cylinder head gaskets over the guide bushes on the cylinder block. Check that they are correctly located. The right and left-hand gaskets are different. The gaskets are marked FRONT TOP (photo).
4   Carefully lower the cylinder heads onto the cylinder block. Oil the

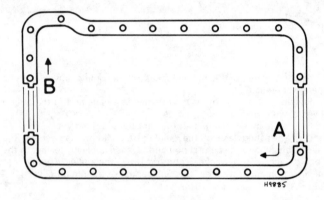

Fig. 1.30 Sump bolt tightening sequence. For 'A' and 'B' see text (Sec 91)

threads and contact faces of the cylinder head bolts and insert them into their holes.
5   Tighten the cylinder head bolts, in the order shown in Fig. 1.31, to the Stage 1 specified torque. Repeat in the same order for Stages 2 and 3 (photo). Final tightening, when required, is done after warm-up (Section 96).

92.1 Fitting a tappet in the block

92.3 Cylinder head gasket markings

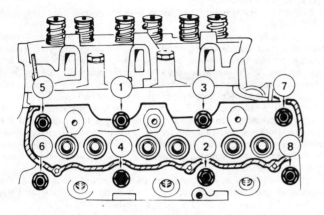

**Fig. 1.31 Cylinder head bolt tightening sequence (Sec 92)**

6 Lubricate the pushrods with engine oil and insert them in the cylinder block (photo).
7 Place the oil splash shields in position on the cylinder heads and fit the rocker shaft assemblies. Guide the rocker arm adjusting screws into the pushrod sockets (photos).
8 Tighten the rocker shaft securing bolts progressively to the specified torque.
9 Refit the inlet manifold, using a new gasket, as described in Chapter 3, Section 32. Do not refit the rocker covers yet.
10 Adjust the valve clearances as described in the next Section.
11 Refit the spark plugs.
12 Refit the rocker covers, using new gaskets. The adhesive side of the gaskets should face the rocker cover.
13 If the engine is in the vehicle, reverse the preliminary steps (Section 62).

## 93 Valve clearances – checking and adjustment

1 If the engine is in the vehicle, carry out the preliminary steps:

   (a) *Disconnect the battery negative lead*
   (b) *Remove the throttle mechanism cover, air cleaner cover, airflow meters and inlet trunking (Chapter 3, Section 29)*
   (c) *Remove the HT leads from the spark plugs and unclip them from the rocker cover*
   (d) *Unbolt and remove the rocker covers*

92.5 Tightening the cylinder head bolts

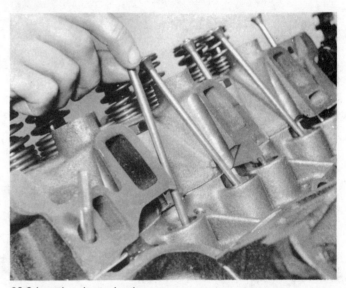

92.6 Inserting the pushrods

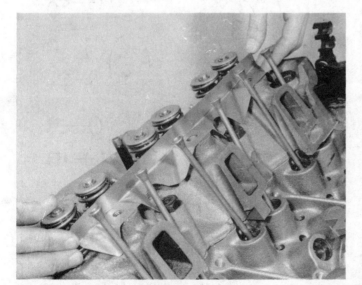

92.7A Fitting the oil splash shields

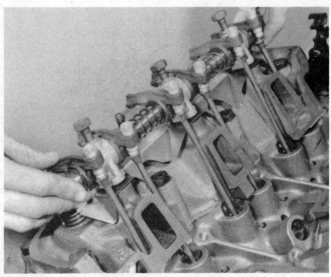

92.7B Fitting an assembled rocker shaft

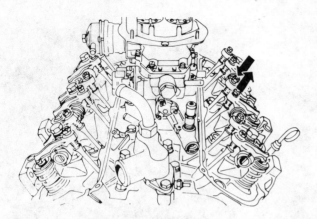

**Fig. 1.32 Valves of No. 5 cylinder overlapping – exhaust closing and inlet opening (arrows) (Sec 93)**

93.5 Adjusting a valve clearance

2   Although not essential, it will be easier to turn the engine if the spark plugs are removed.
3   Valve clearances must be adjusted with the engine cold (less than 40°C/104°F).
4   Turn the engine, using a spanner on the crankshaft pulley bolt, until the crankshaft pulley timing mark is aligned with the TDC (zero) pointer on the timing cover and the valves of No. 5 cylinder are overlapping, *ie* the exhaust valve is closing and the inlet valve is opening, (No. 5 cylinder is the middle one on the left-hand bank – left being the vehicles left, not necessarily to operator's.)
5   When the valves of No. 5 cylinder are in this position, check the valve clearances of No.1 cylinder by inserting a feeler gauge of the specified thickness between the rocker arm and the valve stem. Adjust the clearance, if necessary, by turning the rocker arm adjusting screw until the specified clearance is obtained (photo). Inlet and exhaust valve are different.
6   If the engine is now rotated one-third of a turn clockwise at the crankshaft, the valves of No. 3 cylinder will be overlapping and the valves of No.4 cylinder can be checked and adjusted.
7   Proceed to adjust the clearances according to the firing order as follows. The cylinders are numbered as shown in Fig. 1.33; the valves are listed in their correct order, working from the front of the engine (see Fig. 1.34):

| Valves overlapping | Valves to adjust |
|---|---|
| *No 5 cylinder* | *No 1 cylinder (in, ex)* |
| *No 3 cylinder* | *No 4 cylinder (in, ex)* |
| *No 6 cylinder* | *No 2 cylinder (in, ex)* |
| *No 1 cylinder* | *No 5 cylinder (ex, in)* |
| *No 4 cylinder* | *No 3 cylinder (ex, in)* |
| *No 2 cylinder* | *No 6 cylinder (ex, in)* |

8   Refit the rocker covers, using new gaskets if necesssary. Tighten the rocker cover bolts to the specified torque.
9   If the engine is in the vehicle, refit the other displaced components.

## 94 Ancilliary components – refitting

1   Refer to Section 61 and refit the items listed, referring to the Chapters indicated when necessary.
2   If the oil cooler and its threaded bush were removed, refit them as follows.
3   Screw the new bush into the cylinder block. Apply Omnifit Activator 'Rapid' (to Ford specification SSM-99B-9000-AA) to the exposed threads of the bush and to the inside of the threaded sleeve.

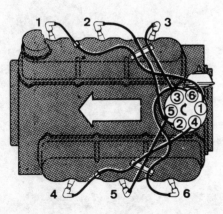

**Fig. 1.33 Cylinder numbering and HT lead connections. White arrow points to front of engine (Sec 93)**

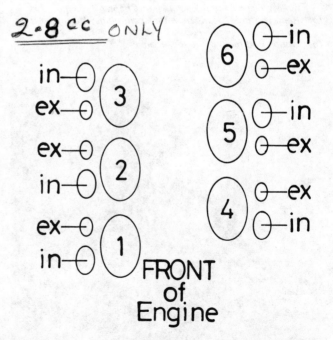

**Fig. 1.34 Location of inlet and exhaust valves (Sec 93)**

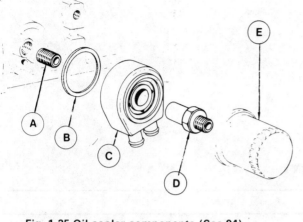

**Fig. 1.35 Oil cooler components (Sec 94)**

| | | | |
|---|---|---|---|
| A | Threaded bush | D | Sleeve |
| B | Seal | E | Oil filter |
| C | Cooler | | |

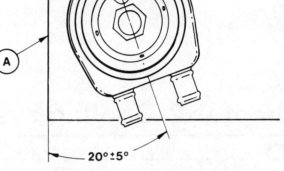

**Fig. 1.36 Oil cooler installation angle (Sec 94)**

*A Rear face of cylinder block*

4  Apply one drop of Omnifit Sealant '300 Rapid' (to Ford specification SSM-4G-9003-AA) to the leading threads of the bush. **Do not** use more than one drop, otherwise sealant may get into the lubrication circuit.
5  Fit the cooler, using a new gasket, and secure with the threaded bush. Make sure that the coolant pipes are positioned at the correct angle (Fig. 1.36), then tighten the threaded sleeve to the specified torque.
6  Fit a new oil filter element, oiling its sealing ring prior to installation. Tighten the filter approximately three-quarters of a turn beyond the point where the seal contacts the cooler face. Do not use any tool to tighten the filter.

## 95 Engine – refitting

1  Refer to Section 50, paragraphs 1 to 9
2  Before starting the engine, refer to Sections 52 and 96.

## 96 Initial start-up after overhaul or major reapiar

1  Refer to Section 52.
2  When conventional (hexagon-headed) cylinder head bolts are fitted, they must be re-tightened after the engine has warmed up. Proceed as follows.
3  Stop the engine and remove the rocker covers.
4  Working in the sequence used for tightening (Fig. 1.31), slacken one cylinder head bolt a quarter turn, then re-tighten it to the Stage 4 specified torque. Repeat in sequence for all the cylinder head bolts.
5  Tighten the inlet manifold bolts (Chapter 3, Section 32).
6  Check the valve clearances (Section 93).
7  Refit the rocker covers and other disturbed components.

## 97 Compression test – description and interpretation

1  When engine performance is down, or if misfiring occurs which cannot be attributed to the ignition or fuel system, a compression test can provide diagnostic clues. If the test is performed regularly it can give warning of trouble before any other symptoms become apparent.
2  The engine must be at operating temperature, the battery must be fully charged and the spark plugs must be removed. The services of an assistant will also be required.
3  Disable the ignition system by dismantling the coil LT feed. Fit the compression tester to No. 1 spark plug hole. (The type of tester which screws into the spark plug hole is to be preferred.)
4  Have the assistant hold the throttle wide open and crank the engine on the starter. Record the highest reading obtained on the compression tester.
5  Repeat the test on the remaining cylinders, recording the pressure developed in each.
6  Desired pressures are given in the Specifications. If the pressure in any cylinder is low, introduce a teaspoonful of clean engine oil into the spark plug hole and repeat the test.
7  If the addition of oil temporarily improves the compression pressure, this indicates that bore or piston wear was responsible for the pressure loss. No improvement suggests that leaking or burnt valves, or a blown head gasket, may be to blame.
8  A low reading from two adjacent cylinders is almost certainly due to the head gasket between them having blown.
9  On completion of the test, refit the spark plugs and reconnect the coil LT feed.

## 98 Fault diagnosis – engine

Refer to Section 53.

2·4 & 2·9 CHAPTER 13

# Chapter 2 Cooling system

## Contents

## Specifications

### General

| | |
|---|---|
| System type | Sealed, pressurised, thermostatically controlled |
| Fan type | Mechanical, temperature-sensitive viscous clutch |

### Coolant

| | |
|---|---|
| Type | See 'Recommended lubricants and fluids' |
| Capacity: | |
| ohc | 8.0 litres (14.1 pints) approx |
| V6 | 8.5 litres (15.0 pints) approx |
| Specific gravity at 45 to 50% antifreeze concentration | 1.069 to 1.077 |

### Pressure cap

| | |
|---|---|
| Blow-off pressure | 0.85 to 1.10 bar (12 to 16 lbf/in²) |

### Thermostat

| | |
|---|---|
| Nominal rating: | |
| ohc | 88°C (190°F) |
| V6 | 82°C (180°F) |
| Actual opening temperature: | |
| ohc | 85° to 89°C (185° to 192°F) |
| V6 | 79° to 83°C (174° to 181°F) |

### Water pump drivebelt

| | |
|---|---|
| Deflection | 10 mm (0.4 in) approx under normal fingertip pressure at mid-point of longest run |

### Torque wrench settings

| | Nm | lbf ft |
|---|---|---|
| Radiator lower mountings | 8 to 12 | 6 to 9 |
| Thermostat housing bolts | 17 to 20 | 13 to 15 |
| Water pump bolts: | | |
| V6 | 9 to 13 | 7 to 10 |
| ohc, M8 bolts | 17 to 21 | 13 to 16 |
| ohc, M10 bolts | 35 to 42 | 26 to 31 |
| Fan shroud bolts | 8 to 11 | 6 to 8 |
| Water pump pulley bolts | 21 to 26 | 16 to 19 |
| Fan-to-viscous clutch bolts: | | |
| ohc | 8 to 10 | 6 to 7 |
| V6 | 17 to 23 | 13 to 17 |
| Cylinder block drain plug | 21 to 25 | 16 to 18 |

## 1  General description

The cooling system is of pressurised type and includes a front mounted crossflow radiator, belt-driven water pump, temperature conscious thermo-viscous fan, wax type thermostat, and an expansion and degas tank.

The radiator matrix is of copper and brass construction and the end tanks are of plastic. On automatic transmission models the right-hand side end tank incorporates the transmission oil cooler.

The thermostat is located behind the water outlet elbow at the front of the cylinder head on ohc models, and on the front of the water pump on V6 models. Its purpose is to ensure rapid engine warm-up by restricting the flow of coolant in the engine when cold, and also to assist in regulating the normal operating temperature of the engine.

The expansion tank incorporates a pressure cap which effectively pressurises the cooling system as the coolant temperature rises thereby increasing the boiling point temperature of the coolant. The tank also has a further degas function. Any accumulation of air bubbles in the coolant, in particular in the thermostat housing and the radiator, is returned to the tank and released in the air space thus maintaining the efficiency of the coolant.

On models fitted with the auxiliary warning system, the expansion tank contains a level sensor which operates a warning light if the coolant level falls significantly.

When the engine is started from cold, the water pump circulates coolant around the cylinder block, cylinder head(s) and inlet manifold. The warm coolant passes through the automatic choke housing (when applicable) and through the heater matrix before returning to the engine. As the coolant expands, the level in the expansion tank rises. Circulation of coolant through the radiator is prevented while the thermostat is shut.

When the coolant reaches the predetermined temperature the thermostat opens and hot water passes through the top hose to the top of the radiator. As the water circulates down through the radiator, it is cooled by the passage of air past the radiator when the car is in forward motion, supplemented by the action of the thermo-viscous fan when necessary. Having reached the bottom of the radiator, the water is now cool and the cycle is repeated. Circulation of water continues through the expansion tank, inlet manifold and heater at all times, the heater temperature control being by an air flap.

The thermo-viscous fan is controlled by the temperature of air behind the radiator. When the air temperature reaches a predetermined level, a bi-metallic coil commences to open a valve within the unit and

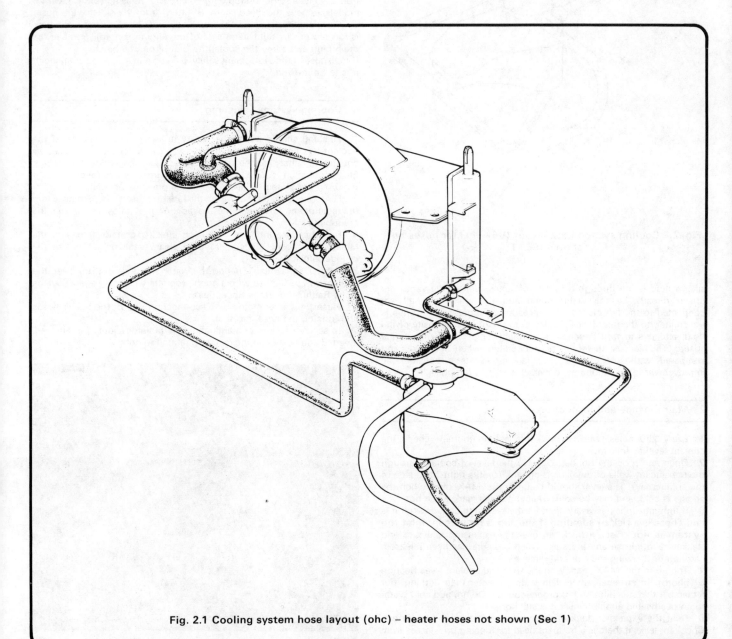

Fig. 2.1 Cooling system hose layout (ohc) – heater hoses not shown (Sec 1)

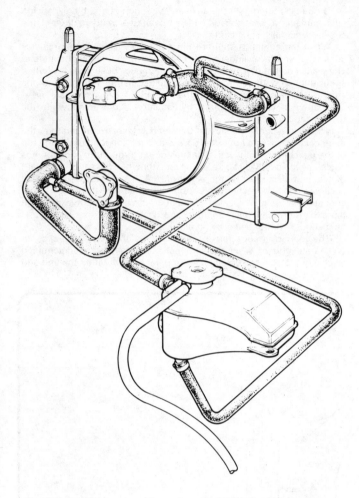

**Fig. 2.2 Cooling system hose layout (V6) – heater hoses not shown (Sec 1)**

silicon fluid is fed through a system of vanes. Half of the vanes are driven directly by the water pump and the remaining half are connected to the fan blades. The vanes are arranged so that drive is transmitted to the fan blades in relation to the drag or viscosity of the fluid, and this in turn depends on ambient temperature and engine speed. The fan is therefore only operated when required, and compared with direct drive type fan represents a considerable improvement in fuel economy, drivebelt wear and fan noise.

## 2  Maintenance and inspection

1   Every 250 miles, weekly, or before a long journey, check the coolant level as follows.
2   Open and prop the bonnet. Observe the level of coolant through the translucent walls of the expansion tank (on the right-hand side of the engine bay). The level should be up to the 'MAX' mark when the engine is cold, and may be somewhat above the mark when hot.
3   If topping-up is necessary, wait for the system to cool down if it is hot. **There is a risk of scalding if the cap is removed whilst the system is hot.** Place a thick rag over the expansion tank cap and slacken it to release any pressure. When pressure has been released, carry on unscrewing the cap and remove it.
4   Top up to the 'MAX' mark with the specified coolant – see Section 6 (photo). In an emergency plain water is better than nothing, but remember that it is diluting the proper coolant. Do not add cold water to an overheated engine whilst it is still hot.
5   Refit the expansion tank cap securely when the level is correct. Check for leaks if there is a frequent need for topping up – losses from this type of system are normally minimal.

6   Every 12 000 miles or annually, inspect the water pump drivebelt(s) for fraying, glazing or other damage. Re-tension or renew as necessary – see Section 13.
7   Every two years, regardless of mileage, renew the coolant. The necessary information will be found in Sections 3 to 6. At the same time inspect all the coolant hoses and hose clips with a critical eye. It is worth renewing the hoses as a precautionary measure if suspect, rather than have one burst on the road.
8   Occasionally clean insects and road debris from the radiator fins, using an air jet or a soft brush.

## 3  Cooling system – draining

1   Disconnect the battery negative lead.
2   Remove the expansion tank cap. Take precautions against scalding if the system is hot.
3   Place a drain pan of adequate capacity beneath the radiator drain plug. Unscrew the plug, without removing it, and allow the coolant to drain (photo).
4   On ohc models, release the hose clip and remove the rubber cap from the bleed spigot on top of the thermostat housing (photo). On V6 models, remove the bleed screw (if fitted) from the radiator top hose.
5   Place another drain pan below the cylinder block drain plug, which is located on the right-hand side of the engine (photo). Remove the drain plug and allow the coolant to drain from the block.
6   Dispose of the old coolant safely, or keep it in a covered container if it is to be re-used.

## 4  Cooling system – flushing

1   Flushing should not be necessary unless periodic renewal of the coolant has been neglected, or unless plain water has been used as coolant. In either case the coolant will appear rusty and dark in colour. Flushing is then required and should be carried out as follows.
2   Drain the system as described in the previous Section.
3   Disconnect the top hose from the radiator. Insert a garden hose into the radiator and run water into the radiator until it flows clear from the drain plug.
4   Run the hose into the expansion tank (ohc models) or into the radiator top hose (V6 models) until clean water comes out of the cylinder block drain plug.
5   If, after a reasonable period the water still does not run clear, the radiator can be flushed with a good proprietary cleaning agent such as Holts Radflush or Holts Speedflush.
6   Flush the heater matrix by disconnecting one of the heater hoses and running the hose into that.
7   In severe cases of contamination the radiator should be removed, inverted and flushed in the reverse direction to normal flow, *ie* with the

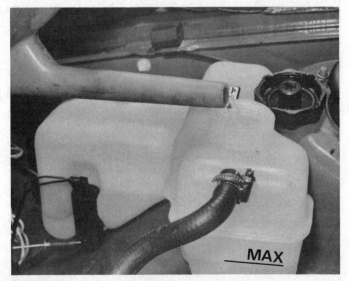

2.4  Topping-up the cooling system expansion tank

3.3 Radiator drain plug (arrowed)

3.4 Releasing the hose clip which secures the bleed spigot cap (ohc)

3.5 Cylinder block drain plug location (ohc shown)

water going in at the bottom and out at the top. Shake the radiator gently while doing this to dislodge any deposits.

## 5  Cooling system – filling

1   Refit any hoses which were disturbed, making sure that they and their clips are in good condition. Refit the cylinder block drain plug and tighten the radiator drain plug.
2   On ohc models, make sure that the bleed spigot cap is still removed. On V6 models, check, if applicable, that the bleed screw is still removed.
3   Pour coolant in through the expansion tank filler hole until the level is up to the 'MAX' line.
4   Refit the bleed spigot cap or screw when coolant starts to emerge from the spigot. Tighten the clip.
5   Squeeze the radiator hoses to help disperse airlocks. Top up the coolant further if necessary, then refit and tighten the expansion tank cap.
6   Run the engine up to operating temperature, checking for coolant leaks. Stop the engine and allow it to cool, then top up the coolant again to the 'MAX' mark if necessary.

## 6  Antifreeze mixture – general

**Warning:** *Antifreeze mixture is poisonous. Keep it out of reach of children and pets. Wash splashes off skin and clothing with plenty of water. Wash splashes off vehicle paintwork, too, to avoid discolouration.*

1   The antifreeze/water mixture must be renewed every two years to preserve its anti-corrosive properties. In climates where antifreeze protection is unnecessary, a corrosion inhibitor may be used instead – consult a Ford dealer. Never run the engine for long periods with plain water as coolant.
2   Only use the specified antifreeze (see *'Recommended lubricants and fluids'*). Inferior brands may not contain the necessary corrosion inhibitors, or may break down at high temperatures. Antifreeze containing methanol is particularly to be avoided, as the methanol evaporates.
3   The specified mixture is 45 to 50% antifreeze and 50 to 55% clean soft water (by volume). Mix the required quantity in a clean container and then fill the system as described in Section 5. Save any surplus mixture for topping-up.

## 7  Radiator – removal and refitting

1   Drain the radiator as described in Section 3. (There is no need to drain the cylinder block).
2   Disconnect the top and bottom hoses from the radiator by slackening the hose clips and pulling off the hoses with a twisting motion (photos). Do not use excessive force – remember the radiator side tanks are made of plastic.
3   On ohc models, disconnect the small hose which runs from the expansion tank to the radiator.
4   On automatic transmission models, clean around the transmission fluid cooler unions on the radiator and disconnect them (photo). Be prepared for fluid spillage; plug or cap the cooler lines to keep dirt out.
5   On models with air conditioning, disconnect the auxiliary fan thermo-switch. If the thermo-switch is mounted in the radiator, remove it.
6   Remove the upper half of the fan shroud by removing the two bolts and four clips (photos).
7   Release the two radiator top mounting clips by pulling out the plastic plugs (photos).
8   Raise and support the front of the vehicle. Support the radiator and remove the two bottom mounting bolts (photo).
9   Carefully lower the radiator slightly to free the top mountings, then remove it from under the vehicle.

7.2A Radiator top hose

7.2B Radiator bottom hose (A). Also shown are automatic transmission fluid cooler lower union (B) and hose to expansion tank (C)

7.4 Transmission fluid cooler upper union

7.6A Fan shroud bolt

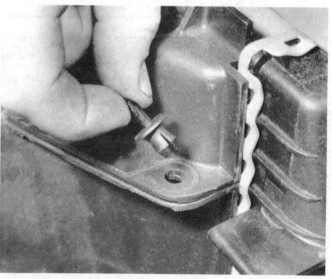

7.6B Fan shroud clip

7.7A Pull out the plug ...

7.7B ... to release the radiator top mounting

7.8 One of the radiator bottom mounting bolts (arrowed)

10 If a new radiator is being fitted, transfer the fan shrouds and mounting hardware from the old one.
11 Refit by reversing the removal operations, then refill the cooling system as described in Section 5.
12 On automatic transmission models, check the transmission fluid level as described in Chapter 6, Section 11.

## 8 Radiator – inspection and repair

1 If the radiator has been removed because of suspected blockage, reverse-flush it as described in Section 4.
2 Clean dirt and debris from the radiator fins, using an air jet or water and a soft brush. Be careful not to damage the fins, or cut your fingers.
3 A radiator specialist can perform a 'flow test' on the radiator to establish whether an internal blockage exists.
4 A leaking radiator must be referred to a specialist for permanent repair. Do not attempt to weld or solder a leaking radiator, as damage to the plastic parts may result.
5 In an emergency, minor leaks from the radiator can be cured by using a radiator sealant such as Holts Radweld while the radiator is *in situ*.

## 9 Thermostat – removal and refitting

### ohc models
1 Disconnect the battery negative lead.
2 Drain the cooling system as described in Section 3. As it is not necessary to completely drain the radiator, the bottom hose can be disconnected from the water pump.
3 Disconnect the top hose from the thermostat housing at the front of the cylinder head (photo).
4 Unscrew the bolts and remove the housing and gasket (photo).
5 Using a screwdriver prise the retaining clip from the housing, and extract the thermostat and sealing ring (photos).
6 Clean the thermostat housing and cylinder head mating surfaces. Obtain a new gasket for reassembly, and if necessary a new sealing ring too.
7 Refit by reversing the removal operations. Make sure that the thermostat is the right way round – the wax capsule fits into the cylinder head, with the direction of flow arrow facing forwards (photo).
8 Refill the cooling system as described in Section 5.

### V6 models
9 The thermostat is removed in the course of water pump removal. Refer to Section 12.

9.3 Top hose attachment to the thermostat housing (ohc)

9.4 Removing the thermostat housing (ohc)

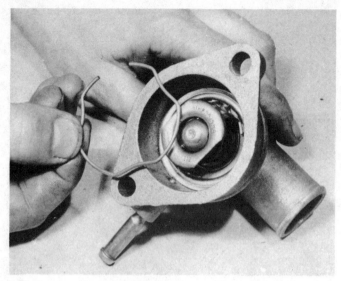

9.5A Remove the retaining clip ...

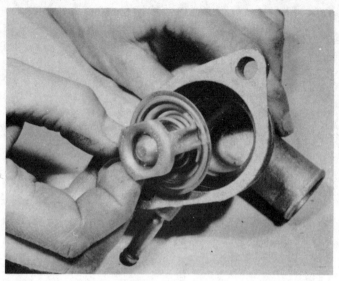

9.5B ... extract the thermostat ...

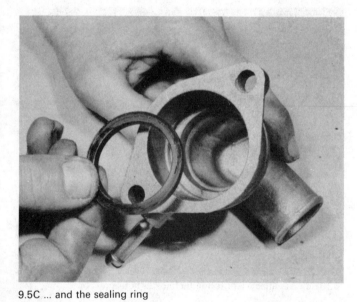

9.5C ... and the sealing ring

9.7 Thermostat direction of flow arrow

## 10 Thermostat – testing

1    A rough test of the thermostat may be made by suspending it with a piece of string in a saucepan full of water. Bring the water to the boil: the thermostat must open by the time the water boils. If not, renew it.
2    If a thermometer is available, the precise opening temperature of the thermostat may be determined and compared with that given in the Specifications.
3    A thermostat which fails to close as the water cools must also be renewed.

## 11 Viscous-coupled fan – removal and refitting

1    Disconnect the battery negative lead.
2    Remove the upper half of the fan shroud (two bolts, four clips).
3    Undo the nut which secures the fan clutch to the water pump. **This nut has a left-hand thread,** *ie* it is undone in a clockwise direction. A thin cranked spanner, 32 mm (ohc) or 36 mm (V6) AF is needed (Fig. 2.4); alternatively, if two of the pulley bolts are removed, a normal

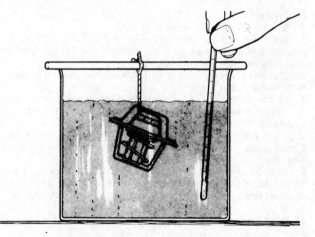

**Fig. 2.3 Checking the thermostat opening temperature (Sec 10)**

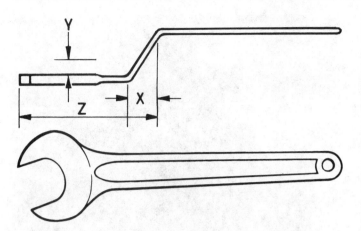

**Fig. 2.4 Dimensions of spanner for undoing fan clutch nut. Spanner thickness must not exceed 5 mm (0.2 in) (Sec 11)**

X = 10 mm (0.4 in)          Z = 50 mm (2.0 in)
Y = 10 mm (0.4 in)

thickness or even an adjustable spanner can be used (photos). If problems are experienced with the pulley turning as the nut is undone, remove the drivebelt and clamp an old drivebelt round the pulley to restrain it, using self-locking pliers. Tap the spanner with a mallet if need be to release the nut.

4   The fan can now be unbolted from the viscous clutch if required. Do not overtighten the bolts when refitting.

5   Refit by reversing the removal operations.

## 12 Water pump – removal and refitting

1   Disconnect the battery negative lead.
2   Drain the cooling system as described in Section 3.
3   Remove the fan and viscous coupling as described in Section 11.
4   If not already done, remove the pump drivebelt(s) as described in Section 13, then unbolt and remove the water pump pulley (photo).

*ohc models*

5   Disconnect the radiator bottom hose and the heater return hose from the pump.
6   Remove the timing belt cover, which is secured by three bolts.
7   Remove the three securing bolts and withdraw the water pump (photos).

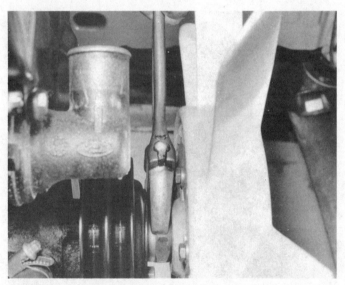

11.3A Undoing the viscous fan clutch nut

11.3B Removing the fan and clutch

12.4 Undoing a water pump pulley bolt (ohc)

12.7A Removing one of the water pump securing bolts

12.7B This water pump bolt also secures the alternator strap

12.7C Water pump removed

### V6 models

8   Disconnect the radiator bottom hose and the heater return hose from the thermostat housing.
9   Remove the three bolts which secure the thermostat housing to the water pump. Remove the housing and the thermostat.
10  Remove the twelve securing bolts and withdraw the water pump (photo).

### All models

11  A leaking, noisy or otherwise defective pump must be renewed.
12  Clean the mating faces and obtain a new gasket for reassembly (photo). On V6 models use a new thermostat housing gasket too.
13  Refit by reversing the removal operation, tightening all fastenings to the correct torque (where specified).
14  Refill the cooling system as described in Section 5.

### 13 Water pump/alternator drivebelt(s) – inspection, renewal and adjustment

1   All models have one or two drivebelts which drive the water pump and alternator from the crankshaft pulley. When power steering is fitted, the same belts drive the steering pump. The air conditioning compressor, when fitted, is driven independently.
2   Periodically inspect the drivebelt(s) for fraying, cracks, glazing or other damage. Turn the engine so that the full length of the belt(s) can be viewed. Renew belts which are in poor condition. When twin drivebelts are fitted, both must be renewed together, even if only one is damaged.
3   Check the tension of the drivebelt(s) by pressing firmly with the fingers in the middle of the longest belt run (engine stopped). Tension is correct when the belt can be deflected by 10 mm (0.4 in) under firm finger pressure (photo).
4   Renewal and adjustment procedures for models with power steering are given in Chapter 10, Section 14. For other models proceed as follows.
5   Disconnect the battery negative lead.
6   On models with air conditioning, remove the compressor drivebelt (Chapter 11, Section 56).
7   Slacken the alternator pivot and adjusting bolts. Swing the alternator towards the engine and slip the belt(s) off the pulleys.
8   Fit the new belt(s) over the pulleys. Move the alternator away from the engine until the belt tension is correct (paragraph 3), then tighten the alternator adjusting strap and pivot bolts. If it is necessary to lever against the alternator to achieve the correct tension, only do so using a wooden or plastic lever (photo).

12.10 Removing the water pump (V6)

12.12 Fitting a new gasket to the water pump

13.3 Checking drivebelt tension

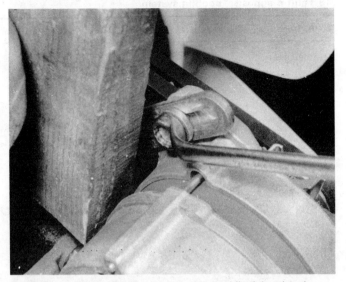

13.8 Using a wooden lever on the alternator while tightening the strap bolt

9   Refit and tension the air conditioning compressor drivebelt, when applicable.
10  Reconnect the battery. If a new drivebelt has been fitted, run the engine for a few minutes, then stop it and recheck the tension.
11  Check the tension of new belts again after a few hundred miles.

## 14 Expansion tank – removal and refitting

1   Disconnect the battery negative lead.
2   Depressurize the cooling system by unscrewing the expansion tank cap. **Take precautions against scalding if the system is hot.**
3   Slacken the hose clips on all the hoses which are connected to the tank. Pull off and plug those hoses which are above the waterline.
4   Remove the two screws which secure the tank. Tilt the tank so that the coolant lies away from the outlets, then disconnect and plug the remaining hose.
5   Disconnect the coolant level sensor, when fitted, and remove the tank.
6   Refit by reversing the removal operations. Top up the cooling system on completion.

## 15 Temperature gauge sender – removal and refitting

1   The temperature gauge sender is located towards the front of the engine. On ohc models it is just below the inlet manifold (photo); on V6 models it is just below the top hose connection on the front of the left-hand cylinder head.
2   Slacken the expansion tank cap to release pressure in the cooling system, **taking precautions against scalding if the system is hot.** Tighten the cap again to minimise coolant loss.

3   Disconnect the wiring from the sender unit. Unscrew and remove it, being prepared for some coolant spillage.
4   Smear sealant on the sender unit threads before refitting, then insert and tighten it. Reconnect the wiring.
5   Top up the cooling system if necessary, then run the engine and check the operation of the temperature gauge.

15.1 Temperature gauge sender (ohc – manifold removed)

**Fault diagnosis overleaf**

## 16 Fault diagnosis – cooling system

| Symptom | Reason(s) |
| --- | --- |
| Overheating | Coolant level low |
| | Drivebelt slipping or broken |
| | Radiator blocked |
| | Coolant hose collapsed |
| | Thermostat stuck shut |
| | Viscous-coupled fan not working |
| | Ignition timing incorrect |
| | Fuel system fault (weak mixture) |
| | Exhaust system restricted |
| | Engine oil level low |
| | Cylinder head gasket blown |
| | Brakes binding |
| | New engine not yet run-in |
| Overcooling | Thermostat missing, jammed open or incorrect rating |
| Loss of coolant* | External leakage |
| | Overheating |
| | Pressure cap defective |
| | Cylinder head gasket blown |
| | Cylinder head or block cracked |
| Oil and/or combustion gases in coolant | Cylinder head gasket blown |
| | Cylinder head or block cracked |

*If the reason for loss of coolant is not obvious, have the cooling system pressure tested by a Ford dealer or other specialist.*

# Chapter 3 Fuel and exhaust systems

*For modifications, and information applicable to later models, see Supplement at end of manual*

## Contents

## Specifications

### General

System type:
| | |
|---|---|
| 1.8 litre (REC) ................................................... | Twin choke Pierburg carburettor |
| 2.0 litre (NEL) ................................................... | Twin choke Weber carburettor |
| 2.0 litre (NRA) and 2.8 litre (PRE) ................ | Electronic fuel-injection (EFI) |
| Fuel tank capacity ............................................ | 70 litres (15.4 gallons) approx |

Fuel grade:
| | |
|---|---|
| Leaded ................................................................ | 97 octane RON (UK 4-star) |
| Unleaded (see Section 4) ................................. | 95 octane RON/85 octane MON |

### Idle adjustments

Idle speed:
| | |
|---|---|
| 1.8 litre (REC) ................................................... | 800 ± 20 rpm |
| 2.0 litre (NEL)* ................................................. | 800 or 875 rpm |
| 2.0 litre (NRA)* ................................................. | 800 ot 875 rpm |
| 2.8 litre (PRE)* ................................................. | 850 rpm |

Idle CO level:
| | |
|---|---|
| 1.8 litre (REC) ................................................... | 1.3% |
| 2.0 litre (NEL) ................................................... | 0.75 to 1.50% |
| 2.0 litre (NRA) and 2.8 litre (PRE) ................ | 0.5 to 1.0% |

*Electronically controlled – see Chapter 4*

### Air cleaner element

Application:
| | |
|---|---|
| 1.8 OHC (carburettor) ...................................... | Champion W118 |
| 2.0 OHC (carburettor) ...................................... | Champion W152 |
| 2.0 OHC (injection) ........................................... | Champion U507 |
| 2.8 OHV (injection) ........................................... | Champion U507 |

### Fuel filter

Type:
| | |
|---|---|
| 2.0 litre injection ............................................... | Champion L204 |
| 2.8 litre injection ............................................... | Champion L204 |

### Pierburg carburettor

Venturi diameter:
| | |
|---|---|
| Primary ................................................................ | 23 mm (0.906 in) |
| Secondary ........................................................... | 26 mm (1.024 in) |

Jet sizes:
| | |
|---|---|
| Idle (fuel) ........................................................... | 45 |
| Idle (air bleed) .................................................. | 115 |
| Primary main ...................................................... | 107.5 |
| Secondary main ................................................. | 130 |

Adjustments:
Fast idle speed (engine warm) ..................................................... 1800 ± 100 rpm (on second highest step of cam)
Choke pull-down ........................................................................... 3 mm (0.12 in)
Throttle damper setting ............................................................... 2 ± 0.5 mm (0.08 ± 0.02 in)
Float level ..................................................................................... Not adjustable
Automatic choke setting .............................................................. Index

## Weber carburettor

| | Primary | Secondary |
|---|---|---|
| Barrel diameter | 30 mm (1.181 in) | 34 mm (1.339 in) |
| Venturi diameter: | | |
| 85HFCA and –DA | 25 mm (0.984 in) | 27 mm (1.063 in) |
| 85HFGA, –HA, –MA and –NA | 23 mm (0.906 in) | 25 mm (0.984 in) |
| Jet sizes – 85HFCA: | | |
| Main jet | 112 | 135 |
| Air correction jet | 165 | 150 |
| Emulsion tube | F22 | F22 |
| Idle jet | 45 | 45 |
| Jet sizes – 85HFDA: | | |
| Main jet | 110 | 135 |
| Air correction jet | 160 | 150 |
| Emulsion tube | F22 | F22 |
| Idle jet | 45 | 45 |
| Jet sizes – 85HFGA and –HA: | | |
| Main jet | 107 | 125 |
| Air correction jet | 180 | 160 |
| Emulsion tube | F59 | F59 |
| Idle jet | 45 | 50 |
| Jet sizes – 85HFMA: | | |
| Main jet | 105 | 130 |
| Air correction jet | 200 | 160 |
| Emulsion tube | F59 | F59 |
| Idle jet | 45 | 50 |
| Jet sizes – 85HFNA: | | |
| Main jet | 110 | 125 |
| Air correction jet | 180 | 160 |
| Emulsion tube | F59 | F59 |
| Idle jet | 45 | 50 |
| Adjustments: | | |
| Choke pull-down (maximum): | | |
| 85HFCA | 9.0 mm (0.35 in) | |
| 85HFDA | 8.0 mm (0.32 in) | |
| All others | 7.5 mm (0.30 in) | |
| Bimetal housing setting: | | |
| 85HFCA, –DA, –HA and –MA | Index | |
| 85HFGA and –NA | 3 mm (0.12 in) lean | |
| Float level | 7.5 to 8.5 mm (0.30 to 0.34 in) | |

## Fuel-injection system
Make ............................................................................................. Bosch
Fuel pump type ............................................................................. Roller cell, electric
Fuel pump output pressure .......................................................... Greater than 5 bar (73 lbf/in²) at 12 volts, no flow
System control pressure ............................................................... 2.5 bar (36 lbf/in²)

## Torque wrench settings

| | Nm | lbf ft |
|---|---|---|
| Inlet manifold – ohc | 17 to 21 | 13 to 16 |
| Inlet manifold – V6: | | |
| Stage 1 | 4 to 8 | 3 to 6 |
| Stage 2 | 8 to 15 | 6 to 11 |
| Stage 3 | 15 to 21 | 11 to 16 |
| Stage 4 | 21 to 25 | 16 to 18 |
| Stage 5 (after warm-up) | 21 to 25 | 16 to 18 |
| Plenum chamber to inlet manifold (V6) | 7 to 10 | 5 to 7 |
| Exhaust manifold: | | |
| ohc | 21 to 25 | 16 to 18 |
| V6 | 25 to 30 | 18 to 22 |
| Fuel pump bolts (mechanical pump) | 14 to 18 | 10 to 13 |
| Fuel pipe to fuel-injection pressure regulator: | | |
| ohc | 15 to 20 | 11 to 15 |
| V6 | 10 to 12 | 7 to 9 |
| Pressure regulator base nut: | | |
| ohc | 20 to 25 | 15 to 18 |
| V6 | 15 to 20 | 11 to 15 |
| Fuel rail bolts (ohc) | 9 to 11 | 7 to 8 |
| Exhaust downpipe flange nuts | 35 to 40 | 26 to 30 |
| Exhaust clamps and U-bolts | 38 to 45 | 28 to 33 |

## 1  General description

All models are fitted with a rear-mounted fuel tank. Fuel is conveyed from the tank by a mechanical or electrical fuel pump, according to model and equipment, to the carburettor or fuel-injection system. The delivery capacity of the fuel pump exceeds the maximum demands of the system, so excess fuel is constantly returned to the tank. This helps to avoid the problems of vapour locks in the fuel lines.

Carburettor models have a twin venturi downdraught carburettor, of Pierburg manufacture on 1.8 litre models and Weber on 2.0 litre models. Both makes of carburettor have an automatic choke. The Weber carburettor also carries a stepper motor which controls idle speed, anti-dieseling and start-up; this is dealt with in Chapter 4.

Fuel-injection, when fitted, is of the Bosch L-Jetronic type. The system is described in detail in Section 25. It is under the control of the EEC IV module (Chapter 4).

The exhaust system fitted in production is made of aluminised steel, with stainless steel used in the endplates and baffles of the rear silencer. Individual sections of the system are easily renewed in service.

Emission control for the UK market is achieved largely by the inherent efficiency of the fuel, ignition and engine management systems. A welcome spin-off from such efficiency is remarkably good fuel economy for a vehicle of such size and weight.

**Warning: Fuel hazards**

*Petrol offers multiple hazards – fire, explosion and toxicity. Do not smoke when working on the fuel system, or allow naked flames nearby. Ensure adequate ventilation if fuel vapour is likely to be produced. Refer to 'Safety first' at the beginning of the manual for more details.*

## 2  Maintenance and inspection

1  Keep an adequate supply of fuel in the tank at all times. A full tank is less likely to suffer from rust and condensation, both of which can cause problems by contaminating the fuel.
2  Every 6000 miles or six months, inspect the exhaust system as described in Section 34. At the same time check the fuel tank and fuel lines for security and freedom from leakage or corrosion.
3  At the first 6000 mile service only, check the idle mixture (CO level) on carburettor models. See Section 16 or 21 as applicable.
4  On 1.8 litre models only, check the idle speed every 6000 miles as described in Section 16. (On all other models the idle speed is electronically controlled.)
5  Every 12 000 miles or annually, check the tightness of the inlet manifold bolts on V6 models (Section 32, paragraph 53 onwards).
6  Every 12 000 miles or annually, remove the air cleaner cover on carburettor models and check that the automatic choke is opening fully when the engine is hot.
7  Every 24 000 miles or two years, renew the air cleaner element as described in Section 5. (More frequent renewal may be necessary in very dusty conditions.)
8  Every 24 000 miles or two years, renew the fuel filter on fuel-injection models (Section 9).

## 3  Tamperproof adjustment screws – caution

1  Certain adjustment points in the fuel system (and elsewhere) are protected by 'tamperproof' caps, plugs or seals. The purpose of such tamperproofing is to discourage, and to detent, adjustment by unqualified operators.
2  In some EEC countries (though not yet in the UK) it is an offence to drive a vehicle with missing or broken tamperproof seals.
3  Before disturbing a tamperproof seal, satisfy yourself that you will not be breaking local or national anti-pollution regulations by doing so. Fit a new seal when adjustment is complete when this is required by law.
4  Do not break tamperproof seals on a vehicle which is still under warranty.

## 4  Unleaded fuel – general

1  Unleaded fuel will theoretically be available in all EEC countries as time progresses, and may eventually replace leaded fuel completely.
2  It is generally believed that continuous use of unleaded fuel can cause rapid wear of conventional valve seats. Valve seat inserts which can tolerate unleaded fuel are fitted to some engines. These engines are identified as follows:

| | |
|---|---|
| *1.8 litre:* | *'S' stamped adjacent to No 4 spark plug* |
| *2.0 litre:* | *'A', 'L', 'P', 'PP', or 'R', stamped adjacent to No 4 spark plug* |
| *2.8 litre:* | *'D' or 'E' stamped in centre of cylinder head exhaust flange* |

3  Engines which are marked as above can be run entirely on unleaded fuel.
4  Engines which are not fitted with the special valve seat inserts can still be run on unleaded fuel, but one tankful of leaded fuel should be used for every three tankfuls of unleaded. This will protect the valve seats.
5  On all models, the ignition timing may have to be retarded when unleaded fuel is used. See Chapter 4, Specifications and Section 15.
6  These recommendations may change as unleaded fuel becomes more common. For up-to-date information consult a Ford dealer.

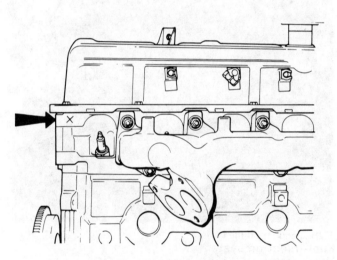

**Fig. 3.1 Identification letter position (arrowed) for cylinder heads with valve seat inserts: ohc shown (Sec 4)**

## 5  Air cleaner and element – removal and refitting

### Carburettor models

1  Remove the screws from the air cleaner cover (photo).
2  Release the spring clips (when fitted), then lift off the cover (photos).
3  Lift out the air cleaner element (photo). Wipe clean inside the air cleaner housing, but be careful not to sweep dirt into the carburettor throat.
4  To remove the air cleaner body, first disconnect the cold air inlet trunking from the spout (photo).
5  Disconnect the vacuum pipe from the inlet manifold, and the hot air trunking from the spout or exhaust manifold shroud (photo).
6  Remove the remaining screw which secures the air cleaner to the valve cover, then lift off the air cleaner.
7  Refit by reversing the removal operations.

### Fuel-injection models

8  Release the four spring clips which secure the air cleaner cover (photo).

5.1 Removing an air cleaner cover screw (carburettor models)

5.2A Release the clip ...

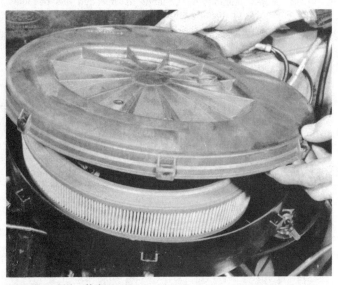

5.2B ... and lift off the cover

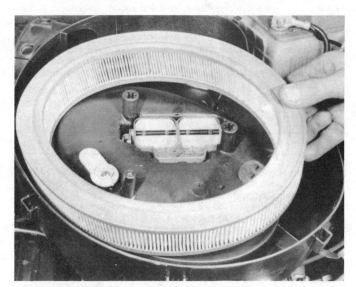

5.3 Removing the air cleaner element

5.4 Disconnecting the air cleaner cold air inlet trunking

5.5 Air cleaner hot air trunking and manifold shroud

**Fig. 3.2 Air cleaner retaining screws (arrowed) (Sec 5)**

5.8 Air cleaner cover spring clip (fuel-injection models)

5.9 Bolts (arrowed) securing the airflow meter to the cover

5.10 Removing the air cleaner element

9  Lift off the cover and move it aside. It is attached to the vane airflow meter(s): be careful not to strain the air trunking or meter wiring. To remove the cover completely, disconnect the meter(s) or unbolt the cover (photo).
10  Remove the air cleaner element, noting which way up it is fitted (photo). Wipe clean inside the air cleaner body.
11  To remove the air cleaner body, remove the three securing nuts which are accessible from inside the left-hand wheel arch. Disengage the body from the air pick-up hose and remove it.
12  Refit by reversing the removal operations.

## 6  Air cleaner temperature control – description and testing

1  On carburettor models only, the air cleaner can take in both hot and cold air. Hot air is obtained from a shroud bolted to the exhaust manifold.
2  A flap valve in the air cleaner spout determines the mix of hot and cold air. The valve is operated by a vacuum diaphragm. Vacuum is obtained from the inlet manifold and is applied via a heat sensing valve, which cuts off the vacuum as the temperature of the incoming air rises. Thus the air cleaner takes in only hot air on starting from cold, changing progressively to cold air as the engine warms up (photos).
3  If the system fails, either the engine will take a long time to warm up (flap stuck in 'cold' position), or it may run roughly and not develop full power when warm (flap stuck in 'hot' position). Check it as follows.
4  With the engine cold, disconnect the cold air inlet trunking from the spout. Look into the spout and check that the flap valve is covering the hot air intake.
5  Start the engine and allow it to idle. Check that the flap moves to cover the cold air intake. If the flap does not move, check the diaphragm and heat sensor as follows.
6  Stop the engine. Disconnect the diaphragm vacuum pipe from the heat sensor. Apply vacuum to the diaphragm, using a vacuum head pump or by connecting the pipe directly to manifold vacuum. If the flap now moves, the heat sensor or vacuum line was faulty. If the flap still does not move, the diaphragm is faulty or the flap is jammed.
7  On completion reconnect the vacuum pipe and the cold air trunking.

6.2A Air cleaner heat sensor from below

6.2B Air cleaner heat sensor from above

6.2C Air cleaner vacuum diaphragm unit

## 7  Fuel pump (mechanical) – testing, removal and refitting

1   Carburettor models without air conditioning are fitted with a mechanical fuel pump, located on the left-hand side of the engine block.

2   To test the pump, disconnect the ignition coil LT lead. Disconnect the outlet hose from the pump and place a wad of rag next to the pump outlet. Take appropriate fire precautions.

3   Have an assistant crank the engine on the starter. Well-defined spurts of fuel must be ejected from the pump outlet – if not, the pump is probably faulty (or the tank is empty). Dispose of the fuel-soaked rag safely.

4   To remove the fuel pump, first disconnect the battery negative lead.

5   Disconnect and plug the pump inlet and outlet hoses. Be prepared for fuel spillage.

6   Unscrew the two bolts and withdraw the pump from the cylinder block. Remove the gasket. If necessary extract the pushrod (photos).

7   Clean the exterior of the pump in paraffin and wipe dry. Clean all traces of gasket from the cylinder block and pump flange.

8   If the fuel pump has a removable cover, remove the screw and withdraw the cover and nylon mesh filter with seal (photos). Clean the

7.6A Removing the mechanical fuel pump

7.6B Fuel pump pushrod

7.8A Removing the fuel pump cover – note alignment indentations

7.8B Fuel pump cover and filter screen

filter, cover and pump in fuel. Locate the filter in the cover and fit the cover to the pump so that the pip and indentation are aligned. Tighten the screw.

9 Refitting is a reversal of removal, but fit a new gasket and tighten the bolts to the specified torque. If necessary discard the crimped type hose clips and fit screw type clips.

## 8 Fuel pump (electrical) – testing, removal and refitting

1 All fuel-injection models, and carburettor models when fitted with air conditioning, have an electric fuel pump. The two types of pump are not the same, although both are mounted under the vehicle next to the fuel tank.

2 If the fuel pump appears to have failed completely, check the appropriate fuse and relay. On fuel-injection models, also check the inertia switch (when fitted) – see Section 25.

3 To test the carburettor type pump, disconnect the fuel supply hose from the pressure regulator or vapour separator in the engine compartment. Lead the hose into a measuring cylinder.

4 Take appropriate fire precautions. Switch on the ignition for 30 seconds and measure the quantity of fuel delivered: it should be at least 400 ml (0.7 pint).

5 To test the fuel-injection type pump, special equipment is required. Consult a Ford dealer or other fuel-injection specialist. The problem may be due to a clogged filter (Section 9).

6 To remove a pump, first disconnect the battery negative lead. Take appropriate fire precautions.

7 Raise and support the rear of the vehicle. Clean the fuel pump and its surroundings.

8 Clamp the tank-to-pump hose, or make arrangements to collect the contents of the fuel tank which will otherwise be released.

9 Place a drain pan beneath the pump. Disconnect the inlet and outlet hoses; be prepared for fuel spillage. **Caution:** *Fuel under pressure may spray out of the outlet hose union as it is slackened.*

10 Disconnect the wiring plug from the pump.

11 Slacken the pump bracket clamp bolt and slide the pump out of the bracket.

12 Refit by reversing the removal operations. Make sure that all hoses and unions are in good condition.

13 Run the engine and check for leaks.

## 9 Fuel filter (fuel-injection models) – renewal

1 Disconnect the battery negative lead.
2 Raise and support the rear of the vehicle.

9.4 Fuel filter outlet union (arrowed)

3 Place a drain pan under the fuel filter. Take adequate fire precautions.

4 Wipe clean the area around the filter inlet and outlet unions, then disconnect them (photo). **Caution:** *Fuel under pressure may spray out as the unions are slackened.*

5 Slacken the filter clamp bolt and withdraw the filter from the clamp. Dispose of the filter safely, remember it is full of fuel.

6 Fit the new filter into the clamp, observing the arrows on the filter indicating the direction of fuel flow. If there is a plastic band or sleeve on the filter, position the clamp over the sleeve to prevent chafing. Tighten the clamp bolt.

7 Refit the inlet and outlet unions, using new sealing washers. Tighten the union bolts.

8 Reconnect the battery. Have an assistant switch the ignition on and off a few times to pressurise the system; watch the filter for leakage as this is done.

9 Lower the vehicle on completion.

## 10 Fuel tank – removal and refitting

1 Run the fuel level as low as possible before removing the tank.
2 Disconnect the battery negative lead.

10.7 Fuel tank supply (left) and return hoses

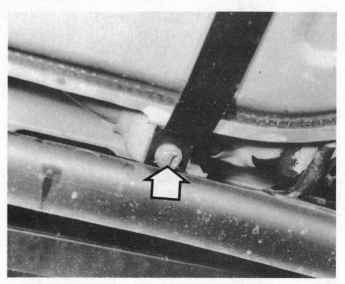

10.8 Fuel tank supporting strap bolt (arrowed)

3   Remove the fuel filler cap. Siphon or pump the remaining fuel out of the tank. Store the fuel in a suitable sealed container.
4   Remove the two screws on either side of the filler neck.
5   Raise and support the rear of the vehicle.
6   Remove the shield from the right-hand rear inner wheel arch. Also remove the rear bumper undershield, which is secured by six screws.
7   Disconnect the fuel supply and return lines from the tank (photo). Drain the fuel in the lines into a suitable container and remove it.
8   Support the fuel tank. Remove the two bolts which secure the rear ends of the fuel tank supporting straps (photo).
9   Lower the tank and supporting straps, unhooking the front ends of the straps from their locations. Disconnect the wiring and the vent hose from the tank. Remove the tank with filler pipe attached.
10 Fuel tank repairs including soldering or welding must be left to specialists. Even when empty, the tank may contain explosive vapour. Proprietary compounds are available for making temporary 'cold' repairs.
11 Refit the fuel tank in the reverse order to removal. Check for leaks on completion.

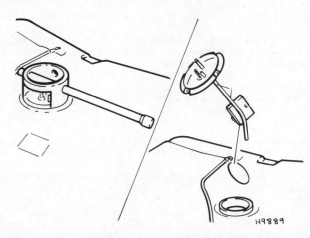

Fig. 3.3 Removing the fuel gauge sender unit (Sec 11)

### 11 Fuel gauge sender unit – removal and refitting

1   Remove the fuel tank as described in the previous Section.
2   Unscrew the sender unit from the tank. There is a Ford tool (No. 23-014) which engages with the lugs on the unit, but with patience a pair of crossed screwdrivers or similar items can be used instead.
3   Remove the sender unit, taking care not to damage the float or bend the float arm. Recover the seal.
4   A defective sender unit must be renewed; spares are not available. Renew the seal in any case.
5   Refit by reversing the removal operations.

### 12 Throttle pedal – removal and refitting

1   Disconnect the battery negative lead.
2   Unclip the under-dash insulation on the driver's side.
3   Disconnect the cable from the pedal. The cable may be secured by a clip, or it may slot into a 'keyhole' fitting (photo).

4   Remove the two nuts which secure the throttle pedal bracket to the bulkhead. Remove the pedal and bracket.
5   Refit by reversing the removal operations.

### 13 Throttle cable – removal and refitting

1   Disconnect the battery negative lead.
2   Disconnect the cable from the pedal as described in the previous Section.
3   Working under the bonnet, free the cable outer from the bulkhead and pull the cable into the engine bay.
4   On carburettor models, remove the air cleaner (Section 5).
5   On V6 models, remove the throttle linkage cover, which is secured by three screws (photos).
6   Disconnect the cable inner from the throttle lever on the carburettor or fuel-injection linkage. The cable may be secured by a spring clip, or by a simple barrel and slot arrangement (photo).
7   Disconnect the cable outer from its bracket. It may be secured by a spring clip, or by four plastic lugs. The lugs are most easily released with a tool made up as shown in Fig. 3.4.
8   Refit by reversing the removal operations. Adjust the threaded

12.3 Throttle pedal showing 'keyhole' cable fitting (arrowed)

13.5A Three screws (arrowed) secure the throttle linkage cover

13.5B Throttle linkage with cover removed

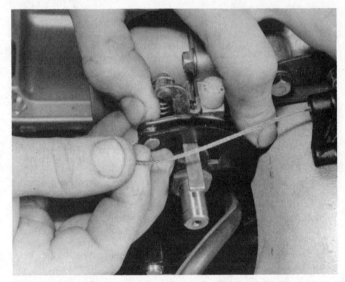

13.6 Dismantling a throttle cable inner – barrel and slot type

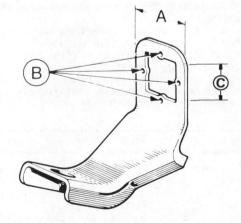

Fig. 3.4 Tool for releasing accelerator cable lugs (Sec 13)

A   25 mm (1 in)    B   Centre punch indents    C   16 mm (0.63 in)

sleeve on the cable outer so that there is a small amount of slack with the pedal released; have an assistant operate the throttle pedal and check that the throttle lever moves over its full range of travel.

9   On automatic transmission models, check the adjustment of the kickdown (downshift) cable as described in Chapter 6, Section 15.

## 14 Vapour separator (carburettor models) – removal and refitting

1   All carburettor models are fitted with a vapour separator, mounted on the left-hand inner wing. On 1.8 litre models the separator incorporates a pressure regulator (photo).

2   Disconnect the battery negative lead.

3   Identify the three hoses connected to the separator. Disconnect the hoses, cutting off the hose clips if they are of the crimped type.

4   Remove the two securing screws and lift out the separator. Remember it is full of fuel.

5   Refit by reversing the removal operations. Make sure that the different hoses are connected to the correct stubs on the regulator. Use new hose clips when necessary.

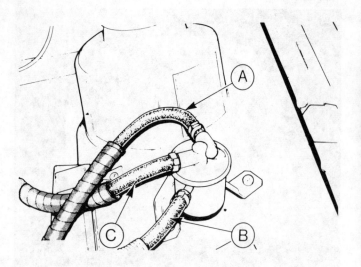

**Fig. 3.5 Fuel vapour separator without pressure regulator (Sec 14)**

A   Fuel return              C   Carburettor supply
B   Fuel supply

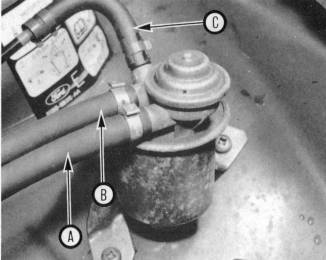

14.1 Fuel vapour separator and pressure regulator
A   Fuel supply              C   Fuel return
B   Carburettor supply

## 15 Pierburg 2V carburettor – description

The Pierburg twin venturi (2V) carburettor is fitted to 1.8 litre models. It is a downdraught type with an automatic choke. Opening of the throttle valves is sequential, the secondary throttle valve opening being controlled by vacuum developed in the primary venturi.

The automatic choke is heated both electrically and by coolant. Electrical heating is controlled by a manifold-mounted thermo-switch, which opens when the coolant temperature reaches a certain value. An external pull-down unit opens the choke valve under the influence of manifold vacuum.

An accelerator pump delivers extra fuel when the throttle is opened suddenly; a power valve provides mixture enrichment under sustained full throttle conditions. A throttle damper may be fitted to some models: its function is to improve smoothness and reduce exhaust emissions by preventing the throttle from suddenly snapping shut when the pedal is released.

An unusual feature is that the float level cannot be adjusted.

## 16 Pierburg 2V carburettor – idle speed and mixture adjustments

1   An accurate tachometer (rev. counter) will be needed to adjust the idle speed, and an exhaust gas analyser (CO meter) or other proprietary device will be needed to adjust the mixture.
2   The engine must be at operating temperature, the air cleaner element must be clean and the vacuum hoses fitted, and the engine valve clearances must be correct. The ignition system must also be in good condition.
3   Connect the tachometer to the engine as instructed by the manufacturers. Start the engine and allow it to idle. Read the speed from the tachometer and compare it with the value in the Specifications.
4   If adjustment is necessary, turn the idle speed adjustment screw (Fig. 3.7). Turn the screw clockwise to increase the speed, and anti-clockwise to decrease the speed.
5   Mixture adjustment is not required on a routine basis. If the CO level is incorrect, proceed as follows.
6   Connect an exhaust gas analyser as instructed by the manufacturers.
7   Raise the engine speed to 3000 rpm approximately and hold it at this speed for 30 seconds, then allow it to idle. Repeat this procedure every 60 seconds until adjustment is complete.
8   Read the CO level when it has stabilised after the 3000 rpm burst.

The desired level is given in the Specifications.
9   If the idle mixture needs adjustment, turn the mixture adjusting screw. The screw may be covered by a tamperproof plug – see Section 3.
10  Recheck the idle speed after adjusting the mixture.
11  Stop the engine and disconnect the test gear.
12  Fit a new tamperproof plug to the mixture adjusting screw if required.

## 17 Pierburg 2V carburettor – removal and refitting

1   Disconnect the battery negative lead.
2   Remove the air cleaner (Section 5).
3   Disconnect the automatic choke electrical lead from the manifold thermo-switch.
4   Unclip the throttle arm from the throttle lever (photo).
5   Disconnect the fuel hose from the carburettor and plug it. If a crimped hose clip is fitted, cut it off and use a worm drive clip when refitting (photo).
6   Depressurise the cooling system by removing the expansion tank filler cap. Take precautions against scalding if the system is hot.
7   Disconnect and plug the automatic choke coolant hoses (photo). Be prepared for coolant spillage.
8   Remove the three 'Torx' screws which secure the carburettor to the manifold (photo).
9   Check that no attachments have been overlooked, then lift the carburettor off the manifold. Recover the gasket.
10  Clean the carburettor and manifold mating surfaces, being careful not to get dirt into the manifold.
11  Refit by reversing the removal operations. Top up the cooling system if necessary on completion, then check the idle speed and mixture as described in the previous Section.

## 18 Pierburg 2V carburettor – dismantling and reassembly

1   Check the cost and availability of spare parts before deciding to dismantle the carburettor. If the unit has seen much service, a new or reconditioned carburettor may prove more satisfactory than attempts at overhaul.
2   Obtain a carburettor repair kit, which will contain the necessary gaskets, diaphragms and other renewable items.
3   With the carburettor removed from the vehicle, clean it thoroughly externally.

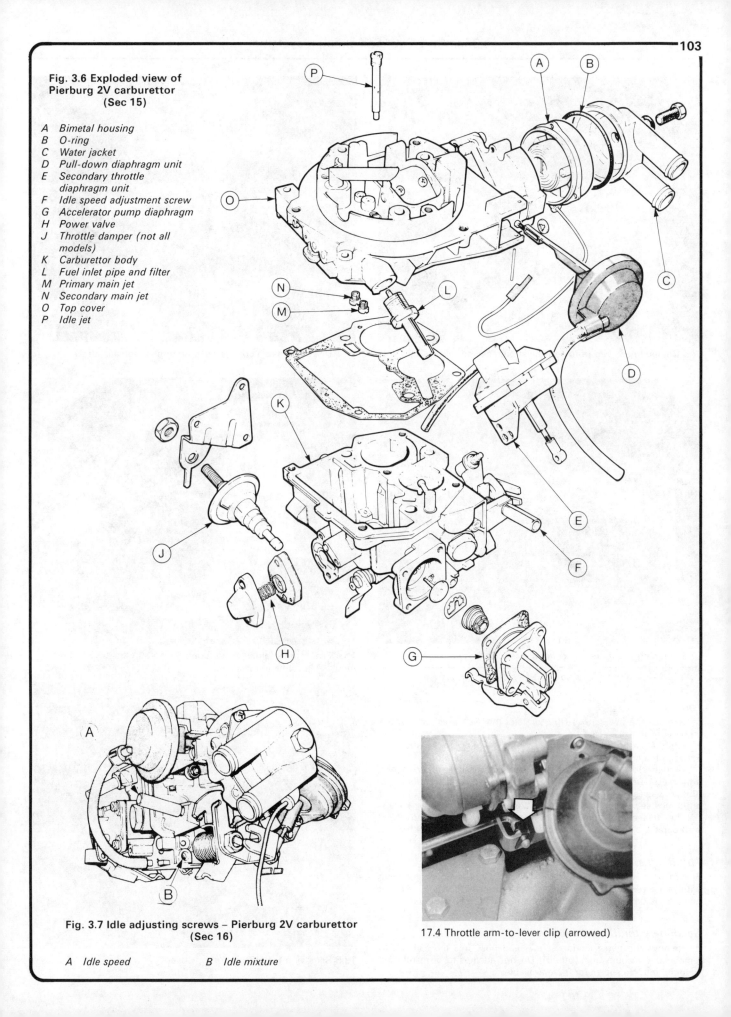

Fig. 3.6 Exploded view of
Pierburg 2V carburettor
(Sec 15)

A   Bimetal housing
B   O-ring
C   Water jacket
D   Pull-down diaphragm unit
E   Secondary throttle
    diaphragm unit
F   Idle speed adjustment screw
G   Accelerator pump diaphragm
H   Power valve
J   Throttle damper (not all
    models)
K   Carburettor body
L   Fuel inlet pipe and filter
M   Primary main jet
N   Secondary main jet
O   Top cover
P   Idle jet

Fig. 3.7 Idle adjusting screws – Pierburg 2V carburettor
(Sec 16)

A   Idle speed          B   Idle mixture

17.4 Throttle arm-to-lever clip (arrowed)

17.5 Crimped hose clip (arrowed) must be renewed

17.7 Disconnecting a coolant hose from the automatic choke

17.8 Undoing a carburettor securing screw. Other two screws are arrowed

18.4 Five screws (arrowed) securing the carburettor cover. Later models have only four screws

### Top cover

4   Remove the five screws (four on later models) which secure the top cover (photo).
5   Lift the cover off the carburettor body, noting the relationship between the fast idle cam and the throttle linkage (photo).
6   With the cover removed, the main jets are accessible (photo). Apart from these jets and the idle jet (on top of the cover), no other jets, tubes or valves should be removed. Do not attempt to remove the float or the needle valve unless new ones are included in the repair kit.
7   The fuel inlet pipe may be removed by unscrewing it. It incorporates a filter which cannot be renewed separately (photo).

### Throttle damper

8   When so equipped, the throttle damper can be removed complete with bracket by undoing the three bracket retaining screws. Do not remove the damper from the bracket unless it is to be renewed.

### Secondary throttle vacuum unit

9   Remove the two securing screws and prise free the balljoint to remove the vacuum unit (photo). Do not attempt to dismantle the vacuum unit. No spares for it are available.

18.5 Removing the carburettor top cover

18.6 Primary (A) and secondary (B) main jets

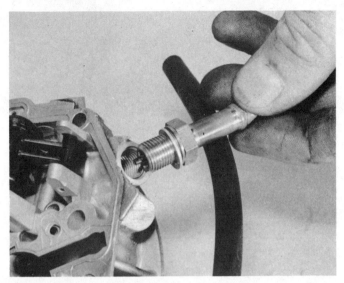

18.7 Fuel inlet pipe with built-in filter

### Accelerator pump

10 Remove the four retaining screws from the pump cover (photo).
11 Remove the cover, diaphragm, spring, seal retainer and seal. Note the orientation of the seal retainer (photos).

### Power valve

12 Remove the two securing screws and remove the valve complete (photo).
13 Carefully release the nylon clips with a small screwdriver and separate the valve into its component parts (photo).

### Automatic choke

14 Remove the central bolt from the water jacket and take off the jacket. Note the O-rings under the head of the bolt and round the rim of the jacket (photo).
15 Look for alignment marks on the bimetal housing and the choke lever carrier. If none are present, make some. Remove the three screws which secure the clamp ring and take off the clamp ring and bimetal housing (photos).
16 The choke lever carrier can be removed from the carburettor body, either with or without the bimetal housing and water jacket, after removing its securing screws (photo).

18.9 Removing the secondary throttle vacuum unit

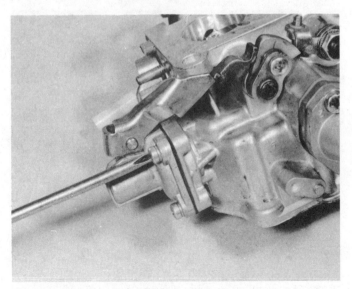

18.10 Removing an accelerator pump cover screw

18.11A Accelerator pump diaphragm

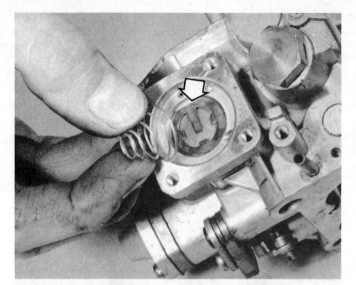

18.11B Accelerator pump spring – note seal retainer flat (arrowed)

18.11C Accelerator pump seal

18.12 Removing the power valve

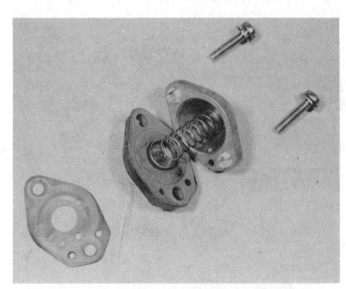

18.13 Power valve components

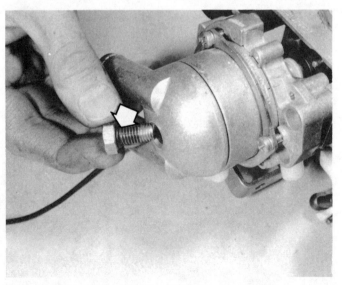

18.14 Choke cover central bolt – note O-ring (arrowed)

18.15A Choke housing-to-carrier alignment marks (arrowed)

18.15B Removing the choke clamp ring and bimetal housing

18.16 Removing the choke lever carrier

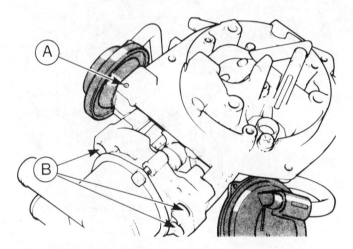

Fig. 3.8 Choke pull-down diaphragm unit removal –
Pierburg 2V carburettor (Sec 18)

*A   Roll pin*          *B   Choke lever housing screws*

17  The choke pull-down diaphragm assembly can be removed after
removal of the choke lever carrier by driving out its roll pin and prising
off the star clip.

## Reassembly and adjustments

18  Reassemble in the reverse order to dismantling, using new gaskets,
O-rings etc.
19  When refitting the top cover, make sure that the gasket is the right
way round and that the fuel riser enters the pick-up channel.
20  When refitting the choke lever carrier, make sure that the linkage is
correctly engaged. Observe the alignment marks when securing the
bimetal housing. Any three of the six clamp ring screw holes can be
used.
21  Accelerator pump delivery is determined by the position of the
lever operating cam (photo). This should not be adjusted, not least
because the desired delivery quantity is not known.
22  To check the choke pull-down, position the fast idle screw on the
highest step of the cam. Press the pull-down adjusting screw towards
the pull-down diaphragm and measure the choke valve opening with a
twist drill or gauge rod of the specified diameter. Adjust if necessary
using a 2 mm Allen key (photo).

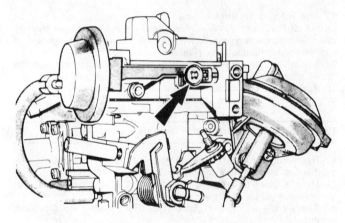

Fig. 3.9 Choke pull-down unit removal. Star clip (arrowed)
must be prised off (Sec 18)

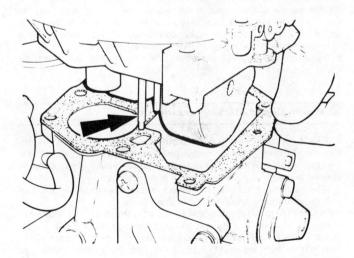

Fig. 3.10 Fuel riser (arrowed) must enter its pick-up channel
– Pierburg 2V carburettor (Sec 18)

18.21 Accelerator pump operating cam (arrowed)

18.22 Choke pull-down adjustment

23  After refitting the throttle damper, adjust its position in the bracket so that with a 2 mm (0.08 in) feeler blade inserted between the idle speed adjusting screw and the throttle lever, the damper plunger is just touching the actuating lever (Fig. 3.11).
24  Adjust the idle speed and mixture, and if necessary the fast idle speed, after refitting the carburettor, see Sections 16 and 19.
25  Recheck the throttle damper adjustment, when applicable.

## 19  Pierburg 2V carburettor – fast idle adjustment

1  This is not a routine operation. It should only be necessary after overhaul, or when a new carburettor is fitted.
2  The idle speed and mixture must be correctly set (Section 16) and the engine must be at operating temperature.
3  Remove the air cleaner (Section 5). Plug the manifold vacuum connection.
4  With the engine running, position the fast idle screw on the second highest step of the fast idle cam. Measure the engine speed and compare it with that given in the Specifications.
5  If adjustment is necessary, remove the tamperproof plug from the fast idle screw by crushing it with pliers. Stop the engine and open the throttle to gain access to the screw with a small screwdriver. Turn the screw a small amount clockwise to increase the speed, anti-clockwise to reduce it, then reseat the screw on the second highest step of the cam and recheck the engine speed. Repeat as necessary.
6  Fit a new tamperproof cap where this is required by law, then refit the air cleaner.

## 20  Weber 2V carburettor – description

The Weber twin venturi (2V) carburettor is fitted to 2.0 litre models. Like the Pierburg it is a downdraught type with an automatic choke. Throttle valve opening is sequential, the secondary throttle being opened by vacuum developed in the primary venturi.

The automatic choke is heated electrically only. A vacuum pull-down unit is integral with the choke housing.

As well as an accelerator pump and a power valve, which deal with transient and full-throttle enrichment, some models have a low vacuum enrichment device. This device responds to a rapid decrease in manifold vacuum by squirting more fuel into the primary venturi, so preventing stalling at low speeds.

A unique feature of this carburettor is the stepper motor attached to the throttle linkage. This motor, under the control of the ESC II module, maintains a steady idle speed; it also controls the throttle position

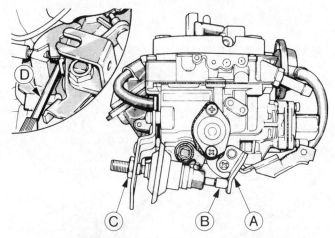

**Fig. 3.11 Throttle damper adjustment – Pierburg 2V carburettor (Sec 18)**

A   Actuating lever            C   Damper locknut
B   Damper plunger             D   Feeler blade

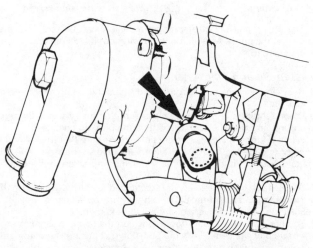

**Fig. 3.12 Fast idle adjustment – Pierburg 2V carburettor. Tip of fast idle screw is arrowed (Sec 19)**

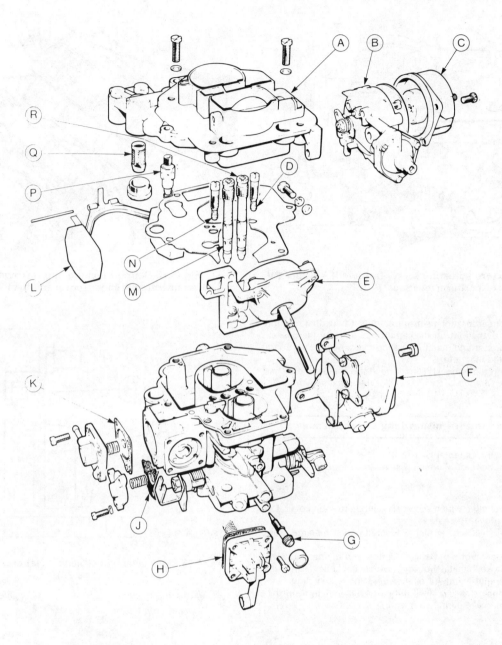

**Fig. 3.13 Exploded view of Weber 2V carburettor (Sec 20)**

A   Top cover
B   Choke lever housing
C   Choke bimetal housing
D   Secondary idle jet

E   Secondary throttle vacuum
    unit
F   Stepper motor
G   Idle mixture adjustment
    screw

H   Accelerator pump diaphragm
J   Power valve diaphragm
K   Low vacuum enrichment
    diaphragm
L   Float

M   Primary emulsion tube
N   Primary idle jet
P   Needle valve
Q   Fuel inlet filter
R   Secondary emulsion tube

during deceleration, start-up and immediately after shut-off. Optimum fuel economy and good emission levels are thereby achieved.

## 21 Weber 2V carburettor – idle speed and mixture adjustments

1   Idle speed cannot be adjusted in the usual way on this carburettor, as it is controlled by the ESC II module. See Chapter 4 for further details.
2   If mixture adjustment is required, proceed as described in Section 16 for the Pierburg carburettor, ignoring the references to idle speed adjustment. The location of the mixture adjusting screw on the Weber carburettor is shown in Fig. 3.14.

## 22 Weber 2V carburettor – removal and refitting

1   Disconnect the battery negative lead.
2   Remove the air cleaner (Section 5).
3   Disconnect the choke and stepper motor wirings. The stepper motor multi-plug locking device must be depressed to release the plug.
4   Unclip the throttle arm from the throttle lever and remove the throttle cable bracket.
5   Disconnect the fuel hose from the carburettor and plug it. If a crimped type hose clip is fitted, cut it off and use a worm drive clip when refitting.
6   Disconnect the vacuum pipe(s) from the carburettor, noting their connecting points if there is any possibility of confusion.

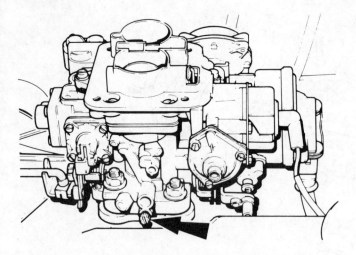

Fig. 3.14 Idle mixture adjusting screw (arrowed) – Weber 2V carburettor (Sec 21)

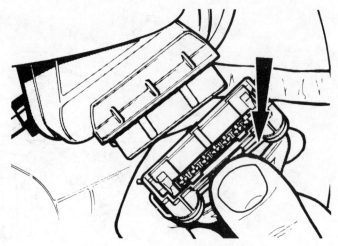

Fig. 3.15 Depress locking clip (arrowed) when disconnecting stepper motor multi-plug (Sec 22)

7   Remove the four carburettor-to-manifold nuts. Check that nothing has been overlooked, then lift off the carburettor. Recover the gasket.
8   Clean the carburettor and manifold mating faces, being careful not to sweep dirt into the manifold.
9   Refit by reversing the removal operations. If the stepper motor has been disturbed, see Chapter 4, Section 11 for the initial adjustment.

## 23 Weber 2V carburettor – dismantling and reassembly

1   Refer to Section 17, paragraphs 1 to 3.
2   Remove the stepper motor, which is secured by four screws.

### Top cover

3   Remove the six screws which secure the carburettor top cover. Lift off the cover and recover the gasket.
4   Remove the fuel inlet filter, which is located under the large brass nut next to the inlet pipe.
5   Drive out the float pivot pin. Detach the float and the needle valve.
6   Remove the choke bimetal housing, which is secured by three screws. Make alignment marks for reference when reassembling.
7   Remove the choke housing itself, which is secured by a further three screws. Again, make alignment marks.

### Main body

8   Unscrew the jets and jet plugs from the carburettor body, noting the position in which they are fitted.
9   Unscrew the primary and secondary emulsion tubes, again noting their positions.
10  Remove the accelerator pump cover, which is secured by four screws. Recover the diaphragm and the spring.
11  Remove the secondary throttle vacuum unit securing screws. Disconnect the link rod and remove the unit.
12  Remove the power valve cover, spring and diaphragm.
13  When fitted, remove the low vacuum enrichment device cover, spring and diaphragm.

### Inspection

14  Clean the float chamber. Blow through all jets and clean their seats. Renew gaskets and diaphragms as a matter of course, and other components as necessary.

### Reassembly and adjustments

15  Reassemble the main body components by reversing the dismantling procedure. Be careful not to kink the diaphragms.
16  Reassemble the top cover components, then check the float level as follows.

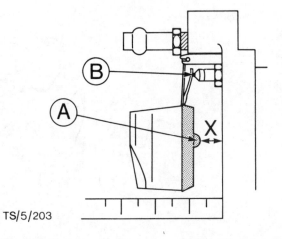

TS/5/203

Fig. 3.16 Float level adjustment – Weber 2V carburettor (Sec 23)

A   Rib on float                    X   Level measurement
B   Adjusting tag

17  Hold the top cover vertically so that the needle valve is closed by the float. Measure the dimension from the gasket face of the cover (with the gasket fitted) to the top rib on the float. The correct value is given in the Specifications. Correct if necessary by bending the tag on the float arm.
18  Refit the top cover, using a new gasket, and secure it with the six screws.
19  Refit the stepper motor.
20  For adjustment of the automatic choke, refer to the next Section.

## 24 Weber 2V carburettor – automatic choke adjustment

1   Disconnect the battery negative lead.
2   Remove the air cleaner (Section 5).
3   Disconnect the feed wire from the choke bimetal housing.
4   Make alignment marks if necessary, then remove the three screws which secure the bimetal housing. Detach the housing and recover the heat sheild.
5   Fit a rubber band over the choke valve lever and tension the rubber band to hold the choke valve closed.

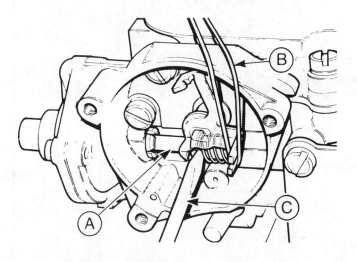

Fig. 3.17 Choke vacuum pull-down check – Weber 2V carburettor (Sec 24)

A  Pull-down diaphragm rod          C  Screwdriver
B  Rubber band

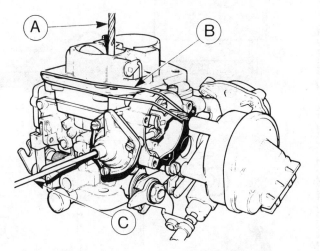

Fig. 3.18 Adjusting the vacuum pull-down – Weber 2V carburettor (Sec 24)

A  Twist drill                              C  Screwdriver
B  Rubber band

6  Using a small screwdriver, press the vacuum pull-down rod into the pull-down housing as far as it will go. Hold the rod in this position and use a drill shank or similar item to measure the clearance between the choke valve and the wall of the primary venturi. Measure the clearance on the down side of the valve. The desired pull-down clearance is given in the Specifications.

7  If adjustment is necessary, remove the end plug from the pull-down diaphragm cover. Turn the adjusting screw located under the plug. Refit the plug when adjustment is correct.

8  Remove the drill and the rubber band.

9  Refit the heat shield, making sure it is properly located.

10  Refit the bimetal housing, engaging the end of the spring with the choke valve lever. Fit the three screws, position the housing in its original alignment (paragraph 4) and tighten the screws.

11  If the bimetal housing has been lost, refer to the Specifications and to Fig. 3.19. Small deviations from the specified setting may be made to correct over or under-choking.

12  Reconnect the choke feed wire, refit the air cleaner and reconnect the battery.

13  Check the idle mixture adjustment (Section 21).

Fig. 3.19 Bimetal housing alignment marks – Weber 2V carburettor (Sec 24)

A  Rich                                       C  Lean
B  Index

## 25 Fuel-injection system – description

The fuel injection system is of the Bosch L-Jetronic type. The system is under the overall control of the EEC IV (electronic engine control) module, which also regulates ignition timing.

Fuel is supplied by an electronic pump via a pressure regulator. The fuel injectors receive an electrical pulse once per crankshaft revolution. The lengh of the pulse determines the amount of fuel injected; pulse length is computed by the EEC IV module on the basis of information received from the various sensors. There is one fuel injector for each cylinder.

Inducted air passes through a vane airflow meter (VAF). On V6 models there are two such meters. A flap in the meter is deflected in proportion to the airflow; this deflection is converted into an electrical signal for the EEC IV module. An adjustable bypass channel provides the means of idle mixture adjustment.

A throttle position sensor (TPS) enables the EEC IV module to read not only throttle position but also its rate of change. Extra fuel can thus be provided for acceleration when the throttle is opened suddenly. Information from the TPS is also used in applying fuel cut-off on the overrun.

Idle speed is controlled by a variable oriface solenoid valve which regulates the passage of air bypasssing the throttle valve. The valve is under the control of the EEC IV module; there is no provision for direct adjustment of the idle speed.

Other sensors inform the EEC IV module of coolant and air temperature; on automatic transmission models another sensor registers the change from P or N to a drive range, causes the idle speed to be adjusted accordingly.

When air conditioning is fitted, a signal from the compressor clutch to the EEC IV module enables idle speed to be maintained despite the load imposed by the compressor.

From mid-1986, all models are fitted with a fuel pump inertia switch. This switch breaks the pump electrical circuit in the event of an accident or similar impact. The switch is located to the left of the tailgate latch striker under the plastic cover. It may be reset by pressing down the button on top of the switch.

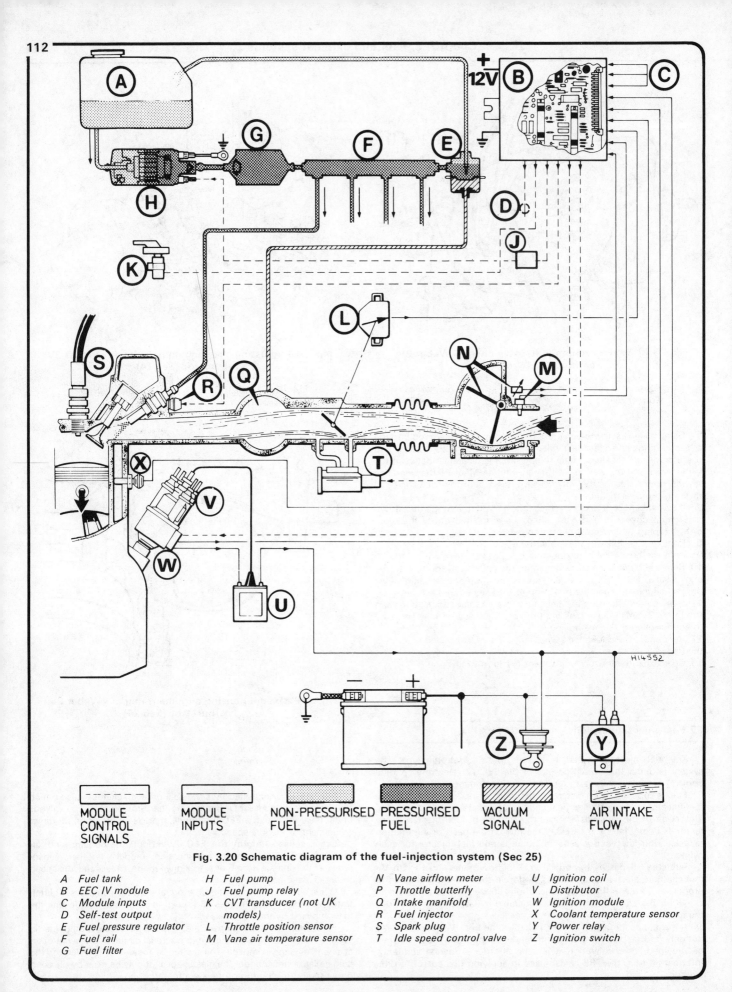

Fig. 3.20 Schematic diagram of the fuel-injection system (Sec 25)

| | | | |
|---|---|---|---|
| A | Fuel tank | H | Fuel pump | N | Vane airflow meter | U | Ignition coil |
| B | EEC IV module | J | Fuel pump relay | P | Throttle butterfly | V | Distributor |
| C | Module inputs | K | CVT transducer (not UK | Q | Intake manifold | W | Ignition module |
| D | Self-test output | | models) | R | Fuel injector | X | Coolant temperature sensor |
| E | Fuel pressure regulator | L | Throttle position sensor | S | Spark plug | Y | Power relay |
| F | Fuel rail | M | Vane air temperature sensor | T | Idle speed control valve | Z | Ignition switch |
| G | Fuel filter | | | | | | |

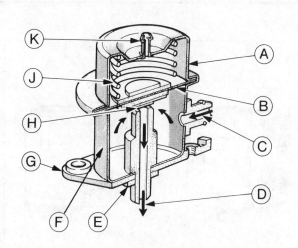

Fig. 3.21 Cutaway view of fuel pressure regulator (Sec 25)

| A | Upper housing | F | Lower housing |
|---|---|---|---|
| B | Diaphragm | G | Baseplate |
| C | Fuel inlet | H | Valve |
| D | Fuel outlet | J | Spring |
| E | Gasket | K | Vacuum supply |

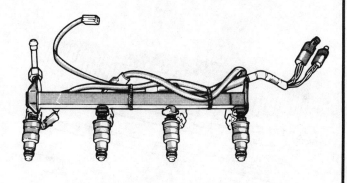

Fig. 3.22 Fuel rail and injectors (ohc) (Sec 25)

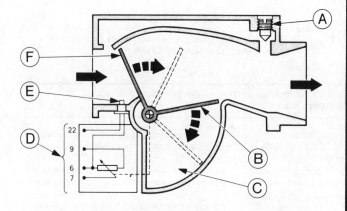

Fig. 3.24 Schematic view of a vane airflow meter (Sec 25)

| A | Mixture adjustment screw | D | Multi-plug connector |
|---|---|---|---|
| B | Compensator flap | E | Air temperature sensor |
| C | Damping chamber | F | Sensor flap |

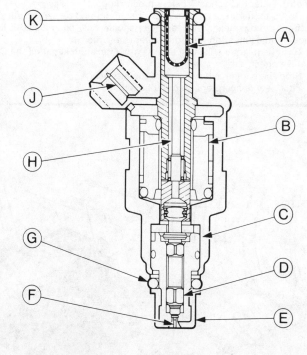

Fig. 3.23 Sectional view of a fuel injector (Sec 25)

| A | Inlet filter | F | Pintle |
|---|---|---|---|
| B | Coil | G | O-ring |
| C | Body | H | Armature |
| D | Needle valve | J | Electrical connection |
| E | Pintle case | K | O-ring |

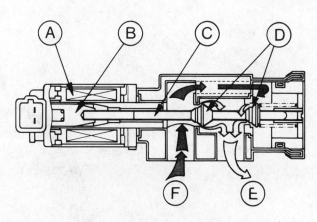

Fig. 3.25 Sectional view of the idle speed control valve (Sec 25)

| A | Coil | D | Valve seats |
|---|---|---|---|
| B | Armature | E | Air out |
| C | Valve stem | F | Air in |

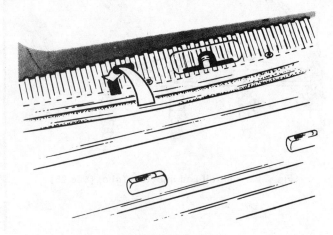

**Fig. 3.26 Fuel pump inertia switch location (arrowed) to the left of the tailgate latch (Sec 25)**

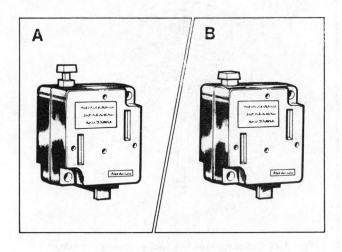

**Fig. 3.27 Inertia switch states (Sec 25)**

*A   Tripped (button out)        B   Normal running (button in)*

### 26 Fuel-injection system – idle speed and mixture adjustments

1   As mentioned in the previous Section, idle speed is controlled by the EEC IV module and no direct adjustment is possible. See Chapter 4 for more details.
2   Idle mixture adjustment should not be necesary on a routine basis. After component renewal or a similar circumstance it may be checked and adjusted as follows.
3   The engine must be at operating temperature. The valve clearances must be correct, the air cleaner element must be clean and the ignition system must be in good condition.
4   Connect an exhaust gas analyser (CO meter) and a tachometer (rev. counter) to the engine as instructed by their makers.

5   Run the engine at 3000 rpm for 15 seconds, then allow it to idle. Repeat the procedure every 60 seconds until adjustment is complete.
6   With the engine idling after the 3000 rpm burst, record the CO level when the reading has stabilised. The desired value is given in the Specifications.
7   If adjustment is necessary, remove the tamperproof plug from the mixture adjusting screw on the underside of the vane airflow meter (photo). Refer to Section 3 before proceeding.
8   On V6 models, note that adjustment should first be carried out on the front airflow meter. The rear meter should only be adjusted if the range of adjustment on the front meter is insufficient.
9   Turn the mixture adjusting screw with a hexagon key until the CO level is correct.
10  Stop the engine and disconnect the test gear.
11  Fit a new tamperproof plug if required.

26.7 Tamperproof plug (arrowed) covering mixture adjusting screw. Airflow meter is inverted for photo

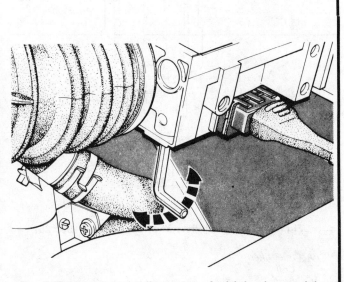

**Fig. 3.28 Idle mixture adjustment – fuel-injection models (Sec 26)**

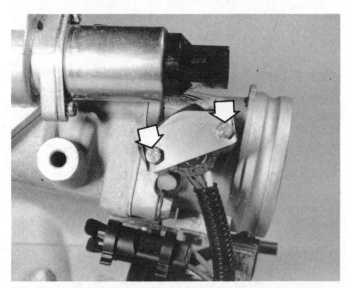

27.3 Throttle position sensor retaining bolts (arrowed)

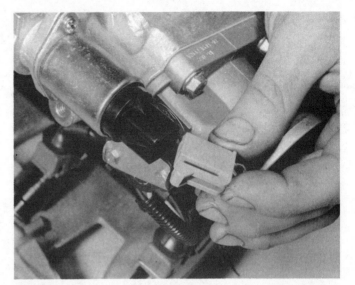

28.2 Disconnecting the idle speed control valve

## 27 Throttle position sensor – removal and refitting

1   Disconnect the battery negative lead.
2   Free the throttle position sensor multi-plug from its clip. On the ohc models this is below the idle speed control valve, on the underside of the inlet manifold; on V6 models it is located below the throttle valve housing.
3   Relieve the locktabs and unbolt the throttle position sensor (photo). Pull the sensor off the throttle valve shaft, disconnect the multi-plug and remove the sensor.
4   Do not rotate the centre part of the sensor beyond its normal range of movement, or damage may result.
5   When refitting, line up the flat on the throttle valve shaft with the flat on the centre of the sensor. Make sure that the sensor is the right way round and fit it over the shaft.
6   Fit and tighten the two bolts and secure it with the locktabs.
7   Reconnect and secure the multi-plug, then reconnect the battery.

## 28 Idle speed control valve – removal and refitting

1   Disconnect the battery negative lead.
2   Disconnect the multi-plug from the idle speed control valve by prising up the retaining lug and pulling the plug, not the wires (photo)
3   Remove the two securing nuts (ohc) or bolts (V6) and withdraw the valve (photo). Recover the gasket.
4   If necessary, the solenoid can be separated from the valve block by removing the two screws to enable the parts to be cleaned. Contamination or air leaks in this area will cause unstable idling. After careful cleaning, the parts can be reassembled.
5   Refit the valve, using a new gasket, and tighten the retaining nuts or bolts. Reconnect the multi-plug and the battery.
6   Start the engine and check that the idle is steady. Bring the engine to operating temperature, then switch on all possible electrical loads (headlights, heated screens, heater blower etc) and check that the idle remains steady. This confirms that the valve is working.

## 29 Vane airflow meter(s) – removal and refitting

### ohc models

1   Disconnect the battery negative lead.
2   Release the locking clip and disconnect the multi-plug from the meter (photo).
3   Release the hose clip and disconnect the air trunking from the meter (photo).

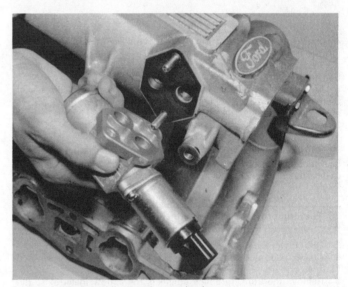

28.3 Removing the idle speed control valve

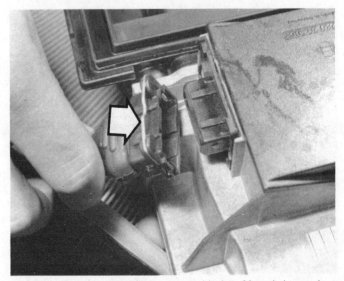

29.2 Disconnecting the airflow meter multi-plug. Meter is inverted to show locking clip (arrowed)

29.3 Releasing an air trunking hose clip

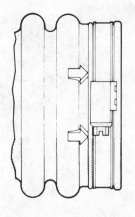

Fig. 3.29 Correct alignment of air inlet trunking and hose clip (Sec 29)

4   Unclip the air cleaner cover and remove it with the meter. Do not drop or jar it.
5   To separate the meter from the cover, remove the four retaining bolts.
6   Refit by reversing the removal operations. Make sure that the seal in the air cleaner cover is correctly located, and align the hose clip as shown in Fig. 3.29.
7   Check the exhaust CO level on completion (Section 26).

## V6 models

8   Proceed as described in paragraphs 1 to 7, except that there are two meters instead of one.

## 30 Fuel injectors – removal and refitting

1   Disconnect the battery negative lead.
2   On V6 models, remove the throttle linkage cover, which is secured by three screws.
3   Remove the trunking which connects the airflow meter(s) to the inlet manifold.

4   On ohc models, release the distributor cap and place it clear of the fuel rail. It will be necessary to disconnect the cap-to-coil HT lead at the coil.
5   Disconnect the multi-plugs from the idle speed control valve, the throttle position sensor and the coolant temperature sensor.
6   On V6 models, unclip the HT leads from the fuel pressure regulator bracket.
7   Disconnect the vacuum and fuel pipes from the fuel pressure regulator, and the fuel feed union from the fuel rail (photo). Be prepared for fuel spillage.
8   On V6 models, disconnect the throttle cable(s). Remove the plenum chamber and throttle body.
9   Disconnect the injector wiring harness.
10  Unbolt the fuel rail and remove it with the injectors (photos). It will be necessary to pull on the rail in order to free the injectors from the manifold.
11  Disconnect the multi-plugs from the injectors (photo).
12  Extract the retaining clips and pull the injectors out of the fuel rail.
13  The sealing rings and retaining clips on **all** injectors must be renewed, even if only one injector has been removed from the rail. The lower seal fits between the thick and thin washers at the tip of the injector (photos).
14  Commence refitting by coating the injector sealing rings with silicone grease to Ford spec ESEM 1C171A.
15  Press the injectors into the fuel rail and secure them with the new retaining clips. Press the clips home.

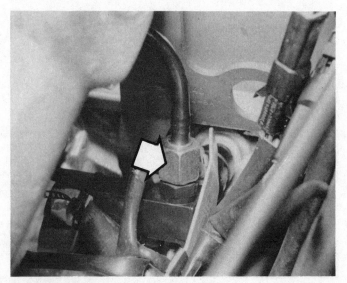

30.7 Fuel feed union (arrowed) on fuel rail

30.10A Undoing a fuel rail-to-manifold bolt (ohc)

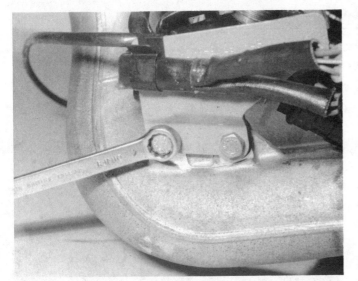

30.10B Two more fuel rail-to-manifold bolts (ohc)

30.11 Disconnecting a fuel injector multi-plug

30.13A Injector showing details of lower seal

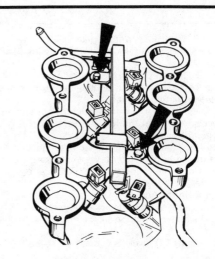

Fig. 3.30 Fuel rail retaining bolts (arrowed) on V6 inlet manifold (Sec 30)

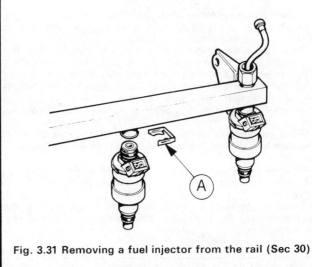

Fig. 3.31 Removing a fuel injector from the rail (Sec 30)

A   Retaining clip

30.13B Injector with seals removed

16  Reconnect the multi-plugs to the injectors.
17  Place the assembled fuel rail on the inlet manifold and press the injectors into their holes.
18  On V6 models, fit and tighten the fuel rail bolts. Refit the plenum chamber, using new gaskets, and tighten the bolts to the specified torque. Reconnect the throttle cable(s).
19  On ohc models, fit the fuel rail bolts but do not tighten them yet.
20  On all models, reconnect the fuel and vacuum pipes. Tighten the fuel pipe unions.
21  On ohc models, tighten the fuel rail bolts to the specified torque.
22  Reconnect the multi-plugs which were displaced during removal. On V6 models, secure the HT leads to the pressure regulator bracket.
23  On ohc models, refit the distributor cap.
24  Refit the air inlet trunking.
25  On V6 models, refit the throttle linkage cover.
26  Reconnect the battery. Run the engine and check that there are no fuel leaks.
27  Check the exhaust CO level (Section 26).

## 31  Fuel pressure regulator – removal and refitting

1  Disconnect the battery negative lead.
2  On V6 models, unclip the HT leads from the fuel pressure regulator bracket.
3  Place a drain pan or plenty of rags beneath the regulator, then disconnect the fuel return pipe (photo). Be prepared for fuel spillage.
4  Disconnect the vacuum pipe from the regulator (photo).
5  Slacken the fuel feed union nut (photo). Wait until any residual fuel pressure has decayed, then unscrew the nut.
6  Unscrew the nut from the base of the regulator. Remove the regulator (photo).
7  When refitting, only tighten the regulator base nut lightly at first. Secure the fuel feed union and tighten its nut, then fully tighten the base nut.
8  Reconnect the vacuum and fuel return pipes.
9  Remove the drain pan or rags. On V6 models, secure the HT leads to their clip.
10  Reconnect the battery. Switch the ignition on and off five times (without cranking the engine) and check that there are no fuel leaks from the regulator.

## 32  Inlet manifold – removal and refitting

*Carburettor models*

1  Remove the carburettor as described in Section 17 or 22. (If preferred, the final removal of the carburettor from the manifold can be left until the manifold has been removed).

31.3 Disconnecting the fuel return pipe from the fuel pressure regulator

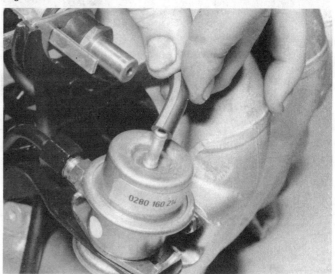

31.4 Disconnecting the vacuum pipe from the fuel pressure regulator

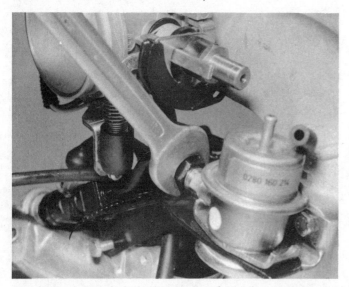

31.5 Slackening the fuel pressure regulator feed union nut

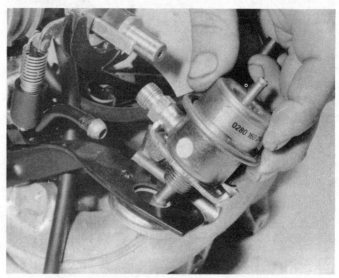

31.6 Removing the fuel pressure regulator

2   Drain the cooling system as described in Chapter 2.
3   Disconnect the coolant and vacuum pipes from the manifold, noting their positions if there is any possibility of confusion.
4   Disconnect the wires from the manifold heater and the coolant temperature sender unit.
5   Disconnect the crankcase ventilation hose from the manifold.
6   Unscrew the six nuts and bolts which secure the manifold and withdraw it. (If the distributor blocks removal, see paragraph 24.) Recover the gasket.
7   Before refitting the manifold, make sure that the mating surfaces are perfectly clean.
8   Apply a bead of sealant at least 5 mm (0.2 in) wide around the central coolant aperture on both sides of a new gasket.
9   Place the gasket over the studs, then fit the manifold and secure it with the six nuts and bolts. Tighten the nuts and bolts evenly to the specified torque.
10  The remainder of refitting is a reversal of the removal procedure. Refill the cooling system on completion as described in Chapter 2.

*Fuel-injection models – ohc*

11  Disconnect the battery negative lead.
12  Drain the cooling system as described in Chapter 2.

13  Disconnect the vacuum pipe(s) from the manifold. The number of pipes varies according to equipment. Label the pipes if necessary (photo).
14  Disconnect the fuel-injection harness multi-plugs at the bulkhead end of the manifold (photo).
15  Disconnect the oil pressure warning light sender wire from below the manifold.
16  Release the hose clips and move the airflow meter-to-manifold trunking clear of the manifold.
17  Remove the distributor cap, unclip the HT leads and move the cap out of the way.
18  Remove the strut which runs from the manifold to the right-hand side of the cylinder head. It is secured by two nuts (photo).
19  Remove the bracket which joins the base of the manifold to the left-hand side of the block. It is secured by four bolts (photo).
20  Unbolt the throttle cable bracket. Unhook the cable inner and move the bracket and cable(s) aside (photo).
21  Disconnect the fuel feed pipe from the injector rail, and the return pipe from the fuel pressure regulator. Be prepared for fuel spillage.
22  Disconnect the coolant pipe from the base of the manifold. Be prepared for coolant spillage.
23  Remove the six nuts and bolts which secure the manifold to the

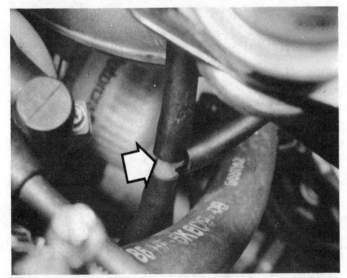

32.13 Manifold vacuum pipe T-piece (arrowed)

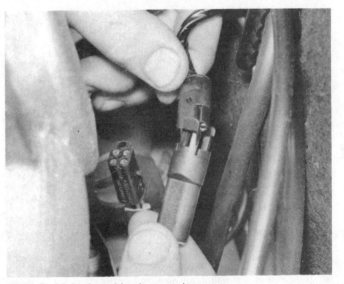

32.14 Fuel-injection wiring harness plugs

32.18 Inlet manifold-to-cylinder head bracing strut

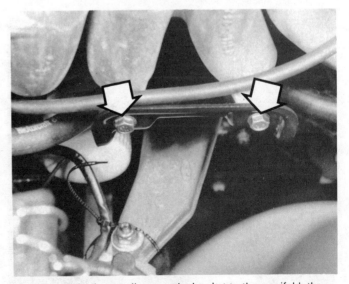

32.19 Two bolts (arrowed) secure the bracket to the manifold; the bolts securing it to the block are hidden

32.20 Unbolting the throttle cable bracket

32.24A Removing the inlet manifold

cylinder head. There may be an earth strap attached to one of the studs by an extra nut.

24  Carefully withdraw the manifold from the cylinder head, complete with its associated fuel-injection components (photo). If the distributor obstructs removal, extract the manifold front stud by locking two nuts together on it and thus unscrewing the stud (photo). Alternatively, remove the distributor.

25  Recover the gasket from the cylinder head (photo).

26  With the manifold removed, items such as the fuel injector rail and the throttle body housing can be removed if required (photos).

27  Clean the mating faces of the manifold and cylinder head. Keep dirt out of the ports and other orifices.

28  Commence refitting by applying a bead of sealant at least 5 mm (0.2 in) wide around the central coolant aperture on both sides of a new gasket.

29  Fit the gasket over the studs, refit the manifold and secure with the six nuts and bolts. Tighten them evenly to the specified torque.

30  The remainder of refitting is a reversal of the removal procedure. Refill the cooling system on completion as described in Chapter 2.

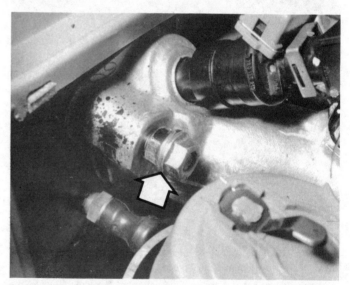

32.24B Use two nuts locked together (arrowed) to remove the stud

32.25 Inlet manifold gasket on the cylinder head

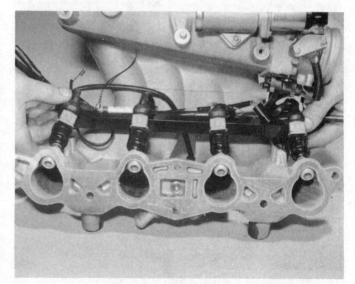

32.26A Removing the fuel rail and injectors from the manifold

32.26B Removing a throttle body housing bolt

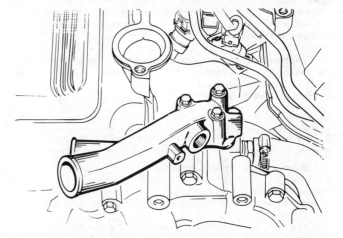

32.26C Removing the throttle body housing

*Fuel-injection models – V6*

31 Disconnect the battery negative lead.
32 Drain the cooling system as described in Chapter 2.
33 Remove the throttle linkage cover.
34 Release the hose clips and move the airflow meter-to-manifold trunking aside. Unclip or remove the crankcase ventilation hose.
35 Disconnect the radiator top hose and the heater hose from the outlet at the front of the manifold. Be prepared for some coolant spillage.
36 Disconnect the multi-plugs from the idle speed control valve, the temperature gauge sender unit; the coolant temperature sensor and the throttle position sensor. Also disconnect the injector wiring harness.
37 Disconnect the throttle cable from the linkage, unclip it and move it aside. On automatic transmission models, also disconnect the downshift cable or multi-plug, as applicable.
38 Disconnect the fuel feed and return pipes. Be prepared for fuel spillage.
39 Remove the HT leads and the distributor as described in Chapter 4.
40 Remove the plenum chamber, which is secured by eight bolts.
41 Remove the rocker covers, which are each secured by seven bolts.
42 Disconnect the water pump bypass hose from the inlet manifold.
43 Remove the eight bolts which secure the inlet manifold to the cylinder heads.
44 Lift off the manifold complete with fuel pressure regulator, fuel rail, throttle body housing etc. If it is stuck, carefully lever it free. **Do not apply leverage at the mating faces.** Recover the gasket.
45 Clean all mating faces, being careful to keep dirt out of ports and other orifices. Obtain new gaskets for both the cylinder head and plenum chamber sides of the manifold, and for the rocker covers.
46 Commence refitting by applying sealant (Ford part No. A70X-19554-BA, or equivalent) around the ports and coolant passages on the cylinder head.
47 Apply sealant around the apertures on both sides of the gasket, then fit the gasket to the cylinder heads.
48 Refit the manifold and insert the securing bolts. Tighten the bolts, in the order shown in Fig.3.34, through the first four stages given in the Specifications.
49 Refit the water pump bypass hose.
50 Refit the rocker covers, using new gaskets. The adhesive sides of the gaskets must face the covers.
51 Reverse the remaining removal operations, but do not refit the throttle linkage cover yet.
52 When the cooling system has been refilled, reconnect the battery and start the engine. Check for fuel and other leaks.
53 Bring the engine to operating temperature, then stop it and carry out the final tightening of the inlet manifold bolts as follows.
54 Release the air inlet trunking. Unplug the idle speed control valve and the throttle position sensor. Unbolt the plenum chamber and move it aside, disconnecting vacuum and breather hoses as necessary.

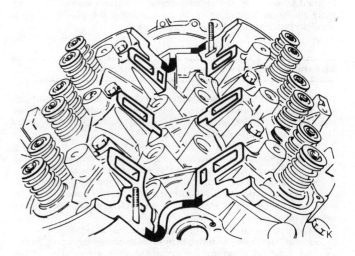

Fig. 3.32 Coolant outlet connector on V6 engine inlet manifold (Sec 32)

Fig. 3.33 Apply sealant to the mating faces (Sec 32)

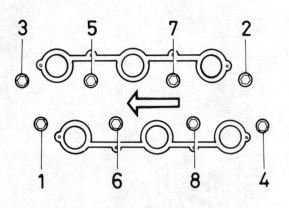

Fig. 3.34 Inlet manifold bolt tightening sequence. Arrow points to front of engine (Sec 32)

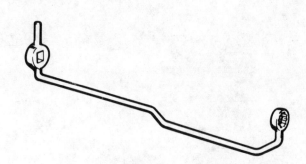

Fig. 3.35 Cranked spanner needed for tightening V6 inlet manifold bolt with distributor fitted (Sec 32)

55  Slacken, but do not remove, the two bolts which secure the fuel rail to the manifold.
56  Tighten the inlet manifold bolts to the Stage 5 specified torque, again following the sequence in Fig. 3.34. A special cranked spanner (Ford tool No. 21-079, or equivalent) will be needed to tighten No. 4 bolt when the distributor is fitted. In the absence of such a spanner, remove the distributor again.
57  Tighten the fuel rail securing bolts.
58  Refit the disturbed components. Run the engine again and check the ignition timing (Chapter 4, Section 6) and the exhaust CO level (Section 26 of this Chapter).
59  Refit the throttle linkage cover.

## 33 Exhaust manifold(s) – removal and refitting

1  Disconnect the battery negative lead.
2  Apply copious quantities of penetrating oil to the manifold and exhaust pipe flange nuts and bolts.
3  On carburettor models, remove the air cleaner and the hot air pick-up pipe (Section 5).
4  Unbolt any heat shields or shrouds from the manifold.
5  Unbolt the exhaust pipe(s) from the manifold flange. Support the exhaust system if necessary.
6  Unbolt the manifold from the cylinder head and remove it. Recover the gasket.
7  Refit by reversing the removal operations. Use a new gasket, and apply anti-seize compound to the various nuts and bolts. Tighten the manifold fastenings to the specified torque.

## 34 Exhaust system – inspection, repair and renewal

1  Periodically inspect the exhaust system for freedom from corrosion and security of mountings. Large holes will be obvious; small holes may be found more easily by letting the engine idle and partly obstructing the tailpipe with a wad of cloth.
2  Check the condition of the rubber mountings by applying downward pressure on the exhaust system and observing the mountings for splits or cracks. Renew deteriorated mountings.
3  Holts Flexiwrap and Holts Gun Gum exhaust repair systems can be used for effective repairs to exhaust pipes and silencer boxes, including ends and bends. Holts Flexiwrap is an MOT approved permanent exhaust repair.
4  As will be seen from Fig. 3.36, the exhaust systems fitted in production have fewer sections than those available for repair. Repair sections may be fitted to production systems by cutting at the appropriate point.
5  As noted in Section 1, the production exhaust systems are made of

aluminised and stainless steel. Repair systems are available to the same standard, or in standard quality (SQ) painted mild steel.
6  It is recommended that the whole exhaust system be removed even if only part requires renewal, since separation of old joints, cutting pipes etc is much easier away from the vehicle. Proceed as follows.
7  Disconnect the battery negative lead. Raise and support the vehicle.
8  Unbolt the manifold-to-downpipe flanged joint(s).
9  On V6 models, unbolt the left-hand front silencer mounting (photo).
10  Release any earth straps (photo).
11  With the help of an assistant, unhook the system from its mountings and remove it.
12  Renew sections as necessary. Apply exhaust jointing compound to sliding and flanged joints, but do not tighten their clamps yet. Use new sealing rings where necessary.
13  Offer the system to the vehicle and hook it onto the mountings.
14  Refit any earth straps. On V6 models, also refit the left-hand front silencer mounting.
15  Loosely fit the manifold flange nuts. Correct the alignment of the system, then tighten all clamp nuts and bolts, starting at the manifold flange(s) and working rearwards (photos).
16  Check that the system alignment is still satisfactory then reconnect the battery. Run the engine and check for leaks.
17  When the system has warmed up, stop the engine and carefully check the tightness of the clamp nuts and bolts.

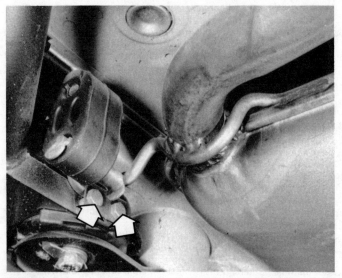

34.9 Left-hand front silencer mounting bolts (arrowed) – V6

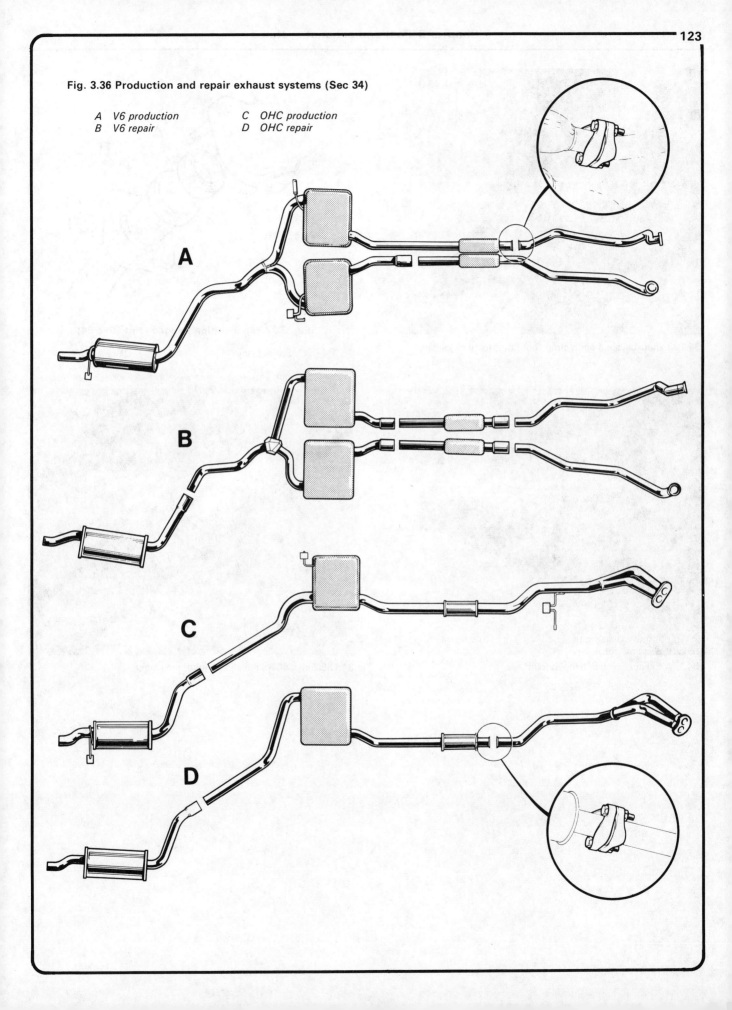

**Fig. 3.36 Production and repair exhaust systems (Sec 34)**

A   V6 production      C   OHC production
B   V6 repair          D   OHC repair

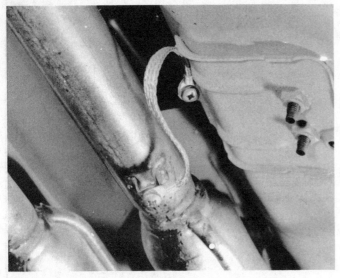

34.10 Exhaust system earth strap (not fitted to all models)

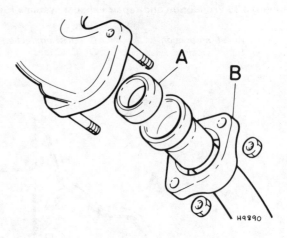

Fig. 3.37 Exhaust pipe flanged joint (Sec 34)

A   Sealing ring                              B   Flange

34.15A Exhaust system flanged joint

34.15B Exhaust system sliding joint and clamp

**35 Fault diagnosis – fuel and exhaust systems**

**Note**: *Excessive fuel consumption or poor performance cannot necessarily be blamed on the carburettor or fuel-injection system. Check first that the ignition system adjustments are correct and that the engine itself is in good mechanical condition. Items such as binding brakes or under-inflated tyres should not be overlooked.*
*Faults relating to the fuel-injection and engine management systems should generally be referred to a Ford dealer or other competent specialist.*

| Symptom | Reason(s) |
|---|---|
| Fuel starvation | Tank empty |
| | Fuel pipe faulty |
| | Electric pump fuse blown |
| | Electric pump inertia switch tripped (when fitted) |
| | Fuel filter blocked |
| Fuel consumption excessive | Leakage from tank, pump or pipes |
| | Air cleaner element choked |
| | Carburettor float level incorrect, or needle valve leaking |
| | Mixture adjustment incorrect |
| | Carburettor generally worn |
| | Engine management system fault |
| | Unsympathetic driving style |
| Lack of power | Air cleaner element choked |
| | Exhaust system kinked or otherwise restricted |
| | Mixture adjustment too weak |
| | Fuel pump delivery inadequate |
| | Air leaks at inlet manifold |
| | Engine management system fault |
| Difficult starting | Incorrect technique (see operator's handbook) |
| | Faulty or maladjusted automatic choke |
| | Air leaks at inlet manifold |
| | Engine management system fault |
| Unstable idle speed | Air leaks at inlet manifold |
| | Air leaks around idle speed control valve (fuel-injection) |
| | Idle speed control valve contaminated (fuel injection) |
| | Carburettor stepper motor plunger dirty (see Chapter 4, Section 11) |
| Backfiring in exhaust | Air leaks in exhaust system |
| | Ignition timing incorrect |
| | Mixture grossly incorrect |
| | Exhaust valve(s) burnt or sticking, or valve clearance too small |
| Spitting back in inlet manifold or carburettor | Mixture very weak |
| | Ignition timing incorrect |
| | Inlet valve(s) burnt or sticking, or valve clearance too small |

# Chapter 4
# Ignition and engine management systems

*For modifications, and information applicable to later models, see Supplement at end of manual*

## Contents

## Specifications

### General
Ignition system type ..................................................................... Breakerless, Hall effect, with electronic control of advance
Firing order:
    ohc ..................................................................................... 1-3-4-2 (No. 1 at pulley end)
    V6 ....................................................................................... 1-4-2-5-3-6 (No. 1 at front of right-hand back)

### Ignition coil
Make ......................................................................................... Bosch, Femsa or Polmot
Primary resistance ...................................................................... 0.72 to 0.86 ohm
Secondary resistance ................................................................... 4.5 to 7.0 k ohms
Output voltage (open-circuit) ........................................................ 25 kV minimum

### HT leads
Resistance .................................................................................. 30 k ohms maximum per lead
Type:
    1.8, 2.0 carburettor and injection ........................................... Champion CLS 10 boxed set
    2.8 ...................................................................................... Champion CLS 6 boxed set

### Spark plugs
Make and type:
    1.8 litre (REC) ...................................................................... Champion RF7YCC or RF7YC
    2.0 litre (NEL) ...................................................................... Champion RF7YCC or RF7YC
    2.0 litre (NRA) ..................................................................... Champion RF7YCC or RF7YC
    2.8 litre (PRE) ...................................................................... Champion RN7YCC or RN7YC
Electrode gap:
    Champion RF7YCC and RN7YCC ............................................ 0.8 mm (0.032 in)
    Champion RF7YC and RN7YC ................................................. 0.7 mm (0.028 in)

### Distributor
Make ......................................................................................... Bosch or Motorcraft
Rotation ..................................................................................... Clockwise (viewed from above)
Automatic advance ...................................................................... Controlled by module
Dwell angle ................................................................................ Controlled by module

### Ignition timing (see text)
Leaded fuel (97 octane):
    Carburettor models ............................................................... 10° BTDC
    Fuel-injection models ............................................................ 12°BTDC
Unleaded fuel (95 octane):*
    Carburettor models ............................................................... 6°BTDC
    Fuel-injection models:
        2.0 litre ......................................................................... 8°BTDC
        2.8 litre ......................................................................... 12°BTDC (no change)

* See also Chapter 3, Section 4

## Torque wrench settings

| Spark plugs: | Nm | lbf ft |
|---|---|---|
| OHC ................................................................ | 20 to 28 | 15 to 21 |
| V6 .................................................................... | 30 to 40 | 22 to 30 |

## 1 General description

The ignition system is responsible for igniting the fuel/air charge in each cylinder at the correct moment. The components of the system are the spark plugs, ignition coil, distributor and connecting leads. Overall control of the system is one of the functions of the engine management module. Fuel-injection models have a subsidiary ignition module mounted on the distributor.

There are no contact breaker points in the distributor. A square wave signal is generated by the distributor electro-magnetically; this signal is used by the engine management module as a basis for switching the coil LT current. Speed-related (centrifugal) advance is also handled by the module. On carburettor models, ignition timing is also advanced under conditions of high inlet manifold vacuum.

The engine management models are 'black boxes' which regulate both the fuel and the ignition systems to obtain the best power, economy and emission levels. The module fitted to carburettor models is known as the ESC II (Electronic Spark Control Mk II) module. On fuel-injection models the more powerful EEC IV (Electronic Engine Control Mk IV) module is used.

Both types of module receive inputs from sensors monitoring coolant temperature, distributor rotor position and (on some models)

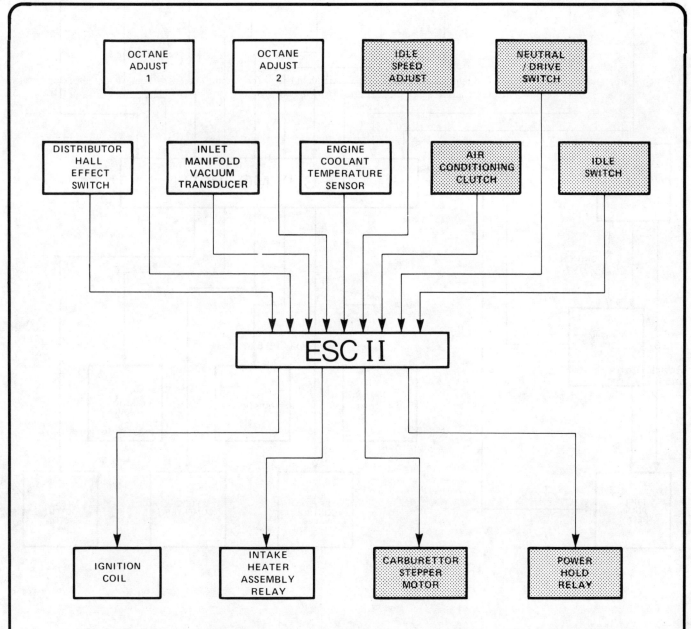

Fig. 4.1 Schematic of ESC II module operation. Shaded areas do not apply to 1.8 litre models (Sec 1)

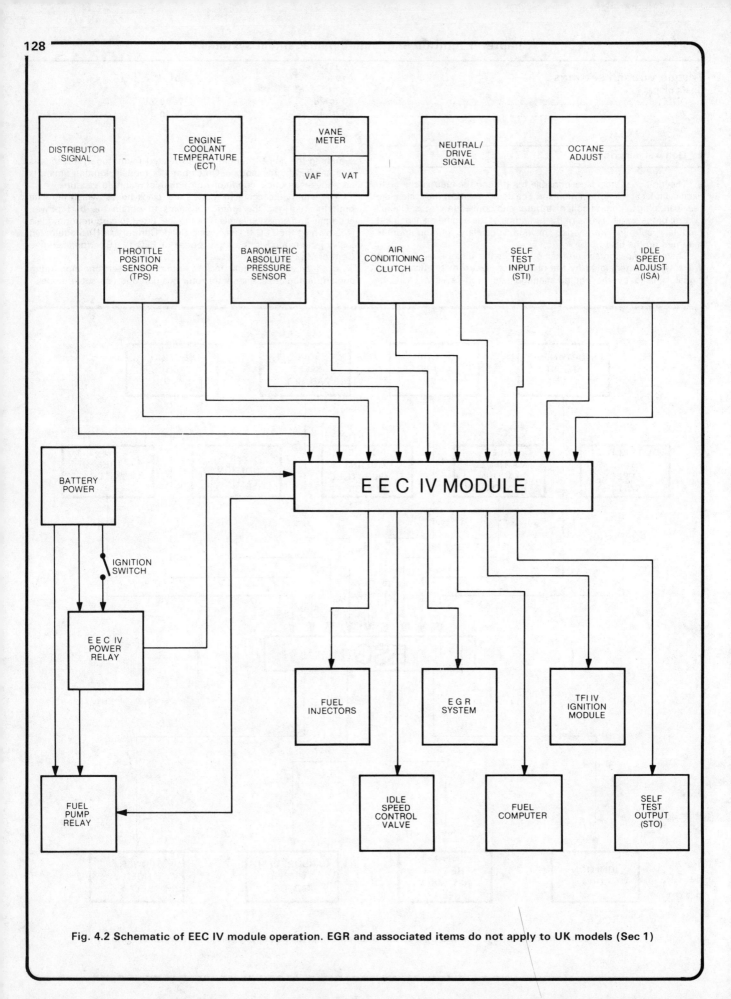

**Fig. 4.2 Schematic of EEC IV module operation. EGR and associated items do not apply to UK models (Sec 1)**

manifold vacuum (photo). Outputs from the module control ignition timing, inlet manifold heating and (except on 1.8 litre models) idle speed. The EEC IV module also has overall control of the fuel-injection system, from which it receives information.

Provision is made for the ignition timing to be retarded to allow the use of low octane fuel if necessary. On all except 1.8 litre models there is also a facility for raising the idle speed.

The EEC IV module contains self-test circuitry which enables a technician with the appropriate test equipment to diagnose faults in a very short time. A 'limited operation strategy' (LOS) means that the car is still driveable, albeit at reduced power and efficiency, in the event of a failure in the module or its sensors.

Due to the complexity and expense of the test equipment dedicated to the engine management system, suspected faults should be investigated by a Ford dealer or other competent specialist. This Chapter deals with component removal and refitting, and with some simple checks and adjustments.

### ESC II module – caution

Although it will tolerate all normal under-bonnet conditions, the ESC II module may be adversely affected by water entry during steam cleaning or pressure washing of the engine bay.

If cleaning the engine bay, therefore, take care not to direct jets of water or steam at the ESC II module. If this cannot be avoided, remove the module completely, and protect its multi-plug with a plastic bag.

### Ignition system HT voltage – warning

Take care to avoid receiving electric shocks from the HT side of the ignition system. Do not handle HT leads, or touch the distributor or coil, when the engine is running. When tracing faults in the HT system, use well insulated tools to manipulate live leads. **Electronic ignition HT voltage could prove fatal.**

### 2  Maintenance and inspection

1   Every 12 000 miles or annually, renew the spark plugs as described in Section 3. (If the time can be spared, it would do no harm to inspect and re-gap the plugs at the 6000 mile/6 month service).
2   Every 24 000 miles or two years, clean and inspect the HT leads and distributor cap as described in Section 4.
3   Inspect the electrical and vacuum connections of the ignition and engine management systems periodically and make sure that they are clean and tight.

### 3  Spark plugs – removal, inspection and refitting

1   The correct functioning of the spark plugs is vital for the correct running and efficiency of the engine. It is essential that the plugs fitted are appropriate for the engine, and the suitable type is specified at the beginning of this Chapter. If this type is used and the engine is in good condition, the spark plugs should not need attention between scheduled replacement intervals. Spark plug cleaning is rarely necessary and should not be attempted unless specialised equipment is available as damage can easily be caused to the firing ends.
2   Make sure that the ignition is switched off before inspecting the HT leads to see if they carry their cylinder numbers – if not, number each

1.0 Vacuum sensor (arrowed) fitted to some models

lead using sticky tape or paint. For cylinder numbering see Fig 4.3 or 4.4.
3   Pull the HT lead connectors off the plugs. Pull on the connectors, not on the leads (photo).

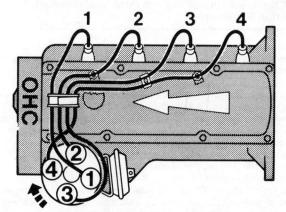

Fig. 4.3 HT lead layout – ohc engine. White arrow points to front (Sec 3)

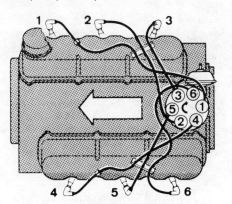

Fig. 4.4 HT lead layout – V6 engine. White arrow points to front (Sec 3)

3.3 Disconnecting an HT lead from a spark plug

4   Blow away any dirt from around the spark plug recesses in the cylinder head(s), using a bicycle pump or an air line.

5   Unscrew and remove the plugs, using a proprietary plug spanner or a spark plug socket, extension and ratchet.

6   Inspect the plugs and compare them with those illustrated by the coloured photographs in this Chapter. The condition of the plugs will tell much about the overall condition of the engine.

7   Apply a smear of anti-seize compound to the spark plug threads. Make sure that the plug insulators are clean and that the screwed HT lead adaptors are tight. Pay particular attention to the plug seating surfaces on ohc engines, since these plugs have no sealing washers ('taper seat' type) and any dirt will cause a bad seal.

8   Screw each plug into its hole by hand. If a plug is reluctant to go in, do not force it with a spanner, but unscrew it and try again. If the plug is cross-threaded, it is the cylinder head which will be damaged.

9   Final tightening of the spark plugs should ideally be carried out using a torque wrench (photo). The tightening torques are given in the Specifications. If a torque wrench is not available, tighten the plugs beyond the point where they contact the head as follows:

*ohc (taper seat plugs) – One-sixteenth of a turn maximum*
*V6 (plugs with washers) – One-quarter of a turn maximum*

10  If the taper seat type of plug is overtightened, the sealing faces will bite together and removal will be very difficult.

11  Refit the HT leads to the plugs, paying attention to the cylinder numbers. Push each connector firmly onto its plug.

12  Run the engine to verify that the HT leads have been refitted correctly.

3.9 Tightening a spark plug with a torque wrench

---

### 4   HT leads, distributor cap and rotor arm – removal, inspection and refitting

1   Disconnect the battery negative lead.

2   Identify the HT leads and disconnect them from the spark plugs as described in the previous Section.

3   On V6 models, remove the screening can lid (photo).

4   Remove the coil-to-distributor HT lead (sometimes called the king lead) by disconnecting it from the coil tower and the distributor cap.

5   Disconnect the other HT leads from the distributor cap, making a sketch if necessary so that they can be reconnected to the same terminals. Remove the leads.

6   On V6 models, remove the distributor screening can (photo).

7   Release the two clips or screws which secure the distributor cap. Remove the cap (photo).

8   Note that if the distributor cap is secured by clips, the engine must not be cranked with the cap removed. This is because it is possible for a spring clip to foul the rotating parts of the distributor and cause damage.

9   Remove the rotor arm. It may simply pull off, or it may be secured by two screws (photo). The rotor arm tips may be coated with silicone grease – if so, do not rub it off.

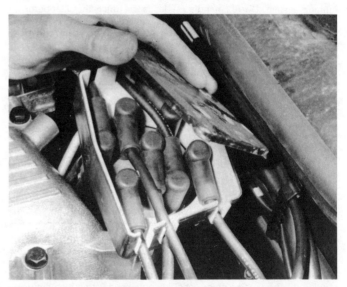

4.3 Removing a distributor can screening lid

4.6 Removing a distributor screening can

4.7 Removing a distributor cap

4.9 Removing a rotor arm

# Are your plugs trying to tell you something?

**Normal.**
Grey-brown deposits, lightly coated core nose. Plugs ideally suited to engine, and engine in good condition.

**Heavy Deposits.**
A build up of crusty deposits, light-grey sandy colour in appearance.
Fault: Often caused by worn valve guides, excessive use of upper cylinder lubricant, or idling for long periods.

**Lead Glazing.**
Plug insulator firing tip appears yellow or green/yellow and shiny in appearance.
Fault: Often caused by incorrect carburation, excessive idling followed by sharp acceleration. Also check ignition timing.

**Carbon fouling.**
Dry, black, sooty deposits.
Fault: over-rich fuel mixture.
Check: carburettor mixture settings, float level, choke operation, air filter.

**Oil fouling.**
Wet, oily deposits. Fault: worn bores/piston rings or valve guides; sometimes occurs (temporarily) during running-in period.

**Overheating.**
Electrodes have glazed appearance, core nose very white – few deposits. Fault: plug overheating. Check: plug value, ignition timing, fuel octane rating (too low) and fuel mixture (too weak).

**Electrode damage.**
Electrodes burned away; core nose has burned, glazed appearance. Fault: pre-ignition. Check: for correct heat range and as for 'overheating'.

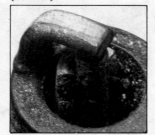

**Split core nose.**
(May appear initially as a crack). Fault: detonation or wrong gap-setting technique. Check: ignition timing, cooling system, fuel mixture (too weak).

# WHY DOUBLE COPPER IS BETTER FOR YOUR ENGINE.

Unique Trapezoidal Copper Cored Earth Electrode

50% Larger Spark Area

Copper Cored Centre Electrode

Champion Double Copper plugs are the first in the world to have copper core in both centre and earth electrode. This innovative design means that they run cooler by up to 100°C – giving greater efficiency and longer life. These double copper cores transfer heat away from the tip of the plug faster and more efficiently. Therefore, Double Copper runs at cooler temperatures than conventional plugs giving improved acceleration response and high speed performance with no fear of pre-ignition.

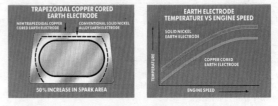

TRAPEZOIDAL COPPER CORED EARTH ELECTRODE

NEW TRAPEZOIDAL COPPER CORED EARTH ELECTRODE / CONVENTIONAL SOLID NICKEL ALLOY EARTH ELECTRODE

50% INCREASE IN SPARK AREA

EARTH ELECTRODE TEMPERATURE VS ENGINE SPEED

TEMPERATURE / SOLID NICKEL EARTH ELECTRODE / COPPER CORED EARTH ELECTRODE / ENGINE SPEED

Champion Double Copper plugs also feature a unique trapezoidal earth electrode giving a 50% increase in spark area. This, together with the double copper cores, offers greatly reduced electrode wear, so the spark stays stronger for longer.

- **FASTER COLD STARTING**
- **FOR UNLEADED OR LEADED FUEL**
- **ELECTRODES UP TO 100°C COOLER**
- **BETTER ACCELERATION RESPONSE**
- **LOWER EMISSIONS**
- **50% BIGGER SPARK AREA**
- **THE LONGER LIFE PLUG**

**Plug Tips/Hot and Cold.**
Spark plugs must operate within well-defined temperature limits to avoid cold fouling at one extreme and overheating at the other.
Champion and the car manufacturers work out the best plugs for an engine to give optimum performance under all conditions, from freezing cold starts to sustained high speed motorway cruising.
Plugs are often referred to as hot or cold. With Champion, the higher the number on its body, the hotter the plug, and the lower the number the cooler the plug. For the correct plug for your car refer to the specifications at the beginning of this chapter.

**Plug Cleaning**
Modern plug design and materials mean that Champion no longer recommends periodic plug cleaning. Certainly don't clean your plugs with a wire brush as this can cause metal conductive paths across the nose of the insulator so impairing its performance and resulting in loss of acceleration and reduced m.p.g.
However, if plugs are removed, always carefully clean the area where the plug seats in the cylinder head as grit and dirt can sometimes cause gas leakage.
Also wipe any traces of oil or grease from plug leads as this may lead to arcing.

10 Clean the HT leads and distributor cap with a dry cloth. Scrape any corrosion or other deposits from the connectors and terminals. Also clean the coil tower.
11 Renew the HT leads if they are cracked, burnt or otherwise damaged. If a multi-meter is available, measure the resistance of the leads. The desired value is given in the Specifications.
12 Renew the distributor cap if it is cracked or badly burnt inside, or if there is evidence of 'tracking' (black lines marking the path of HT leakage). If there is a carbon brush at the centre of the cap, make sure that it moves freely, and is not excessively worn.
13 Clean the metal track of the rotor arm with abrasive paper (but see paragraph 9 first). Renew the arm if it is cracked or badly burnt.
14 Commence reassembly by fitting the rotor arm to the distributor. It is positively located by a notch or shaped pegs so it cannot be fitted the wrong way round. Tighten the securing screws, when applicable.
15 Refit the distributor cap and secure it with the clips or screws.
16 On V6 models, refit the screening can.
17 Reconnect the HT leads to the distributor cap, making sure that they are correctly fitted. The No. 1 connector on the cap is marked (photos).
18 On V6 models, refit the screening can lid.
19 Reconnect the HT leads to the spark plugs and coil.
20 Reconnect the battery and run the engine.

## 5  Distributor – removal and refitting

**Note:** *The distributor should not be removed without good cause, since the accuracy of ignition timing achieved in production is unlikely to be regained.*

1 Disconnect the battery negative lead.
2 Remove the distributor cap as described in the previous Section. Depending on model, it may be possible to move the cap aside without disconnecting the HT leads.
3 Using a spanner on the crankshaft pulley bolt, turn the engine to bring No. 1 cylinder to firing point. (If the distributor cap is secured by clips, make sure the clips stay clear of the distributor moving parts.) No. 1 cylinder is at firing point when:

(a) The timing marks are in alignment (Section 6)
(b) The tip of the rotor arm is pointing to the place occupied by the No. 1 HT lead connector in the distributor cap

4 With No. 1 cylinder at firing point, the tip of the rotor arm should also be aligned with a notch in the distributor body. Mark the notch for reference when refitting.

5 Depress the locking tab on the distributor multi-plug. Disconnect the plug, pulling on the plug itself, not the wires (photo).
6 Make alignment marks between the distributor body and the engine, then remove the distributor clamp bolt and clamp plate (photo). On V6 models access is poor, and a crow's-foot spanner will be needed. The clamp bolt may be covered in sealant to discourage tampering – if so, scrape it off. Unbolt the support bracket, when fitted.
7 Lift out the distributor (photo). Mark the position taken up by the rotor arm after removal.
8 If the distributor is mechanically or electrically defective, it must be renewed. The only spares available are the cap, rotor arm, module (when applicable) and the shaft O-ring (photo).
9 Commence refitting by positioning the rotor arm to the point noted in paragraph 7. This will be approximately 20° clockwise from the No. 1 firing point (paragraph 4).
10 Make sure that the engine is still positioned at the firing point for No.1 cylinder.
11 Offer the distributor to the engine, observing the distributor body-to-engine alignment marks. As the drivegear meshes, the distributor shaft will turn anti-clockwise. The rotor arm should end up in the correct position for No.1 firing – if not, withdraw the distributor, re-position the shaft and try again.

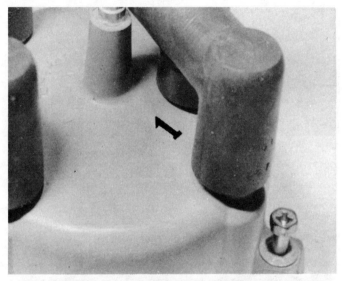

4.17A Distributor cap (4-cylinder), showing No. 1 terminal marking

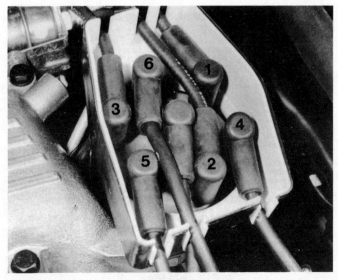

4.17B HT lead identification at distributor cap (V6)

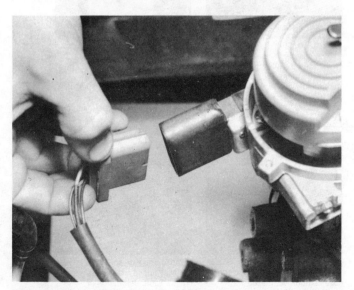

5.5 Disconnecting a distributor multi-plug

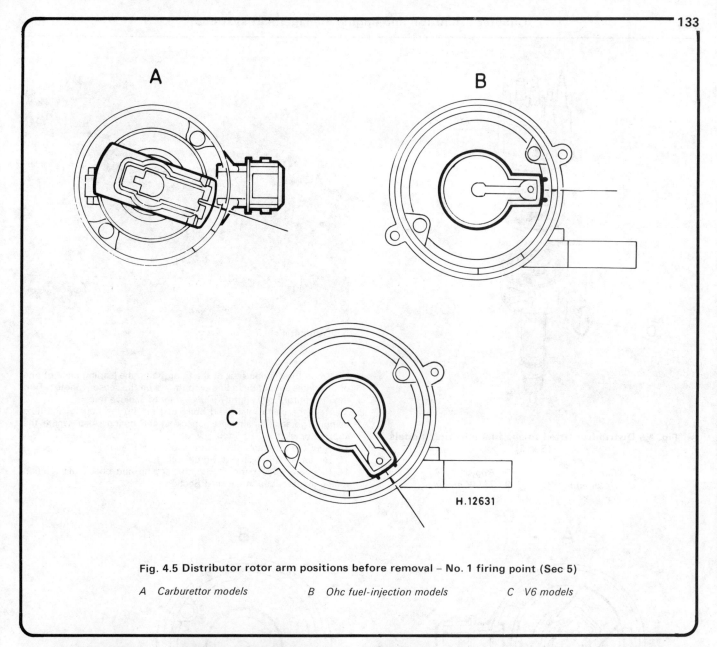

Fig. 4.5 Distributor rotor arm positions before removal – No. 1 firing point (Sec 5)

A   Carburettor models          B   Ohc fuel-injection models          C   V6 models

H.12631

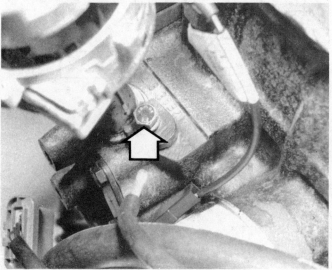

5.6 Distributor clamp bolt (arrowed)

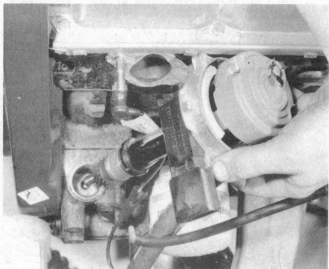

5.7 Removing the distributor (ohc)

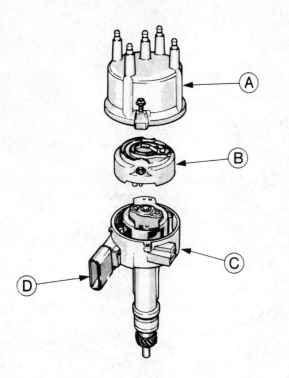

**Fig. 4.6 Distributor fitted to ohc fuel-injection models
(Sec 5)**

| A | Cap | C | Body |
|---|---|---|---|
| B | Rotor arm | D | TFI IV module |

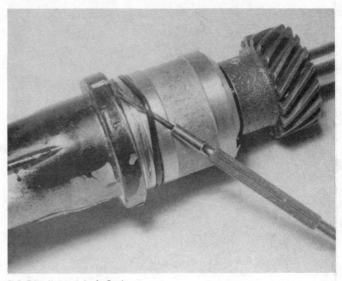

5.8 Distributor shaft O-ring

12 When the distributor is at the firing point, the leading edge of one of the vanes should be in line with the rib on the sensor (photo). Turn the distributor body slightly if necessary to achieve this.
13 Refit the clamp plate and bolt. Just nip up the bolt for the time being. Tighten it finally after checking the timing. Also secure the support bracket, when fitted.
14 Refit the rotor arm, distributor cap and HT leads.
15 Reconnect the distributor multi-plug.
16 Reconnect the battery. Run the engine and check the ignition timing as described in the next Section.

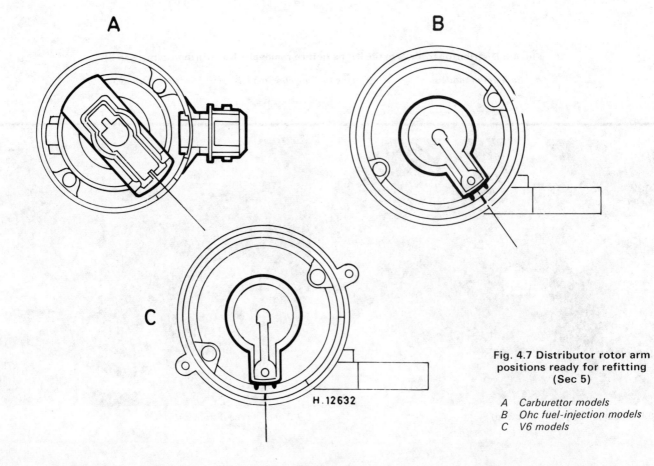

H.12632

**Fig. 4.7 Distributor rotor arm
positions ready for refitting
(Sec 5)**

| A | Carburettor models |
|---|---|
| B | Ohc fuel-injection models |
| C | V6 models |

5.12 Vane leading edge and sensor rib (arrows) are aligned at firing point

6.3 Timing marks and pointer (ohc). Cast pulley shown

## 6 Ignition timing – checking

1  Ignition timing is set very accurately in production. It does not need to be checked or adjusted on a routine basis. Adjustment will only be necessary if the distributor, or an associated component such as the timing belt, has been disturbed. (For temporary adjustment see Section 15).

2  Before checking the timing, the following conditions must be met:

(a)  The engine must be warmed up

(b)  On carburettor models, the vacuum pipe must be disconnected from the manifold and the manifold hole be plugged

(c)  Idle speed must be below 900 rpm

(d)  Any earthed 'octane adjustment' wires must be temporarily isolated (see Section 15)

3  Locate the timing marks. On ohc engines the timing scale is on the crankshaft pulley, and a pointer on the timing cover must be aligned with the appropriate mark on the pulley (photo). Note that two alternative types of pulley may be fitted – see Fig. 4.8. On V6 engines

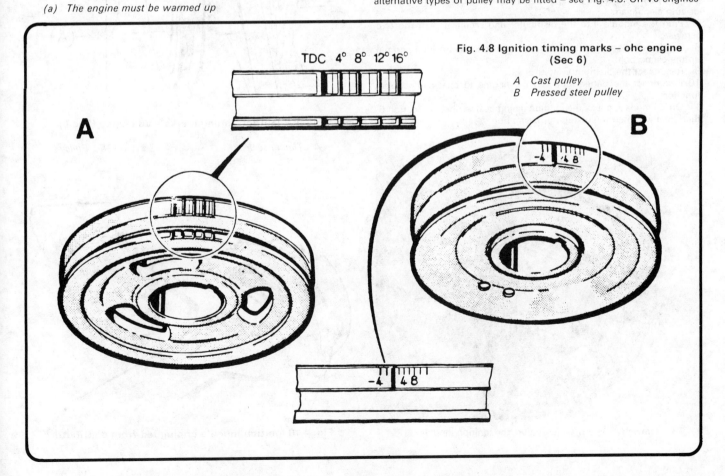

TDC 4° 8° 12° 16°

**Fig. 4.8 Ignition timing marks – ohc engine (Sec 6)**

A  Cast pulley
B  Pressed steel pulley

there is a single notch on the pulley and the timing scale is on the timing cover (Fig. 4.9). The desired values are given in the Specifications. Highlight the appropriate marks with white paint.

4   Connect a timing light (strobe) to No. 1 HT lead, following the maker's instructions. Some lights require additional power connections to be made, either to the mains or to the battery.

5   Run the engine at idle and shine the timing light onto the marks. Take care not to get the timing light leads, clothing etc tangled in the fan blades or other moving parts. The timing marks will appear stationary and (if the timing is correct) in alignment.

6   If adjustment is necessary, stop the engine. Slacken the distributor clamp bolt and turn the distributor body slightly. To retard the ignition (move the mark nearer TDC) turn the distributor body clockwise, and vice versa to advance the ignition. Tighten the clamp bolt and re-check the timing.

7   When adjustment is correct, stop the engine and disconnect the timing light. Reconnect the vacuum pipe, when applicable, and reconnect any 'octane adjustment' wires.

## 7   Ignition module (fuel-injection models) – removal and refitting

1   Disconnect the battery negative lead.

2   Disconnect the distributor multi-plug.

3   On V6 models only, make alignment marks between the distributor body and the engine. Slacken the distributor clamp bolt and swivel the distributor to make the module securing screws accessible.

4   Remove the two screws which secure the module (photo). These screws are deeply recessed. The screws seen here have 'Torx' heads; ordinary hexagon heads have also been encountered, and to undo these a thin socket or box spanner will be required.

5   Pull the module downwards and remove it.

6   When refitting, coat the rear face of the module with heat sink compound to Ford spec 815F-12103-AA. This is extremely expensive, so it may be worthwhile trying to obtain a smear from a friendly dealer or auto electrician.

7   Plug the module into the distributor and secure it with the two screws.

8   On V6 models, return the distributor to its original position and nip up the clamp bolt.

9   Reconnect the distributor multi-plug.

10   Reconnect the battery and run the engine to check for correct function.

11   On V6 models, check the ignition timing as described in Section 6, then finally tighten the distributor clamp bolt.

## 8   Ignition coil – testing, removal and refitting

1   The ignition coil is mounted on the left-hand inner wing (photo). If it fails, there will be no spark and the engine will stop.

2   To test the coil an ohmmeter will be required. Disconnect the LT and HT leads from the coil and measure the resistance between the two LT terminals (primary resistance), then between the HT terminal and either LT terminal (secondary resistance). Desired values are given in the Specifications. In fact most test gear will not be able to distinguish between a normal primary resistance (which is very low) and a short-circuit.

3   In the absence of am ohmmeter, test the coil by substitution of a known good unit.

4   To remove the coil, disconnect the LT and HT leads, then remove the two screws which secure the coil clamp. Lift out the coil.

5   Refit by reversing the removal operations.

## 9   Fuel trap (carburettor models) – removal and refitting

1   On carburettor models, a fuel trap is fitted in the vacuum pipe between the inlet manifold and the ESC II module.

2   Disconnect the battery negative lead.

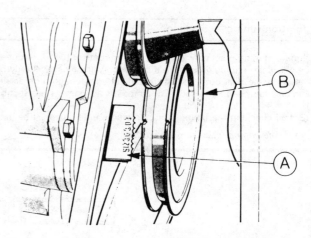

**Fig. 4.9 Ignition timing marks – V6 engine (Sec 6)**

A   Timing scale                              B   Pulley

7.4 Two screws (arrowed) which secure the ignition module

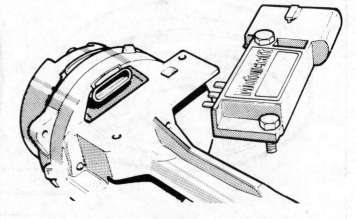

**Fig. 4.10 Ignition module unplugged from distributor (Sec 7)**

3   Disconnect the vacuum pipes from the trap and remove it. Dispose of it carefully, it may contain fuel.
4   When refitting, note that the end of the trap marked 'CARB' goes towards the manifold, and the end marked 'DIST' towards the module.
5   Reconnect the battery.

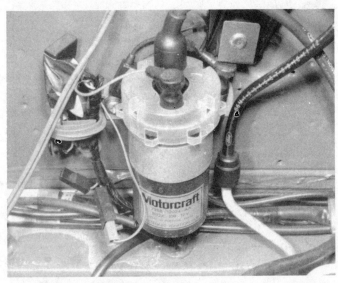

8.1 Ignition coil location

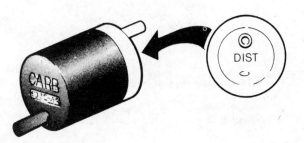

**Fig. 4.11 Fuel trap markings (Sec 9)**

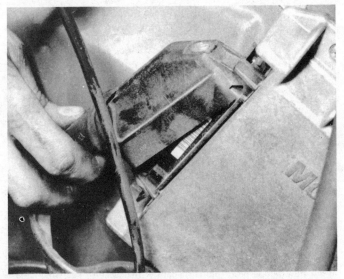

10.3 ESC II module multi-plug

## 10 Engine management control module – removal and refitting

### ESC II module (carburettor models)
1   Disconnect the battery negative lead.
2   Disconnect the vacuum pipe from the module (photo).
3   Release the locking catch and disconnect the multi-plug from the module (photo).
4   Remove the three securing screws and detach the module and bracket from the left-hand inner wing.
5   Refit by reversing the removal operations. Make sure that the multi-plug is securely fitted and the locking catch engaged.

### EEC IV module (fuel-injection models)
6   Disconnect the battery negative lead.
7   Remove the under-dash trim on the passenger side.
8   Unclip the module and lower it onto the vehicle floor.
9   Remove the control bolt from the multi-plug and disconnect the plug from the module.
10  Refit by reversing the removal operations.

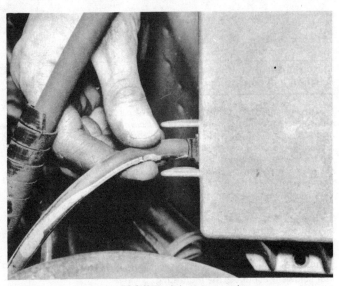

10.2 Disconnecting the ESC II module vacuum pipe

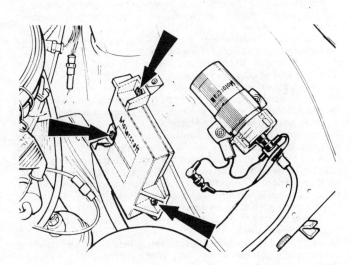

**Fig. 4.12 ESC II module retaining screws (arrowed) (Sec 10)**

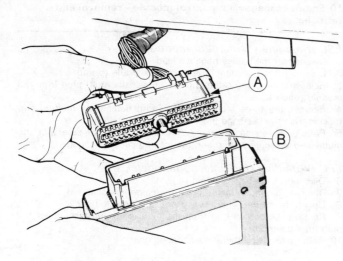

Fig. 4.13 Disconnecting the EEC IV module (Sec 10)

A   Multi-plug                    B   Securing bolt

Fig. 4.14 Carburettor stepper motor and mounting bracket
(Sec 11)

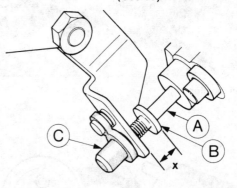

Fig. 4.15 Throttle lever initial adjustment (Sec 11)

A   Plunger                       X   7.5 ± 1.0 mm
B   Adjusting screw                   (0.30 ± 0.04 in)
C   Cap

## 11 Carburettor stepper motor (2.0 litre models) – removal, refitting and adjustment

**Note:** *Irregular idle is not necessarily caused by a faulty or badly adjusted stepper motor. Good electrical contact between the stepper motor plunger and the adjusting screw is essential. Before attempting adjustment or renewal of the motor, try the effect of cleaning the plunger and adjusting screw contact faces with abrasive paper followed by switch cleaning fluid. Switch cleaning fluid is available from electronic component shops.*

1   Disconnect the battery negative lead.

2   Remove the air cleaner (Chapter 3, Section 5).

3   Disconnect the multi-plug from the stepper motor. Release the locking clip and pull on the plug, not on the wires.

4   Remove the four screws which secure the stepper motor bracket to the carburettor. Remove the motor and bracket and separate them.

5   Refit the motor and bracket to the carburettor and secure with the four screws. Reconnect the multi-plug.

6   Make an initial adjustment to the throttle lever adjusting screw if necessary so that it protrudes from the lever by dimension 'X' as shown in Fig. 4.15.

7   Reconnect the air cleaner vacuum hose. Position the air cleaner to one side so that there is still access to the carburettor and stepper motor.

8   Connect a tachometer (rev. counter) to the engine as instructed by the manufacturers. Reconnect the battery.

9   Run the engine. Check the idle mixture (CO level) as described in Chapter 3 and adjust if necessary.

10  Switch off all electrical loads (headlights, heater blower etc). If the idle speed adjustment lead is earthed, temporarily isolate it – see Section 15. Make sure that the automatic transmission selector is in the 'N' or 'P' position (where applicable).

11  Accelerate the engine to a speed greater then 2500 rpm, allow it to return to idle, then repeat. Insert a feeler blade of thickness 1.0 mm (0.04 in) between the stepper motor plunger and the adjusting screw. With the feeler blade in place, engine speed should be 875 ± 25 rpm.

12  If adjustment is necessary, remove the tamperproof cap from the adjusting screw locknut. Release the locknut, turn the adjusting screw to achieve the correct speed and tighten the locknut.

13  Repeat paragraph 11 and check that the speed is still correct. Readjust if necessary.

14  Remove the feeler blade. Stop and restart the engine, observing the stepper motor plunger. Immediately after switching off, the plunger should move to the 'anti-dieseling' position; after a few seconds it should extend to the 'vent manifold/start' position.

15  Disconnect the test gear and refit the air cleaner.

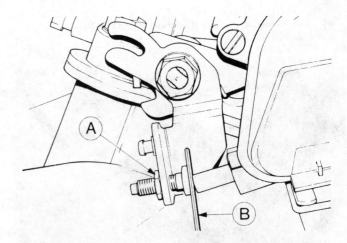

Fig. 4.16 Stepper motor adjustment (Sec 11)

A   Locknut                       B   Feeler blade

16  Recheck the idle mixture.

17  Fit new tamperproof plugs or caps if necessary – see Chapter 3, Section 3.

18  Reconnect the idle speed adjustment lead if it was earthed.

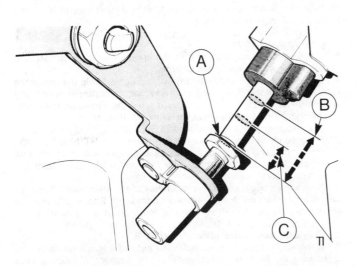

**Fig. 4.17 Stepper motor plunger positions (Sec 11)**

A  *Vent manifold/start*        C  *Idle*
B  *Anti-dieseling*

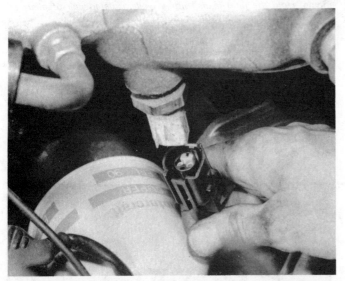

12.4 Coolant temperature sensor multi-plug

13.5 Removing the manifold heater

## 12 Coolant temperature sensor – removal and refitting

1   The engine management system temperature sensor is located on the underside of the inlet manifold (ohc) or on the front face of the cylinder block (V6).
2   Disconnect the battery negative lead.
3   Drain the cooling system as described in Chapter 2, Section 3. Save the coolant if it is fit for re-use.
4   Disconnect the multi-plug from the sensor. Pull on the plug, not on the wiring (photo).
5   Unscrew the sensor and remove it.
6   Refit by reversing the removal operations. Refill the cooling system as described in Chapter 2, Section 5.

## 13 Manifold heater (carburettor models) – removal and refitting

**Note:** *The manifold heater must not be removed while it is hot.*
1   Disconnect the battery negative lead.
2   Remove the air cleaner to improve access.
3   Remove the three bolts which secure the heater to the underside of the manifold.
4   Disconnect the electrical feed from the heater.
5   Remove the heater. Recover the gasket and O-ring (photo).
6   Use a new gasket and O-ring when refitting. Offer the heater to the manifold, insert the three bolts and tighten them evenly, making sure that the heater does not tip or jam.
7   Reconnect the electrical feed.
8   Refit the air cleaner and reconnect the battery.

## 14 Engine management system relays – general

1   On carburettor models, one relay handles the current for the intake manifold heater. On 2.0 litre models another relay, known as the power hold relay, supplies the ESC II module. The power hold relay is needed so that the carburettor stopper motor can perform its anti-diesel/vent manifold cycle after switching off. When the cycle is complete, the relay is de-energised.
2   Carburettor models with an electric fuel pump also have a fuel pump relay.
3   Fuel-injection models have one relay supplying the EEC IV module and another supplying the fuel pump.
4   All these relays are located behind the facia panel. Access is gained by removing the facia top – see Chapter 11, Section 39.
5   Testing of a suspect relay is by substitution of a known good unit.

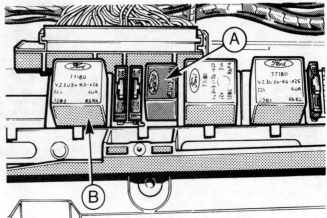

**Fig. 4.18 Engine management system relays (Sec 14)**

A  *Power hold*                    B  *Manifold heater*

## 15 Ignition timing and idle speed adjustments

1   All models have a facility for retarding the ignition timing by up to six degrees without physically disturbing the distributor. The adjustment is intended for use when the correct grade of fuel is not available.

2   Adjustment is made by earthing one or two leads (sometimes called octane adjustment leads) which terminate in a multi-plug next to the ignition coil (photo). Ideally a service adjustment lead, available from a Ford dealer, should be used. Cut and insulate the wires in the adjustment lead which are not to be earthed.

3   The amount of ignition retardation is as follows:

| Wire(s) earthed | Degrees retard | | |
| --- | --- | --- | --- |
| | 1.8/2.0 carburettor | 2.0 injection | V6 models |
| Blue | 2 | 4 | 6 |
| Red | 4 | 2 | 3 |
| Blue and red | 6 | 6 | Forbidden |

4   Performance and efficiency will suffer as a result of this adjustment. Normal timing should be restored (by isolating the adjustment leads) when the correct grade of fuel is available.

5   If the yellow adjustment lead is earthed, this will raise the idle speed by 75 rpm (ohc) or 50 rpm (V6). It may be found that the yellow lead has already been earthed in production, in whch case disconnecting it will lower the idle speed by the same amount. This adjustment does not apply to 1.8 litre carburettor models.

## 16 Fault diagnosis – ignition system

The electronic ignition fitted is far less likely to cause trouble than the contact breaker type fitted to many cars, largely because the low tension circuit is electronically controlled. However the high tension circuit remains identical and therefore the associated faults are the same. There are two main symptoms indicating ignition faults. Either the engine will not start or fire, or the engine is difficult to start and misfires. If it is a regular misfire, the fault is almost sure to be in the secondary or high tension circuit.

### Engine fails to start

1   If the starter motor fails to turn the engine check the battery and starter motor with reference to Chapter 12.

2   Disconnect an HT lead from any spark plug and hold the end of the cable approximately 5 mm (0.2 in) away from the cylinder head using *well insulated pliers*. While an assistant spins the engine on the starter motor, check that a regular blue spark occurs. If so, remove, clean, and re-gap the spark plugs as described in Section 3.

3   If no spark occurs, disconnect the main feed HT lead from the distributor cap and check for a spark as in paragraph 2. If sparks now occur, check the distributor cap, rotor arm, and HT leads as described in Section 4 and renew them as necessary.

4   If no sparks occur check the resistance of the main feed HT lead as described in Section 4 and renew as necessary. Should the lead be serviceable check that all wiring and multi-plugs are secure on the electronic module and distributor.

5   Check the coil as described in Section 8.

6   If the above checks reveal no faults but there is still no spark, the distributor or the control module must be suspect. Consult a Ford dealer for further testing, or test by substitution.

### Engine misfires

7   If the engine misfires regularly, run it at a fast idling speed. Pull off each of the plug HT leads in turn and and listen to the note of the engine. *Hold the plug leads with a well insulated pair of pliers as protection against a shock from the HT supply.*

8   No difference in engine running will be noticed when the lead from the defective circuit is removed. Removing the lead from one of the good cylinders will accentuate the misfire.

9   Remove the plug lead from the end of the defective plug and hold it about 5 mm (0.2 in) away from the cylinder head. Restart the engine. If the sparking is fairly strong and regular, the fault must lie in the spark plug.

10  The plug may be loose, the insulation may be cracked, or the points may have burnt away, giving too wide a gap for the spark to jump. Worse still, one of the points may have broken off. Either renew the plug, or clean it, reset the gap, and then test it.

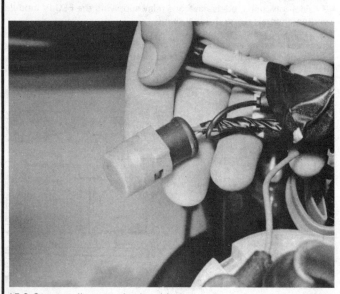

15.2 Octane adjustment lead multi-plug

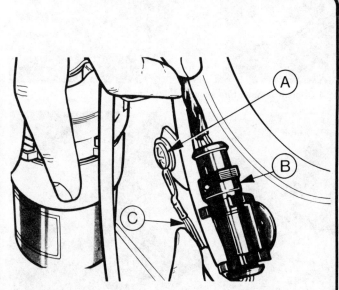

**Fig. 4.19 Service adjustment lead for timing and idle adjustment (Sec 15)**

A   Earthing point (coil screw)     C   Cut wires not to be earthed
B   Multi-plug

11 If there is no spark at the end of the plug lead, or if it is weak and intermittent check the HT lead from the distributor to the plug. If the insulation is cracked or perished or if its resistance is incorrect, renew the lead. Check the connections at the distributor cap.

12 If there is still no spark, examine the distributor cap carefully for tracking. This can be recognised by a very thin black line running between two or more electrodes, or between an electrode and some other part of the distributor. These lines are paths which now conduct electricity across the cap, thus letting it run to earth. The only answer in this case is a new distributor cap. Tracking will also occur if the inside or outside of the distributor cap is damp. If the engine fails to start due to either damp HT leads or distributor cap, a moisture dispersant, such as Holts Wet Start, can be very effective. To prevent the problem recurring, Holts Damp Start can be used to provide a sealing coat, so excluding any further moisture from the ignition system. In extreme difficulty, Holts Cold Start will help to start a car when only a very poor spark occurs.

## 17 Fault diagnosis – engine management system

1 If a fault is suspected in an engine management system do not immediately blame the 'black box'. Check first that all wiring is in good condition and that all multi-plugs are securely fitted.

2 Unless components are freely available for testing by substitution, further investigation should be left to a Ford dealer or other competent specialist.

3 Note that relays, modules and similar components cannot necessarily be substituted from another vehicle. The control modules in particular are dedicated to particular engine, transmission and territory combinations.

# Chapter 5 Clutch

## Contents

## Specifications

### General

| | |
|---|---|
| Clutch type .................................................................... | Single dry plate, diaphragm spring, cable actuation |
| Adjustment .................................................................... | Automatic in use |

### Driven plate

Nominal diameter:
| | |
|---|---|
| 1.8 litre and 2.0 litre ................................................... | 216 mm (8.5 in) |
| V6 ................................................................................ | 241 mm (9.5 in) |

Lining thickness (new):
| | |
|---|---|
| 1.8 litre and 2.0 litre ................................................... | 3.85 mm (0.152 in) |
| V6 ................................................................................ | 3.81 mm (0.150 in) |

### Torque wrench setting

| | Nm | lbf ft |
|---|---|---|
| Clutch pressure plate bolts ............................................ | 22 to 33 | 16 to 24 |

## 1 General description

The clutch is of single dry plate type with a diaphragm spring pressure plate. The unit is dowelled and bolted to the rear face of the flywheel.

The clutch plate (or disc) is free to slide along the splines of the gearbox input shaft and is held in position between the flywheel and the pressure plate by the pressure of the pressure plate spring. Friction lining material is riveted to the clutch plate and it has a spring cushioned hub to absorb transmission shocks and to help ensure a smooth take off.

The circular diaphagm spring is mounted on shoulder pins and held in place in the cover by two fulcrum rings which are riveted in position.

The clutch is actuated by a cable controlled by the clutch pedal. Wear of the friction linings is compensated for by an automatic pawl

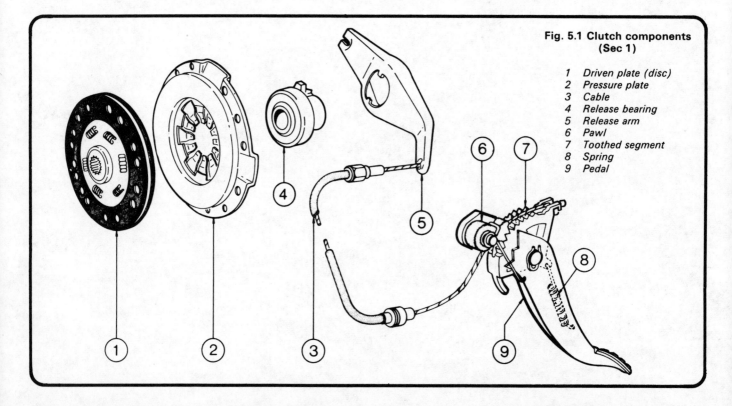

**Fig. 5.1 Clutch components (Sec 1)**

1  Driven plate (disc)
2  Pressure plate
3  Cable
4  Release bearing
5  Release arm
6  Pawl
7  Toothed segment
8  Spring
9  Pedal

and quadrant adjuster on the top of the clutch pedal. The clutch release mechanism consists of a ball bearing which slides on a guide sleeve at the front of the gearbox, and a release arm which pivots inside the clutch bellhousing.

Depressing the clutch pedal actuates the clutch release arm by means of the cable. The release arm pushes the release bearing forwards to bear against the release fingers so moving the centre of the diaphragm spring inwards. The spring is sandwiched between two annular rings which act as fulcrum points. As the centre of the spring is pushed in, the outside of the spring is pushed out, so moving the pressure plate backwards and disengaging the pressure plate from the clutch plate.

When the clutch pedal is released the diaphragm spring forces the pressure plate into contact with the friction linings on the clutch plate and at the same time pushes the clutch plate a fraction of an inch forwards on its splines so engaging the clutch plate with the flywheel. The clutch plate is now firmly sandwiched between the pressure plate and the flywheel so the drive is taken up.

## 2 Maintenance and inspection

1 Every 1000 miles or so, or whenever excessive free play is evident in the clutch pedal, lift the pedal upwards against its stop and then

release it. This will allow the self-adjusting mechanism to take up any free play in the cable.
2 No other maintenance is specified for the clutch. All the working components will have to be renewed sooner or later – depending on driving style and conditions – and if slipping, screeching or other symptoms of wear become evident, prompt attention may save more extensive damage.
3 Inspect the clutch cable occasionally at its attachment to the clutch release arm. Lubricate the cable if it is dry, and renew it if it is frayed, or stiff in operation.

## 3 Clutch pedal – removal, overhaul and refitting

1 Disconnect the clutch cable from the release arm and clutch pedal as described in Section 4, but do not remove the cable.
2 Disconnect the wiring from the stop light switch. On models with cruise control, also disconnect the brake and clutch vacuum dump switches.
3 Disconnect the brake hydraulic unit pushrod from the brake pedal.
4 Remove the two nuts and one bolt which secure the pedal bracket to the bulkhead.
5 Remove the spring clip from the pedal shaft. Push the shaft through the brake and clutch pedals and remove the clutch pedal, complete with adjuster components.
6 Prise the bushes from each side of the pedal and extract the toothed segment. Unhook the spring.
7 Prise one of the clips from the pawl pin, withdraw the pin and remove the pawl and spring.
8 Clean all the components and examine them for wear and damage. Renew them as necessary.
9 Lubricate the bores of the pawl and segment with graphite grease.
10 Assemble the pawl, spring and pin to the pedal with reference to Fig. 5.2, then refit the clip.
11 Attach the spring to the toothed segment, then insert the segment into the pedal and press in the two pivot bushes.
12 Lift the pawl and turn the segment so that the pawl rests on the smooth curved surface at the end of the teeth.
13 Attach the segment spring to the pedal.
14 Lubricate the pedal shaft with a molybdenum-based grease. Pass the shaft through the pedals and secure it with the spring clip.
15 Secure the pedal bracket to the bulkhead, then reconnect the brake unit pushrod, the stop light switch and (when applicable) the cruise control switches. See Chapter 12, Section 25.
16 Reconnect the clutch cable as described in Section 4.

## 4 Clutch cable – removal and refitting

1 Raise and securely support the front of the vehicle.
2 Inside the vehicle, lift up the clutch pedal as far as possible and jam it in this position with a piece of wood.
3 Underneath the vehicle, unclip the rubber gaiter which protects the end of the clutch cable and the release arm. Pull the cable down in

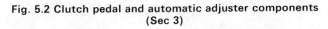

**Fig. 5.2 Clutch pedal and automatic adjuster components
(Sec 3)**

A  Pawl
B  Spring
C  Pawl pin and clip
D  Bush

E  Clutch pedal
F  Toothed segment tension
   spring
G  Toothed segment

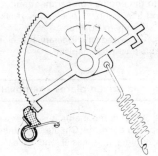

**Fig. 5.3 Clutch pedal toothed segment at initial setting
(Sec 3)**

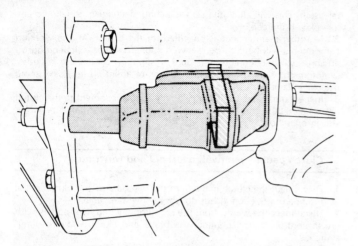

Fig. 5.4 Rubber gaiter clipped over the release arm (Sec 4)

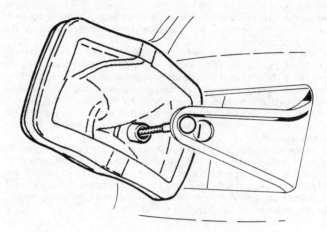

Fig. 5.5 Clutch cable attachment to release arm (Sec 4)

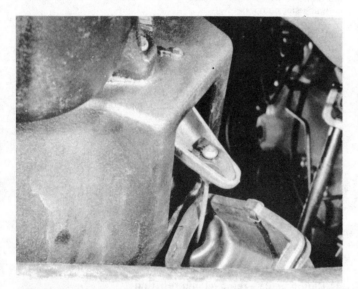

4.3A Clutch cable attachment to release arm

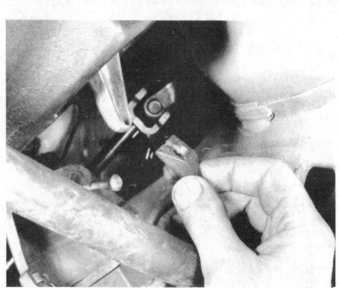

4.3B Removing the clutch cable rubber insulator

front of the release arm and unhook the cable inner from the release arm with pliers. Remove the rubber insulator (photos).
4  Pull the gaiter off the cable and free the cable at the gearbox end.
5  Inside the vehicle, unclip the under-dash insulation on the driver's side. Unhook the cable inner from the toothed segment.
6  Pull the cable into the engine compartment and remove it.
7  Refit by reversing the removal operations. Make sure that the release arm gaiter is securely in position.
8  Remove the piece of wood and operate the clutch pedal a few times to settle the adjustment mechanism.

## 5  Clutch pressure and driven plates – removal

1  For access to the clutch components it is necessary to remove the engine (Chapter 1) or the gearbox (Chapter 6). Unless there is other work to do on the engine, it is easier and quicker to remove the gearbox.
2  If the pressure plate may be re-used, mark its position relative to the flywheel, using a scriber or dabs of paint.
3  Slacken the six bolts which secure the pressure plate to the flywheel. Undo each bolt a little at a time, in a 'criss-cross' sequence, until the spring pressure is released. Remove the bolts and washers.

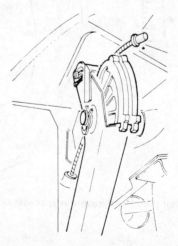

Fig. 5.6 Disconnecting the clutch cable inner from the toothed segment (Sec 4)

4   Lift the pressure plate off the dowels on the flywheel. Note which way round the driven plate is fitted and lift it from the pressure plate or flywheel (photo).

5   Clean off dust and dirt using a damp cloth or an old damp paintbrush. **Do not disperse the dust into the air, and take care not to to inhale it, as it may contain asbestos.**

## 6   Clutch components – inspection

1   Examine the friction surfaces of the flywheel and the pressure plate for scoring or cracks. Light scoring may be ignored. Excessive scoring or cracks can sometimes be machined off the flywheel face – consult a specialist. The pressure plate must be renewed if it is badly scored.

2   Inspect the pressure plate cover and the diaphragm spring for damage, or blue discolouration suggesting overheating. Pay attention to the tips of the spring fingers where the release bearing operates. Renew the pressure plate if in doubt.

3   Renew the driven plate if the friction linings are worn down to, or approaching, the rivets. If the linings are oil-soaked or have a hard black glaze, the source of oil contamination – the crankshaft rear oil seal or gearbox input shaft oil seal – must be dealt with before the plate is renewed. Also inspect the driven plate springs, hub and splines.

4   Note that if the driven plate only is renewed, problems may be experienced related to the bedding-in of the driven plate and old pressure plate. It is certainly better practice to renew the driven plate and pressure plate together, if finances permit.

5   Spin the release bearing in the clutch bellhousing and feel for roughness or shake. The bearing should be renewed without question unless it is known to be in perfect condition. For renewal see Section 7.

## 7   Clutch release bearing and arm – removal and refitting

1   With the gearbox and engine separated to provide access to the clutch, attention can be given to the release bearing located in the clutch housing, over the input shaft.

2   If the gearbox is still in the car, remove the rubber boot and disconnect the clutch cable from the release arm with reference to Section 4.

3   Free the release bearing from the release arm and withdraw it from the guide sleeve (photo).

4   Pull the release arm from the fulcrum pin, then withdraw the arm over the input shaft (photo).

5   Check the release bearing as described in Section 6. If there are any signs of grease leakage, renew the bearing (photo).

6   Refitting is a reversal of removal.

5.4 Removing the pressure plate and the driven plate from the flywheel

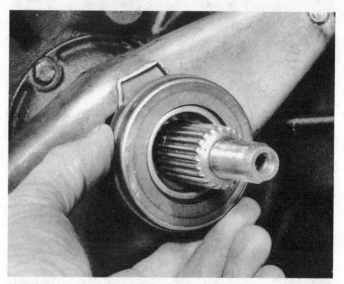

7.3 Removing the clutch release bearing

7.4 Clutch release arm, showing fulcrum pin (arrowed)

7.5 The release bearing removed

## 8  Clutch pressure and driven plates – refitting

1   It is important that no oil or grease gets on the clutch plate friction linings, or the pressure plate and flywheel faces. It is advisable to refit the clutch with clean hands and to wipe down the pressure plate and flywheel faces with a clean rag before assembly begins.
2   Place the driven plate against the flywheel, making sure it is the right way round. The flatter side of the plate (marked 'FLYWHEEL SIDE') must go towards the flywheel (photo).
3   Fit the pressure plate loosely on the flywheel dowels, aligning the previously made marks if the original plate is being refitted. Insert the six bolts and spring washers. Tighten the bolts finger tight, so that the driven plate is just gripped but can still be moved.

4   The driven plate must now be centralised so that when the engine and gearbox are mated, the gearbox input shaft splines will pass through the splines in the centre of the plate. Ideally a universal clutch centralising tool should be used, or if available an old gearbox input shaft. Alternatively a wooden mandrel can be made.
5   Make sure that the centralising tool is located correctly in the driven plate and in the crankshaft pilot bearing, then tighten the pressure plate bolts progressively to the specified torque. Remove the tool and check the centralisation of the driven plate visually (photos).
6   Make sure that the release bearing and arm have been refitted, then refit the engine or gearbox as described in the appropriate Chapter.
7   If a new driven plate has been fitted, it may take 30 or 40 starts before the new plate beds in and operates satisfactorily.

8.2 Clutch plate is marked 'FLYWHEEL SIDE'

Fig. 5.7 Centralising the clutch driven plate (Sec 8)

8.5A Tightening the pressure plate bolts

8.5B Clutch fitted to flywheel and driven plate centred

## 9 Fault diagnosis – clutch

| Symptom | Reason(s) |
| --- | --- |
| Judder when taking up drive | Clutch friction surfaces worn |
| | Oil contamination of clutch |
| | Splines on driven plate or input shaft worn |
| | Pressure plate defective |
| | Engine/gearbox mountings worn |
| Clutch drag (failure to release) | Driven plate sticking on splines |
| | *Driven plate rusted to flywheel (after long periods of disuse) |
| | Cable free play excessive (due to stretch or faulty adjuster mechanism) |
| | Input shaft seized in crankshaft pilot bearing |
| Clutch slip (engine speed increases without increasing vehicle speed) | Friction surfaces worn or oil contaminated |
| | Pressure plate defective |
| | Insufficient free play in cable |
| Noise when depressing clutch pedal (engine stopped) | Pedal shaft or adjuster component dry |
| | Clutch cable or release arm pivot dry |
| Noise when clutch pedal held depressed (engine running) | Release bearing dry or worn |
| | Pressure plate spring fingers damaged |

*It is possible to free it by applying the handbrake, depressing the clutch pedal, engaging top gear and operating the starter motor. If really badly corroded, then the engine will not turn over, but in the majority of cases the driven plate will free. Once the engine starts, rev it up and slip the clutch several times to clear the rust deposits.

# Chapter 6
# Manual gearbox and automatic transmission

*For modifications, and information applicable to later models, see Supplement at end of manual*

## Contents

## Specifications

*Manual gearbox*

### General

| | |
|---|---|
| Gearbox type | 5 forward speeds and 1 reverse. Synchro on all forward gears |
| Maker's designation | Type N |

### Ratios

| | 1.8 litre/2.0 litre | 2.8 litre |
|---|---|---|
| 1st | 3.650 : 1 | 3.360 : 1 |
| 2nd | 1.970 : 1 | 1.810 : 1 |
| 3rd | 1.370 : 1 | 1.260 : 1 |
| 4th | 1.000 : 1 | 1.000 : 1 |
| 5th | 0.816 : 1 | 0.825 : 1 |
| Reverse | 3.660 : 1 | 3.365 : 1 |

### Lubrication

| | |
|---|---|
| Lubricant type | See 'Recommended lubricants and fluids' |
| Lubricant capacity | 1.25 litres (2.2 pints) approx |

### Torque wrench settings

| | Nm | lbf ft |
|---|---|---|
| Clutch housing to gear housing | 70 to 90 | 52 to 66 |
| Clutch housing to engine | 40 to 51 | 30 to 38 |
| Clutch release bearing guide sleeve | 9 to 11 | 7 to 8 |
| Extension housing to gear housing | 45 to 49 | 33 to 36 |
| Crossmember to floor | 20 to 25 | 15 to 18 |
| Crossmember to mounting | 16 to 20 | 12 to 15 |
| Mounting to gearbox | 50 to 57 | 37 to 42 |
| Reversing light switch | 1 to 2 | 0.7 to 1.5 |
| Selector locking mechanism | 17 to 19 | 13 to 14 |
| Oil filler plug | 23 to 27 | 17 to 20 |
| 5th gear layshaft nut | 120 to 150 | 89 to 111 |
| 5th gear locking plate | 21 to 26 | 16 to 19 |
| Gear lever to extension housing | 20 to 27 | 15 to 20 |
| Air deflector plate nut | 21 to 26 | 16 to 19 |
| Gearbox top cover bolts | 9 to 11 | 7 to 8 |

*Automatic transmission*

## General

| | |
|---|---|
| Transmission type ............................................................................. | 4 forward speeds and 1 reverse |
| Maker's designation ......................................................................... | A4LD |
| Torque converter type ..................................................................... | Trilock (hydraulic, with lock-up facility) |

## Ratios

| | |
|---|---|
| 1st ..................................................................................................... | 2.47 : 1 |
| 2nd .................................................................................................... | 1.47 : 1 |
| 3rd ..................................................................................................... | 1.00 : 1 |
| 4th ..................................................................................................... | 0.75 : 1 |
| Reverse ............................................................................................ | 2.11 : 1 |
| Converter: | |
|     2.0 litre .................................................................................. | 2.35 : 1 |
|     2.8 litre .................................................................................. | 2.15 : 1 |

## Lubrication

| | |
|---|---|
| Lubricant type .................................................................................. | See *'Recommended lubricants and fluids'* |
| Lubricant capacity (from dry) ........................................................ | 8.5 litres (15 pints) approx |

## Torque wrench settings

| | Nm | lbf ft |
|---|---|---|
| Converter housing to transmission housing ................................... | 40 to 48 | 30 to 35 |
| Extension housing to transmission housing .................................. | 40 to 48 | 30 to 35 |
| Driveplate to torque converter ........................................................ | 32 to 38 | 24 to 28 |
| Sump bolts: | | |
|     Polyacrylic gasket ............................................................... | 8 to 11 | 6 to 8 |
|     Cork gasket .......................................................................... | 15 to 18 | 11 to 13 |
| Downshift cable bracket ................................................................. | 18 to 22 | 13 to 16 |
| Selector lever nut ............................................................................ | 11 to 14 | 8 to 10 |
| Downshift lever nut ......................................................................... | 45 to 50 | 33 to 37 |
| Starter inhibitor switch .................................................................... | 10 to 14 | 7 to 10 |
| Brake band adjusting screw locknut .............................................. | 50 to 58 | 37 to 43 |
| Oil cooler unions: | | |
|     Pipe to connector ................................................................ | 22 to 24 | 16 to 18 |
|     Connector to transmission housing ................................... | 24 to 30 | 18 to 22 |
| Converter housing to engine .......................................................... | 30 to 36 | 22 to 27 |
| Centre carrier bolt ........................................................................... | 9 to 12 | 7 to 9 |

## 1 Manual gearbox – general description

A five-speed manual gearbox is fitted to these models. It is known by the makers as the type 'N' gearbox and is essentially the same as that fitted to some Sierra, Capri and 'old' Granada models.

The gearbox follows conventional rear wheel drive practice. Drive from the clutch is picked up by the input shaft, which runs in line with the mainshaft. The input shaft gear and mainshaft gears are in constant mesh with the layshaft gear cluster. Selection of gears is by sliding synchromesh hubs, which lock the appropriate mainshaft gear to the mainshaft. Drive in 4th gear is direct, ie the input shaft is locked to the mainshaft.

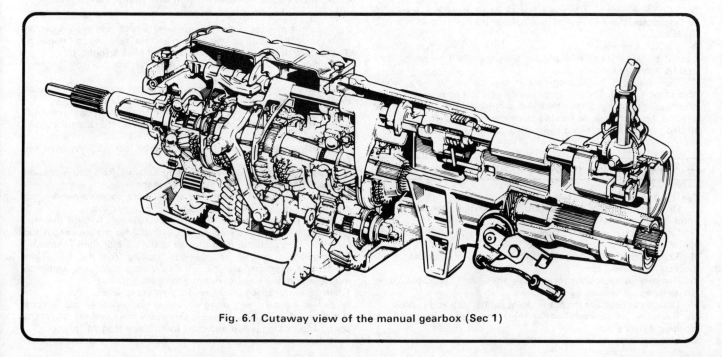

**Fig. 6.1 Cutaway view of the manual gearbox (Sec 1)**

Reverse gear is obtained by sliding an idler gear into mesh with two straight-cut gears on the mainshaft and layshaft. All the forward gear teeth are helically cut to reduce noise and improve wear characteristics.

Drive from the gearbox is picked up by the propeller shaft, which mates with the mainshaft tail.

## 2  Manual gearbox – maintenance and inspection

1   Maintenance is limited to checking the oil level periodically, and looking for leaks if it is low. Proceed as follows.

2   Place the vehicle over a pit, or raise and support it at front and rear. The vehicle must be level for an accurate check.

3   If the transmission is hot after a run, allow it to cool for a few minutes. This is necessary because the oil can foam when hot and give a false level reading.

4   Wipe clean around the filler/level plug, which is located on the left-hand side of the gearbox. Unscrew the plug with a square drive key and remove it.

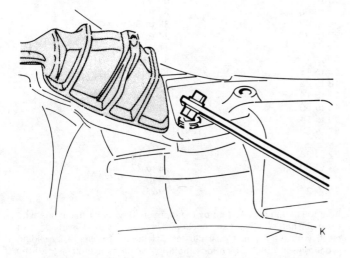

**Fig. 6.2 Removing the gearbox filler/level plug (Sec 2)**

5   Using a piece of bent wire as a dipstick, check that the oil level is up to the bottom of the filler/level plug hole, or no more than 5 mm (0.2 in) below it.

6   Top up if necessary using clean oil of the specified type. Do not overfill; allow excess oil to drip out of the plug hole if necessary. Refit and tighten the filler/level plug.

7   Frequent need for topping-up can only be due to leaks, which should be rectified. The rear extension oil seal can be renewed *in situ* after removing the propeller shaft. For renewal of the input shaft oil seal (in the clutch release bearing guide sleeve) see Section 5.

8   No periodic oil changing is specified, and no drain plug is fitted.

## 3  Manual gearbox – removal and refitting

1   Disconnect the battery negative lead.

2   On V6 models only, remove the distributor screening can, cap and rotor.

3   On all models, unscrew the gear lever knob and remove the outer gaiter.

4   Remove the centre console and its bracket. Refer to Chapter 11, Section 40, if necessary.

5   Remove the gear lever inner gaiter, frame and sound insulation. These items are secured by four screws.

6   Unbolt the gear lever from the extension housing and remove it.

7   Raise the vehicle both front and rear and support it securely, or position it over a pit.

8   Unbolt the front anti-roll bar brackets.

9   Unbolt the exhaust heat shield, when fitted (V6 only).

10  Unhook the exhaust system rear mountings and tie the system out of the way. It may be preferable to remove the system completely. On V6 models, remove the left-hand exhaust hanger bracket.

11  Remove the propeller shaft (Chapter 7, Section 3).

12  Support the engine, either with a hoist or bar from above, or with a jack and a block of wood from below. The support should be adjustable to enable the best position to be assumed, especially when refitting.

13  Remove the gearbox crossmember. This is secured by five bolts – two on each side and one in the centre.

14  Disconnect the reversing light switch and the speedometer sender multi-plugs.

15  Remove the starter motor (Chapter 12, Section 11).

16  Disconnect the clutch cable from the release arm. Also unbolt the clutch housing adaptor plate.

17  On ohc models only, unbolt the engine/gearbox bracing strap.

18  Remove the six bolts which secure the clutch housing to the engine. On V6 models, also remove the air deflector plate, if fitted.

19  The services of an assistant may now be required. Alternatively, a home-made gearbox cradle mounted on a trolley jack may be used.

20  Take the weight of the gearbox and carefully draw it rearwards off the engine. Once the locating dowels have been cleared, the gearbox will try to drop – *do not let the weight of the gearbox hang on the input shaft, or damage to the shaft and clutch may occur.*

21  When the input shaft is clear of the clutch, lower the gearbox and remove it from under the vehicle.

22  Commence refitting by making sure that the clutch driven plate is accurately centred (Chapter 5, Section 8). Apply a smear of grease or anti-seize compound to the input shaft splines, and secure the clutch release arm with wire or string to stop the release bearing falling forwards during refitting.

23  Offer the gearbox to the engine, making sure that the input shaft is entering the clutch driven plate and that the gearbox is well supported. Some adjustment of the engine or gearbox position may be needed to get the two units aligned correctly. Rocking the gearbox slightly, or having an assistant turn the crankshaft back and forth, can help to engage the shaft splines with the clutch plate.

24  When the gearbox is snug against the engine, refit the engine-to-clutch housing bolts and tighten them to the specified torque.

25  The remainder of refitting is a reversal of the removal procedure. Tighten fastenings to the correct torque, when specified. Before lowering the vehicle, check the gearbox oil level and top up if necessary (Section 2).

## 4  Manual gearbox – dismantling into major assemblies

1   Clean the exterior of the gearbox with paraffin and wipe dry.

2   Remove the clutch release bearing and arm referring to Chapter 5.

3   Unscrew and remove the reversing light switch (photo).

4   Unbolt the clutch bellhousing from the front of the gearbox. Remove the gasket.

5   Unscrew the bolts and withdraw the clutch release bearing guide sleeve and gasket from the front of the gearbox (photo).

6   Unscrew the bolts and remove the top cover and gasket (photo).

7   Invert the gearbox and allow the oil to drain, then turn it upright again.

8   Unscrew the bolts and lift the 5th gear locking plate from the extension housing (photo).

9   Extract the 5th gear locking spring and pin from the extension housing (photos). Use a screw to remove the pin.

10  Working through the gear lever aperture, use a screwdriver or small drift to tap out the extension housing rear cover (photo).

11  Select reverse gear and pull the selector shaft fully to the rear. Support the shaft with a piece of wood, then drive out the roll pin and withdraw the connector from the rear of the selector shaft (photos).

12  Unbolt and remove the extension housing from the rear of the gearbox. If necessary tap the housing with a soft-faced mallet to release it from the dowels. Remove the gasket (photo).

13  Remove the speedometer sender unit and drivegear.

14  Select neutral, then using an Allen key, unscrew the selector locking mechanism plug from the side of the main casing. Extract the spring and locking pin, if necessary using a pen magnet (photos).

15  Drive the roll pin from the selector boss and selector shaft.

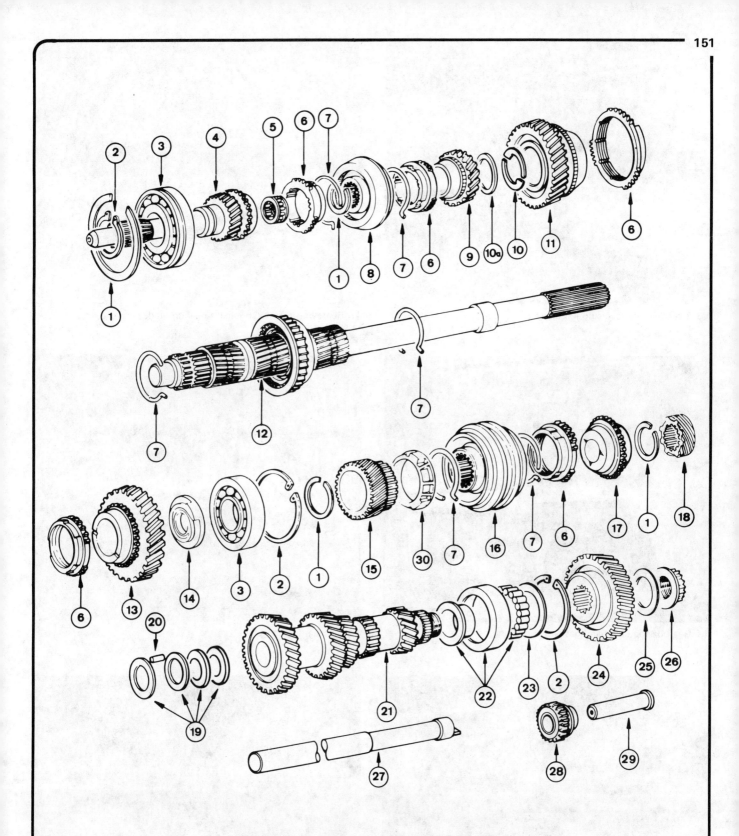

**Fig. 6.3 Manual gearbox internal components (Sec 4)**

| | | | | |
|---|---|---|---|---|
| 1 | Circlips | 10 | Thrust washer segments | 15 | 5th gear | 23 | Spacer |
| 2 | Circlips | 10a | Thrust washer retaining | 16 | 5th gear synchro sleeve | 24 | Layshaft 5th gear |
| 3 | Ball-bearings | | ring | 17 | 5th gear synchro hub | 25 | Washer |
| 4 | Input shaft | 11 | 2nd gear | 18 | Speedometer drivegear | 26 | 5th gear nut |
| 5 | Needle roller bearing | 12 | Mainshaft and 1st/2nd | 19 | Layshaft spacers | 27 | Layshaft |
| 6 | Synchro rings | | synchro hub | 20 | Needle rollers | 28 | Reverse idler gear |
| 7 | Synchro springs | 13 | 1st gear | 21 | Layshaft gear cluster | 29 | Idler shaft |
| 8 | 3rd/4th synchro sleeve | 14 | Oil scoop ring | 22 | Roller bearing | 30 | Synchro key retainer |
| 9 | 3rd gear | | | | | | |

4.3 Removing the reversing light switch

4.5 Removing the clutch release bearing guide sleeve

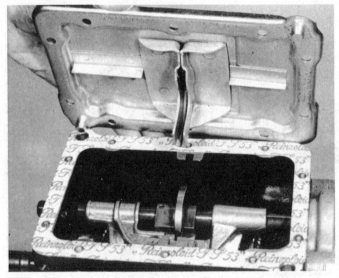

4.6 Gearbox top cover and gasket

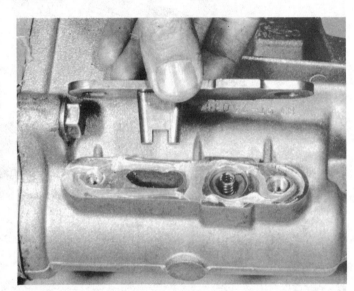

4.8 5th gear locking plate

4.9A 5th gear locking spring

4.9B 5th gear locking pin

4.10 Extension housing rear cover

4.11A Driving out the selector shaft roll pin

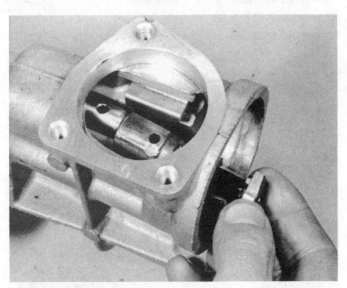
4.11B Removing the selector shaft connector

4.12 Removing the extension housing

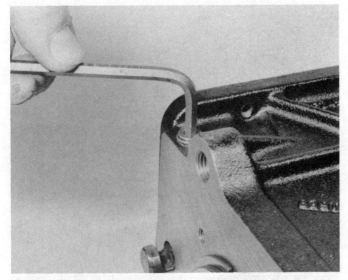
4.14A Removing the selector locking mechanism plug

4.14B Selector locking spring and pin

16 If necessary the selector shaft centralising spring and 5th gear locking control may be removed. Using a small screwdriver push out the pin and plug and slide the control from the selector shaft (photos).

17 Note the location of the selector components, then withdraw the selector shaft from the rear of the gearbox and remove the selector boss and locking plate, 1st/2nd and 3rd/4th selector forks, and 5th gear selector fork and sleeve. Note that the roll pin hole in the selector boss is towards the front (photos).

18 Extract the circlip and pull the 5th gear synchroniser unit from the main casing, leaving it loose on the mainshaft (photos).

19 Slide the 5th driven gear from the synchroniser unit hub (photo).

20 Select 3rd gear and either 1st or 2nd gear by pushing the respective synchroniser sleeves – this will lock the mainshaft and layshaft gear cluster.

21 Unscrew and remove the 5th driving gear retaining nut while an assistant holds the gearbox stationary (photo). The nut is tightened to a high torque setting and an additional extension may be required to achieve the necessary leverage.

22 Remove the washer and pull the 5th driving gear from the layshaft gear cluster using a two-legged puller and socket in contact with the cluster. Remove the spacer ring (photos). Select neutral.

23 Extract the circlip retaining the layshaft gear cluster bearing in the intermediate housing (photo).

4.16A 5th gear locking control plug ...

4.16B ... and roll pin

4.17A Selector boss and locking plate

4.17B 1st/2nd selector fork

4.17C 3rd/4th selector fork

4.17D 5th gear interlock sleeve

4.17E 5th gear selector fork

4.18A Removing 5th gear synchro circlip

4.18B 5th gear synchro hub

4.18C 5th gear synchro sleeve

4.19 Removing 5th speed driven gear

4.21 Removing 5th gear retaining nut from layshaft

4.22A Pulling 5th gear off the layshaft

4.22B 5th gear spacer ring

4.23 Removing the layshaft bearing circlip

24  Using a soft faced mallet, tap the intermediate housing free of the main casing and pull the intermediate housing rearwards as far as possible. Using a screwdriver inserted between the intermediate housing and main casing, prise the bearing from the shoulder on the layshaft gear cluster and remove it from the intermediate housing (photo).

25  Using a soft metal drift from the front of the main casing, drive the layshaft rearwards to allow the gear cluster to be lowered to the bottom of the casing.

26  Ease the input shaft from the front of the casing, if necessary using a small drift inside the gearbox to move the bearing slightly forwards, then using levers beneath the bearing circlip (photo).

27  Remove the 4th gear synchroniser ring. Remove the input shaft needle roller bearing from the end of the mainshaft or from the centre of the input shaft (photos).

28  Remove the mainshaft and intermediate housing from the main casing (photo). Remove the gasket.

29  Withdraw the layshaft and gear cluster from the main casing (photo).

30  Insert a suitable bolt (M8 x 60) into the reverse gear idler shaft, and using a nut, washer and socket pull out the idler shaft. Note the fitted position of the reverse idler gear, then remove it (photos).

4.24 Extracting the layshaft gear rear bearing

4.26 Removing the input shaft

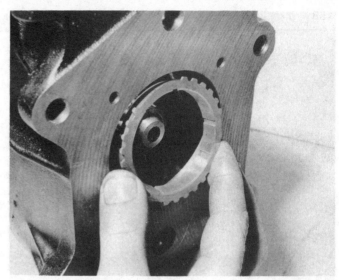

4.27A 4th gear synchro ring

4.27B Input shaft needle roller bearing

4.28 Removing the mainshaft and the intermediate housing

4.29 Removing the layshaft and gear cluster

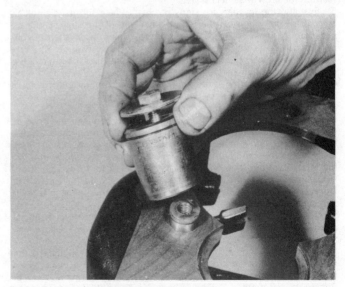

4.30A Pulling out the reverse idler gear shaft

4.30B Reverse idler gear

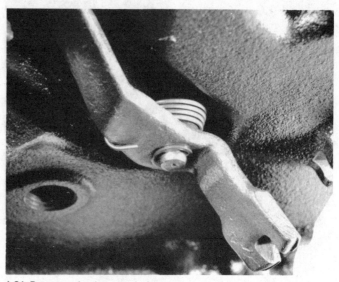

4.31 Reverse relay lever and pivot

31 Remove the guide from the reverse relay lever, then extract the circlip and remove the relay lever from the pivot (photo).
32 Remove the magnetic disc from the bottom of the main casing. Also remove any needle rollers which may have been displaced from the layshaft gear cluster (photo).

## 5   Manual gearbox components – inspection

1   Before embarking on the overhaul of a gearbox, check the cost and availability of spares and the cost of a new or reconditioned gearbox. If the old gearbox has seen much service a complete new unit may be the most satisfactory solution, particularly as it should have a guarantee.
2   Thoroughly clean the interior of the gearbox, and check for dropped needle rollers and spring pins.
3   Carefully clean and then examine all the component parts for general wear, distortion, slackness of fit, and damage to the machined faces and threads.
4   Examine the gearwheels for excessive wear and chipping of the teeth. Renew them as necessary.
5   Examine the layshaft for signs of wear, where the needle rollers bear. If a small ridge can be felt at either end of the shaft it will be necessary to renew it. If it is necessary to renew the layshaft needle rollers, make sure that the rollers used for any one location all come from the same pack. If more than one pack is purchased, do not mix the needle rollers from separate packs.
6   The synchroniser rings are bound to be badly worn and it is false economy not to renew them. New rings will improve the smoothness and speed of the gearchange considerably.
7   The needle roller bearing and cage, located between the nose of the mainshaft and the annulus in the rear of the input shaft, is also liable to wear, and should be renewed as a matter of course.
8   Examine the condition of the two ball bearing assemblies, one on the input shaft and one on the mainshaft. Check for noisy operation, looseness between the inner and outer races, and for general wear. Normally they should be renewed on a gearbox that is being rebuilt. The same applies to the layshaft roller bearing.
9   If either synchroniser unit is worn it will be necessary to buy a complete assembly as the parts are not sold individually. Also check the sliding keys for wear.
10   Examine the ends of the selector forks where they rub against the channels in the synchroniser units. If possible compare the selector forks with new units to help determine the wear that has occurred. Renew them if worn.
11   If the bearing bush in the extension is badly worn it is best to take the extension to your local Ford garage to have the bearing pulled out

4.32 Swarf-collecting magnetic disc in the bottom of the main casing

and a new one fitted. **Note:** *This is normally done with the mainshaft assembly still located in the extension housing.*
12   The oil seals in the extension housing and clutch release bearing sleeve should be renewed as a matter of course. Drive out the old seal with the air of a drift or broad screwdriver. It will be found that the seal comes out quite easily (photo).
13   With a piece of wood or suitable sized tube to spread the load evenly, carefully tap a new seal into place, ensuring that it enters the bore squarely (photo).

## 6   Manual gearbox input shaft – dismantling and reassembly

1   Extract the small circlip from the input shaft (photo).
2   Locate the bearing outer track on top of an open vice, then using a soft-faced mallet, drive the input shaft down through the bearing.
3   Remove the bearing from the input shaft, noting that the groove in the outer track is towards the front splined end of the shaft (photo).
4   Place the input shaft on a block of wood and lightly grease the bearing location shoulder.

5.12 Prising out the oil seal from the clutch release bearing sleeve

5.13 Fitting a new oil seal to the clutch release bearing sleeve

6.1 Removing the circlip from the input shaft

6.3 Removing the input shaft bearing

5   Locate the new bearing on the input shaft with the circlip groove facing the correct way. Then using a metal tube on the inner track, drive the bearing fully home (photo).
6   Refit the small circlip.

### 7   Manual gearbox mainshaft – dismantling and reassembly

1   Extract the circlip and slide the 3rd/4th synchroniser unit together with the 3rd gear from the front of the mainshaft, using a two-legged puller where necessary. Separate the gear and unit, then remove the 3rd gear synchroniser ring (photos).
2   Remove the outer ring from the 2nd gear, then extract the thrust washer halves (photos).
3   Slide the 2nd gear from the front of the mainshaft and remove the 2nd gear synchroniser ring (photos).
4   Mark the 1st/2nd synchroniser unit hub and sleeve in relation to each other and note the location of the selector fork groove, then slide the sleeve forward from the hub and remove the sliding keys and springs. Note that the synchroniser hub cannot be removed from the mainshaft (photos).
5   Using a suitable puller, pull the speedometer drivegear off the rear of the mainshaft (photo).

6.5 Using a metal tube to fit the input shaft bearing

7.1A Removing 3rd/4th synchro circlip

7.1B Removing 3rd/4th synchro ring and sleeve

7.1C 3rd speed mainshaft gear

7.2A 2nd gear thrust washer retaining ring

7.2B 2nd gear thrust washer half

7.3A 2nd speed mainshaft gear

7.3B 2nd gear synchro ring

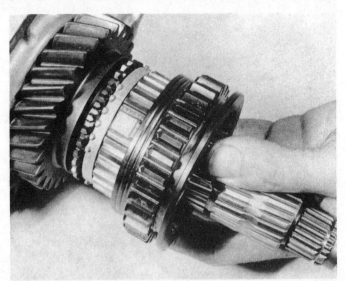

7.4A 1st/2nd synchro sleeve with reverse gear teeth

7.4B Removing a synchro sliding key

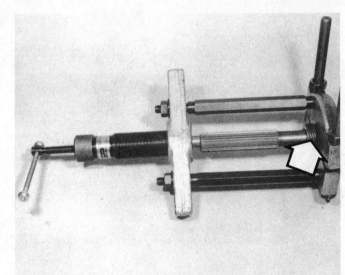

7.5 Pulling off the speedometer drivegear

6   Remove the circlip which retains the 5th gear components on the mainshaft. Remove the 5th synchro unit and 5th driven gear.
7   Extract the circlip retaining the mainshaft bearing, then support the intermediate housing on blocks of wood and drive the mainshaft through the bearing with a soft-faced mallet (photo).
8   Remove the oil scoop ring, 1st gear, and 1st gear synchroniser ring (photo).
9   If necessary, extract the circlip and drive the ball bearing from the intermediate housing using a metal tube (photo). Also the synchroniser units may be dismantled, but first mark the hub and sleeve in relation to each other. Slide the sleeve from the hub and remove the sliding keys and springs.
10  Clean all the components in paraffin, wipe dry and examine them for wear and damage. Obtain new components as necessary. During reassembly lubricate the components with gearbox oil, and where new parts are being fitted, lightly grease contact surfaces.
11  Commence reassembly by assembling the synchroniser units. Slide the sleeves on the hubs in their previously noted positions, then insert the sliding keys and fit the springs as shown in Fig. 6.5.
12  Support the intermediate housing then, using a tube on the outer track, drive in the new bearing and fit the circlip.

7.7 Removing the mainshaft bearing circlip

7.8 Mainshaft oil scoop ring

7.9 Intermediate housing bearing circlip

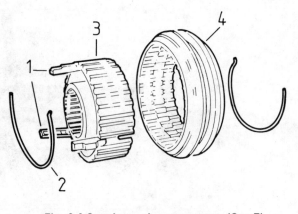

**Fig. 6.4 Synchro unit components (Sec 7)**

| 1 | Sliding key | 3 | Hub |
| 2 | Spring | 4 | Sleeve |

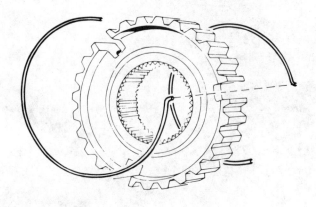

**Fig. 6.5 Relative positions of synchro springs (Sec 7)**

13  Fit the spring to the rear of the 1st/2nd synchroniser hub followed by the 1st gear synchroniser ring (photo).

14  Slide the 1st gear and oil scoop ring (with the oil groove towards 1st gear) onto the mainshaft.

15  Using a metal tube on the mainshaft bearing inner track, drive the intermediate housing onto the mainshaft and fit the circlip, Make sure that the large circlip is towards the rear of the mainshaft.

16  Locate the 5th driven gear and 5th gear synchroniser with circlip, loose on the mainshaft. Tap the speedometer drivegear lightly onto its shoulder – its final position will be determined later (photo).

17  Fit the 1st/2nd synchroniser sleeve to the hub in its previously noted position with the selector groove facing forward, then insert the sliding keys and fit the springs as shown in Fig. 6.5.

18  Fit the 2nd gear synchroniser ring to the 1st/2nd synchroniser unit with the sliding keys located in the slots.

19  Slide the 2nd gear onto the front of the mainshaft and retain with the thrust washer halves and outer ring (photo).

20  Slide the 3rd gear onto the front of the mainshaft, then locate the synchroniser ring on the gear cone.

21  Locate the 3rd/4th synchroniser unit on the mainshaft splines with the long side of the hub facing the front (photo). Tap the unit fully home using a metal tube, then fit the circlip. Make sure that the slots in the 3rd gear synchroniser ring are aligned with the sliding keys as the synchroniser unit is being fitted.

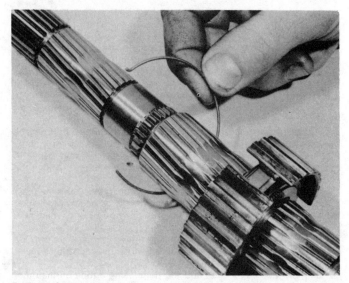

7.13 1st/2nd synchro spring

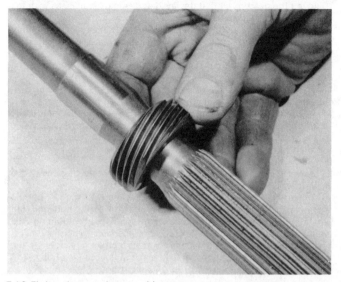

7.16 Fitting the speedometer drivegear

7.19 Thrust washer tab locating hole (arrowed)

7.21 3rd/4th synchro sleeve

## 8  Manual gearbox – reassembly

1    Locate the magnetic disc in the bottom of the main casing.
2    Fit the reverse relay lever onto the pivot and retain with the circlip. Fit the guide to the lever.
3    Position the reverse idler gear in the main casing with the long shoulder facing the rear and engaged with the relay lever. Slide in the idler shaft and tap fully home with a soft-faced mallet.
4    Smear grease inside the end of the layshaft gear cluster, then fit the three spacers, 21 needle rollers and another spacer. The grease will hold the rollers in position while the layshaft is fitted.
5    Insert the layshaft in the gear cluster until the front of the shaft is flush with the front gear on the cluster.
6    Locate the layshaft and gear cluster in the bottom of the main casing.
7    Position a new gasket on the main casing, then fit the mainshaft and intermediate housing, and temporarily secure with two bolts.
8    Fit the input shaft needle roller bearing to the end of the mainshaft or in the centre of the input shaft (photo).
9    Fit the 4th gear synchroniser ring to the 3rd/4th synchroniser unit with the cut-outs over the sliding keys, then fit the input shaft assembly and tap the bearing fully into the casing up to the retaining circlip (photo).

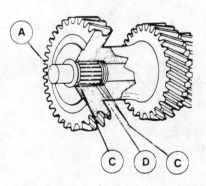

Fig. 6.6 Layshaft needle roller bearing (Sec 8)

A   Layshaft                    D   Needle rollers
C   Spacers

8.8 Input shaft needle roller bearing

8.9 Fitting the input shaft

10  Invert the gearbox so that the layshaft gear cluster meshes with the input shaft and mainshaft gears.

11  Using a soft metal drift, drive the layshaft into the main casing until flush at the front face – the flat on the rear end of the layshaft must be horizontal (photo).

12  Using a metal tube tap the layshaft gear cluster bearing into the intermediate housing and secure with the circlip (photo).

13  Fit the spacer ring then, using a metal tube, tap the 5th driving gear onto the splines of the layshaft gear cluster.

14  Fit the thrust washer and retaining nut. Select 3rd gear and either 1st or 2nd gear by pushing the respective synchroniser sleeve. While an assistant holds the gearbox stationary, tighten the nut to the specified torque, then lock it by peening the collar on the nut into the slot in the gear cluster (photos).

15  Select neutral, then slide the 5th driven gear into mesh with the driving gear.

16  Slide the 5th gear synchroniser unit complete with spacer onto the 5th driven gear. Then using a metal tube, drive the hub and 5th synchroniser ring onto the mainshaft splies while guiding the synchroniser ring onto the sliding keys. Fit the circlip (photos).

17  Tap the speedometer drivegear into its correct position on the mainshaft – the distance between the gear and the 5th gear hub circlip should be $122 \pm 0.5$ mm ($4.80 \pm 0.02$ in) (photo).

8.11 Layshaft correctly positioned before installation

8.12 Fitting the layshaft bearing

8.14A Tightening 5th gear layshaft nut ...

8.14B ... and peening the nut in position

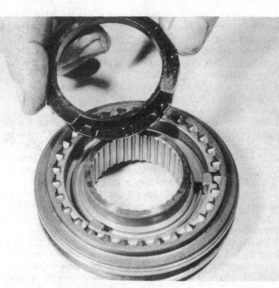

8.16A 5th gear synchro and spacer

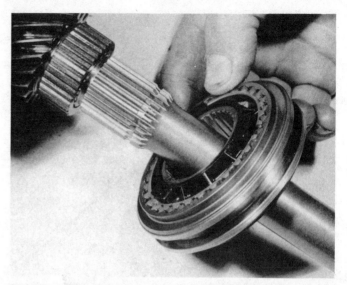

8.16B Fitting 5th gear synchro sleeve to the mainshaft

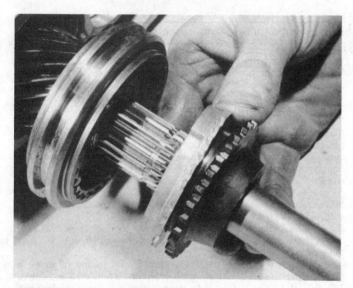

8.16C 5th gear synchro ring and hub

8.16D 5th gear synchro circlip

8.17 Measuring the distance between the circlip and the speedometer drivegear

18 Locate the 5th gear selector fork in its synchroniser sleeve and the interlock sleeve in the groove (short shoulder to front), then insert the selector shaft through the sleeve and selector fork into the main casing (photo).

19 Locate the 1st/2nd and 3rd/4th selector forks in their respective synchroniser sleeves, position the selector boss and locking plate, and insert the selector shaft through the components into the front of the main casing. The roll pin hole in the selector boss must be towards the front.

20 If removed, refit the selector shaft centralising spring and 5th gear locking control by inserting the pin and plug.

21 Align the holes, then drive the roll pin into the selector boss and selector shaft (photo).

22 Insert the selector locking pin and spring, apply sealer to the plug threads, then insert and tighten the plug using an Allen key.

23 Refit and secure the speedometer drivegear and sender unit.

24 Remove the temporarily fitted bolts from the intermediate housing, then select 4th gear.

25 If not already done, fit a new selector shaft oil seal and a new rear oil seal to the extension housing.

26 Stick a new gasket to the extension housing with grease, and fit the housing to the intermediate housing. Take care not to damage the rear oil seal, and make sure that the selector shaft centralising spring locates on the pin (photo).

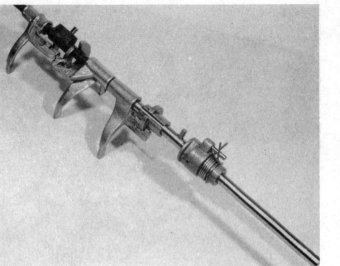

8.18 Selector shaft and forks assembled

8.21 Pinning the boss to the selector shaft

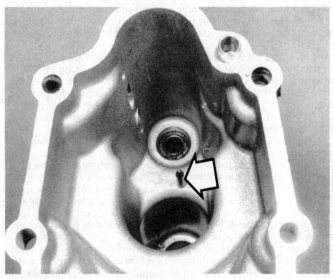

8.26 Selector shaft spring pin (arrowed)

27  Insert the bolts and tighten them to the specified torque in diagonal sequence. Before inserting the three bolts which go right through the main casing, apply sealer to their threads.
28  Select reverse gear and locate the connector on the rear of the selector rod. Support the rod with a piece of wood, then drive in the roll pin. Select neutral.
29  Press the rear cover into the extension housing.
30  Check that the 5th gear interlock sleeve is correctly aligned, then insert the 5th gear locking pin and spring.
31  Apply some sealer to the 5th gear locking plate, locate it on the extension housing, and insert and tighten the bolts finger tight. Check that all gears engage freely – reposition the locking plate if necessary. When satisfied, tighten the locking plate bolts to the specified torque.
32  Fit the gearbox top cover together with a new gasket and tighten the bolts to the specified torque in diagonal sequence.
33  Fit the clutch release bearing guide sleeve (oil slot downwards) together with a new gasket and tighten the bolts to the specified torque in diagonal sequence. Where necessary apply sealer to the bolt threads.
34  Fit the clutch bellhousing to the front of the gearbox together with a new gasket. Apply sealer to the bolt threads, then insert the bolts and tighten them to the specified torque in diagonal sequence.
35  Insert and tighten the reversing light switch in the extension housing.
36  Fit the clutch release bearing and arm as described in Chapter 5.

## 9  Automatic transmission – general description

1    The automatic transmission is known as the type A4LD. It has four forward gears and one reverse. The torque converter locks up in 3rd and 4th gears, so avoiding losses due to converter slip. 4th gear is an overdrive, maximum speed and acceleration being obtained in 3rd.
2    The gear selector has seven positions: 'P', 'R', 'N', 'D', '3', '2' and '1'. (On early models positions 'D' and '3' are labelled 'DE' and 'D', but their functions are the same). The engine can only be started in positions 'P' and 'N'. In position 'D' the transmission will change automatically through all four forward gears, according to speed, load and throttle position. In position '3', top (overdrive) gear will not be engaged. Position '2' engages 2nd gear only, position '1' engages 1st gear only, but if these positions are selected while travelling at speed, the transmission will not change down until speed has reduced sufficiently to avoid damage.
3    Engine braking in the lower gears is only obtained in positions '1' and '2'; in position '3' and 'D' there is a freewheel effect in the first three gears.
4    A 'kickdown' facility causes the transmission to change down a gear (subject to speed) if the throttle is depressed fully and held down. This is useful when rapid acceleration is required, for example when overtaking. Kickdown is controlled either by a cable linked to the transmission and the throttle cable, or by a throttle-operated switch and a solenoid actuator on the transmission (photos).
5    The automatic transmission is a complex unit, but if it is not abused it is reliable and long-lasting. Repair or overhaul operations are beyond the scope of many dealers, let alone the home mechanic; specialist advice should be sought if problems arise which cannot be solved by the procedures given in this Chapter.

## 10  Automatic transmission – maintenance and inspection

1    Every 12 000 miles or annually, or at the first sign of any malfunction, check the fluid level as described in Section 11.
2    At the same intervals, lubricate the selector and kickdown linkages with engine oil or aerosol lubricant.
3    Every 24 000 miles or two years, adjust the brake bands as described in Section 13.
4    Regularly inspect the transmission and the fluid cooler unions for leaks. The rear extension oil seal can be renewed with the transmission installed after removal of the propeller shaft.
5    Periodic fluid changing is not specified, neither is a drain plug provided. If it is wished to change the fluid it will be necessary to remove the sump.
6    Always take great care not to introduce dirt or foreign matter into the transmission.

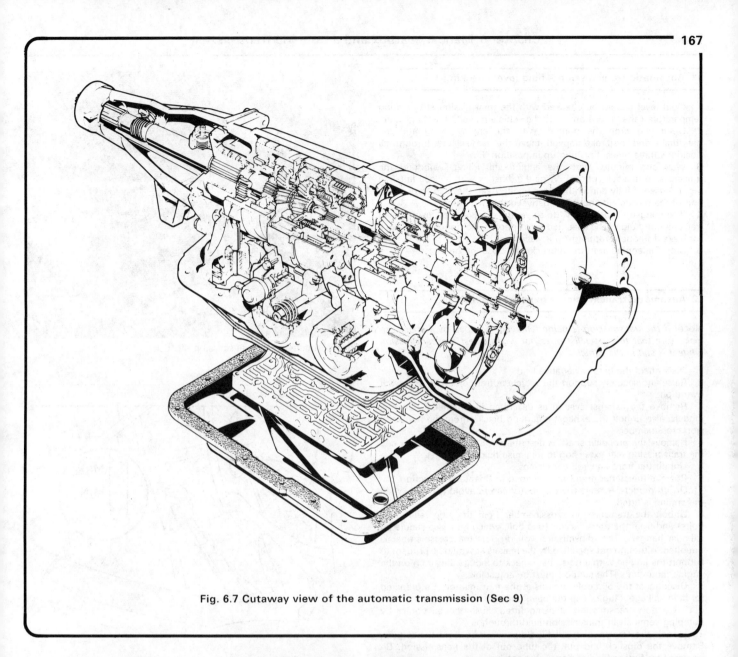

Fig. 6.7 Cutaway view of the automatic transmission (Sec 9)

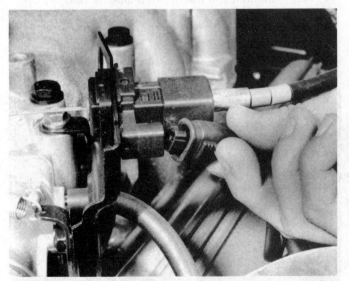

9.4A Kickdown switch multi-plug

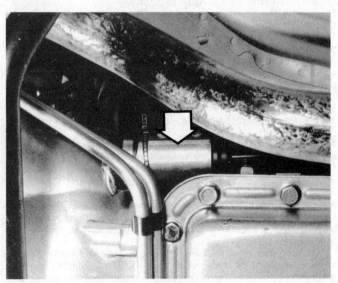

9.4B Kickdown solenoid actuator (arrowed)

## 11 Automatic transmission – fluid level checking

1   Fluid level should be checked with the transmission at operating temperature (after a run) and with the vehicle parked on level ground.
2   Open and prop the bonnet. With the engine idling and the handbrake and footbrake applied, move the gear selector through all positions three times, finishing up in position 'P'.
3   Wait one minute. With the engine still idling, withdraw the transmission dipstick (photo). Wipe the dipstick with a clean lint-free rag, re-insert it fully and withdraw it again. Read the fluid level at the end of the dipstick: it should be between the two notches.
4   If topping-up is necessary, do so via the dipstick tube, using clean transmission fluid of the specified type (photo). Do not overfill. Check for leaks if frequent topping-up is necessary.
5   Stop the engine, refit the dipstick and close the bonnet.

## 12 Automatic transmission – removal and refitting

**Note:** *If the transmission is being removed for repair by a specialist, make sure that the specialist does not wish to test the transmission while it is still in the vehicle.*

1   Disconnect the battery negative lead.
2   Raise and securely support the vehicle at front and rear, or drive it over a pit.
3   Remove the exhaust system as described in Chapter 3. On ohc models, also unbolt the exhaust mounting bracket from the transmission crossmember.
4   Remove the propeller shaft as described in Chapter 7. Plug or cap the transmission rear extension to minimise fluid loss.
5   Unbolt the front anti-roll bar clamps.
6   Remove the starter motor as described in Chapter 12, Section 11.
7   On V6 models, remove the distributor cap to avoid damage when the engine is fitted.
8   Unbolt the transmission crossmember from the side rails (four bolts) and from the transmission (one bolt, which may also secure an exhaust hanger). The transmission will drop as the crossmember is unbolted. Although not specified by the makers, it would be prudent to support the engine with a hoist, bar or jack to reduce the strain on the engine mountings. The support must be adjustable.
9   Disconnect the oil cooler unions at the transmission. Be prepared for fluid spillage. Plug or cap the open unions to keep fluid in and dirt out. If a new transmission is being fitted, flush the oil cooler by pumping some clean transmission fluid through it.
10  Unbolt the transmission oil filler/dipstick tube from the engine. Remove the dipstick and pull the tube out of the transmission. Be prepared for further fluid spillage; plug the hole.
11  Remove the transmission selector rod by releasing the bayonet clips which secure each end of it.
12  Disconnect the downshift (kickdown) cable from the lever on the transmission. On models where kickdown is electrically-operated, disconnect the kickdown solenoid wiring.
13  Disconnect the multi-plug from the starter inhibitor/reversing light switch.
14  Remove the speedometer sender unit and move it aside. Plug the hole to keep dirt out.
15  Disconnect the pipe from the vacuum diaphragm. Unclip the pipe and move it aside.
16  Unbolt the adaptor plate from the bottom of the engine. On ohc models, also unbolt the engine/transmission bracing strap.
17  Working through the starter motor aperture, remove the four nuts which secure the driveplate to the torque converter. Turn the crankshaft to bring each nut into view, using a spanner on the crankshaft pulley or by prising on the starter ring gear.
18  Remove the remaining bolts which secure the torque converter housing to the engine. The transmission is now hanging on the dowels.
19  With the help of an assistant, or using a cradle and a trolley jack, take the weight of the transmission and withdraw it from the engine. As the transmission comes clear, push the torque converter rearwards and hold it secure as the transmission is removed.
20  Commence refitting by checking that the torque converter is fully engaged in the transmission oil pump. Correct engagement is

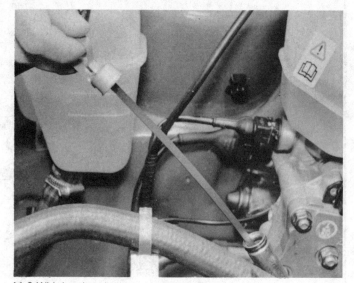

11.3 Withdrawing the transmission dipstick

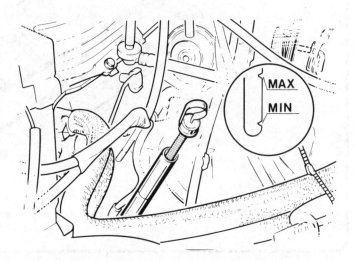

**Fig. 6.8 Automatic transmission dipstick (Sec 11)**

11.4 Topping-up the transmission fluid

indicated when the nose of the converter is positioned a distance 'A' from the converter housing flange – see Fig. 6.10. Rotate the converter and push it into mesh with the oil pump if necessary. **Damage will result if the transmission is refitted with the converter improperly engaged.**

21 Make sure that the adaptor plate is located on the dowels at the rear of the engine.

22 Offer the transmission to the engine. Do not allow the torque converter to fall forwards. The studs on the torque converter must pass through the holes in the driveplate. Support the transmission until it is engaged with the dowels.

23 Insert the torque converter housing-to-engine bolts, omitting the one which secures the dipstick/filler tube. Before tightening the bolts, make sure that the torque converter has perceptible endfloat – if not, it is not properly engaged (paragraph 20). When satisfied, tighten the bolts evenly to the specified torque.

24 Fit the driveplate-to-torque converter nuts, rotating the crankshaft to bring them into position. Just nip each nut up at first, then go round again and tighten them to the specified torque.

25 Secure the adaptor plate and (on ohc models) the bracing strap.

26 Reconnect the vacuum pipe.

27 Refit the speedometer sender unit.

28 Reconnect the starter inhibitor/reversing light switch.

29 Reconnect the downshift cable to the operating lever, or reconnect the solenoid, as appropriate.

30 Refit the selector rod and secure it with the clips. If adjustment is necessary, refer to Section 16.

31 Reconnect the oil cooler pipes to the transmission.

32 Insert the dipstick/oil filler tube into the transmission and secure it to the engine with the remaining converter housing-to-engine bolt.

33 Refit the transmission crossmember.

34 Refit the propeller shaft as described in Chapter 7.

35 Refit the starter motor as described in Chapter 12, Section 11.

36 Secure the front anti-roll bar clamps, tightening the bolts to the specified torque (Chapter 10 Specifications).

37 Refit the exhaust system as described in Chapter 3.

38 Lower the vehicle to the ground. Refit the distributor cap if it was removed, then reconnect the battery negative lead.

39 Fill the transmission with fluid up to the 'MIN' mark on the dipstick.

40 Road test the vehicle to check for correct operation of the selector and kickdown mechanism. Adjust if necessary (Sections 15 and 16).

41 With the transmission warmed up, recheck the fluid level and top up if necessary (Section 11). Also check for leaks at the fluid cooler unions, the bottom of the dipstick/filler tube and at any other disturbed components.

## 13 Automatic transmission – brake band adjustment

**Note** : *A brake band torque wrench – Ford tool No. 17-005, or equivalent – will be required for this job.*

1 Raise and support the front of the vehicle.

2 Disconnect the downshift (kickdown) cable from the transmission, when so equipped.

3 Release the locknuts on the two brake band adjuster screws. Back off each adjuster screw a couple of turns (photo).

4 Using the torque wrench, tighten one adjusting screw to 13 Nm (10 lbf ft). Remove the torque wrench and back off the adjuster screw exactly two full turns from this position, then hold the screw and tighten the locknut.

5 Repeat the operations on the other adjuster.

6 Reconnect the downshift cable, when applicable, then lower the vehicle.

## 14 Starter inhibitor/reversing light switch (automatic transmission) – removal and refitting

1 Raise and support the front of the vehicle.

2 Disconnect the multi-plug from the switch (on the left-end side of the transmission, towards the front).

3 Unscrew the switch from the transmission. Recover the O-ring.

4 Use a new O-ring when refitting. Screw in the switch and tighten it to the specified torque.

5 Reconnect the multi-plug and check the operation of the switch.

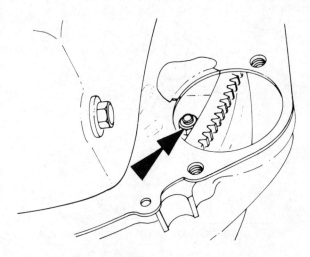

Fig. 6.9 One of the driveplate nuts (arrowed) seen through the starter motor aperture (Sec 12)

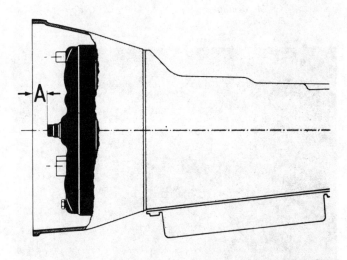

Fig. 6.10 With torque converter correctly fitted, dimension 'A' must be at least 8 mm (0.32 in) (Sec 12)

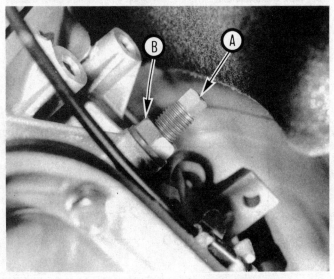

13.3 Brake band adjuster screw (A) and locknut (B)

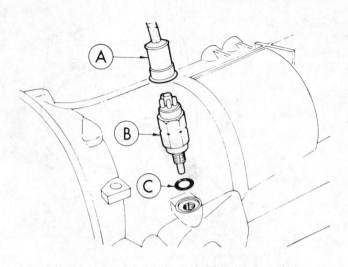

**Fig. 6.11 Starter inhibitor switch (Sec 14)**

A   Multi-plug                    C   O-ring
B   Switch

15.2 Throttle cable and downshift cable bracket and adjusters

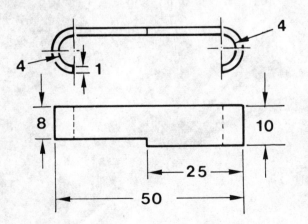

**Fig. 6.12 Downshift cable setting gauge – dimensions in mm (Sec 15)**

The starter motor must only operate in positions 'P' and 'N', and the reversing lights must only come on in position 'R'. Any adjustment can only be to the selector linkage (Section 16); the switch itself is not adjustable.

6   Lower the vehicle.

## 15 Downshift mechanism (automatic transmission) – adjustment

1   On models built up to mid-1986, the downshift (kickdown) linkage is by mechanical cable. On later models a throttle switch and a solenoid actuator are used.

### Cable adjustment

2   Adjustment takes place at the throttle cable bracket under the bonnet (photo).
3   Make up a setting gauge to the dimensions shown in Fig. 6.12.
4   Release the downshift cable adjusting nut and locknut and unscrew them to the end of their thread.
5   Have an assistant depress the throttle pedal as far as it will go. Make sure that the pedal travel is not restricted by mats or carpets.
6   Turn the throttle cable adjusting nut to achieve a dimension 'X' (Fig. 6.13) of 10 mm (0.39 in). Use the 10 mm end of the setting gauge to check this gap. Make sure that the spring and the spring cup do not turn when turning the adjusting nut.
7   Remove the setting gauge and re-insert it with the 8 mm end in gap 'X'. Have the assistant release the throttle pedal: the gauge will be clamped in position.
8   Pull the downshift cable outer sleeve in the direction arrowed (Fig. 6.13) to take up any slack. Hold the sleeve in this position and secure it with the downshift cable adjusting nut and locknut. Tighten the nuts.
9   Remove the setting gauge. Adjustment is now complete.

### Solenoid adjustment

10  Raise and support the vehicle.
11  Slacken the two screws which secure the solenoid bracket.
12  Have an assistant switch on the ignition and press the throttle pedal to the floor. **Do not start the engine.**
13  Move the downshift lever on the transmission anti-clockwise as far as possible, and position the solenoid so that its cable is under slight tension.
14  Tighten the bracket screws, bottom one first, to retain the solenoid in this position.
15  Have the assistant release and reapply the throttle several times. Each time that the pedal is fully depressed, the downshift lever should be drawn anti-clockwise to within 0.2 mm (0.008 in) of its stop. Do not try to adjust the solenoid to eliminate this very small amount of free play.
16  Switch off the ignition and lower the vehicle.

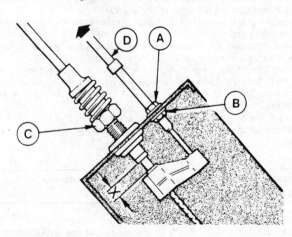

**Fig. 6.13 Downshaft cable adjustment (Sec 15)**

A   Downshift cable adjusting        C   Throttle cable adjusting nut
    nut                              D   Downshift cable
B   Downshift cable locknut          X   See text

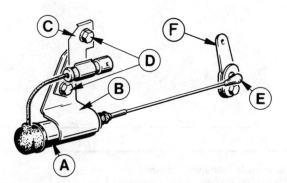

Fig. 6.14 Downshift solenoid mounting details (Sec 15)

| | | | |
|---|---|---|---|
| A | Solenoid | D | Bracket screws |
| B | Bracket | E | Cable end |
| C | Multi-plug clip | F | Downshift lever |

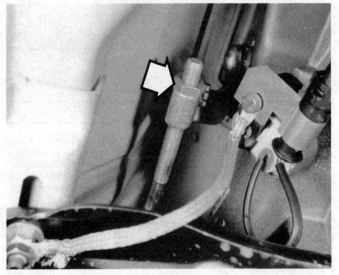

Fig. 6.15 Selector rod adjustment position (Sec 16)

## 16 Selector rod (automatic transmission) – removal, refitting and adjustment

1   Raise and support the front of the vehicle.
2   Remove the selector rod by releasing the bayonet clip at each end of it. The rod bushes can now be renewed if necessary.
3   Commence refitting by moving the gear selector to position 'DE' (or 'D' on later models). Move the selector lever on the transmission to the same position.
4   Connect the rod to the selector lever on the transmission and secure it with the clip.
5   Offer the other end of the rod to the gear selector. If it will fit without strain, and without disturbing the gear selector or the selector lever, adjustment is correct.
6   If adjustment is necessary, slacken the selector rod locknut (photo). Rotate the rod end-piece to lengthen or shorten the rod until it is a comfortable fit in the selector, then tighten the locknut.
7   Secure the selector rod to the gear selector with the spring clip.
8   Lower the vehicle. Check that the gear selector accurately engages each function. Pay particular attention to the engagement of the parking pawl in position 'P', and the correct operation of the starter inhibitor/reversing light switch (Section 14). Readjust the selector rod if necessary.

16.6 Selector rod locknut (arrowed)

## 17 Fault diagnosis – manual gearbox and automatic transmission

| Symptom | Reason(s) |
|---|---|
| *Manual gearbox* | |
| Noisy operation | Oil level low, or incorrect grade |
| | Worn bearings or gears |
| Ineffective synchromesh | Worn synchro rings |
| Jumps out of gear | Worn synchro units |
| | Worn gears |
| | Worn selector forks |
| | Worn locking pins and springs |
| Difficulty in engaging gears | Clutch fault |
| | Worn selector components |
| | Seized input shaft pilot bearing |

*Automatic transmission*

Faults in these units are nearly always the result of low fluid level or incorrect adjustment of the selector linkage or downshift mechanism. Internal faults should be diagnosed by a main Ford dealer who has the necessary equipment to carry out the work.

# Chapter 7 Propeller shaft

## Contents

## Specifications

### General
Shaft type ........................................................................ Tubular, three-piece, with centre bearing and rubber coupling
Number of universal joints ............................................... 2

### Torque wrench settings

|  | Nm | lbf ft |
|---|---|---|
| Pinion flange bolts | 57 to 75 | 42 to 55 |
| Centre bearing carrier to floor | 18 to 23 | 13 to 17 |
| Universal joint bolt | 34 to 39 | 25 to 29 |

## 1 General description

The propeller shaft is in three parts. The front part is splined and mates with the gearbox output shaft. It is joined to the centre part by a rubber 'doughnut' coupling. The centre part of the shaft joins the rear part by means of a universal joint. Another universal joint, which carries the flange which bolts to the final drive pinion flange, terminates the rear part of the shaft.

A self-aligning ball bearing supports the centre part of the shaft. The bearing is mounted in a carrier which is bolted to the vehicle floor.

The parts of the shaft are carefully balanced during manufacture. If it is necessary to separate the parts – as when renewing the centre bearing – it is important that alignment marks be made so that the original balance can be maintained. Attempts to repair worn universal joints are likely to upset the balance of the shaft; in any case, spares are not supplied by the manufacturers.

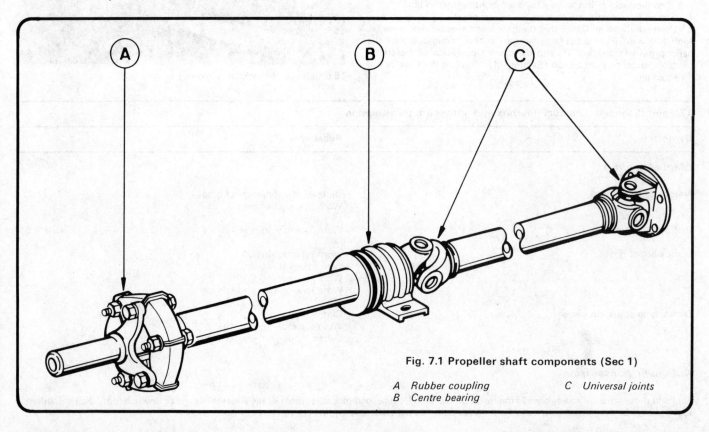

Fig. 7.1 Propeller shaft components (Sec 1)

A   Rubber coupling  
B   Centre bearing  
C   Universal joints

## 2  Maintenance and inspection

1  No periodic maintenance is specified for the propeller shaft. Check occasionally that the centre bearing and final drive flange bolts are tight.

2  Wear in the universal joints may be suspected if there is vibration in the transmission, or a knocking or clunking on going from drive to overrun or vice versa.

3  To test a universal joint, jack up the car and support it on axle stands. Then attempt to turn the propeller shaft either side of the joint in alternate opposite directions. Also attempt to lift each side of the joint. Any movement within the universal joint is indicative of considerable wear, and if evident the complete propeller shaft must be renewed.

4  Wear in the centre bearing is characterised by noise in the transmission.

5  The centre bearing is a little more difficult to test for wear. If bearing movement (as distinct from universal joint or rubber insulator movement) can be felt when lifting the propeller shaft front section next to the mounting bracket, the bearing should be removed as described in Section 4 and checked for roughness while spinning the outer race by hand. If excessive wear is evident, renew the bearing.

6  Deterioration of the rubber coupling will be self-evident on inspection. If a new coupling is available it can be fitted after unbolting the old one. A couple of long worm drive hose clips or similar will be needed to compress the coupling when removing or inserting the bolts.

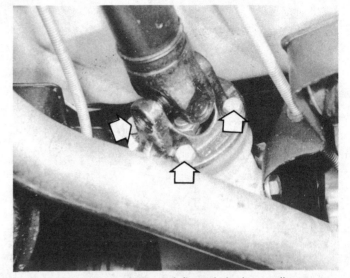

3.3 Three of the four propeller shaft flange bolts (arrowed)

## 3  Propeller shaft – removal and refitting

1  Chock the front wheels. Raise and support the rear of the vehicle.

2  Make alignment marks between the propeller shaft and final drive pinion flanges.

3  Remove the four bolts which hold the flanges together (photo).

4  Remove the two bolts which hold the centre bearing carrier to the floor (photo). Lower the shaft and bearing carrier, noting the number and location of any shims and washers.

5  Pull the shaft rearwards and out of the transmission extension. Be prepared for oil spillage: insert a chamfered plastic cap into the extension, or cover it with a plastic bag secured with a rubber band.

6  Withdraw the propeller shaft from under the vehicle.

7  Commence refitting by removing the plastic bag or cap from the transmission extension.

8  Clean and lubricate the front section of the propeller shaft. Enter the front section into the transmission, being careful not to damage the oil seal.

9  Refit the centre bearing carrier to the floor, remembering the shims and washers. Fit the bolts but do not tighten them yet.

10  Align the flange mating marks, when applicable, then insert the flange bolts and tighten them to the specified torque.

11  Tighten the bearing carrier bolts to the specified torque.

12  Check the transmission oil or fluid level and top up if necessary.

13  Lower the vehicle.

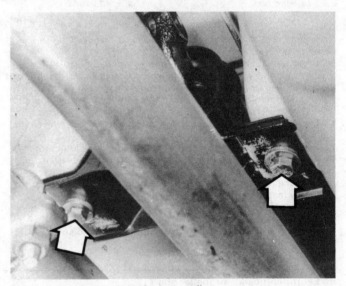

3.4 Centre bearing carrier bolts (arrowed)

## 4  Propeller shaft centre bearing – renewal

1  Remove the propeller shaft as described in Section 3.

2  Mark the front and rear sections of the propeller shaft in relation to each other. Mark also the exact position of the U-shaped washer beneath the bolt located in the central universal joint.

3  Bend back the locking plate and loosen the bolt in the central universal joint so that the U-shaped washer can be removed (photo).

4  With the U-shaped washer removed, slide the rear section from the front section.

5  Pull the centre bearing bracket together with the insulator rubber from the centre bearing.

6  Remove the outer protective dust cap then, using a suitable puller, pull the centre bearing and inner dust cap from the front propeller shaft section.

7  Wipe clean the centre bearing components. Fit the inner protective

4.3 Propeller shaft centre bearing. Retaining bolt is arrowed

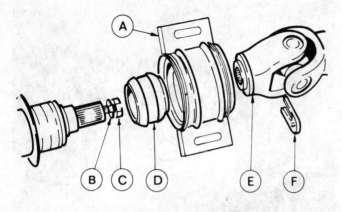

Fig. 7.2 Centre bearing components (Sec 4)

A   Mounting bracket with       D   Ball bearing and dust caps
    rubber insulator            E   Splined universal joint yoke
B   Locking plate               F   U-shaped washer
C   Bolt

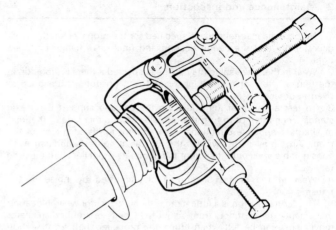

Fig. 7.3 Pulling off the centre bearing (Sec 4)

dust cap to the new bearing and pack the cavity between the cap and bearing with grease.

8   Using a suitable metal tube on the inner race, push the centre bearing and inner cap onto the front propeller shaft section. Note that the red double seal end of the bearing must face forward.

9   Fit the outer dust cap and pack the cavity between the cap and bearing with grease.

10  Ease the bracket together with the insulator rubber over the centre bearing.

11  Screw the bolt and locking plate into the end of the front propeller shaft section leaving a sufficient gap for the U-shaped washer to be inserted.

12  Slide the rear section onto the front section, making sure that the previously made marks are aligned.

13  Refit the U-shaped washer in its previously noted position with the small peg towards to the splines.

14  Tighten the bolts and bend over the locking plate to secure.

15  Refit the propeller shaft (Section 3).

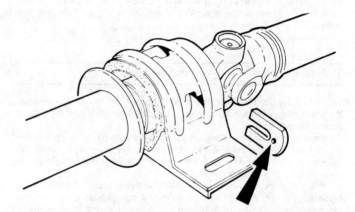

Fig. 7.4 Correct position of peg (arrowed) when refitting the U-shaped washer (Sec 4)

## 5   Fault diagnosis – propeller shaft

| Symptom | Reason(s) |
| --- | --- |
| Vibration | Worn universal joints or centre bearing |
|  | Propeller shaft out of balance |
|  | Deteriorated rubber insulator on centre bearing |
| Knock or 'clunk' when taking up drive | Worn universal joints |
|  | Loose flange bolt |
| Excessive 'rumble' increasing with road speed | Worn centre bearing |

# Chapter 8 Final drive and driveshafts

*For modifications, and information applicable to later models, see Supplement at end of manual*

## Contents

## Specifications

### General

| | |
|---|---|
| Final drive type ............................................................... | Hypoid, bolted to rear underbody and to rear axle beam |
| Driveshaft type ............................................................... | Open, tubular, constant velocity (CV) joint at each end |

### Final drive ratio

| | |
|---|---|
| Standard, manual gearbox: | |
| 1.8 litre (REC) and 2.0 litre (NRA) ....................... | 3.92 : 1 |
| 2.0 litre (NEL) ........................................................ | 3.62 : 1 |
| 2.8 litre (PRE) ........................................................ | 3.36 : 1 |
| Standard, automatic transmission: | |
| 2.0 litre (NRA and NEL) ......................................... | 3.62 : 1 |
| 2.8 litre (PRE) ........................................................ | 3.36 : 1 |
| Trailer package, manual gearbox: | |
| 2.0 litre (NEL) ........................................................ | 3.92 : 1 |
| 2.8 litre (PRE) ........................................................ | 3.64 : 1 |
| Limited slip differential: | |
| 2.0 litre (NRA and NEL) ......................................... | 3.64 : 1 |
| 2.8 litre (PRE) ........................................................ | 3.36 : 1 |

### Final drive lubrication

| | |
|---|---|
| Lubricant type ................................................................. | See 'Recommended lubricants and fluids' |
| Lubricant capacity: | |
| 7 inch crownwheel (all 1.8 litre and some 2.0 litre) ..... | 0.9 litres (1.6 pints) approx |
| 7.5 inch crownwheel (all 2.8 litre and some 2.0 litre) ... | 1.3 litres (2.3 pints) approx |

### Final drive adjustment

| | |
|---|---|
| Crownwheel and pinion backlash .................................... | 0.08 to 0.15 mm (0.003 to 0.006 in) |
| Pinion turning torque ...................................................... | 1.6 to 2.1 Nm (1.2 to 1.6 lbf ft) |

### Driveshaft joint lubrication

| | |
|---|---|
| Lubricant type ................................................................. | Grease to Ford spec. SQM 1C 9104 A |
| Lubricant capacity .......................................................... | 70 ± 10 g (2.45 ± 0.35 oz) per joint |

### Torque wrench settings

| | Nm | lbf ft |
|---|---|---|
| Pinion flange nut | 110 to 130 | 81 to 96 |
| Final drive mountings: | | |
| To crossmember ...................................................... | 70 to 90 | 52 to 66 |
| Rear mounting to casing ......................................... | 40 to 50 | 30 to 37 |
| Rear mounting to floor ............................................ | 20 to 25 | 15 to 18 |
| Final drive cover screws ............................................... | 45 to 60 | 33 to 44 |
| Final drive oil filler/level plug ....................................... | 35 to 45 | 26 to 33 |
| Driveshaft flange screws ............................................... | 38 to 43 | 28 to 32 |

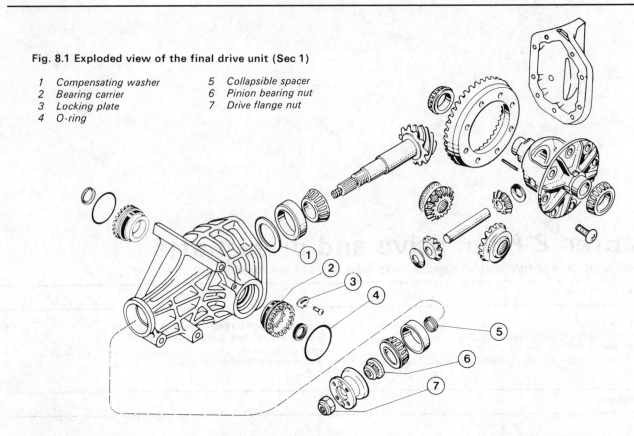

**Fig. 8.1 Exploded view of the final drive unit (Sec 1)**

1  Compensating washer
2  Bearing carrier
3  Locking plate
4  O-ring
5  Collapsible spacer
6  Pinion bearing nut
7  Drive flange nut

## 1  General description

The final drive assembly is bolted to the floor and to the rear axle crossmember, so reducing unsprung weight. It is enclosed in a light alloy housing. Oil seals protect the pinion and output shafts.

A conventional crownwheel end pinion set-up is used. A two-pinion differential is standard, with both the differential and the pinion running in taper roller bearings. Preload of the differential bearings is by means of adjustable cups, whilst that for the pinion bearings is determined by a collapsible spacer. A shim under the head of the pinion controls its depth of mesh with the crownwheel.

A viscous-coupled limited slip differential is available on some models. This type of differential is unlike earlier friction plate limited slip units, which had inherent problems of increased tyre wear, noise and adverse effects on handling. The viscous-coupled unit is silent, causes no extra tyre wear and needs no special lubricant. It operates by virtue of the shear force set up between the viscous coupling plates when one rear wheel is turning faster than the other.

Drive from the differential is taken to the wheels by two open driveshafts with a constant velocity (CV) joint at each end. Connection to the final drive unit and hubs is by bolted flanges.

Overhaul of the final drive unit is not covered in this book, because of the need for various specified tools and fixtures not normally available to the home mechanic. Overhaul should therefore be referred to a Ford dealer.

## 2  Maintenance and inspection

1  Every 12 000 miles or twelve months, or sooner if leakage is suspected, check the final drive oil level as follows.
2  Position the vehicle over a pit, or raise it at front and rear on ramps or axle stands. The vehicle must be level.
3  Wipe clean around the final drive filler/level plug (photo). Unscrew the plug with a hexagon key. Using a piece of bent wire as a dipstick, check that the oil is no more than 10 mm (0.4 in) below the plug hole.
4  If topping-up is necessary, use clean gear oil of the specified type. Do not overfill. Frequent need for topping-up can only be due to leaks, which should be rectified.

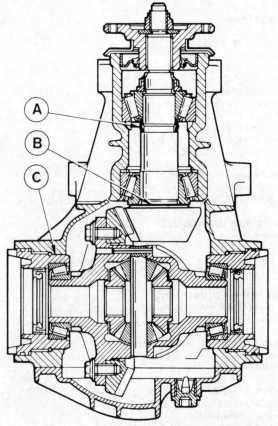

**Fig. 8.2 Sectional view of the final drive unit (Sec 1)**

A  Collapsible spacer
B  Shim
C  Bearing carrier

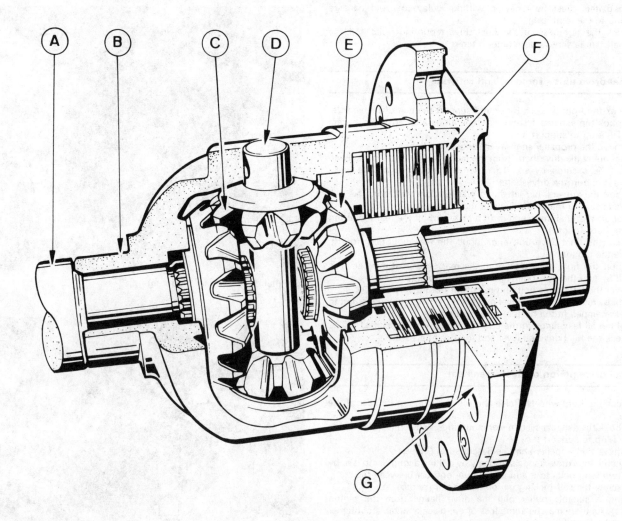

Fig. 8.3 Cutaway view of the limited slip differential (Sec 1)

| | | | |
|---|---|---|---|
| A Output stub | C Differential pinion | E Side gear | G Crownwheel flange |
| B Differential cage | D Pinion shaft | F Coupling plates and fluid | |

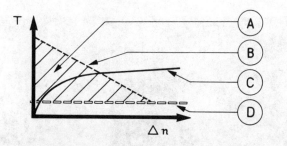

Fig. 8.4 Comparison of friction plate and viscous-coupled
limited slip differentials (Sec 1)

A Locking force
B Friction plate differential
C Viscous-coupled differential

D Pre-loading
n Speed
T Time

5    When the level is correct, refit the filler/level plug and tighten it.
6    There is no requirement for periodic oil changing, and no drain plug
is provided.
7    At the same intervals, examine the driveshaft joint rubber gaiters.
Flex the gaiters by hand and inspect the folds and clips. Damaged or

2.3 Final drive oil filler/level plug (arrowed)

leaking gaiters must be renewed without delay to avoid damage occurring to the joint itself.

8   Check the tightness of the final drive mounting bolts and the driveshaft flange screws from time to time.

### 3   Final drive unit – removal and refitting

1   Chock the front wheels. Raise and support the rear of the vehicle.
2   Unhook the exhaust system rear mountings and move the system aside. Tie it up to support it.
3   Remove the propeller shaft as described in Chapter 2.
4   Disconnect the driveshafts from the final drive output flanges. Each driveshaft is secured by six 'Torx' screws and three double lock-washers. Support the driveshafts.
5   Unbolt the anti-roll bar left-hand bracket from the floor. This will improve access to the final drive rear mounting.
6   Support the final drive unit with a jack. Unbolt the rear mounting from the floor (photo).
7   Lower the final drive unit and unbolt the rear mounting from it. Remove the mountings.
8   Unbolt the final drive unit from the rear axle crossmember. It is secured by two through-bolts and two short bolts (photo).
9   Lower the final drive unit and remove it from the vehicle.
10   Refit by reversing the removal operations. When offering the unit to the crossmember, fit the bottom through-bolt first.
11   Tighten all fastenings to the correct torque, when specified.
12   Check the final drive oil level and top up if necessary.

### 4   Final drive pinion oil seal – renewal

1   Chock the front wheels. Raise and securely support the rear of the vehicle.
2   Unhook the exhaust system rear mountings. Move the system aside and tie it up to support it.
3   Remove the propeller shaft as described in Chapter 7.
4   Hold the final drive flange stationary by bolting a long bar to it or by fitting two long bolts to it and inserting a long bar between them.
5   Unscrew the self-locking pinion flange nut (photo).
6   Using a suitable puller pull the drive flange from the pinion (photos). As there may be some loss of oil, place a suitable container beneath the final drive unit.
7   Using a screwdriver, lever the oil seal from the final drive unit (photo).
8   Clean the oil seal seating within the housing, the drive flange, and the end of the pinion.
9   Pack the lips of the new oil seal with grease. (The seal may be supplied already greased, in which case do not disturb it). Fit the seal

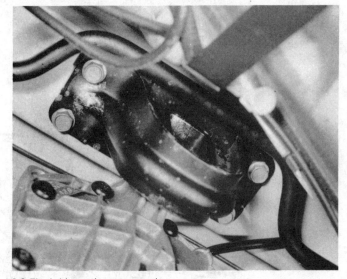

3.6 Final drive unit rear mounting

3.8 The two through-bolts and one of the short bolts (all arrowed) which secure the final drive unit to the rear axle crossmember

4.5 Removing the pinion flange nut

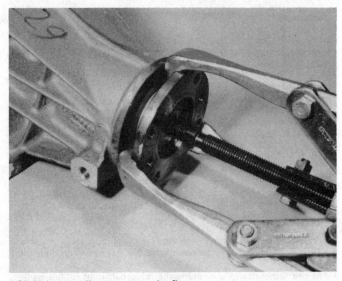

4.6A Using a puller to remove the flange

4.6B Removing the drive flange

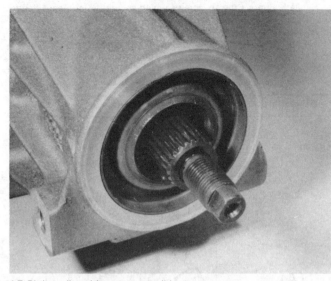

4.7 Pinion oil seal is now accessible

to the housing, lips inwards, and drive it in until flush using a tube or a wooden block with a hole in it.

10 Slide the drive flange onto the pinion splines, taking care not to damage the oil seal.

11 Fit the self-locking nut and tighten it to the specified torque while holding the drive flange stationary using the method described in paragraph 4 (photo). Ideally a new self-locking nut should be used, and it should not be unscrewed and tightened more than three times otherwise it will lose its self-locking characteristic.

12 Refit the propeller shaft as described in Chapter 7.

13 Top up the final drive oil as described in Section 2.

## 5 Final drive output flange oil seals – renewal

1 Remove the final drive unit as described in Section 3.

2 Remove the rear cover from the final drive unit. This is secured by nine 'Torx' screws. Any oil left inside the unit will be released when the cover is removed.

3 Clean old sealant from the cover mating faces, taking care to keep it out of the interior of the unit.

4 Remove the circlips which secure the output flanges inside the differential. *Do not get the circlips mixed up,* as their thickness is selected and may differ from left to right.

5 Withdraw the output flanges and stubs. Clean the seal rubbing faces.

6 Measure the fitted depths of the old oil seals, then prise them from their locations. Clean the seal seats.

7 Pack the lips of the new seals with grease (if they are not supplied ready-greased). Fit the seals, lips inwards, and drive them in to the depth previously noted, using a piece of tube.

8 Refit the output flanges and stubs, being careful not to damage the seal lips. Secure them with the same circlips.

9 Apply liquid sealant (to Ford spec. SQM 4G 9523 A) to the mating faces of the final drive unit and the rear cover.

10 Fit the rear cover. Insert the cover screws and tighten them evenly to the specified torque.

11 Refit the final drive unit as described in Section 3. Remember to refill it with oil on completion.

## 6 Driveshaft – removal and refitting

1 Chock the front wheels. Raise and support the rear of the vehicle.

2 Remove the six 'Torx' screws which secure the inboard flange to the final drive unit (photo). Recover the three double lockwashers. Support the driveshaft.

4.11 Tightening the pinion flange nut

6.2 Undoing a driveshaft flange screw

3   Similarly remove the six screws which secure the outboard flange to the rear hub. Remove the driveshaft.

4   At all times, avoid bending the CV joints to excessive angles, and do not allow the shaft to hang down from one end.

5   Refit by reversing the removal operations. Tighten the flange screws to the specified torque.

## 7   Driveshaft – overhaul

1   The CV joints cannot be overhauled, but they can be renewed separately, as can the rubber gaiters. Check when purchasing gaiters

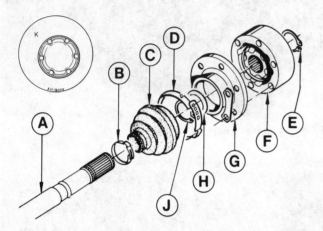

**Fig. 8.5 Driveshaft CV joint assembly (Sec 7)**

| A | Shaft | F | Constant velocity joint |
|---|---|---|---|
| B | Wire clip | G | Protective cover |
| C | Gaiter | H | Dished washer (if fitted) |
| D | Clip | J | Inner circlip |
| E | Outer circlip | K | Sealant application |

whether the grease required for the CV joints is included.

2   Remove the driveshaft as described in the previous Section.

3   Undo or cut the clips which secure the rubber gaiters. Peel the gaiters back from the CV joints.

4   Release the CV joints by removing the outer circlips (one per joint) which secure them to the shaft. Pull off the joints and remove the inner circlips.

5   The gaiters can now be removed from the shaft.

6   Renew components as necessary. The gaiter clips must be renewed in any case.

7   Pack the CV joints with the specified type and quantity of grease.

8   Fit the gaiters and the CV joint inner covers to the shaft. Fit the inner circlips. Apply sealant to the protective cover face where it will meet the CV joint (inset in Fig. 8.5). Clean any grease off the corresponding face of the joint.

9   Fit the CV joints, grooves outermost, and secure them with the outer circlips.

10  Secure the gaiters with the new clips.

11  Refit the driveshaft.

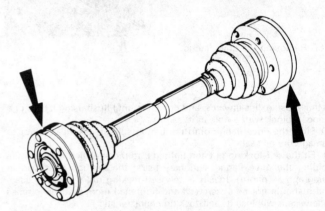

**Fig. 8.6 Correct fitting of CV joints with grooves (arrowed) outermost (Sec 7)**

## 8   Fault diagnosis – final drive and driveshaft

| Symptom | Reason(s) |
|---|---|
| Excessive final drive noise | Oil level low, or incorrect grade<br>Worn bearings<br>Worn or badly adjusted crownwheel and pinion<br>Loose or deteriorated final drive mountings |
| Oil leakage from final drive | Pinion or output flange oil seal leaking<br>Rear cover leaking<br>Cover or casing cracked |
| Grating, knocking or vibration from driveshafts | Flange screws loose<br>CV joints worn<br>Driveshaft bent |

# Chapter 9 Braking system

*For modifications, and information applicable to later models, see Supplement at end of manual*

## Contents

## Specifications

### General
System type ............................................................................. Discs all round, hydraulic operation, anti-lock braking system (ABS)
Handbrake ............................................................................... Mechanical operation of rear calipers

### Hydraulic system
Fluid type ................................................................................ See *'Recommended lubricants and fluids'*
Operating pressure .................................................................. 130 to 190 bar (1885 to 2755 lbf/in²)
Pressure warning switch operates at ........................................... 100 to 110 bar (1450 to 1595 lbf/in²)

### Brake pads
Lining minimum thickness ......................................................... 1.5 mm (0.06 in)

### Brake discs
Run-out ................................................................................... 0.15 mm (0.006 in) maximum
Thickness variation .................................................................. 0.015 mm (0.0006 in) maximum
Minimum thickness:
  Front ................................................................................. 22 mm (0.87 in)
  Rear .................................................................................. Cast into outer rim (typically 8.9 mm/0.35 in)

### Torque wrench settings

| | Nm | lbf ft |
|---|---|---|
| Front caliper: | | |
|   To stub axle carrier | 51 to 61 | 38 to 45 |
|   Slide bolts | 20 to 25 | 15 to 18 |
| Rear caliper: | | |
|   Bracket to carrier plate | 51 to 61 | 38 to 45 |
|   Slide bolts | 31 to 35 | 23 to 26 |
| Hydraulic unit to bulkhead | 41 to 51 | 30 to 38 |
| Accumulator to pump body | 35 to 45 | 26 to 33 |
| Pump mounting bolts | 7 to 9 | 5 to 7 |
| High pressure hose banjo bolts | 16 to 24 | 12 to 18 |
| Reservoir mounting bolts | 4 to 6 | 3 to 4 |
| Wheel sensor fixing bolts | 8.5 to 11 | 6.3 to 8 |

## 1  General description

Disc brakes are fitted all round. The footbrake operates hydraulically on all four wheels, and the handbrake operates mechanically on the rear wheels. Both footbrake and handbrake are self-adjusting in use.

Ford's anti-lock braking system (ABS) is fitted to all models. The system monitors the rotational speed of each roadwheel. When a wheel begins to lock under heavy braking, the ABS reduces the hydraulic pressure to that wheel, so preventing it from locking. When this happens a pulsating effect will be noticed at the brake pedal. On some road surfaces the tyres may squeal when braking hard even though the wheels are not locked.

The main components of the system are the hydraulic unit, the calipers, pads and discs, the wheel sensors and the 'brain' or control module. The hydraulic unit contains the elements of a traditional master cylinder, plus an electric motor and pump, a pressure accumulator and control valves. The pump is the source of pressure for the system and does away with the need for a vacuum servo.

The hydraulic circuit is split front and rear, as is normal practice with rear wheel drive vehicles. In the event that the hydraulic pump fails, unassisted braking effort is still available on the front calipers only.

Warning lights inform the driver of low brake fluid level, ABS failure and (on some models) brake pad wear. The low fluid level light doubles as a 'handbrake on' light; if it illuminates at the same time as the ABS warning light, it warns of low hydraulic pressure.

ABS cannot overturn the laws of physics: stopping distances will inevitably be greater on loose or slippery surfaces. However, the system should allow even inexperienced drivers to retain directional control under panic braking.

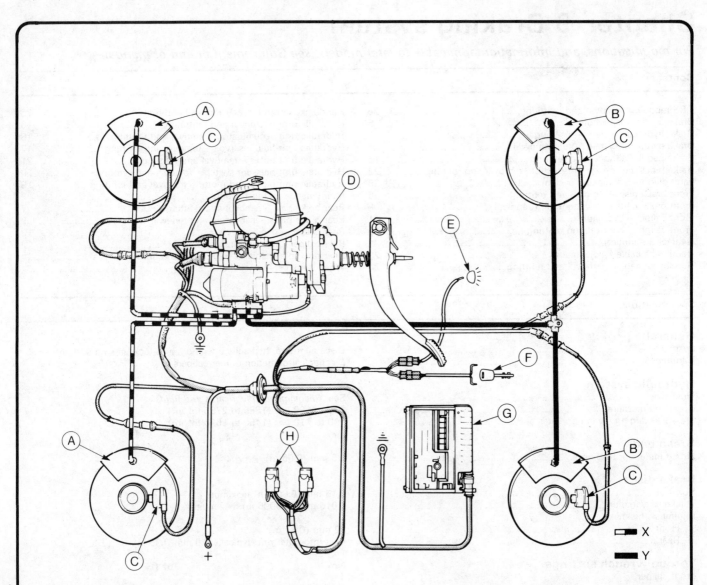

**Fig. 9.1 Schematic of anti-lock braking system (Sec 1)**

| A | Front calipers | D | Hydraulic unit | G | ABS module | X | Front hydraulic circuit |
|---|---|---|---|---|---|---|---|
| B | Rear calipers | E | Warning light | H | Relays and diodes | Y | Rear hydraulic circuit |
| C | Wheel sensors | F | Ignition switch | | | | |

## 2  Maintenance and inspection

1  Check the brake fluid level frequently. The procedure is as follows.

2  With the vehicles parked on level ground and the ignition switched off, pump the brake pedal at least 20 times or until the pedal feels hard.

3  Open the bonnet. Switch on the ignition: the hydraulic unit pump will be heard running. Wait until the pump stops, then switch off the ignition.

4  The fluid level in the reservoir should now be between the 'MAX' and 'MIN' marks. If topping-up is necessary, unplug the electrical connectors from the cap, then unscrew and remove it (photos). Catch the hydraulic fluid which will drip off the level sensor with a piece of rag. If any brake fluid gets onto paintwork, wash it off immediately with clean water.

5  Top up with fresh brake fluid of the specified type (photo). Do not overfill. Refit and reconnect the reservoir cap immediately; again, wash any spilled fluid off paintwork.

6  Frequent need for topping-up can only be due to a leak, which must be rectified without delay.

7  Every 6000 miles or six months, or at once if prompted by the wear warning light, inspect the front and rear brake pads for wear. Refer to Sections 8 and 9.

8  At the same interval, check the function of the brake fluid level warning light. Chock the wheels, release the handbrake and switch on the ignition. Unscrew and raise the brake fluid reservoir cap whilst an assistant observes the warning light: it should come on as the level sensor is withdrawn from the fluid. Refit the cap.

9  Every 12 000 miles or annually, or whenever leakage is suspected, inspect the hydraulic pipes, flexible hoses and unions. Refer to Section 22.

10  Periodically inspect the handbrake cable and linkage and lubricate the exposed parts. Adjustment should only be necessary to compensate for cable stretch or after fitting a new cable – see Section 23.

11  Inspect the brake discs whenever new pads are fitted – see Section 5.

12  Every 36 000 miles or three years, renew the hydraulic fluid as described in Section 4. At the same time, consider renewing the flexible hoses and caliper rubber seals as a precautionary measure.

13  Observe scrupulous cleanliness at all times when working on the hydraulic system. Even small particles of dirt can have a devastating affect. Only use clean hydraulic fluid, preferably from a sealed can, for topping-up and refilling the system. Avoid using old fluid which has been standing in part-used cans for long periods. Never re-use fluid which has been bled from the system.

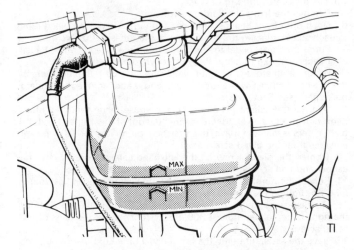

Fig. 9.2 Brake fluid reservoir (Sec 2)

2.4A Unplugging an electrical connector from the brake fluid reservoir cap

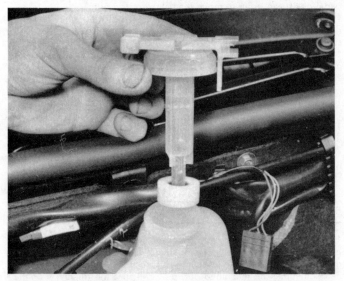

2.4B Removing the brake fluid reservoir cap

2.5 Topping-up the brake fluid reservoir

### 3  Brake hydraulic system – bleeding

1   Bleeding is necessary whenever air has entered the hydraulic system – for instance after component renewal. Because the hydraulic circuits are split, if only the front or rear circuit has been disturbed it will normally only be necessary to bleed the front or rear calipers. If the hydraulic unit has been disturbed, or the fluid level has been allowed to fall so low that air has entered the system, both front and rear circuits must be bled, starting with the front.
2   The services of an assistant will be required. As far as is known, pressure bleeding or other 'one-man' equipment cannot be used. In addition a supply of fresh brake fluid of the correct type will be needed, together with a length of flexible tube to fit the bleed screws and a clean glass or plastic container.
3   Do not allow the hydraulic unit pump motor to run for more than two minutes at a time. The motor must be allowed to cool (with the ignition off) for at least ten minutes after each two minute spell of running.
4   Remember that brake fluid is poisonous and that the rear brake hydraulic system may be under considerable pressure. *Take care not to allow hydraulic fluid to spray into the face or eyes.*
5   Keep the reservoir topped up to the 'MAX' mark during bleeding.
6   Discard the fluid bled out of the system as it is unfit for re-use.

### Front brakes

7   Remove the dust cap (if fitted) from the left-hand caliper bleed screw. Slacken the bleed screw, then nip it up again. Make sure that the ignition is off.
8   Fit the bleed tube over the bleed screw. Place the other end of the tube in the bleed jar (glass or plastic container). Pour sufficient brake fluid into the jar to cover the end of the tube.
9   Open the bleed screw one full turn. Have the assistant depress the brake pedal as far as it will go, and hold it depressed. Tighten the bleed screw, then tell the assistant to release the pedal.
10  Repeat paragraph 9 until clean fluid, free of air bubbles, flows from the bleed screw during the downstrokes. Remember to keep the fluid reservoir topped up.
11  Repeat the operations on the right-hand caliper. Refit the bleed screw dust caps (if applicable) on completion.

### Rear brakes

12  Remove the dust cap (if fitted) from the rear left-hand caliper bleed screw. Open the bleed screw one full turn.
13  Fit the bleed tube over the bleed screw. Place the other end of the tube in the bleed jar (photo).

3.13 Bleeding a rear brake caliper

14  Have the assistant depress the brake pedal as far as it will go and hold it down. Switch on the ignition: the hydraulic unit pump will start and fluid will flow from the bleed screw.
15  When clean fluid, free of air bubbles, emerges from the bleed screw, tighten the bleed screw and have the assistant release the pedal.
16  Wait for the hydraulic unit pump to stop, then top up the reservoir and repeat the procedure on the right-hand caliper. This time the brake pedal should only be depressed half-way.
17  Switch off the ignition, top up the reservoir again and refit the reservoir cap. Refit the bleed screw dust caps (if applicable).

### 4  Brake hydraulic system – fluid renewal

1   Periodic renewal of the brake fluid is necessary because the fluid absorbs water from the atmosphere. This water lowers the boiling point of the fluid, so increasing the risk of vapour locks, and causes rust and corrosion in braking system components.
2   Simple bleeding of the hydraulic system as described in the previous Section is not adequate for fluid renewal because of the large quantity of fluid which is normally present in the front calipers.
3   An assistant and the rest of the bleeding equipment will be needed, together with an extra bleed tube and jar. A considerable quantity of hydraulic fluid will be required – probably about 2 litres (nearly half a gallon).
4   Slacken the front wheel nuts. Raise and support the front of the vehicle and remove the front wheels.
5   Remove the hydraulic fluid reservoir cap.
6   Open both front bleed screws one full turn. Attach one bleed tube to each screw, placing the other ends of the tubes in the jars.
7   Pump the brake pedal to expel fluid from the bleed screws. Pause after each upstroke to allow the master cylinder to refill.
8   When air emerges from both bleed screws, stop pumping. Detach the left-hand caliper without disconnecting it and remove the inboard brake pad (see Section 8).
9   Depress the caliper piston, using a purpose-made tool or a blunt item such as a tyre lever, to force more fluid out of the caliper. Hold the piston depressed and have the assistant pump the pedal until air emerges from the bleed screw again.
10  Tighten the bleed screw on the left-hand caliper. Loosely refit the caliper and pad so that the piston is not accidentally ejected.
11  Repeat the purging operation on the right-hand caliper, but do not refit it or tighten the bleed screw yet.
12  Fill the reservoir with fresh hydraulic fluid. Position the bleed jar for the right-hand caliper at least 300 mm (1 foot) above the level of the bleed screw.
13  Have the assistant pump the brake pedal until fluid free of bubbles emerges from the bleed screw. Tighten the bleed screw at the end of a downstroke.
14  Place a piece of wood in the caliper jaws to limit piston travel. Keep your fingers clear of the piston. Have the assistant depress the brake pedal **gently** in order to move the caliper piston out.
15  With the pedal held depressed, slacken the bleed screw on the right-hand caliper and again depress the piston. Tighten the bleed screw when the piston is retracted. The pedal can now be released.
16  Disconnect the bleed tube. Refit the right-hand brake pad and caliper.
17  Remove the left-hand caliper and inboard pad again. Carry out the operations in paragraphs 12 to 16 on the left-hand caliper.
18  Bleed the rear brakes as described in Section 3, paragraph 12 onwards.
19  Refit the front wheels, lower the vehicle and tighten the wheel nuts.
20  Pump the brake pedal to bring the pads up to the discs, then make a final check of the hydraulic fluid level. Top up and refit the reservoir cap.

### 5  Brake discs – inspection

1   Whenever the brake pads are inspected, also inspect the brake discs for deep scratches, scores or cracks. Light scoring is normal and may be ignored. A cracked disc must be renewed; scratches and scores can sometimes be machined out, provided that the thickness of the disc is not reduced below the specified minimum.

2   When the brake pads are renewed, or if brake judder or snatch is noticed, check the discs for run-out and thickness variation. (Note that wheel bearing wear can cause disc run-out).

3   Position a dial test indicator probe against the disc wear face, approximately 15 mm (0.6 in) in from the outer circumference. Zero the indicator, rotate the disc and read the run-out from the indicator. Maximum run-out is given in the Specifications. If a dial test indicator is not available, use a fixed pointer and feeler blades.

4   Measure the thickness of the disc, using a micrometer, in eight evenly spaced positions around the disc. Maximum thickness variation is given in the Specifications. Renew the disc if the variation is out of limits.

### 6   Front brake disc – removal and refitting

1   Slacken the front wheel nuts, raise and support the vehicle and remove the relevant front wheel.

2   Remove the two bolts which hold the caliper bracket to the stub axle carrier. Lift the caliper and bracket off the disc and tie them up out of the way. Do not allow the caliper to hang on the flexible hose.

3   Remove the spring clip which secures the disc (photo).

4   Mark the relationship of the disc to the hub if it is to be re-used, then remove the disc from the hub.

5   Refit by reversing the removal operations. Tighten the caliper bracket bolts to the specified torque, and check that the brake flexible hose is not kinked or fouling in any position of the steering wheel.

6   Pump the brake pedal to bring the pads up to the disc.

### 7   Rear brake disc – removal and refitting

1   Chock the front wheels and release the handbrake. Slacken the rear wheel nuts, raise and support the vehicle and remove the relevant rear wheel.

2   Free the handbrake cable from its clip in the suspension lower arm.

3   Remove the two bolts which secure the caliper bracket to the hub. Lift the caliper and bracket off the disc and suspend it without straining the flexible hose.

4   Remove the spring clip from the wheel stud. Mark the disc-to-hub relationship and remove the disc.

5   Refit by reversing the removal operations.

6   Pump the brake pedal to bring the pads up to the disc.

### 8   Front brake pads – inspection and renewal

1   Disc pads can be inspected without removing the front wheels, using a mirror and a torch through the aperture in the rear face of the caliper. If any one pad is worn down to the minimum specified, all four pads (on both front wheels) must be renewed.

2   To renew the pads, first remove the front wheels, then prise free the spring clip from the outboard face of a caliper (photo).

3   Disconnect the pad wear warning wires, when fitted (photo).

4   Unscrew the two caliper slide bolts, using a 7 mm hexagon key, until the caliper is free of the bracket (photo).

5   Lift the caliper off the disc and remove the pads (photo). Support the caliper so that the flexible hose is not strained. *Do not press the brake pedal with the caliper removed.*

6   Clean the dust and dirt from the caliper, bracket and disc, using a damp cloth or old paintbrush which can be thrown away afterwards. **Take care not to disperse the dust into the air, or to inhale it, since it may contain asbestos.** Scrape any scale or rust from the disc. Investigate any hydraulic fluid leaks.

7   Push the caliper piston back into its housing, using the fingers or a blunt instrument, to accommodate the extra thickness of the new pads.

8   Fit the new pads to the caliper, being careful not to contaminate the friction surfaces with oil or grease. The inboard pad has a spring clip which fits into the piston recess; the outboard pad must have its backing paper peeled off, after which the pad should be stuck to the other side of the caliper (photos).

9   Fit the caliper and pads over the disc and onto the caliper bracket. Tighten the slide bolts to the specified torque.

10  Reconnect the wear warning wires, when fitted.

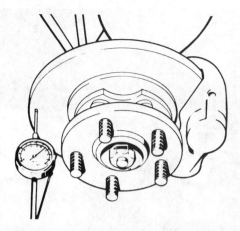

**Fig. 9.3 Measuring brake disc run-out (Sec 5)**

6.3 Disc-securing spring clip

8.2 Spring clip fitted to outboard face of front caliper

8.3 Pad wear warning multi-plug (arrowed) on front caliper

8.4 Undoing a caliper slide bolt

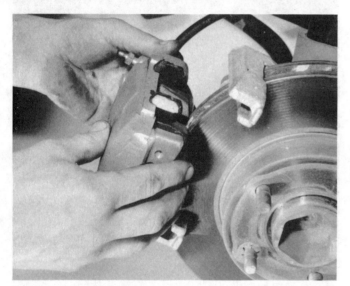

8.5 Lifting a front caliper off the disc

8.8A Clipping the inboard front pad into the piston

11  Refit the spring clip to the caliper.
12  Repeat the operations on the other caliper, then refit the wheels and lower the vehicle. Tighten the wheel nuts.
13  Pump the brake pedal several times to bring the pads up to the disc, then check the brake fluid level.
14  Avoid heavy braking as far as possible for the first hundred miles or so to allow the new pads to bed in.

## 9  Rear brake pads – inspection and renewal

1  It is necessary to remove the rear wheels in order to inspect the rear pads. The pads can be viewed through the top of the caliper after removing the spring clip. If any one pad is worn down to the minimum specified, all four pads (on both rear wheels) must be renewed.
2  Free the handbrake cable from its clip on the suspension lower arm. Release the handbrake.
3  Remove the caliper slide bolt nearest the front, counterholding the slide pin with another spanner (photo).
4  Disconnect the pad wear warning wires, when fitted (photo).
5  Swing the caliper rearwards and remove the pads (photo). *Do not press the brake pedal with the caliper removed.*

8.8B Both pads fitted to a front caliper

9.3 Undoing a rear caliper front slide bolt

9.4 Pad wear warning multi-plug (arrowed) on rear caliper

6   Clean the caliper and surrounding components, referring to paragraph 6 of the previous Section.

7   Retract the caliper piston, by turning it clockwise, to accommodate the extra thickness of the new pads. There is a Ford tool (No. 12-006) for this purpose, but a pair of circlip pliers or any similar tool can be used instead (photo).

8   Remove any backing paper from the new pads, then fit them to the caliper bracket. Be careful not to contaminate the friction surfaces with oil or grease.

9   Swing the caliper over the pads. Refit and tighten the slide bolt.

10   Reconnect the wear warning wires, when fitted.

11   Repeat the operations on the other rear caliper.

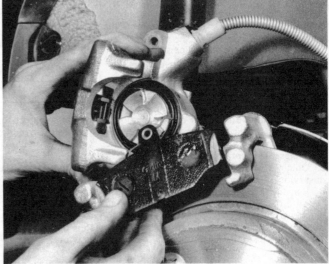

9.5 Removing a rear brake pad

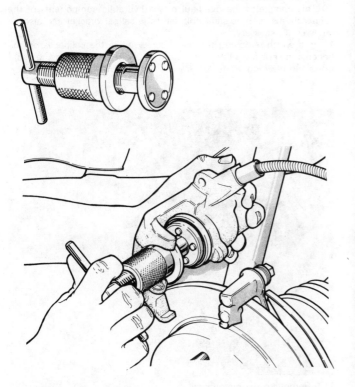

Fig. 9.4 Ford tool 12-006 for winding back the rear caliper
pistons (Sec 9)

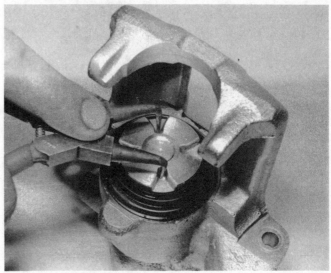

9.7 Rotating the caliper piston to retract it

12 Secure the handbrake cable, refit the wheels and lower the vehicle. Tighten the wheel nuts.
13 Switch on the ignition and pump the brake pedal several times to bring the pads up to the discs. Switch off the ignition and check the operation of the handbrake.
14 Allow the new pads to bed in – see paragraph 14 of the previous Section.

## 10 Front caliper – removal and refitting

1 With the ignition off, pump the brake pedal at least 20 times (or until it becomes hard) to depressurise the hydraulic system.
2 Slacken the front wheel nuts, raise and support the vehicle and remove the relevant front wheel.
3 Slacken the flexible hose hydraulic union at the caliper by no more than a quarter turn.
4 Remove the brake pads as described in Section 8.
5 The caliper can now be removed by holding the flexible hose stationary and rotating the caliper to unscrew it. Be prepared for hydraulic fluid spillage: plug or cap the caliper and hose. A brake hose clamp may be used if available (photo). Take great care to keep dirt out of the hydraulic system.
6 The caliper bracket may be unbolted from the stub axle carrier if wished.
7 Refit by reversing the removal operations, but before refitting the wheel, check the positioning of the flexible hose. It must not be kinked, nor foul adjacent components, in any position of the steering wheel. Release the other end of the hose from its bracket if necessary and reposition it.
8 Bleed both front brake calipers as described in Section 3.

## 11 Front caliper – overhaul

1 It is possible to carry out these operations without disconnecting the caliper hydraulic hose, but this is not recommended because of the risk of introducing dirt into the hydraulic system. Scrupulous cleanliness is essential.
2 Obtain a caliper repair kit, which will contain a piston seal and a dust boot. (The piston itself can also be renewed if necessary).
3 Remove the piston from the caliper. This is best done with low air pressure (eg from a foot pump) applied to the hydraulic inlet union. Place a piece of wood opposite the piston to prevent damage, and keep your fingers clear as the piston may be ejected with some force.
4 With the piston removed, pull off the dust boot (photo).

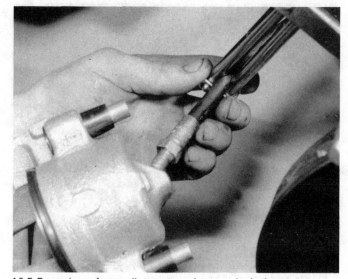

10.5 Removing a front caliper – note clamp on brake hose

5 Extract the piston seal from the groove in the bore, using a blunt or non-metallic instrument (photo). Discard the seal and dust boot.
6 Clean the piston and bore with methylated spirit and inspect them for scuffs, scores or other damage. If the piston is corroded it must be renewed. Slight imperfections in the bore can be polished out with wire wool.
7 Place the clean component on a clean surface ready for reassembly (photo). Lubricate the caliper hose with clean hydraulic fluid.
8 Fit the new piston seal to the groove in the bore, using the fingers only to work it into position.
9 Lubricate the piston with clean hydraulic fluid and fit the dust boot over the piston, making sure it is the right way up. Insert the piston into the bore and press it home, engaging the dust boot lip with the groove on the caliper (photo).
10 This completes the overhaul of the hydraulic components of the caliper. Items such as slide bolts and the caliper bracket can also be renewed if necessary.
11 It is worth removing the bleed screw while the caliper is on the bench and applying a little anti-seize compound to its threads, to avoid trouble in undoing it later.

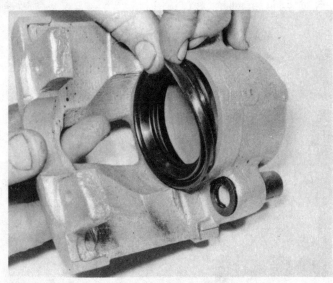

11.4 Removing the dust boot from a front caliper

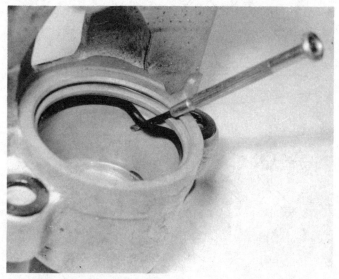

11.5 Removing the piston seal

11.7 Front caliper components

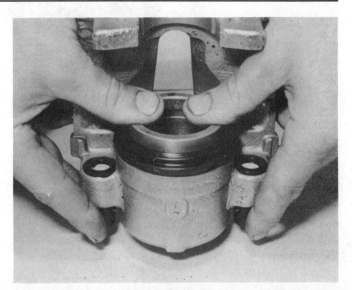

11.9 Pressing the piston into the bore

## 12 Rear caliper – removal and refitting

1   With the ignition off, pump the brake pedal at least 20 times (or until it becomes hard) to depressurise the system.
2   Chock the front wheels and release the handbrake. Slacken the rear wheel nuts, raise and support the vehicle and remove the relevant wheel.
3   Disconnect the pad wear warning wires, when fitted.
4   Disconnect the flexible hose from the brake pipe. Plug or cap the open unions to reduce spillage and to keep dirt out. Unscrew the flexible hose from the caliper and remove it.
5   Remove the two slide bolts. Lift the caliper off the pads and bracket, at the same time unhooking the handbrake cable (photos). Alternatively, the two bracket-to-hub bolts can be removed and the caliper and bracket separated on the bench.
6   Refit by reversing the removal operations, but before refitting the wheel, bleed both rear calipers as described in Section 3.
7   When bleeding is complete, pump the brake pedal several times to bring the pads up to the disc, then check the operation of the handbrake.

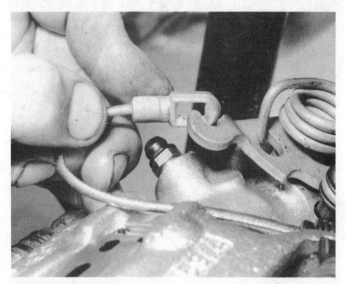

12.5A Unhook the handbrake cable ...

## 13 Rear caliper – overhaul

**Note**: *Complete dismantling of the rear caliper should not be attempted unless Ford spring compressor (tool No. 12-007) is available, or unless the problems likely to arise in the absence of the tool are understood. Renewal of the piston seal and dust boot requires no special tools.*

1   Clean the caliper externally and mount it in a soft-jawed vice.
2   Rotate the piston anti-clockwsie until it is protruding from the bore by about 20 mm (0.8 in). Free the dust boot from the groove in the piston, then carry on unscrewing the piston and remove it. Remove and discard the dust boot.
3   The piston and bore may now be cleaned and examined, and the piston seal and dust boot renewed, as described for the front caliper (Section 11).
4   The piston adjuster nut seal should also be renewed. Remove the circlip from the piston, then extract the thrust washers, wave washer and thrust bearing. Note the fitted sequence of these components. Finally remove the nut (photos).
5   Remove the seal from the nut, noting which way round it is fitted. Clean the nut with methylated spirit. Lubricate the new seal with clean hydraulic fluid and fit it to the nut.

12.5B ... and remove the rear caliper

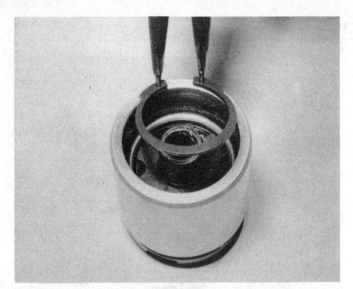

13.4A Removing the circlip from a rear caliper piston ...

13.4B ... followed by a thrust washer ...

13.4C ... a wave washer and (not shown) another thrust washer ...

13.4D ... the thrust bearing ...

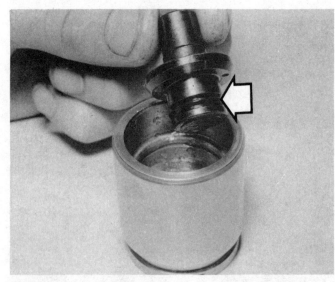

13.4E ... and the adjuster nut itself. Note seal (arrowed) on nut

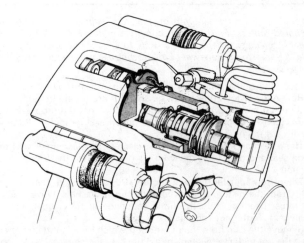

Fig. 9.5 Sectional view of a rear caliper (Sec 13)

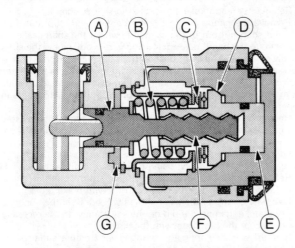

Fig. 9.6 Part section of rear caliper showing self-adjusting mechanism (brakes released) (Sec 13)

A  Handbrake pushrod
B  Preload spring
C  Preload washer
D  Clutch face
E  Adjuster nut
F  Quick thread
G  Key plate

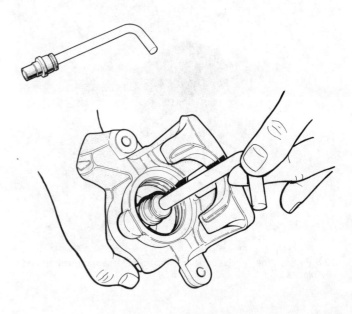

Fig. 9.7 Ford tool 12-007 for compressing the rear caliper spring (Sec 13)

6  For further dismantling it is virtually essential to have Ford tool 12-007. This tool appears to be a cut-down adjuster nut with a handle for turning it. In the workshop it was found that the actual piston adjuster nut could be used to compress the spring if it were turned with circlip pliers (photo). This works well enough for dismantling, but reassembly proved extremely difficult because of the limited clearance between the skirt of the nut and the caliper bore.
7  Having compressed the adjuster spring just enough to take the load off the circlip, release the circlip inside the caliper bore. Remove the

spring compressor, then extract the circlip, spring cover, spring and washer (photos).
8  A long thin pair of circlip pliers will now be needed to release the key plate retaining circlip from the caliper bore (photo). With the circlip removed, the pushrod and key plate can be pulled out.

13.6 Using the adjuster nut to compress the caliper spring

13.7A Extract the circlip ...

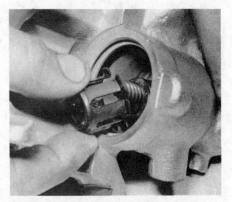

13.7B ... the spring cover ...

13.7C ... the spring itself ...

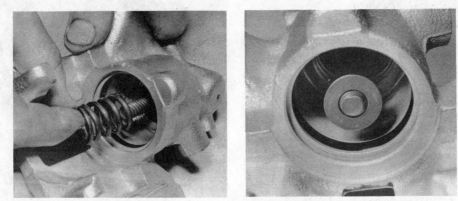

13.7D ... and the washer

13.8 Remove the circlip (ends arrowed) to release the pushrod and key plate

9   Remove the handbrake strut from the caliper bore.

10  Remove the handbrake lever return spring and stop bolt. Pull the lever and shaft nut out of the caliper. Prise out the shaft seal.

11  Clean up the handbrake shaft using wire wool; renew the shaft if it is badly corroded. The shaft bush in the caliper can also be renewed if necessary. Pull out the old bush with an internal puller or slide hammer; press in the new bush to 7.5 mm (0.30 in) below the shaft seal lip. The slot in the side of the bush must line up with the pushrod bore in the caliper.

12  Having renewed components as necessary, commence reassembly by smearing a little brake grease or anti-seize compound on the handbrake shaft and bush.

13  Fit a new handbrake shaft seal to the caliper. Pass the shaft through the seal and into the caliper, being careful not to damage the seal lips.

14  Refit the handbrake lever stop bolt and return spring.

15  Refit the handbrake strut, lubricating it with brake grease.

16  Fit a new O-ring to the base of the pushrod. Refit the pushrod and the key plate, engaging the pip on the key plate with the recess in the caliper. Secure the key plate with the circlip.

17  Refit the washer, spring and spring cover. Compress the spring and refit the circlip, then release the spring compressor.

18  Lubricate the caliper bore with clean hydraulic fluid and fit a new piston seal.

19  Reassemble the piston components. Lubricate the contact face of the adjuster nut with a little brake grease, then fit the adjuster nut (with new seal), thrust bearing, thrust washer, wave washer and the second thrust washer. Secure with the circlip.

20  Fit a new dust boot. the manufacturers recommend that it be fitted to the caliper groove and the piston fitted afterwards; it is also possible to fit the boot to the piston first and engage it in the caliper groove afterwards. Either way it is a fiddly business.

21  Refit the piston and screw it into the caliper, then fit whichever lip of the dust boot was left free (photo).

22  Renew the slide pin gaiters and apply a little anti-seize compound to the slide pins when reassembling the caliper to the bracket.

---

**14  Rear disc splash shield – removal and refitting**

The splash shield is retained by the rear hub bolts. Proceed as described in Chapter 10, Section 29, for removal and refitting of the rear hub.

---

**15  Brake pedal – removal and refitting**

1   Disconnect the battery negative lead.

2   Depressurise the hydraulic system by pumping the brake pedal at least 20 times, or until it becomes hard.

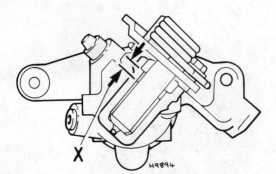

H9893

**Fig. 9.8 Handbrake lever and associated components (Sec 13)**

**Fig. 9.9 Handbrake shaft bush correctly fitted (Sec 13)**

H9894

X = 7.5 mm (0.30 in)

13.21 Dust boot fitted to caliper and piston

3   Remove the under-dash trim on the driver's side.
4   Remove the spring clip which secures the hydralic unit pushrod to the brake pedal. Also remove the clip from the brake pedal shaft (photo).
5   Withdraw the brake pedal shaft towards the left of the vehicle – through the clutch pedal, when applicable – until the brake pedal is free.
6   Remove the pedal, noting the fitted sequence of bushes, spacers and washers.
7   Refit by reversing the removal operations. Check the correct functioning of the stop light and (if applicable) cruise control switches before refitting the trim. See Chapter 12, Sections 25 and 43.

## 16  Hydraulic unit – removal and refitting

1   Disconnect the battery negative lead.
2   Depressurise the hydraulic system by pumping the brake pedal at least 20 times, or until it becomes hard.
3   Disconnect the six multi-plugs from the hydraulic unit. They are all different, so there is no need to label them. When a plug has a spring clip retainer, lift the clip before pulling out the plug. To release the pump plug, pull back the rubber boot and the plug sleeve (photos).
4   Unbolt the earth strap from the unit (photo).
5   Make arrangements to catch spilt hydraulic fluid. Identify the

15.4 Pushrod spring clip (A) and brake pedal shaft clip (B)

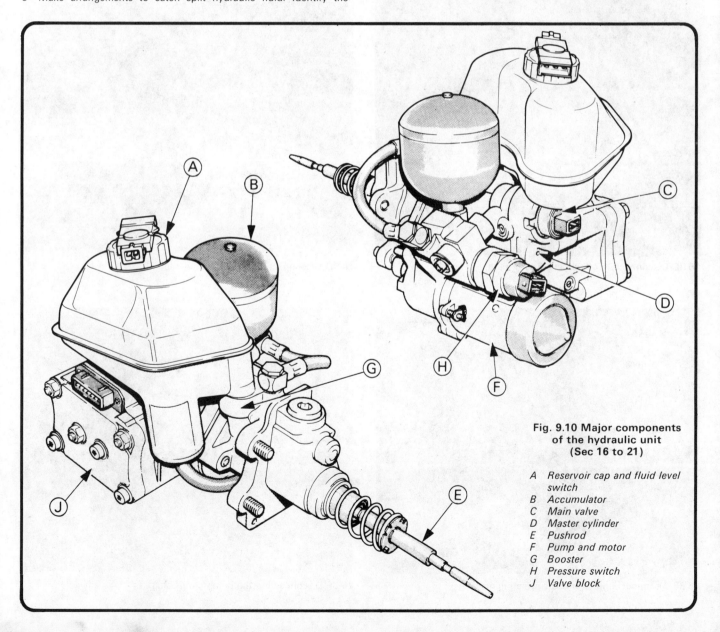

Fig. 9.10 Major components
of the hydraulic unit
(Sec 16 to 21)

A   Reservoir cap and fluid level
    switch
B   Accumulator
C   Main valve
D   Master cylinder
E   Pushrod
F   Pump and motor
G   Booster
H   Pressure switch
J   Valve block

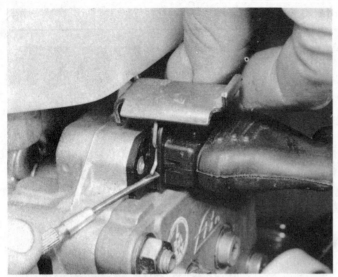

16.3A Disconnecting the valve block multi-plug. Lift the spring clip ...

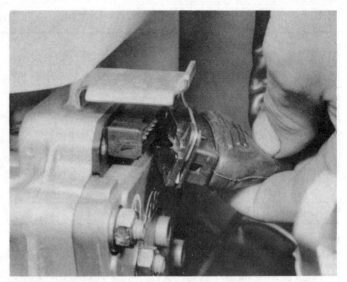

16.3B ... and pull off the plug

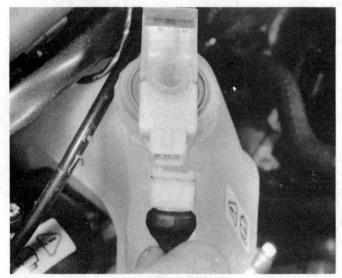

16.3C Disconnecting a fluid level sensor plug

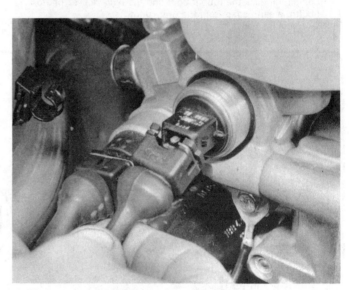

16.3D Disconnecting the main valve plug

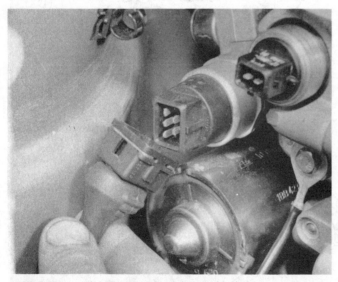

16.3E Disconnecting the pressure switch multi-plug

16.3F Disconnecting the pump motor plug

16.4 Earth strap (arrowed) bolted to hydraulic unit

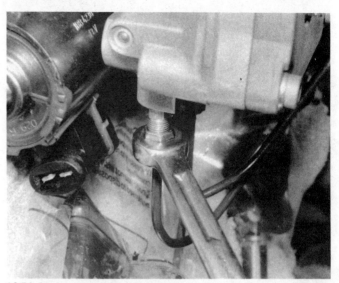

16.5A Disconnecting a hydraulic pipe

16.5B One way to cap an open hydraulic union

hydraulic pipes and disconnect them from the base of the unit. Plug or cap the open unions to keep fluid in and dirt out (photos).

6   Remove the under-dash trim on the driver's side. Disconnect the spring clip which secures the hydraulic unit pushrod to the brake pedal.

7   Have an assistant support the hydraulic unit. Remove the four nuts which hold the unit to the bulkhead (photo). Withdraw the unit from under the bonnet.

8   Recover the sealing compound from the unit and the bulkhead.

9   Drain the hydraulic fluid from the reservoir. *Do not actuate the pushrod with the unit removed.*

10 Dismantling of the hydraulic unit should be limited to the operations described in the following Sections. These operations can all be carried out without removing the unit from the vehicle if wished.

11 Refit by reversing the removal operations, noting the following points:

(a)  Do not refill the reservoir until the end of refitting
(b)  Use new sealing compound between the unit and the bulkhead
(c)  Make sure that the hydraulic pipes are reconnected to the correct unions
(d)  Bleed the complete hydraulic system on completion – see Section 3

## 17 Hydraulic unit fluid reservoir – removal and refitting

1   Disconnect the battery negative lead.

2   Depressurise the hydraulic system by pumping the brake pedal at least 20 times, or until it becomes hard.

3   Disconnect the multi-plugs and remove the reservoir cap.

4   Remove the reservoir securing screw, which is located just above the valve block mutli-plug (photo).

5   Make arrangements to catch spilt fluid, then disconnect the low pressure hose from its connections to the pump. the hose is secured by a spring clip (photos). Allow the brake fluid to drain out of the hose.

6   Pull the reservoir out of the seals on the hydraulic unit and remove it (photo).

7   Note the spigot locating bush on the rear inlet union, which may stay in the hydraulic unit or may come out with the reservoir (photo).

8   Refit by reversing the removal operations. Use new seals between the hydraulic unit and the reservoir.

9   Bleed the complete hydraulic system on completion (Section 3). Check for leaks around the disturbed components.

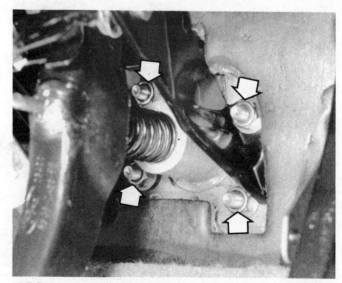

16.7 Four nuts (arrowed) which hold the hydraulic unit to the bulkhead

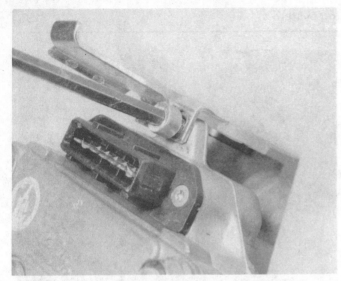

17.4 Undoing the reservoir securing screw

17.5A Extract the spring clip ...

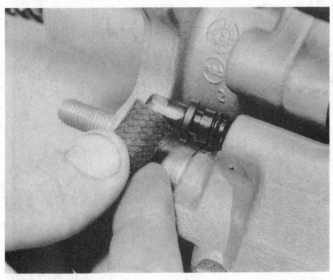

17.5B ... and disconnect the hose

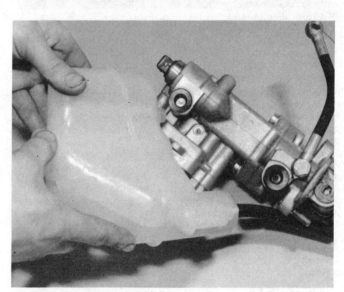

17.6 Removing the hydraulic fluid reservoir

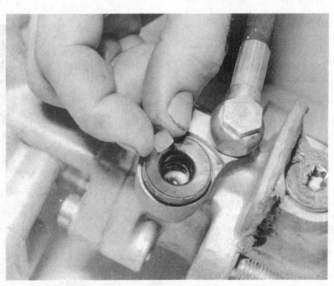

17.7 The spigot locating bush fits into this union

## 18 Hydraulic unit accumulator – removal and refitting

1 Disconnect the battery negative lead.
2 Depressurise the hydraulic system by pumping the brake pedal at least 20 times, or until it becomes hard.
3 Wrap a clean rag round the base of the accumulator to catch any spilt fluid.
4 Unscrew the accumulator using a hexagon key. Remove the accumulator, being prepared for fluid spillage (photos).
5 When refitting, fit a new O-ring to the base of the accumulator. Fit the accumulator and tighten it.
6 Reconnect the battery. Switch on the ignition and check that the hydraulic unit pump stops within 60 seconds. If not, there may be something wrong with the accumulator.
7 Bleed the complete hydraulic system (Section 3).

## 19 Hydraulic unit pump and motor – removal and refitting

1 Remove the accumulator as described in the previous Section.
2 Disconnect the high pressure hose from the pump. Be prepared for fluid spillage.
3 Disconnect the low pressure hose from the pump. Allow the fluid to drain out of the reservoir through the hose.
4 Disconnect the multi-plugs from the pressure switch and the pump motor.
5 Remove the pump mounting bolt (photo).
6 Pull the pump and motor assembly off the mounting spigot and remove it.
7 Recover the mounting bushes and renew them if necessary.
8 If a new pump is to be fitted, transfer the pressure switch to it, using a new O-ring.
9 Commence refitting by offering the pump to the spigot, then reconnecting the low pressure hose.
10 Refit and tighten the pump mounting bolt.
11 Reconnect the high pressure hose, using new sealing washers on the banjo union.
12 Refit the accumulator, using a new O-ring.
13 Reconnect the multi-plugs and the battery.
14 Refill the reservoir, then switch on the ignition and allow the pump to prime itself. Do not let the pump run for more than two minutes – see Section 3. Check for leaks around the disturbed components.
15 Bleed the complete hydraulic system (Section 3).

## 20 Hydraulic unit pressure switch – removal and refitting

**Note:** *To remove the pressure switch from the hydraulic unit in situ, Ford tool No. 12-008, or equivalent, will be required. The switch may be removed without special tools after removing the hydraulic unit complete (Section 16) or the pump (Section 19).*

1 Disconnect the battery negative lead.
2 Depressurise the hydraulic system by pumping the brake pedal at least 20 times, or until it becomes hard.
3 Disconnect the multi-plug from the switch, then unscrew and remove it (photo).
4 When refitting, use a new O-ring on the switch. Position the plastic sleeve so that the hole in the sleeve is facing the pump motor (photo). Tighten the switch.
5 Reconnect the multi-plug and the battery.
6 Bleed the complete hydraulic system (Section 3).

18.4A Unscrewing the accumulator

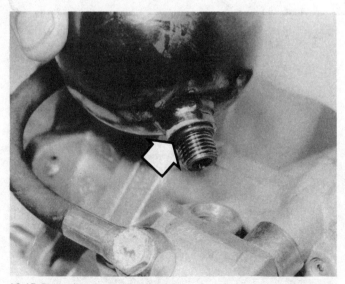

18.4B Removing the accumulator. Note O-ring (arrowed)

19.5 Hydraulic unit pump mounting bolt

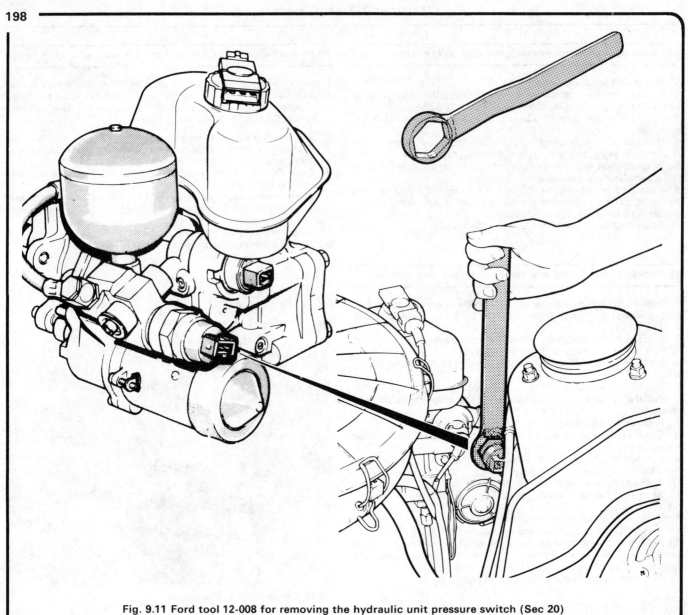

Fig. 9.11 Ford tool 12-008 for removing the hydraulic unit pressure switch (Sec 20)

20.3 Unscrewing the pressure switch

20.4 Refitting the pressure switch. Hole (arrowed) in plastic sleeve must face pump motor

## 21 Hydraulic unit hoses – removal and refitting

1 There are two hoses on the hydraulic unit. The low pressure hose connects the reservoir to the pump intake; the high pressure hose connects the pump outlet to the booster and valve block.
2 To remove either hose, first disconnect the battery. Depressurise the hydraulic system by pumping the brake pedal at least 20 times, or until it becomes hard.

*Low pressure hose*
3 Have ready a container to catch spilt fluid. Remove the spring clip and pull the hose off the pump intake. Allow the contents of the reservoir to drain out of the hose and into the container.
4 Pull the hose off the reservoir and remove it.
5 Refit by connecting the hose to the reservoir and pump intake. Secure the hose to the pump with the spring clip.
6 Refill the reservoir, reconnect the battery and bleed the complete hydraulic system (Section 3). Check for leaks.

*High pressure hose*
7 Remove the banjo bolts which secure the hose (photo). Be prepared for fluid spillage.
8 Remove the hose and recover the sealing washers.
9 Refit by reversing the removal operations, using new sealing washers on both sides of each union (photo).
10 Reconnect the battery and bleed the complete hydraulic system (Section 3). Check for leaks.

## 22 Brake pipes and hoses – inspection, removal and refitting

1 Periodically inspect the rigid brake pipes for rust and other damage, and the flexible hoses for cracks, splits or 'ballooning'. Have an assistant depress the brake pedal (ignition on) and inspect the hose and pipe unions for leaks. Renew defective items without delay.
2 Before removing any pipe or hose, depressurise the hydraulic system by switching off the ignition and pumping the brake pedal 20 times, or until it becomes hard.
3 To remove a flexible hose, first undo the union nut which secures the rigid pipe to it. The use of a split ring spanner, sold for this purpose, is recommended (photo). Be prepared for hydraulic fluid spillage, and take precautions to keep dirt out.
4 Having disconnected the rigid pipe, release the hose from the bracket by removing the locknut and washer (photo).

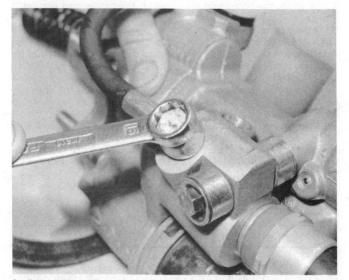

21.7 Undoing a high pressure hose union

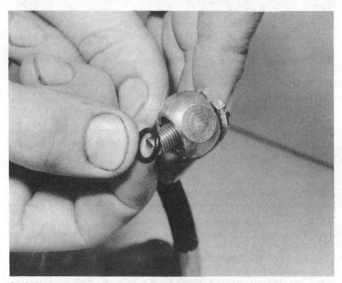

21.9 Fitting new sealing washers to a banjo union

22.3 Undoing a rigid pipe union nut. Flexible hose locknut is just above

22.4 Removing a flexible hose from its bracket

5  Unscrew the hose from its union on the caliper and remove it (photo).

6  Refit by reversing the removal operations, then bleed the appropriate part of the hydraulic system (Section 3). In the case of the front hoses, check that they are not kinked or twisted, and that they do not contact other components when the steering is moved from lock to lock. Reposition the hose in the bracket if necessary.

7  To remove a rigid pipe, simply undo the union nuts at the hydraulic unit, hose bracket or T-piece (photo). Free the pipe from any retaining clips and remove it.

8  New pipes can be bought ready-made, with the unions attached. Some garages and motor factors will make up pipes to order, using the old pipe as a pattern. If purchasing proprietary pipes made of copper alloy or similar material, follow the manufacturer's instructions carefully concerning bending, provision of extra clips etc.

9  Fit and secure the new pipe and tighten the union nuts. bleed the appropriate part of the hydraulic system (Section 3).

## 23 Handbrake cable – adjustment

1  The handbrake is normally self-adjusting in use. Adjustment may be required to compensate for cable stretch over a long period, and is also necessary after fitting a new cable.

2  Chock the front wheels, release the handbrake and raise and support the rear of the vehicle.

3  Release the adjuster locknut from the adjuster nut. Back off the adjuster nut, slackening the cable until both handbrake levers on the calipers are resting against their stops (photo).

4  Paint alignment marks between each handbrake lever and the caliper body (photo).

5  Tighten the adjuster nut until either handbrake lever just starts to move – as shown by the alignment marks.

6  Apply the handbrake and release it a few times to equalise the cable runs.

7  Tighten the locknut onto the adjuster nut finger tight, then tighten a further three to six 'clicks' using self-locking pliers or a peg spanner.

8  Lower the vehicle.

## 24 Handbrake cable – removal and refitting

1  Slacken the rear wheel nuts and chock the front wheels. Raise and support the rear of the vehicle and remove both rear wheels. Release the handbrake.

2  Slacken off the handbrake cable adjuster locknut and adjuster nut.

3  Free the cable from the equaliser yoke by removing the circlip and clevis pin (photo). Beware of self-tapping screws protruding through the floor in this area.

22.5 Disconnecting the hose from the caliper

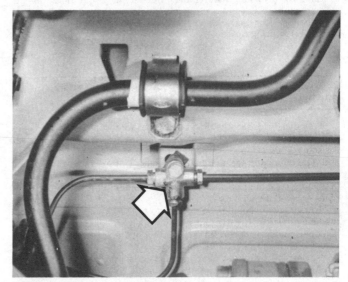

22.7 Brake pipe union T-piece (arrowed)

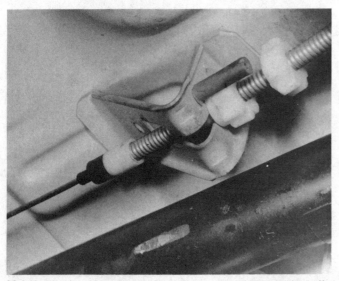

23.3 Handbrake cable adjuster. Locknut has already been backed off adjuster nut

23.4 Alignment marks painted on lever and body

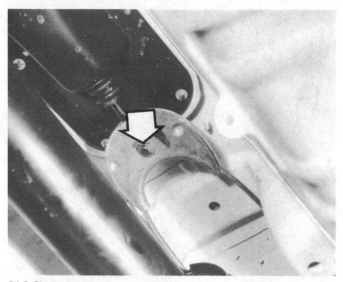

24.3 Circlip (arrowed) on equaliser yoke. Note protruding screws in transmission tunnel

24.4A Handbrake cable inner attached to lever on caliper

4   Unhook the cable inner from the handbrake levers on the calipers. Free the cable outer from the caliper brackets (photo).
5   Free the cable from the lower arm and underbody brackets and remove it.
6   Refit by reversing the removal operations, but before refitting the rear wheels, adjust the cable as described in the previous Section.

## 25 Handbrake control lever – removal and refitting

1   Chock the front wheels and release the handbrake. Raise and support the rear of the vehicle.
2   Disconnect the battery negative lead.
3   Disconnect the handbrake cable equaliser yoke by removing the circlip and clevis pin.
4   Remove the centre console (Chapter 11, Section 40).
5   Remove the handbrake control lever boot (photo).
6   Disconnect the wiring from the handbrake warning switch.
7   Unbolt the handbrake lever and remove it, complete with switch. Remove the switch if necessary.
8   Refit by reversing the removal operations.

24.4B Handbrake cable outer attached to caliper bracket

## 26 ABS module – removal and refitting

1   Remove the under-dash trim on the passenger's side.
2   Push the module upwards and then swing it forwards to release it from its clip.
3   Press the multi-plug locking lever, disconnect the multi-plug and unhook it from the module. Remove the module.
4   Refit by reversing the removal operations. Make sure that the multi-plug is properly engaged before refitting the module.

## 27 Wheel sensors – removal and refitting

### Front

1   Ensure that the handbrake is applied. Raise and support the front of the vehicle.
2   From under the bonnet disconnect the wheel sensor wiring multi-plug. Unclip the wiring, working towards the sensor.
3   Remove the securing bolt and withdraw the sensor from the stub axle carrier (photos).
4   Unclip the wire from the bracket on the strut. Remove the sensor and its wiring (photo).

25.5 Removing the handbrake lever boot

27.3A Removing a front sensor securing bolt

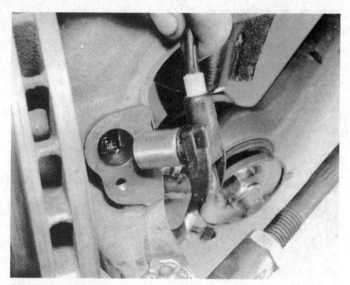

27.3B Removing a front sensor

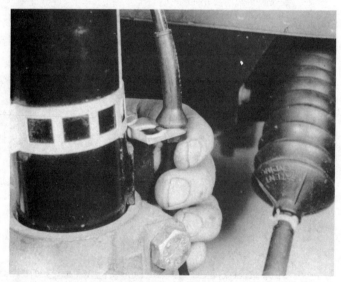

27.4 Unclipping the sensor wire from the strut

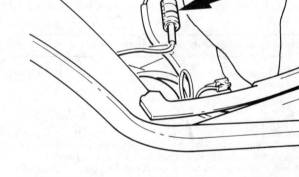

Fig. 9.12 Rear wheel sensor multi-plug (arrowed) (Sec 27)

5   Clean any rust or debris from the sensor bore in the stub axle carrier. Pack the bore with clean wheel bearing grease.
6   Renew the O-ring on the sensor and smear it with grease.
7   Refit by reversing the removal operations.

*Rear*
8   Chock the front wheels and release the handbrake. Slacken the rear wheel nuts, raise and support the rear of the vehicle and remove the rear wheel.
9   Fold the rear seat cushion forwards, remove the side kick panel and roll back the carpet to gain access to the sensor multi-plug.
10  Disconnect the multi-plug, release the floor grommet and pass the cable through the floor.
11  Unclip the handbrake cable from the suspension lower arm.
12  Remove the caliper front slide bolt and pivot the caliper rearwards to gain access to the sensor.
13  Remove the sensor securing bolt and withdraw the sensor.
14  Clean up the sensor bore, pack it with grease and renew the sensor O-ring.
15  Refit by reversing the removal operations.

## 28 Fault diagnosis – braking system

Faults in the ABS system which cannot readily be diagnosed from this chart should be referred to a Ford dealer or other competent specialist.

| Symptom | Reason(s) |
| --- | --- |
| Excessive pedal travel | Air in hydraulic system<br>Disc run-out excessive<br>Flexible hoses 'ballooning' |
| Vehicle pulls to one side | Tyre pressures incorrect<br>Pads contaminated<br>Pads renewed on one side only<br>Caliper piston seized |
| Pedal pulsates when braking hard | Normal feature of ABS – no fault |
| Brake judder | Disc run-out or thickness variation excessive<br>Pads badly worn or contaminated<br>Worn front suspension lower balljoint |
| Excessive effort needed to stop vehicle | Hydraulic pump not working<br>Excessively hard linings fitted<br>New linings not yet bedded-in<br>Failure of front or rear hydraulic circuit |
| Rear brake pad wear excessive | Stop-light switch (or cruise control switch, when applicable) incorrectly fitted – see Chapter 12, Sections 25 and 43. |

# Chapter 10 Steering and suspension

*For modifications, and information applicable to later models, see Supplement at end of manual*

## Contents

## Specifications

### General

Suspension type:

 Front ................................................................. Independent, MacPherson struts and anti-roll bar

 Rear .................................................................. Independent, semi-trailing arms and anti-roll bar; ride height control optionally available

Steering type ........................................................... Rack and pinion, power-assisted on some models

### Front wheel alignment

Toe:

 Setting value ...................................................... 2 ± 1 mm (0.08 ± 0.04 in) toe-in

 Tolerance in service ............................................. 0.5 mm (0.02 in) toe-out to 4.5 mm (0.18 in) toe-in

Castor:

 Standard, without ride height control ....................... + 1°51′ ± 1°00′

 Standard, with ride height control ........................... + 1°58′ ± 1°00′

 Heavy duty ........................................................ + 1°46′ ± 1°00′

Camber:

 Standard ............................................................ − 0°23′ ± 1°00′

 Heavy duty ........................................................ 0°00′ ± 1°00′

Difference between left-hand and right-hand sides:

 Castor ............................................................... 1°00′ maximum

 Camber .............................................................. 1°15′ maximum

### Steering gear

Make:

 Manual ............................................................... Cam Gears

 Power-assisted .................................................... Cam Gears or ZF

Power steering fluid type ............................................. See 'Recommended lubricants and fluids'

## Tyres

| | | |
|---|---|---|
| Tyre sizes ........................ | 175 SR/TR/HR 14, 185/70 HR/TR/VR 14, 195/65 HR 15, 205/60 VR 15 | |
| | **Front** | **Rear** |
| Tyre pressures: | | |
| Normal load ........................ | 1.8 bar (26 lbf/in²) | 1.8 bar (26 lbf/in²) |
| Full load ........................ | 2.1 bar (30 lbf/in²) | 2.9 bar (42 lbf/in²) |

## Torque wrench settings

| | Nm | lbf ft |
|---|---|---|
| *Steering* | | |
| Steering gear-to-crossmember bolts: | | |
| Stage 1 (clamping) ........................ | 45 | 33 |
| Slacken, then Stage 2 (snug) ........................ | 15 | 11 |
| Stage 3 ........................ | Tighten 90° further | Tighten 90° further |
| Track rod end balljoint nut ........................ | 25 to 30 | 18 to 22 |
| Track rod end locknut ........................ | 57 to 68 | 42 to 50 |
| Track rod inner balljoint nut ........................ | 75 | 55 |
| Intermediate shaft coupling pinch-bolts ........................ | 20 | 15 |
| Pinion retaining nut (manual steering) ........................ | 70 to 100 | 52 to 74 |
| Pinion shaft nut (power steering) ........................ | 37 to 47 | 27 to 34 |
| Slipper yoke plug (see text): | | |
| Manual steering ........................ | 4 to 5 | 3 to 4 |
| Power steering ........................ | 3 to 4 | 2 to 3 |
| Steering wheel nut ........................ | 45 to 55 | 33 to 41 |
| Steering column mounting nuts ........................ | 17 to 24 | 13 to 18 |
| Steering column adjuster pivot nut ........................ | 10 to 13 | 7 to 10 |
| Steering pump bracket to block ........................ | 52 to 64 | 38 to 47 |
| Steering pump pulley hub bolt ........................ | 10 to 12 | 7 to 9 |
| Pressure hose to steering pump ........................ | 26 to 31 | 19 to 23 |
| Steering pump bracket-to-engine mounting ........................ | 41 to 58 | 30 to 43 |
| Steering pump to bracket (V6) ........................ | 22 to 29 | 16 to 21 |
| *Front suspension* | | |
| Hub nut ........................ | 390 to 450 | 288 to 332 |
| Lower arm balljoint nut ........................ | 65 to 85 | 48 to 63 |
| Top mount retaining nuts ........................ | 20 to 24 | 15 to 18 |
| Stub axle carrier pinch-bolt ........................ | 80 to 90 | 59 to 66 |
| Anti-roll bar clamps ........................ | 70 to 90 | 52 to 66 |
| Anti-roll bar to lower arms ........................ | 70 to 110 | 52 to 81 |
| Crossmember to frame ........................ | 70 to 90 | 52 to 66 |
| Suspension strut to turret ........................ | 40 to 52 | 30 to 38 |
| Lower arm pivot: | | |
| Stage 1 (clamping) ........................ | 45 | 33 |
| Slacken, then Stage 2 (snug) ........................ | 15 | 11 |
| Stage 3 ........................ | Tighten 90° further | Tighten 90° further |
| *Rear suspension* | | |
| Final drive mounting to floor ........................ | 20 to 25 | 15 to 18 |
| Final drive mounting to rear cover ........................ | 40 to 50 | 30 to 37 |
| Guide plate-to-floor bolts ........................ | 41 to 51 | 30 to 38 |
| Guide plate insulator bolt ........................ | 69 to 88 | 51 to 65 |
| Lower arm to crossmember ........................ | 80 to 95 | 59 to 70 |
| Brake anchor plate to lower arm ........................ | 52 to 64 | 38 to 47 |
| Anti-roll bar bracket bolts ........................ | 20 to 25 | 15 to 18 |
| Shock absorber mountings: | | |
| Top ........................ | 73 to 97 | 54 to 72 |
| Bottom ........................ | 68 to 92 | 50 to 68 |
| Rear hub bolts ........................ | 80 to 100 | 59 to 74 |
| *Wheels* | | |
| Wheel nuts (steel or alloy wheels) ........................ | 70 to 100 | 52 to 74 |

## 1 General description

The steering gear is of rack-and-pinion type. Power assistance is standard on V6 models and optional on others. The power-assisted steering gear has a 'variable ratio' effect which increases the steering ratio about the straight-ahead position: this provides quick lock-to-lock action without the penalty of over-responsiveness in open road driving.

The steering wheel is adjustable both up-and-down and fore-and-aft. Both steering column and shaft are designed to collapse under impact. The steering shaft is connected to the pinion by an intermediate shaft, which has a universal joint at its upper end and a flexible coupling at the lower end.

Front suspension is independent, of the MacPherson strut type, with coil springs and concentric telescopic shock absorbers. The struts are attached to the tops of the stub axle carriers, which are located at their lower ends by balljoints incorporated in the lower suspension arms. The lower suspension arms pivot at their inner ends, where they are attached to a central crossmember. The anti-roll bar is attached to the rear of the arms and serves to control fore-and-aft movement as well as reducing roll.

Suspension geometry has been designed to give good steering 'feel', resistance to pulling caused by uneven braking effort or tyre deflation, and (in the case of manual steering) acceptably low steering wheel effort at parking speeds. Only toe is adjustable in service.

The rear suspension is also independent. It is of the semi-trailing arm type, with coil springs and separate telescopic shock absorbers. An optionally available ride height control system keeps the rear suspension height constant, regardless of vehicle load.

Both front and rear wheel bearings are of a special taper-roller type and require no periodic adjustment in service.

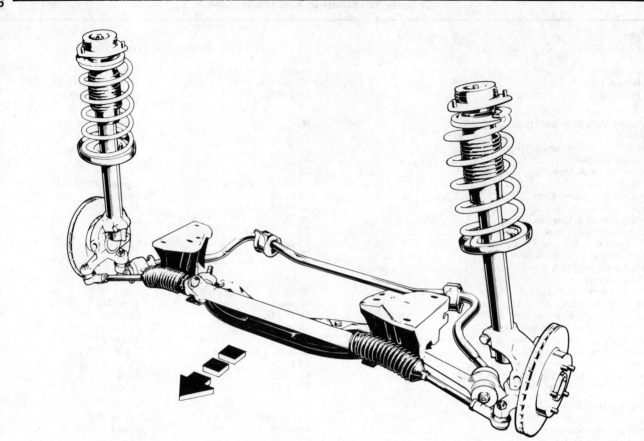

Fig. 10.1 Front suspension and steering components. Arrow points to front of vehicle (Sec 1)

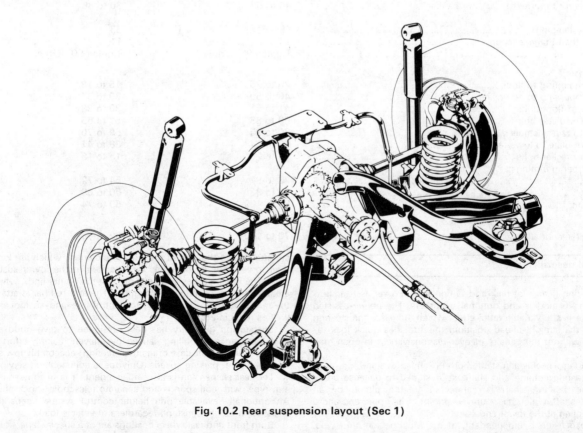

Fig. 10.2 Rear suspension layout (Sec 1)

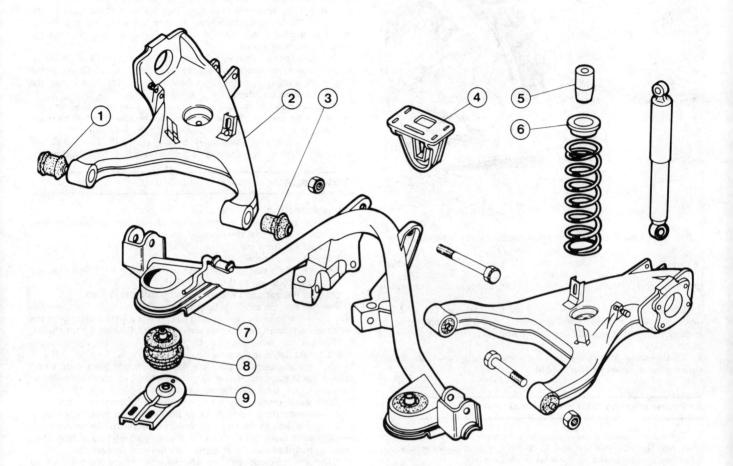

**Fig. 10.3 Rear suspension components (Sec 1)**

| | | | |
|---|---|---|---|
| 1 | Lower arm outer bush | 4 | Final drive rear mounting |
| 2 | Lower arm | 5 | Buffer |
| 3 | Lower arm inner bush | 6 | Spring seat |

| | | |
|---|---|---|
| 7 | Crossmember |
| 8 | Insulator |
| 9 | Guide plate |

## 2 Maintenance and inspection

1   Check the tyre pressures and inspect the tyres frequently – see Section 40 for details.

2   Make a thorough inspection of the tyres, preferably by removing the wheels, every 6000 miles or six months.

3   At the same intervals, if the wheels are not removed for tyre inspection the wheel nuts should be checked for tightness. With the wheels on the ground, slacken one wheel nut by a quarter turn, then retighten it immediately to the specified torque (photo). Repeat for all the wheel nuts.

4   Every 12 000 miles or twelve months, examine all steering and suspension components for wear and damage. Pay particular attention to dust covers and gaiters, which if renewed promptly when damaged can save further damage to the component protected.

5   At the same intervals, check the front suspension lower arm balljoints for wear by levering up the arms (see Fig. 10.4). Balljoint free movement must not exceed 0.5 mm (0.02 in). The track rod end balljoints can be checked in a similar manner, or by observing them whilst an assistant rocks the steering wheel back and forth. If the lower arm balljoint is worn, the complete lower arm must be renewed (Section 23). Track rod end renewal is described in Section 18.

6   Check the shock absorbers by bouncing the vehicle up and down at each corner in turn. When released, it should come to rest within one complete oscillation. Continued movement, or squeaking and

2.3 Tightening a wheel nut with a torque wrench

**Fig. 10.4 Checking a front suspension lower arm balljoint for wear (Sec 2)**

groaning noises from the shock absorber, suggest that renewal is required (Section 27 or 36).

7  On models with power steering, check the fluid level every 12 000 miles or twelve months. See Section 3 for details. If topping-up is needed, inspect the steering gear, hoses and pump for leaks and repair as necessary.

8  At the same intervals check the tension and condition of the steering pump drivebelt (Section 14).

## 3  Power steering fluid – level check and bleeding

1  The power steering fluid dipstick is incorporated in the reservoir filler cap. The reservoir is mounted on the pump. Observe scrupulous cleanliness when checking the level or topping-up.

2  The system should be at operating temperature and the engine switched off. Wipe clean around the reservoir filler cap. Unscrew the cap, withdraw the dipstick and wipe it with a clean lint-free rag. Reinsert the dipstick, screw the cap home, then unscrew it again and read the level on the dipstick. It should be up to the 'MAX' or upper 'HOT' mark (depending on the dipstick markings) (photo).

3  Top up if necessary with clean fluid of the specified type. Check for leaks if topping-up is frequently required.

4  If the level is checked cold, use the 'MIN' or 'FULL COLD' mark on the dipstick for reference. Recheck the level at operating temperature.

3.2 Removing the power steering fluid dipstick

5  If the fluid level falls so low that air enters the pump, or after component renewal, the system must be bled as follows.

6  Remove the reservoir filler cap. Top up with clean fluid to the appropriate 'cold' level (paragraph 4). It is important that the fluid is free of air bubbles, so do not shake the container when topping-up, and pour the fluid slowly.

7  Disconnect the negative LT lead from the ignition coil. Have an assistant crank the engine on the starter in two second bursts, at the same time turning the steering wheel from lock to lock. Keep the reservoir topped up whilst this is going on.

8  When air bubbles no longer appear in the fluid, stop the cranking. Reconnect the coil negative lead and run the engine for a few seconds, then stop it and check the level again. Refit the filler cap.

9  Run the vehicle for a few miles to warm up the fluid and expel any remaining air, then stop the engine and make a final fluid level check.

## 4  Steering gear – removal and refitting

### Manual steering

1  Position the steering in the straight-ahead position, then remove the ignition key so that the steering is locked.

2  Slacken the front wheel nuts. Raise and support the front of the vehicle and remove the front wheels.

3  Remove the pinch-bolt and nut which secure the intermediate shaft flexible coupling to the pinion shaft.

4  Slacken the track rod end locknuts by half a turn each.

5  Remove the splitpin from the track rod balljoint nuts. Unscrew the nuts, break the balljoint tapers using a separator tool and disengage the track rod ends from the steering arms. Refer to Section 18 for details.

6  Remove the two bolts which secure the steering gear to the crossmember. Lift out the steering gear.

7  Mark the positions of the track rod ends on the track rods, using paint or sticky tape, so that they can be refitted in approximately the same positions. Unscrew the track rod ends and locknuts.

8  Commence refitting by screwing on the locknuts and track rod ends, observing the previously made position marks when applicable.

9  Bring the rack to the straight-ahead position. Do this by counting the number of turns of the pinion needed to go from lock to lock, then applying half that number of turns from full lock on one side.

10 Offer the steering gear to the vehicle, engaging the flexible coupling and loosely fitting the securing bolts. Note that the master spline on the pinion shaft mates with the corresponding groove in the flexible coupling.

11 Tighten the two steering gear-to-crossmember bolts to the specified Stage 1 torque. Slacken the bolts and retighten to the Stage 2 torque. Finally tighten the bolts through the angle specified for Stage 3.

12 Make sure that the flexible coupling and pinion shaft are properly engaged, then fit the pinch-bolt and nut. Tighten the pinch-bolt to the specified torque.

13 Refit the track rod ends to the steering arms. Fit the balljoint nuts and tighten them to the specified torque, then secure with new split pins.

14 Nip up the track rod end locknuts, but do not tighten them fully yet.

15 Refit the front wheels and wheel nuts. Lower the vehicle and tighten the wheel nuts to the specified torque.

16 Check the toe setting as described in Section 19. When toe is correct, tighten the track rod end locknuts fully.

### Power-assisted steering

17 Proceed as described for manual steering gear, but before removing the steering gear-to-crossmember bolts, remove the clamp plate bolt from the steering gear valve body (photo).

18 Pull the fluid pipes out of the valve body. Be prepared for fluid spillage. Plug or cap the open pipes and orifices.

19 The steering gear may now be removed.

20 Refit in the reverse order to removal, using new O-rings on the fluid pipes.

21 Bleed the steering gear hydraulic system on completion (Sec 3).

## 5  Steering gear (manual) – overhaul

1  Before deciding to overhaul the steering gear, check the price and availability of components and the price of a new or reconditioned

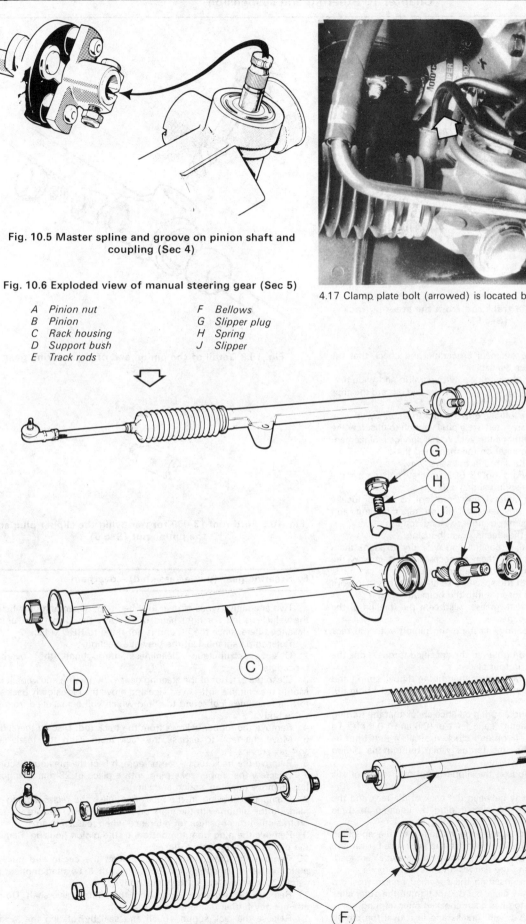

Fig. 10.5 Master spline and groove on pinion shaft and coupling (Sec 4)

Fig. 10.6 Exploded view of manual steering gear (Sec 5)

A  Pinion nut
B  Pinion
C  Rack housing
D  Support bush
E  Track rods

F  Bellows
G  Slipper plug
H  Spring
J  Slipper

4.17 Clamp plate bolt (arrowed) is located between two fluid pipes

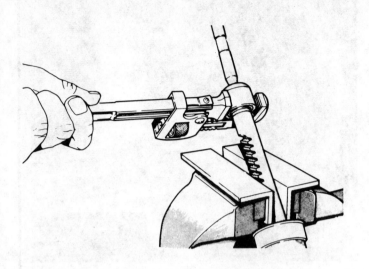

**Fig. 10.7 Unscrewing a track rod from the steering rack (Sec 5)**

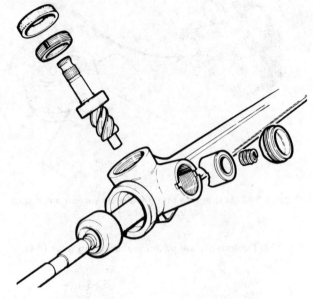

**Fig. 10.8 Detail of the pinion end of the steering gear (Sec 5)**

**Fig. 10.9 Ford tool 13-009 for removing the slipper plug and the pinion nut (Sec 5)**

unit. Also read through the overhaul procedure and check that the tools and facilities needed are available.

2　Clean the exterior of the steering gear with paraffin and wipe dry.

3　Mount the steering gear in a vice, then remove and discard the clips and slide the rubber bellows off the track rods.

4　Move the rack fully to the left and grip the rack in a soft jawed vice.

5　If the original track rods are fitted use a pipe wrench to unscrew the balljoint from the rack and remove the track rod. If service replacement track rods are fitted use a spanner on the machined flats.

6　Remove the right-hand track rod in the same way.

7　Using a hexagon key, or Ford tool 13-009, unscrew and remove the slipper plug and remove the spring and slipper.

8　Remove the pinion dust cover. Using Ford tool 13-009 or locally made four segment tool, unscrew the pinion retaining nut and withdraw the pinion and bearing using a twisting action.

9　Withdraw the rack from the steering gear housing.

10　Clean all the components in paraffin and wipe dry. Examine them for wear and damage and renew them as necessary. If necessary the rack support bush in the housing can be renewed.

11　Lightly coat the rack with the specified semi-fluid grease (to Ford spec. SLM-1C-9110A) and insert it into the housing.

12　Fill the pinion housing with grease. Also coat the threads of the pinion retaining nut with the grease.

13　Refit the pinion and bearing, meshing the pinion with the rack teeth.

14　Fit the remaining nut and tighten to the specified torque. Lock the nut by peening the housing in four places.

15　Move the rack to its central position then fit the slipper, spring and plug, and tighten the plug to the specified torque. Loosen the plug 60° to 70°.

16　Using a piece of string and a spring balance check that the turning torque of the pinion is between 0.8 and 1.4 Nm (0.6 and 1.0 lbf ft). To do this accurately turn the pinion anti-clockwise half a turn from its central position and measure the torque while turning the pinion clockwise through one complete turn.

17　If necessary tighten or loosen the slipper plug until the torque is correct.

18　There must be no free play between the back of the rack and the slipper. When satisfied, lock the slipper plug by peening in three places.

19　Refit the track rods and tighten the balljoints to the specified torque. When doing this, make sure that the rack itself (not the housing) is clamped in the vice, otherwise the pinion may be damaged. Lock the balljoints by peening the flanges into the rack groove.

20　Refit the rubber bellows, inserting the specified grease (to Ford spec. SM1C-1021-A). Fit new clips, but do not tighten the outer clips yet – leave them slack until toe has been checked after refitting.

21　Load the pinion dust cover with grease and fit it over the pinion shaft.

## 6　Steering gear (power-assisted) – overhaul

Two alternative types of gear may be fitted, depending on whether the vehicle is left- or right-hand drive. Only the Cam Gears unit is described here, since the ZF unit is not fitted to RHD vehicles.

1　Refer to paragraph 1 of the previous Section.

2　Observe scrupulous cleanliness throughout the overhaul procedure.

3　Clean the exterior of the steering gear with paraffin and wipe it dry. Mount the unit in a soft-jawed vice and move the rack slowly back and forth a few times, collecting the fluid which will be expelled from the valve body.

4　Remove the rubber bellows from the track rod. Discard the clips.

5　Move the rack to expose the rack teeth. Grip the teeth in a soft-jawed vice.

6　Remove the track rods – see paragraph 5 of the previous Section.

7　Unscrew the slipper yoke plug with a piece of 28 mm hexagonal bar. Remove the plug, spring and slipper.

8　Clamp the housing in the vice. Centralise the rack, aligning the mark on the pinion with the mark on the valve body. Record the rack protrusion in this position for reference when reassembling.

9　Remove the plug from the bottom of the pinion housing. Remove the pinion shaft nut now exposed.

10　Remove the pinion dust cover. Extract the circlip and pull the pinion/valve shaft out of the housing with a twisting motion. Be careful to keep dirt out of the valve body.

11　Remove the seal and bearing from the pinion/valve shaft. Do not attempt any further dismantling of this item.

12　Release the rack support bush and seal by rotating the locking collar anti-clockwise with a hammer and punch. Prise the locking wire

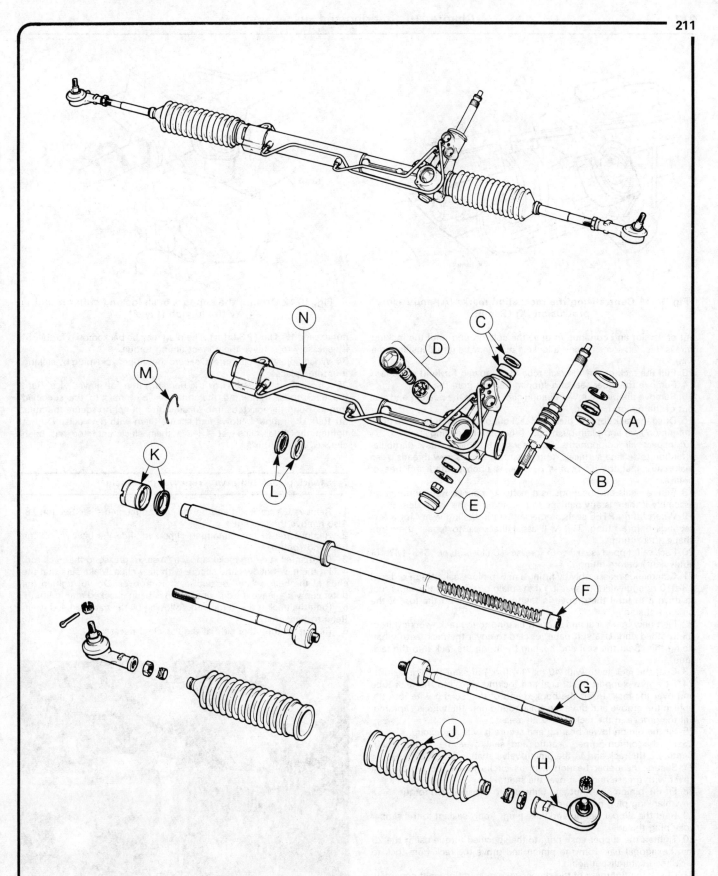

**Fig. 10.10 Exploded view of the power steering gear (Sec 6)**

A  Pinion dust cover, circlip  
   and seal  
B  Pinion  
C  Pinion upper bearing  

D  Slipper assembly  
E  Pinion lower bearing  
F  Rack  
G  Track rod  

H  Track rod end  
J  Bellows  
K  Rack support bush and seal  

L  Inner seals  
M  Locking wire  
N  Rack tube

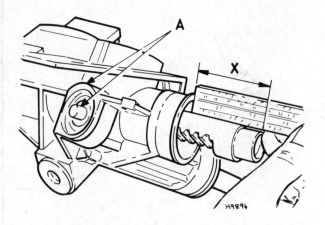

Fig. 10.11 Centralising the rack: align marks (A) and record protrusion (X) (Sec 6)

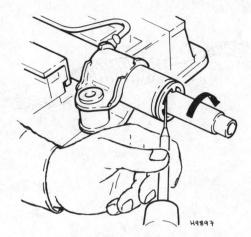

Fig. 10.12 Driving the support bush locking collar round with a punch (Sec 6)

out of its slot and continue to drive the collar round until the locking wire is free. On some models a locking plug may be found instead of a wire.

13  Pull the rack out of the rack tube. Be prepared for fluid spillage.

14  Remove the inner seal and support bearing from the rack.

15  Remove the pinion lower bearing circlip. Drive the bearing and seal out of the pinion housing.

16  Drive the rack support bush and seal out of the rack tube. Also drive the pinion seal and plain bush out of the pinion housing.

17  Inspect all components for wear and damage. Pay particular attention to sealing surfaces, rubbing surfaces and screw threads. Also make sure that the air bypass passage is unobstructed and free of grease.

18  Renew seals and bearings as a matter of course. Renew the valve assembly if there is any damage to the pinion or the valve sleeve.

19  When fitting PTFE seals, immerse them in boiling water for a few seconds before fitting. This will assist the seals to regain their true shape after fitting.

20  Pack all lipped seals with grease (Calipsol type SF3-137, or equivalent) before fitting.

21  Commence reassembly by fitting a new pinion seal, using Ford tool 13-010 or equivalent to seat it. Fit the plain bush, using the same tool to drive it in until the groove in the tool is level with the top of the pinion housing.

22  Fit a new inner seal and support bearing to the rack, working from the toothed end. Use stiff paper or card to cover the rack teeth when doing this. Seat the seal and bearing by fitting the rack into the rack tube.

23  Coat the rack teeth with 40 ml (1.4 fl oz) of semi-fluid grease.

24  Fit a new support bush, seal and locking wire into the rack tube and over the rack. Insert the hooked end of the locking wire into the hole in the groove and drive the collar round until the wire is captured. Fill the groove in the rack tube with grease.

25  Fit the pinion lower bearing and secure it with the circlip.

26  Fit the pinion upper bearing and seal over the pinion shaft. Centralise the rack and fit the pinion/valve shaft.

27  Secure the upper bearing with its circlip. Load the pinion dust cover with grease and fit it over the shaft.

28  Fit the pinion shaft nut and tighten it to the specified torque. Fit a new blanking plug over the nut.

29  Refit the slipper, spring and yoke plug. Apply sealant to the slipper yoke plug threads.

30  Tighten the slipper yoke plug to the specified torque using the 28 mm hexagonal bar. Turn the pinion and move the rack from lock to lock, then centralise it again.

31  Check the tightness of the slipper yoke plug; retighten if necessary to the specified torque.

32  Check the pinion turning torque, using a piece of cord and a spring balance or similar equipment. It should be not less than 1.4 Nm (1.0 lbf ft).

33  Unscrew the slipper yoke plug by 22° to 27° (approximately one-sixteenth of a turn). Check the pinion turning torque again: it must

not exceed 1.7 Nm (1.3 lbf ft). The plug may be backed off a further 5° if necessary to achieve the correct timing torque.

34  When adjustment is correct, secure the slipper yoke plug by staking it in three places.

35  Clamp the rack teeth (**not** the housing) in a soft-jawed vice. Refit the track rods, tightening the inner balljoint nuts to the specified torque. Bend the locktabs into place with a punch to secure the nuts.

36  Refit the rubber bellows and secure them with new clips. Do not tighten the outer clips yet – leave them slack until toe has been checked after refitting.

## 7  Steering rack bellows – renewal in vehicle

1  Remove the track rod end on the side concerned – see Section 18. Also remove the locknut.

2  Remove the bellows retaining clips and slide the bellows off the track rod (photo).

3  On manual steering racks, apply a smear of grease to the track rod.

4  Fit the new bellows and secure with new clips. Make sure that the ends of the bellows are located in their grooves. Do not tighten the outer clip yet – leave it slack until toe has been checked after refitting.

5  Refit the track rod end locknut, followed by the track rod end itself. Refer to Section 18.

6  Repeat on the other side of the vehicle if necessary.

7.2 Steering rack bellows retaining clips (arrowed)

## 8  Steering wheel – removal and refitting

1   Disconnect the battery negative lead.
2   Prise off the horn push pad from the centre of the steering wheel.
3   Remove the three screws which secure the horn switch plate. Withdraw the plate, disconnect its wires and remove it.
4   Engage the steering lock, then undo and remove the steering wheel nut (photo). Unlock the steering again.
5   Mark the relationship of the wheel to the shaft, then pull the wheel off the shaft. Use a puller if it cannot be removed by hand. Do not use hammer blows, which may damage the collapsible parts of the column and shaft.
6   Recover the spacer from below the steering wheel (photo).
7   Refit by reversing the removal operations. Tighten the steering wheel nut to the specified torque.

## 9  Steering wheel – centralising

1   This operation is for correcting small errors in steering wheel centralisation – up to 60°. For larger errors, remove the steering wheel and make a rough correction by repositioning the wheel on refitting.
2   Drive the vehicle in a straight line on a level surface. Note the angle by which the steering wheel deviates from the desired straight-ahead position.
3   Raise the front of the vehicle by driving it onto ramps, or with a jack and axle stands.
4   Slacken both track rod end locknuts. Also slacken the steering rack bellows outer clips.
5   Make alignment marks between each track rod end and its rod, so that the amount of rotation applied can be accurately determined.
6   Turn both track rods **in the same direction** to correct the steering wheel position. As a rough guide, 19° of track rod rotation will change the steering wheel position by 1°. To correct error at the steering wheel, rotate both track rods anti-clockwise (viewed from the left-hand side of the vehicle), and the reverse to correct as anti-clockwise errors. *Both track rods must be rotated by the same amount.*
7   Tighten the bellows clips and the track rod end locknuts when adjustment is correct. Lower the vehicle.

## 10  Steering column – removal and refitting

1   Disconnect the battery negative lead.
2   Position the steering in the straight-ahead position.
3   Remove the steering wheel as described in Section 8. (This is not essential, but will improve access.)
4   Working under the bonnet, disconnect the intermediate shaft universal joint from the steering column shaft. Make alignment marks between the two shafts for reference when reassembling.
5   Remove the steering column shrouds and disconnect the switch multi-plugs. Do not forget the ignition/starter switch.
6   Disconnect the bonnet release cable from the operating lever on the underside of the column.
7   Prise out the driver's side air vent. Remove the under-dash insulation and trim panel on the driver's side, unclipping the bulb failure module, where applicable.
8   Remove the three nuts which secure the column height adjuster to the mounting bracket (photo). Remove the column assembly by drawing it into the vehicle. Do not drop it or otherwise mistreat it if it is to be re-used.
9   When refitting, have an assistant guide the column shaft into the intermediate shaft universal joint. Secure the column with the three nuts inside the vehicle and adjust it to the minimum length position, then tighten the coupling pinch-bolt.
10  Complete refitting by reversing the removal operations.

## 11  Steering column – dismantling and reassembly

1   Before dismantling the steering column for repair, check the cost and availability of spare parts.
2   With the column removed from the vehicle and the steering wheel removed, begin by slackening the height adjuster pinch-bolt.

8.4 Undoing the steering wheel nut

8.6 Spacer ring (arrowed) fits below steering wheel

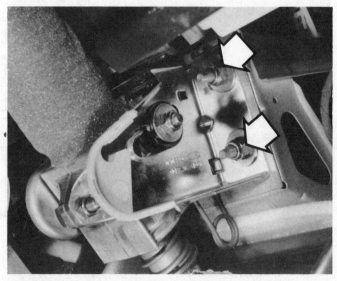
10.8 Two of the three nuts (arrowed) which secure the column height adjuster

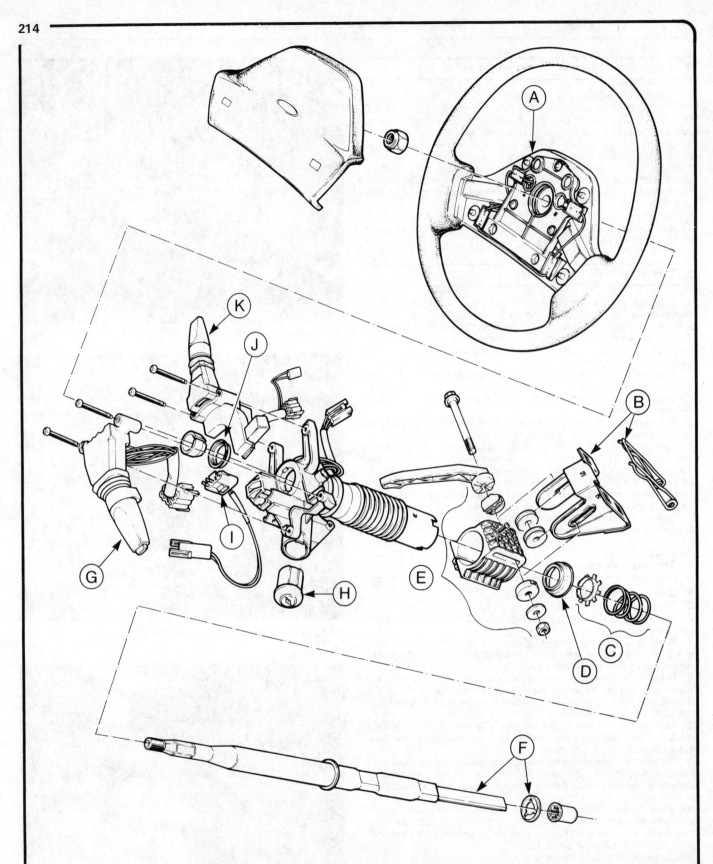

**Fig. 10.13 Exploded view of steering wheel and column (Sec 11)**

A   Steering wheel
B   Mounting bracket and spring
C   Thrust washer and spring

D   Lower bearing
E   Height adjuster
F   Column shaft and spire washer

G   Multi-function switch
H   Ignition/steering lock
I   Horn brush unit

J   Upper bearing
K   Multi-function switch

3   Spread the adjuster by inserting a screwdriver into its slot. Separate the shaft lower bearing from the adjuster.

4   Slacken the adjuster body screw so that it protrudes by approximately 5 mm (0.2 in). Draw the shaft out of the column tube.

5   The spire washer, spring and lower bearing can now be slid off the shaft.

6   From the bottom of the shaft remove the bulkhead bush and spire washer.

7   If not already done, remove the multi-function switches from the steering column.

8   Remove the steering column lock as described in the next Section. Also remove the ignition/starter switch.

9   Unclip the horn brush unit and remove it.

10  Separate the height adjuster and its bracket from the column tube.

11  The upper bearing can now be prised out of the column tube.

12  If it is wished to dismantle the height adjuster, take care when releasing the spring as it is under tension. Remove the pivot bolt and adjusting lever, followed by the spring and slides. Note the fitted sequence of the various washers. Use thread locking compound on the pivot nut when reassembling.

13  Commence reassembly by fitting the assembled height adjuster to the column tube.

14  Refit the lower bearing to the adjuster, again using a scerwdriver to spread the adjuster.

15  Fit the upper bearing, using a tube or socket to seat it.

16  Refit the horn brush unit.

17  Refit the ignition/starter switch, the steering column lock and the multi-function switches.

18  Fit a new spire washer and the bulkhead bush. Hold the triangular part of the shaft and push the bush up the shaft until the lower end of the bush is 54 ± 1 mm (2.13 ± 0.04 in) from the lower end of the shaft.

19  Fit the spring and a new spire washer to the shaft. Insert the shaft into the column tube.

20  Tighten the height adjuster body screw.

21  Refit the steering column assembly to the vehicle.

## 12  Steering column lock – removal and refitting

1   Remove the steering column as described in Section 10.

2   Insert the key into the lock and turn it to position I. (If the lock has failed so that the key will not enter, destructive methods will have to be used).

3   Depress the locking button with a small screwdriver. Draw the lock barrel out of its housing using the key (photos).

4   Refit by reversing the removal operations.

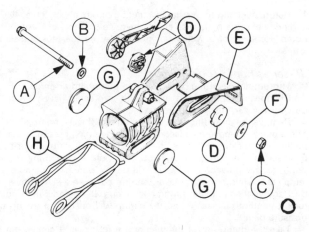

**Fig. 10.14 Exploded view of column height adjuster (Sec 11)**

| | |
|---|---|
| A   *Pivot bolt* | E   *Bracket* |
| B   *Plastic washer (not fitted to* | F   *Washer* |
|     *all models)* | G   *Slides* |
| C   *Nut* | H   *Spring* |
| D   *Guides* | |

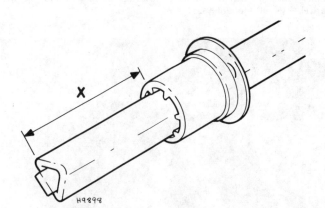

**Fig. 10.15 Spire washer and bulkhead bush correctly fitted (Sec 11)**

$X = 54 \pm 1$ mm $(2.13 \pm 0.04$ in$)$

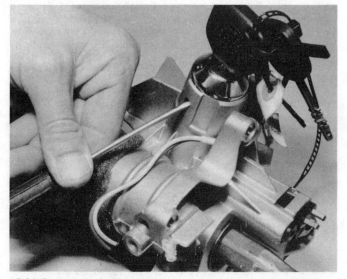

12.3A Depress the locking button ...

12.3B ... and withdraw the lock

### 13 Steering intermediate shaft and flexible coupling – removal and refitting

1   The intermediate shaft and flexible coupling are not available separately, and so must be renewed as a unit.
2   Disconnect the battery negative lead.
3   Position the steering straight-ahead.
4   Remove the pinch-bolts which secure the upper and lower ends of the intermediate shaft. Free the universal joint from the column shaft, then pull the flexible coupling off the pinion shaft.
5   When refitting, engage the master spline on the pinion shaft with the groove in the flexible coupling.
6   Tighten the pinch-bolts to the specified torque.
7   Reconnect the battery.

### 14 Steering pump drivebelt – removal, refitting and tensioning

1   Disconnect the battery negative lead.
2   On models with air conditioning, remove the compressor drivebelt.
3   On ohc models, slacken the alternator adjusting strap and pivot bolts. Push the alternator in towards the engine and slip the drivebelt(s) off the pulleys.
4   On V6 models, slacken the steering pump adjusting strap and pivot bolts (photo). Push the pump in towards the engine and slip the drivebelt(s) off the pulleys.

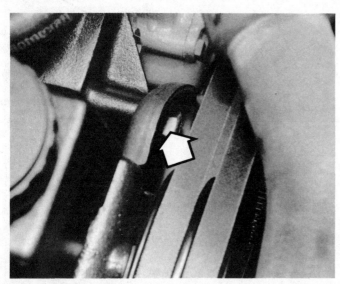

14.4 Steering pump pivot bolt (arrowed) – V6

5   On all models, examine the drivebelt(s) for cracks, fraying or other damage. Renew the belt if in doubt. When twin drivebelts are fitted, both must be renewed together even if only one is damaged or broken.
6   Feed the belt(s) over the pulleys, then adjust the tension as follows.
7   Nip up the alternator or steering pump fastenings so that the component can be moved by hand but will not move under its own weight.
8   Push or lever the alternator or steering pump away from the engine until the belt tension is correct, then tighten the adjusting strap and pivot bolts. Only use a wooden or plastic lever; do not lever against the steering pump reservoir.
9   Belt tension is correct when the belt can be deflected by 10 to 13 mm (0.4 to 0.5 in) under firm finger pressure in the middle of the longest run.
10  On models so equipped, refit and tension the air conditioning compressor drivebelt.

11  Reconnect the battery and run the engine for a few minutes, then stop the engine and recheck the belt tension.
12  Recheck the tension of a new drivebelt after a few hundred miles.

### 15 Steering pump – removal and refitting

1   Disconnect the battery negative lead.
2   Wipe clean around the unions, then disconnect the high pressure and return pipes from the pump and the reservoir. Be prepared for fluid spillage; take steps to keep fluid out of the alternator.
3   Remove the pump drivebelt(s) as described in the previous Section.
4   Remove the pump mounting, pivot and adjustment bolts (as applicable) and lift the pump from the engine.
5   If a new pump is to be fitted, recover the pulley and mounting plate from the old pump.
6   Refit by reversing the removal operations. Adjust the drivebelt tension on completion (Section 14) and bleed the steering hydraulic system (Section 3).

### 16 Steering pump – overhaul

1   Before deciding to overhaul a steering pump, check the availability and price of spare parts; also check the price of a new or reconditioned pump. Renewal of a well worn pump may be the most satisfactory course.

*'P' series pump (ohc models)*
2   Thoroughly clean the outside of the pump and reservoir.
3   Clamp the pump in a vice with protected jaws, shaft side downwards. **Do not** clamp on the reservoir.
4   Remove the mounting stud, the union and the O-ring from the back of the pump. Remove the reservoir from the pump housing by carefully pulling and rocking it free. Retrieve the O-rings from the housing.
5   Insert a pin punch or nail into the hole in the pump housing opposite the flow control valve. Press the punch to compress the endplate retaining ring and lever the ring out with a screwdriver.
6   Remove the endplate, spring and O-ring. If the endplate is not free rock it gently to release it and the spring will push it up. Remove the pressure plate.
7   Take the pump out of the vice and turn it over. Remove the flow control valve and its spring.
8   Remove the circlip from the pump shaft and push out the shaft. Do not attempt to separate the pulley flange from the shaft.
9   Remove the pump ring, vanes, rotor and thrust plate. Extract the pressure plate O-ring.
10  Extract the two dowel pins from the housing and remove the shaft seal, taking care not to damage the seal housing.
11  Remove the magnet and clean it, noting its location for reassembly. Keep it away from ferrous metal filings.
12  Clean all metal components in a suitable solvent and dry them. Scrupulous cleanliness must be observed from now on.
13  Fit a new pump shaft seal to the housing, using a socket or tube and a hammer to drive it home. Refit the shaft.
14  Fit a new pressure plate O-ring into the third groove from the rear of the housing (Fig. 10.20). Lubricate the O-ring with power steering fluid.
15  Mount the housing in the vice and fit the two dowel pins.
16  Fit the thrust plate and rotor onto the shaft, with the countersunk side of the rotor facing the thrust plate. Make sure the thrust plate holes engage with the dowel pins.
17  Fit the pump ring onto the dowel pins with the arrow on the rim of the ring uppermost (Fig. 10.21). Fit the ten vanes into the rotor slots, rounded ends outwards. Make sure the vanes slide freely.
18  Refit the circlip to the end of the pump shaft. Refit the magnet in the housing.
19  Lubricate the pressure plate with power steering fluid and fit it over the dowel pins. Make sure the spring seat is uppermost. Press the plate a little way below the O-ring to seat it.
20  Lubricate and fit the endplate O-ring in the second groove from the end. Fit the endplate spring, lubricate the endplate and press it into position so that the retaining ring can be fitted. (It may be necessary to use a G-clamp or similar device to keep the endplate depressed whilst the ring is fitted. Do not depress the plate further than necessary).

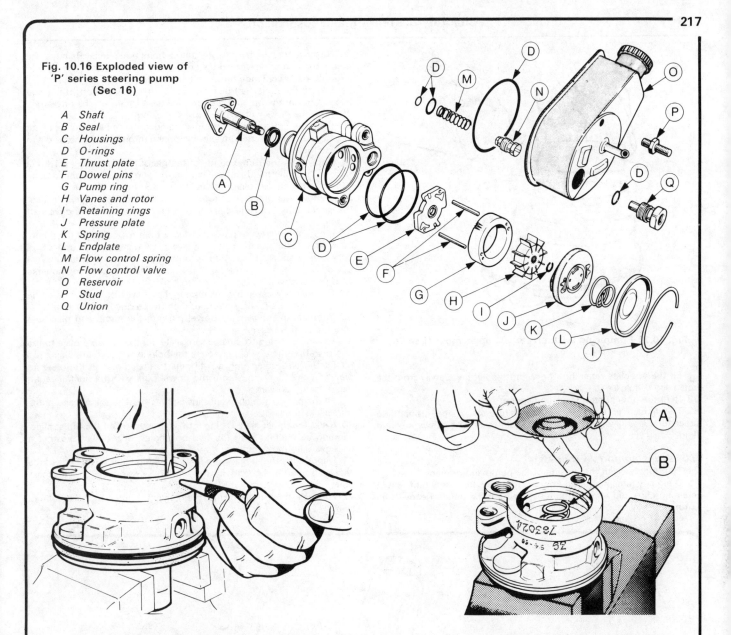

Fig. 10.16 Exploded view of 'P' series steering pump (Sec 16)

A  Shaft
B  Seal
C  Housings
D  O-rings
E  Thrust plate
F  Dowel pins
G  Pump ring
H  Vanes and rotor
I  Retaining rings
J  Pressure plate
K  Spring
L  Endplate
M  Flow control spring
N  Flow control valve
O  Reservoir
P  Stud
Q  Union

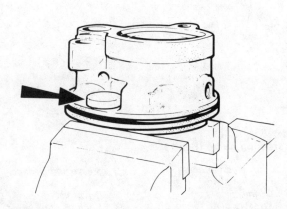

Fig. 10.17 Removing the steering pump endplate retaining ring (Sec 16)

Fig. 10.18 Removing the steering pump endplate (A) and spring (B) (Sec 16)

Fig. 10.19 Steering pump magnet (arrowed) (Sec 16)

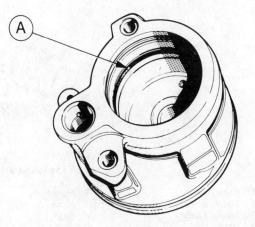

Fig. 10.20 Pressure plate O-ring (A) in third groove (Sec 16)

**Fig. 10.21 Pump ring with arrow (A) uppermost (Sec 16)**

21 Fit the endplate retaining ring with its open ends away from the hole used to release it.
22 Refit the flow control valve and spring.
23 The remainder of reassembly is a reversal of the dismantling procedure. Use new O-rings and lubricate them with power steering fluid.

### 'TC' series pump (V6 models)

24 Thoroughly clean the outside of the pump and reservoir.
25 Drain any remaining fluid from the reservoir, then slide off the two retaining clips and remove the reservoir from the pump. Recover the O-ring.

26 Unscrew the high pressure union from the pump. Remove the union, the control valve and the spring.
27 Pull the drive flange off the pump driveshaft.
28 Extract the driveshaft bearing circlip, then pull the driveshaft and bearing out of the pump. Press or drive the bearing off the driveshaft.
29 Prise the driveshaft seal out of its housing.
30 From the other side of the pump, remove the thrust plate retaining circlip. Use a small screwdriver or pin punch through the access hole to release the circlip.
31 Apply pressure to the centre of the pressure plate, using a 13 mm (0.5 in) bar from the driveshaft side of the pump, until the thrust plate can be removed. Recover the thrust plate O-ring.
32 Remove the pump ring, rotor, vanes and pressure plate. Recover the dowel pins, pressure plate O-ring and spring, and the driveshaft O-ring.
33 If necessary, drive or press the sleeve from the centre of the pump.
34 Examine all components for wear or damage and renew as necessary. Renew all seals and O-rings as a matter of course. Observe scrupulous cleanliness during reassembly and lubricate components with power steering fluid.
35 Commence reassembly by pressing the sleeve into the centre of the pump. Make sure it is fully seated, then fit the driveshaft O-ring.
36 Insert the pressure plate dowel pin into the pump and place the spring over the sleeve.
37 Fit a new O-ring to the pressure plate. Fit the pressure plate to the pump so that the dowel pin enters the hole in the pressure plate.
38 Fit the two pump ring dowel pins to their holes in the pressure plate. Fit the pump ring onto the dowel pins with the identification marks facing upwards.
39 Fit the pump rotor and vanes inside the ring. The splined end of the rotor faces upwards.
40 Insert the thrust plate O-ring into its groove. Insert the thrust plate, aligning its dimples with the two bolt holes; also make sure that it engages with the pump ring dowel pins.
41 Depress the thrust plate and fit its retaining circlip. The ends of the circlip should be aligned with the bolt hole nearest the circlip access hole.
42 Fit a new driveshaft seal into the housing, using a socket or tube to seat it.

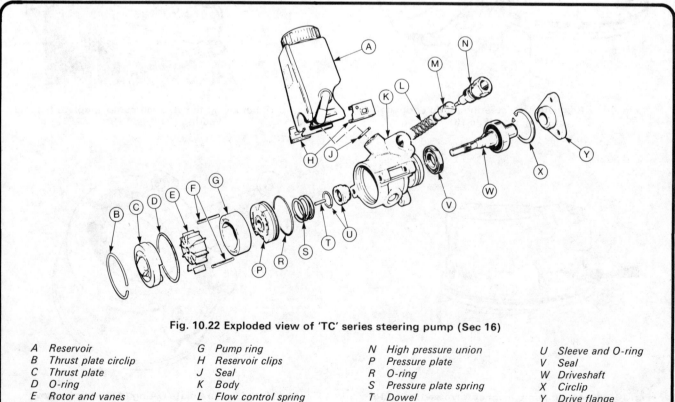

**Fig. 10.22 Exploded view of 'TC' series steering pump (Sec 16)**

| | | | |
|---|---|---|---|
| A  Reservoir | G  Pump ring | N  High pressure union | U  Sleeve and O-ring |
| B  Thrust plate circlip | H  Reservoir clips | P  Pressure plate | V  Seal |
| C  Thrust plate | J  Seal | R  O-ring | W  Driveshaft |
| D  O-ring | K  Body | S  Pressure plate spring | X  Circlip |
| E  Rotor and vanes | L  Flow control spring | T  Dowel | Y  Drive flange |
| F  Dowels | M  Control valve | | |

43 Press a new bearing onto the driveshaft, applying pressure to the bearing inner race. Insert the driveshaft into the pump, turning it to engage the splines.
44 Fit the bearing retaining circlip, chamfered edge outwards.
45 Fit the control valve spring, control valve and high pressure union. Use a new O-ring on the union.
46 Fit the flange to the driveshaft. Draw it onto the driveshaft using a bolt screwed into the driveshaft and some spacers.
47 Fit a new reservoir O-ring to the pump housing.
48 Refit the reservoir and secure it with the spring clips.

## 17 Power steering hoses – removal and refitting

1 Disconnect the battery negative lead.
2 Clean around the hose unions on the steering gear. Remove the single securing bolt, withdraw the hoses and catch the fluid which will drain from the reservoir.
3 Clean around the hose unions on the pump. Disconnect the unions and remove the hoses.
4 Refit in the reverse order to removal, using new O-rings.
5 Top up the steering fluid and bleed the system (Section 3).

## 18 Track rod end – removal and refitting

1 Slacken the front wheel nuts, raise and support the vehicle and remove the front wheel on the side concerned.
2 Slacken the track rod end locknut by half a turn.
3 Remove the split pin from the track rod end balljoint nut. Unscrew the nut a few turns (photo).
4 Break the balljoint taper with a proprietary balljoint separator (photo). Remove the separator and the nut and disengage the track rod end from the steering arm.
5 Unscrew the track rod end from the track rod, being careful not to disturb the locknut.
6 When refitting, screw the track rod end onto the track rod as far as the locknut, then back it off half a turn.
7 Insert the ball-pin into the steering arm. Tighten the balljoint nut to the specified torque and secure with a new split pin. Nip up the track rod end locknut, but do not tighten it fully yet.
8 Refit the roadwheel, lower the vehicle and tighten the wheel nuts to the specified torque.
9 Check the toe setting as described in Section 19. (This may not be strictly necessary if the same track rod end has been refitted, but is certainly advisable if any components have been renewed.)
10 Tighten the track rod end locknut when toe it correct.

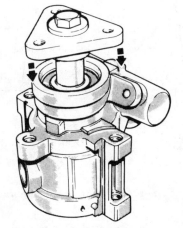

**Fig. 10.23 Drawing on the pump driveshaft flange (Sec 16)**

## 19 Front wheel alignment – checking and adjusting

1 Front wheel alignment is defined by camber, castor, steering axis inclination and toe setting. The first three factors are determined in production; only toe can be adjusted in service. Incorrect toe will cause rapid tyre wear.
2 Toe is defined as the amount by which the distance between the front wheels, measured at hub height, differs from the front edges to the rear edges. If the distance between the front edges is less than that at the rear, the wheels are said to toe-in; the opposite case is known as toe-out.
3 To measure toe, it will be necesary to obtain or make a tracking gauge. These are available in motor accessory shops, or one can be made from a length of rigid pipe or bar with some kind of threaded adjustment facility at one end. Many tyre specialists will also check toe free, or for a nominal sum.
4 Before measuring toe, check that all steering and suspension components are undamaged and that tyre pressures are correct. The vehicle must be at approximately kerb weight, with the spare wheel and jack in their normal positions and any abnormal loads removed.
5 Park the vehicle on level ground and bounce it a few times to settle the suspension.

18.3 Track rod end balljoint nut unscrewed

18.4 Using a balljoint separator

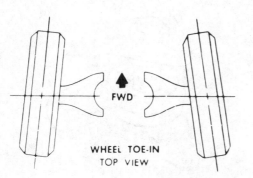

**Fig. 10.24 Front wheel toe-in (greatly exaggerated) (Sec 19)**

6   Use the tracking gauge to measure the distance between the inside faces of the front wheel rims, at hub height, at the rear of the front wheels. Record this distance; call it measurement 'A'.
7   Push the vehicle forwards or backwards so that the wheels rotate exactly 180° (half a turn). Measure the distance between the front wheel rims again, this time at the front of the wheels. Record this distance; call it measurement 'B'.
8   Subtract measurement 'B' from measurement 'A'. If the answer is positive it is the amount of toe-in; if negative it is the amount of toe-out. Permissible values are given in the Specifications.
9   If adjustment is necessary loosen the track rod end locknuts and the outer bellows clips, then rotate each track rod by equal amounts until the setting is correct. Hold the track rod ends in their horizontal position with a spanner while making the adjustment.
10  Tighten the locknuts and outer bellows clips.
11  Provided the track rods have been adjusted by equal amounts the steering wheel should be central when moving straight-ahead. The amount of visible thread on each track rod should also be equal. If necessary refer to Section 9.

## 20 Front suspension crossmember – removal and refitting

1   Disconnect the battery negative lead.
2   Raise and securely support the front of the vehicle.
3   Remove the suspension lower arm pivot nuts and bolts (photo). Disengage the arms from the crossmember.

4   Disconnect the steering column shaft from the intermedaiate shaft universal joint.
5   Remove the two bolts which secure the steering gear to the crossmember. Draw the steering gear forwards so that it.is clear of the crossmember and support it by wiring it to the frame rails.
6   It is now necessary to support the engine, preferably from above, using a hoist or an adjustable support bar resting on the wings or suspension turrets. Alternatively a jack and some wooden blocks may be used from below, but this is bound to obstruct access to some extent.
7   Remove the engine mounting lower securing nuts. Raise the engine until the mountings are just clear of the crossmember.
8   Release the brake pipe clips from the crossmember and slide the brake pipes from their slots. Be careful not to strain the pipes.
9   Support the crossmember and remove its four securing bolts. Lower the crossmember and remove it from the vehicle.
10  Commence refitting by offering the crossmember to the frame rails. Insert the four securing bolts and tighten them to the specified torque.
11  Secure the brake pipes to the crossmember.
12  Refit the steering gear to the crossmember. Tighten its securing bolts to the specified torque.
13  Insert the suspension arms into the crossmember and secure them with the pivot bolts and nuts. Do not tighten the nuts and bolts yet, just nip them up.
14  Lower the engine onto the crossmember. Make sure that the engine mountings locate correctly into the holes in the crossmember. Tighten the engine mounting nuts. The engine support bar or hoist can now be removed.
15  Reconnect the steering column shaft to the intermediate shaft. Tighten the pinch-bolt to the specified torque.
16  Lower the vehicle onto its wheels, then tighten the lower arm pivot bolts to the specified torque.
17  Reconnect the battery.

## 21 Front stub axle carrier – removal and refitting

1   Slacken the front wheel nuts. Raise and support the front of the vehicle and remove the front wheel.
2   Separate the track rod end from the steering arm. Refer to Section 18 if necessary.
3   Unbolt the brake caliper, pull it off the disc and tie it up out of the way. Do not allow it to hang by its hose.
4   Remove the split pin from the suspension lower arm balljoint nut. Slacken the nut a few times, then use a proprietary balljoint separator to break the taper (photo).
5   Use a stout piece of wood to lever the lower arm downwards and free the balljoint from the stub axle carrier.

20.3 Front suspension lower arm pivot bolt

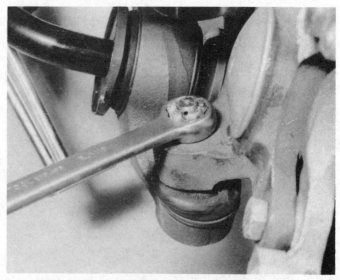

21.4 Slackening the front suspension lower arm balljoint nut

6   Remove the ABS wheel sensor from its hole.
7   Remove the spring clip from one of the wheel studs and pull the brake disc off the hub.
8   Remove the stub axle carrier pinch-bolt. Spread the stub axle carrier by carefully introducing a chisel or blunt instrument into its slot. Draw the stub axle carrier off the suspension strut and remove it.
9   Refit by reversing the removal operations, noting the following points:

(a)  Tighten all fastenings to the specified torque
(b)  Use new split pins, when applicable
(c)  Renew the wheel sensor O-ring if necessary; clean the sensor and its bore, and smear them with wheel bearing grease

## 22 Front wheel bearings – renewal

1   Remove the stub axle carrier as described in the previous Section.
2   Screw the wheel nuts onto the studs to protect the threads. Clamp the stub axle carrier in a vice by means of the studs and nuts; do not overtighten.
3   Remove the dust cap from the hub nut, carefully levering it free (photo). A new cap and a new hub nut will be required for reassembly.
4   Undo the hub nut (photo). This nut is very tight. The right-hand hub nut has a **left-hand** thread, therefore it is undone in a **clockwise** direction.
5   Remove the ABS rotor from below the hub nut.
6   Lift the carrier off the stub axle, tapping it with a mallet if necessary to free it. Remove the bearing inner race from the carrier.
7   Prise the oil seal out of the carrier and recover the bearing outer race.
8   Drive the bearing tracks out of the stub axle carrier using a blunt drift and a hammer. Be careful not to mark the bearing seats.
9   Clean all old grease and debris from the stub axle carrier.
10  New bearing components are matched in production and must only be fitted as a set. Only the manufacturer's approved components should be used in order to obtain the required long service life and freedom from adjustment.
11  Drive the new bearing tracks into the carrier, preferably using a suitable diameter tube to seat them. Make sure the tracks are fully seated.
12  Work some clean grease into the bearing races. Use high melting-point lithium-based grease (to Ford spec. SAMIC-9111A or equivalent). Make sure all the spaces between the rollers are filled; do not pack grease into the space between the inner and outer bearings however.
13  Fit the bearing outer race. Grease the lips of a new oil seal and fit it to the stub axle carrier, lips facing inwards. Seat the seal with a pipe or large socket and a mallet.
14  Offer the carrier to the stub axle, tapping it home if necessary. Fit the bearing inner race over the stub axle.
15  Refit the ABS rotor, dished face uppermost.
16  Fit a new hub nut (left-hand thread on the right-hand hub) and tighten it to the specified torque.
17  Fit a new dust cap and seat it by tapping round the rim (photo).
18  Refit the stub axle carrier.

## 23 Front suspension lower arm – removal, overhaul and refitting

1   Raise the vehicle on ramps or on a hoist, so that the weight is still on the wheels.
2   Remove the lower arm pivot nut and bolt.
3   Remove the anti-roll bar end nut, dished washer and plastic cover. Note which way round these components are fitted.
4   Now raise and support the vehicle so that the front wheels are off the ground.
5   Remove the split pin from the lower arm balljoint nut. Back off the nut a few turns, break the taper with a balljoint separator, then remove the nut and free the balljoint from the stub axle carrier.
6   Pull the lower arm off the anti-roll bar and remove it.
7   If the balljoint is defective, the whole arm must be renewed. The dust boot can be renewed separately if required.
8   The anti-roll bar bushes (compliance bushes) can be removed by cutting off their flanges with a chisel, then pressing or tapping out the

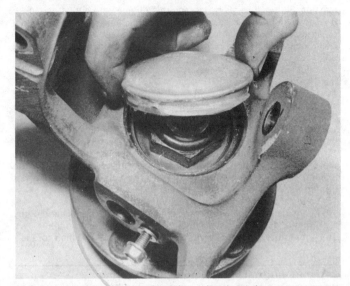

22.3 Removing the dust cap from the stub axle carrier

22.4 Front wheel bearing hub nut

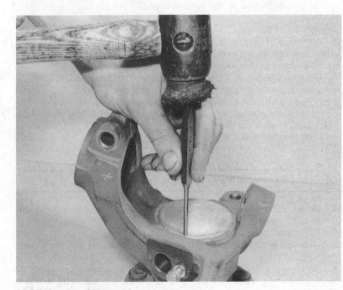

22.17 Seating the new dust cap

remains. Fit new bushes by tapping them home with a tube or socket.

9   The pivot bush can be pressed out using a bench vice and a couple of large sockets or suitable pieces of tube. The new pivot bush should be lubricated with soap or glycerine (**not** oil or grease) before being fitted in a similar fashion. Do not keep the new bush compressed in the tube for longer than necessary, in case it becomes permanently distorted.

10  Commence refitting by offering the arm ot the anti-roll bar. Make sure that the shallow dished washer and the plastic cover are fitted on the inboard side of the bar (furthest from the nut).

11  Refit the balljoint to the stub axle carrier. Tighten the castellated nut to the specified torque and secure it with a new split pin.

12  Fit the pivot end of the arm into the crossmember and secure it with the pivot nut and bolt. Jacking the vehicle up or down to vary the loading on the wheels may help to get the holes lined up. Do not tighten the pivot nut and bolt yet.

13  Lower the vehicle back onto its wheels.

14  Fit the deep dished washer and the plastic cover over the end of the anti-roll bar. Fit the nut and tighten it to the specified torque.

15  Tighten the lower arm pivot nut and bolt to the specified torque.

## 24  Front anti-roll bar – removal and refitting

1   Raise the vehicle on ramps or a hoist, so that the weight is still on the wheels.

2   Unbolt the two anti-roll bar clamps (photo).

3   Now raise and support the vehicle with the wheels free.

4   Remove the two nuts which hold the ends of the anti-roll bar to the lower arms. Recover the plastic covers and deep dished washers.

5   Remove one lower arm pivot nut and bolt. Prise the lower arm out of the crossmember and work the anti-roll bar free from it.

6   Pull the anti-roll bar out of the other lower arm and remove it. Recover the other compliance bush covers and washers.

7   Refit by reversing the removal operations, but do not finally tighten any fastenings until the weight of the vehicle is back on the wheels. Tighten in the following order:

   (a)  Anti-roll bar clamps
   (b)  Anti-roll bar-to-lower arm nuts
   (c)  Lower arm pivot nut and bolt

8   Make sure that the anti-roll bar clamp bushes are not twisted on completion.

## 25  Front anti-roll bar bushes – renewal

### Compliance bushes

1   These are described in Section 23. It is not strictly necessary to remove the lower arms to renew these bushes, though obviously access is not good with the arms installed.

### Clamp bushes

2   Although it is possible to remove and refit the clamp bushes without removing the anti-roll bar, since the bushes are split, this is not recommended by the makers.

3   Remove the anti-roll bar as described in the previous Section.

4   Slide the clamp bushes off the anti-roll bar, if necessary prising them open a little first.

5   Lubricate the new bushes with glycerine or soap and slide them into position with the split facing forwards.

6   Refit the anti-roll bar.

## 26  Front suspension strut – removal and refitting

1   Slacken the front wheel nuts, raise and support the vehicle and remove the front wheel.

2   Disconnect the battery negative lead.

3   Unbolt the brake caliper and suspend it nearby so that the flexible hose is not strained.

4   Remove the ABS sensor from the stub axle carrier.

5   Separate the track rod end and suspension lower arm balljoints from the stub axle carrier. Refer to Sections 18 and 23 if necessary.

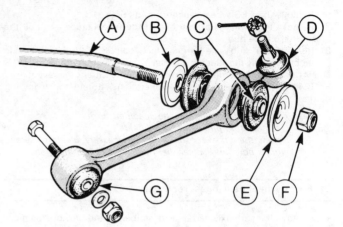

**Fig. 10.25 Front suspension lower arm components (Sec 23)**

A   Anti-roll bar
B   Rear dished washer and
    cover
C   Bushes
D   Balljoint

E   Front dished washer and
    cover
F   Locknut
G   Pivot bush

24.2 A front anti-roll bar clamp

6   Unclip the ABS/brake pad wear wiring from the strut.

7   Remove the dust cover from the top of the strut.

8   Have an assistant support the strut. Remove the three nuts which secure the strut to the turret (photo). **Do not** undo the centre nut.

9   Lower the strut out of the turret and remove it.

10  Refit by reversing the removal operations. Do not fully tighten the strut-to-turret nuts until the weight of the vehicle is back on its wheels.

## 27  Front suspension strut – dismantling and reassembly

**Warning:** *Spring compressors of adequate rating must be used for this job. The use of makeshift or inadequate equipment may result in damage and personal injury.*

1   With the strut removed, clamp it in a vice with protected jaws.

2   Remove the stub axle carrier pinch-bolts. Spread the carrier by carefully introducing a chisel or blunt screwdriver into the crack, then slide it off the strut (photo).

3   Fit spring compressors to the strut. Compress the spring until it is no longer tensioning the strut. Make sure that the compressors are secure.

26.8 Two of the three nuts (arrowed) which secure the front suspension strut to the turret

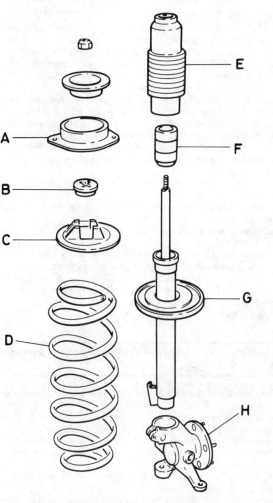

Fig. 10.26 Front suspension strut components (Sec 27)

A  Top mount
B  Bearing
C  Spring upper seat
D  Spring
E  Gaiter
F  Bump stop
G  Shock absorber and spring lower seat
H  Stub axle

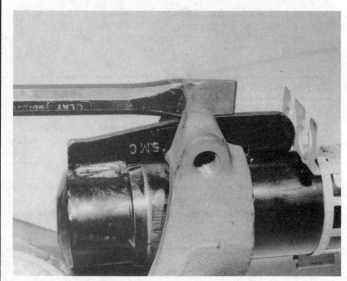

27.2 Speading the stub axle carrier clamp

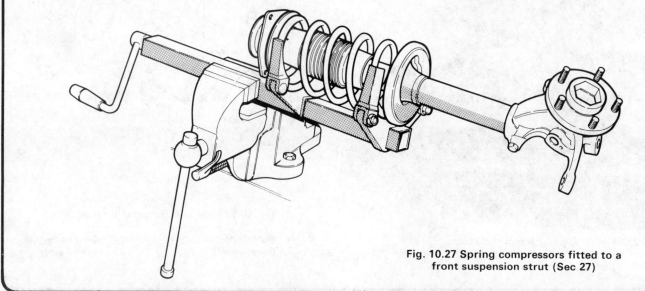

Fig. 10.27 Spring compressors fitted to a front suspension strut (Sec 27)

4   Hold the piston rod with a hexagon key and remove the piston rod nut. Also remove the dished retainer.

5   Remove the top mount, the bearing and the spring upper seat.

6   Carefully lift off the compressed spring. Place it where it will not be knocked or jarred.

7   Remove the shock absorber gaiter and bump stop.

8   Examine all components for wear and damage and renew as necessary. The shock absorber must be renewed if it is leaking, or if it shows uneven resistance when 'worked' with its lower end clamped in a vice. In theory springs and shock absorbers should be renewed in pairs in order to maintain balanced handling characteristics.

9   Commence reassembly by sliding the bump stop onto the shock absorber piston rod. Refit the gaiter.

10  Make sure that the spring seats are clean, then fit the compressed spring to the lower seat.

11  Refit the spring upper seat, the bearing (small hole upwards) and the top mount.

12  Refit the dished retainer and the piston rod nut. Hold the piston rod and tighten the nut.

13  Carefully release the spring compressors. Make sure that the ends of the spring are correctly located in the spring seats.

14  Spread the stub axle carrier again. Slide it onto the strut, remove the spreader and refit the pinch-bolt. Tighten the pinch-bolt to the specified torque.

15  Refit the strut to the vehicle.

### 28 Rear suspension and final drive assembly – removal and refitting

1   Raise the rear of the vehicle and support it securely under the frame rails.

2   Remove the exhaust system as described in Chapter 3.

3   Remove the propeller shaft as described in Chapter 7.

4   Release the handbrake cable from the equaliser yoke by removing the circlip from the handbrake lever pin. Release the cable from its floor brackets.

5   Disconnect the brake flexible hoses from the rear brake pipes, referring if necessary to Chapter 9.

6   Disconnect the ABS and brake pad wear sensor wires (as applicable). Free the wires from the suspension lower arms.

7   Unbolt the two anti-roll bar brackets from the floors.

8   Disconnect the ride height control sensor and the shock absorber air lines, when so equipped.

9   Lower the vehicle onto its wheels in order to load the rear springs a little. Place a jack under the final drive unit and support it.

10  Unbolt and remove the two guide plates (photo). The centre bolt on each plate is retained by a lockwasher which must be released first.

11  Unbolt the final drive unit rear mounting from the floor.

12  Remove the luggage area side trim, then remove the rear shock absorber upper mounting bolts.

13  Raise and support the rear of the vehicle again. Withdraw the rear suspension and final drive assembly.

14  Refit by reversing the removal operations. Tighten all fastenings to the specified torque, when known. When applicable use new O-rings on the ride height control line unions.

15  Bleed the brake hydraulic system and adjust the handbrake on completion.

### 29 Rear hub – removal and refitting

1   Remove the wheel trim. Apply the handbrake and chock the front wheels.

2   Slacken the driveshaft stub axle. This nut is very tight. The left-hand nut has a **left-hand** thread, therefore it is undone **clockwise.**

3   Remove the brake disc (Chapter 9, Section 7).

4   Remove the driveshaft stub axle.

5   Remove the four bolts which secure the hub. Pull the hub off the driveshaft stub, leaving the disc splash shield loose.

6   Refit by reversing the removal operations. Carry out the final tightening of the driveshaft stub nut with the wheels on the ground.

### 30 Rear wheel bearings – renewal

1   Remove the rear hub as described in the previous Section.

2   Prise out both oil seals from the hub. Recover the bearing races.

3   Drive the bearing tracks out of the hub with a hammer and a blunt drift.

4   Clean grease and debris from the hub and clean up any burrs or nicks.

5   Fit the new bearing tracks, pressing them in squarely with the help of a piece of pipe or tube.

6   Thoroughly grease the bearing races and pack the lips of the oil seals with grease.

28.10 One of the rear suspension guide plates

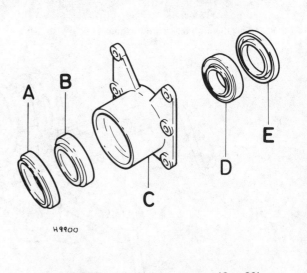

**Fig. 10.28 Rear hub components (Sec 30)**

A   Outer oil seal          D   Inner bearing
B   Outer bearing          E   Inner oil seal
C   Hub

7   Fit the races and the oil seals, lips inwards. Seat the oil seals with a mallet and the pipe or tube.
8   Refit the rear hub.

## 31  Wheel stud – renewal

1   This procedure is only specified by the manufacturers as applying to the rear wheels, but there is no reason to believe that it will not work on the front.
2   Remove the rear wheel, brake caliper and brake disc.
3   Drive the wheel stud out of the hub flange.
4   Insert the new stud from the inboard side of the flange. Engage the splines by hand pressure, then draw the stud into place with a wheel nut and progressively thicker spacers.
5   Refit the brake disc, caliper and wheel.

## 32  Rear spring – removal and refitting

1   Raise and support the rear of the vehicle.
2   Unbolt the driveshaft outboard flange from the stub. It is secured by six 'Torx' screws.
3   Disconnect the anti-roll bar from the link rod by prising it free. On models with ride height control, also disconnect the height sensor from the anti-roll bar link rod.
4   Free the brake pipe and flexible hose from the brackets next to the spring. If it is the left-hand spring which is being removed, also unbolt the brake pipe T-piece from the floor.
5   Raise a jack under the rear suspension lower arm to load the spring.
6   Unbolt the shock absorber from the lower arm.
7   Unbolt the guide plate from the body on the side concerned.
8   Carefully lower the jack until the spring is no longer under tension. Remove the spring and the rubber buffer.
9   Refit by reversing the removal operations, tightening all fastenings to the specified torque when known.

## 33  Rear crossmember insulator – removal and refitting

**Note:** *Ford tool No. 15-014, or locally made equivalent, will be required for this job.*

1   Raise and support the rear of the vehicle.
2   Flatten the lockwasher which secures the guide plate centre bolt. Remove the centre bolt and the two bolts which hold the guide plate to the floor; remove the guide plate.
3   Wedge a piece of wood between the crossmember and the floor.
4   Draw the insulator out with the special tool.
5   Smear the new insulator with glycerine or liquid soap, then press it in as follows.
6   Use the special tool spindle or other long M12 bolt. Screw a nut up to the bolt head, then fit a plain washer and the insulator onto the bolt. Pass the bolt through the hole in the crossmember and screw it into the floor, then press the insulator home by winding the nut and washer up the bolt.
7   Remove the installation tool and the piece of wood.
8   Refit the guide plate, tightening the bolts to the specified torque. Secure the centre bolt with the lockwasher.
9   Lower the vehicle.

## 34  Rear suspension lower arm – removal and refitting

1   Remove the rear hub as described in Section 29.
2   Disconnect both rear brake flexible hoses from the brake pipes. Free the brake pipes from the brackets on the lower arms.
3   Unclip the handbrake cable from the lower arm.
4   Remove the rear spring as described in Section 32.
5   Remove the lower arm-to-crossmember bolts. Withdraw the lower arm.
6   Renew the rubber bushes if wished, using lengths of tube or sockets and a vice, or large nuts and bolts. Lubricate the new bushes with glycerine or liquid soap.

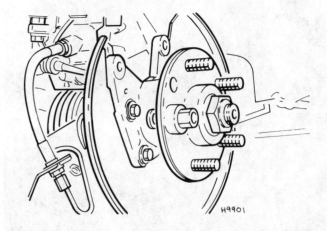

Fig. 10.29 Fitting a new wheel stud using a nut and spacer (Sec 31)

Fig. 10.30 Ford tool 15-014 for removal and refitting of the rear crossmember insulators (Sec 33)

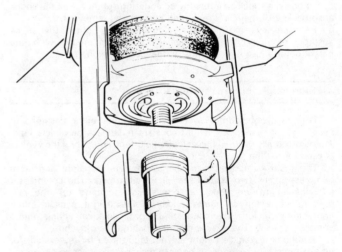

Fig. 10.31 Drawing out an insulator with the special tool (Sec 33)

7   Refit by reversing the removal operations, tightening the lower arm-to-crossmember bolts with the weight of the vehicle back on its wheels. Bleed the brake hydraulic system on completion.

## 35  Rear anti-roll bar – removal and refitting

1   Raise and support the rear of the vehicle.
2   Separate the anti-roll bar from the link rods on each side by prising them free (photo).
3   Unbolt the two anti-roll bar brackets. Remove the bar, brackets and bushes (photo).
4   Refit by reversing the removal operations. Tighten the bracket bolts to the specified torque.

35.2 Rear anti-roll bar link rod

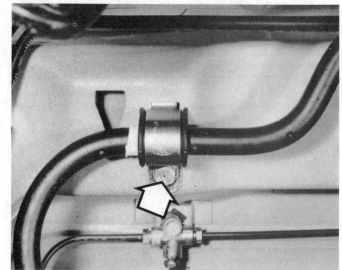

35.3 A rear anti-roll bar bracket – bolt arrowed

## 36 Rear shock absorber – removal and refitting

1   Working inside the vehicle, remove the luggage area side trim to gain access to the shock absorber top mounting.
2   Raise and support the rear of the vehicle. Raise a jack under the rear suspension lower arm to take the load off the shock absorber.
3   On models with ride height control, disconnect the air line from the shock absorber.
4   Unbolt the shock absorber top mounting (photo).
5   Unbolt the shock absorber lower mounting (photo). Pull the shock absorber out of the lower mounting bracket and remove it.
6   Refit by reversing the removal operations. Tighten the shock absorber mountings to the specified torque. On models with ride height control, use new O-rings on the air line union.

## 37 Ride height control system – general

The ride height control system is an optional extra, designed to keep the rear suspension height constant regardless of vehicle load. This is obviously useful if heavy loads are often carried, or if the vehicle is used for towing.

The main components of the system are a height sensor, a compressor and two special rear shock absorbers. The compressor supplies air to the shock absorbers, so 'pumping up' the rear suspension, when so commanded by the height sensor. Other components include the connecting pipes, electrical wiring and a compressor relay. The relay is mounted behind the glovebox.

Variations in vehicle height are not recognised by the system for approximately 20 seconds, in order to prevent responses to temporary changes such as those induced by cornering or braking. Control circuitry also prevents the compressor being energised for more than five minutes continuously, as could otherwise happen if the system sprang a leak.

No repairs to individual components are possible. Apparent control faults should be referred to a Ford dealer before embarking on an expensive programme of testing by substitution. Always use new O-rings on the pipe unions once they have been disturbed.

## 38 Ride height control compressor – removal and refitting

1   Disconnect the battery negative lead.
2   Raise and support the front of the vehicle.
3   Remove the compressor cover, which is secured by four screws.
4   Disconnect the air pipe and the power supply leads from the compressor.

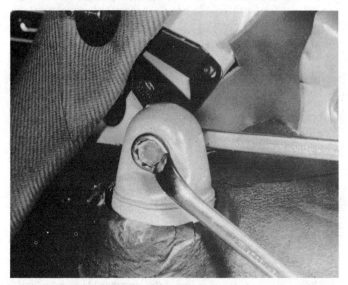

36.4 Undoing a rear shock absorber top mounting

36.5 Undoing a rear shock absorber lower mounting

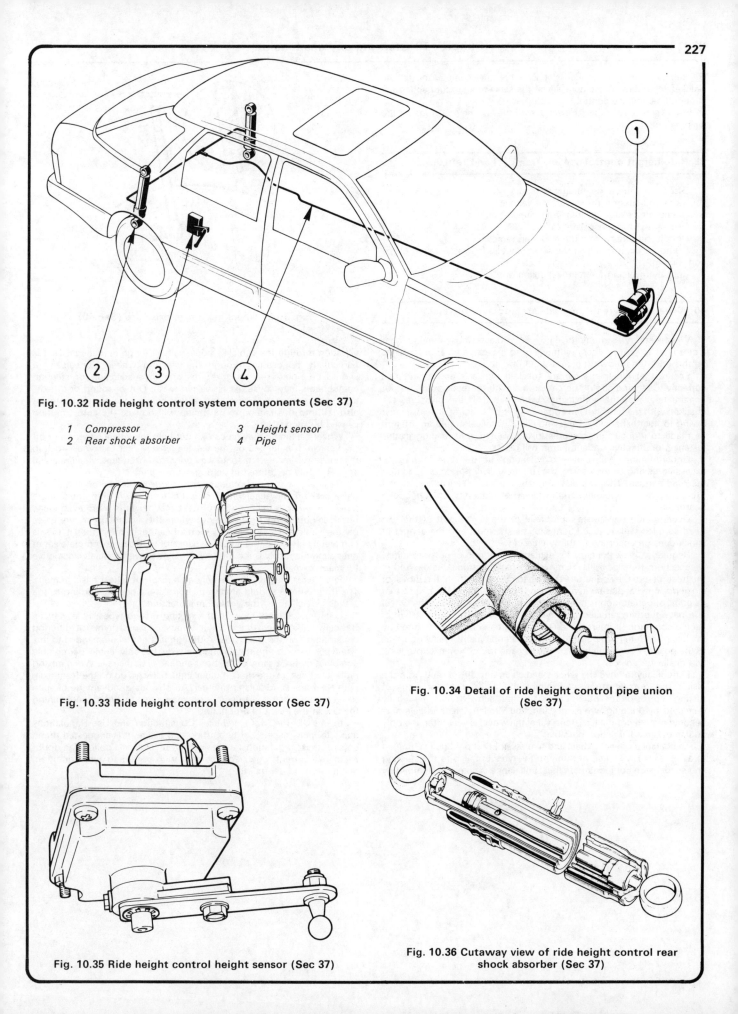

**Fig. 10.32 Ride height control system components (Sec 37)**

1  *Compressor*
2  *Rear shock absorber*
3  *Height sensor*
4  *Pipe*

**Fig. 10.33 Ride height control compressor (Sec 37)**

**Fig. 10.34 Detail of ride height control pipe union (Sec 37)**

**Fig. 10.35 Ride height control height sensor (Sec 37)**

**Fig. 10.36 Cutaway view of ride height control rear shock absorber (Sec 37)**

5   Remove the three bolts which secure the compressor to the bracket. Withdraw the compressor, at the same time disconnecting the suction line and the control multi-plug.
6   Refit by reversing the removal operations; use new O-rings on the air pipe union.

## 39 Ride height control sensor – removal and refitting

1   Disconnect the battery negative lead.
2   Raise and support the rear of the vehicle.
3   Unclip the linkage balljoint from the sensor.
4   Disconnect the sensor multi-plug.
5   Unbolt the sensor from the floor and remove it.
6   Do not attempt to adjust the sensor by altering the position of the control arm.
7   Refit by reversing the removal operations.

## 40 Wheels and tyres – general care and maintenance

Wheels and tyres should give no real problems in use provided that a close eye is kept on them with regard to excessive wear or damage. To this end, the following points should be noted.

Ensure that tyre pressures are checked regularly and maintained correctly. Checking should be carried out with the tyres cold and not immediately after the vehicle has been in use. If the pressures are checked with the tyres hot, an apparently high reading will be obtained owing to heat expansion. Under no circumstances should an attempt be made to reduce the pressures to the quoted cold reading in this instance, or effective underinflation will result.

Underinflation will cause overheating of the tyre owing to excessive flexing of the casing, and the tread will not sit correctly on the road surface. This will cause a consequent loss of adhesion and excessive wear, not to mention the danger of sudden tyre failure due to heat build-up.

Overinflation will cause rapid wear of the centre part of the tyre tread coupled with reduced adhesion, harsher ride, and the danger of shock damage occurring in the tyre casing.

Regularly check the tyres for damage in the form of cuts or bulges, especially in the sidewalls. Remove any nails or stones embedded in the tread before they penetrate the tyre to cause deflation. If removal of a nail *does* reveal that the tyre has been punctured, refit the nail so that its point of penetration is marked. Then immediately change the wheel and have the tyre repaired by a tyre dealer. Do *not* drive on a tyre in such a condition. In many cases a puncture can be simply repaired by the use of an inner tube of the correct size and type. If in any doubt as to the possible consequences of any damage found, consult your local tyre dealer for advice.

Periodically remove the wheels and clean any dirt or mud from the inside and outside surfaces. Examine the wheel rims for signs of rusting, corrosion or other damage. Light alloy wheels are easily damaged by 'kerbing' whilst parking, and similarly steel wheels may become dented or buckled. Renewal of the wheel is very often the only course of remedial action possible.

The balance of each wheel and tyre assembly should be maintained to avoid excessive wear, not only to the tyres but also to the steering and suspension components. Wheel imbalance is normally signified by

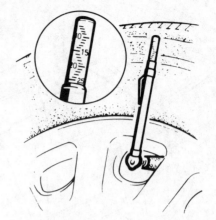

Fig. 10.37 Checking a tyre pressure (Sec 40)

vibration through the vehicle's bodyshell, although in many cases it is particularly noticeable through the steering wheel. Conversely, it should be noted that wear or damage in suspension or steering components may cause excessive tyre wear. Out-of-round or out-of-true tyres, damaged wheels and wheel bearing wear/maladjustment also fall into this category. Balancing will not usually cure vibration caused by such wear.

Wheel balancing may be carried out with the wheel either on or off the vehicle. If balanced on the vehicle, ensure that the wheel-to-hub relationship is marked in some way prior to subsequent wheel removal so that it may be refitted in its original position.

General tyre wear is influenced to a large degree by driving style – harsh braking and acceleration or fast cornering will all produce more rapid tyre wear. Interchanging of tyres may result in more even wear, but this should only be carried out where there is no mix of tyre types on the vehicle. However, it is worth bearing in mind that if this is completely effective, the added expense of replacing a complete set of tyres simultaneously is incurred, which may prove financially restrictive for many owners.

Front tyres may wear unevenly as a result of wheel misalignment. The front wheels should always be correctly aligned according to the settings specified by the vehicle manufacturer.

Legal restrictions apply to the mixing of tyre types on a vehicle. Basically this means that a vehicle must not have tyres of differing construction on the same axle. Although it is not recommended to mix tyre types between front axle and rear axle, the only legally permissible combination is crossply at the front and radial at the rear. When mixing radial ply tyres, textile braced radials must always go on the front axle, with steel braced radials at the rear. An obvious disadvantage of such mixing is the necessity to carry two spare tyres to avoid contravening the law in the event of a puncture.

In the UK, the Motor Vehicles Construction and Use Regulations apply to many aspects of tyre fitting and usage. It is suggested that a copy of these regulations is obtained from your local police if in doubt as to the current legal requirements with regard to tyre condition, minimum tread depth, etc.

## 41 Fault diagnosis – steering and suspension

| Symptom | Reason(s) |
| --- | --- |
| Excessive play at steering wheel | Worn track rod end balljoints<br>Worn lower suspension arm balljoints<br>Worn intermediate shaft coupling<br>Worn steering gear |
| Vehicle wanders or pulls to one side | Uneven tyre pressures<br>Incorrect wheel alignment<br>Worn track rod end balljoints<br>Worn lower suspension arm balljoints<br>Faulty shock absorber<br>Accident damage |
| Steering heavy or stiff | Low tyre pressures<br>Seized balljoint<br>Seized strut top bearing<br>Incorrect wheel alignment<br>Steering gear damaged or lacking lubricant<br>Power steering fault (see below) |
| Lack of power assistance | Fluid level low<br>Pump drivebelt slack or broken<br>Pump or steering gear defective |
| Wheel wobble and vibration | Wheel nuts loose<br>Wheels out of balance or damaged<br>Wheel bearings worn<br>Worn track rod end balljoints<br>Worn lower suspension arm balljoints<br>Faulty shock absorber |
| Excessive tyre wear | Incorrect tyre pressures<br>Wheels out of balance<br>Incorrect wheel alignment<br>Faulty shock absorbers<br>Unsympathetic driving style |

# Chapter 11 Bodywork and fittings

*For modifications, and information applicable to later models, see Supplement at end of manual*

## Contents

## Specifications

### Torque wrench settings

| | Nm | lbf ft |
| --- | --- | --- |
| Front seat belt buckle to seat frame | 51 to 64 | 38 to 47 |
| Seat belt retractor bolts (front and rear) | 25 to 45 | 18 to 33 |
| Other seat belt anchorages | 25 to 45 | 18 to 33 |
| Rear seat back hinge to body | 21 to 25 | 16 to 18 |
| Rear seat back latch striker | 40 to 60 | 30 to 44 |
| Front seat retaining bolts | 25 to 32 | 18 to 24 |
| Front seat frame-to-slide bolts | 25 to 32 | 18 to 24 |
| Rear bumper mountings | 21 | 16 |
| Front bumper adjuster lockbolt | 21 | 16 |

## 1 General description

The bodyshell and floorpan are of pressed steel, and form an integral part of the vehicle's structure. Various reinforcing and mounting components beneath the floorpan are made of HSLA (High Strength Low Alloy) and REPHOS (rephosphorised) steels, which have superior strength-to-weight characteristics when compared with conventional steels.

Extensive use is made of plastic for peripheral components such as the radiator grille, bumpers and wheel trims, and for much of the interior trim.

Interior fittings are to the high standard expected in a vehicle of this class, with even the basic level models well equipped. A wide range of options is available, including air conditioning and leather upholstery.

## 2 Maintenance – bodywork and underframe

1 The general condition of a vehicle's bodywork is the one thing that significantly affects its value. Maintenance is easy but needs to be regular. Neglect, particularly after minor damage, can lead quickly to further deterioration and costly repair bills. It is important also to keep watch on those parts of the vehicle not immediately visible, for instance the underside, inside all the wheel arches and the lower part of the engine compartment.

2 The basic maintenance routine for the bodywork is washing – preferably with a lot of water, from a hose. This will remove all the loose solids which may have stuck to the vehicle. It is important to flush these off in such a way as to prevent grit from scratching the finish. The wheel arches and underframe need washing in the same way to remove any accumulated mud which will retain moisture and tend to encourage rust. Paradoxically enough, the best time to clean the underframe and wheel arches is in wet weather when the mud is thoroughly wet and soft. In very wet weather the underframe is usually cleaned of large accumulations automatically and this is a good time for inspection.

3 Periodically, except on vehicles with a wax-based underbody protective coating, it is a good idea to have the whole of the underframe of the vehicle steam cleaned, engine compartment included, so that a thorough inspection can be carried out to see what minor repairs and renovations are necessary. Steam cleaning is available at many garages and is necessary for removal of the accumulation of oily grime which sometimes is allowed to become thick in certain areas. If steam cleaning facilities are not available, there are one or two excellent grease solvents available such as Holts Engine Cleaner or Holts Foambrite which can be brush applied. The dirt can then be simply hosed off. Note that these methods should not be used on vehicles with wax-based underbody protective coating or the

coating will be removed. Such vehicles should be inspected annually, preferably just prior to winter, when the underbody should be washed down and any damage to the wax coating repaired using Holts Undershield. Ideally, a completely fresh coat should be applied. It would also be worth considering the use of such wax-based protection for injection into door panels, sills, box sections, etc, as an additional safeguard against rust damage where such protection is not provided by the vehicle manufacturer.

4    After washing paintwork, wipe off with a chamois leather to give an unspotted clear finish. A coat of clear protective wax polish, like the many excellent Turtle Wax polishes, will give added protection against chemical pollutants in the air. If the paintwork sheen has dulled or oxidised, use a cleaner/polisher combination such as Turtle Extra to restore the brilliance of the shine. This requires a little effort, but such dulling is usually caused because regular washing has been neglected. Care needs to be taken with metallic paintwork, as special non-abrasive cleaner/polisher is required to avoid damage to the finish. Always check that the door and ventilator opening drain holes and pipes are completely clear so that water can be drained out·

Bright work should be treated in the same way as paint work. Windscreens and windows can be kept clear of the smeary film which often appears, by the use of a proprietary glass cleaner like Holts Mixra. Never use any form of wax or other body or chromium polish on glass.

### 3   Maintenance – upholstery and carpets

Mats and carpets should be brushed or vacuum cleaned regularly to keep them free of grit. If they are badly stained remove them from the vehicle for scrubbing or sponging and make quite sure they are dry before refitting. Seats and interior trim panels can be kept clean by wiping with a damp cloth and Turtle Wax Carisma. If they do become stained (which can be more apparent on light coloured upholstery) use a little liquid detergent and a soft nail brush to scour the grime out of the grain of the material. Do not forget to keep the headlining clean in the same way as the upholstery. When using liquid cleaners inside the vehicle do not over-wet the surfaces being cleaned. Excessive damp could get into the seams and padded interior causing stains, offensive odours or even rot. If the inside of the vehicle gets wet accidentally it is worthwhile taking some trouble to dry it out properly, particularly where carpets are involved. *Do not leave oil or electric heaters inside the vehicle for this purpose.*

### 4   Minor body damage – repair

*The photographic sequences on pages 238 and 239 illustrate the operations detailed in the following sub-sections.*
**Note**: *For more detailed information about bodywork repair, the Haynes Publishing Group publish a book by Lindsay Porter called The Car Bodywork Repair Manual. This incorporates information on such aspects as rust treatment, painting and glass fibre repairs, as well as details on more ambitious repairs involving welding and panel beating.*

#### Repair of minor scratches in bodywork
If the scratch is very superficial, and does not penetrate to the metal of the bodywork, repair is very simple. Lightly rub the area of the scratch with a paintwork renovator like Turtle Wax New Color Back, or a very fine cutting paste like Holts Body + Plus Rubbing Compound, to remove loose paint from the scratch and to clear the surrounding bodywork of wax polish. Rinse the area with clean water.

Apply touch-up paint, such as Holts Dupli-Color Color Touch or a paint film like Holts Autofilm, to the scratch using a fine paint brush; continue to apply fine layers of paint until the surface of the paint in the scratch is level with the surrounding paintwork. Allow the new paint at least two weeks to harden: then blend it into the surrounding paintwork by rubbing the scratch area with a paintwork renovator or a very fine cutting paste, such as Holts Body + Plus Rubbing Compound or Turtle Wax New Color Back. Finally, apply wax polish from one of the Turtle Wax range of wax polishes.

Where the scratch has penetrated right through to the metal of the bodywork, causing the metal to rust, a different repair technique is required. Remove any loose rust from the bottom of the scratch with a penknife, then apply rust inhibiting paint, such as Turtle Wax Rust Master, to prevent the formation of rust in the future. Using a rubber or nylon applicator fill the scratch with bodystopper paste like Holts

Body + Plus Knifing Putty. If required, this paste can be mixed with cellulose thinners, such as Holts Body + Plus Cellulose Thinners, to provide a very thin paste which is ideal for filling narrow scratches. Before the stopper-paste in the scratch hardens, wrap a piece of smooth cotton rag around the top of a finger. Dip the finger in cellulose thinners, such as Holts Body + Plus Cellulose Thinners, and then quickly sweep it across the surface of the stopper-paste in the scratch; this will ensure that the surface of the stopper-paste is slightly hollowed. The scratch can now be painted over as described earlier in this Section.

#### Repair of dents in bodywork
When deep denting of the vehicle's bodywork has taken place, the first task is to pull the dent out, until the affected bodywork almost attains its original shape. There is little point in trying to restore the original shape completely, as the metal in the damaged area will have stretched on impact and cannot be reshaped fully to its original contour. It is better to bring the level of the dent up to a point which is about ⅛ in (3 mm) below the level of the surrounding bodywork. In cases where the dent is very shallow anyway, it is not worth trying to pull it out at all. If the underside of the dent is accessible, it can be hammered out gently from behind, using a mallet with a wooden or plastic head. Whilst doing this, hold a suitable block of wood firmly against the outside of the panel to absorb the impact from the hammer blows and thus prevent a large area of the bodywork from being 'belled-out'.

Should the dent be in a section of the bodywork which has a double skin or some other factor making it inaccessible from behind, a different technique is called for. Drill several small holes through the metal inside the area – particularly in the deeper section. Then screw long self-tapping screws into the holes just sufficiently for them to gain a good purchase in the metal. Now the dent can be pulled out by pulling on the protruding heads of the screws with a pair of pliers.

The next stage of the repair is the removal of the paint from the damaged area, and from an inch or so of the surrounding 'sound' bodywork. This is accomplished most easily by using a wire brush or abrasive pad on a power drill, although it can be done just as effectively by hand using sheets of abrasive paper. To complete the preparation for filling, score the surface of the bare metal with a screwdriver or the tang of a file, or alternatively, drill small holes in the affected area. This will provide a really good 'key' for the filler paste.

To complete the repair see the Section on filling and re-spraying.

#### Repair of rust holes or gashes in bodywork
Remove all paint from the affected area and from an inch or so of the surrounding 'sound' bodywork, using an abrasive pad or a wire brush on a power drill. If these are not available a few sheets of abrasive paper will do the job just as effectively. With the paint removed you will be able to gauge the severity of the corrosion and therefore decide whether to renew the whole panel (if this is possible) or to repair the affected area. New body panels are not as expensive as most people think and it is often quicker and more satisfactory to fit a new panel than to attempt to repair large areas of corrosion.

Remove all fittings from the affected area except those which will act as a guide to the original shape of the damaged bodywork (eg headlamp shells etc). Then, using tin snips or a hacksaw blade, remove all loose metal and any other metal badly affected by corrosion. Hammer the edges of the hole inwards in order to create a slight depression for the filler paste.

Wire brush the affected area to remove the powdery rust from the surface of the remaining metal. Paint the affected area with rust inhibiting paint like Turtle Wax Rust Master; if the back of the rusted area is accessible treat this also.

Before filling can take place it will be necessary to block the hole in some way. This can be achieved by the use of aluminium or plastic mesh, or aluminium tape.

Aluminium or plastic mesh or glass fibre matting, such as the Holts Body + Plus Glass Fibre Matting, is probably the best material to use for a large hole. Cut a piece to the approximate size and shape of the hole to be filled, then position it in the hole so that its edges are below the level of the surrounding bodywork. It can be retained in position by several blobs of filler paste around its periphery.

Aluminium tape should be used for small or very narrow holes. Pull a piece off the roll and trim it to the approximate size and shape required, then pull off the backing paper (if used) and stick the tape over the hole; it can be overlapped if the thickness of one piece is insufficient. Burnish down the edges of the tape with the handle of a screwdriver or similar, to ensure that the tape is securely attached to the metal underneath.

### Bodywork repairs – filling and re-spraying

Before using this Section, see the Sections on dent, deep scratch, rust holes and gash repairs.

Many types of bodyfiller are available, but generally speaking those proprietary kits which contain a tin of filler paste and a tube of resin hardener are best for this type of repair, like Holts Body + Plus or Holts No Mix which can be used directly from the tube. A wide, flexible plastic or nylon applicator will be found invaluable for imparting a smooth and well contoured finish to the surface of the filler.

Mix up a little filler on a clean piece of card or board – measure the hardener carefully (follow the maker's instructions on the pack) otherwise the filler will set too rapidly or too slowly. Alternatively, Holts No Mix can be used straight from the tube without mixing, but daylight is required to cure it. Using the applicator apply the filler paste to the prepared area; draw the applicator across the surface of the filler to achieve the correct contour and to level the filler surface. As soon as a contour that approximates to the correct one is achieved, stop working the paste – if you carry on too long the paste will become sticky and begin to 'pick up' on the applicator. Continue to add thin layers of filler paste at twenty-minute intervals until the level of the filler is just proud of the surrounding bodywork.

Once the filler has hardened, excess can be removed using a metal plane or file. From then on, progressively finer grades of abrasive paper should be used, starting with a 40 grade production paper and finishing with 400 grade wet-and-dry paper. Always wrap the abrasive paper around a flat rubber, cork, or wooden block – otherwise the surface of the filler will not be completely flat. During the smoothing of the filler surface the wet-and-dry paper should be periodically rinsed in water. This will ensure that a very smooth finish is imparted to the filler at the final stage.

At this stage the 'dent' should be surrounded by a ring of bare metal, which in turn should be encircled by the finely 'feathered' edge of the good paintwork. Rinse the repair area with clean water, until all of the dust produced by the rubbing-down operation has gone.

Spray the whole repair area with a light coat of primer, either Holts Body + Plus Grey or Red Oxide Primer – this will show up any imperfections in the surface of the filler. Repair these imperfections with fresh filler paste or bodystopper, and once more smooth the surface with abrasive paper. If bodystopper is used, it can be mixed with cellulose thinners to form a really thin paste which is ideal for filling small holes. Repeat this spray and repair procedure until you are satisfied that the surface of the filler, and the feathered edge of the paintwork are perfect. Clean the repair area with clean water and allow to dry fully.

The repair area is now ready for final spraying. Paint spraying must be carried out in a warm, dry, windless and dust free atmosphere. This condition can be created artificially if you have access to a large indoor working area, but if you are forced to work in the open, you will have to pick your day very carefully. If you are working indoors, dousing the floor in the work area with water will help to settle the dust which would otherwise be in the atmosphere. If the repair area is confined to one body panel, mask off the surrounding panels; this will help to minimise the effects of a slight mis-match in paint colours. Bodywork fittings (eg chrome strips, door handles etc) will also need to be masked off. Use genuine masking tape and several thicknesses of newspaper for the masking operations.

Before commencing to spray, agitate the aerosol can thoroughly, then spray a test area (an old tin, or similar) until the technique is mastered. Cover the repair area with a thick coat of primer; the thickness should be built up using several thin layers of paint rather than one thick one. Using 400 grade wet-and-dry paper, rub down the surface of the primer until it is really smooth. While doing this, the work area should be thoroughly doused with water, and the wet-and-dry paper periodically rinsed in water. Allow to dry before spraying on more paint.

Spray on the top coat using Holts Dupli-Color Autospray, again building up the thickness by using several thin layers of paint. Start spraying in the centre of the repair area and then work outwards, with a side-to-side motion, until the whole repair area and about 2 inches of the surrounding original paintwork is covered. Remove all masking material 10 to 15 minutes after spraying on the final coat of paint.

Allow the new paint at least two weeks to harden, then, using a paintwork renovator or a very fine cutting paste such as Turtle Wax New Color Back or Holts Body + Plus Rubbing Compound, blend the edges of the paint into the existing paintwork. Finally, apply wax polish.

### Plastic components

With the use of more and more plastic body components by the vehicle manufacturers (eg bumpers, spoilers, and in some cases major body panels), rectification of more serious damage to such items has become a matter of either entrusting repair work to a specialist in this field, or renewing complete components. Repair of such damage by the DIY owner is not really feasible owing to the cost of the equipment and materials required for effecting such repairs. The basic technique involves making a groove along the line of the crack in the plastic using a rotary burr in a power drill. The damaged part is then welded back together by using a hot air gun to heat up and fuse a plastic filler rod into the groove. Any excess plastic is then removed and the area rubbed down to a smooth finish. It is important that a filler rod of the correct plastic is used, as body components can be made of a variety of different types (eg polycarbonate, ABS, polypropylene).

Damage of a less serious nature (abrasions, minor cracks etc) can be repaired by the DIY owner using a two-part epoxy filler repair material, like Holts Body + Plus or Holts No Mix which can be used directly from the tube. Once mixed in equal proportions (or applied direct from the tube in the case of Holts No Mix), this is used in similar fashion to the bodywork filler used on metal panels. The filler is usually cured in twenty to thirty minutes, ready for sanding and painting.

If the owner is renewing a complete component himself, or if he has repaired it with epoxy filler, he will be left with the problem of finding a suitable paint for finishing which is compatible with the type of plastic used. At one time the use of a universal paint was not possible owing to the complex range of plastics encountered in body component applications. Standard paints, generally speaking, will not bond to plastic or rubber satisfactorily, but Holts Professional Spraymatch paints to match any plastic or rubber finish can be obtained from dealers. However, it is now possible to obtain a plastic body parts finishing kit which consists of a pre-primer treatment, a primer and coloured top coat. Full instructions are normally supplied with a kit, but basically the method of use is to first apply the pre-primer to the component concerned and allow it to dry for up to 30 minutes. Then the primer is applied and left to dry for about an hour before finally applying the special coloured top coat. The result is a correctly coloured component where the paint will flex with the plastic or rubber, a property that standard paint does not normally possess.

---

### 5   Major body damage – repair

---

Where serious damage has occurred or large areas need renewal due to neglect, it means certainly that completely new sections or panels will need welding in and this is best left to professionals. If the damage is due to impact, it will also be necessary to completely check the alignment of the bodyshell structure. Due to the principle of construction, the strength and shape of the whole car can be affected by damage to one part. In such instances the services of a Ford agent with specialist checking jigs are essential. If a body is left misaligned, it is first of all dangerous as the car will not handle properly, and secondly uneven stresses will be imposed on the steering, engine and transmission, causing abnormal wear or complete failure. Tyre wear may also be excessive.

---

### 6   Bonnet – removal and refitting

---

1   Open and prop the bonnet.
2   Mark around the bonnet hinge bolts, using soft pencil or a washable marker pen, to provide a guide when refitting (photos).
3   Disconnect the windscreen washer hose at the non-return valve or washer pump. Be prepared for fluid spillage.
4   Disconnect the under-bonnet light (when fitted).
5   Free the insulation from around the left-hand hinge bolts. With the help of an assistant, support the bonnet and remove the hinge bolts. Unhook the bonnet from the pump and remove it.
6   Refit by reversing the removal operations. Make sure that the gap between the bonnet and the wings is equal on both sides when the bonnet is shut; adjust if necessary at the hinge bolts.
7   Adjust the bump stops and bonnet lock striker if necessary to obtain satisfactory opening and closing of the bonnet (photo).

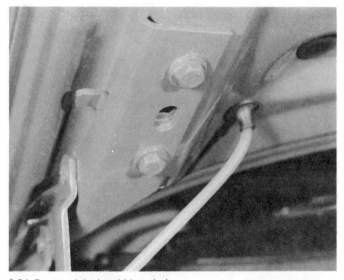

6.2A Bonnet right-hand hinge bolts

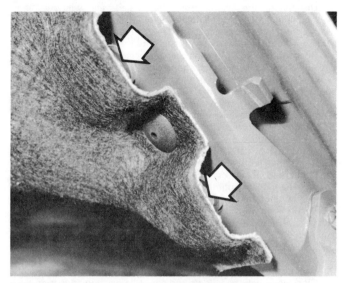

6.2B Left-hand hinge bolts (arrowed) are obscured by insulation

6.7 Bonnet lock striker and safety catch

## 7 Door – removal and refitting

1   Open the door and disconnect the wiring multi-plug from the door pillar (photo).
2   Unbolt the door check strap.
3   Slacken, but do not remove, the hinge cotter pin nuts (photo).
4   Open the door to approximately 60° from the vehicle body and lift it off the hinges. If the door is reluctant to move, make sure that it is opened to the correct angle and that the cotter pin nuts are adequately slackened.
5   Refit by reversing the removal operations. Adjust the door striker plate if necessary as described in Section 11.
6   If a new door is to be fitted, new hinges will have to be welded to it after trial fitting. Consult a Ford dealer for details.

## 8 Tailgate – removal and refitting

1   Open the tailgate and remove the interior trim panel, which is retained by eleven screws.

7.1 Door wiring multi-plug

7.3 One of the hinge cotter pin nuts (arrowed)

2  Disconnect the wiring from the heated rear window, aerial pre-amplifier and lock solenoid. Tie some string to each piece of wiring, then free the grommet and draw the wiring out of the tailgate. Untie the string and leave it in the tailgate for use when refitting.
3  Repeat paragraph 2 for the rear wiper motor and the rear washer tube, and any other electrical equipment.
4  Have an assistant support the tailgate. Disconnect the struts from the tailgate – refer to Section 18 if necessary.
5  Jam the tailgate latch with a piece of wood or cardboard so that the tailgate cannot shut. Lower the tailgate.
6  Working inside the vehicle, prise out the hinge covers from the headlining. Remove the hinge nuts and recover the washers (photo).
7  With the aid of an assistant, lift the tailgate away from the vehicle.
8  Commence refitting by offering the tailgate to its aperture, aligning the hinges and reconnecting the struts. Do not allow the struts alone to support the tailgate until the hinge nuts have been fitted.
9  Fit the hinge nuts and washers. Do not fully tighten the nuts yet.
10  Secure any wiring looms and the washer tube to the pieces of string used during removal. (It is to be hoped that a new tailgate will be supplied with wiring or string in place). Draw the wires and tube into position. Tape up the connectors if necessary to prevent them snagging.
11  Reconnect the wires and the washer tube and refit the grommets.
12  Close and latch the tailgate and adjust its position so that an even gap exists all round it, then tighten the hinge nuts.
13  Refit the hinge covers and the interior trim panel.

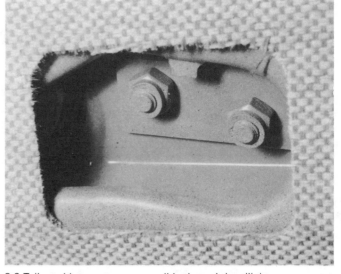

8.6 Tailgate hinge nuts are accessible through headlining

## 9  Sliding roof – removal and refitting

1  This procedure applies to the manually-operated roof. For removal of the electrically-operated roof motor, see Chapter 12, Section 32.
2  Open the roof. Remove the four setscrews and ten self-tapping screws which secure the sliding roof frame.
3  Apply masking tape to the front and sides of the roof aperture to protect the paintwork.
4  Close the roof. Remove the 'Torx' screw which secures the operating handle, counterholding the handle whilst slackening the screw (photo). Remove the operating handle.
5  With the aid of an assistant, remove the sliding roof assembly by pushing it up from inside and drawing it forwards from outside. Support the rear of the roof as it is removed.
6  Refit by reversing the removal operations.

## 10  Bonnet release cable – removal and refitting

1  If the release cable has broken, the bonnet catch can be released from below with the aid of a long screwdriver. It will be necessary to raise and support the front of the vehicle for access. With the bonnet open, proceed as follows.
2  Remove the steering column lower shroud.
3  Disconnect the cable from the release lever by pulling the cable outer from the bracket, then unhooking the inner from the lever (photo).
4  Pull the cable through the bulkhead grommet into the engine bay. Release the cable from any clips or ties.
5  Disengage the inner and outer cables from the bonnet catch (photo). Remove the cable.
6  Refit by reversing the removal operations, being careful not to kink the cable or bend it sharply. Check that operation of the release lever causes the catch to move before closing the bonnet.

## 11  Door striker plate – adjustment

1  Open the door and slacken the two 'Torx' screws which secure the striker plate. The screws should be loosened until the plate can be moved by tapping, but not by hand pressure.
2  Move the striker plate if necessary until it is aligned with the centre of the latch opening (Fig. 11.2).
3  Open and close the door a few times until the locking action is smooth and the door position when shut is satisfactory.
4  Open the door again and tighten the striker plate screws.

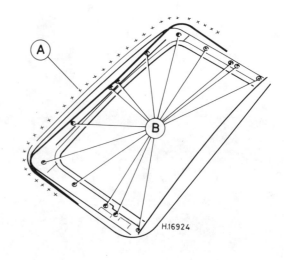

H.16924

**Fig. 11.1 Sliding roof removal (Sec 9)**

A  Masking tape　　　　　　　B  Frame screws

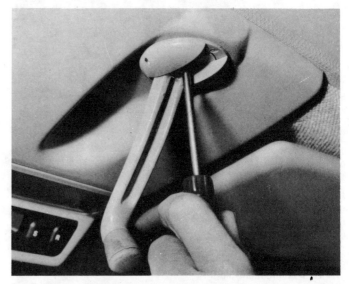

9.4 Removing the sliding roof operating handle

10.3A Bonnet release cable connected to release lever

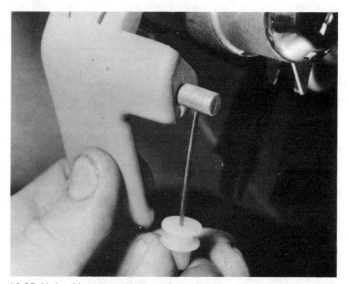

10.3B Unhooking the cable inner from the release lever

10.5 Bonnet release cable connected to catch

## 12 Door exterior handle – removal and refitting

1   Remove the door interior trim panel (Section 20).
2   Carefully peel away the foam rubber sheet in the area of the door handle operating rod. Disconnect the rod from the handle.
3   Remove the two screws which secure the handle to the door, then remove the handle.
4   Refit by reversing the removal operations.

## 13 Door lock barrel – removal and refitting

1   Remove the door interior trim panel (Section 20).
2   Carefully peel away the foam rubber sheet in the area of the lock barrel. Unhook the operating rod from the lock barrel lever (photo).
3   When so equipped, unclip the switch from the lock barrel and disconnect its wiring.
4   Remove the large U-clip which secures the lock barrel to the door. Remove the barrel.

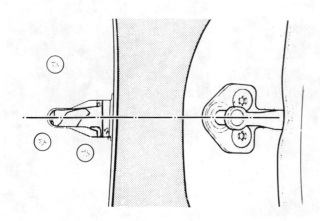

Fig. 11.2 Door latch striker in line with centre of opening (Sec 11)

13.2 Unhook the operating rod (arrowed) from the lock barrel lever

5   Refit by reversing the removal operations. Check the lock for
correct operation before refitting the door trim.

## 14 Door latch assembly – removal and refitting

1   Remove the door interior trim panel (Section 20).
2   Carefully peel away the foam rubber sheet in the area of the door
latch. Unhook the lock barrel operating rod from the latch. Also
unhook the exterior handle operating rod.
3   Disconnect the lock motor multi-plug (when fitted). Remove the
two screws to release the lock motor. Pivot the motor to release the
operating rod from it.
4   Remove the door interior handle securing screw (photo). Slide the
handle rearwards to release it from the door. Unhook the rods from the
handle and release them from their bushes.
5   When door latch switches are fitted, disconnect the switch
multi-plug.
6   Remove the three screws which secure the door latch (photo).
Manoeuvre the latch behind the window channel and out of the door
through the large cut-out. Further displacement or removal of the foam
rubber sheet may be necessary.
7   Refit in the reverse order to removal, noting the following points:

   (a)  *Apply a little grease to the interior handle rods where they
        pass through the plastic bushes*
   (b)  *When securing the interior handle, have the locking lever in
        the 'unlocked' position, hold the assembly forwards as far as it
        will go and tighten the securing screw*
   (c)  *Check all functions before refitting the trim panel*

## 15 Door weatherstrip – removal and refitting

### Door weatherstrip
1   Open the door and remove the weatherstrip securing screw from
the latch end. In the case of the rear door, also remove the screw from
the hinge end.
2   Carefully lift the latch end of the weatherstrip and pull it off the
door.
3   Refit by reversing the removal operations, using the palm of the
hand to seat the weatherstrip.

### Aperture weatherstrip
4   Open the door. Remove the scuff plate securing screws from the
bottom of the door aperture.
5   Pull the old weatherstrip out of the door aperture.
6   Fit the new weatherstrip, starting at the right-angled corner at the
top. Fit the weatherstrip to the other corners and bends, leaving the
straight sections until last.
7   Refit the scuff, plate securing screws.

## 16 Tailgate lock barrel – removal and refitting

1   Disconnect the battery negative lead.
2   Remove the tailgate interior trim panel, which is secured by eleven
screws.
3   Remove the six nuts which secure the tailgate handle. Remove the
handle and recover the gasket.
4   Disconnect the tailgate lock switch multi-plug. Release the switch
locking tab and remove the switch.
5   Disconnect the operating rod from the lock lever (photo). Extract
the U-clip and remove the lock barrel.
6   Refit by reversing the removal operations.

## 17 Tailgate latch assembly – removal and refitting

1   Disconnect the battery negative lead.
2   Remove the tailgate interior trim panel, which is secured by eleven
screws.
3   Unhook the operating rod from the tailgate latch. Also disconnect
the lock switch and solenoid multi-plugs.

14.4 Door interior handle securing screw (arrowed)

14.6 Door latch securing screws

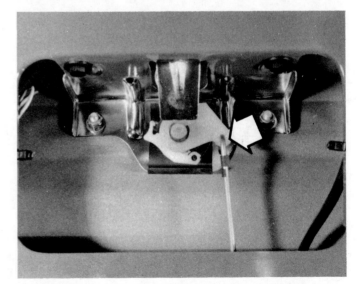

16.5 Operating rod (arrowed) connected to tailgate lock lever

4    Remove the three bolts which secure the tailgate latch. Remove the latch.
5    Refit by reversing the removal operations.

### 18 Tailgate strut – removal and refitting

1    Open the tailgate and support it with a piece of wood.
2    Release the strut from its mountings by raising the spring clips with a small screwdriver, then pulling the strut off the ball-stands. Do not raise the clips more than 4 mm (0.16 in) if the strut is to be re-used (photo).
3    Do not attempt to dismantle a strut, and dispose of it safely. It contains gas under pressure.
4    To refit a strut, position it over the ball-studs. Push on each end in turn until it snaps home.

### 19 Fuel filler lock barrel – removal and refitting

1    Open the fuel filler flap. Remove the key.
2    Apply pressure to the lock barrel at the key slot, using the thumb of one hand. With the other hand insert a screwdriver into the cut-out in the filler flap to release the lock barrel retaining spring. As the spring is released, thumb pressure will eject the lock barrel into the petrol tank.
3    To refit, push the lock barrel into the flap until the retaining spring clicks home.

### 20 Door interior trim panel – removal and refitting

*Front door*
1    Open the door and remove the screws which secure the front and rear edges of the trim panel (photo).

2    Remove the two screws from under the covers on the door pocket. Unclip and remove the pocket.
3    On models with electrically-operated windows and mirrors, prise out and disconnect the window and mirror switches. The window switch multi-plugs on the driver's side are colour coded: the blue plug is outermost. On models with manually-operated windows, remove the window winder handle, which is secured by a single screw (photos).
4    Remove the two screws located under the arm-rest. One of these screws will be accessible through the window switch aperture, (on higher level trim models) when applicable (photos).

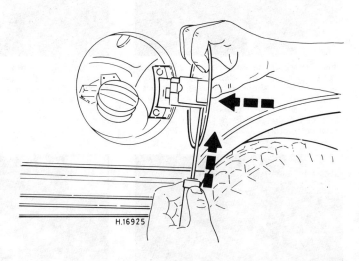

**Fig. 11.3 Removing the fuel filler flap lock barrel (Sec 19)**

18.2 Releasing a tailgate strut by prising up the spring clip

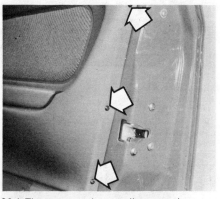

20.1 Three screws (arrowed) secure the rear edge of the front door trim panel

20.3A Prise the cap off the window winder handle ...

20.3B ... and remove the screw

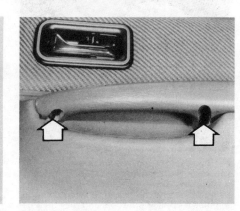

20.4A The two armrest screws (arrowed) – low level trim

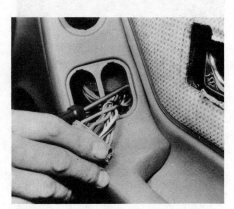

20.4B Access to this screw is through the window switch aperture

**1**

This photographic sequence shows the steps taken to repair the dent and paintwork damage shown above. In general, the procedure for repairing a hole will be similar; where there are substantial differences, the procedure is clearly described and shown in a separate photograph.

**2**

First remove any trim around the dent, then hammer out the dent where access is possible. This will minimise filling. Here, after the large dent has been hammered out, the damaged area is being made slightly concave.

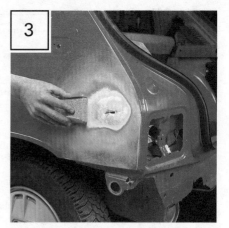

**3**

Next, remove all paint from the damaged area by rubbing with coarse abrasive paper or using a power drill fitted with a wire brush or abrasive pad. 'Feather' the edge of the boundary with good paintwork using a finer grade of abrasive paper.

**4**

Where there are holes or other damage, the sheet metal should be cut away before proceeding further. The damaged area and any signs of rust should be treated with Turtle Wax Hi-Tech Rust Eater, which will also inhibit further rust formation.

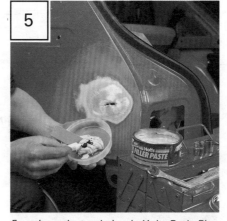

**5**

*For a large dent or hole* mix Holts Body Plus Resin and Hardener according to the manufacturer's instructions and apply around the edge of the repair. Press Glass Fibre Matting over the repair area and leave for 20-30 minutes to harden. Then ...

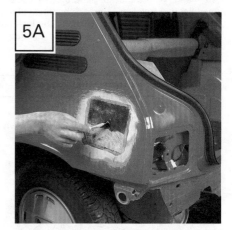

**5A**

... brush more Holts Body Plus Resin and Hardener onto the matting and leave to harden. Repeat the sequence with two or three layers of matting, checking that the final layer is lower than the surrounding area. Apply Holts Body Plus Filler Paste as shown in Step 5B.

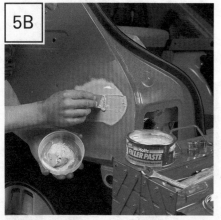

**5B**

*For a medium dent*, mix Holts Body Plus Filler Paste and Hardener according to the manufacturer's instructions and apply it with a flexible applicator. Apply thin layers of filler at 20-minute intervals, until the filler surface is slightly proud of the surrounding bodywork.

**5C**

*For small dents and scratches* use Holts No Mix Filler Paste straight from the tube. Apply it according to the instructions in thin layers, using the spatula provided. It will harden in minutes if applied outdoors and may then be used as its own knifing putty.

**6**

Use a plane or file for initial shaping. Then, using progressively finer grades of wet-and-dry paper, wrapped round a sanding block, and copious amounts of clean water, rub down the filler until glass smooth. 'Feather' the edges of adjoining paintwork.

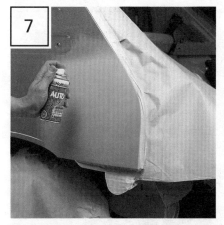

**7**

Protect adjoining areas before spraying the whole repair area and at least one inch of the surrounding sound paintwork with Holts Dupli-Color primer.

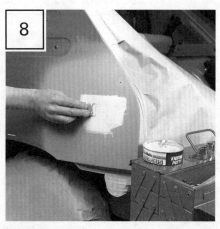

**8**

Fill any imperfections in the filler surface with a small amount of Holts Body Plus Knifing Putty. Using plenty of clean water, rub down the surface with a fine grade wet-and-dry paper – 400 grade is recommended – until it is really smooth.

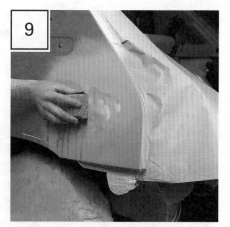

**9**

Carefully fill any remaining imperfections with knifing putty before applying the last coat of primer. Then rub down the surface with Holts Body Plus Rubbing Compound to ensure a really smooth surface.

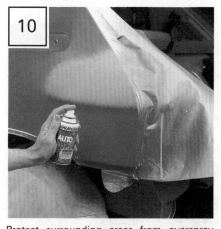

**10**

Protect surrounding areas from overspray before applying the topcoat in several thin layers. Agitate Holts Dupli-Color aerosol thoroughly. Start at the repair centre, spraying outwards with a side-to-side motion.

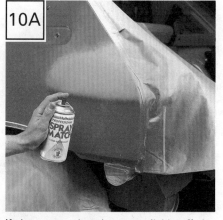

**10A**

If the exact colour is not available off the shelf, local Holts Professional Spraymatch Centres will custom fill an aerosol to match perfectly.

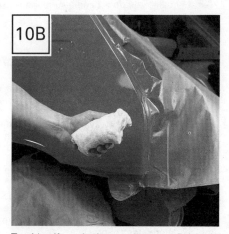

**10B**

To identify whether a lacquer finish is required, rub a painted unrepaired part of the body with wax and a clean cloth.

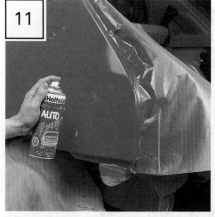

**11**

If *no* traces of paint appear on the cloth, spray Holts Dupli-Color clear lacquer over the repaired area to achieve the correct gloss level.

**12**

**13**

The paint will take about two weeks to harden fully. After this time it can be 'cut' with a mild cutting compound such as Turtle Wax Minute Cut prior to polishing with a final coating of Turtle Wax Extra.

**14**

When carrying out bodywork repairs, remember that the quality of the finished job is proportional to the time and effort expended.

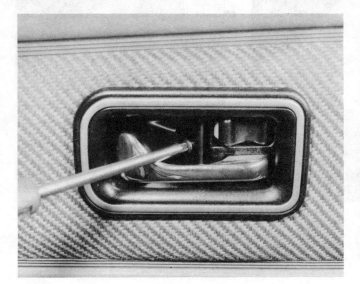

20.5 Removing the door handle surround screw

20.6 Removing the mirror mounting trim screw

5  Remove the door interior handle surround, which is retained by a single screw (photo).
6  Remove the triangular trim panel which covers the door mirror mountings. This trim panel is secured by a single screw concealed under a cover (photo).
7  Pull the trim panel away from the door at the top to free the push-in clips, then lift it to free it from the lower mountings. A certain amount of jerking and thumping may be necessary to release the clips and mountings.
8  To gain access to the components within the door it will be necessary to peel back the foam rubber sheet. This sheet is secured by a bead of powerful adhesive around its edge, and some of the door hardware may be riveted through it. To remove the sheet from around a riveted fitting, carefully cut it free with a sharp knife, then glue it back in place afterwards (photos).
9  Refit by reversing the removal operations.

### Rear door
10  Operations are similar to those just described for the front door. Note that the interior handle surround is secured by two screws, one of which is accessible after removing the ashtray.

20.8A Peeling back the rubber sheet

## 21  Door window glass – removal and refitting

1  Remove the door interior trim panel as described in the previous Sections. Peel back the foam rubber sheet.
2  Remove the door weather strip, referring if necessary to Section 15.

### Front door
3  Raise and support the window. Undo the two screws which secure the glass to the regulator mechanism and lower the glass into the door.
4  Remove the three screws (one front, two rear) which secure the window channels.
5  Free the glass from the channels. Carefully remove the glass upwards through the window aperture.
6  Refit by reversing the removal operations. Note that the channels are adjustable: wind the window up and down after securing the channels and adjust them if necessary for smooth operation. The regulator mechanism can also be adjusted (Fig. 11.5).

### Rear door
7  Remove the two screws which secure the window channel.
8  Remove the two screws which secure the glass to the regulator mechanism. Free the glass from the channel and carefully lift it out through the window aperature.
9  When refitting, secure the glass and the channel, then make sure

20.8B Front door with rubber sheet peeled back

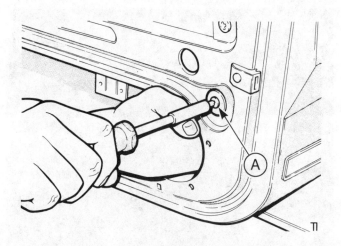

**Fig. 11.4 One of the front door window channel screws (A) (Sec 21)**

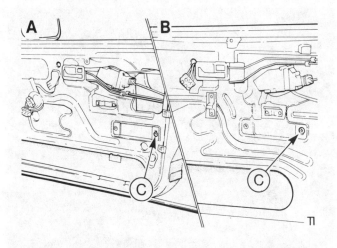

**Fig. 11.5 Window regulator adjustment screws (C) (Sec 21)**

A  *Front door*                     B  *Rear door*

that the window can wind up and down smoothly before proceeding further. Adjust the channel or regulator if necessary.
10  Refit the weatherstrip and trim panel.

## 22  Door window regulator mechanism – removal and refitting

1  The window regulator mechanism is riveted to the door skin. A blind rivet gun will therefore be needed for successful refitting.
2  Remove the door interior trim panel as described in Section 20. Peel back the foam rubber sheet.
3  Support the glass and remove the two screws which secure it to the regulator mechanism. Wedge or tape the glass in the raised position.
4  When applicable, disconnect the window motor multi-plug (photo).
5  Remove the two slide screws and drill out the four rivets which secure the regulator (photos). Remove the regulator through the large lower aperture in the door.
6  When refitting, secure the regulator with the two slide screws, then fit four new rivets in the rivet holes (photo).
7  The remainder of refitting is a reversal of removal.

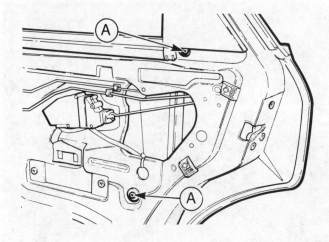

**Fig. 11.6 Rear door window channel screws (A) (Sec 21)**

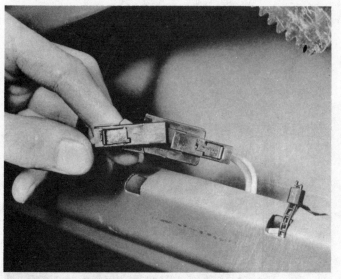

22.4 Window motor multi-plug

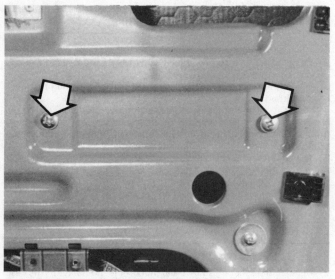

22.5A The two regulator slide screws (arrowed)

22.5B Two of the rivets (arrowed) which secure the regulator. Two other rivets are out of shot to right

22.6 Fitting new rivets with a blind rivet gun

### 23 Windscreen and fixed glass – removal and refitting

The windscreen, the rear (tailgate) window and the rear quarter windows are all secured and weatherproofed by special adhesives. The equipment and skills required to remove and refit this type of window are beyond the scope of this book. Consult a Ford dealer or a windscreen specialist.

### 24 Bonnet insulation panel – removal and refitting

1   Open and prop the bonnet.
2   When an under-bonnet light is fitted, disconnect its wire. Remove the screw which secures the light, pull the wire through the insulation panel and remove it.
3   Remove the centre screws from the plastic fittings which secure the insulation (photo). Prise the outer parts of the fittings out of the bonnet and remove the insulation panel.
4   Refit by reversing the removal operations. Feed the under-bonnet light wire into place before finally securing the insulation panel.

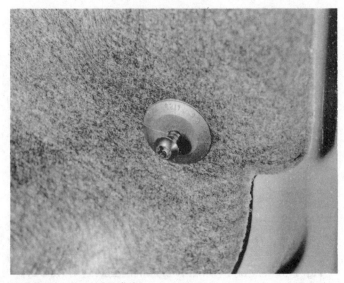

24.3 Bonnet insulation fitting

### 25 Radiator grille – removal and refitting

1   Open and prop the bonnet.
2   Remove the two screws which secure the centre section of the grille.
3   When fitted, remove the headlight washer jets by pulling them out of their fittings.
4   Release one end of the grille side section from its fixing next to the direction indicator lens (photo). Carefully pull the side section away from its mountings until it can be separated from the grille centre section.
5   The centre section can now be released from the other side section by raising the tang on the catch which holds the sections together, then twisting them apart.
6   Refit by reversing the removal operations.

### 26 Side mouldings – removal and refitting

1   Prise the centre insert out of the moulding with a screwdriver.
2   Remove the securing screws and pull off the moulding. In the case of the door mouldings, note that the ends are also secured with adhesive tape.

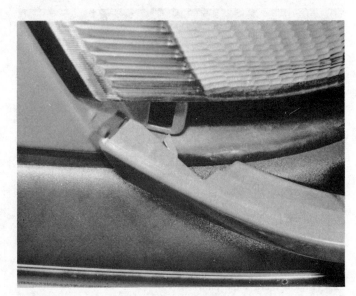

25.4 Removing a grille side section

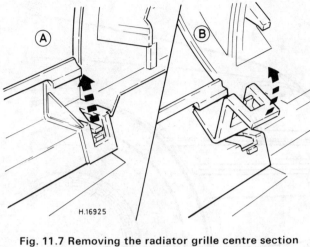

Fig. 11.7 Removing the radiator grille centre section (Sec 25)

A   Raise tang                    B   Twist apart

3   Refit by reversing the removal operations. Use new adhesive tape when necessary.

## 27 Windscreen mouldings – removal and refitting

1   A blind rivet gun will be needed for this job.
2   Open the front doors. Remove the gutter weatherstrip, making sure to release the bottom flap which is glued to the 'A' pillar.
3   Drill out the five rivets which secure the side moulding. The side moulding can now be removed.
4   Repeat the operations on the other side of the vehicle, then remove the upper moulding by pulling it upwards.
5   Commence refitting by pushing the upper moulding onto its clips. Make sure it is centrally aligned.
6   Refit the side mouldings and secure them with new blind rivets.
7   Clean and degrease the gutter weatherstrip flaps, then glue them in position and refit the weatherstrips.

## 28 Tailgate window mouldings – removal and refitting

1   Open the tailgate. From inside remove the two nuts which secure the upper moulding and the two screws which secure the lower moulding. Close the tailgate.
2   Prise off the lower moulding and fittings.
3   Pull off the side mouldings, which are clipped to the edge of the glass.
4   To remove the upper moulding, carefully lift one end. Free the moulding from its clips, working from the lifted end, and remove it.
5   To remove the lower moulding, simply pull it from its clips.
6   Refit by reversing the removal operations. Make sure that the upper and lower mouldings are centred before securing them.

## 29 Door window frame mouldings – removal and refitting

1   A blind rivet gun will be needed to refit some of these mouldings.
2   Commence by removing the door weatherstrip (Section 15).

### Front door

3   Remove the nut which secures the upper moulding. Carefully prise the upper moulding off the door.
4   Prise the edge moulding out of the window channel, then twist it and remove it.
5   Remove the door mirror (Section 37).
6   Drill out the rivet which secures the front corner moulding. Remove the moulding.

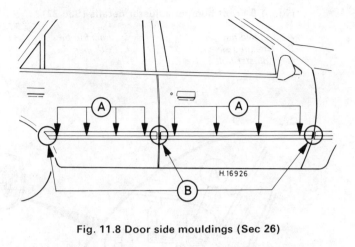

Fig. 11.8 Door side mouldings (Sec 26)

A   Screws                    B   Adhesive tape

7   Refit by reversing the removal operations, using a new blind rivet to secure the corner moulding.

### Rear door

8   Remove the nut which secures the upper moulding to the front top corner of the door. Carefully pull the moulding from the door, separating the stud and bush fitting at the rear end.
9   Drill out the rivet which secures the rear moulding to the top of the door. Separate the rear moulding flange from the door and window channel and remove it by twisting it.
10   Remove the front moulding by separating the weatherstrip from the back of it and lifting the moulding from the door.
11   Refit by reversing the removal operations. Use a new rivet to secure the rear moulding.

## 30 Rear quarter window moulding – removal and refitting

1   A blind rivet gun will be needed to refit the moulding.
2   Open the rear door. Drill out the rivets which secure the weatherstrip to the mouldings.
3   Drill out the top rivet and remove the upper moulding from its studs.
4   Open the tailgate, drill out the lower moulding rivet and remove the lower moulding from its clips.
5   Drill out the three rivets which secure the side moulding. Remove the side moulding.
6   Refit by reversing the removal operations, using new rivets to secure the mouldings.

## 31 Motifs and emblems – removal and refitting

1   The bonnet emblem, tailgate motif and other badges are glued in place. They may be removed by using a piece of thin braided nylon cord, making a back-and-forth motion to cut through the adhesive.
2   Clean old adhesive from the bonnet or boot lid using methylated spirit.
3   If a new emblem is to be fitted, warm it (for instance with a hairdryer) until it is warm to the touch. Peel the backing paper off the adhesive surface and press the emblem into position, making sure that it is properly aligned. Hold the emblem in place for at least half a minute to allow the glue to set.

## 32 Front bumper – height adjustment

1   Front bumper height is easily adjusted by means of the two adjusters incorporated in the front mountings (photo). A 'Torx' key to fit the locking bolt and a 24 mm socket will be required.

**Fig. 11.9 Front bumper adjuster details (Sec 32)**

A  Captive nut          D  Locking bolt
B  Threaded sleeve      E  Bumper
C  Adjuster bolt

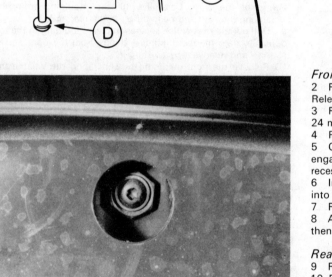

32.1 One of the front bumper height adjusters, seen from below

2  Slacken the locking bolts by half a turn each using the 'Torx' key.
3  Turn the adjuster bolts, using the 24 mm socket, until the bumper height is correct and the same on each side. As a guide, bumper height is correct when the gap between the top of the bumper and the bottom of the radiator grille side extensions is 7 mm (0.28 in),.
4  Tighten the locking bolts when adjustment is correct.

## 33 Bumpers – removal and refitting

1  Raise the front or rear of the vehicle (as applicable) and support it securely.

### Front

2  Release the side fasteners by turning them through 90° (photo). Release the lateral supports by pulling them off the bumper.
3  Remove the locking bolts completely, using a 'Torx' key, then use a 24 mm socket to remove the adjuster bolts.
4  Pull the bumper away from the front of the vehicle and remove it.
5  Commence refitting by offering the bumper to the vehicle, engaging the side pins and the front mounting brackets in their recesses.
6  Insert the locking bolts into the adjuster bolts. Screw the adjusters into place, but do not tighten them yet.
7  Refit the lateral supports and side fasteners.
8  Adjust the bumper height as described in the previous Section, then lower the vehicle.

### Rear

9  Release the side fasteners by turning them though 90°.
10  Remove the two 'Torx' screws which secure the rear bumper to its mountings (photo).
11  Disconnect the number plate light wiring and free the wiring from the bumper.
12  Pull the bumper away from the rear of the vehicle and remove it.
13  If a new bumper is being fitted, adjust the mounting brackets so that the distance between the bumper and bracket top faces is 111 mm (4.4 in).
14  Refit by reversing the removal operations. Lower the vehicle on completion.

## 34 Bumper mouldings – removal and refitting

1  Remove the bumper as described in the previous Section

### All models except Ghia

2  Prise the old moulding out of the bumper.
3  Scrape all remains of adhesive from the moulding groove in the bumper. Clean the groove with methylated spirit and allow it to dry.
4  Apply adhesive primer (to Ford spec. ESK-M2G-264A) to the bumper groove and allow it to dry. This primer should be obtained with the new moulding from a Ford dealer.

33.2 Bumper side fastener – twist to release

33.10 A rear bumper mounting screw

5   Heat the new moulding with (for instance) a hair dryer or fan heater until it is warm to the touch. Do not coil the moulding tighter than 300 mm (11.8 in) in diameter.
6   Peel the backing paper off the moulding. Insert one end into the slot at one end of the groove so that approximately 10 mm (0.4 in) protrudes through the slot. Press the moulding into the groove, working along the bumper, and tuck the other end of the moulding into the slot at the far end. *Do not cut off the ends of the moulding: they are sealed to prevent water entering.*
7   Seat the moulding by running a hand-held roller along it.
8   Refit the bumper.

*Ghia only*
9   The procedure is similar to that just described, but with the following differences:

(a)  *The moulding is secured with studs and nuts as well as with adhesive.*
(b)  *The adhesive tape is supplied separately from the moulding, and both bumper and moulding must be primed.*

10  When purchasing the new moulding, also obtain the correct type of adhesive tape and primer.

## 35  Front spoiler – removal and refitting

1   A blind rivet gun will be needed to refit the spoiler.
2   Raise and support the front of the vehicle.
3   Drill out the two rivets at each end which secure the spoiler to the bumper.
4   Remove the twelve nuts and washers which secure the line of the spoiler to the bumper. Lift off the spoiler; it can be separated into two halves if wished.
5   When refitting, secure the ends of the spoiler first. Use new rivets and make sure that the bumper and spoiler are correctly aligned.
6   Refit and tighten the twelve nuts and washers. Lower the vehicle on completion.

## 36  Headlining – removal and refitting

1   Open the doors, the tailgate, the sliding roof (when fitted) and the bonnet.
2   Disconnect the battery negative lead.
3   Free the weatherstrips from the tops of the door apertures and from around the pillars.

4   On models with a sliding roof, remove the edge trim from the aperture.
5   Remove the tailgate hinge covers.
6   If a rear interior light is fitted, remove it.
7   Remove the grab handles and the sun visors.
8   Remove the front interior light, the sliding roof handle and the overhead console (as applicable).
9   Unbolt the front seat belt upper anchors. Remove the upper trim from the 'B' pillars. This trim is secured by a single screw on each side of the vehicle.
10  Remove the securing screws and detach the 'C' and 'D' pillar trim panels.
11  Remove the top of the facia panel – see Section 39.
12  Remove the securing screw from the base of the 'A' pillar trim on each side. Detach the 'A' pillar trim panels.
13  Remove the headlining through the tailgate, peeling it back from around the sliding roof (when applicable – see paragraph 15).
14  Refitting is essentially a reversal of the removal procedure. The services of an assistant will be required during the initial stages of refitting.
15  When a sliding roof is fitted, the headlining is secured around the aperture with double-sided adhesive tape.

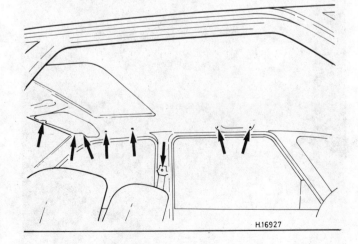

Fig. 11.10 Grab handle, seat belt anchor and sun visor retaining screws (arrowed) (Sec 36)

## 37 Exterior mirror – removal and refitting

1   To remove a manually-adjusted mirror, first pull off the operating lever cover. Remove the triangular trim panel which covers the mirror mounting: this panel is secured by a single screw concealed under a cover. Pull out the control retaining clip (photos).
2   For electrically-adjusted mirrors, remove the door interior trim panel (including the triangular trim panel) and peel back the top part of the foam sheet for access to the mirror multi-plug. Refer to Section 20. Disconnect the multi-plug.
3   For all mirrors, support the mirror and remove the three securing screws. Lift the mirror off the door, disengaging the base from the rubber seal (photos).
4   Refit by reversing the removal operations.

## 38 Interior mirror – removal and refitting

1   Remove the mirror from the windscreen by 'sawing' through the adhesive bond with a piece of nylon cord.

2   Clean the mirror base and the mounting area on the windscreen with methylated spirit. Both items must be perfectly clean, and the windscreen must be at room temperature (20°C/68°F approx).
3   Peel off the backing paper from one side of the special adhesive patch. Press the sticky side of the patch firmly onto the mirror base.
4   Warm the mirror base and patch to 50° to 70°C (122° to 158°F). Immediately remove the backing paper from the other side of the patch and press the mirror firmly onto the mounting area. Hold it in position for at least two minutes, and do not attempt to adjust the mirror for at least half an hour.
5   Beware of using proprietary adhesives to attach the mirror to the windscreen: not all are suitable and some may leave residues which are difficult to remove.

## 39 Facia panels and trim – removal and refitting

1   Disconnect the battery negative lead.
2   Remove the instrument panel surround, which is secured by four screws. Pull out the heater louvre panel.
3   Remove the facia top (crash pad), which is secured by five screws

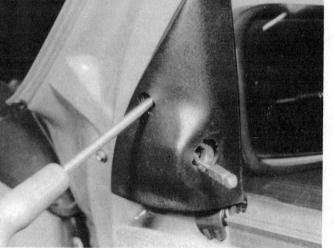

37.1A Removing the mirror mounting trim screw

37.1B Pull out the clip (arrowed) to release the mirror control

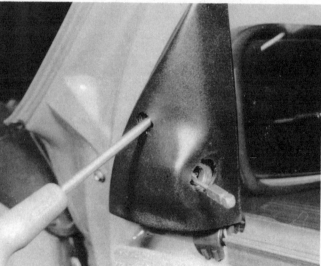

37.3A Removing a mirror securing screw. Other two screws are arrowed

37.3B Removing a mirror from the door

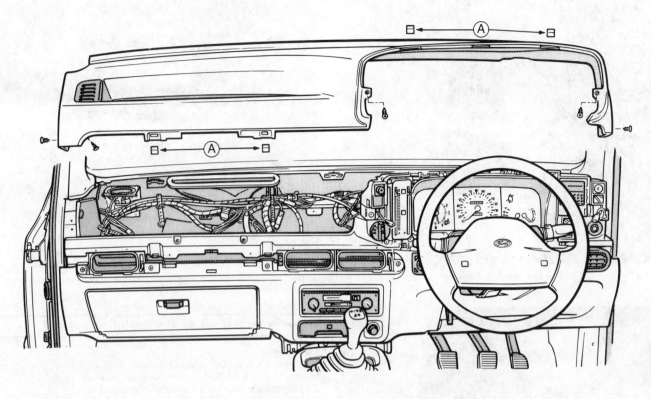

Fig. 11.11 Facia top retaining screws and spring clips (A) (Sec 39)

and four spring clips. With the screws and clip removed, a good tug will free the top from the clips next to the windscreen (photos).
4  Remove the carpet and soft trim from below the facia on both sides. It is clipped in place.
5  Remove the driver's side lower trim panel, which is secured by six screws. One of the screws is only accessible after removing the air vent grille. Unclip the AWS bulb failure warning module, when fitted (photos).
6  Disconnect the glovebox arms and hinges. Withdraw the hinge pins and remove the lid.
7  Slide the auxiliary fuse panel off its mounting and remove the

glovebox light (when fitted).
8  Remove the ABS and ESC/EEC modules (Chapter 12, Section 27). Remove the two nuts and washers from inside the glovebox.
9  Remove the radio, stowage box or graphic equaliser, ashtray, cigarette lighter panel and (when applicable) the gear lever gaiter.
10 Remove the centre console, disconnecting switches, rear heater controls etc as necessary. See Section 40.
11 Remove the six screws which secure the passenger's side lower panel. Remove the panel.
12 Refit by reversing the removal operations, transferring the brackets, captive nuts or other fittings to any new panels being fitted.

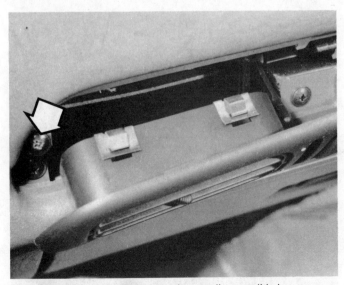

39.3A One of the facia top screws (arrowed) accessible by removing the heater louvre panel

39.3B One of the facia top spring clips

39.3C Releasing the facia top (seen through windscreen)

39.5A One of the screws which secures the driver's side lower trim panel

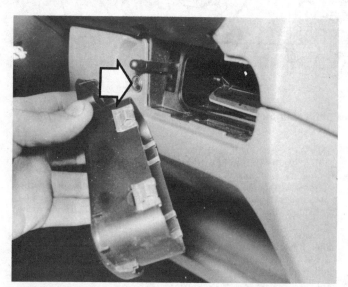

39.5B Remove the grille for access to the screw (arrowed)

## 40 Centre console – removal and refitting

### Low series

1   Remove the rubber mat and the two screw cover plugs from the front of the console. Remove the two front screws (photos).
2   Remove the gear lever knob by unscrewing it.
3   Remove the central securing screw, which is also concealed by a cover plug, and the two rear screws (one each side of the handbrake) (photos).
4   Lift off the console, moving the handbrake and gear lever as necessary.
5   Refit by reversing the removal operations.

### High series

6   Disconnect the battery negative lead.
7   Open the cassette box. Remove the two screws, accessible from under the lid, which secure the switch panel (photo). Raise the rear of the panel, disconnect the multi-plugs and remove it.
8   Remove the cassette box liner and the box itself, which is secured by two screws (photo).
9   Remove the rear control panel by undoing the two screws in the

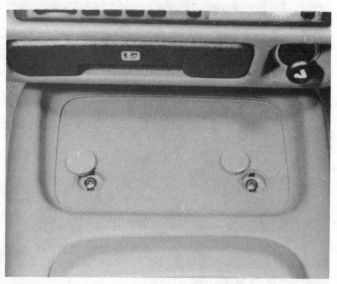

40.1 The two front screws which secure the low series console

40.3A The central securing screw ...

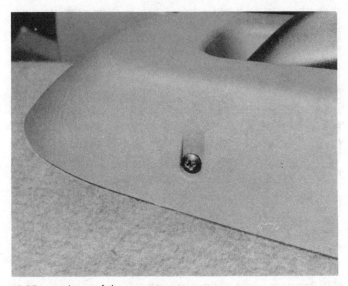

40.3B ... and one of the rear screws

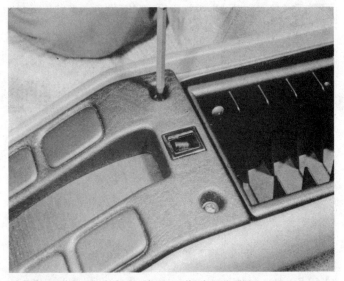

40.7 Removing a switch panel screw (high series)

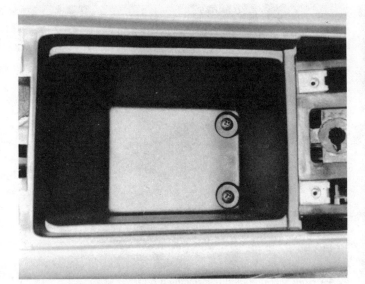

40.8 Cassette box, showing securing screws

40.12 Removing a front securing screw

top corners and pulling off the heater control knob. Disconnect the cigarette lighter, and other wiring when applicable.
10  Remove the two screws which secure the rear heater control.
11  Remove the gear selector knob by unscrewing it.
12  Remove the four remaining screws (two at the front and one on each side) (photo). It may be necessary to cut the carpet to gain access to the side screws.
13  Remove the console, freeing it from the facia lower trim, the gear selector and the handbrake.
14  Refit by reversing the removal operations.

## 41  Overhead console – removal and refitting

1  Disconnect the battery negative lead.
2  Remove the interior light by carefully prising it out of the console and disconnecting it.
3  Remove the sliding roof control handle or switches (as applicable).
4  Remove the two retaining screws from the front of the console. Pull the front of the console down and then slide the assembly rearwards to release it from the two clips (photos). These clips may be quite tight. Disconnect the clock.
5  Refit by reversing the removal operations.

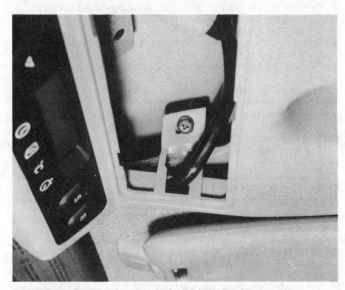

41.4A One of the overhead console retaining screws

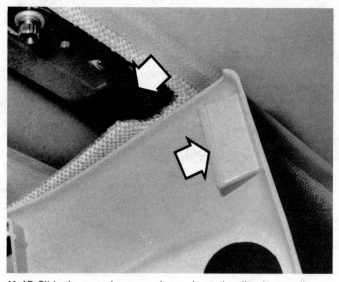

41.4B Slide the console rearwards to release the clips (arrowed)

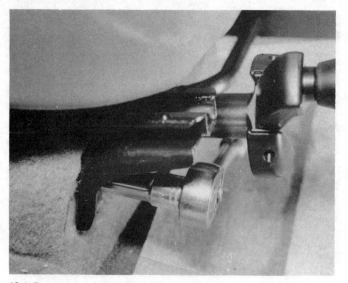

42.1 Removing a front seat retaining bolt

## 42 Front seat – removal and refitting

1　Move the seat rearwards as far as possible, then remove the two front retaining bolts (photo).
2　Disconnect the assist spring from under the driver's seat. (Moving the seat forwards will reduce the tension on this spring, but also makes it harder to get at).
3　When applicable, disconnect the seat heating and/or adjustment motor multi-plugs.
4　Move the seat fully forwards and remove the three rear retaining bolts. These bolts are under plastic covers (photos).
5　Lift out the seat, complete with adjustment mechanism and seat belt buckle.
6　If a new seat is being fitted, transfer the adjustment mechanism and other components to it.
7　Refit by reversing the removal operations. Tighten the seat retaining bolts to the specified torque.

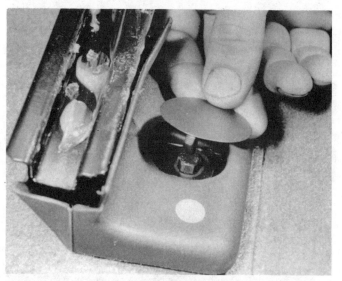

42.4A Front seat outboard rear retaining bolt

## 43 Front seat air cushion – removal and refitting

1　Remove the front seat as described in the previous Section.
2　Remove the side trim pieces from the seat. Free the air tube by removing its two securing screws.
3　Separate the backrest from the base of the seat by removing the four retaining bolts.
4　Remove the backrest cover by unbending its retaining tags and sliding it off.
5　Expose the air cushion by lifting up the foam padding. Cut the hog rings (wire loops) which secure the corners of the cushion and remove it with the air hoses.
6　When refitting, use new hog rings. Position the cut-out in the cushion level with the second spring in the backrest.
7　The remainder of refitting is a reversal of the removal procedure.

## 44 Seat belts – care and maintenance

1　All models are fitted with inertia reel front seat belts as standard. Rear seat belts are available as an extra.
2　Maintenance is limited to periodic inspection of the belts for fraying or other damage. Also check the operation of the buckles and retractor mechanisms. In case of damage or malfunction the belt must be renewed.
3　If it is wished to clean the belts, use only an approved upholstery cleaner or a weak solution of detergent, followed by rinsing with water.

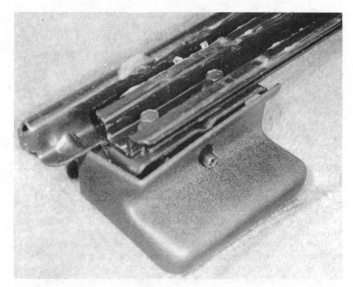

42.4B The other two rear retaining bolts are under the cover

Do not use solvents, strong detergents, dyes or bleaches. Keep the belt extended until it is dry.

4  Belts which have been subjected to impact loads must be renewed.

## 45  Front seats belts – removal and refitting

1  Remove the cover from the belt top anchor. With the adjustable type of anchor, the cover is removed by levering out the adjuster button and removing two screws.

2  Remove the anchor bolt or nut and detach the seat belt runner from it. Note the position of any washers or spacers (photo).

3  Carefully pull out the door aperture weatherstrips (front and rear) from the 'B' pillar (photo). Unclip the pillar trim.

4  Remove the screws which secure the retractor cover trim, pull away more of the weatherstrips and remove the trim. Also remove the webbing guide, which is secured by two screws.

5  Unbolt the lower anchor and the retractor, again noting the position of any washers or spacers. Remove the retractor and webbing (photo).

6  The seat belt buckle is secured to the seat frame by two 'Torx' screws. There is no need to renew the buckle just because the retractor

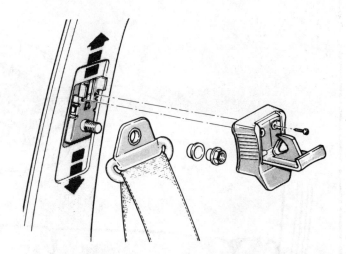

Fig. 11.12 Front seat belt adjustable top anchor (Sec 45)

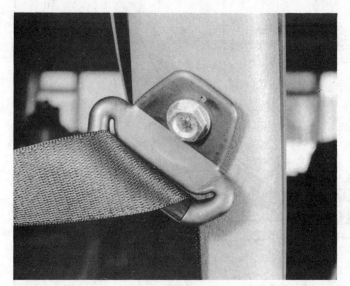

45.2 Front seat bolt runner and top anchor (non-adjustable type)

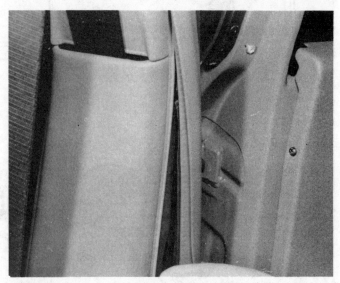

45.3 Removing the weatherstrip from the 'B' pillar

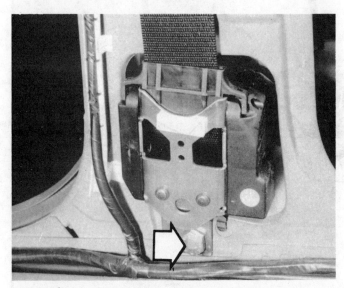

45.5 Seat belt retractor mechanism – securing bolt arrowed

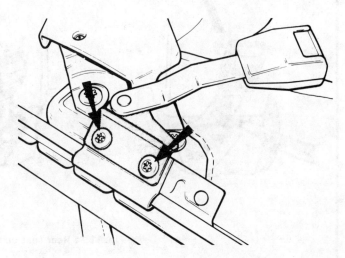

Fig. 11.13 Front seat belt buckle secured by two 'Torx' screws (arrowed) (Sec 45)

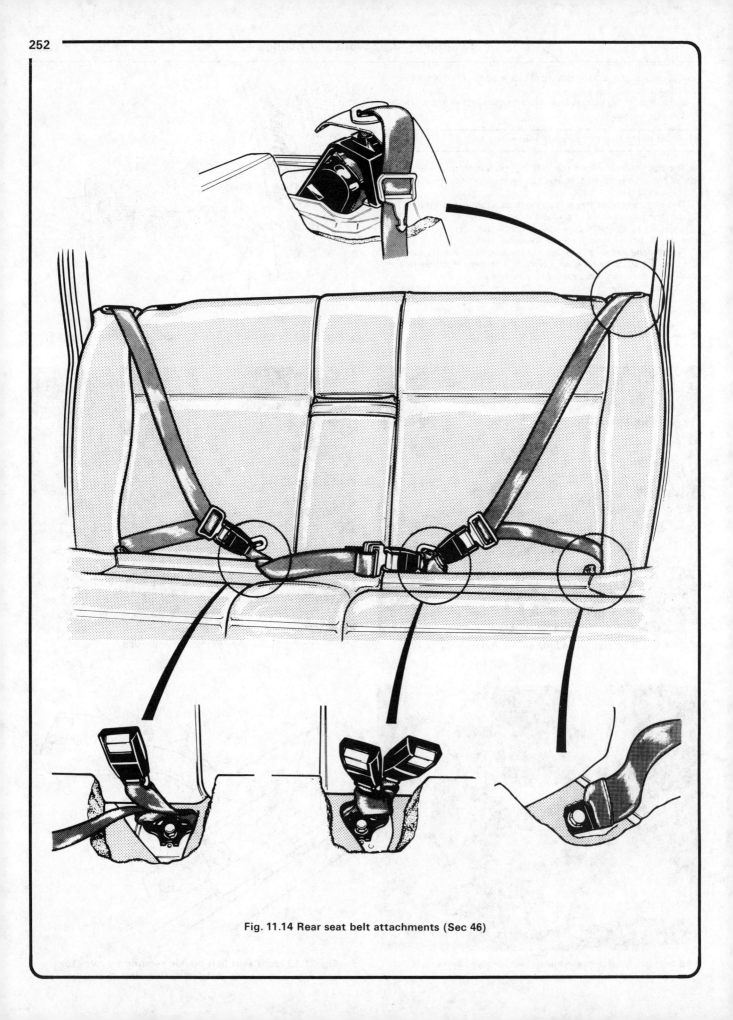

Fig. 11.14 Rear seat belt attachments (Sec 46)

and webbing are being renewed. If it is wished to remove the buckle, first remove the seat as described in Section 42.

7   Refit by reversing the removal operations. Tighten all anchorages to the specified torque, and make sure that the belt is not twisted.

## 46  Rear seat belts – removal and refitting

1   This Section described the removal and refitting of factory or dealer-installed rear seat belts. A rear belt kit can be purchased from a Ford dealer and should be found to correspond with the items shown here. If a proprietary kit is purchased, make sure it is suitable for the vehicle in question and follow the manufacturer's instructions.
2   Fold the rear seat cushion forwards.
3   Feed the buckle webbing through the slits in the carpet. Remove the buckle securing bolt, remove the pins from the buckle elastic straps and remove the buckles.
4   Remove the lower anchor bolts, then fold the seat backrests forwards. Fold back the luggage area carpet and remove the backrest hinges.
5   Remove the seat back striker pins (low series) or adjuster mechanism cover (high series) (photo).
6   Prise the webbing guides from each side cushion.
7   Remove the side cushions. Each one is retained by a single nut and washer located near the loudspeaker (photo). With the nut and washer removed, the cushion is then released by prising open the metal tags which secure its bottom wire. Pull the bottom of the cushion forwards and upwards to free it from the retractor.
8   The retractor can now be unbolted and the webbing withdrawn through the side cushions.
9   Commence refitting by fitting the retractor. First fit the rear bolt and tighten it by a few turns only, so that the retractor is still free to move. Push the retractor rearwards and then downwards so that it takes up its fitted positions, then fit the front bolt. Tighten both bolts to the specified torque.
10 The remainder of refitting is a reversal of the removal procedure. Tighten the belt and buckle anchor bolts to the specified torque.

## 47  Rear seat components – removal and refitting

### Cushion
1   Fold the seat cushion forwards and remove the hinge retaining screws. To remove the hinges as well, unbolt the hinges from the body instead (photos).

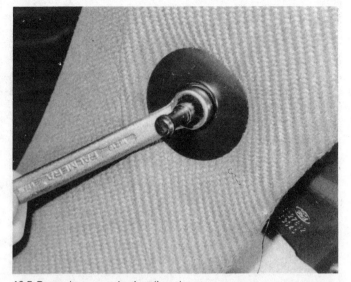

46.5 Removing a seat back striker pin

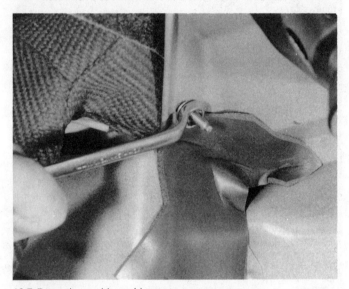

46.7 Removing a side cushion nut

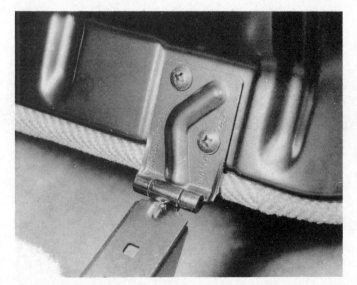

47.1A Rear seat hinge-to-cushion screws

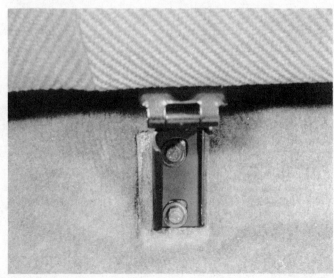

47.1B Rear seat hinge-to-body bolts

47.3 Rear seat backrest hinges. One of the backrests has been removed

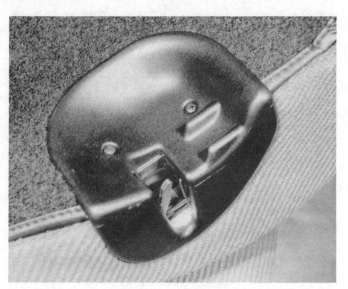

47.6 Backrest catch cover, showing securing screws

2   When refitting, just nip up the hinge screws or bolts and check the fit of the cushions. Tighten the screws or bolts fully when satisfied.

### Backrests
3   Fold the backrests forward and peel back the carpet to expose the hinges (photo).
4   Remove the hinge screws, free the seat belt webbing clips (when applicable) and remove the backrests.
5   Refit by reversing the removal operations.

### Backrest catch
6   Fold the backrest forwards. Remove the catch cover, which is secured by two screws (photo).
7   Remove the two 'Torx' screws which secure the catch. Unhook the operating rod from the catch and remove it.
8   The operating rod and button can now be withdrawn if wished. When refitting, position the rod with the hooked end facing inwards.
9   Refit the catch, engage it with the operating rod and secure it with the 'Torx' screws.
10  Refit and secure the catch cover. Check the catch for correct operation.

## 48  Heater controls – removal and refitting

### Front
1   Disconnect the battery negative lead.
2   Remove the instrument cluster (Chapter 12, Section 17).
3   Remove the facia top (Section 39 in this Chapter).
4   Unclip the two control cables from the control levers (photo).
5   On air conditioned models, disconnect the hoses from the vacuum switch.
6   Remove the four screws which secure the heater control assembly. Withdraw the assembly from the facia.
7   When refitting, secure the control assembly with the four screws. Reconnect the vacuum switch (when applicable) and the control cables. Adjust the control cables if necessary by altering the positions of the cable clips.
8   When satisfied with the operation of the cables, refit the other disturbed components.

### Rear
9   Remove the centre console (Section 40).
10  Unclip the control cables and remove the control unit.
11  Refit in the reverse order to removal.

## 49  Heater control cables – removal and refitting

### Front
1   Remove the heater controls as described in the previous Section.
2   Remove the centre console as described in Section 40. Also remove the console bracket and the gear lever inner gaiter.
3   Unclip the under-dash trim on both sides. Remove the glovebox lid.
4   Remove the radio (Chapter 12, Section 45).
5   Remove the ABS and (when applicable) the EEC IV modules (Chapter 9, Section 26, and Chapter 12, Section 27).
6   Remove the remaining lower trim on the passenger side to expose the heater casing.
7   Remove the two securing screws and release the cables from the heater.
8   When refitting, place the air distribution and temperature control valve levers in their uppermost positions, then connect the cables.
9   The remainder of refitting is a reversal of the removal procedure.

48.4 Heater control cable clip (arrowed) viewed through windscreen

*Rear*

10  Remove the centre console as described in Section 40.
11  Remove the front seat on the side concerned (Section 42). Also remove the rear seat cushion (Section 47).
12  Remove the front panel belt lower anchor bolt.
13  Remove the front scuff plate, which is secured by three screws. Remove the front screw from the rear scuff plate.

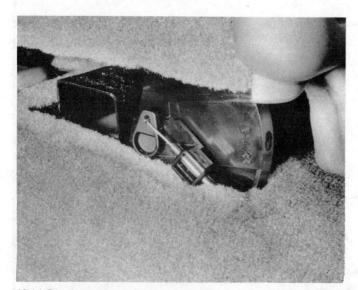

49.14 Rear heater control cable at nozzle

14  Roll back the front carpet from the scuff plates to expose the heater cable. Release the cable from its ties and disconnect it from the control unit and the nozzle (photo).
15  Refit by reversing the removal operations.

## 50  Heater assembly – removal and refitting

1  Disconnect the battery negative lead.
2  Depressurise the cooling system by slackening the expansion tank cap. Take precautions against scalding if the system is hot.
3  Disconnect the two heater hoses from the stubs on the bulkhead. Be prepared for some coolant spillage: catch the coolant in a clean container if it is fit for re-use. Plug the hoses, or tie them up with their open ends raised.
4  Expel as much coolant as possible from the heater matrix by blowing through it.
5  Remove the matrix connector plate and gasket from the bulkhead.
6  Working inside the vehicle, remove the centre console and other trim as described for access to the heater control cables (Section 49, paragraphs 2 to 7).
7  Remove the instrument cluster surround, which is secured by four screws. Also pull out the heater louvre panel.
8  Remove the facia panel top, which is secured by five screws and four clips.
9  Detach the air trunking from the heater casing. Release the trunking from the bulkhead when necessary.
10  Remove the two nuts which secure the heater unit. Pull the unit into the vehicle until the pipe stubs are clear of the bulkhead, then remove it sideways. Be prepared for coolant spillage.
11  Check the condition of the foam gasket on the bulkhead and renew it if necessary.
12  Refit by reversing the removal operations.
13  Top up the cooling system on completion, and check the level again after the engine has been run.

## 51  Heater assembly – dismantling and reassembly

1  Remove the heater assembly as described in the previous Section.
2  Remove the two screws which secure the heater matrix. Withdraw the matrix.
3  Release the clips which secure the casing halves together, using a screwdriver. Carefully prise the halves apart and separate them.
4  Remove the flap valves and operating levers from the casing halves, noting how they are fitted for reference when reassembling.
5  Flush the matrix with clean water to remove any debris. A leaking matrix must be renewed, unless a radiator specialist can repair it.
6  Reassembly is a reversal of dismantling. Additional clips may be needed to secure the casing halves once they have been separated.

## 52  Demister nozzle – removal and refitting

1  Disconnect the battery negative lead.
2  Remove the instrument cluster (Chapter 12, Section 17). Pull out the heater louvre panel.
3  Remove the facia panel top, which is secured by five screws and four clips.
4  Remove the under-dash trim and unclip the wiring loom as necessary to gain access to the demister nozzle on the side concerned. Remove the two securing screws and withdraw the nozzle.
5  Refit by reversing the removal operations.

## 53  Facia air vents – removal and refitting

1  Access to the facia air vents is obtained by removing the facia panel components as described in Section 39. The precise extent of dismantling required will depend on which vent is being removed.
2  Having gained access, the vent is removed by disconnecting its trunking and removing the securing screws. The passenger's side vent is secured by two screws; the centre and driver's side vents are secured by four screws.
3  Refit by reversing the removal operations.

## 54  Rear heater nozzles and hoses – removal and refitting

1  Access to the rear heater nozzles is obtained by removing the front seat on the side concerned. Each nozzle is secured by three screws. After removing the screws, unclip the control cable and remove the nozzle.
2  When refitting the nozzle, tighten the two lower screws first, followed by the upper screw.
3  Access to the rear heater hoses is gained by removing the facia panel components as described in Section 39. Additionally the centre console and front seat(s) must be removed, and the carpet moved away as described for removal of the rear heater control cables (Section 49).
4  Having gained access, the heater hose is simply pulled off the heater assembly and the nozzle.
5  Refit by reversing the removal operations.

## 55  Air conditioning system – description and precautions

1  Air conditioning is fitted as standard on Scorpio models and is optionally available on some other models. In conjunction with the heater the system enables any reasonable air temperature to be achieved inside the car, it also reduces the humidity of the incoming air, aiding demisting even when cooling is not required.
2  The refrigeration side of the air conditioning system functions in a similar way to a domestic regrigerator. A compressor, belt-driven from the crankshaft pulley, draws refrigerant in its gaseous phase from an evaporator. The compressed refrigerant passes through a condenser where it loses heat and enters its liquid phase. After dehydration the refrigerant returns to the evaporator where it absorbs heat from air passing over the evaporator fins. The refrigerant becomes a gas again and the cycle is repeated.

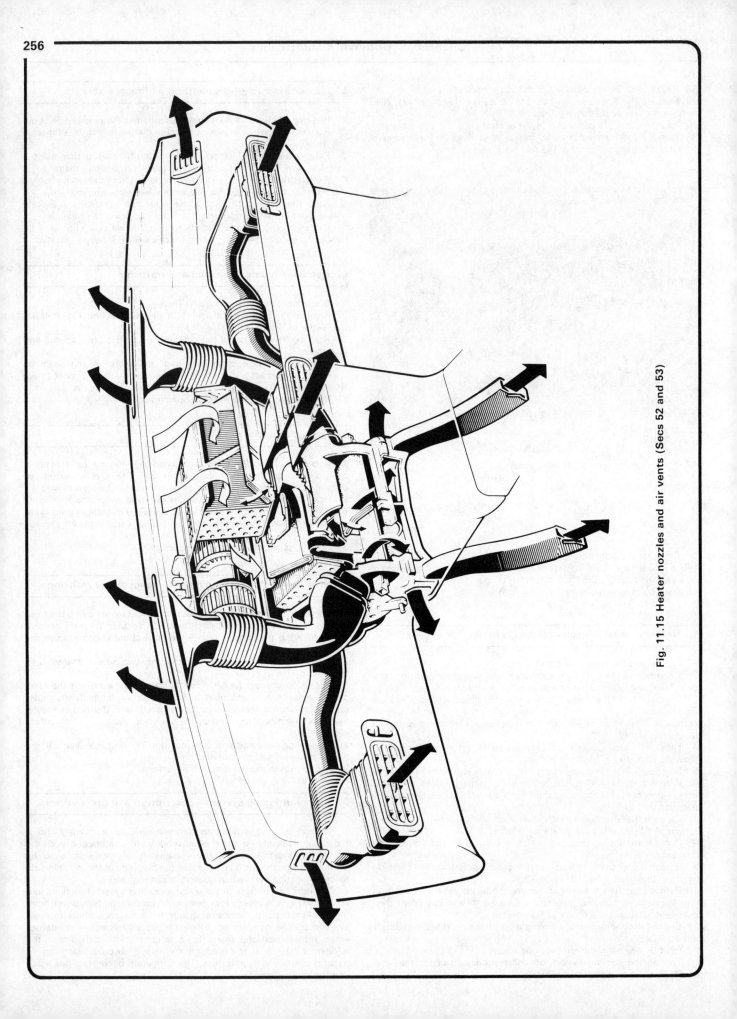

Fig. 11.15 Heater nozzles and air vents (Secs 52 and 53)

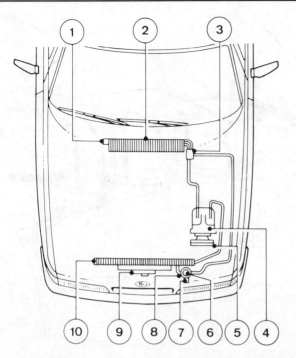

Fig. 11.16 Air conditioning system component locations
(Sec 55)

| 1 | De-ice thermostat | 6 | Pressure switch |
| 2 | Evaporator | 7 | Sight glass |
| 3 | Expansion valve | 8 | Dehydrator |
| 4 | Compressor | 9 | Cooling fan |
| 5 | Compressor clutch | 10 | Condenser |

3   Various subsidiary controls and sensors protect the system against
excessive temperature and pressures. Additionally, engine idle speed is
increased when the system is in use to compensate for the additional
load imposed by the compressor.

*Precautions*
4   Although the refrigerant is not itself toxic, in the presence of a
naked flame (or a lighted cigarette) it forms a highly toxic gas. Liquid
refrigerant spilled on the skin will cause frostbite. If refrigerant enters
the eyes, rinse them with a dilute solution of boric acid and seek
medical advice immediately.
5   In view of the above points, and of the need for specialised
equipment for evacuating and recharging the system, any work which
requires the disconnection of a refrigerant line must be left to a
specialist.
6   Do not allow refrigerant lines to be exposed to temperatures above
230°F (110°C) – eg during welding or paint drying operations.
7   Do not operate the air conditioning system if it is known to be short
of refrigerant, or further damage may result.

## 56 Air conditioning system – maintenance

1   Regularly inspect the compressor drivebelt for correct tension and
good condition. Tension is adjusted in the same way as for the
alternator drivebelt.
2   At the 12 000 mile/12 monthly service, remove the radiator grille
and clean any leaves, insects etc from the condenser coil and fins. Be
very careful not to damage the condenser fins: use a soft brush, or a
compressed air jet, along (not across) the fins.
3   Before refitting the grille, check the refrigerant charge as follows.
The engine should be cold and the ambient temperature should be
between 64° and 77°F (18° and 25°C).
4   Start the engine and allow it to idle. Observe the refrigerant sight
glass and have an assistant switch on the air conditioning to fan speed
III. A few bubbles should be seen in the sight glass as the system starts
up, but all bubbles should disappear within 10 seconds. Persistent

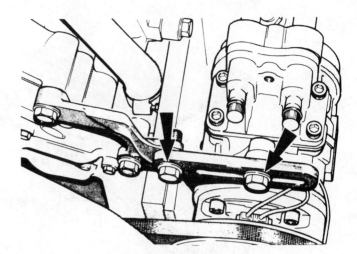

Fig. 11.17 Air conditioning compressor adjuster strap bolts
(arrowed) (Sec 56)

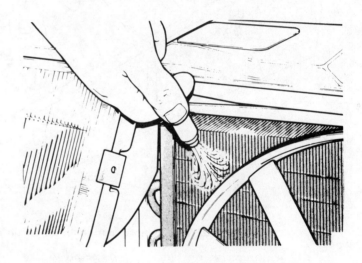

Fig. 11.18 Cleaning the condenser fins with an air jet
(Sec 56)

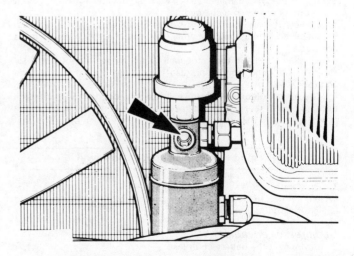

Fig. 11.19 Refrigerant sight glass (arrowed) (Sec 56)

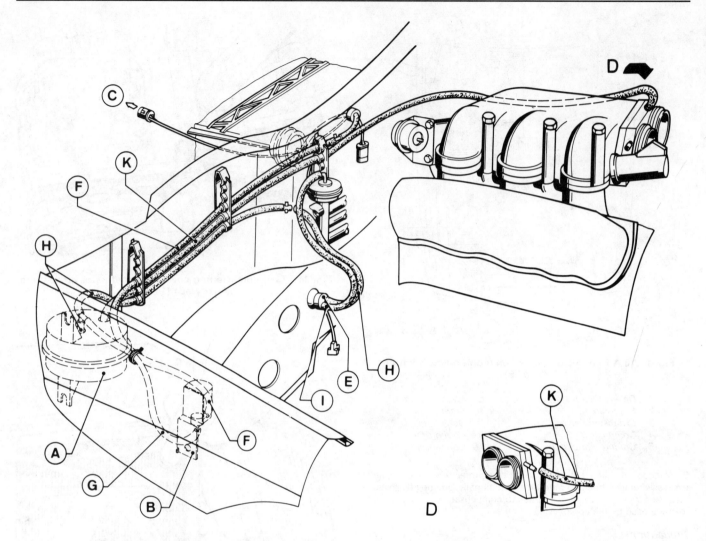

**Fig. 11.20 Vacuum hose routing for air conditioning system. V6 shown, ohc similar (Sec 56)**

| A | Vacuum reservoir | D | Alternative view | G | White | I | Green |
|---|---|---|---|---|---|---|---|
| B | Air recirculation valve | E | From control unit | H | Black | K | Yellow |
| C | To de-ice thermostat | F | Blue | | | | |

bubbles, or no bubbles at all, mean that the refrigerant charge is low. Switch off the system immediately if the charge is low and do not use it again until it has been recharged.

5   Operate the air conditioning system for at least 10 minutes each month, even during cold weather, to keep the seals etc in good condition.

6   Regularly inspect the refrigerant pipes, hoses and unions for security and good condition. Also inspect the vacuum hoses and control cables.

7   The air conditioning system will lose a proportion of its charge through normal seepage – typically up to 100 g (4 oz) per year – so it it as well to regard periodic recharging as a maintenance operation.

## 57 Air conditioning system – component renewal

1   Only those items which can be renewed without discharging the system are described here. Other items must be dealt with by a Ford dealer or air conditioning specialist.

*Compressor drivebelt*

2   Disconnect the battery earth lead.

3   On ohc engines, remove the radiator cooling fan. See Chapter 2, Section 11.

4   Slacken the compressor strap and pivot bolts, move the compressor towards the engine and remove the old drivebelt.

5   Fit the new drivebelt, position the compressor to achieve the correct belt tension and tighten the strap and pivot bolts.

6   Refit and secure the fan, when applicable, and reconnect the battery.

7   Recheck the belt tension after it has run for at least 10 minutes under load.

*Condenser fan and motor*

8   Disconnect the battery earth lead and remove the radiator grille.

9   Disconnect the fan wiring connector at the right-hand side of the condenser.

10   Remove the three securing bolts and remove the fan and motor. Turn the frame to position the fan wiring on the dehydrator side to avoid damaging the wiring. Take care also not to damage the condenser fins or tube.

11   Unclip the fan guard from the top of the frame.

12   To remove the fan blades from the motor, remove the retaining nut and circlip. **The nut has a left-hand thread,** ie it is undone clockwise.

13   With the blades removed, the motor can be unscrewed from the frame.

14   Reassemble and refit in the reverse order of dismantling and removal.

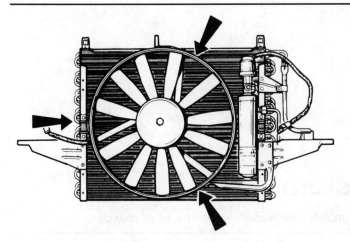

**Fig. 11.21 Condenser fan securing bolts (arrowed) (Sec 57)**

### De-ice thermostat

15 Disconnect the battery negative lead.

16 Disconnect the vacuum hoses from the plenum chamber cover. Pull off the rubber seal and remove the plenum chamber cover: it is secured by four screws and one nut.

17 Disconnect the thermostat from the evaporator casing and remove it. Also remove the thermostat probe.

18 Refit by reversing the removal operations.

### Heater water valve

19 The heater water valve used with air conditioning is vacuum-operated. It is located on the right-hand side of the engine bay, near the bulkhead.

20 Drain the cooling system (Chapter 2, Section 3).

21 Slacken the hose clips and detach the coolant hoses from the valve, noting how they are connected.

22 Disconnect the vacuum hose from the top of the valve.

23 Unclip the valve from its bracket and remove it.

24 Refit by reversing the removal operations. Refill the cooling system as described in Chapter 2, Section 3.

# Chapter 12 Electrical system

For modifications, and information applicable to later models, see Supplement at end of manual

## Contents

---

## Specifications

### General

System type ................................................................. 12 volt, negative earth
Battery type ................................................................. Lead acid

### Alternator

Make and type ............................................................ Bosch KI-55A, NI-70A or NI-90A
Rated output at 13.5 volts and 6000 engine rpm ...... 55, 70 or 90 amps
Rotor winding resistance at 20°C/68°F:
  KI-55A ..................................................................... 3.4 to 3.7 ohms
  NI-70A and NI-90A .................................................. 2.8 to 3.1 ohms
Brush wear limit .......................................................... 5 mm (0.2 in)
Regulated voltage at 4000 engine rpm and 3 to 7 amp load ...... 13.7 to 14.6 volts
Voltage regulator type ................................................ Solid state, integral

### Starter Motor

Make and type ............................................................ Bosch short frame, long frame or reduction gear
Rating:
  Short frame .............................................................. 0.85 or 0.95 kW
  Long frame ............................................................... 1.1 kW
  Reduction gear ......................................................... 1.4kW

Brush wear limit:
    Short frame and reduction gear ............................................ 8 mm (0.32 in)
    Long frame ................................................................................ 10 mm (0.39 in)
Commutator minimum diameter ..................................................... 32.8 mm (1.29 in)
Armature endfloat .......................................................................... 0.3 mm (0.012 in)

## Wiper blades ....................................................................... Champion C-5101

## Light bulbs (typical)

| | Fitting | Wattage |
|---|---|---|
| Headlights ................................................. | H4 | 60/55 |
| Auxiliary driving lights ............................. | H3 | 55 |
| Front foglights .......................................... | H3 | 55 |
| Side/parking lights ................................... | Glass base | 5 |
| Direction indicators ................................. | Bayonet | 21 |
| Stop and tail lights .................................. | Bayonet | 21/5 |
| Reversing light ......................................... | Bayonet | 21 |
| Rear foglight ............................................ | Bayonet | 21 |
| Door open/kerb illumination lights ......... | Bayonet | 5 |
| Number plate lights ................................. | Glass base | 5 |
| Engine bay light ...................................... | Bayonet | 10 |
| Luggage area light .................................. | Bayonet | 5 |
| Interior lights .......................................... | Festoon | 10 |
| Reading light ........................................... | Glass base | 5 |
| Footwell lights ........................................ | Glass base | 5 |
| Vanity mirror light .................................. | Festoon | 3 |
| Glovebox light ........................................ | Glass base | 3 |
| Ashtray light ........................................... | Glass base | 1.2 |
| Pilot and warning lights ......................... | Glass base | 1.2/2.5 |
| Instrument illumination ........................... | Glass base | 1.2/2.5 |
| Heater control light ............................... | Glass base | 1 |
| Automatic transmission selector light ... | Bayonet | 1.4 |
| Clock light ............................................... | Bayonet | 1.4 |

## Fuses and circuit breakers – main fuse box

| Fuse No. | Rating (A) | Circuit(s) protected |
|---|---|---|
| 1 | 20 | LH main beam, LH auxiliary driving light |
| 2 | 20 | RH main beam, LH auxiliary driving light |
| 3 | 10 | LH dipped beam |
| 4 | 10 | RH dipped beam |
| 5 | 10 | LH side and tail lights |
| 6 | 10 | RH side and tail lights |
| 7 | 15 | Instrument illumination, number plate lights |
| 8 | 10 | Control circuits for air conditioning, heated windscreen and ride height control |
| 9 | 30 | Headlight washer pump, tailgate and fuel filler flap release |
| 10 | 20 | Central locking system, interior lights, clock, mirror adjustment |
| 11 | 20 | Fuel pump (with air conditioning), taxi circuits |
| 12 | 10 | Hazard warning flasher |
| 13 | 30 | Heated seats, cigarette lighters |
| 14 | 30 | Horn |
| 15 | 30 | Wiper motors and screen washer pumps |
| 16 | 30 | Heated rear window, heated mirrors |
| 17 | 20 | Front foglights |
| 18 | 30 | Heater blower |
| 19 | 10 | Accessory circuits |
| 20 | 15 | Direction indicators, reversing lights |
| 21 | 15 | Stop-lights |
| 22 | 10 | Instrument and controls |
| 23 | C20 | Power windows (front) and sliding roof |
| 24 | C20 | Power windows (rear) and rear seat adjustment |

*C = Circuit breaker*

## Fuses and circuit breakers – auxiliary fuse box

| Colour | Rating (A) | Circuit(s) protected |
|---|---|---|
| Black | 20 | Fuel-injection pump |
| Pink | 20 | Air conditioning cooling fan |
| Yellow | 20 | Anti-lock braking system control circuitry |
| Green | 30 | Anti-lock braking system pump |
| Brown | 30 | Heated windscreen (left-hand side) |
| Brown | 30 | Heated windscreen (right-hand side) |
| Grey | C20 | Front seat adjustment |
| Orange | 20 | Ride height control |

*C = Circuit breaker*

## Relays in main fuse box
### Identification

| | Function |
|---|---|
| I | Ignition circuit |
| II | Heated rear window and mirrors |
| III | Power windows and sliding roof |
| IV | Seat belt warning |
| V | Intermittent wipe – front |
| VI | Intermittent wipe – rear |
| VII | Headlight washer |
| VIII | Interior light delay |
| IX | Rear seat adjustment |
| X | Headlights (main beam) |
| XI | Engine auxiliary |
| XII | Automatic transmission inhibitor |
| A | Spare |
| B | Radio |
| C | Horn |
| D | Tailgate release |
| E | Spare |
| F | Headlights (dipped beam) |
| G | Seat heaters |
| H | Front foglights |

## Other relays and modules
### Identification

| | Function |
|---|---|
| **Behind facia (centre):** | |
| L1 | Lights on buzzer |
| L2 | Rear foglight control |
| L3 | Automatic transmission kickdown time |
| L4 | Fuel pump (with air conditioning) |
| L5 | Hydraulic switch |
| L6 | Anti-theft alarm |
| **Behind facia (passenger side):** | |
| M1 | Manifold heater (carburettor) or fuel pump (fuel-injection) |
| M2 | Power hold (carburettor) or inspection valve (fuel-injection) |
| M3 | Heated windscreen (power) |
| M4 | Heated windscreen (timer) |
| M5 | Air conditioning cooling fan |
| M6 | ABS pump relay |
| M7 | ABS main relay |
| M8 | ABS control unit |
| M9 | Ride height control |
| **Below instrument panel (driver's side):** | |
| N1 | Bulb failure warning unit |
| **Below facia (passenger side):** | |
| P1 | ABS module |
| P2 | Fuel-injection system module |
| **Behind facia (passenger side):** | |
| R1 | Speed control system module |
| R2 | Auxiliary warning system module |
| R3 | Rear audio console module |

## Torque wrench settings

| | Nm | lbf ft |
|---|---|---|
| Alternator adjusting strap: | | |
| To steering pump bracket (ohc) | 21 to 26 | 16 to 19 |
| To front cover (V6) | 41 to 51 | 30 to 38 |

## 1 General description

The electrical system is of the 12 volt, negative earth type. Electricity is generated by an alternator, belt-driven from the crankshaft pulley. A lead-acid storage battery provides a reserve of power for use when the demands of the system temporarily exceed the alternator output, and for starting.

The battery negative terminal is connected to 'earth' – vehicle metal – and most electrical system components are wired so that they only receive a positive feed, the current returning via vehicle metal. This means that the component mounting forms part of the circuit. Loose or corroded mountings can therefore cause apparent electrical faults.

Many semiconductor devices are used in the electrical system, both in the 'black boxes' which control vehicle functions and in other components. Semiconductors are very sensitive to excessive (or wrong polarity) voltage, and to extremes of heat. Observe the appropriate precautions to avoid damage.

Although some repair procedures are given in this Chapter, sometimes renewal of a well-used item will prove more satisfactory. The reader whose interests extend beyond component renewal should obtain a copy of the 'Automobile Electrical Manual,' available from the publishers of this book.

Before starting work on the electrical system, read the precautions listed in 'Safety first!' at the beginning of the manual.

## 2 Maintenance and inspection

1 Weekly, before a long journey, or when prompted by the appropriate warning light, check that all exterior lights are working. Renew blown bulbs as necessary (Section 13).
2 At every 12 000 mile service, or whenever poor output from the alternator is suspected, check the tension and condition of the alternator drivebelt(s). See Chapter 2, Section 13.

3   At the same interval, check the tightness of the battery terminals and clean them if necessary (Section 3).

## 3   Battery – maintenance

1   The battery fitted as original equipment is 'maintenance-free', and requires no maintenance apart from having the case kept clean, and the terminals clean and tight.
2   To clean the battery terminals, disconnect them, negative (earth) first (photos). Use a wire brush or abrasive paper to clean the terminals. Bad corrosion or 'fungus' should be treated with a solution of bicarbonate of soda, applied with an old toothbrush. Do not let this solution get inside the battery.
3   Coat the battery terminals with petroleum jelly or a proprietary anti-corrosive compound before reconnecting them. Reconnect and tighten the positive (live) lead first, followed by the negative (earth) lead. Do not overtighten.
4   Keep the top of the battery clean and dry. Periodically inspect the battery tray for corrosion, and make good as necessary.
5   If a 'traditional' type battery is fitted as a replacement, remove the old cell covers at major service intervals and check that the plate separators in each cell are covered by approximately 6 mm (0.25 in) of electrolyte. If the battery case is translucent, the cell covers need not be removed to check the level. Top up if necessary with distilled or de-ionized water; do not overfill, and mop up any spillage at once (photo).
6   Persistent need for topping-up the battery electrolyte suggests either that the alternator output is excessive, or that the battery is approaching the end of its life.

## 4   Battery – charging

1   In normal use the battery should not require charging from an external source, unless the vehicle is laid up for long periods, when it should be recharged every six weeks or so. If vehicle use consists entirely of short runs in darkness it is also possible for the battery to become discharged. Otherwise, a regular need for recharging points to a fault in the battery or elsewhere in the charging system.
2   There is no need to disconnect the battery from the vehicle wiring when using a battery charger, but switch off the ignition and leave the bonnet open.
3   Domestic battery chargers (up to about 6 amps output) may safely be used overnight without special precautions. Make sure that the charger is set to deliver 12 volts before connecting it. Connect the leads (red or positive to the positive terminal, black or negative to the negative terminal) **before** switching the charger on at the mains.
4   When charging is complete, switch off at the mains **before** disconnecting the charger from the battery. Remember that the battery will be giving off hydrogen gas, which is potentially explosive.
5   Charging at a higher rate should only be carried out under carefully controlled conditions. Very rapid or 'boost' charging should be avoided if possible, as it is liable to cause permanent damage to the battery through overheating.
6   During any sort of charging, battery electrolyte temperature should never exceed 38°C (100°F). If the battery becomes hot, or the electrolyte is effervescing vigorously, charging should be stopped.

## 5   Battery – removal and refitting

1   Disconnect the battery negative (earth) lead.
2   Disconnect the battery positive leads. These may be protected by a plastic cover. Do not allow the spanner to bridge the positive and negative terminals.
3   Release the battery hold-down clamp. Lift out the battery. Keep it upright and be careful not to drop it – it is heavy.
4   Commence by placing the battery in its tray, making sure it is the right way round. Secure it with the hold-down clamp.
5   Clean the battery terminals if necessary (Section 3), then reconnect them. Connect the positive lead first, then the negative lead.

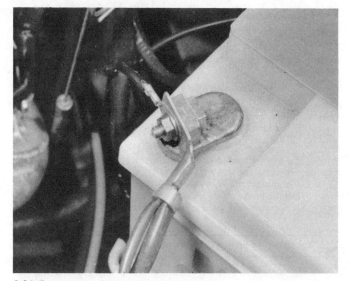

3.2A Battery negative terminal

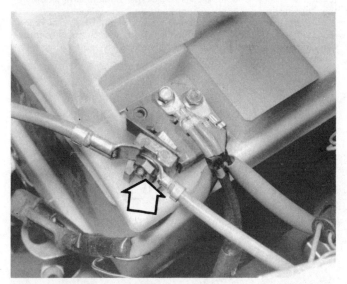

3.2B Battery positive terminal. Remove the large nut (arrowed) to release the heavy leads and the terminal plate

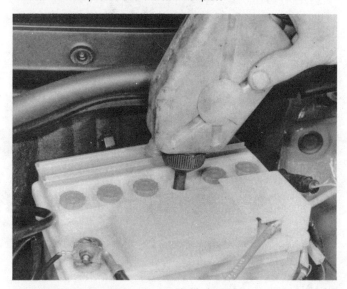

3.5 Topping-up a battery cell with distilled water

## 6 Alternator – precautions

1 To avoid damage to the alternator semiconductors, and indeed to many other components, the following precautions should be observed:

   (a) *Do not disconnect the battery or the alternator whilst the engine is running*
   (b) *Do not allow the engine to turn the alternator when the latter is not connected*
   (c) *Do not test for output from the alternator by 'flashing' the output lead to earth*
   (d) *Do not use a battery charger of more than 12 volts output, even as a starting aid*
   (e) *Disconnect the battery and the alternator before carrying out electric arc welding on the vehicle*
   (f) *Always observe correct battery polarity*

## 7 Alternator – testing on the vehicle

1 Should it appear that the alternator is not charging the battery, check first that the drivebelt is intact and in good condition and that its tension is correct (Chapter 2). Also check the condition and security of the alternator electrical connections and the battery leads.

2 Accurate assessment of alternator output requires special equipment and a degree of skill. A rough idea of whether output is adequate can be gained by using a voltmeter (range 0 to 15 or 0 to 20 volts) as follows.

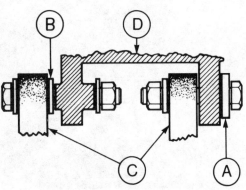

**Fig. 12.1 Alternator mounting details – two pivot bolt type (Sec 8)**

A  Large washer
B  Small washer (not always fitted)
C  Mounting bracket
D  Alternator

3 Connect the voltmeter across the battery terminals. Switch on the headlights and note the voltage reading: it should be between 12 and 13 volts.

4 Start the engine and run it at a fast idle (approx 1500 rpm). Read the voltmeter: it should indicate 13 to 14 volts.

5 With the engine still running at a fast idle, switch on as many electrical consumers as possible (heated rear window, heater blower etc). The voltage at the battery should be maintained at 13 to 14 volts. Increase the engine speed slightly if necessary to keep the voltage up.

6 If alternator output is low or zero, check the brushes, as described in Section 9. If the brushes are OK, seek expert advice.

7 Occasionally the condition may arise where the alternator output is excessive. Clues to this condition are constantly blowing bulbs; brightness of lights vary considerably with engine speed; overheating of alternator and battery, possible with steam or fumes coming from the battery. This condition is almost certainly due to a defective voltage regulator, but expert advice should be sought.

8 Note that the alternator voltage regulator can be renewed without removing the alternator from the vehicle. The procedure is part of brush renewal (Section 9).

## 8 Alternator – removal and refitting

1 Disconnect the battery negative lead.

2 Disconnect the multi-plug from the rear of the alternator. It may be secured by a wire clip.

3 Slacken the alternator adjusting and pivot nuts and bolts. Swing the alternator towards the engine and slip the drivebelt(s) off the pulley.

4 Support the alternator. Remove the adjusting and pivot nuts, bolts and washers, noting the fitted positions of the washers. Lift out the alternator. Do not drop it, it is fragile.

5 Refit by reversing the removal operations. Tension the drivebelt(s) (Chapter 2), then tighten the adjustment strap bolt followed by the pivot nut and bolt. If there are two pivot bolts, tighten the front one first.

6 Refit the multi-plug and reconnect the battery.

## 9 Alternator – brush renewal

1 The alternator brushes can be inspected or renewed without removing the alternator from the vehicle, but disconnect the battery negative lead first.

2 From the rear of the alternator remove the two screws which secure the voltage regulator/brush carrier assembly. Withdraw the assembly (photos).

3 Measure the length of each brush protruding from the carrier (photo). If they are worn down to, or below, the minimum specified, the old brushes will have to be unsoldered and new ones soldered into place. Some skill with a soldering iron will be required; excess heat from the soldering iron could damage the voltage regulator. When fitted, the new brushes must move freely in their holders.

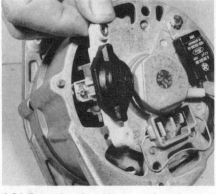

9.2A Removing the voltage regulator/brush carrier

9.2B Voltage regulator/brush carrier removed

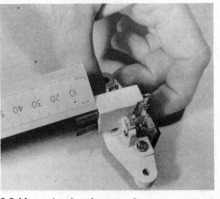

9.3 Measuring brush protrusion

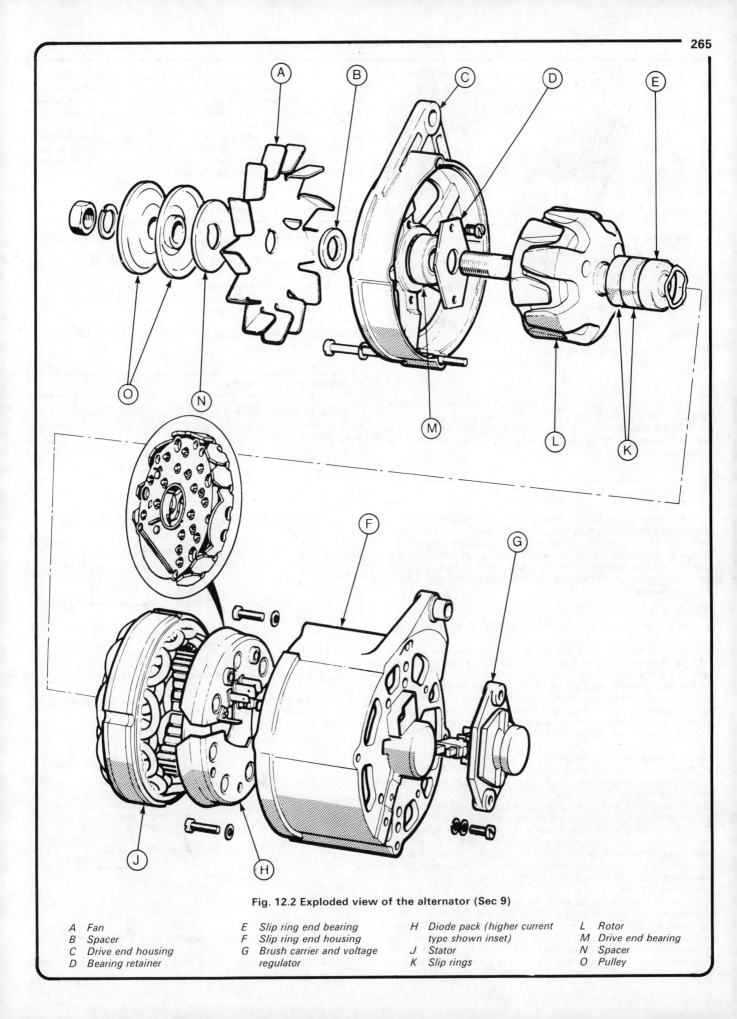

**Fig. 12.2 Exploded view of the alternator (Sec 9)**

A  Fan
B  Spacer
C  Drive end housing
D  Bearing retainer

E  Slip ring end bearing
F  Slip ring end housing
G  Brush carrier and voltage
   regulator

H  Diode pack (higher current
   type shown inset)
J  Stator
K  Slip rings

L  Rotor
M  Drive end bearing
N  Spacer
O  Pulley

9.4 Clean the slip rings (arrowed)

4   Clean the slip rings with a cloth moistened with methylated spirit (photo). If they are badly burnt or damaged, seek expert advice.
5   Refit the assembled brush carrier/voltage regulator and secure it with the two screws. If the alternator is on the vehicle, reconnect the battery negative lead.

## 10 Starter motor – testing on the vehicle

1   If the starter motor fails to operate, first check that the battery is charged by switching on the headlights. If the headlights do not come on, or rapidly become dim, the battery or its connections are at fault.
2   Check the security and condition of the battery and starter solenoid connections. Remember that the heavy lead to the solenoid is always 'live' – disconnect the battery negative lead before using tools on the solenoid connections.

### Solenoid check
3   Disconnect the battery negative lead, and all leads from the solenoid.
4   Connect a battery and a 3 watt test lamp between the solenoid body and the solenoid motor terminal (Fig. 12.3). The test lamp should light: if not, the solenoid windings are open-circuit.
5   Connect a battery and an 18 to 21 watt test lamp across the solenoid motor and battery terminals. Connect a further lead from the battery positive terminal to the solenoid spade terminal (Fig. 12.4). The solenoid should be heard to operate and the test lamp should light: if not, the solenoid contacts are defective.

### On load voltage check
6   Remake the original connections to the solenoid and reconnect the battery negative lead. Connect a voltmeter across the battery terminals, then disconnect the low tension lead from the coil positive terminal and operate the starter by turning the ignition switch. Note the reading on the voltmeter which should not be less than 10.5 volts.
7   Now connect the voltmeter between the starter motor terminal on the solenoid and the starter motor body. With the coil low tension lead still disconnected, operate the starter and check that the recorded voltage is not more than 1 volt lower than that noted in paragraph 6. If the voltage drop is more than 1 volt a fault exists in the wiring from the battery to the starter.
8   Connect the voltmeter between the battery positive terminal and the terminal on the starter motor. With the coil low tension lead disconnected operate the starter for two or three seconds. Battery voltage should be indicated initially, then dropping to less than 1 volt. If the reading is more than 1 volt there is a high resistance in the wiring from the battery to the starter and the check in paragraph 9 should be made. If the reading is less than 1 volt proceed to paragraph 10.

9   Connect the voltmeter between the two main solenoid terminals and operate the starter for two or three seconds. Battery voltage should be indicated initially then dropping to less than 0.5 volt. If the reading is more than 0.5 volt, the solenoid and connections may be faulty.
10  Connect the voltmeter between the battery negative terminal and the starter motor body, and operate the starter for two or three seconds. A reading of less than 0.5 volt should be recorded; however, if the reading is more, the earth circuit is faulty and the earth connections to the battery and body should be checked.

## 11 Starter motor – removal and refitting

1   Disconnect the battery negative lead. Raise and support the front of the vehicle.
2   From underneath the vehicle, disconnect the feed (heavy) cable from the solenoid.
3   Disconnect the command lead from the solenoid spade terminal.
4   Undo the starter motor securing bolts and (where fitted) the support bracket fastenings. Withdraw the starter motor from the vehicle.
5   Refit by reversing the removal operations. Check for correct operation on completion.

## 12 Starter motor – overhaul

1   Before embarking on a major overhaul of a starter motor, check the availabiility of spare parts and compare their cost with that of a new or reconditioned motor.

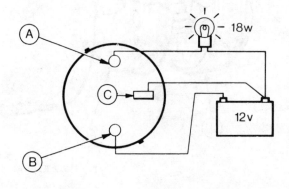

**Fig. 12.3 Solenoid winding check (Sec 10)**

A   Battery terminal              C   Spade terminal
B   Motor terminal

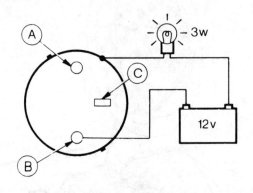

**Fig. 12.4 Solenoid contact check (Sec 10)**

A   Battery terminal              C   Spade terminal
B   Motor terminal

2   Remove the starter motor as described in the previous Section. When fitted, remove the rear support bracket.
3   Disconnect the motor lead from the solenoid terminal (photo).
4   Remove the two screws which secure the armature end cap. Remove the cap, the C-washer and the plain washer(s) (photo).
5   Remove the two through-bolts or studs. If the stud nuts are inaccessible, lock two nuts together on the stud and turn them to unscrew it (photo).
6   Remove the commutator end cover to expose the brushgear (photo). Carefully withdraw the brushplate from the commutator. Be careful to avoid damage to the brushes as they are released.
7   Examine the brushes: they should not be excessively worn (see Specifications) and must slide freely in their holders (photo). Brush renewal varies according to motor type as follows:

*Short frame – the brush lead must be removed from the stand-off connector on the brushplate, and the clip on the new brush lead be soldered to the connector (Fig. 12.5).*
*Long frame – the old brush leads must be cut and the new leads attached by soldering*
*Reduction gear – the brushplate must be renewed complete with brushes, holders and springs*

12.3 Disconnecting the motor lead from the solenoid

12.4 Remove the C-washer (arrowed) from the end of the shaft

12.5 Using two nuts locked together to unscrew a stud

12.6 Starter motor with commutator and cover removed

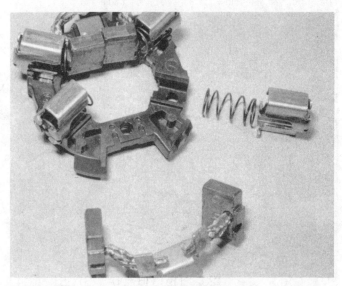
12.7 Brushgear fitted to reduction gear starter motor

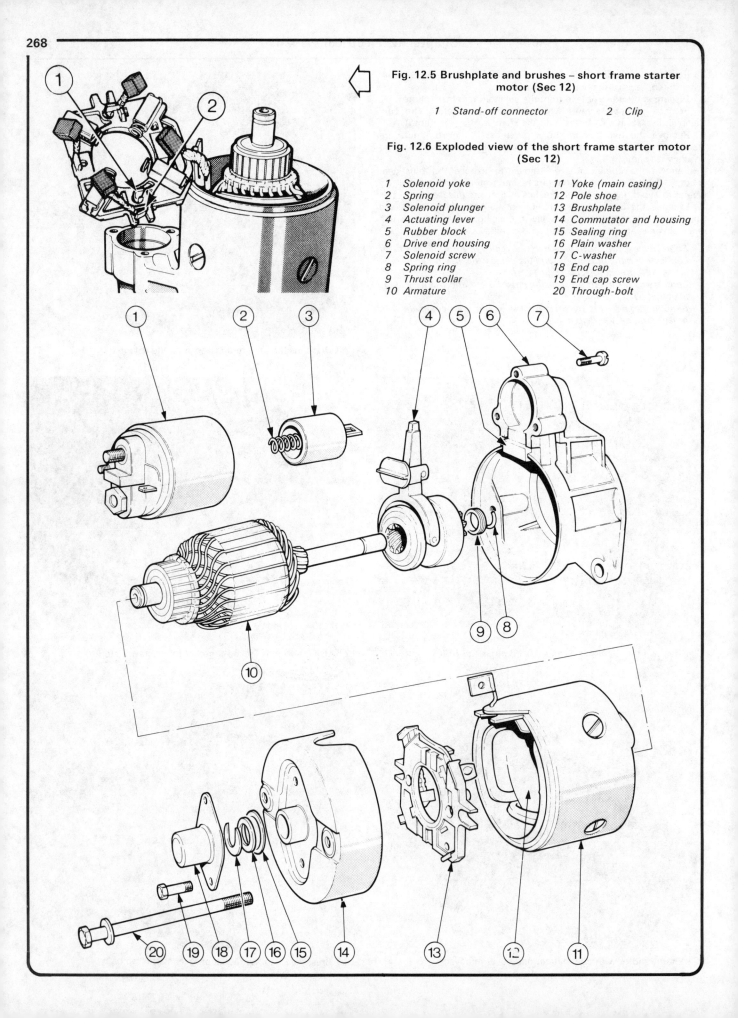

Fig. 12.5 Brushplate and brushes – short frame starter motor (Sec 12)

1   Stand-off connector      2   Clip

Fig. 12.6 Exploded view of the short frame starter motor (Sec 12)

| | | | |
|---|---|---|---|
| 1 | Solenoid yoke | 11 | Yoke (main casing) |
| 2 | Spring | 12 | Pole shoe |
| 3 | Solenoid plunger | 13 | Brushplate |
| 4 | Actuating lever | 14 | Commutator and housing |
| 5 | Rubber block | 15 | Sealing ring |
| 6 | Drive end housing | 16 | Plain washer |
| 7 | Solenoid screw | 17 | C-washer |
| 8 | Spring ring | 18 | End cap |
| 9 | Thrust collar | 19 | End cap screw |
| 10 | Armature | 20 | Through-bolt |

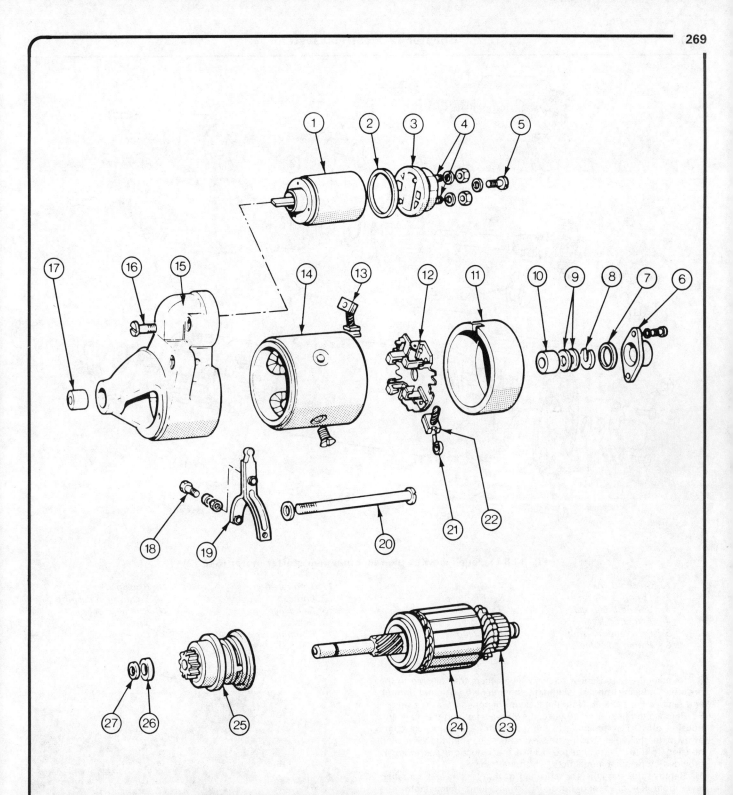

**Fig. 12.7 Exploded view of the long frame starter motor (Sec 12)**

| | | |
|---|---|---|
| 1 Solenoid | 10 Bush | 19 Actuating lever |
| 2 Gasket | 11 Commutator end housing | 20 Through-bolt |
| 3 Switch contacts | 12 Brushplate | 21 Brush spring |
| 4 Terminals | 13 Connector link | 22 Brush |
| 5 Screw | 14 Yoke (main casing) | 23 Commutator |
| 6 End cap | 15 Drive end housing | 24 Armature |
| 7 Seal | 16 Solenoid screw | 25 Pinion and clutch |
| 8 C-washer | 17 Bush | 26 Thrust collar |
| 9 Plain washers | 18 Pivot bolt | 27 Spring ring |

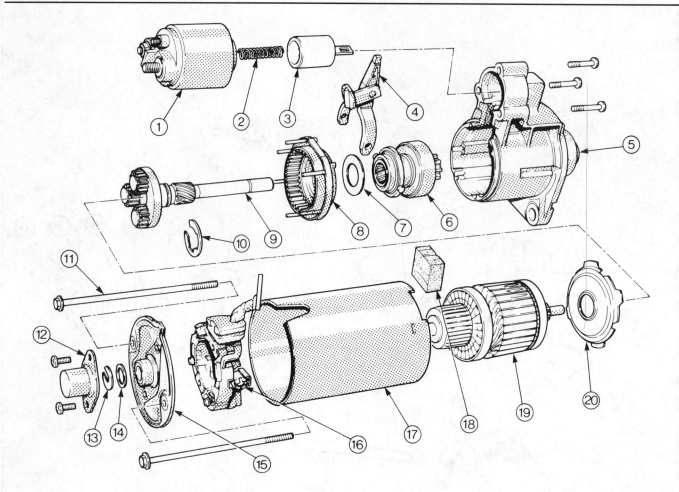

**Fig. 12.8 Exploded view of the reduction gear starter motor (Sec 12)**

| | | | |
|---|---|---|---|
| 1 Solenoid yoke | 7 Spacer | 11 Through-bolt | 16 Brushplate |
| 2 Spring | 8 Ring gear | 12 End cap | 17 Yoke (main casing) |
| 3 Solenoid plunger | 9 Output shaft and planetary | 13 C-washer | 18 Rubber block |
| 4 Actuating lever | gears | 14 Spacer | 19 Armature |
| 5 Drive end housing | 10 Circlip | 15 Commutator end plate | 20 Cover |
| 6 Pinion and clutch | | | |

8   Remove the two or three screws which secure the solenoid to the drive end housing (photo). Withdraw the solenoid yoke and unhook and remove the plunger. Note the location of springs, washers etc.
9   Remove the field winding yoke, if necessary tapping the drive end housing off it. The armature on the reduction gear motor will come away with the yoke, leaving the reduction gears in the drive end housing (photo). Note that the field of the reduction gear motor is provided by permanent magnets, which are fragile.
10  Remove the armature (or reduction gears), pinion and actuating lever from the drive end housing. On the long frame motor the actuating lever is secured by a pivot nut and bolt; on the other motors it is secured by a rubber plug.
11  To remove the pinion and one-way clutch from the armature or reduction gears, carefully grip the armature or gear housing (**not** the clutch) in a vice with padded jaws. Use a tube and hammer to drive the thrust collar down the shaft to expose the spring ring. Remove the spring ring and the thrust collar, then pull off the clutch and pinion (photos).
12  Inspect all components for wear and damage. The armature shaft bushes can be renewed if necessary. If there are signs that the armature has been touching pole pieces, bush wear may be suspected.
13  Simple continuity checks can be made on the armature and (when applicable) the field windings, using a multi-meter or a battery and test lamp. Special test equipment is required for thorough checking, however.

12.8 Removing a solenoid securing screw

**Fig. 12.9 Removing the solenoid – short frame motor (Sec 12)**

A   Plunger         C   Yoke
B   Spring

12.9 Removing the armature from the yoke

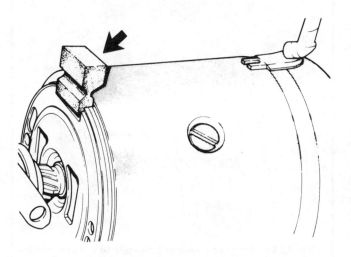

**Fig. 12.10 Correct position of rubber plug (arrowed) – short frame motor (Sec 12)**

12.11A Using a tube and hammer to drive down the thrust collar

12.11B Removing the pinion and clutch

14 A burnt or otherwise damaged commutator can sometimes be reclaimed by machining, providing that the refinishing limit is not exceeded. This is specialist work. Beware of using abrasives to clean the commutator, as particles may become embedded in the copper.

15 Renewal of individual field coils or magnets is not possible without special equipment, even if the parts are available.

16 Commence reassembly by fitting the clutch and pinion to the armature or planet gear shaft. Fit the thrust collar and a new spring clip to the shaft, then use a couple of spanners to lever the collar over the clip (photo).

17 On the reduction gear type motor, remove the cover plate and apply a little silicone-based grease to the reduction gears (photos). Refit the cover plate – it will only go on one way.

18 Reassemble the motor in the reverse order to that followed when dismantling. Note how the solenoid plunger is fitted to the actuating lever on the shoft frame motor (Fig. 12.11).

19 Clean the commutator with a rag moistened with methylated spirit, then refit the brushplate. Either clip the brushes in place after fitting the plate, or use a tube of suitable diameter to keep the brushes retracted during fitting (photo). Make sure that the brushplate is correctly positioned to allow the passage of through-bolts or studs.

12.16 Levering the collar up over the spring clip

12.17A Reduction gears with cover fitted

12.17B Reduction gears engaged

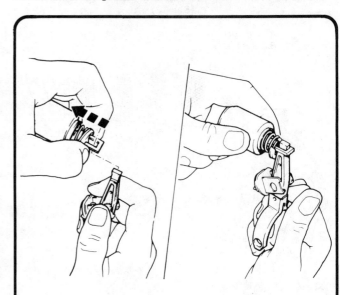
Fig. 12.11 Fitting the solenoid plunger to the actuating lever – short frame motor (Sec 12)

12.19 Using a socket to keep the brushes retracted

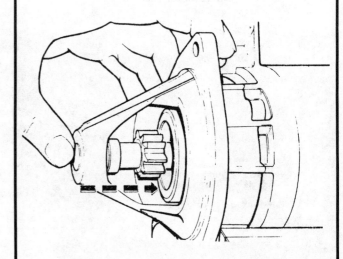
Fig. 12.12 Push the armature in the direction arrowed before checking the endfloat (Sec 12)

20 Adjust the armature endfloat when refitting the plain end C-washers. Add or subtract plain washers so that the endfloat is as near zero as possible, without preloading. Push the armature towards the commutator end to take up any slack before checking the endfloat.
21 Apply a little grease to the armature end before refitting the cap.
22 If a rear support bracket is fitted, only tighten its securing nuts loosely until after the motor has been refitted to the vehicle.

## 13 Exterior lights – bulb renewal

### Headlight
1 Open and prop the bonnet. Remove the cover from the rear of the headlight unit by twisting it anti-clockwise.
2 Disconnect the wiring plug from the headlight bulb. Release the spring clip by squeezing its legs together and move it clear of the bulb (photos).
3 Remove the headlight bulb (photo). **Caution:** *If the lights have just been in use, the bulb may be extremely hot.*
4 When handling the new bulb, use a tissue or clean cloth to avoid touching the glass with the fingers. If the glass is accidentally touched, wipe it clean using methylated spirit. Moisture and grease from the skin can cause blackening and rapid failure of the new bulb.
5 Fit the new bulb, making sure that the legs and cut-outs in the bulb base and the reflector match up. Secure with the spring clip.
6 Reconnect the wiring plug. Check the headlight for correct operation, then refit and secure the rear cover.

### Front parking light (sidelight)
7 Gain access as for the headlight bulb, then pull the parking light bulbholder from the headlight reflector (photo).
8 Extract the wedge base bulb from the holder (photo). Fit the new bulb, refit the bulbholder and check for correct operation.

### Auxiliary driving light (when fitted)
9 From above the auxiliary light unit, release the cover spring clip and remove the cover (photo).
10 Release the spring clip from the bulb. Withdraw the bulb and unplug its wiring connector (photos). **Caution:** *If the lights have just been in use, the bulb may be extremely hot.*
11 Do not touch the glass of the new bulb with the fingers – see paragraph 4.
12 Connect the new bulb, fit it and secure it with the spring clip.
13 Check the light for correct operation, then refit and secure the cover.

13.2A Headlight bulb removal: disconnect the wiring plug ...

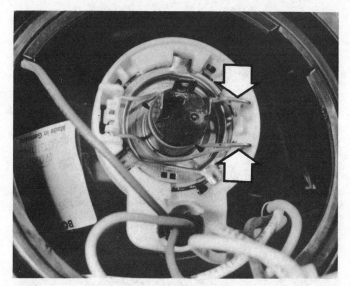
13.2B ... and squeeze the spring clip legs (arrowed)

13.3 Removing a headlight bulb

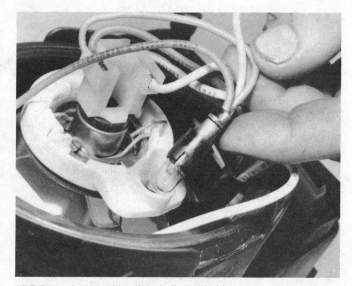
13.7 Removing a parking light bulb and holder

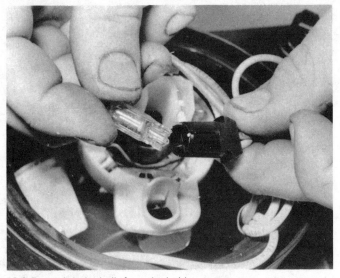

13.8 Removing the bulb from the holder

13.9 Auxiliary driving light cover

13.10A Auxiliary driving light bulb in position

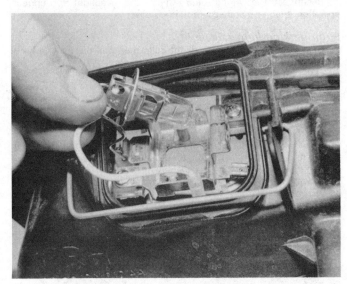

13.10B Removing the auxiliary driving light bulb

### Front foglight (when fitted)

14 Remove the lens and reflector together by undoing the two retaining screws. Do not disturb the alignment screw.

15 Disconnect the wiring from the bulb. Release the spring clip and extract the bulb. **Caution:** *If the lights have just been in use, the bulb may be extremely hot.*

16 Do not touch the glass of the new bulb with the fingers – see paragraph 4.

17 Fit the new bulb and secure it with the spring clip. Reconnect the wiring.

18 Refit the lens and reflector and secure it with the two screws. Check for correct operation.

### Front direction indicator

19 From under the bonnet, unhook the spring which secures the direction indicator light unit (photo).

20 Withdraw the light unit and free the bulbholder from it by twisting it anti-clockwise (photo).

21 Remove the bulb from the holder by pushing and twisting anti-clockwise (photo). Fit the new bulb to the holder, refit the bulb and holder to the light unit and refit and secure the light unit.

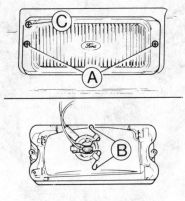

**Fig. 12.13 Front foglight bulb renewal (Sec 13)**

A   Rotating screws                 C   Alignment screw
B   Spring clip

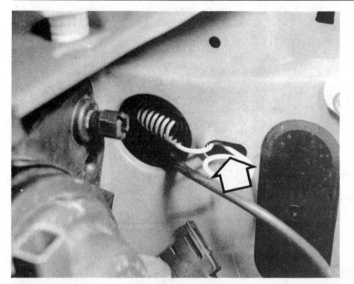

13.19 Unhook the spring (arrowed) to release the front direction indicator light unit

13.20 Removing the bulb and holder from the direction indicator light unit

13.21 Removing a direction indicator bulb

22 Check the direction indicators for correct operation. If renewing the bulb has not solved the problem, refer to Section 26.

### Direction indicator side repeaters

23 Reach up behind the wing and release the light unit by squeezing the two release tags together.
24 Pull the light unit out of the wing. Twist the bulbholder anti-clockwise to release it. Pull out the old bulb and press in the new one (photos).
25 Refit the bulbholder, then insert the light unit into its hole and press it home.

### Rear light cluster

26 Access to rear light cluster bulbs is gained from within the luggage area. First remove the access cover on the side concerned; on the right-hand side, also remove the jack.
27 Grasp the bulbholder in the apertures provided, squeeze the retaining lugs together and withdraw the bulbholder (photo).
28 The appropriate bulb(s) can now be renewed, and the bulbholder refitted.

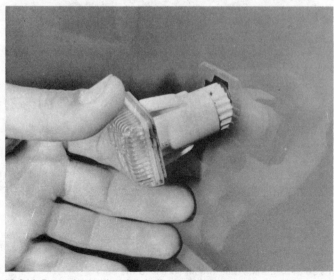

13.24A Removing a direction indicator side repeater

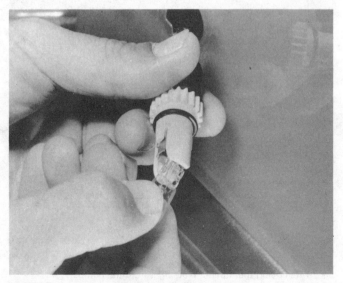

13.24B Fitting a new side repeater bulb

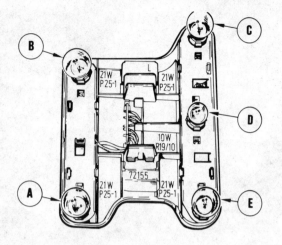

**Fig. 12.14 Identification of rear light bulbs (Sec 13)**

A   Reversing light          D   Tail light
B   Direction indicator      E   Rear foglight
C   Stop-light

13.27A Rear light cluster bulbholder retaining lugs (arrowed)

### Number plate light

29  Carefully prise the light unit out of the bumper with a screwdriver (photo).
30  Twist the light unit and bulbholder anti-clockwise to separate them (photo). Pull out the wedge base bulb and press in the new one.
31  Reassemble the light unit and bulbholder, then push the assembly home.

---

## 14 Exterior light units – removal and refitting

1  For removal and refitting of the front foglights, front direction indicators, direction indicator repeaters and the number plate lights, refer to the previous Section.

### Headlight

2  Unhook the direction indicator light unit retaining spring. Withdraw the direction indicator unit and allow it to hang.

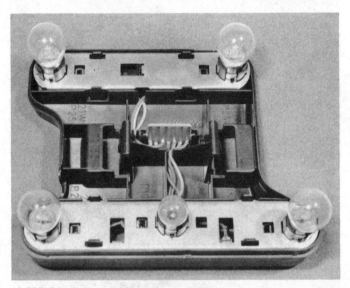

13.27B Rear light bulbholder removed

13.29 Removing the number plate light from the bumper

13.30 Separate the unit to gain access to the bulb

3  Pull out the rubber moulding from between the base of the headlight and the bumper. (This moulding may in fact be stuck to the headlight surround).

4  Release the headlight surround retaining lugs, prising them carefully with a screwdriver. Work from the outside towards the centre of the vehicle. Remove the surround by pulling it forwards and then sideways.

5  Remove the radiator grille, which is secured by two screws (photo).

6  Disconnect the headlight wiring connector. Remove the two retaining screws, and the nut on the side mounting (photos). Draw the headlight unit forwards and twist it to remove it.

7  Refit by reversing the removal operations. Make sure that the locating pin on the outside of the headlight unit engages in the hole in the apron panel.

8  If the new unit has been fitted, or if the adjusting screws have been disturbed, have the beam alignment checked without delay. Refer to Section 15.

9  Note that the headlight lens can be renewed independently of the rest of the unit, once the securing clips have been removed (photo).

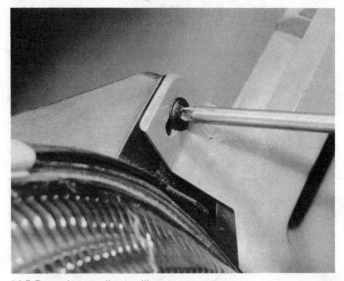

14.5 Removing a radiator grille screw

14.6A Headlight top mounting screw

14.6B Headlight bottom mounting screw

14.6C Headlight side mounting nut

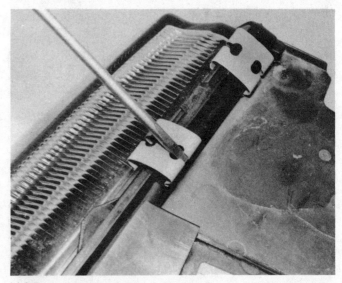

14.9 Removing a headlight lens securing clip

14.12 Four of the rear light unit securing nuts (arrowed) – there are two more out of sight

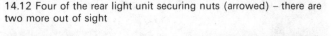

14.13A Removing the rear light unit

14.13B Disconnecting the multi-plug from the rear light unit

*Auxiliary driving light*
10  This is integral with the headlight unit.

*Rear light cluster*
11  Remove the rear light cluster bulbholder as described in the previous Section.
12  Remove the six nuts which secure the rear light unit (photo).
13  Withdraw the light unit from the vehicle and disconnect the multi-plug and wiring harness from it (photos).
14  Fit a new gasket to the light unit if the old one was damaged.
15  Refit by reversing the removal operations.

---

**15  Headlight beam alignment**

1  It is recommended that beam adjustment be carried out by a Ford garage using optical alignment equipment. In an emergency, however, the followng procedure will produce acceptable results.
2  The vehicle should be normally laden and the tyre pressures must be correct. Park the vehicle on level ground, approximately 10 metres (33 feet) in front of a flat wall or garage door.
3  Draw a vertical line on the wall or door corresponding to the centre-line of the vehicle. (The position of this line can be determined by marking the centres of the windscreen and rear window with crayon, then viewing the wall or door from the rear of the vehicle).
4  With the centre-line established, construct the other lines shown in Fig. 12.15.
5  Switch the headlights on to dipped beam. Cover one headlight with cloth and adjust the other, using the two screws at the rear of the unit, to bring the centre of the beam to the point 'C' on the appropriate side of the alignment chart (photo).
6  Transfer the cloth to the headlight already adjusted, and repeat the adjustment on the other headlight.
7  Have the alignment checked professionally at the first opportunity.
8  Holts Amber Lamp is useful for temporarily changing the headlight colour to conform with the normal usage on Continental Europe.

---

**16  Interior lights – bulb renewal**

1  Always switch the light off, or disconnect the battery negative lead, before changing a bulb.

*Courtesy light*
2  Carefully prise the light unit from its location. If reading (spot) lights are fitted, prise from the middle; if not, prise from one end.
3  Renew the bulb(s), detaching the reflector or contact plate as necessary (photo).
4  Reassemble the light unit and press it home.

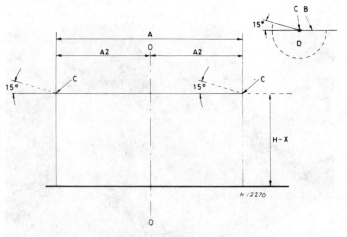

**Fig. 12.15 Headlight beam alignment chart (Sec 15)**

A  Distance between headlamp centres
B  Light-dark boundary
C  Beam centre dipped
D  Dipped beam pattern
H  Height from ground to centre of headlamps
X  = 120 mm (4.7 in)

15.5 Headlight beam adjustment screws (arrowed)

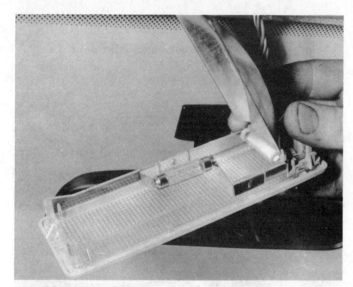

16.3 Detaching the courtesy light from its reflector

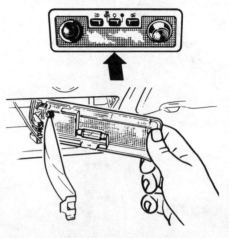

Fig. 12.16 Courtesy light bulb renewal. Prise at points arrowed (Sec 16)

Fig. 12.17 Mirror light bulb renewal. Prise frame at point arrowed (Sec 16)

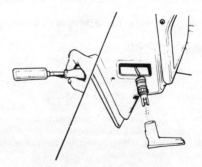

Fig. 12.18 'Door open' light bulb renewal (Sec 16)

### Vanity mirror light

5   Carefully prise the frame off the mirror to expose the bulbs.
6   Unclip the blown bulb(s) and press in the new ones. Make sure that the spring contacts which secure the bulb are clean and tight; bend them slightly to improve their tension if necessary.
7   Check for correct operation, then snap the mirror frame home.

### Door lights

8   The 'door open' warning light can be removed from the edge of the door by prising the lens from the inside edge.
9   Renew the bulb and press the lens home.
10  The kerb illumination light is renewed in a similar way. Prise out the lens using the slot provided, renew the bulb and refit the lens.

### Footwell lights

11  Free the light unit by carefully prising with a screwdriver.
12  Extract the bulbholder by twisting and pulling. Renew the bulb, refit the holder and press the light unit home.

### Luggage area light

13  Carefully prise free the light unit (photo).
14  Pull out the old bulb, press in the new one and refit the light unit.

### Engine bay light

15  This light bulb is directly accessible once the bonnet is opened. It is of the bayonet type.

### Instrument panel lights

16  Remove the instrument cluster as described in Section 17.
17  Extract the appropriate bulb and holder by twisting it 90° anti-clockwise (photo).

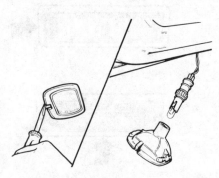

Fig. 12.19 Kerb illumination light bulb renewal (Sec 16)

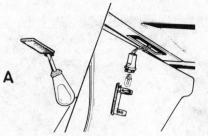

A

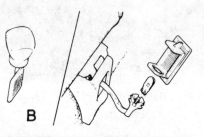

B

Fig. 12.20 Footwell light bulb renewal – front (A) and rear (B) (Sec 16)

16.13 Luggage area light unit

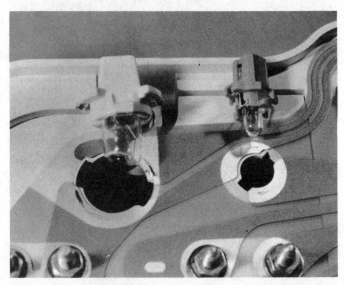

16.17 Instrument panel lights

18 Large bulbs are of the wedge base type and can be pulled out of their holders. Small bulbs and holders cannot be separated, but must be renewed complete.
19 Refit the bulbs and holder, then refit the instrument panel.

### Switch illumination lights
20 The pilot lights in the minor switches cannot be renewed independently of the switch.
21 The bulbs which illuminate the lighting master switch and the heater blower switch can be renewed after pulling off the switch knob (photos).
22 The switch symbols in the instrument panel surround are illuminated by a single bulb. To gain access to the bulb, remove the instrument panel surround, which is secured by four screws. The bulb is of the wedge base type (photo).

### Glovebox light
23 Open the glovebox. Remove the combined switch/light unit, which is secured by two screws (photo).
24 Prise out the switch, renew the bayonet fitting bulb and refit the switch
25 Refit the light unit and secure it with the two screws.

### Ashtray light
26 Remove the storage box or audio unit from just above the ashtray (photo).
27 Free the bulbholder from above the ashtray, either by pulling it outwards (low series trim) or by carefully prising it away from its housing using a screwdriver (high series trim).

28 Renew the wedge base bulb. Refit the bulbholder and the other disturbed components.

### Radio fader light
29 Carefully prise off the fader surround.
30 Extract the bulbholder by twisting it anti-clockwise. Disconnect its wiring plug and remove it.
31 The bulb and holder cannot be separated. Fit the new bulbholder unit, check for correct operation, then refit the fader surround.

### Heater control light
32 Remove the instrument panel surround.
33 Pull off the heater control knobs, then prise the display panel off the heater controls to expose the bulb.
34 Renew the bulb, check for correct operation, then refit the disturbed components (photo).

16.21A Pull off the switch knob ...

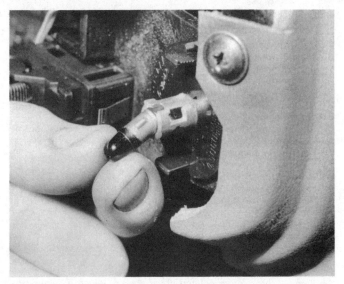

16.21B ... and renew the bulb

16.22 Removing the switch symbol illumination light

16.23 The glovebox light unit

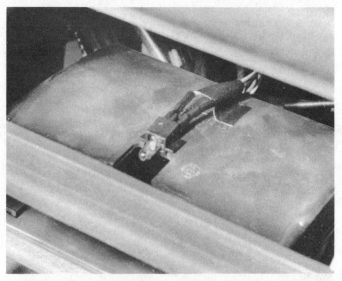

16.26 Ashtray light bulb seen through radio aperture

16.34 Renewing the heater control light bulb

*Automatic transmission selector light*

35  Carefully pull off the selector housing. Remove the selector knob by unscrewing it.

36  Release the selector indicator plate, which is secured by two clips. Remove the indicator plate by sliding it up the selector stalk.

37  Remove the selector guide plate, which is secured by four screws. Extract the bulbholder and renew the bulb (photos).

38  An alternative means of access is by removing the centre console as described in Chapter 11, Section 40.

39  Refit by reversing the removal operations.

*Rear console light*

40  Remove the rear heater control lever knob by pulling it off.

41  Remove the rear console panel, which is secured by two screws at the top.

42  Free the bulbholder by twisting it anti-clockwise. Renew the wedge base bulb.

43  Refit the bulbholder and the other disturbed components.

*Hazard warning switch light*

44  Remove the steering column upper shroud, which is secured by three screws.

45  Make sure that the switch is in the 'off' position, then pull off the switch cap.

46  Pull out the wedge base bulb and press in the new one.

47  Refit the switch cap and the steering column upper shroud.

*Clock light*

48  If the clock is in the instrument panel, renewal is as described for the other instrument panel lights.

49  To renew the light bulb is the overhead type of clock, first remove the overhead console (Chapter 11, Section 41).

50  Remove the back of the clock, which is secured by two screws, for access to the bulb (photo).

51  Renew the bayonet fitting bulb (photo). Refit the back of the clock, then refit the overhead console.

## 17  Instrument cluster – removal and refitting

1  Although not essential, it is wise to disconnect the battery negative lead.

2  Remove the instrument panel surround, which is secured by four screws (photo). Disengage the switch symbol illumination light from the surround.

3  Remove the four screws which secure the instrument cluster (photo).

4  Partly withdraw the instrument cluster, disconnect the multi-plugs and remove the cluster (photos). The multi-plugs are colour coded and not interchangeable; when a graphic display module is fitted, its multi-plug has a red locking mechanism which must be retracted before the plug can be disconnected.

5  Refit by reversing the removal operations.

## 18  Instrument cluster – dismantling and reassembly

1  With the instrument cluster removed, a particular gauge or other component can be renewed by following the appropriate parts of this Section.

2  Remove all the light bulbs and holders from the rear of the panel by twisting them anti-clockwise.

3  To remove the printed circuit, unclip and remove the two multi-plug terminal retainers. Remove all the nuts and washers from the printed circuit terminals, then unclip and remove the printed circuit. Be careful with it, it is fragile (photo).

4  To remove the instrument cluster glass, release the two securing clips from the bottom edge of the glass. Swing the glass upwards and remove it (photo).

5  With the glass removed, the speedometer, fuel and temperature gauges can be removed individually after undoing their securing nuts

16.37 Automatic transmission selector with bulbholder displaced

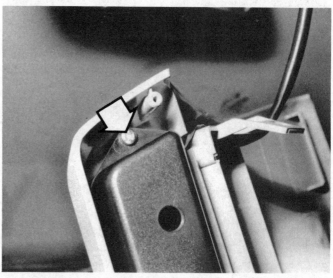

16.50 One of the two screws (arrowed) which secure the back of the clock

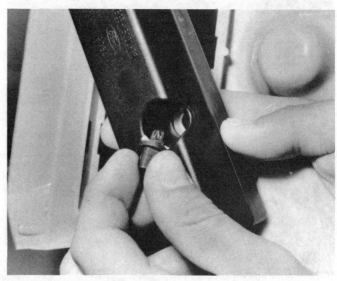

16.51 Renewing the clock bulb

17.2 Two of the instrument panel surround screws

17.3 Removing an instrument panel securing screw

17.4A Instrument cluster viewed through windscreen to show multi-plugs

17.4B Removing the instrument cluster

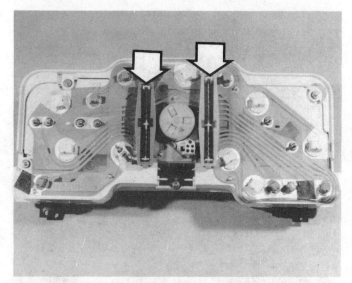

18.3 Instrument cluster printed circuit. Unclip retainers at their top ends (arrowed)

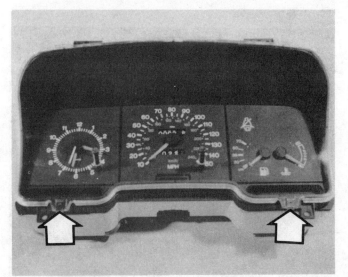

18.4 Instrument cluster glass securing clips (arrowed)

or screws. To remove the clock or tachometer, the printed circuit must be removed as well.
6   When fitted, the low fuel/high temperature warning light bulbs can be renewed after removing the combined gauge unit. Use tweezers to extract the old bulb and to fit the new one.
7   The graphic display module, when fitted, can be removed after undoing its two securing screws.
8   Reassemble the instrument cluster by reversing the dismantling operations.

## 19 Clock – removal and refitting

1   To remove the clock from the instrument panel, refer to the previous Section.
2   To remove the clock from the overhead console, first remove the console.
3   Remove the clock rear cover, which is secured by two screws.
4   Remove the two screws which secure the clock itself, then withdraw the clock.
5   Refit by reversing the removal operations.

## 20 Cigarette lighter – removal and refitting

1   Disconnect the battery negative lead.

### Front lighter
2   On models with high level trim, pull the centre console surround away from the radio to gain access to the lighter. On models with low level trim, remove the radio/cassette unit.
3   Disconnect the wires from the cigarette lighter and push it out of the illuminated ring.
4   Refit by reversing the removal operations.

### Rear lighter
5   Pull off the rear heater control lever knob.
6   Remove the rear console panel, which is secured by two screws.
7   Disconnect the wires from the lighter and push it out of the illuminated ring.
8   Refit by reversing the removal operations.

## 21 Horn – removal and refitting

1   Two horns are fitted as standard. The high tone horn is located to the right of the radiator and is accessible from under the bonnet. The low tone horn is located below and to the left of the radiator and is accessible from below.
2   Remove the horn securing nut or bolt and recover the shakeproof washer.
3   Disconnect the wiring and remove the horn.
4   When refitting the horn, make sure it is correctly positioned before tightening the securing nut or bolt.

## 22 Horn switch plate, slip rings and brushes – removal and refitting

1   Disconnect the battery negative lead.

### Switch plate
2   Pull off the steering wheel centre cover (photo).
3   Undo the three screws which retain the switch plate. Disconnect and remove the switch plate (photo).
4   Refit by reversing the removal operations.

### Slip rings
5   Remove the steering wheel (Chapter 10, Section 8).
6   Release the tangs which secure the slip rings to the underside of the steering wheel. Disconnect the slip rings from the switch plate and remove them.
7   Refit by reversing the removal operations.

### Brushes
8   Remove the steering wheel (Chapter 10, Section 8).
9   Remove the steering column upper and lower shrouds.
10  Disconnect the wiring from the horn brushes. Carefully lever out the brush unit, using a thin screwdriver inserted into the bottom edge of the unit.
11  Refit by reversing the removal operations.

## 23 Seat heating elements – removal and refitting

1   Remove the seat (Chapter 11, Section 42).
2   Remove the seat cushion trim or backrest trim as necessary.
3   Note which way round the heating element is facing, then remove the wire clips and adhesive tape which secure it to the seat. Retrieve the tie-rod and fit it to the new element.
4   Fit the new element with the thermostat facing the cushion foam. Secure the element with wire clips and tape, making sure that it is not too tight – it must be able to flex under load.
5   Refit the cushion or backrest trim.
6   Refit the seat and check the heating elements for correct operation.

22.2 Removing the steering wheel centre cover

22.3 Three screws (arrowed) secure the horn switch plate

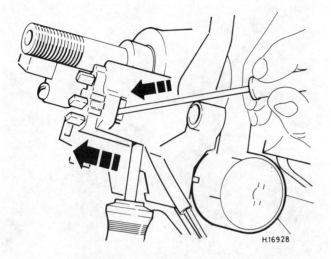

Fig. 12.21 Removing the horn brush unit (Sec 22)

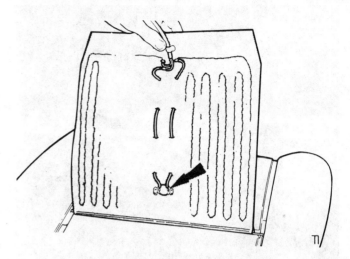

Fig. 12.22 Seat heating element. Thermostat (arrowed) must face the foam (Sec 23)

## 24 Ignition/starter switch – removal and refitting

1  Disconnect the battery negative lead.
2  Remove the steering column upper and lower shrouds.
3  Remove the switch by depressing its two retaining tabs. Unplug the wiring connector and remove the switch (photos).
4  When refitting, make sure that the slot in the centre of the switch is aligned with the driver on the lock.
5  Reconnect the switch and push it home until the retaining tabs click into place.
6  Reconnect the battery and check the switch for correct operation, then refit the steering column shrouds.
7  For removal of the steering/ignition lock barrel, see Chapter 10, Section 12.

## 25 Switches – removal and refitting

1  Disconnect the battery negative lead, or satisfy yourself that there is no risk of a short-circuit, before removing any switch.
2  Except where noted, a switch is refitted by reversing the removal operations.

*Lighting master switch*
3  Pull the knob off the lighting switch.
4  Depress the two retaining lugs and pull the switch out of the instrument panel surround.
5  Disconnect the multi-plug from the switch and remove it.

*Heater blower switch*
6  This is removed in the same way as the lighting master switch.

*Instrument illumination dimmer switch*
7  Remove the instrument panel surround, which is retained by four screws.
8  Pull the dimmer switch from its location and disconnect the multi-plug (photo).
9  Although the switch looks as if it can be dismantled, this should not be attempted unless the switch is surplus to requirements, and a new unit is readily available.

*Mirror control switch*
10 Carefully prise the switch out of the armrest using a thin-bladed screwdriver. Protect the armrest with a piece of cloth or thick card.
11 Disconnect the multi-plug and remove the switch (photo).

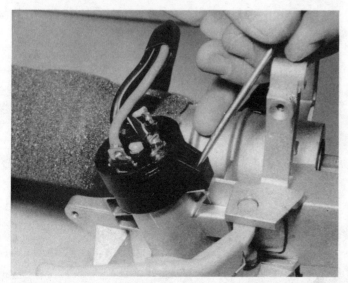

24.3A Ignition/starter switch removal: depress the retaining tabs ...

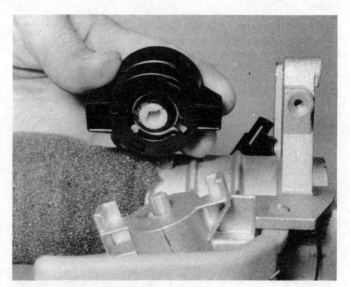

24.3B ... and lift off the switch

25.8 Removing the instrument illumination dimmer switch

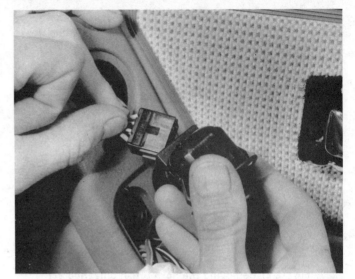

25.11 Removing a mirror control switch

### Direction indicator/headlight flasher switch

12  Remove the steering wheel centre cover.
13  Remove the steering column upper and lower shrouds, which are secured by a total of six screws.
14  Unlock the steering and turn the steering wheel to gain access to the two screws which retain the switch (photo). Remove the screws.
15  Withdraw the switch from the steering column and disconnect its multi-plug (photo). It may be necessary to release some cable ties in order to free the multi-plug.
16  When refitting, check the switch for correct operation before refitting the shrouds and steering wheel centre cover. When fitting the shrouds, be careful not to trap the switch rubber gaiter.

### Windscreen wipe/wash switch

17  Proceed as described in the previous sub-section for the direction indicator switch. Depending on equipment, the wipe/wash switch may have more than one multi-plug connected to it.

### Door pillar switch (for courtesy light)

18  Remove the single securing screw and pull the switch from its location (photo).
19  Retain the wiring with (for instance) string or a clothes peg, so that it cannot fall into the door pillar, then disconnect the switch.
20  Lubricate the plunger of the switch with a little petroleum jelly when refitting

### Reversing light switch (manual gearbox)

21  Raise the front of the vehicle and support it securely.
22  Locate     reversing light switch, which is located on the right-hand     of the gearbox.
23  Disconnect the wiring from the switch, wipe clean around it and unscrew it.
24  When refitting, make sure that the switch wiring is routed sufficiently far from the exhaust system to avoid damage due to heat.

### Window operating switch

25  The window operating switch is removed from the armrest or console in the same way as the mirror control switch previously described in paragraphs 10 and 11 (photo).

### Sliding roof switch

26  Carefully prise the switch from the overhead console using a thin-bladed screwdriver.
27  Disconnect the multi-plug and remove the switch.

### Tailgate lock switch

28  The tailgate lock switch controls the luggage area lights. When appropriate, it also provides inputs to the auxiliary warning and anti-theft systems.

25.14 Two screws (arrowed) secure the direction indicator/headlight flasher switch. Steering wheel removed for clarity

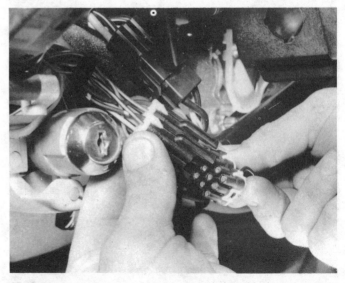

25.15 Disconnecting a steering column switch multi-plug

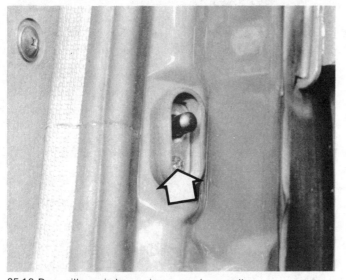

25.18 Door pillar switch securing screw (arrowed)

25.25 Removing a window operating switch

29 To avoid damage to other components, the battery **must** be disconnected before the tailgate lock switch is removed.
30 Remove the tailgate interior trim panel, which is secured by eleven screws.
31 Release the switch locking tab, pivot the switch away from the lock and disconnect it.
32 When refitting, make sure that the slot on the switch engages with the operating lug on the lock barrel.

### Handbrake 'ON' switch

33 Gain access to the base of the handbrake lever by removing the rubber gaiter and (if necessary) the centre console or switch panel (photo).
34 Disconnect the wiring from the handbrake switch. Undo the two securing screws and remove the switch, noting how the screws do not pass through holes in the lever but engage in slots.
35 After refitting the switch, check for correct operation before refitting the surrounding trim.

### Stop-light switch

36 Remove the under-dash trim on the driver's side. The trim is secured by plastic clips.
37 Disconnect the wiring from the switch. Turn the switch 90° anti-clockwise and remove it from the brake pedal bracket (photo).
38 When refitting, hold the pedal in the fully raised position, push in the switch and turn it clockwise to lock it. Release the pedal and check that at least 2 mm (0.08 in) of the switch plunger is visible.

### Oil pressure warning switch

39 This switch is located on the left-hand side of the cylinder block. Access may be impeded by one of the manifolds and associated equipment.
40 Disconnect the wire from the switch, then unscrew the switch and remove it.
41 Clean the switch and its seat before refitting. Apply a little sealant to the switch threads if wished.
42 Run the engine and check that there are no oil leaks from the switch. Stop the engine and check the oil level.

### Heated rear window switch

43 Remove the instrument panel surround, which is secured by four screws.
44 Carefully prise the switch from its location, disconnect the multi-plug and remove it.

### Foglight switch(es)

45 These are removed in the same way as the heated rear window switch (photo).

25.33 Handbrake 'On' switch

25.37 Stop-light switch fitted to brake pedal bracket

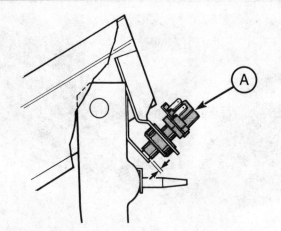

**Fig. 12.23 Fitting the stop-light switch (A). Plunger protrusion (between arrows) must be at least 2 mm (0.08 in) (Sec 25)**

25.45 Removing a foglight switch

*Hazard warning switch*
46  This is integral with the direction indicator switch.

*Front seat adjusting switch*
47  Remove the seat trim panel.
48  Prise the operating levers off the switch with a thin-bladed screwdriver.
49  Remove the two securing screws, withdraw the switch and unplug it.

*Rear seat adjusting switch*
50  This is removed in the same way as the mirror control switch already described in paragraphs 10 and 11.

*Heated seat control switches*
51  These are removed in the same way as the mirror control switch already described in paragraphs 10 and 11.

*Starter inhibitor/reversing light switch (automatic transmission)*
52  Refer to Chapter 6, Section 14.

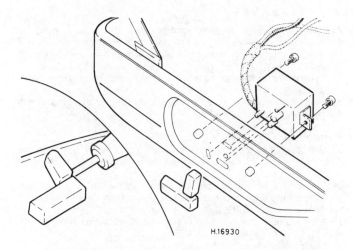

**Fig. 12.24 Removing the front seat adjusting switch (Sec 25)**

### 26  Direction indicator system – general

1  The direction indicator system consists of the flasher unit, control switch, external and repeater lights and the associated wiring. The hazard warning system shares the same flasher unit.
2  If the direction indicators operate abnormally fast or slowly on one side only, check the bulbs and wiring on that side. Incorrect wattage bulbs, dirty bulbholders and poor earth connections can all cause changes in the flashing rate.
3  If the direction indicators do not work at all, check the fuse before suspecting the flasher unit. If the hazard warning system works but the indicators do not, the flasher unit is almost certainly not faulty.
4  The flasher unit is plugged into the direction indicator switch, on the side away from the steering wheel. It can be unplugged after removing the steering column top shroud (photo). Testing is by substitution of a known good unit.

### 27  Fuses, relays and control units – general

*Fuses*
1  The battery positive (live) lead is protected by a fusible link. If this link melts, a major short-circuit is indicated, and expert advice should be sought before repairing it.
2  The main fuse/relay box is located under the bonnet, near the bulkhead on the right-hand side. It contains up to 24 fuses and nearly as many relays (according to equipment). Fuse applications are listed on the underside of the fuse box lid (photo).

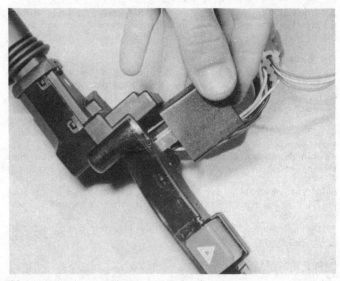

26.4 Unplugging the direction indicator flasher unit

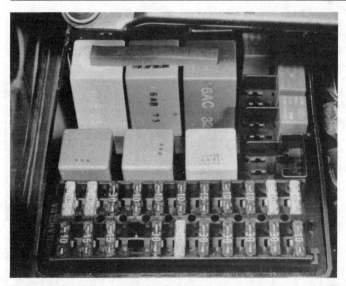

27.2 Main fuse/relay box under the bonnet

27.3 Auxiliary fuse box in the glovebox

3   There is an auxiliary fuse box inside the vehicle, accessible after opening the glovebox (photo). An in-line fuse for the radio is located under the facia on the left-hand side, near the heater.

4   The fuses are of the 'blade' type, and are colour coded to show their current rating. A blown fuse can be recognised by the melted wire link in the middle.

5   To renew a blown fuse, first switch off the circuit concerned. Pull the old fuse out of its holder, using tweezers or long-nosed pliers. Press in a new fuse of the same rating and try the  circuit again.

6   If the new fuse blows immediately or within a short time, do not carry on renewing fuses but look for a short-circuit in the wiring to the item(s) protected by the fuse. When more than one item is protected by a single fuse, switching on one item at a time until the fuse blows will help to isolate the defect.

7   Never fit a fuse of a higher rating (current capacity) than specified, and do not bypass fuses with silver foil or strands of wire. Serious damage, including fire, could result.

8   In some positions (such as for power window and seat adjustment motors) circuit breakers are fitted instead of fuses. These are normally self-resetting once the cause of the overload has been cleared.

*Relays*

9   Relays are electrically-operated switches. They are used for two main reasons:

   (a)  *A relay can switch a heavy current at a distance, thus allowing the use of lighter gauge control switches and wiring*
   (b)  *A relay can receive more than one control input, unlike a mechanical switch*

10  In addition, some relays have a 'timer' function – for example, the intermittent wipe and heated windscreen timer relays.

11  If a circuit or system served by a relay develops a fault, always remember that the problem could be in the relay. Testing is by substitution of a known good unit. Beware of substituting relays which look the same but perform different functions.

12  To renew a relay, simply unplug it from its holder and plug in the new one. Access to the relays in the main fuse box is as described for the fuses. Access to the relays located behind the facia is achieved by removing the facia top (photo) – See Chapter 11, Section 39.

13  The sliding roof relay is located in the overhead console.

*Control units and modules*

14  Control units and modules have similar functions to relays, but can accept more inputs and perform more tasks. For the most part they are completely electronic, rather than electro-mechanical.

15  The two major modules are the EEC IV module (on fuel-injection models) and the ABS control module. These are located below the glovebox on the passenger side, and are accessible after removing the under-dash trim (photo).

27.12 Some of the relays located behind the facia (seen through the windscreen)

27.15 EEC IV and ABS modules unclipped from their locations

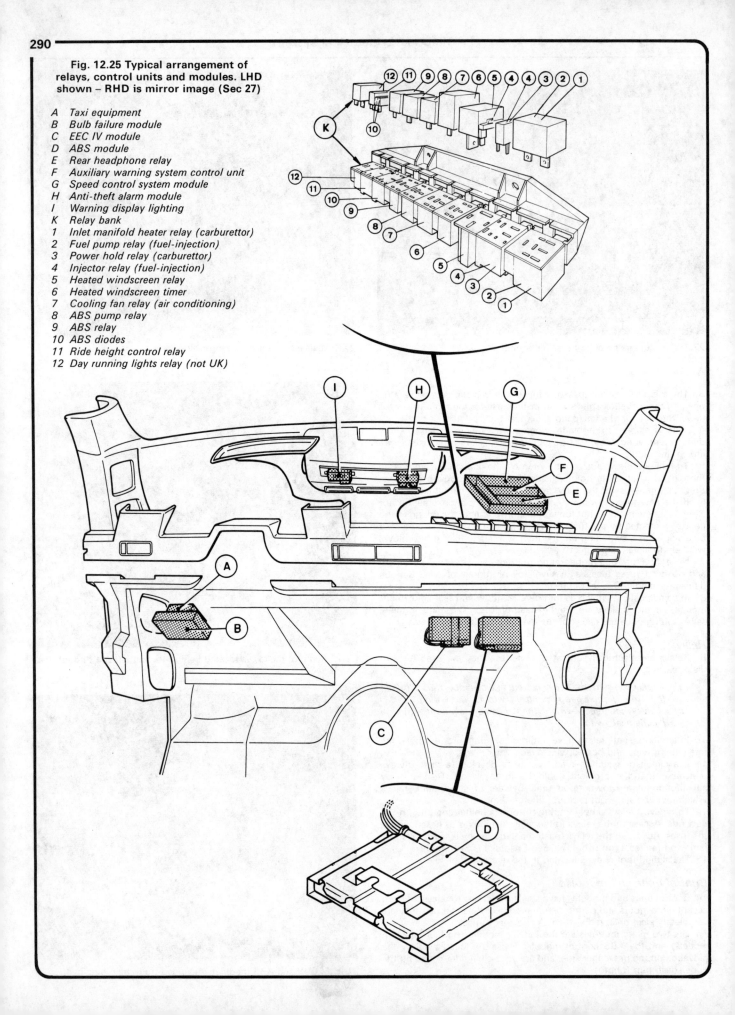

**Fig. 12.25 Typical arrangement of relays, control units and modules. LHD shown – RHD is mirror image (Sec 27)**

A  Taxi equipment
B  Bulb failure module
C  EEC IV module
D  ABS module
E  Rear headphone relay
F  Auxiliary warning system control unit
G  Speed control system module
H  Anti-theft alarm module
I  Warning display lighting
K  Relay bank
1  Inlet manifold heater relay (carburettor)
2  Fuel pump relay (fuel-injection)
3  Power hold relay (carburettor)
4  Injector relay (fuel-injection)
5  Heated windscreen relay
6  Heated windscreen timer
7  Cooling fan relay (air conditioning)
8  ABS pump relay
9  ABS relay
10  ABS diodes
11  Ride height control relay
12  Day running lights relay (not UK)

16 As with relays, testing by the home mechanic is limited to substitution of known good units. This is likely to be prohibitively expensive on a trial and error basis so in case of problems a Ford dealer or other competent specialist should be consulted at an early stage.

## 28 Central locking system – general

1 When fitted, the central locking system causes all door locks (including the tailgate lock) to take up the position of the drivers or front passengers door lock.

2 To reduce the chances of locking the keys in the vehicle, the system will not respond to the operation of a front door locking lever from inside the vehicle if either of the front doors are open.

3 There is no inertia switch to release the locks in case of vehicle impact; it is therefore not advisable to have the doors locked when on the move.

4 Regardless of the state of the central locking system, the tailgate cannot be opened when the engine is running. This is to prevent unauthorised entry whilst the vehicle is stopped in traffic.

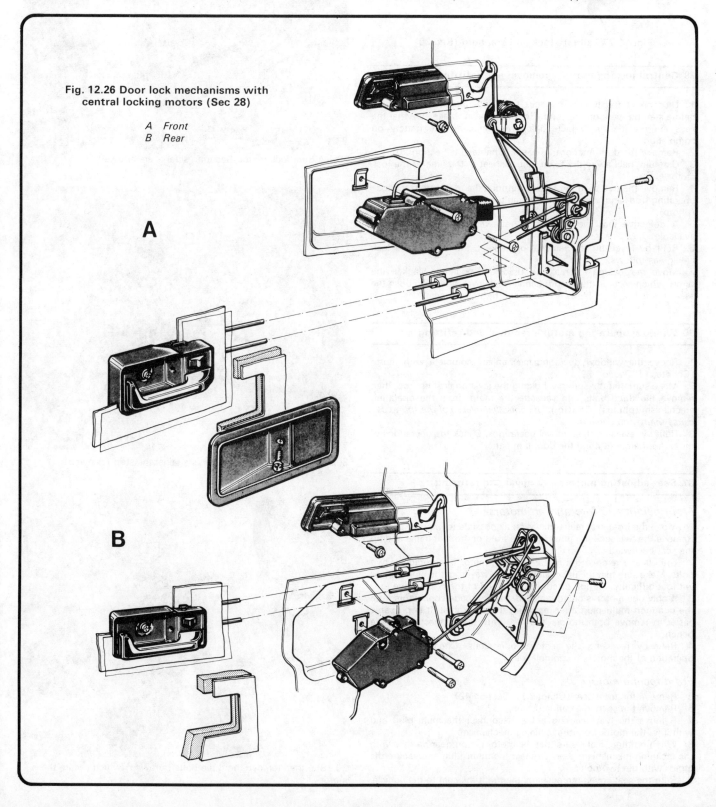

Fig. 12.26 Door lock mechanisms with central locking motors (Sec 28)

A Front
B Rear

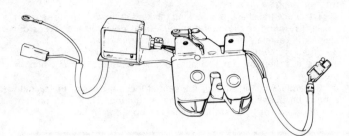

**Fig. 12.27 Tailgate lock and solenoid (Sec 28)**

## 29 Central locking motor – removal and refitting

1   Disconnect the battery negative lead and unlock all the doors before starting work on the central locking system. Make sure that the keys are outside the vehicle before reconnecting the battery on completion.
2   Remove the door interior trim panel (Chapter 11, Section 20).
3   Carefully peel away the foam rubber sheet in the area of the lock motor.
4   Remove the two securing screws, unhook the motor from the lock operating rod and disconnect the multi-plug. Remove the motor (photo).
5   A defective lock motor must be renewed. No spare parts are available.
6   Refit by reversing the removal operations, then adjust the lock linkage as follows.
7   Move the locking lever to the 'unlocked' position. Slacken the screw which secures the interior handle/lock lever assembly, push the assembly forwards as far as it will go and tighten the screw.

## 30 Window operating motor – removal and refitting

1   Reove the window operating mechanism, complete with motor (Chapter 11, Section 22).
2   Make sure that the spring is holding the lever against its stop, then remove the three bolts and separate the motor from the operating mechanism (photos). **Caution:** *Uncontrolled release of the spring can cause injury and damage.*
3   Refit by reversing the removal operations. Check the operations of the motor before refitting the door trim panel.

## 31 Seat adjusting motors – removal and refitting

### Front height and fore-and-aft motors

1   Move the front seat rearwards as far as possible to improve access. Remove the two securing bolts from the front of the seat frame and tip the seat backwards.
2   Unbolt and remove the motor(s). Each motor is secured by two bolts. Make sure that the drive cables come away from the worm drives without difficulty – if not, disconnect one end of the worm drive too.
3   If only one motor is being removed, free its spade connectors from the common multi-plug after removing the plug shell. It is probably easier to remove both motors and deal with the connectors on the bench.
4   Refit by reversing the removal operations. Check for correct operation of the motors on completion.

### Front recline motor

5   Remove the front seat (Chapter 11, Section 42).
6   Remove the seat cover and cushion.
7   Remove the two securing bolts, disconnect the multi-plug and withdraw the motor from the reclining mechanism.
8   When refitting, make sure that the motor pinion gear meshes with the reclining mechanism gear. Connect the multi-plug and secure the motor with the two bolts.
9   Refit the seat cover and cushion, then refit the seat to the vehicle.

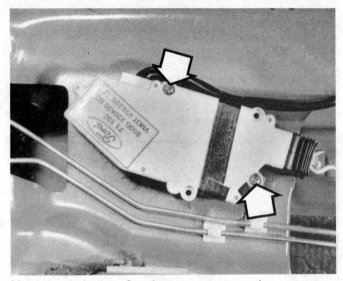

29.4 A door lock motor. Securing screws are arrowed

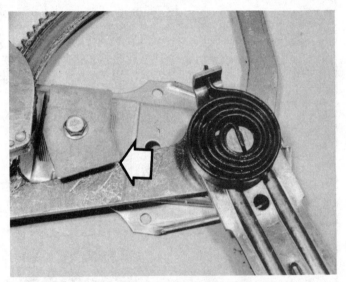

30.2A Make sure that the lever is against the stop (arrowed) ...

30.2B ... then remove the three bolts (arrowed) which secure the motor

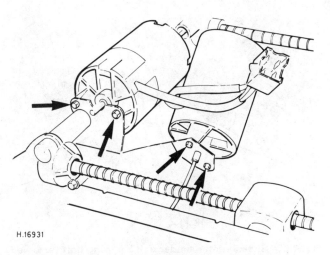

Fig. 12.28 Seat adjusting motor bolts (arrowed) (Sec 31)

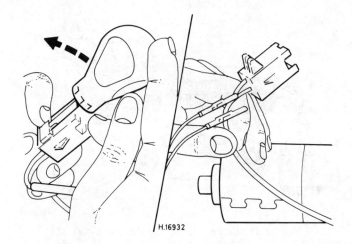

Fig. 12.29 Removing the spade connectors from the multi-plug (Sec 31)

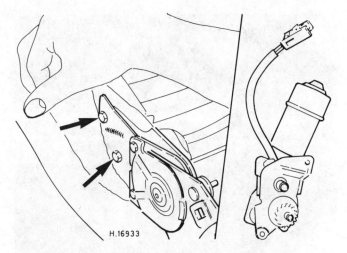

Fig. 12.30 Front seat recline motor bolts (arrowed) (Sec 31)

Fig. 12.31 Rear seat recline motor (Sec 31)

*Rear recline motor*

10 Remove the trim panel fom the left-hand side of the luggage area.
11 Remove the three 'Torx' screws which secure the motor and reclining mechanism. Disconnect the multi-plug (next to the seat squab) and remove the motor.
12 Refit by reversing the removal operations. Check for correct operation before refitting the luggage area trim panel.

## 32 Sliding roof motor – removal and refitting

1   Remove the overhead console.
2   Remove the three bolts which secure the motor. Lower the motor, disconnect the multi-plug and remove it. Recover the relay.
3   When refitting, make sure that the motor drivegear meshes with the roof operating mechanism. Refit the relay, reconnect the multi-plug and secure the motor with the three bolts.
4   Check the operation of the motor, then refit the overhead console.

## 33 Speedometer sender unit – removal and refitting

1   All vehicles are fitted with an electrical speedometer sender unit instead of a mechanical cable. The sender unit it located on the left-hand side of the transmission extension.

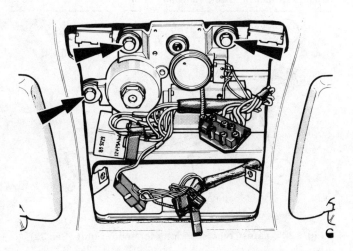

Fig. 12.32 Sliding roof motor retaining bolts (arrowed) (Sec 32)

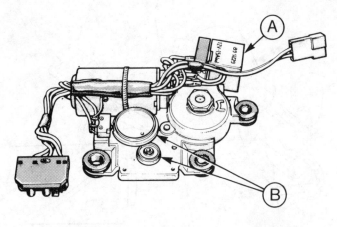

**Fig. 12.33 Sliding roof motor removed (Sec 32)**

A   Relay                    B   Control discs

2   Raise and securely support the front of the vehicle. Place a drain pan underneath the speedometer sender unit.
3   Remove the securing bolt, pull the sender unit out of the transmission and disconnect the multi-plug (photo). Be prepared for some spillage of gearbox oil or ATF (automatic transmission fluid).
4   If a new sender unit is being fitted, transfer the driven gear and circlip from the old unit. On automatic transmission models, also transfer the O-ring.
5   If the old sender unit had two connecting wires and the new unit has three, the brown wire must be cut at the multi-plug and an earth tag fitted. Consult a Ford dealer if in doubt.
6   Fit the new sender unit, using a new bolt (M6 x 25 mm for manual gearbox, M6 x 35 mm for automatic transmission). Besides the sender unit, the bolt also secures the new earth tag (when applicable), the radio earth strap and the multi-plug retaining bracket.
7   Connect the multi-plug and fit it to the bracket.
8   If any spillage of gearbox oil or transmission fluid occurred, top up the level before the vehicle is next run.

## 34  Wiper arms and blades – removal and refitting

1   To remove a windscreen wiper arm, first open the bonnet.
2   Mark the position of the blade on the windscreen or rear window (as applicable) with a piece of masking tape.
3   Lift up the plastic cap and undo the wiper arm retaining nut. Pull the arm off the drive spindle (photos).

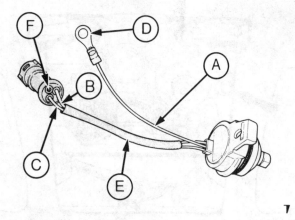

**Fig. 12.35 Latest type speedometer sender unit (Sec 33)**

A   Brown wire                E   Sleeve
B   Brown/yellow wire         F   Cut brown wire here (see
C   Brown/black wire              text)
D   Earth tag (see text)

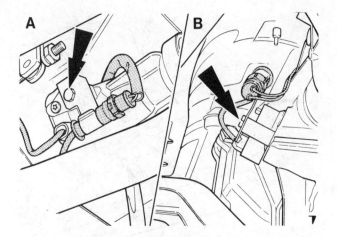

**Fig. 12.34 Speedometer sender unit securing bolt (arrowed) (Sec 33)**

A   Automatic transmission        B   Manual gearbox

33.3 Speedometer sender unit – securing bolt arrowed

34.3A Lift up the cap to expose the nut

34.3B Pull the arm off the spindle

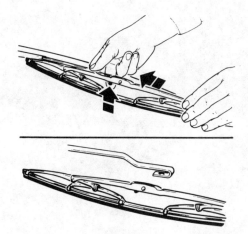

Fig. 12.36 Removing a wiper blade (Sec 34)

4   Refit in the reverse order to removal, using the masking tape to indicate the correct fitted position of the arm and blade.
5   To remove a blade alone, hinge the arm and blade away from the screen. Press the tab on the spring clip in the middle of the blade and unhook the blade from the arm.
6   Refit the blade by sliding it onto the hook on the arm (photo).

## 35 Windscreen wiper motor and linkage – removal and refitting

1   Remove the windscreen wiper arms as described in the previous Section.
2   Undo the eight 'Torx' screws which secure the wiper motor and linkage to the bulkhead (photos).
3   Disconnect the multi-plug and remove the motor and linkage (photo).
4   The linkage arms can be removed by levering them off the pivot pins.

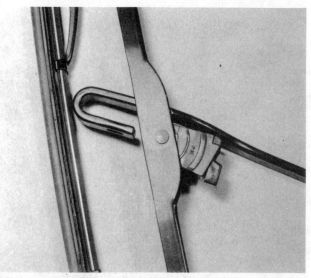

34.6 Fitting a wiper blade to the arm

35.2A Removing the wiper motor and linkage: two screws (arrowed) in front of the motor ...

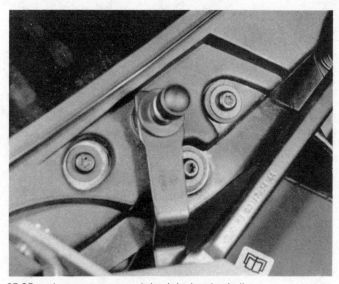

35.2B ... three screws around the right-hand spindle ...

35.2C ... and two screws on the left. Eighth screw is midway between the spindles

35.3 Disconnecting the wiper motor multi-plug

5   To remove the motor, undo the crank arm nut and remove the three securing bolts (photo). The motor cover can then be removed. A defective motor must be renewed.
6   Refit by reversing the removal operations. Before refitting the wiper arms, switch the wipers on and then off so that the motor takes up the 'parked' position.

## 36 Rear window wiper motor – removal and refitting

1   Remove the rear wiper arm from the spindle.
2   Open the tailgate and remove the interior trim panel, which is secured by eleven screws.
3   Remove the three bolts which secure the wiper motor bracket to the tailgate (photo). Also remove the screw which secures the earth tag. Disconnect the wiring plug and remove the motor and bracket.
4   The bracket can be unbolted from the motor if wished. No spare parts for the motor are available.
5   Commence refitting by offering the motor and bracket to the tailgate. Secure the assembly with the three bolts, then reconnect the wiring and secure the earth tag.
6   Switch on the ignition and operate the rear wiper control briefly so that the motor stops in the 'parked' position.
7   Refit the wiper arm and blade. Wet the window and operate the rear wiper control again to check the function of the motor.
8   Switch off the ignition and refit the tailgate interior trim panel.

## 37 Windscreen, rear window and headlight washers – general

1   All models are fitted with an electric windscreen washer pump. Most models also have a rear window washer pump, with a separate rear-mounted reservoir (photo). When headlight washers are fitted, these are supplied by a separate pump which shares a larger reservoir with the windscreen washer pump.
2   Only use water and an approved screen wash additive in the washer reservoirs (photo). In freezing conditions use an additive with antifreeze properties, or add a small amount of methylated spirit to the water. **Do not** use engine antifreeze: it is harmful to the wiper blades and to the vehicle's paintwork.
3   Windscreen and rear washer jets can be adjusted by inserting a pin into the jet nozzle and moving it as necessary. A special tool (Ford No. 32 004) is needed for adjustment of the headlight washer jets.
4   Windscreen and rear washer jets are removed simply by prising or pulling them from their locations (photo). Headlight washer jets can be unclipped from their holders after disconnection of the high pressure hose from the jet.

35.5 To remove the wiper motor, undo the crank arm nut and the three bolts (arrowed)

36.3 Three bolts (arrowed) which secure the rear wiper motor

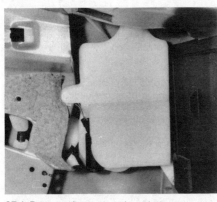

37.1 Rear washer reservoir and pump (luggage area trim removed)

37.2 Topping-up the screen washer reservoir

37.4 A windscreen washer jet prised out of its location in the bonnet

5   There is a check valve in the hose feeding the headlight washer jets. If this valve fails, the reservoir will empty itself through the jets.

6   To remove a washer pump, first syphon out the contents of the reservoir. Disconnect the wiring and the hose from the pump, then pull the pump out of its grommet in the reservoir. Renew the grommet if necessary when refitting the pump.

## 38 Fuel computer – description

When fitted, the fuel computer display and control unit is located to the right of the instrument cluster on RHD models. The driver can select four functions: instantaneous economy, average economy, fuel used and range on fuel remaining. The 'average economy' and 'fuel used' functions can be reset by pressing the 'clear' button. A 'mode' button changes the units from metric to Imperial or vice versa.

The 'range' function will be displayed automatically, and an alarm tone will sound, at 50, 25 and 10 miles to empty. (In fact there should be approximately 5 litres of fuel left in the tank when the calculated range to empty is zero, but it would be unwise to rely on this.)

The computer receives inputs from the fuel tank sender unit, the speedometer sender unit and the EEC IV module (fuel-injected models) or a fuel flow meter (carburettor models). A fuel flow sensor is not needed with fuel-injection because the module can provide the input needed.

## 39 Fuel computer components – removal and refitting

1   The fuel tank sender unit, EEC IV module and speedometer sender unit are not peculiar to the fuel computer. Their removal and refitting procedures are given in Chapter 3, Chapter 4 and this Chapter respectively.

### Computer module and bulb

2   Remove the instrument panel surround, which is secured by four screws.

3   Carefully pull the module from its location. Relese the multi-plug by pressing downwards and disconnect it.

4   The module illumination bulbholder may now be extracted by gripping it with pliers and twisting it anti-clockwise. Extract the old wedge base bulb, press in the new one and refit the bulb and holder.

5   Reconnect the multi-plug and press the module back into its hole. Check for correct operation, then refit the instrument panel surround.

### Fuel flow sensor (carburettor models only)

6   The fuel flow sensor is located under the bonnet, on the left-hand inner wing.

7   Disconnect the battery negative lead.

8   Disconnect the multi-plug and the fuel pipes from the sensor. Be prepared for fuel spillage; plug or cap the pipes.

9   Remove the three screws which secure the sensor bracket. Remove the sensor and bracket together; they can be separated on the bench if wished.

10  Refit by reversing the removal operations. Use new fuel pipe clips if the old ones were damaged during removal.

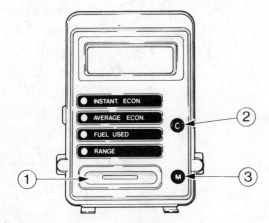

Fig. 12.37 Fuel computer controls (Sec 38)

1   Function select
2   Clear
3   Mode

H.16929

Fig. 12.38 Renewing the fuel computer module bulb (Sec 39)

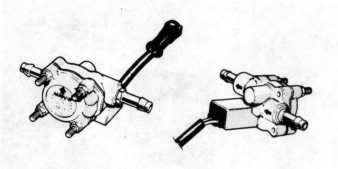

**Fig. 12.39 Fuel flow sensor fitted to carburettor models (Sec 39)**

## 40 Auxiliary warning system – description

When fitted, the auxiliary warning system (AWS) monitors coolant and washer fluid levels, brake pad wear, external air temperature and the function of certain light bulbs. Warning is also given if a door or the fuel filler flap is not properly shut.

Low fluid levels and brake pad wear are indicated by warning lights in the instrument cluster. A graphic display module, also in the instrument cluster, shows a plan view of the car and carries the bulb fail/door ajar warnings. Warning of possible ice hazard is given by two snowflake symbols in the graphic display module; the yellow symbol illuminates at +4°C (+39°F) and the red symbol at 0°C (+32°F). Temperature information is also passed to the digital clock in the overhead console, where it can be displayed if wished.

When the ignition is switched on, the AWS warning lights and the symbols in the graphic display module should all light up for a few seconds, then extinguish. (The stop-light symbols should not extinguish until the brakes have been operated once.) If a light or symbol remains lit, the level or system indicated should be checked as soon as possible. If a light or symbol flashes, a circuit fault is indicated and the level or system should be monitored regularly until the fault is corrected.

The main components of the system, besides the warning lights and display module, are the various sensors and the control assembly. The fluid level sensors are reed switches, operated by floating magnets. Brake pad wear is indicated when a loop of wire, embedded in the pad lining at a predetermined depth, is exposed and broken by the disc. All sensors, including the 'door ajar' switches, incorporate resistors in such an arrangement that the control assembly can read the difference between open and closed sensor contacts, and open or short-circuits in the wiring.

Light bulbs are monitored by the bulb failure module, located below the instrument panel. The lights monitored are the parking lights, tail lights, stop-lights and dipped beam headlights. The bulbs are monitored in pairs, so the fitting of an incorrect wattage bulb on one side of the vehicle may give a false alarm.

The air temperature sensor is located behind the front bumper. It is a resistor which changes resistance with temperature (a thermistor).

The AWS control assembly integrates the inputs from the various sensors and controls the illumination of the warning lights and symbols. Low fluid level warnings are subject to a certain delay to allow for false alarms which could be caused by vehicle movement. The control assembly is located behind the facia on the passenger side.

If a fault develops in the AWS, thorough testing and fault finding should be left to a Ford dealer or other competent specialist. Unskilled or uninformed testing may cause further damage.

When checking wires or sensors for continuity, disconnect the control assembly and bulb failure module first, otherwise damage may be caused.

## 41 Auxiliary warning system components – removal and refitting

### Warning light bulbs
1   Refer to Sections 17 and 18.

### Graphic display module
2   Refer to Sections 17 and 18.
3   The bulbs and light emitting diodes (LEDs) can be removed from the module using tweezers or jeweller's pliers. When renewing the fuel filler warning LED, note that the pip on the LED must align with the yellow dot on the circuit board.

### Fuel filler switch
4   Open the fuel filler flap and remove the filler cap.
5   Inside the luggage area, remove the trim on the right-hand side and disconnect the switch multi-plug.
6   Remove the screw which secures the switch to the filler neck. Remove the switch and withdraw its wires.
7   Refit by reversing the removal operations.

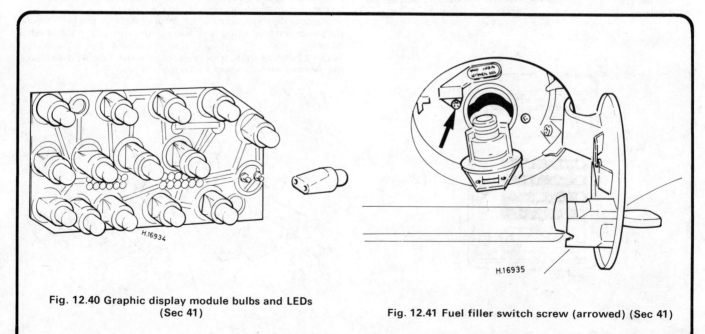

**Fig. 12.40 Graphic display module bulbs and LEDs (Sec 41)**

**Fig. 12.41 Fuel filler switch screw (arrowed) (Sec 41)**

41.9 Removing the air temperature sensor

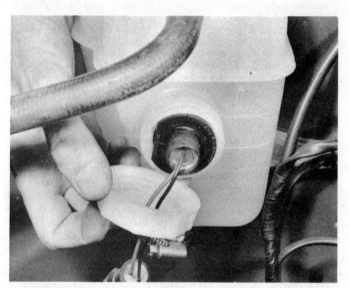

41.16 Removing the coolant level switch

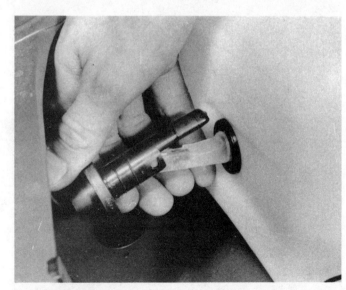

41.19 Removing the washer fluid level switch

### Air temperature sensor

8   From under the front bumper, unclip and disconnect the sensor multi-plug.
9   Unclip the sensor from its slot by pulling the securing tag inwards. Remove the sensor (photo).
10  When refitting, first connect the multi-plug. Fit the hook on the end of the sensor into the slot and press the sensor into place, then secure the multi-plug in its clip.

### Door/tailgate switch

11  Remove the door interior trim panel (Chapter 11, Section 20) or the tailgate interior trim panel (eleven screws).
12  Pull the switch to detach it from the lock and disconnect its multi-plug.
13  Refit by reversing the removal operations.

### Coolant level switch

14  Remove the cap from the coolant expansion tank, taking precautions against scalding if the coolant is hot.
15  Syphon coolant out of the tank if necessary until the level is below the switch.
16  Disconnect the switch multi-plug. Unscrew the retaining ring and pull the switch out of its grommet. Note how flats on the grommet and switch ensure correct fitting (photo).
17  Refit by inserting the switch into the grommet – use a new grommet if necessary – and screwing on the retaining ring. Reconnect the multi-plug and top up the cooling system.

### Washer fluid level switch

18  Syphon the fluid out of the washer reservoir until the level is below the switch.
19  Disconnect the switch multi-plug. Carefully prise the switch out of its grommet and remove it. Note how flats on the grommet and switch ensure correct fitting (photo).
20  When refitting, make sure that the grommet is in good condition (renew if necessary) and is correctly seated. Press the switch home, reconnect the multi-plug and refill the reservoir.

### Control assembly

21  Remove the instrument panel surround and the facia top (Chapter 11, Section 39).
22  Remove the two nuts which secure the assembly. Disconnect the multi-plug by pressing in the locking lever and pulling the plug. Remove the control assembly.
23  Refit by reversing the removal operations. Check the AWS for correct operation before refitting the disturbed trim.

### Bulb failure module

24  Remove the under-dash trim on the driver's side. This is secured by six screws, one of which is only accessible after removing the air vent grille.

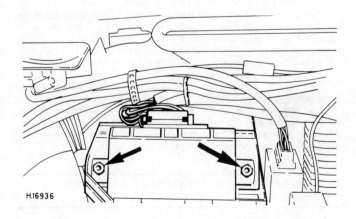

H.16936

**Fig. 12.42 Auxiliary warning system control assembly – retaining nuts arrowed (Sec 41)**

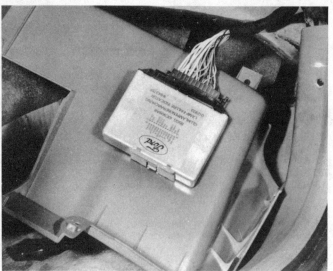

41.25 The bulb failure module secured to the under-dash trim

25 Pull the module from its bracket. Disconnect the multi-plug by pressing in the locking lever and pulling the plug. Remove the module (photo).
26 Refit by reversing the removal operations.

## 42 Speed control system – description

The speed control system is an optional extra on all models. When in use it maintains the vehicle speed at the value set by the driver, without the driver having to use the throttle. The system should only be used in good road conditions.

The main components of the system are the speed control module, a vacuum pump and servo, and one or two vacuum dump valve/switch units. The system control switches are located in the steering wheel. Information on vehicle speed is sent to the control module by the speedometer sender unit.

When the driver switches the system on, a pilot light in the instrument panel illuminates. Subsequent pressing of the '+' switch whilst the vehicle is moving at 25 mph (40 km/h) or more will cause that speed to be maintained by the system until the command is cancelled, either by pressing the '-/=' switch or by operation of the brake or clutch pedals. The set speed is retained in the module memory, and pressing the '-/=' switch again will cause the set speed to be resumed. Switching the system off, either with the 'O' switch or by switching off the ignition, erases the set speed from the memory.

The actual movement of the throttle linkage needed to maintain the set speed is performed by the vacuum servo, which is provided with vacuum by the electrically-driven vacuum pump. Operation of the brake or clutch pedals dumps the vacuum in the system and switches off the pump by means of the vacuum dump valve/switch mounted on the appropriate pedal bracket.

For detailed operating instructions, consult the operator's handbook supplied with the vehicle.

If a fault develops in the system, check that all electrical and vacuum connections are secure. Unless the fault is obviously in one particular component, further investigation should be left to a Ford dealer or other competent specialist.

## 43 Speed control system components – removal and refitting

### Control switches
1 Remove the steering wheel (Chapter 10, Section 8).
2 Remove the three screws which secure the horn contact plate. Disconnect the spade terminals and remove the contact plate.

3 Carefully prise the switch out of the steering wheel. Disconnect the spade terminals and remove it.
4 Refit by reversing the removal operations.

### Vacuum dump valve/switch
5 Remove the under-dash trim on the driver's side.
6 For the brake pedal, slacken the switch top and bottom mounting nuts, then remove the bottom nut completely. Disconnect the wiring plug and vacuum hose from the switch and remove it.
7 The clutch pedal switch is mounted in a spring-loaded bracket to allow for small changes in pedal position with the operation of the self-adjusting mechanism. Disconnect the wiring plug and vacuum hose, then push the switch out of its bracket.
8 Refit by reversing the removal operations. Adjust the switch position so that there is a gap of at least 1.5 mm (0.06 in) between the switch plunger cap and the body of the switch.

### Speed control module
9 Refer to Section 41. The speed control module shares the same mountings as the AWS module; the AWS module is larger.

### Vacuum pump
10 The vacuum pump is located behind the left-hand headlight on carburettor models, and behind the right-hand headlight on fuel-injection models. Start by removing the appropriate headlight unit (Section 14).
11 Disconnect the multi-plug and the vacuum hose from the pump. The multi-plug is released by squeezing and pulling it at the same time.
12 Prise out the three mountings and remove the pump.
13 When refitting, pull the pump mountings into position with pliers.
14 Reconnect the vacuum hose and the multi-plug, then refit the headlight unit.

### Vacuum servo
15 Disconnect the servo-to-throttle linkage cable at one end.
16 Disconnect the vacuum hose from the servo.
17 Undo the servo retaining nut and remove the servo from its bracket.
18 Refit by reversing the removal operations. On all but 2.0 litre carburettor models, adjust the cable so that it is slightly slack when the throttle linkage is in the idle position (pedal released).
19 On 2.0 litre carburettor models, the stepper motor plunger must be withdrawn before the cable is adjusted. Proceed as follows.
20 Observe the stepper motor plunger. Have an assistant switch on the ignition for a few seconds, then switch it off again. When the ignition is switched off, the stepper motor plunger will retract fully ('vent manifold' position).
Disconnect the battery negative lead while the stepper motor plunger is retracted.
21 Adjust the servo cable so that it is slightly slack, then reconnect the battery negative lead.

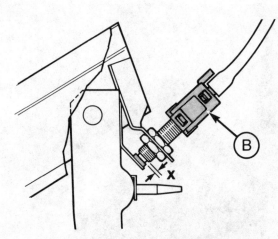

Fig. 12.43 Vacuum dump valve/switch (B) (Sec 43)

X = 1.5 mm (0.06 in) minimum

## Printed circuit board

22  The printed circuit board is located in the steering wheel. It can be removed after detaching the horn contact plate and disconnecting the switch spade terminals as described at the beginning of this Section.

## 44  Heater blower motor – removal and refitting

1  Disconnect the battery negative lead.
2  Pull off the rubber sealing strip from the top of the plenum chamber (photo).
3  Pull the two wiring harness clips from the front of the plenum chamber (photo).
4  Remove the two screws and two clips which secure the plenum chamber cover (photo). Lift out the cover.
5  Disconnect the multi-plug from the blower motor resistor. Also disconnect the motor earth cable (photo).
6  Remove the two nuts which secure the motor assembly. Lift out the motor, casing and resistor together.
7  The casing halves and the resistor can be separated from the motor after prising open the clamp which holds the casing halves together.
8  Refit by reversing the removal operations.

## 45  Radio or radio/cassette player (original equipment) – removal and refitting

1  Two DIN standard extraction tools will be needed to remove the radio/cassette unit. These tools are available from vehicle audio equipment specialists.

## Radio (only)

2  Pull off the control knobs, remove the spindle nuts and washers and remove the radio face plate.
3  Push the two securing lugs inwards, at the same time pulling the radio from its location. The services of an assistant may be required.
4  Withdraw the radio and disconnect the aerial cable and the other wiring plugs from it.
5  If a new radio is to be fitted, transfer the support brackets and locating plate from the old unit to the new one.
6  Refit by reconnecting the wiring to the radio, then sliding it into its aperture. Press it in until the securing lugs click into position.
7  Refit the face plate, spindle nuts and washers and control knobs. The top of the face plate is marked on the side which faces the radio.
8  If a new unit has been fitted, trim it by tuning in a weak medium wave station (around 1500 kHz/200 m) and turning the trimmer screw in either direction until the best reception is obtained. On the radio originally fitted, the trimmer screw is on the front face of the unit; for other types of radio, consult the manufacturer's instructions. Electronic units are normally self-trimming.

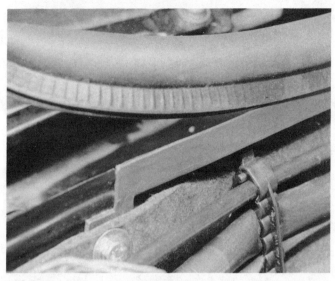

44.2 Pulling off the rubber sealing strip

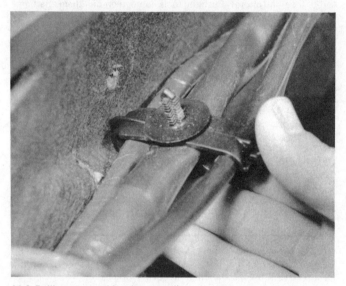

44.3 Pulling out a wiring harness clip

44.4 One of the plenum chamber cover clips

44.5 Blower motor showing wiring connections

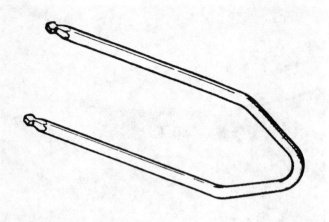

**Fig. 12.44 Radio/cassette DIN extraction tool (Sec 45)**

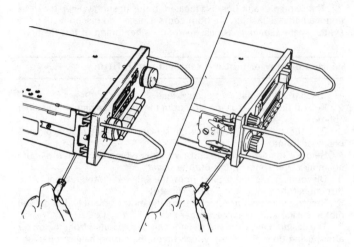

**Fig. 12.45 Releasing a DIN extraction tool (Sec 45)**

### Radio/cassette unit

9   Insert the DIN extraction tools (paragraph 1) into the holes at each end of the unit (photo). Push the tools home, then pull them apart and rearwards to remove the unit. Pull evenly on each side, otherwise the unit may jam in its slide.
10  Disconnect the aerial cable and other wiring plugs (photo).
11  To remove the DIN tools from the unit, push the clips into which they engage rearwards with a screwdriver.
12  If a new unit is being fitted, transfer the support bracket and locating plate to it.
13  Reconnect the wiring to the unit, engage it in its slide and press it home until the retaining clips engage.
14  If it is necessary to trim the new unit, refer to paragraph 8.

### Graphic equaliser

15  When fitted, the graphic equaliser is removed in the same way as described for the radio/cassette unit.

### 46  Loudspeakers (original equipment) – removal and refitting

1   Depending on the level of equipment fitted, loudspeakers may be located in the front door panels, below the rear parcel shelf and in the facia. Those in the facia are high frequency units.

### Front door speakers

2   Remove the door interior trim panel (chapter 11, Section 20).
3   Remove the four screws which secure the loudspeaker. Withdraw the speaker, disconnect the wiring and remove it.
4   Refit by reversing the removal operations; observe the TOP marking when fitting the speaker (photo).

### Rear parcel shelf speakers

5   Remove the speaker cover by twisting it anti-clockwise and pulling it off.
6   Remove the four nuts which secure the speaker, lower the speaker and disconnect the wiring from it. Note that the terminals are different sizes to ensure correct reconnection.
7   Refit by reversing the removal operations.

### High frequency units

8   Remove the instrument panel surround and the facia top (Chapter 11, Section 39).
9   Remove the two screws which secure the speaker bracket. Disconnect the wiring and withdraw the speaker and bracket together. The screws which secure the speaker to the bracket can then be removed (photo).
10  Refit by reversing the removal operations.

### 47  Radio aerial pre-amplifier (original equipment) – removal and refitting

1   On these models the heated rear window element is used as the radio aerial. To produce a good signal at the radio a pre-amplifier, mounted in the tailgate, is used.
2   Remove the tailgate interior trim panel, which is secured by eleven screws.
3   Remove the two screws which secure the pre-amplifier (photo). Disconnect the wiring from the pre-amplifier and remove it.
4   Refit by reversing the removal operations.

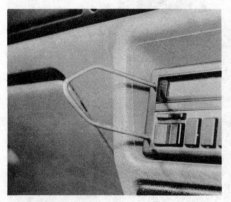

45.9 A DIN extraction tool fitted to a radio/cassette unit

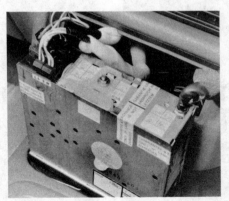

45.10 Radio/cassette unit wiring

46.4 Front door loudspeaker – note 'TOP' marking

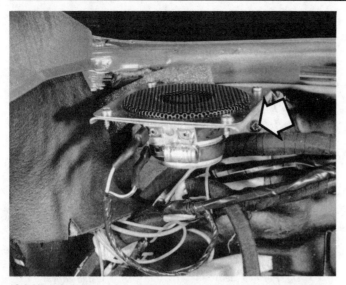

46.9 High frequency loudspeaker located under the facia top. One of the bracket securing screws (arrowed) is visible

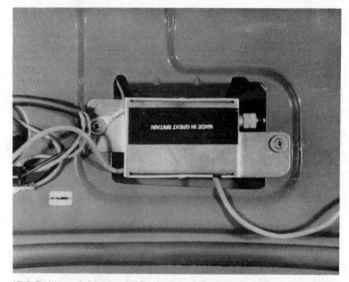

47.3 Radio aerial pre-amplifier mounted in the tailgate

## 48 Joystick fader control – removal and refitting

1   This Section deals with the facia-mounted control. On models with a graphic equaliser, the joystick fader is incorporated in the equaliser.
2   Remove the instrument cluster (Section 17).
3   Prise out the fader surround and detach the bulbholder (photo).
4   Release the fader control by turning its retaining clip anti-clockwise. Withdraw it from the facia and disconnect its multi-plug.
5   Refit by reversing the removal operations.

## 49 Rear entertainment console – removal and refitting

1   Pull the heater control knob off its lever. Remove the two retaining screws from the top corners of the rear console.
2   Pull off the balance and volume control knobs. Withdraw the console and disconnect the wiring from it.
3   The console may be removed from the face plate if wished by undoing the three retaining screws.
4   To renew the console bulbs, extract the bulbholders by grasping with pliers and turning them anti-clockwise.
5   Refit by reversing the removal operations.

## 50 Rear headphone relay – removal and refitting

1   The rear headphone relay is located behind the facia, next to the AWS control assembly and the speed control module (when fitted). Its function is to mute the loudspeakers when the headphones are plugged into the rear entertainment console.
2   To remove the relay, first remove the AWS control assembly and (if applicable) the speed control unit. Refer to Sections 41 and 43.
3   Disconnect the relay multi-plug, undo its securing screw and nut and remove it.
4   Refit by reversing the removal operations.

## 51 Radio equipment – suppression of interference

Adequate interference suppression equipment is installed in production. If interference is a problem, consult a Ford dealer first to make sure that the latest standard HT leads, distributor cap etc are fitted. On V6 models a screening care can be fitted to the distributor, but this also involves modifications to the plenum chamber cover.
Radio equipment which is fitted instead of the original items may

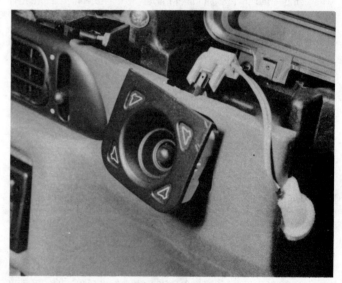

48.3 Removing the joystick fader

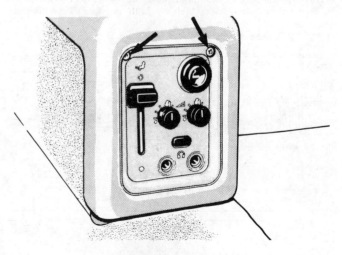

Fig. 12.46 Rear entertainment console. Retaining screws arrowed (Sec 49)

be more sensitive to interference. On early models (built up to May 1985) a radio feed relay may not have been fitted. The installation of such a relay in position 'B' in the fuse/relay box, together with the use of the appropriate wiring connectors, will effectively isolate the radio power supply from the rest of the vehicle's electrical systems. Consult a Ford dealer for the parts required. All models built from June 1985 have a radio feed relay fitted as standard.

## 52 Heated rear window and windscreen – general

1    All models are equipped with a heated rear window. Heating is achieved by passing current through a resistive grid bonded to the inside of the rear window.
2    Do not allow hard or sharp items of luggage to rub against the heating grid. Use a soft cloth or chamois to clean the inside of the window, working along the lines of the grid.
3    The heated rear window draws a high current, so it has its own fuse and relay. (In addition mirror heating, when fitted, uses the same circuit). If the heating function is lost completely, check the switch, relay, fuse and wiring connections.
4    Small breaks in the grid can be repaired using special conductive paint, obtainable from motor accessory shops. Use the paint as directed by the manufacturer.
5    When fitted, the heated windscreen contains two bands of very fine wires embedded in the laminating layer of the screen. A current is passed through these wires when heating is required.
6    The current drawn by the heated windscreen is very high, so each band of wires is protected by a separate fuse. Power and timer relays behind the facia handle the current and limit the period of operation to approximately four minutes. The wiring arrangements are such that the screen will only be heated when the engine is running, so avoiding excessive drain on the battery.
7    If the heated windscreen does not work, check the switch, relays, fuses and wiring connections. Problems which appear to be within the windscreen itself should be referred to a Ford dealer.

## 53 Anti-theft alarm system – description

The alarm system is available as an optional extra. On vehicles so equipped, the alarm is automatically set by locking the driver's or front passenger's door with the key. After a brief delay (approximately 20 seconds), the alarm will be set off if the doors, bonnet or tailgate are opened.

The only way to disarm the alarm system is by unlocking one of the front doors with the key. Even if the key is used to open the tailgate, if the alarm is set it will go off.

The components of the alarm system are a control module, tripping switches, activating switches, an alarm horn and a signal buzzer.

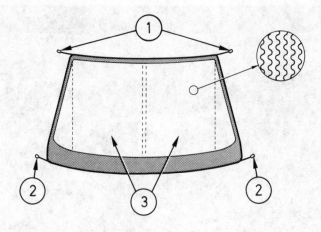

**Fig. 12.47 Heated windscreen details (Sec 52)**

1    *Positive feeds*            3    *Heated zones*
2    *Earth points*

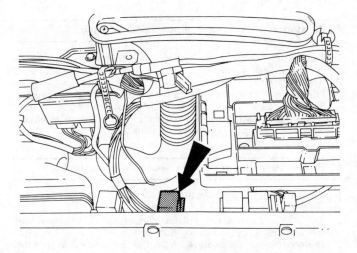

**Fig. 12.48 Heated windscreen relay (arrowed) (Sec 52)**

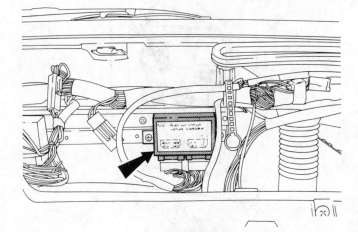

**Fig. 12.49 Anti-theft alarm module (arrowed) (Sec 53)**

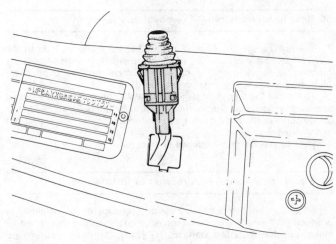

**Fig. 12.50 Bonnet tripping switch (Sec 53)**

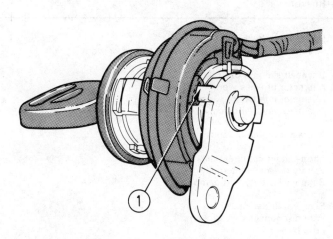

Fig. 12.51 Door lock activating switch (Sec 53)

1   Operating lug

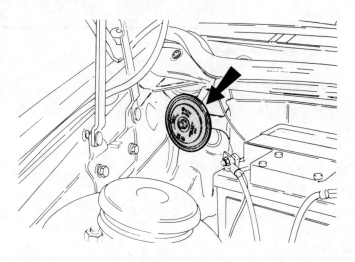

Fig. 12.52 Alarm horn (arrowed) (Sec 53)

The control module is located behind the facia. It determines whether the alarm is set or not, monitors the tripping switches and the ignition circuit, and limits the duration of the alarm to 30 seconds. This last item is a legal requirement. The control module also operates the signal buzzer to tell the driver that the alarm is set, and controls the activation delay.

The tripping switches on the doors and tailgate are the same as those used for 'open door' warnings in the AWS. The bonnet switch is peculiar to the alarm system.

The activating switches are fitted to the front door lock barrels, where they are activated by a lug on the end of the barrel. They only make contact momentarily as the lock is operated.

The alarm horn is mounted next to the battery. Both the horn and its leads are claimed to be inaccessible without opening the bonnet. The signal buzzer is also mounted under the bonnet.

No service, repair or component renewal procedures have yet been published for the alarm system components. Any problems arising which cannot be dealt with by component substitution should therefore be referred to a Ford dealer.

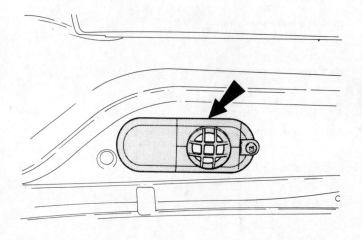

Fig. 12.53 Alarm signal buzzer (arrowed) (Sec 53)

## 54 Wiring diagrams – general

Each wiring diagram covers a particular system of the vehicle; an indication of this is given in the captions. Each diagram also has a number – for example, Fig. 12.55 is diagram No. 2 and covers power distribution. When a number is shown on a diagram inside a box with an arrow symbol, this indicates that the circuit concerned starts, or is continued, in the diagram having that number.

Space limitations mean that not all diagrams have been included. Therefore the diagram numbers are not consecutive, neither is it always possible to follow a particular circuit to completion.

The prefix 'C' indicates a connector or multi-plug, 'S' a soldered joint and 'G' an earthing point (ground). The numbers appearing at the break in each wire indicate the circuit number and wire colour.

## 55 Fault diagnosis – electrical system

| Symptom | Reason(s) |
| --- | --- |
| Starter motor does not turn – no voltage at motor | Battery terminals loose or corroded<br>Battery discharged or defective<br>Starter motor connections loose or broken<br>Starter switch or solenoid faulty<br>Automatic transmission not in 'P' or 'N'<br>Automatic transmission inhibitor switch faulty |
| Starter motor does not turn – voltage at motor | Starter motor internal defect |
| Starter motor turns very slowly | Battery nearly discharged or defective<br>Battey terminals loose or corroded<br>Starter motor internal defect |

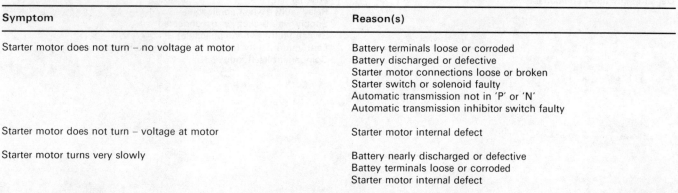

| Symptom | Reasons |
|---|---|
| Starter motor noisy or rough | Mounting bolts loose<br>Pinion or flywheel ring gear teeth damaged or worn |
| Alternator not charging battery | Drivebelt slipping or broken<br>Alternator brushes worn<br>Alternator connections loose or broken<br>Alternator internal defect |
| Alternator overcharging battery | Alternator regulator faulty |
| Battery will not hold charge | Short-circuit continual drain on battery<br>Battery defective internally<br>Battery case dirty and damp |
| Gauge or speedometer gives no reading | Sender unit defective<br>Wire disconnected or broken<br>Fuse blown<br>Gauge or speedometer defective |
| Fuel or temperature gauge reads too high | Sender unit defective<br>Wire earthed<br>Gauge faulty |
| Horn operates continuously | Horn push stuck down<br>Cable to horn push earthed<br>Relay defective |
| Horn does not operate | Fuse blown<br>Cable or connector broken or loose<br>Switch plate, slip rings or brushes dirty or defective<br>Relay defective |
| Lights do not come on | Battery discharged<br>Fuse(s) blown<br>Light switch faulty<br>Bulbs blown<br>Relay defective (when applicable) |
| Lights give poor illumination | Lenses or reflectors dirty<br>Bulbs blackened<br>Incorrect wattage bulbs fitted |
| Wiper motor fails to work | Fuse blown<br>Connections loose or broken<br>Relay defective<br>Switch defective<br>Motor defective |
| Wiper motor works slowly and draws little current | Brushes badly worn<br>Commutator dirty or burnt |
| Wiper motor works slowly and draws heavy current | Linkage seized or otherwise damaged<br>Motor internal fault |
| Wiper motor works, but blades do not move | Linkage broken or disconnected<br>Motor gearbox badly worn |
| Defect in any other components | Fuse blown<br>Relay faulty (when applicable)<br>Supply wire broken or disconnected<br>Switch faulty (when applicable)<br>Earth return faulty (check for loose or corroded mountings)<br>Component itself faulty |

SYMBOL-EXPLANATION:

```
┌─┐
│2│▶  POWER DISTRIBUTION FROM
└─┘    OR CONTINUATION ON        PAGE 2

(GB)  SHOWS SPECIFIC LEGAL
       REQUIREMENT OF THIS COUNTRY.

(||)  CONNECTION DOES NOT EXIST
       IN EVERY VARIATION.
```

COLOR CODE:

```
BLUE....BL        PINK....RS
BROWN...BR        RED.....RT
YELLOW..GE        BLACK...SW
GREY....GR        VIOLET..VI
GREEN...GN        WHITE...WS
```

| Fig. No. | Diagram No. | Subject |
|----------|-------------|---------|
| 12.55 | 2 | Power distribution |
| 12.56 | 3 | Charge, start and run |
| 12.57 | 3A | Charge, start and run |
| 12.58 | 4 | Engine management (1.8 litre) |
| 12.59 | 4A | Engine management (2.0 litre carburettor) |
| 12.60 | 5 | Engine management (2.0 litre fuel-injection) |
| 12.61 | 5C | Engine management (2.8 litre) |
| 12.62 | 7A | Exterior lighting |
| 12.63 | 8A | Front and rear foglights |
| 12.64 | 9 | Signalling and warning systems |
| 12.65 | 10 | Interior lighting |
| 12.66 | 10B | Instrument and control lighting |
| 12.67 | 11 | Heater blower |
| 12.68 | 16 | Power-operated sliding roof |
| 12.69 | 12 | Wipers and washers |
| 12.70 | 14 | Central locking system |
| 12.71 | 15 | Power-operated windows |
| 12.72 | 17 | Front seat adjustment |
| 12.73 | 17A | Rear seat adjustment |
| 12.74 | 24 | Fuel computer |
| 12.75 | 18 | Heated screens and mirror adjustment |
| 12.76 | 21 | ABS |
| 12.77 | 22 | Heated seats |
| 12.78 | 23 | Auxiliary warning system |
| 12.79 | 25 | Door ajar warning system |
| 12.80 | 26 | Bulb failure warning system |
| 12.81 | 27 | Anti-theft alarm |
| 12.82 | 28 | Speed control system |
| 12.83 | 29 | Radio/cassette player and associated circuits (typical) |

*Some of the wiring diagrams are out of sequence. This is to ensure that the halves of the larger diagrams appear on opposite pages.*

**Fig. 12.54 Explanatory notes for wiring diagrams (Sec 54)**

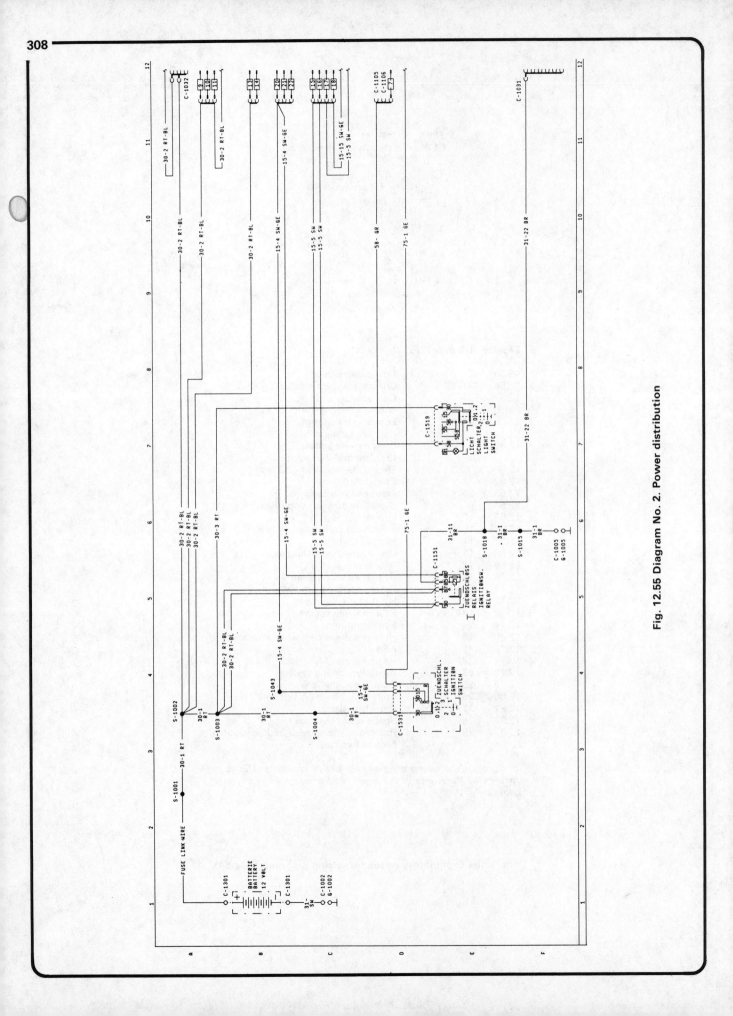

**Fig. 12.55 Diagram No. 2. Power distribution**

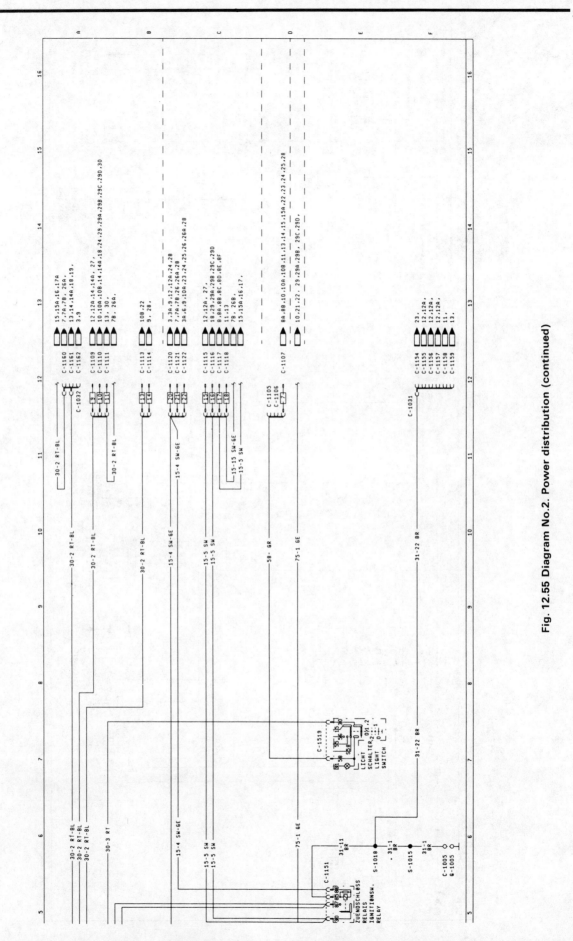

Fig. 12.55 Diagram No.2. Power distribution (continued)

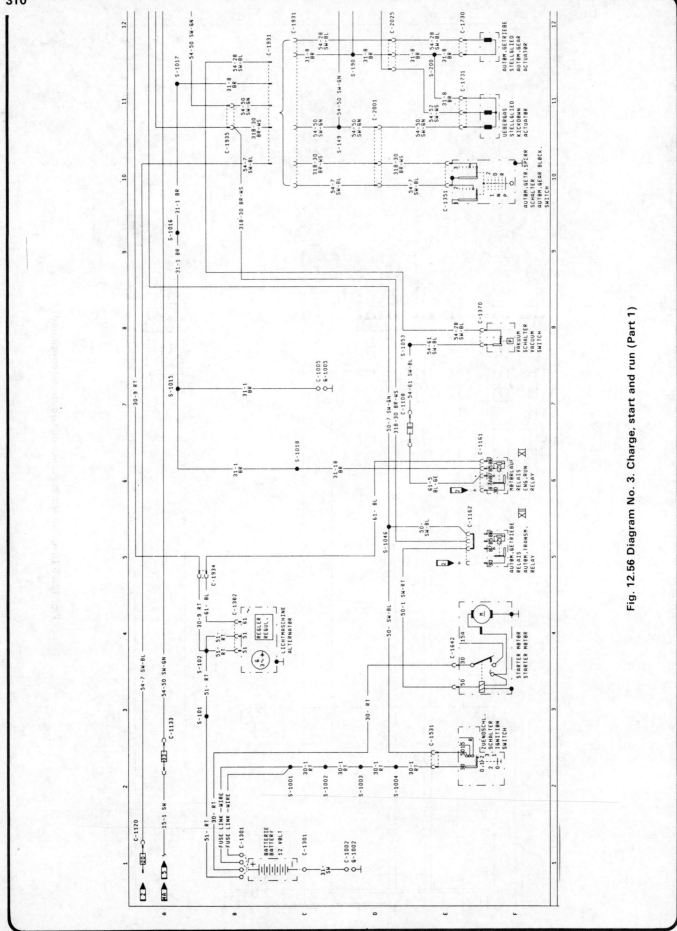

Fig. 12.56 Diagram No. 3. Charge, start and run (Part 1)

311

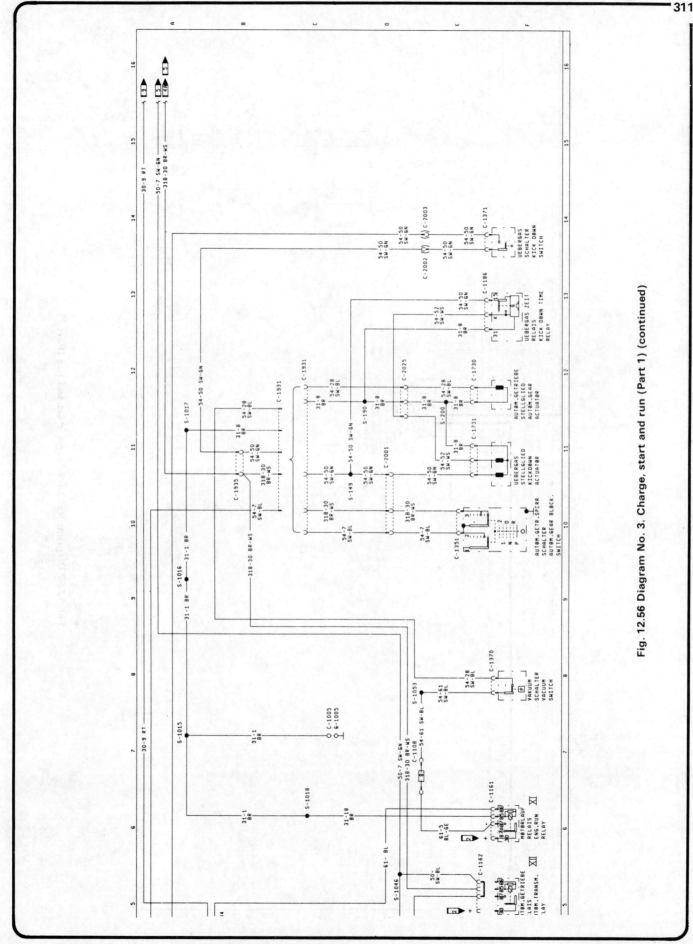

Fig. 12.56 Diagram No. 3. Charge, start and run (Part 1) (continued)

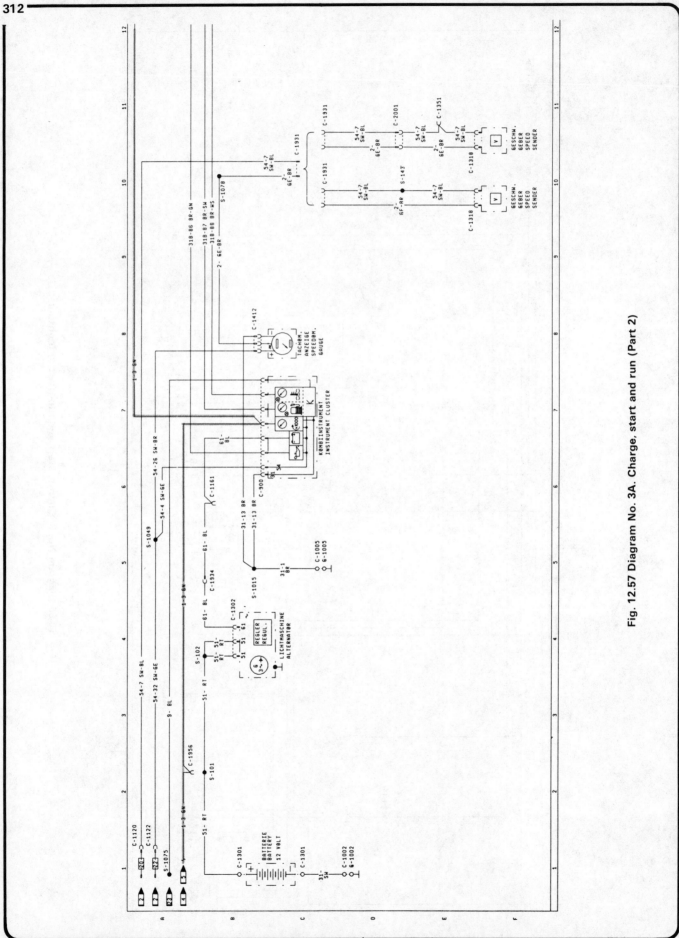

Fig. 12.57 Diagram No. 3A. Charge, start and run (Part 2)

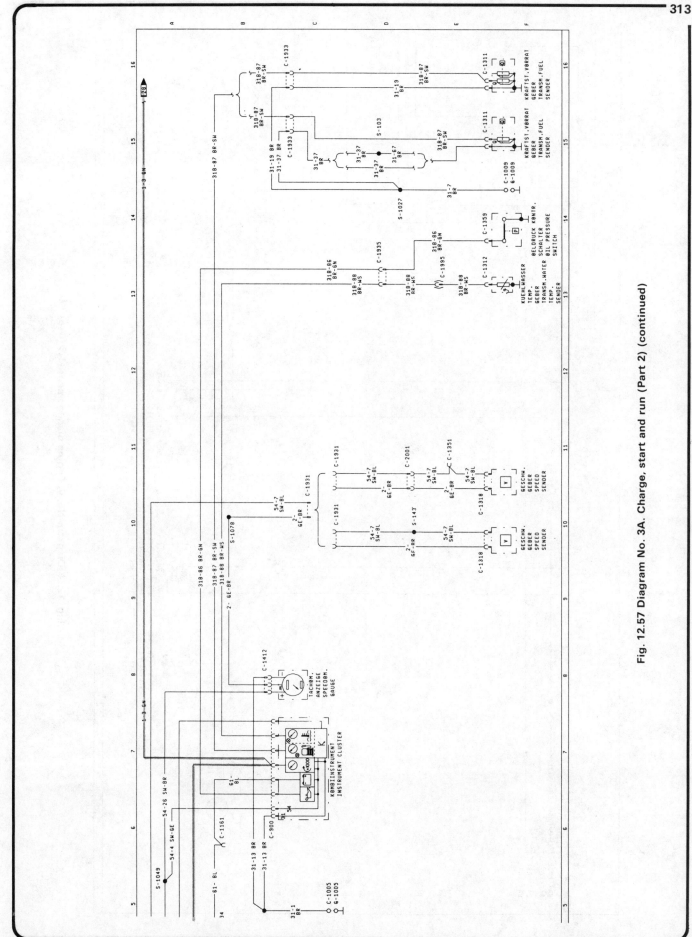

Fig. 12.57 Diagram No. 3A. Charge, start and run (Part 2) (continued)

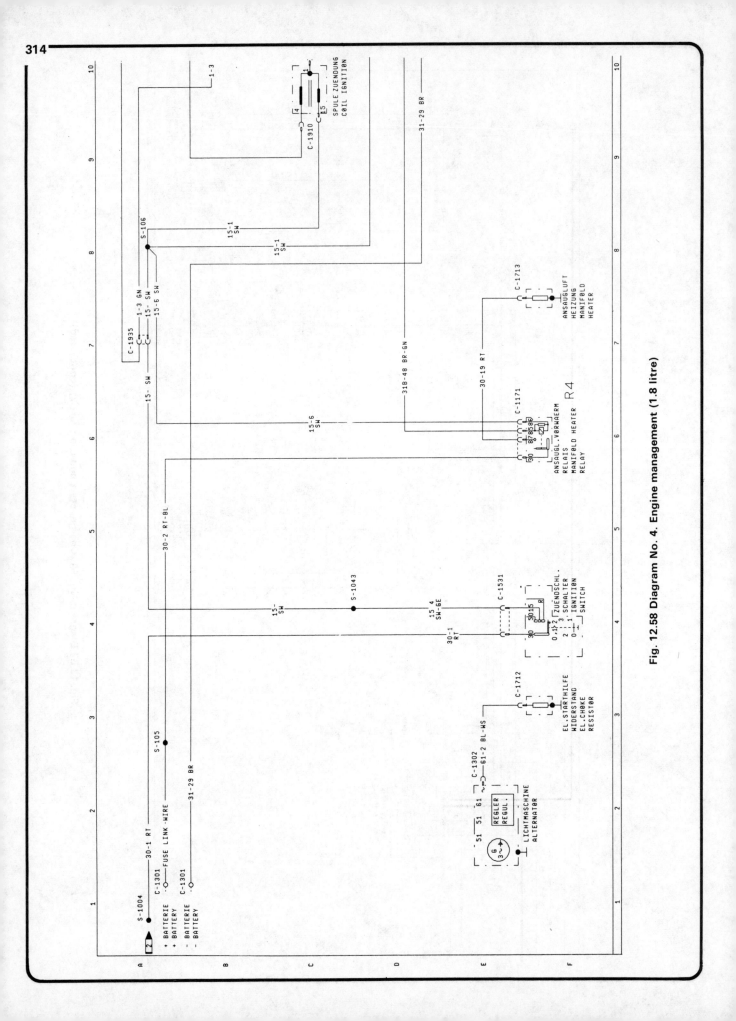

Fig. 12.58 Diagram No. 4. Engine management (1.8 litre)

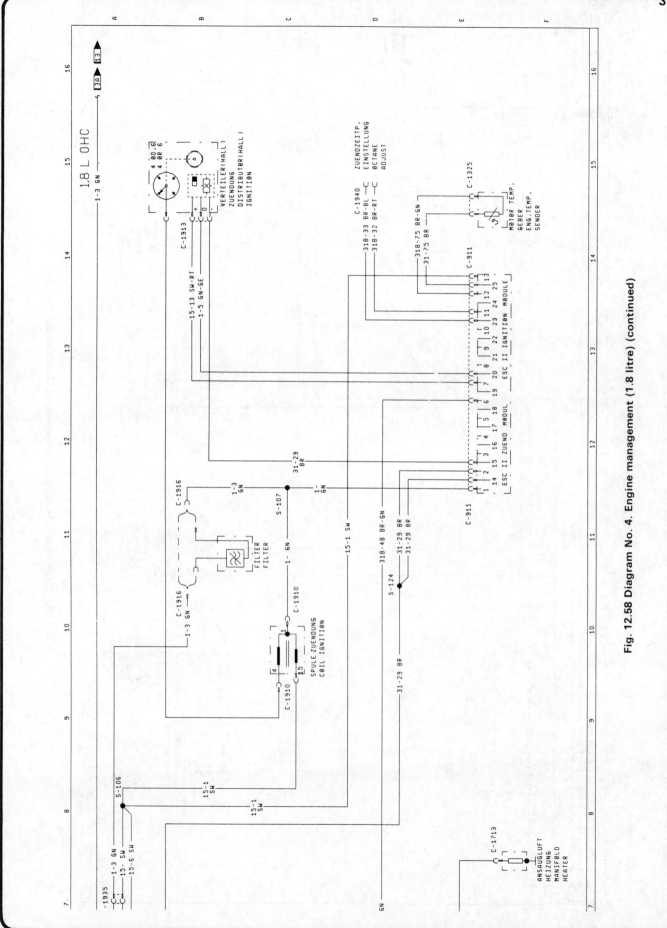

Fig. 12.58 Diagram No. 4. Engine management (1.8 litre) (continued)

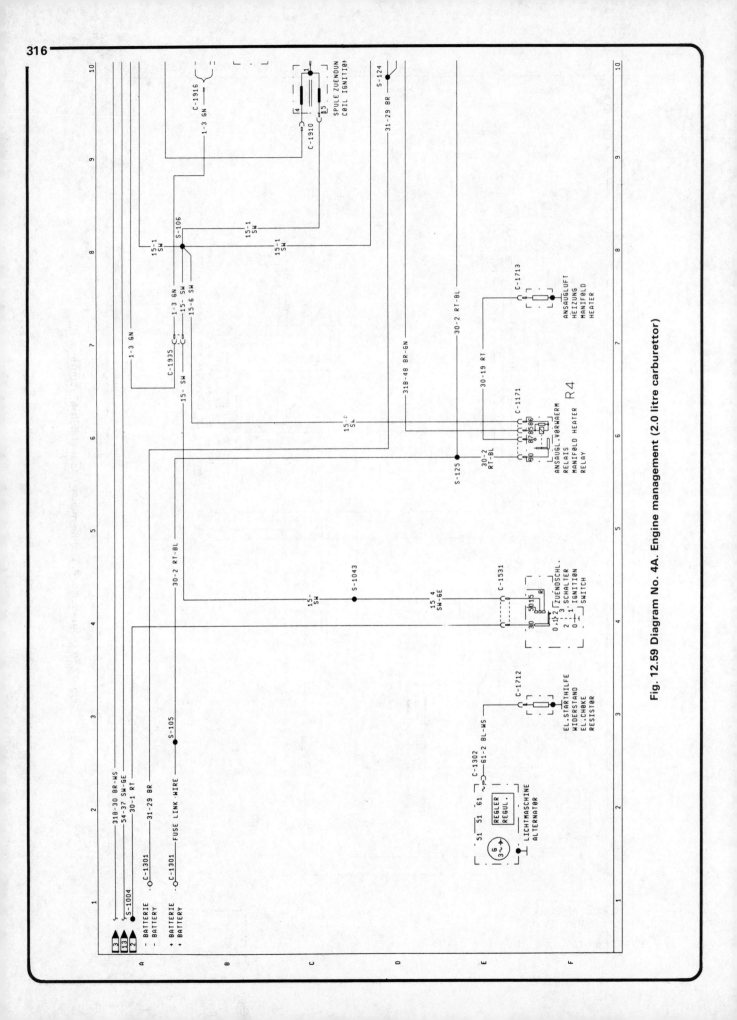

Fig. 12.59 Diagram No. 4A. Engine management (2.0 litre carburettor)

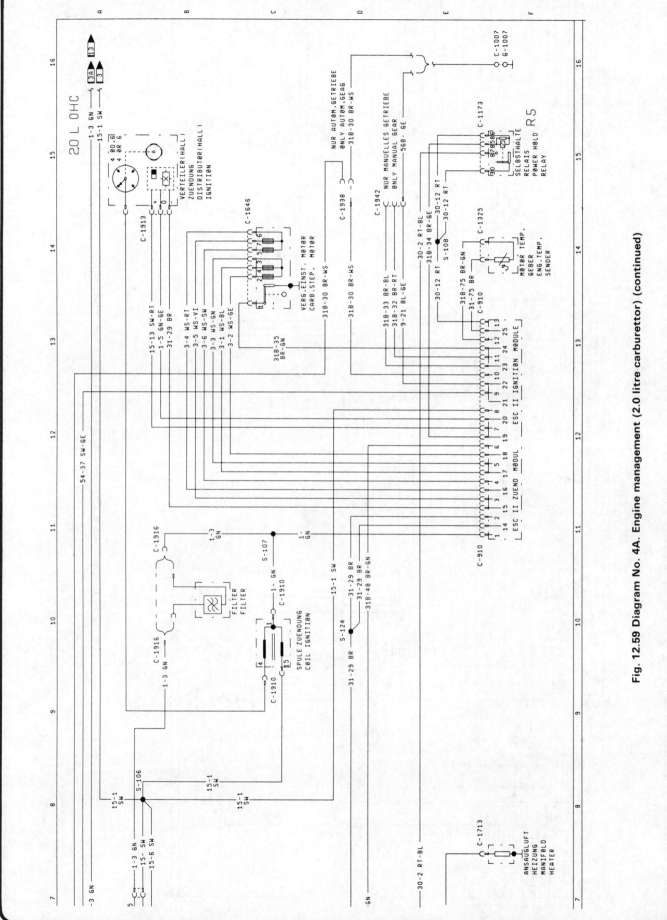

Fig. 12.59 Diagram No. 4A. Engine management (2.0 litre carburettor) (continued)

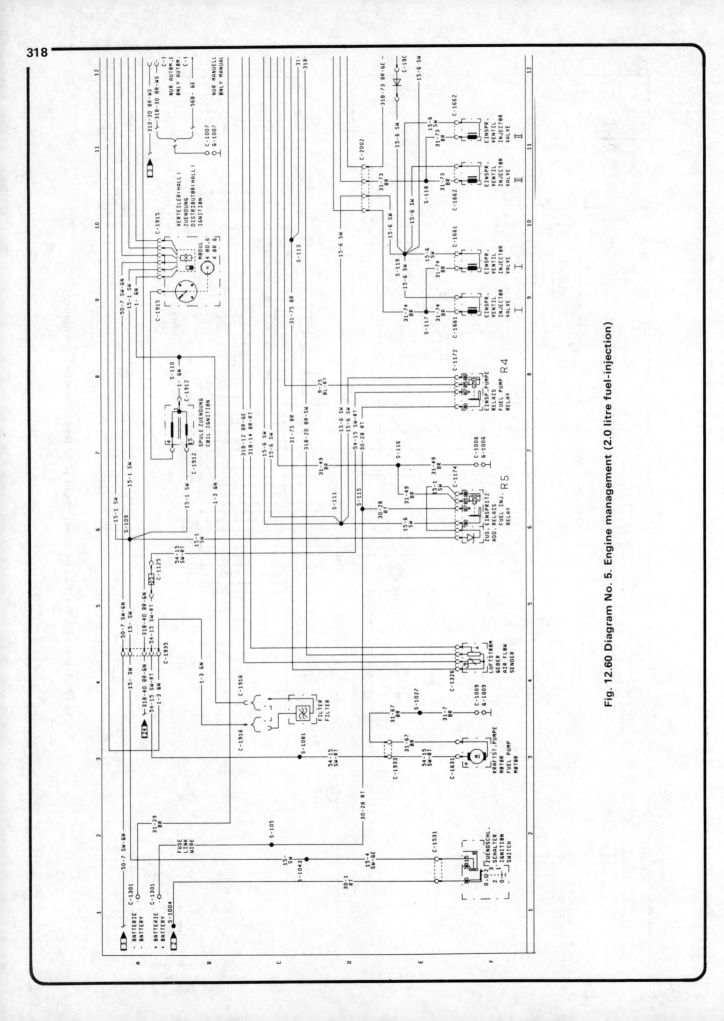

Fig. 12.60 Diagram No. 5. Engine management (2.0 litre fuel-injection)

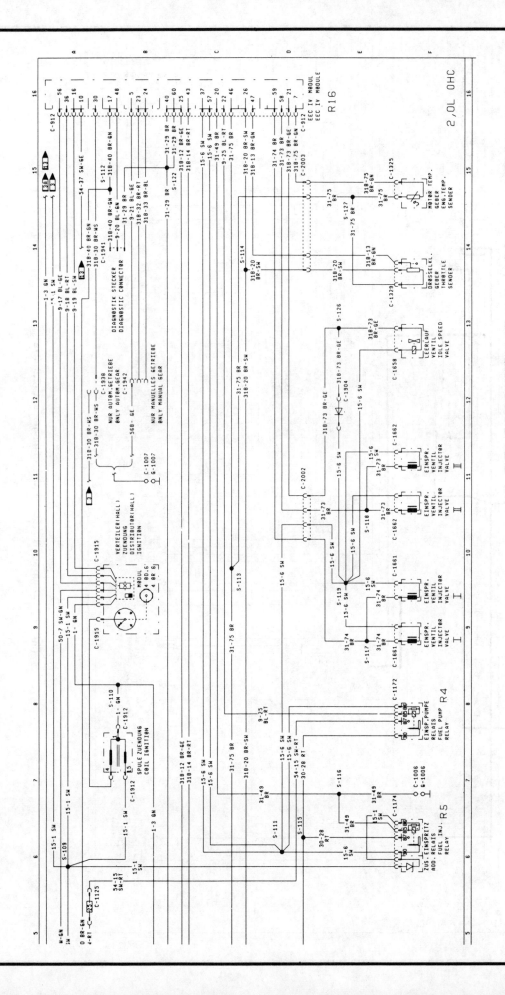

Fig. 12.60 Diagram No. 5. Engine management (2.0 litre fuel-injection) (continued)

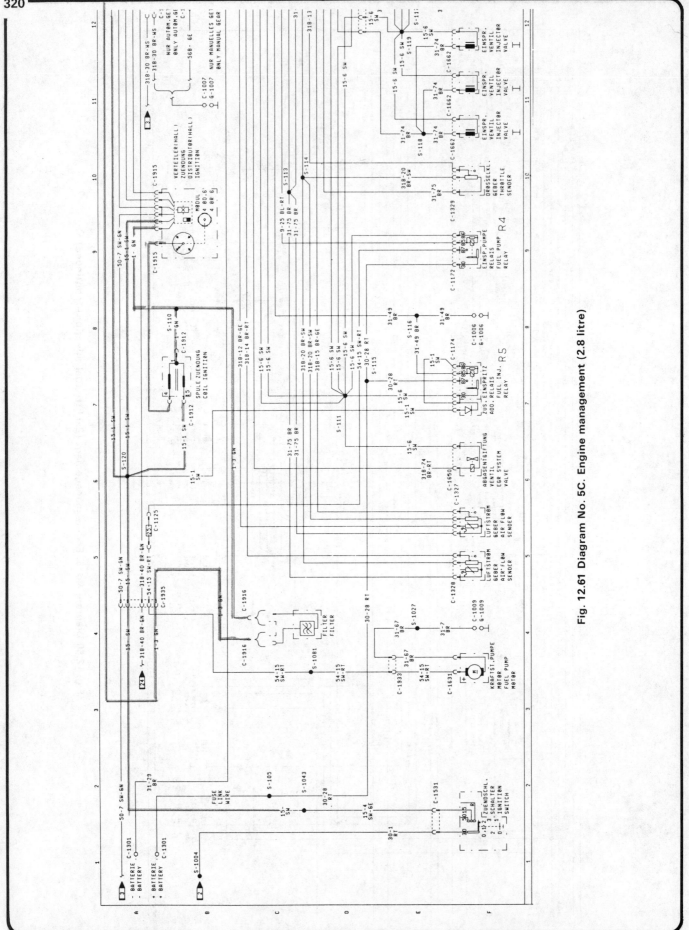

Fig. 12.61 Diagram No. 5C. Engine management (2.8 litre)

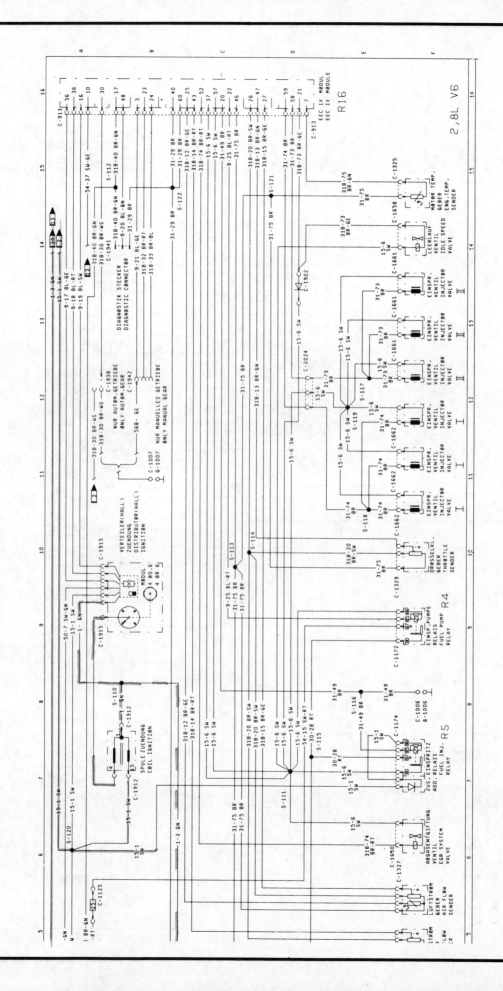

Fig. 12.61 Diagram No. 5C. Engine management (2.8 litre) (continued)

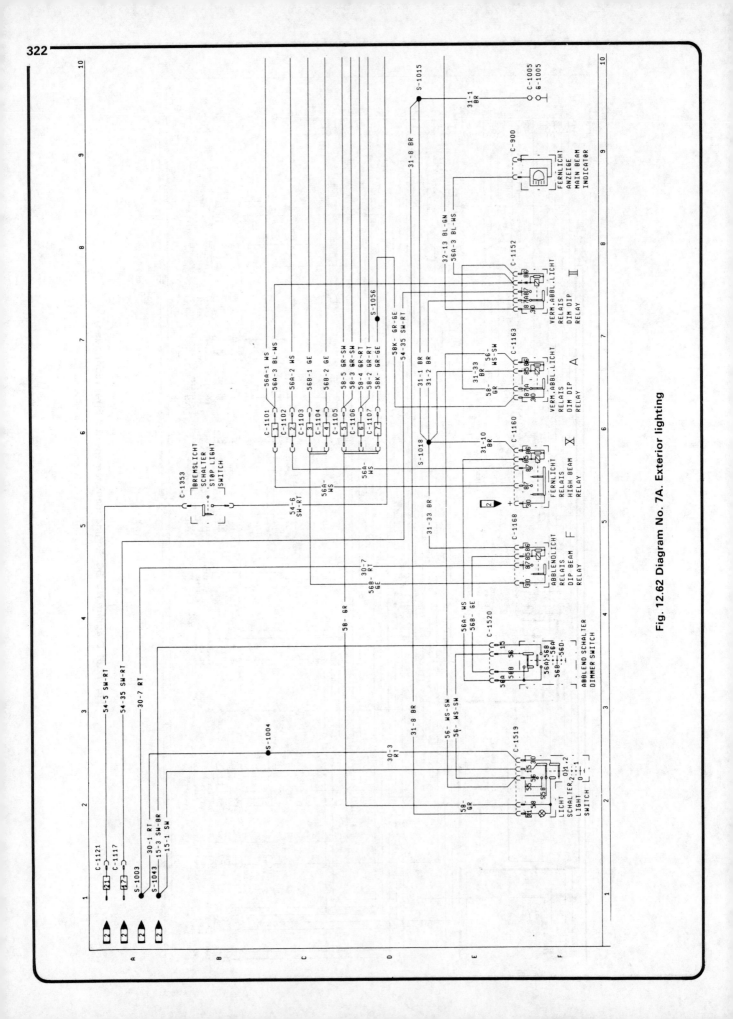

Fig. 12.62 Diagram No. 7A. Exterior lighting

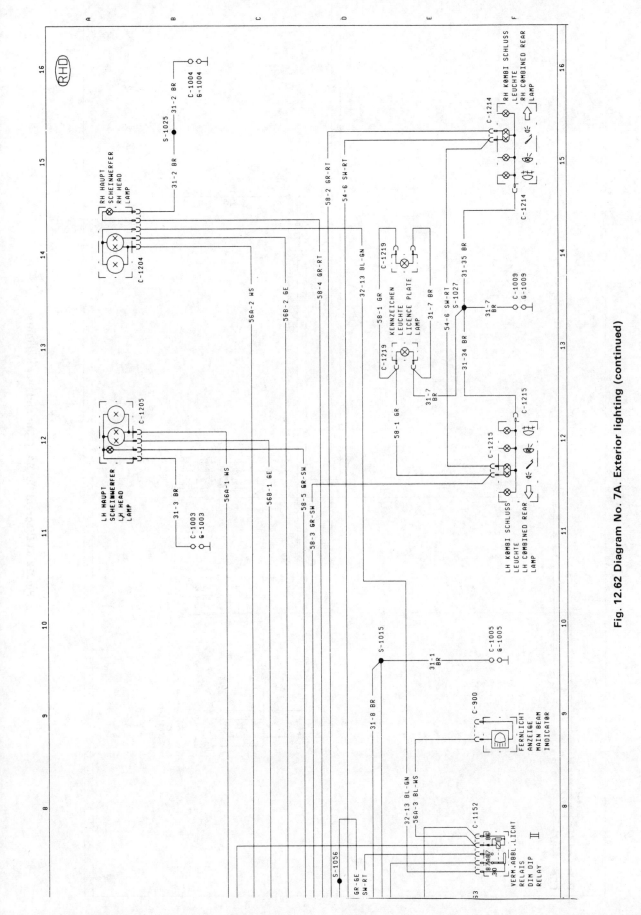

**Fig. 12.62 Diagram No. 7A. Exterior lighting (continued)**

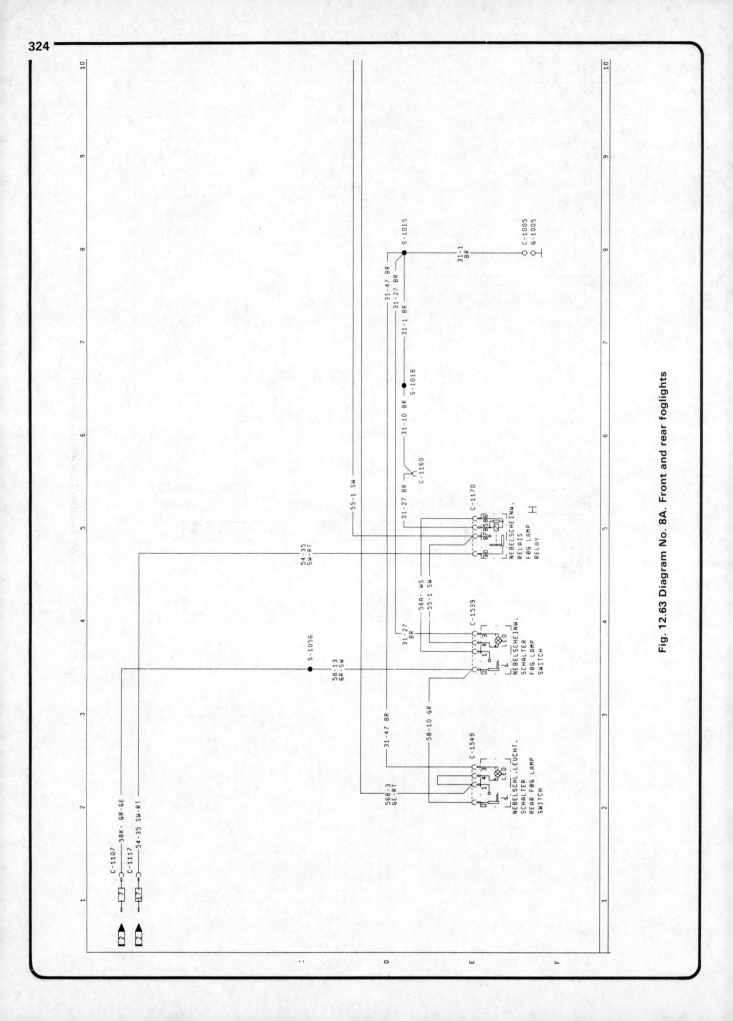

Fig. 12.63 Diagram No. 8A. Front and rear foglights

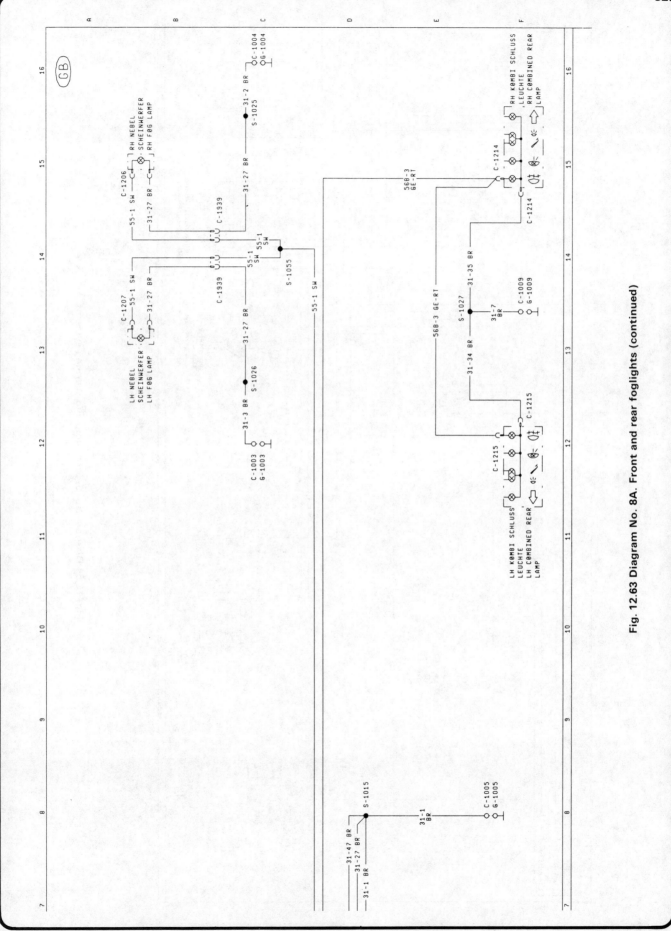

Fig. 12.63 Diagram No. 8A. Front and rear foglights (continued)

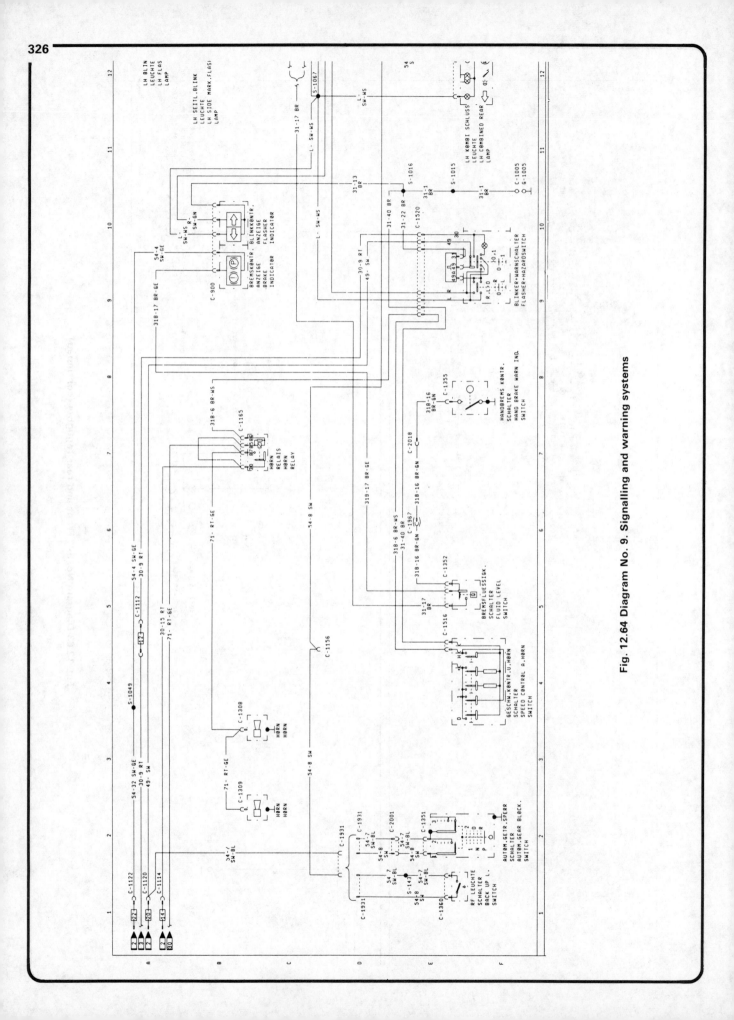

Fig. 12.64 Diagram No. 9. Signalling and warning systems

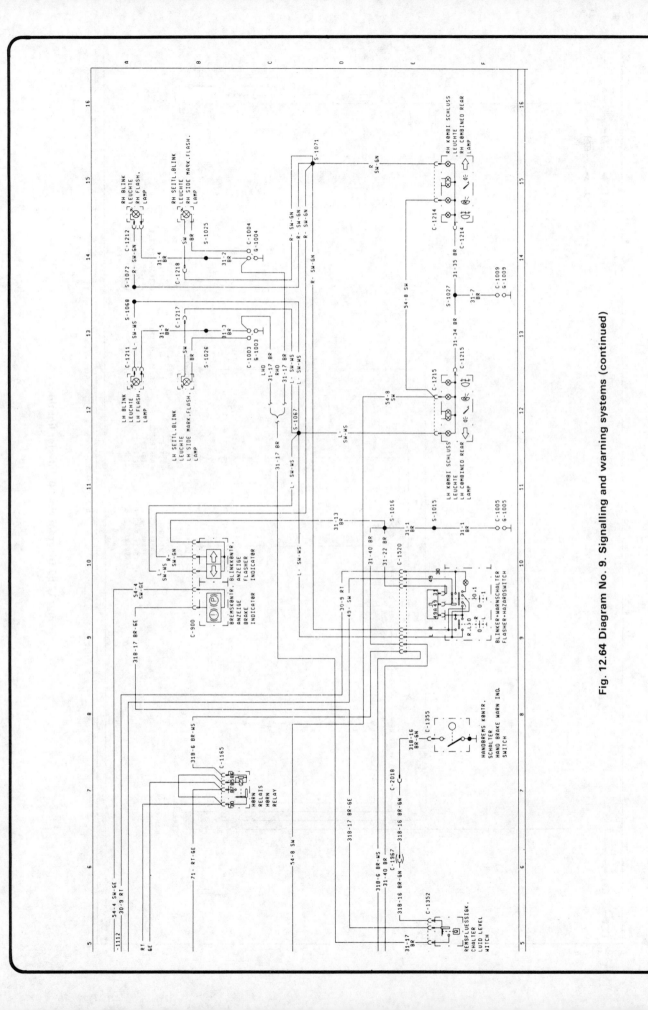

Fig. 12.64 Diagram No. 9. Signalling and warning systems (continued)

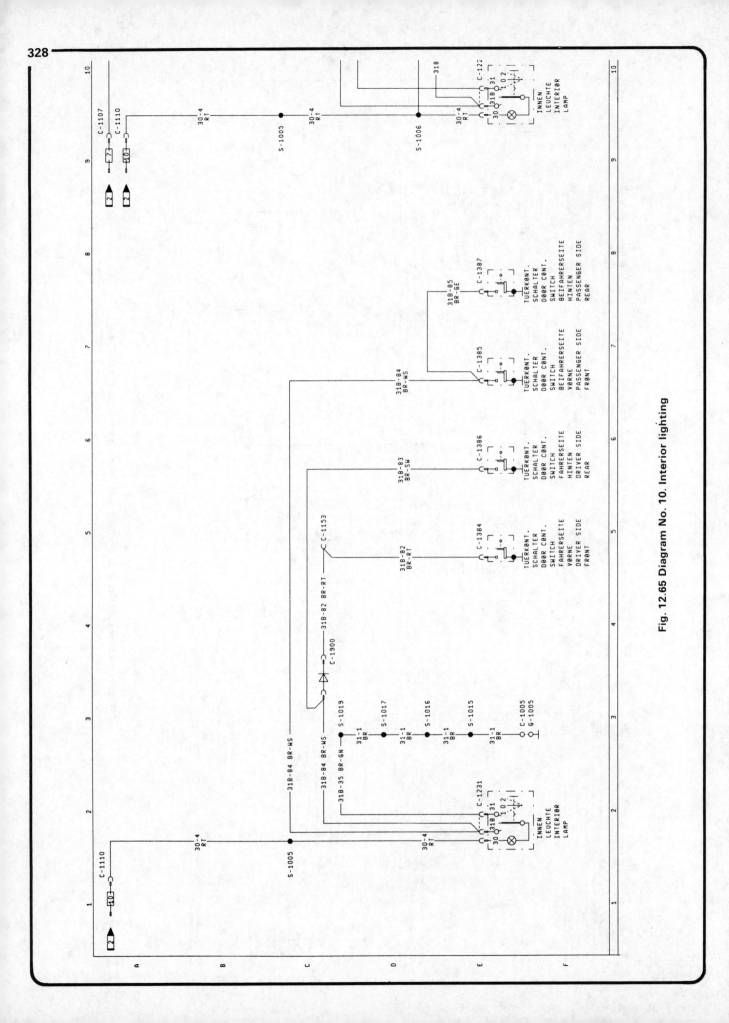

Fig. 12.65 Diagram No. 10. Interior lighting

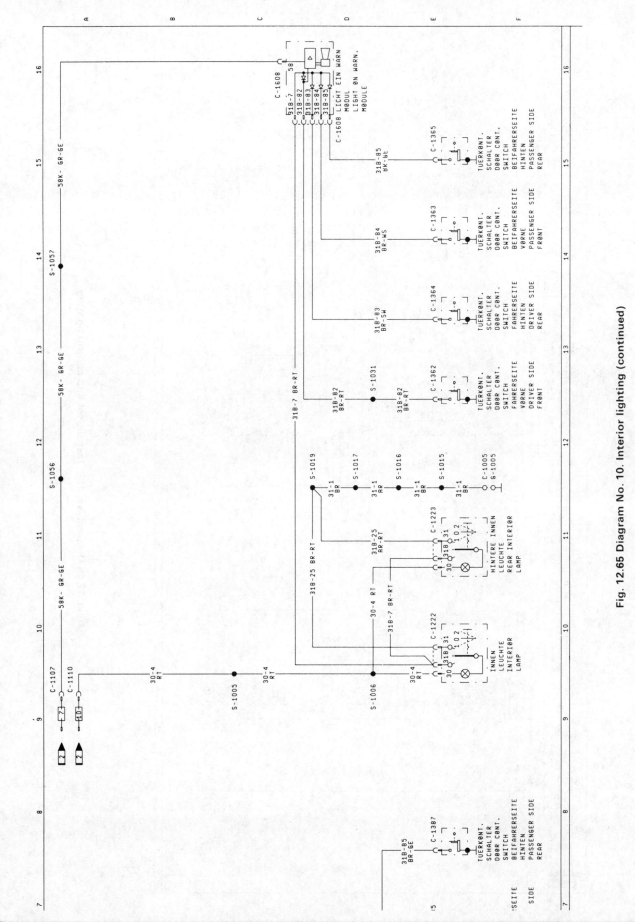

Fig. 12.65 Diagram No. 10. Interior lighting (continued)

330

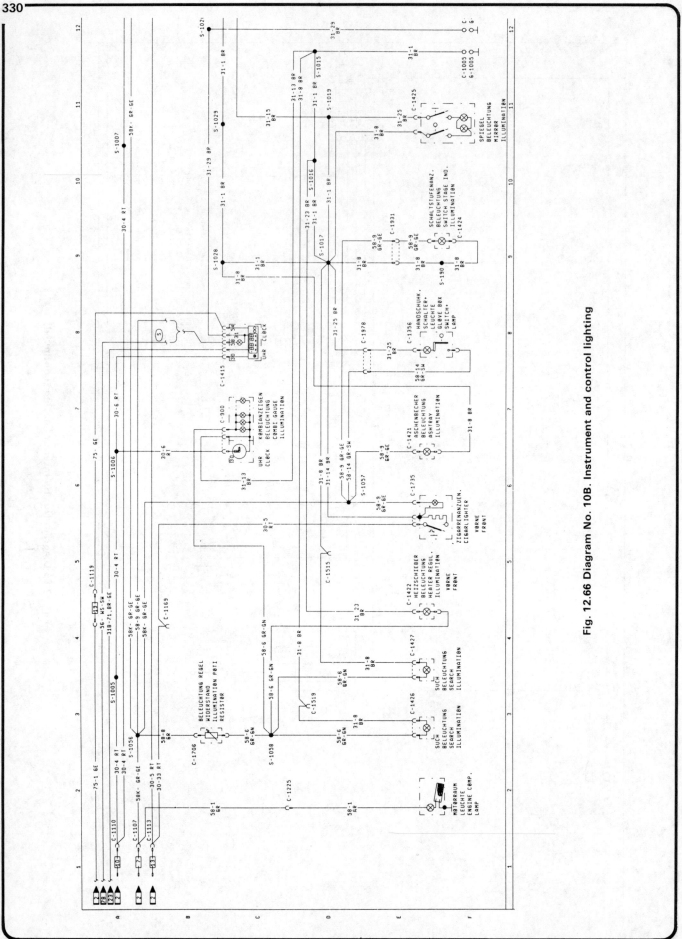

Fig. 12.66 Diagram No. 10B. Instrument and control lighting

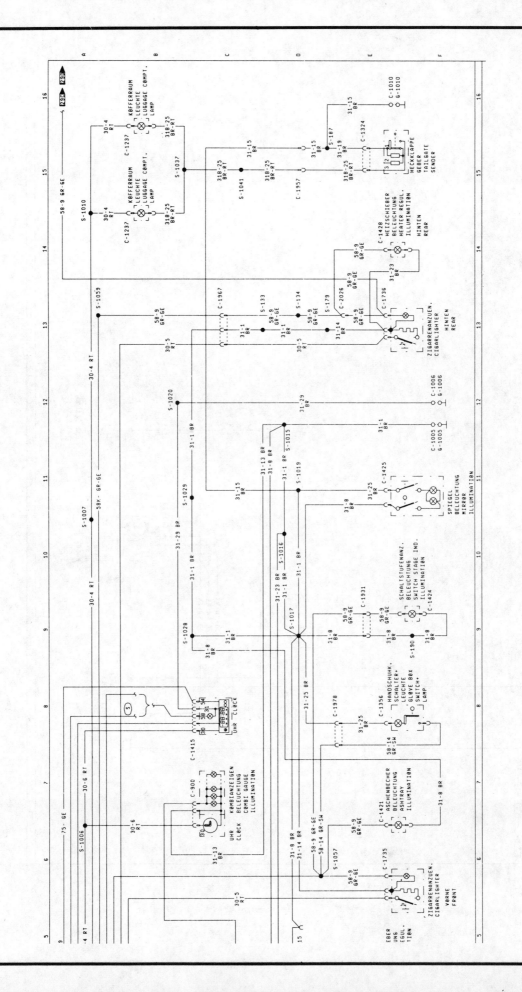

Fig. 12.66 Diagram No. 10B. Instrument and control lighting (continued)

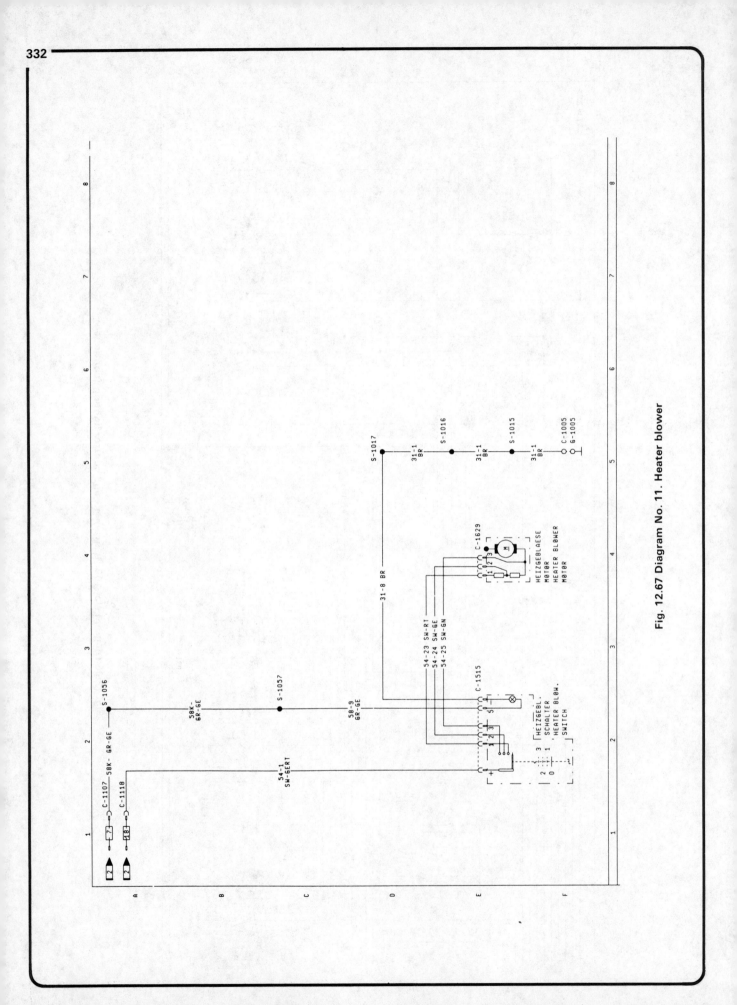

Fig. 12.67 Diagram No. 11. Heater blower

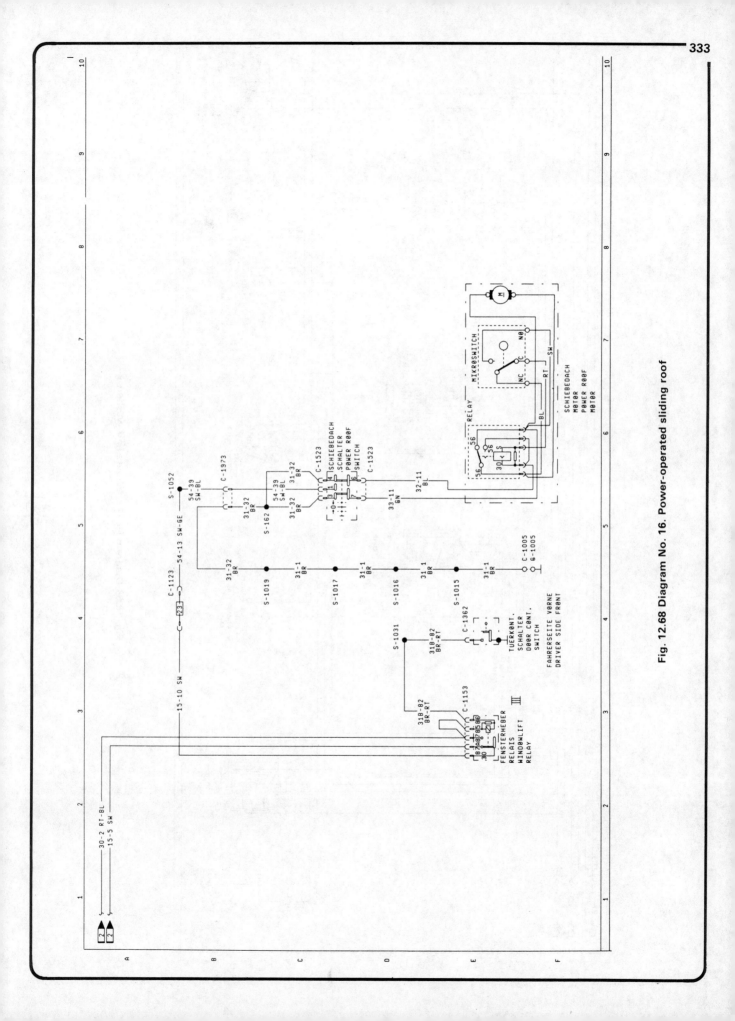

Fig. 12.68 Diagram No. 16. Power-operated sliding roof

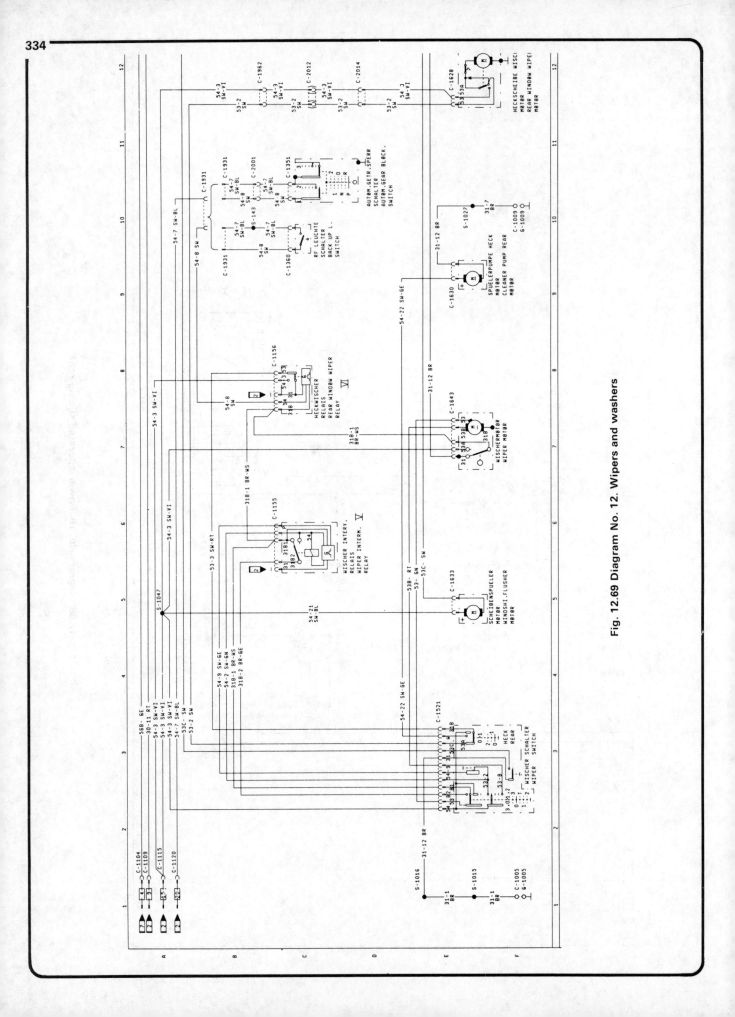

Fig. 12.69 Diagram No. 12. Wipers and washers

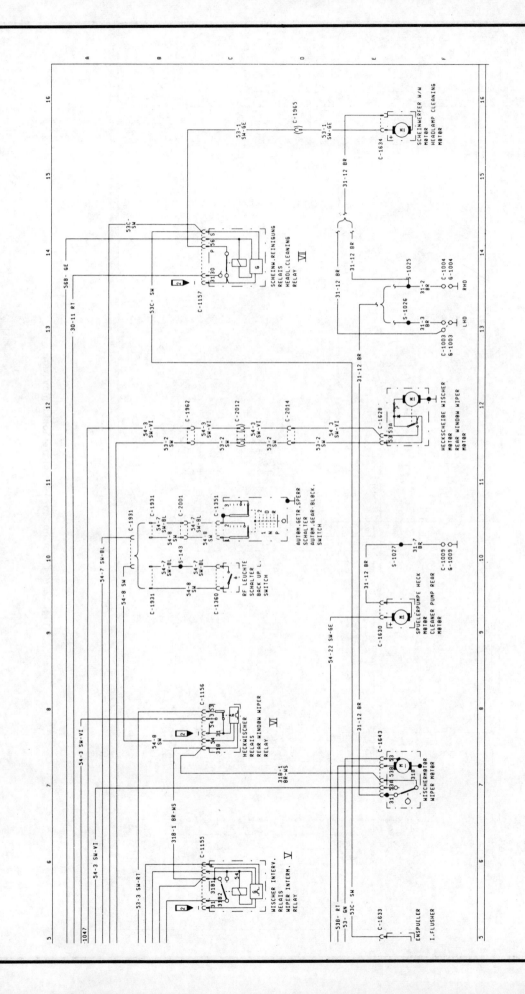

Fig. 12.69 Diagram No. 12. Wipers and washers (continued)

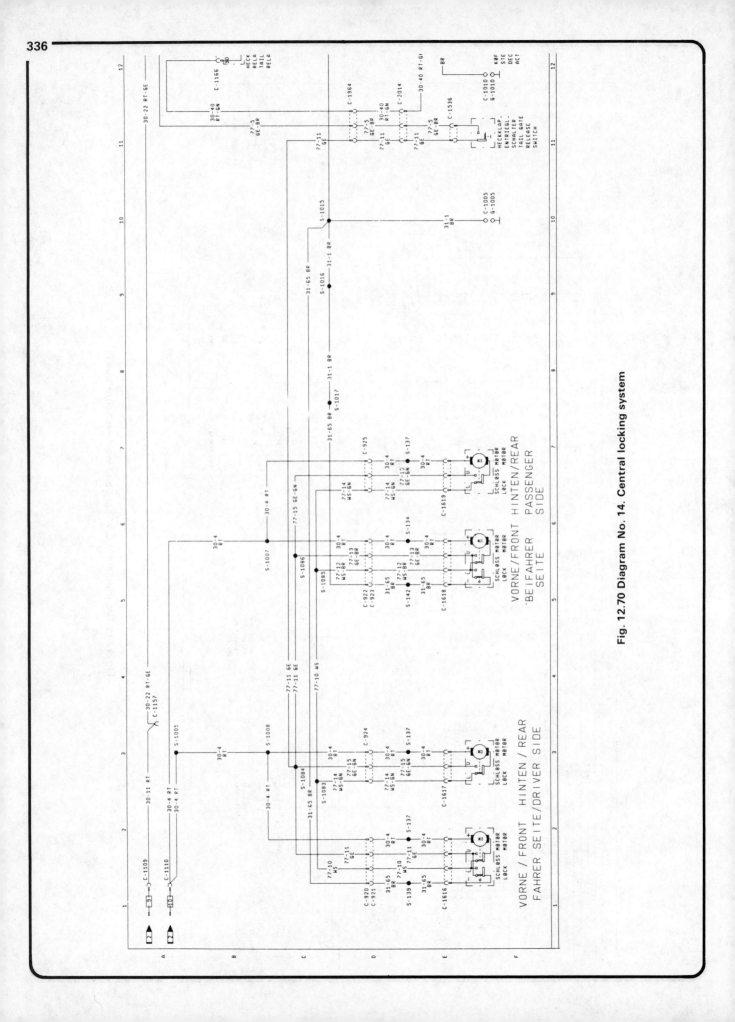

Fig. 12.70 Diagram No. 14. Central locking system

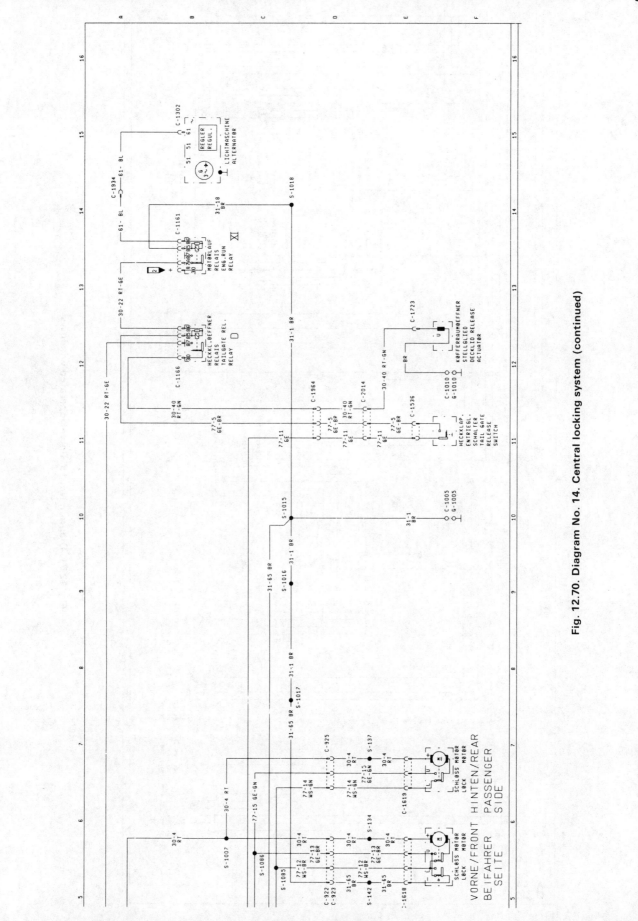

Fig. 12.70. Diagram No. 14. Central locking system (continued)

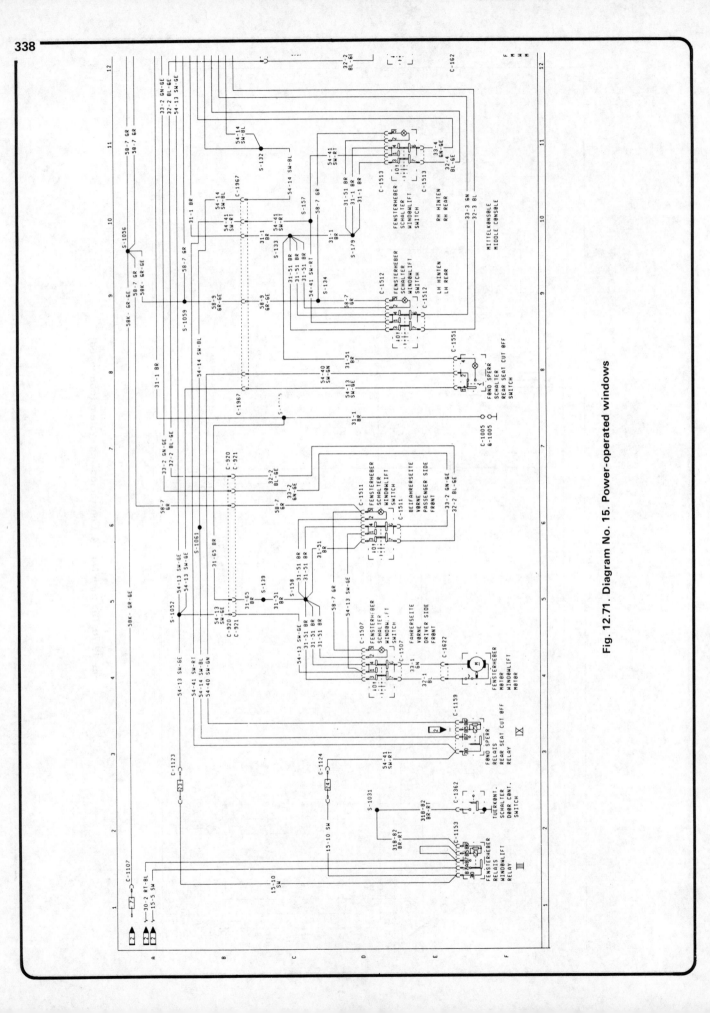

Fig. 12.71. Diagram No. 15. Power-operated windows

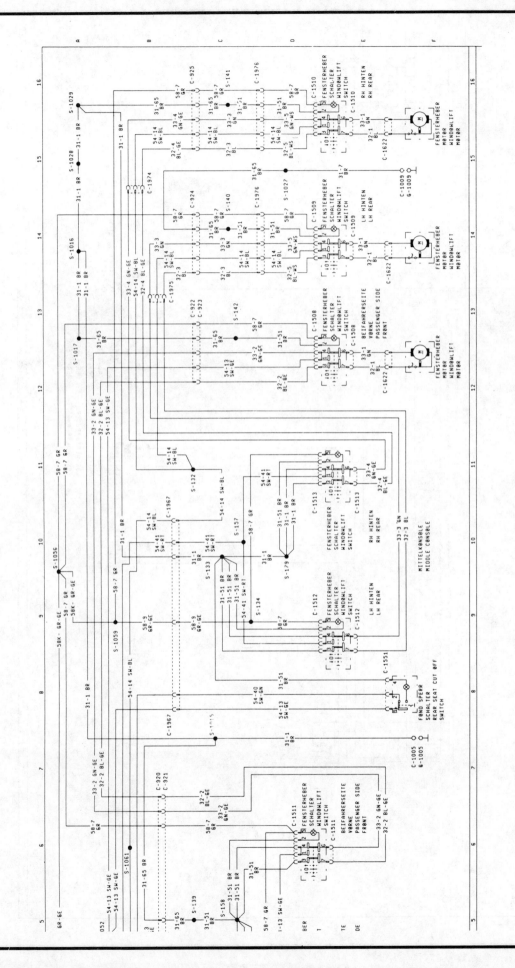

Fig. 12.71 Diagram No. 15. Power-operated windows (continued)

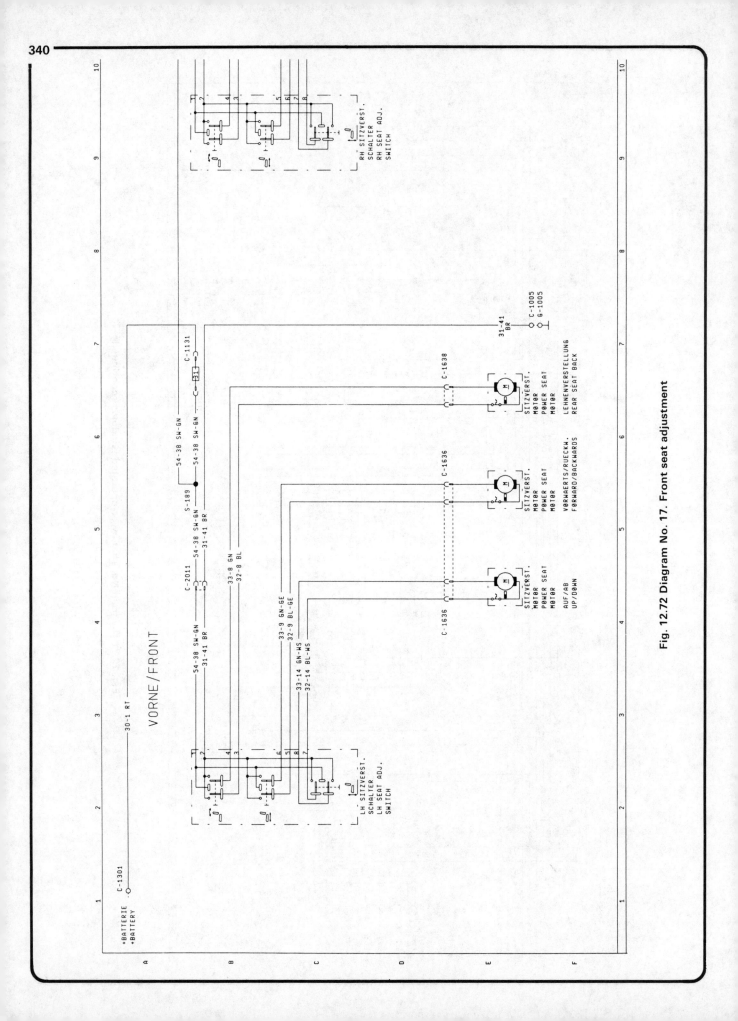

Fig. 12.72 Diagram No. 17. Front seat adjustment

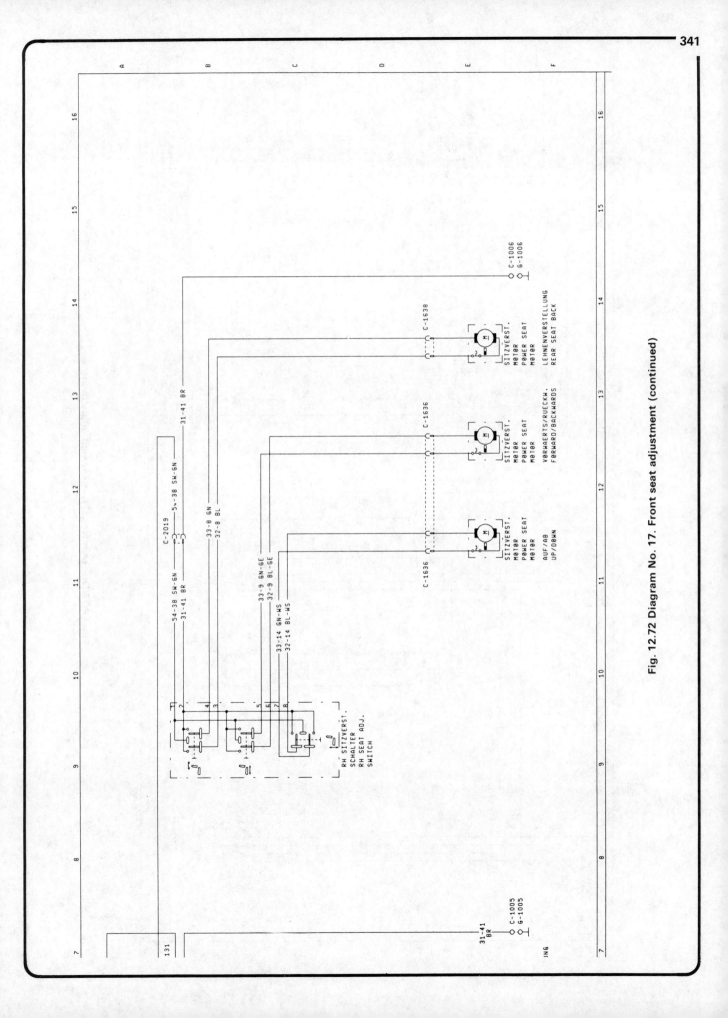

Fig. 12.72 Diagram No. 17. Front seat adjustment (continued)

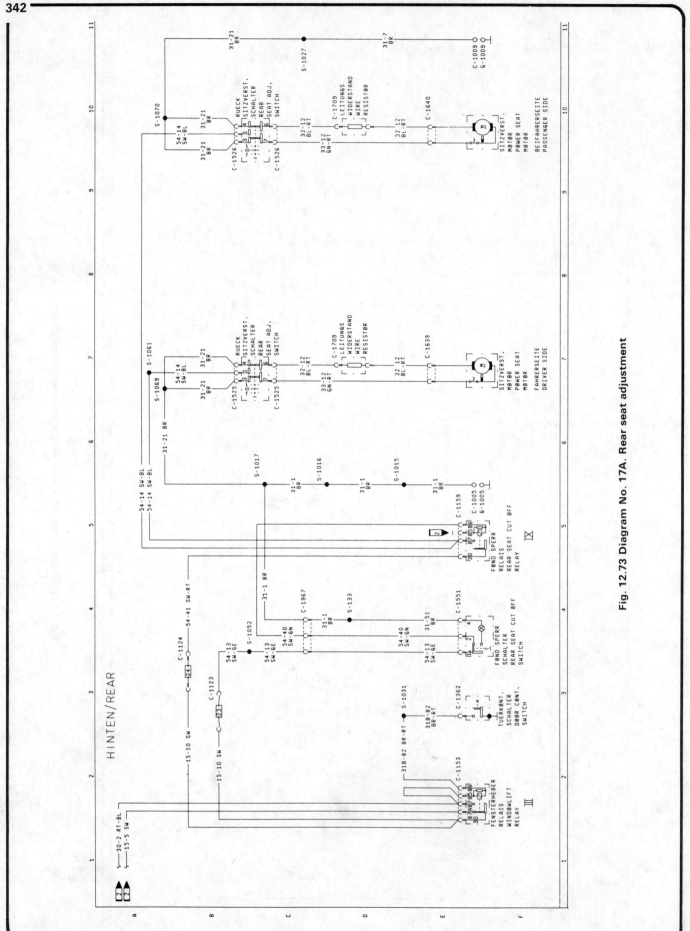

Fig. 12.73 Diagram No. 17A. Rear seat adjustment

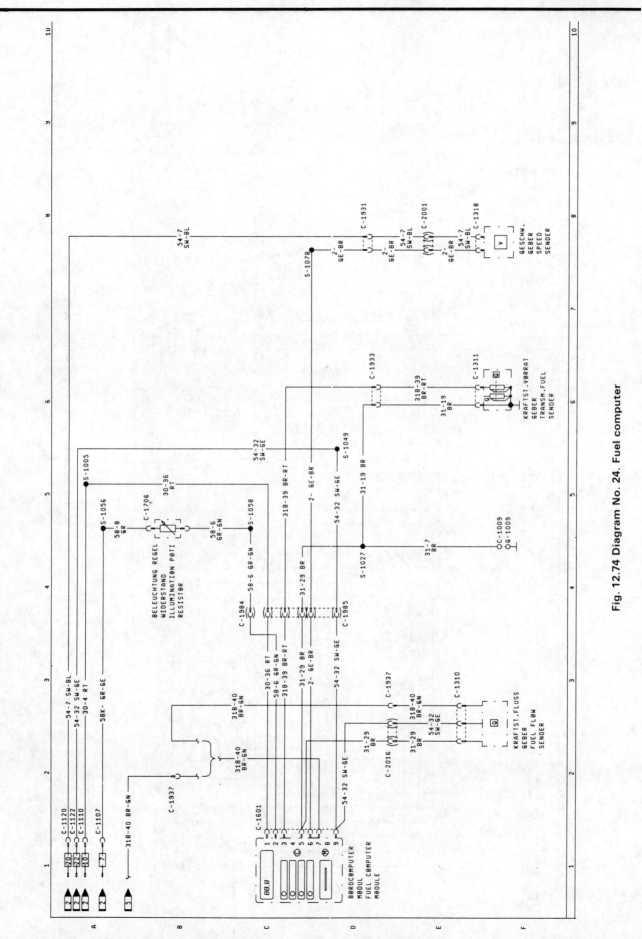

Fig. 12.74 Diagram No. 24. Fuel computer

344

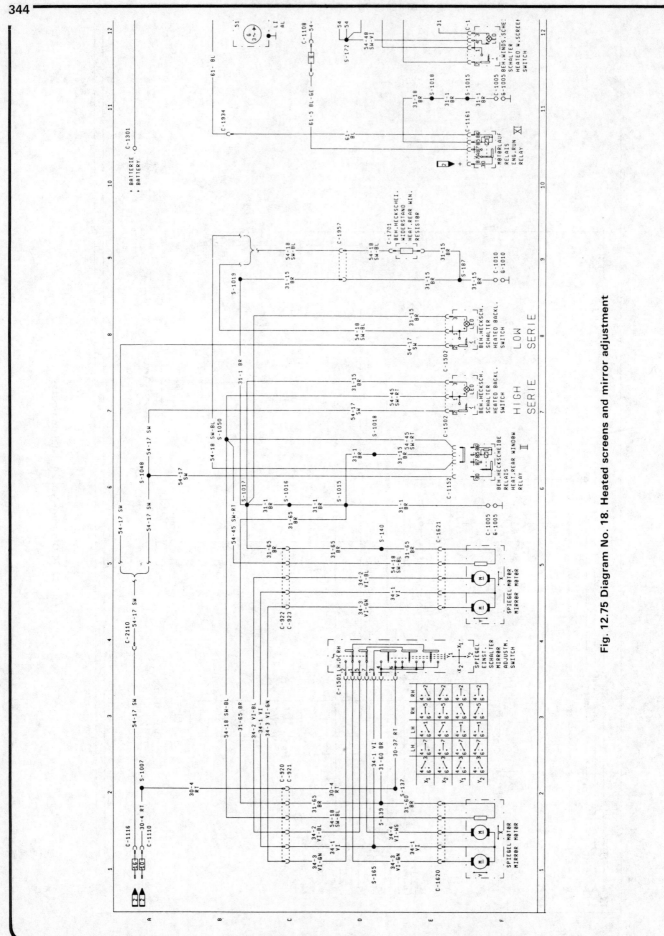

Fig. 12.75 Diagram No. 18. Heated screens and mirror adjustment

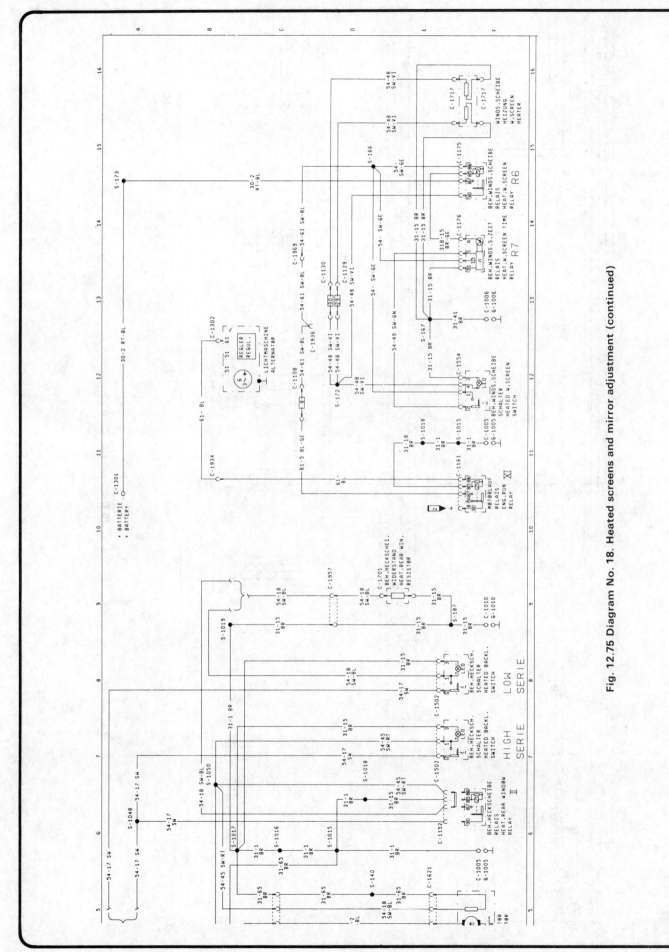

Fig. 12.75 Diagram No. 18. Heated screens and mirror adjustment (continued)

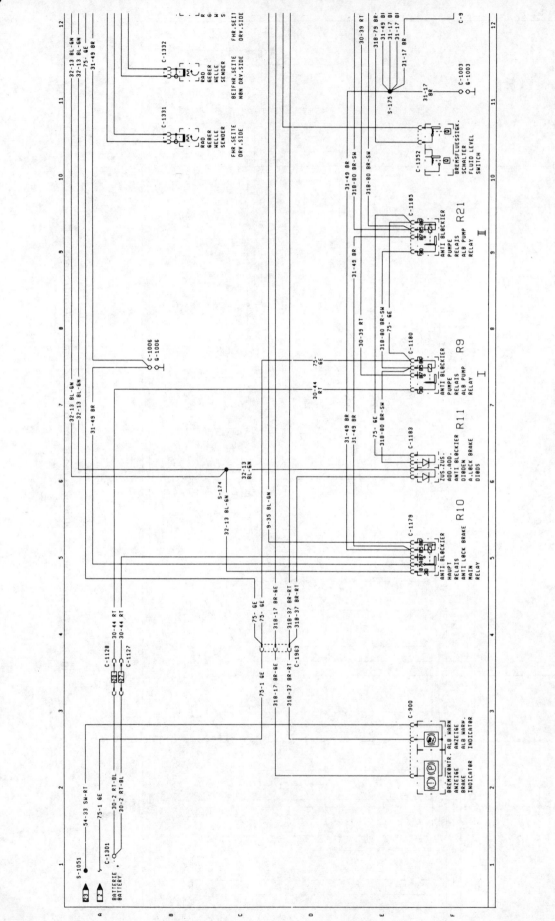

Fig. 12.76 Diagram No. 21. ABS

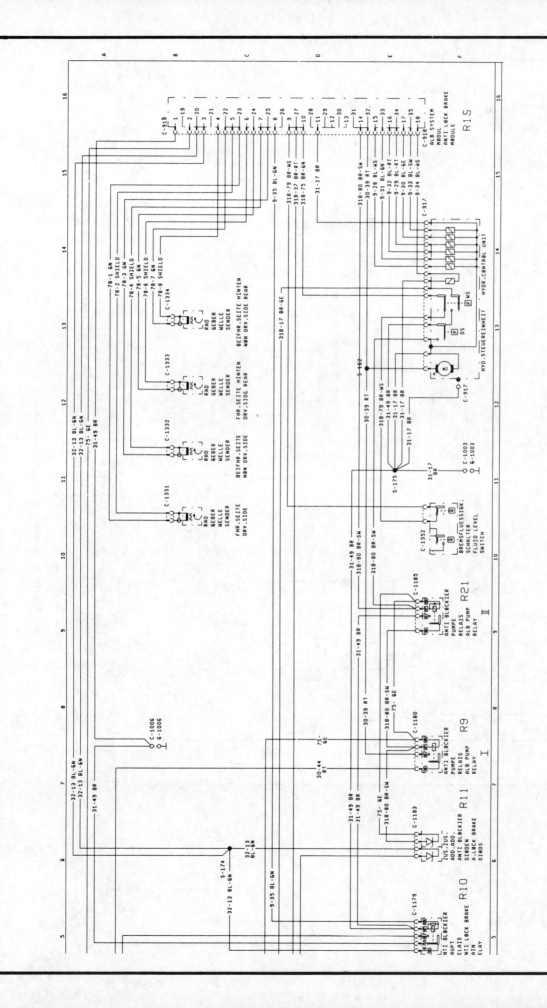

Fig. 12.76 Diagram No. 21. ABS (continued)

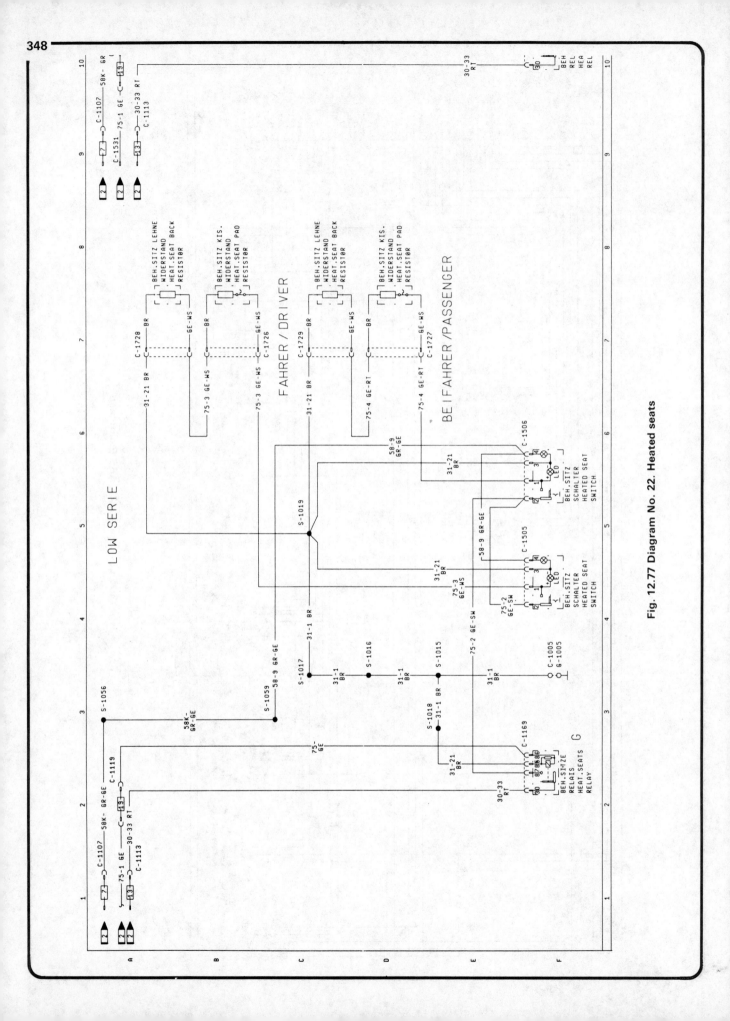

Fig. 12.77 Diagram No. 22. Heated seats

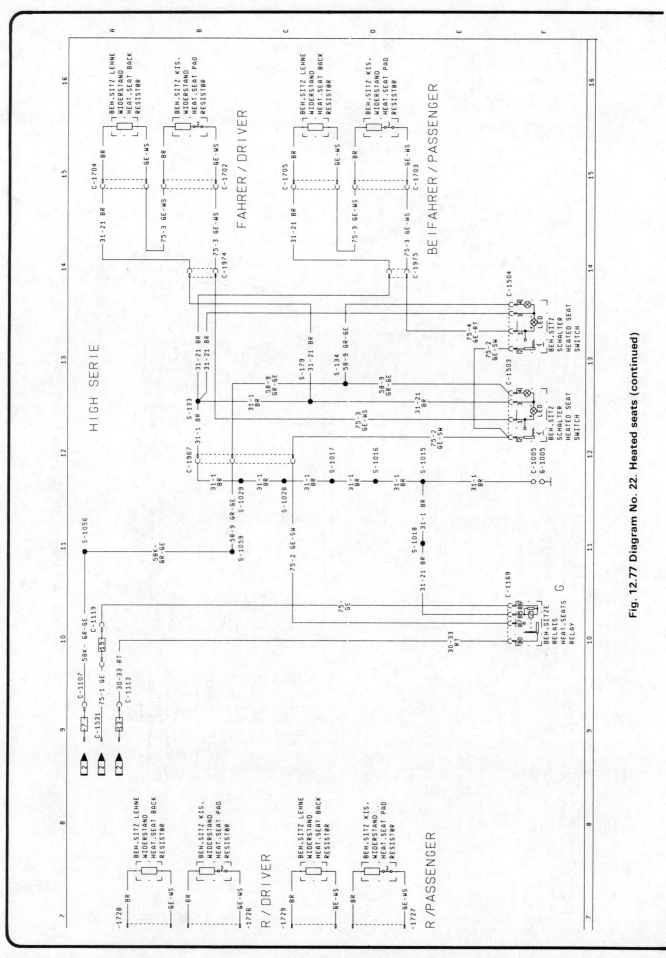

Fig. 12.77 Diagram No. 22. Heated seats (continued)

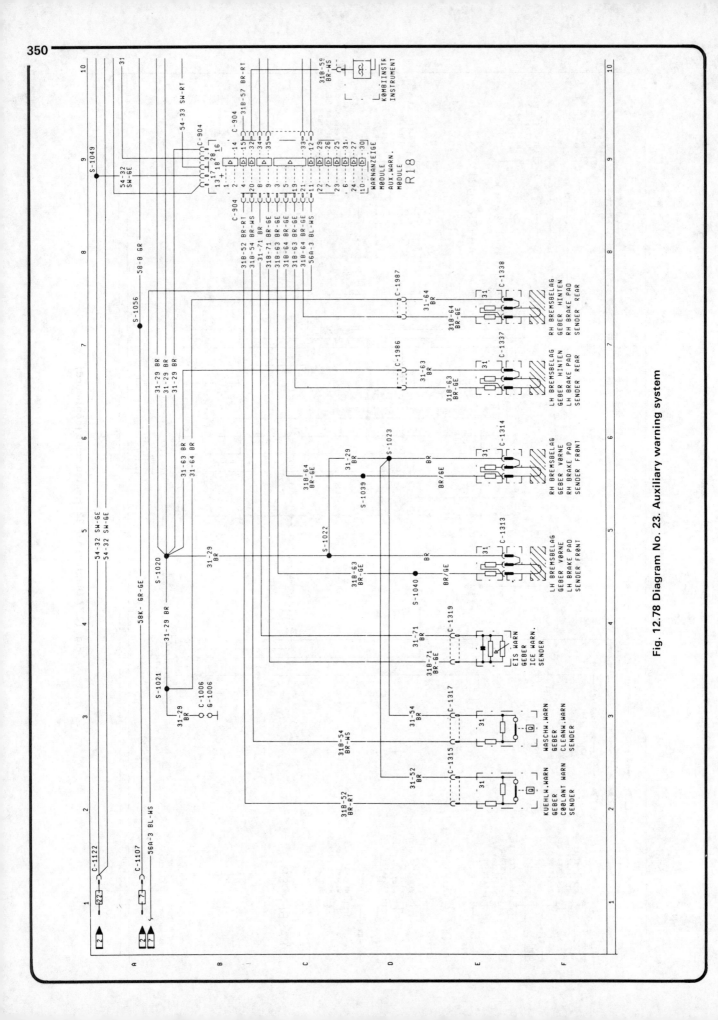

Fig. 12.78 Diagram No. 23. Auxiliary warning system

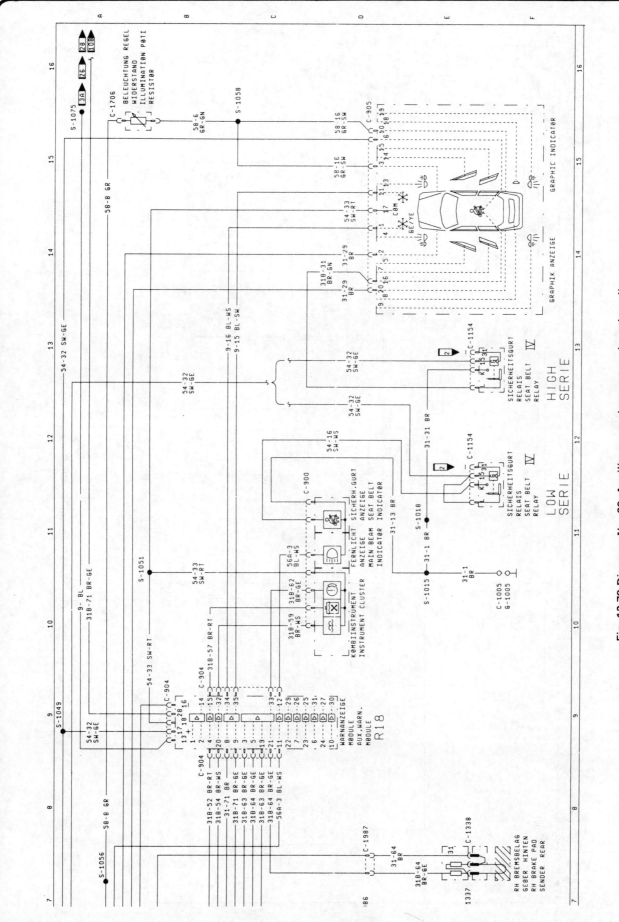

Fig. 12.78 Diagram No. 23. Auxiliary warning system (continued)

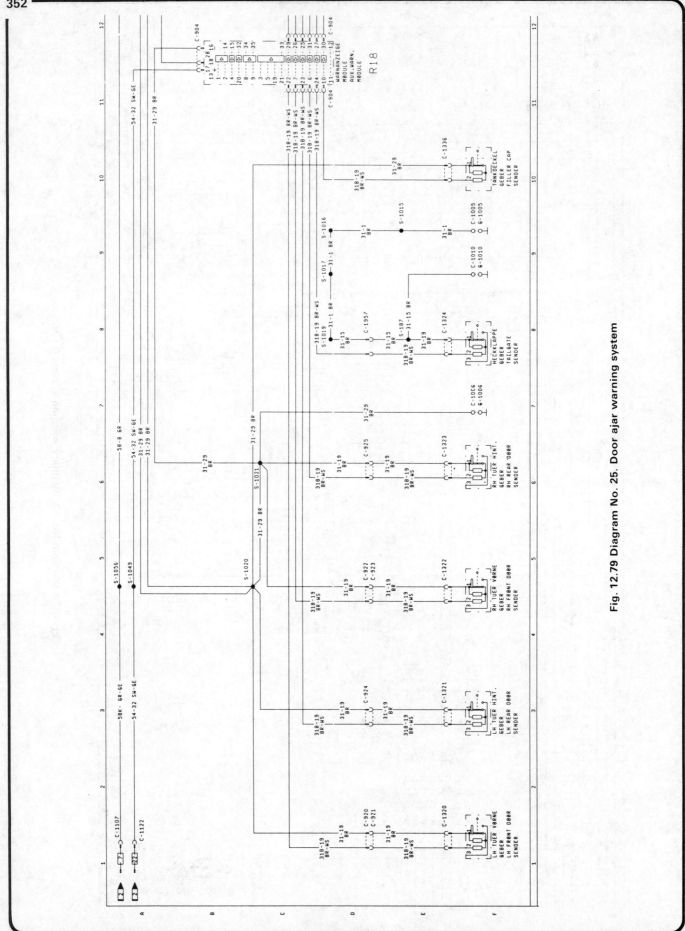

Fig. 12.79 Diagram No. 25. Door ajar warning system

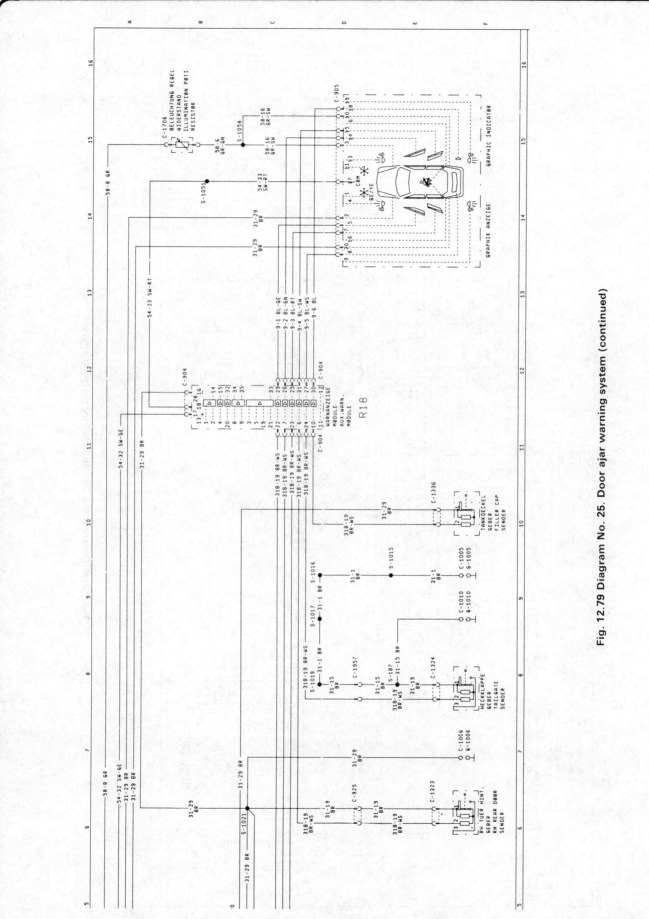

Fig. 12.79 Diagram No. 25. Door ajar warning system (continued)

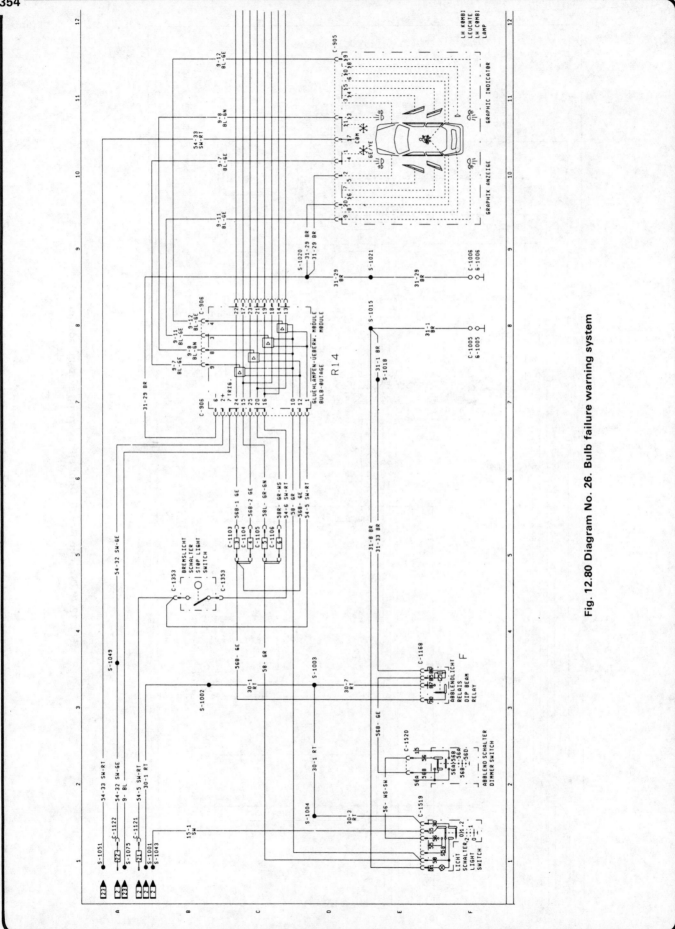

**Fig. 12.80 Diagram No. 26. Bulb failure warning system**

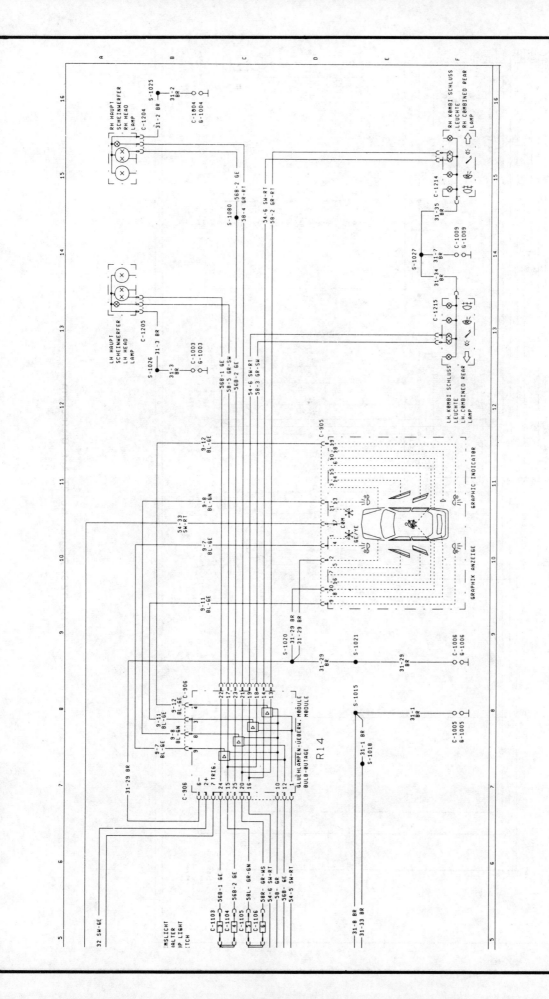

Fig. 12.80 Diagram No. 26. Bulb failure warning system (continued)

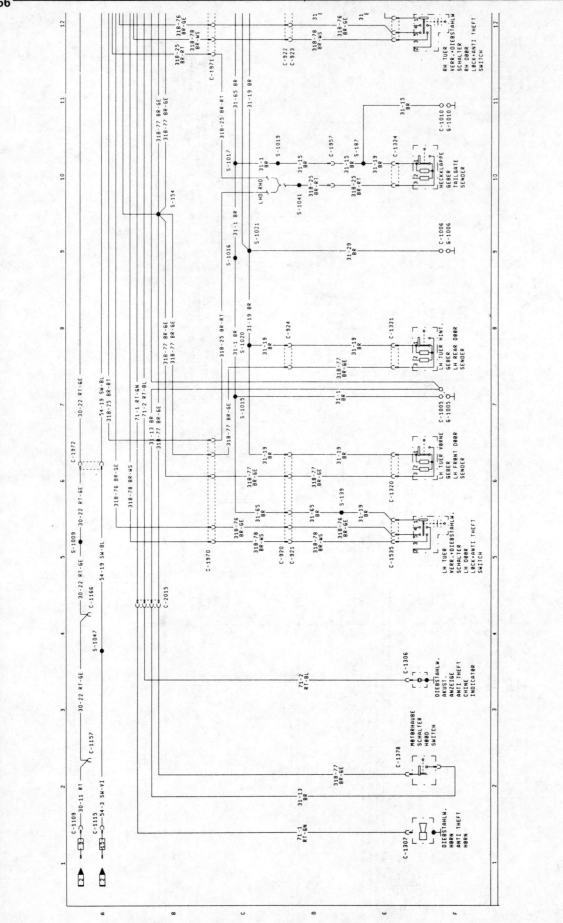

Fig. 12.81 Diagram No. 27. Anti-theft alarm

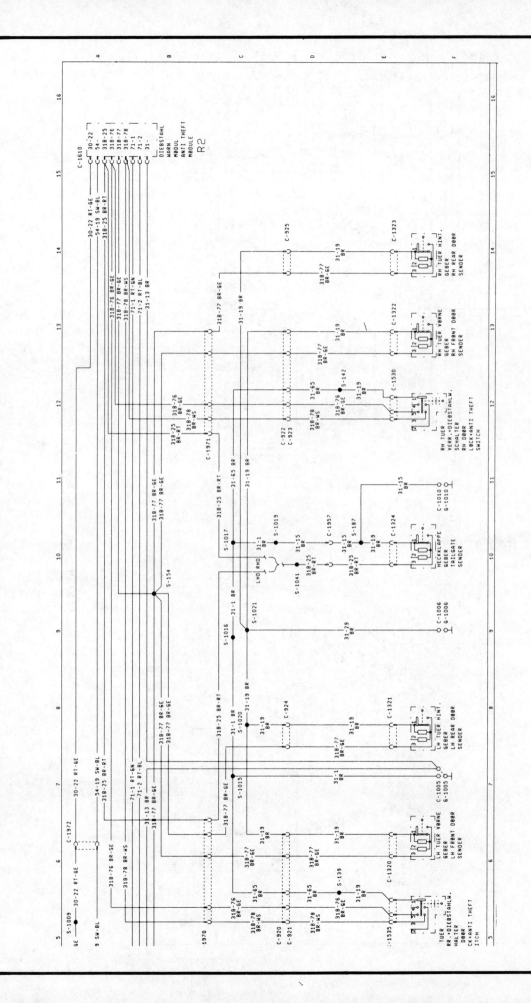

Fig. 12.81 Diagram No. 27. Anti-theft alarm (continued)

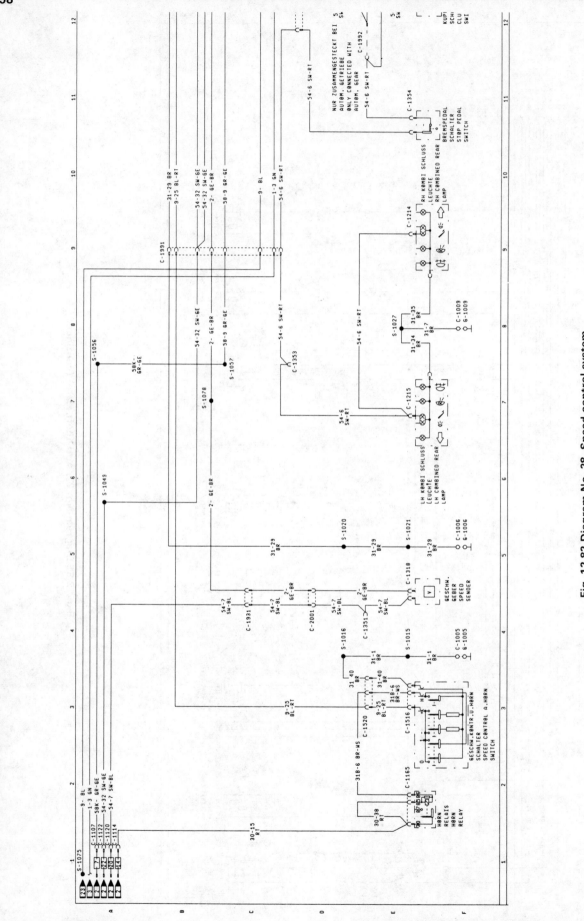

**Fig. 12.82 Diagram No. 28. Speed control system**

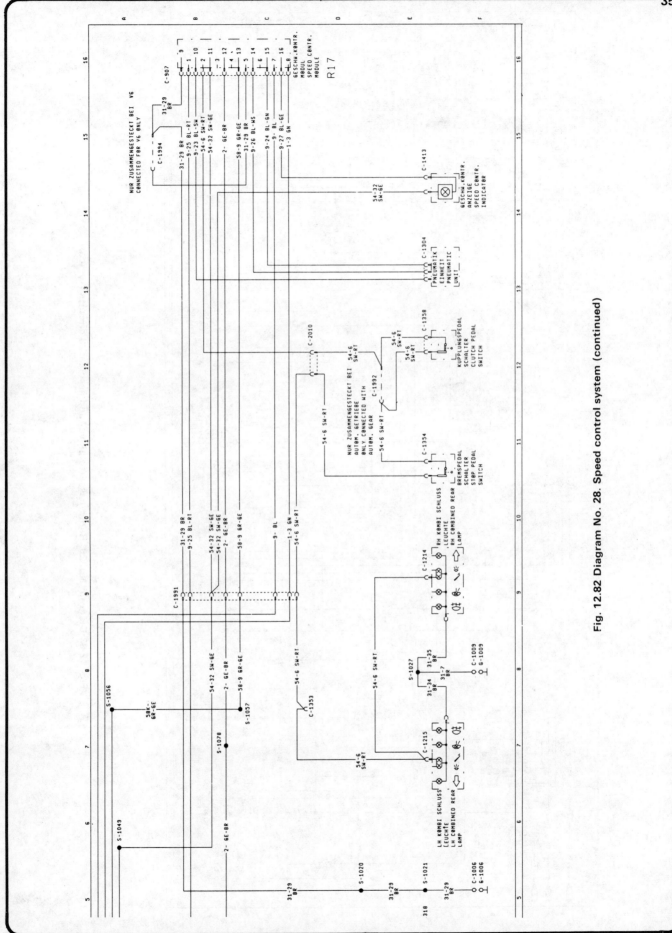

Fig. 12.82 Diagram No. 28. Speed control system (continued)

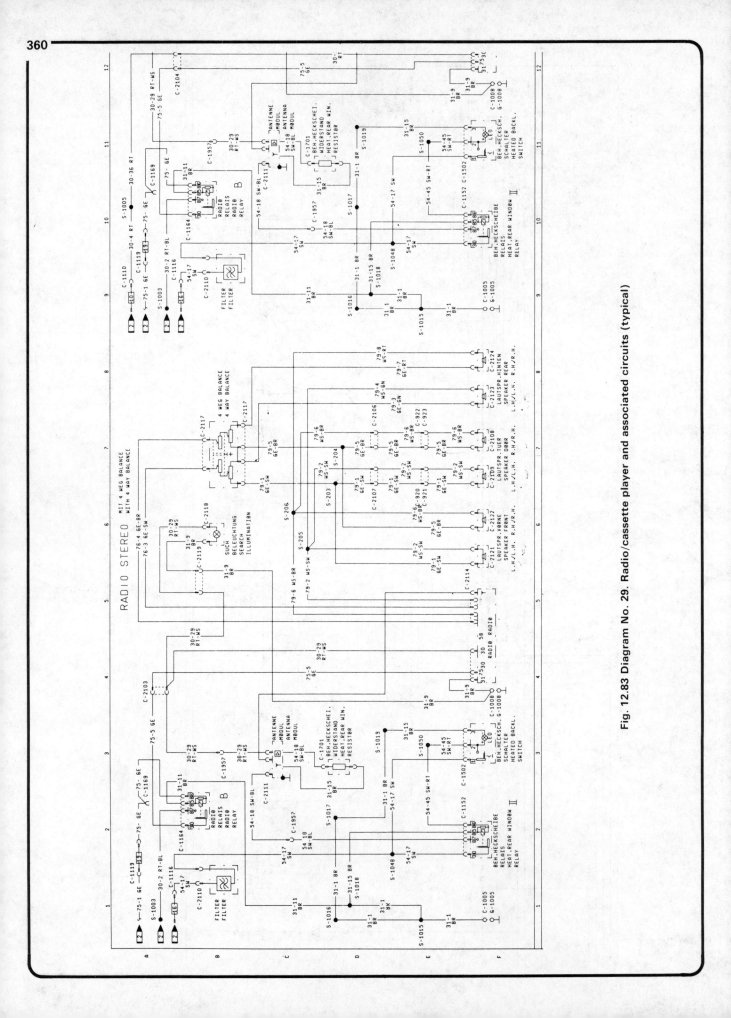

Fig. 12.83 Diagram No. 29. Radio/cassette player and associated circuits (typical)

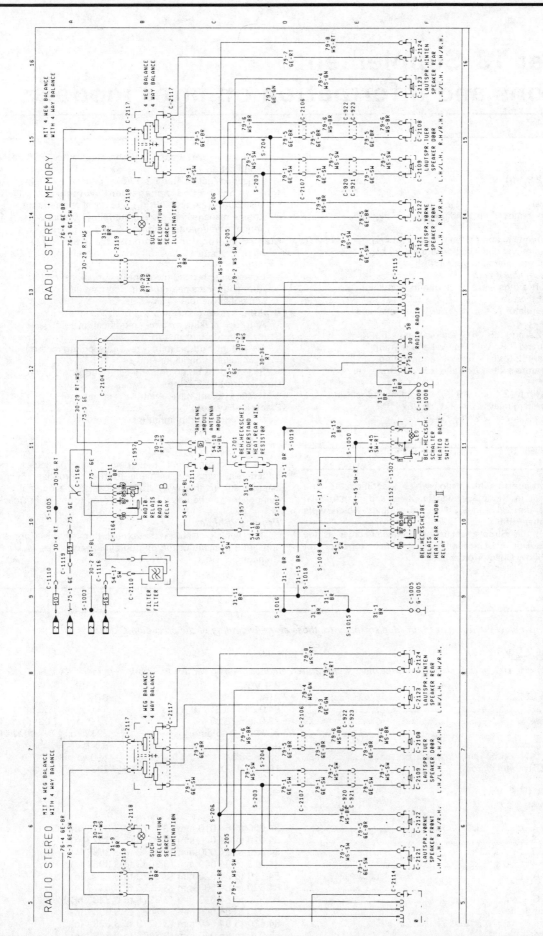

**Fig. 12.83 Diagram No. 29. Radio/cassette player and associated circuits (typical) (continued)**

# Chapter 13 Supplement:
# Revisions and information on later models

## Contents

---

## 1  Introduction

This Supplement contains information which is additional to, or a revision of, material in the preceding Chapters, and in particular features details of the 2.4 and 2.9 litre V6 engines which were introduced in October 1986.

The Sections in this Supplement follow the same order as the original Chapters. The Specifications are grouped together for convenience but follow Chapter order.

It is recommended that before any particular operation is undertaken, reference is made to the appropriate Section of the Supplement. In this way, any changes to the original procedure or component can be noted before referring to the main Chapters.

### Project vehicle

The vehicle used in the preparation of this Supplement, and appearing in many of the photographic sequences, was a 1987 Ford Granada 2.9 Ghia.

---

## 2  Specifications

*The specifications below are revisions of, or supplementary to, those at the beginning of the preceding Chapter*

### Engine (2.4 and 2.9 V6 ohv)

**Note:** *Unless otherwise stated, the specifications for the 2.4 and 2.9 V6 engines are as given for the 2.8 V6 engine in Chapter 1*

#### General

| | 2.4 V6 | 2.9 V6 |
|---|---|---|
| Identification code ................................................................ | ARC | BRC |
| Bore ..................................................................................... | 84.0 mm (3.31 in) | 93.0 mm (3.66 in) |
| Stroke .................................................................................. | 72.0 mm (2.83 in) | 72.0 mm (2.83 in) |
| Cubic capacity ..................................................................... | 2394 cc (146 cu in) | 2933 cc (179 cu in) |
| Compression ratio ............................................................... | 9.5:1 | 9.5:1 |
| Maximum power (DIN, kW @ rpm) ....................................... | 96 @ 5800 | 110 @ 5800 |
| Maximum torque (DIN, Nm @ rpm) ...................................... | 193 @ 3000 | 233 @ 3000 |

#### Cylinder block (2.4 V6)

| | |
|---|---|
| Identification mark ............................................................... | D |
| Bore diameter: | |
|    Standard grade 1 ......................................................... | 84.000 to 84.010 mm (3.3071 to 3.3075 in) |
|    Standard grade 2 ......................................................... | 84.010 to 84.020 mm (3.3075 to 3.3079 in) |
|    Standard grade 3 ......................................................... | 84.020 to 84.030 mm (3.3079 to 3.3083 in) |
|    Standard grade 4 ......................................................... | 84.030 to 84.040 mm (3.3083 to 3.3087 in) |
|    Oversize grade A ......................................................... | 84.510 to 84.520 mm (3.3272 to 3.3276 in) |
|    Oversize grade B ......................................................... | 84.520 to 84.530 mm (3.3276 to 3.3279 in) |
|    Oversize grade C ......................................................... | 84.530 to 84.540 mm (3.3279 to 3.3283 in) |
|    Standard service grade ................................................. | 84.030 to 84.040 mm (3.3083 to 3.3087 in) |
|    Oversize 0.5 mm .......................................................... | 84.530 to 84.540 mm (3.3279 to 3.3283 in) |
|    Oversize 1.0 mm .......................................................... | 85.030 to 85.040 mm (3.3476 to 3.3480 in) |

## Cylinder block (2.9 V6)
Identification mark ................................................................... F

**Note:** *All other specifications for the 2.4 and 2.9 V6 engines are as given for the 2.8 V6 engine in Chapter 1*

## Pistons (2.4 V6)
Diameter:
    Standard grade 1 ........................................................... 83.962 to 83.972 mm (3.3056 to 3.3060 in)
    Standard grade 2 ........................................................... 83.972 to 83.982 mm (3.3060 to 3.3064 in)
    Standard grade 3 ........................................................... 83.982 to 83.992 mm (3.3064 to 3.3068 in)
    Standard grade 4 ........................................................... 83.992 to 84.002 mm (3.3068 to 3.3072 in)
    Service standard ........................................................... 83.978 to 84.002 mm (3.3062 to 3.3072 in)
    Oversize 0.5 mm ........................................................... 84.478 to 84.502 mm (3.3259 to 3.3269 in)
    Oversize 1.0 mm ........................................................... 84.978 to 85.002 mm (3.3456 to 3.3465 in)
Clearance in bore ................................................................. 0.028 to 0.048 mm (0.0011 to 0.0019 in)
Piston ring end gaps:
    Top and centre ............................................................. 0.30 to 0.50 mm (0.012 to 0.020 in)
    Bottom ......................................................................... 0.40 to 1.40 mm (0.016 to 0.055 in)

## Pistons (2.9 V6)
Clearance in bore ................................................................. 0.028 to 0.048 mm (0.0011 to 0.0019 in)
Piston ring end gaps:
    Top and centre ............................................................. 0.30 to 0.50 mm (0.012 to 0.020 in)
    Bottom ......................................................................... 0.40 to 1.40 mm (0.016 to 0.055 in)

**Note:** *All other specifications for the 2.4 and 2.9 V6 engines are as given for the 2.8 V6 engine in Chapter 1*

## Cylinder heads (2.4 and 2.9 V6)
Identification mark:
    2.4 V6 ......................................................................... H
    2.9 V6 ......................................................................... F

**Note:** *All other specifications for the 2.4 and 2.9 V6 engines are as given for the 2.8 V6 engine in Chapter 1*

## Crankshaft (2.4 V6)
Thrust washer thickness:
    Standard ....................................................................... 2.28 to 2.33 mm (0.090 to 0.092 in)
    Oversize ....................................................................... 2.48 to 2.53 mm (0.098 to 0.100 in)
Crankshaft endfloat ............................................................. 0.08 to 0.32 mm (0.003 to 0.013 in)
Permitted undersize for main and big-end journals ............................. 0.254 mm (0.010 in)

## Crankshaft (2.9 V6)
Crankshaft endfloat ............................................................. 0.08 to 0.24 mm (0.003 to 0.009 in)
Permitted undersize for main and big-end journals ............................. 0.254 mm (0.010 in)

**Note:** *All other specifications for the 2.4 and 2.9 V6 engines are as given for the 2.8 V6 engine in Chapter 1*

## Camshaft and valves (2.4 and 2.9 V6)
Camshaft drive ................................................................... Chain
Cam lift, inlet and exhaust ...................................................... 6.72 mm (0.265 in)
Cam length, inlet and exhaust ................................................... 36.08 to 36.25 mm (1.420 to 1.427 in)
Camshaft endfloat ............................................................... 0.065 to 0.165 mm (0.0026 to 0.0065 in)
Thrust plate thickness ........................................................... 4.02 to 4.05 mm (0.158 to 0.160 in)
Valve timing:
    Inlet opens ................................................................... 24° BTDC
    Inlet closes .................................................................. 64° ABDC
    Exhaust opens ............................................................... 66° BBDC
    Exhaust closes .............................................................. 22° ATDC

| | **2.4 V6** | **2.9 V6** |
|---|---|---|
| Inlet valve: | | |
|   Head diameter | 39.67 to 40.06 mm (1.562 to 1.577 in) | 41.85 to 42.24 mm (1.648 to 1.663 in) |
|   Length | 106.2 to 106.9 mm (4.18 to 4.21 in) | 106.2 to 106.9 mm (4.18 to 4.21 in) |
| Exhaust valve: | | |
|   Head diameter | 33.83 to 34.20 mm (1.332 to 1.345 in) | 35.83 to 36.21 mm (1.411 to 1.426 in) |
|   Length | 106.1 to 107.1 mm (4.18 to 4.22 in) | 106.8 to 107.8 mm (4.21 to 4.24 in) |

Valve spring free length .......................................................... 55.12 mm (2.170 in)
Valve stem oil seal type .......................................................... Rubber, one size

**Note:** *All other specifications for the 2.4 and 2.9 V6 engines are as given for the 2.8 V6 engine in Chapter 1*

## Torque wrench settings (2.4 and 2.9 V6)

| | Nm | lbf ft |
|---|---|---|
| Camshaft sprocket bolt | 68 | 50 |
| Camshaft thrust plate bolts | 13 | 10 |
| Chain guide to block bolts | 13 | 10 |
| Oil intake pipe to oil pump bolts | 13 | 10 |
| Oil pump to block bolts | 18 | 13 |
| Crankshaft pulley to vibration damper bolts | 33 | 24 |

**Torque wrench settings (continued)**

| | Nm | lbf ft |
|---|---|---|
| Sump drain plug | 28 | 21 |

Cylinder head (Torx) bolts (new):

| | | |
|---|---|---|
| Stage 1 | 40 | 30 |
| Stage 2 | 75 | 55 |
| Stage 3 | Wait 5 minutes, then tighten a further 90° | |

**Note:** *All other specifications for the 2.4 and 2.9 V6 engines are as given for the 2.8 V6 engine in Chapter 1*

## Cooling system (2.4 and 2.9 V6)

**Torque wrench settings**

| | Nm | lbf ft |
|---|---|---|
| Water pump bolts | 10 | 7 |
| Thermostat housing bolts | 10 | 7 |

## Fuel system (2.4 and 2.9 V6)

### General

| | |
|---|---|
| System type | Electronic fuel injection |
| Idle speed | 850 to 950 rpm |
| Idle CO level | 0.5 to 1.0% |
| Fuel filter | Champion L204 |

### Torque wrench settings

| | Nm | lbf ft |
|---|---|---|
| Idle speed control valve | 10 | 7 |
| Fuel pressure regulator bolts | 10 | 7 |
| Fuel rail temperature switch | 25 | 18 |
| Engine coolant temperature sensor | 25 | 18 |
| Plenum chamber bolts | 10 | 7 |

## Ignition system (2.4 and 2.9 V6)

### Spark plugs

| | |
|---|---|
| Type | Champion RC7YCC or RC7YC |

Electrode gap:

| | |
|---|---|
| Champion RC7YCC | 0.8 mm (0.032 in) |
| Champion RC7YC | 0.7 mm (0.028 in) |

**Ignition timing (static)*** ........................ 12° BTDC

*\*Timing for 97 octane leaded fuel (4-star). For unleaded premium (95 octane) fuel, consult your Ford dealer*

## Manual gearbox

### Gear ratios

| | |
|---|---|
| 2.4 V6 models | As 1.8/2.0 models, in Chapter 6 |
| 2.9 V6 models | As 2.8 models, in Chapter 6 |

### Torque wrench setting

| | Nm | lbf ft |
|---|---|---|
| Layshaft bearing spigot bolts (2.8 and 2.9 V6 models) | 14 to 19 | 10 to 14 |

## Final drive

### Final drive ratio

| | |
|---|---|
| All 2.4 and 2.9 V6 models | 3.64:1 |

### Final drive adjustment

| | |
|---|---|
| Pinion turning torque (1987 on) | 1.8 to 2.4 Nm (1.3 to 1.8 lbf ft) |

### Torque wrench setting

| | Nm | lbf ft |
|---|---|---|
| Pinion flange nut (1987 on) | 100 to 120 | 74 to 89 |

## Steering and suspension

### Rear wheel alignment checking values (all models)

| | |
|---|---|
| Toe-in | 0.3 ± 3.25 mm (0.012 ± 0.128 in) |

Camber angle at ride height given below – mm (in):

| | |
|---|---|
| 340 to 349 (13.4 to 13.7) | −4°20' to −1° 28' |
| 350 to 359 (13.8 to 14.1) | −3° 58' to −1° 05' |
| 360 to 369 (14.2 to 14.5) | −3° 35' to −0° 43' |
| 370 to 379 (14.6 to 14.9) | −3° 13' to −0° 21' |
| 380 to 389 (15.0 to 15.3) | −2° 51' to +0° 01' |
| 390 to 399 (15.4 to 15.7) | −2° 29' to +0° 24' |
| 400 to 409 (15.8 to 16.1) | −2° 06' to +0° 46' |
| 410 to 419 (16.1 to 16.5) | −1° 44' to +1° 09' |
| 420 to 429 (16.5 to 16.9) | −1° 21' to +1° 31' |
| 430 to 439 (16.9 to 17.3) | −0° 59' to +1° 54' |
| Maximum side-to-side variation | 1° 00' |

## Weights (kerb)

### 2.4 V6 models

| | |
|---|---|
| GL | 1265 kg (2789 lb) |
| Ghia | 1295 kg (2855 lb) |
| Ghia X | 1310 kg (2889 lb) |

### 2.9 V6 models

| | |
|---|---|
| Ghia | 1315 kg (2900 lb) |
| Ghia X | 1330 kg (2933 lb) |

**Under-bonnet view of a 2.9 V6 Granada**

1  Windscreen wiper motor
2  Battery
3  Suspension strut top mounting
4  Brake fluid reservoir
5  Ignition distributor
6  Coolant expansion tank
7  Washer fluid reservoir
8  Automatic transmission fluid dipstick
9  Right-hand rocker cover
10  Oil filler cap
11  Plenum chamber
12  Left-hand rocker cover
13  Engine oil dipstick
14  Airflow meters
15  Air cleaner cover
16  Power steering fluid reservoir
17  Idle speed control valve
18  Drivebelts
19  Top hose bleed screw
20  Radiator upper shroud
21  Bonnet prop
22  Main fuse/relay box

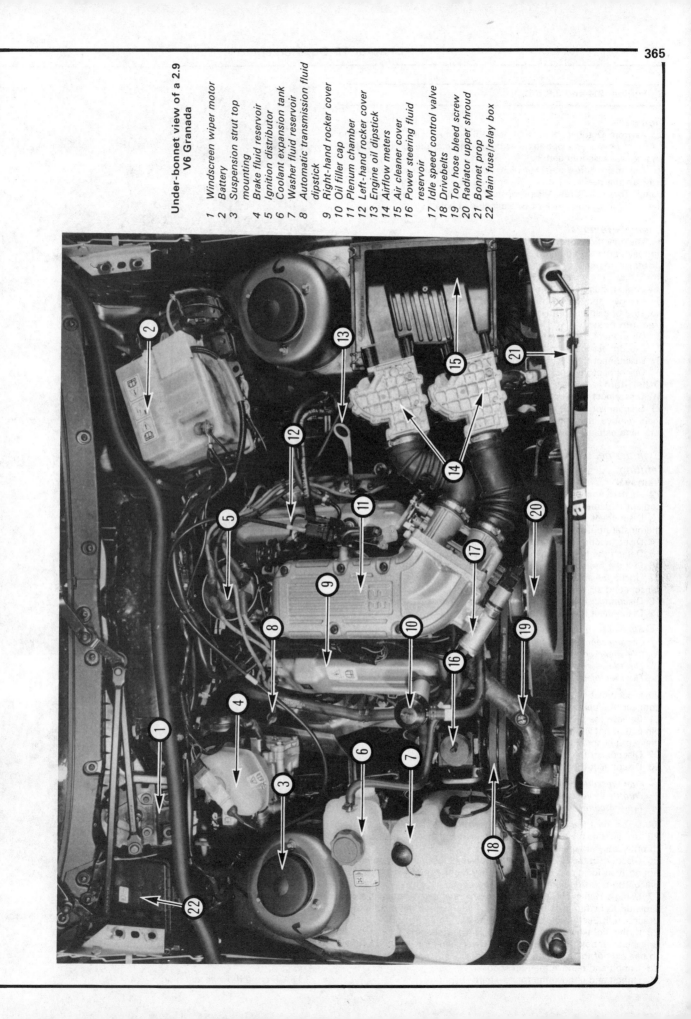

## 3  Engine (2.4 and 2.9 V6)

### General

1  As from October 1986, two new V6 engines were added to the range of power unit options – at the same time, the existing 2.8 V6 engine was discontinued.
2  The main differences between the earlier and later V6 engines concern the design of the cylinder head, the timing gear and the oil pump (photo). Only those operations which differ from those described in Chapter 1, Part B, are included here.

### Engine – removal

3  The operations are essentially as described in Chapter 1, Section 59 but pay particular attention to the following.

**Coolant hoses**

4  Remove the hoses which run between the thermostat housing and the coolant pump, and the cooling system expansion tank.
5  Remove the heater hoses which run between the thermostat housing or distribution pipe and oil cooler (where fitted).

**Vacuum hoses**

6  Disconnect the hose from the fuel pressure regulator.
7  Disconnect the hose from the plenum chamber.
8  Disconnect the hose from the throttle valve.
9  Disconnect the hose from the T-piece connector.

**Other items**

10  Disconnect the throttle cable from the operating lever and bracket.
11  Disconnect the right-hand exhaust downpipe from the manifold, then remove the starter motor, the oil filter, and disconnect the left-hand exhaust downpipe, in that order.

### Cylinder heads – removal, dismantling, reassembly and refitting

**Removal**

12   If the engine is in the car, disconnect the battery and drain the coolant (Chapter 2).
13  Disconnect the radiator top hose and the heater hose from the thermostat housing.
14  Disconnect the air hoses from the throttle valve housing (photo).
15  Detach the two plugs from the airflow sensors (photos).
16  Pull the breather hose from the oil filler cap (photo).
17  Unclip the air cleaner cover and remove it together with the airflow sensors and air hoses.
18  Disconnect the hoses from the coolant expansion tank.
19  Disconnect the leads from the following:

*Alternator (right-hand cylinder head removal only)*
*Coolant temperature sensors*
*Idle speed control valve*
*Throttle valve potentiometer*
*The fuel injector wiring loom (photos)*

20  Disconnect the multi-plug from the ignition distributor. Disconnect the fuel temperature sensor plug (photos).
21  Release the pressure in the fuel distributor pipe by depressing the pin in the vent valve. Cover the valve with a rag during this operation to prevent fuel spray (photo).
22  Disconnect the fuel lines (photo).
23  Disconnect the vacuum hoses from the following:

*Fuel pressure regulator*
*Throttle valve assembly*
*T-piece connector (photo)*

24  Disconnect the rocker cover breather hose (photo).
25  Unbolt the plenum chamber and place it to one side with the throttle cable attached.
26  Disconnect the HT leads from the spark plugs and the ignition coil, noting their locations. Remove the distributor cap (two screws) and place it to one side complete with leads.
27  Using a 19 mm socket on the crankshaft damper centre bolt, set No 1 piston to its firing point (12° BTDC) and remove the distributor as described in Section 5 of this Supplement.
28  If the right-hand cylinder head is being removed, remove the drivebelts, unbolt the alternator and power steering pump and tie them to one side of the engine compartment.
29  Unbolt and remove the rocker cover(s).
30  Unbolt and remove the rocker shaft(s) (photo).

3.2 2.9 V6 cylinder head

3.14 Air hoses disconnected from throttle valve housing

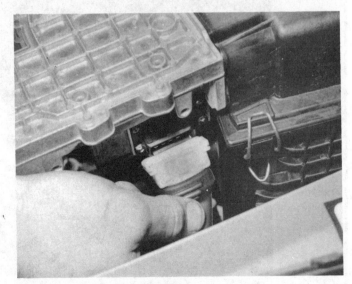

3.15A Front airflow sensor plug

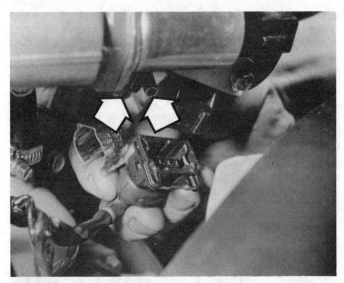

3.15B Rear airflow sensor plug. Vacuum hose nozzles arrowed

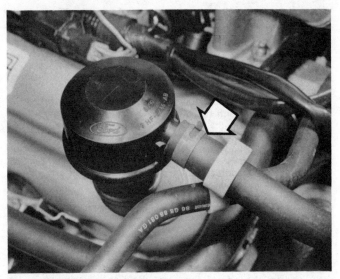

3.16 Oil filler cap breather hose (arrowed)

3.19A Coolant temperature sensors

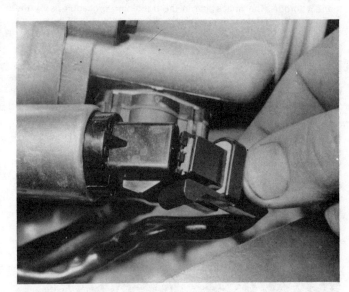

3.19B Idle speed control valve plug

3.20A Ignition distributor wiring plug

3.20B Fuel temperature sensor plug

31 Withdraw the pushrods and keep them in their originally fitted sequence.

32 Disconnect the coolant hose (inlet manifold to timing cover).

33 Unbolt and remove the inlet manifold with fuel rail and injectors. Discard the gasket.

34 Disconnect the exhaust downpipe(s) from the manifold(s).

35 Disconnect the earth straps from the rear of the left-hand cylinder head, and also release the cable clamp.

36 Unscrew and remove the spark plugs.

37 Unscrew the cylinder head bolts using the reverse of the tightening sequence shown in Fig. 1.31. Obtain new bolts for refitting. Remove the cylinder heads and discard the cylinder head gaskets.

**Dismantling and reassembly**

38 The procedures are as described in Chapter 1, Section 77. Disregard the references to oversize exhaust valve stem oil seals.

**Refitting**

39 Refitting the cylinder heads is essentially a reversal of the removal operations but also refer to Chapter 1, Section 92 and then observe the following differences:

40 Always use new Torx type cylinder head bolts. Oil them and allow them to drain. When fitted, the word 'OBEN' should be visible on the new gaskets (photos).

41 Tighten the bolts in the specified sequence (Fig. 1.31) to the correct torque. The final stage in the tightening procedure is by the angular method. Use a disc similar to the one shown or make a paint

3.21 Fuel rail vent valve and cap

3.22 Fuel lines

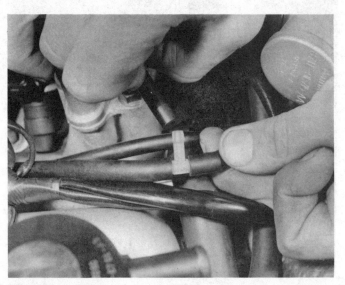

3.23 Vacuum hoses at T-piece connector

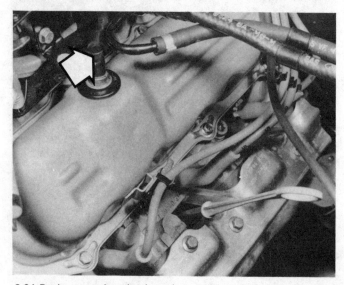

3.24 Rocker cover breather hose (arrowed)

3.30 Removing rocker shaft and pedestals

mark at the same point on each bolt head to ensure that each bolt is turned through exactly the same number of degrees (photo).

42 As a result of the bolt tightening torque used and the elasticity of the bolts, no further tightening is required after the initial running-in period.

43 Apply jointing compound to the areas where the inlet manifold and cylinder heads meet, and locate a new gasket in position. Make sure that it is the correct way round. Tighten the inlet manifold bolts to the specified torque and in the sequence shown in Fig. 13.1 (photos).

44 Check that No 1 piston is still at its firing point (12° BTDC) and fit the distributor as described in Section 5.

45 Adjust the valve clearances as described later in this Section.

46 Fit new rocker cover gaskets, peeling off the self-adhesive shield before sticking the gaskets to the covers. Note the aluminium spacers in the gaskets to prevent overtightening (photo).

47 Use a new gasket at the plenum chamber and tighten the fixing bolts to the specified torque (photos).

48 Refit the alternator and power steering pump (if removed) and tension the drivebelts.

49 Reconnect the fuel lines using new hose clips. Reconnect all coolant and vacuum hoses and electrical leads. Refill the engine with coolant and reconnect the battery.

50 Switch on the ignition and bleed the fuel system by operating the vent valve on the fuel rail.

51 Run the engine to normal operating temperature and then check the ignition timing as described in Chapter 4, Section 6.

52 The inlet manifold bolts should be retightened to the specified torque in the sequence shown in Fig. 13.1. This will mean disconnecting the air hoses from the throttle valve housing, the vacuum hose from the left-hand rocker cover, and the wiring from the idle speed control valve and throttle valve potentiometer. Remove the

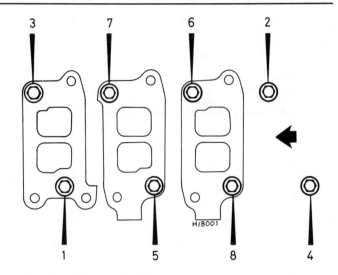

**Fig. 13.1 Inlet manifold bolt tightening sequence (Sec 3)**

*Arrow indicates front of engine*

plenum chamber, place it to one side, then release the fuel rail bolts, but do not disconnect the fuel pipes. It may also be necessary to remove the distributor again, for access to one of the bolts – see Chapter 3, Section 32, paragraph 56.

3.40A LH cylinder head gasket correctly located

3.40B Lowering LH cylinder head onto block

3.41 Cylinder head bolt angular tightening disc

3.43A Inlet manifold gasket correctly located

3.43B Fitting inlet manifold complete with fuel rail and injectors

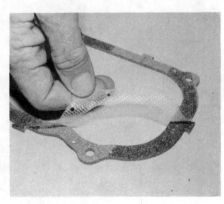

3.46 Peeling off rocker cover gasket protective shield

## Timing chain – removal and refitting (engine in car)

53  Using the crankshaft damper centre bolt, turn the engine until No 1 piston is at its firing point (12° BTDC). This can be verified by removing the distributor cap and checking that the contact end of the rotor is aligned with the No 1 HT lead contact.

54  Disconnect the battery negative terminal lead.

55  Unclip the air cleaner cover and remove it complete with air flow sensors and air hoses. Remove the oil filler cap.

56  Drain the cooling system, disconnect the radiator upper hose from the thermostat housing.

57  Disconnect the hose which runs between the coolant pump and the expansion tank.

58  Remove the radiator upper shroud, then the radiator (photos).

59  Remove the fan from the coolant pump hub (LH thread, see Chapter 2).

60  Disconnect the coolant hoses from the timing cover/coolant pump hose stubs.

61  Remove the alternator and power steering pump drivebelts.

62  Unscrew the four bolts and take off the crankshaft pulley.

63  Lock the crankshaft by jamming the starter ring gear teeth, and unscrew the vibration damper centre bolt. Withdraw the damper from the front of the crankshaft. A puller will be required for this, preferably one which has two screws for the tapped holes provided (photos).

64  Using an engine support bar or a hoist, take the weight of the engine then unscrew the nuts from the top of the engine mounting brackets (photos).

65  Drain the engine oil, retaining it for further use only if it is not contaminated or due for renewal.

66  Unbolt the coolant distribution pipe bracket from the timing cover (photo).

67  Disconnect the leads and remove the starter motor (photo).

68  Ensure that the front roadwheels and the steering wheel are in the straight-ahead position, then remove the bolt from the steering shaft coupling and slide the coupling down the shaft (photo).

69  Unscrew the sump pan nuts and bolts. The rear bolts can only be unscrewed using a box spanner or thin-walled socket (photo).

70  Release the brake hydraulic lines from their support brackets by pulling out the retaining clips.

71  Unscrew the two bolts from each of the crossmember side brackets. Lower the crossmember just enough to be able to remove the

3.47A Plenum chamber gaskets

3.47B Lowering plenum chamber into position

3.58A Radiator upper shroud plastic clip and centre pin

3.58B Removing radiator upper shroud

sump pan. In practice, as the car is standing on its roadwheels, the car body should be raised by placing two jacks under the front jacking points (photos).
72 Extract the nine bolts and remove the timing cover, complete with coolant pump (photo).
73 Removal of the radiator grille will provide better access to the cover bolts.

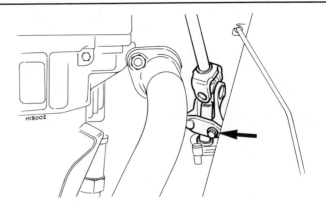

**Fig. 13.2 Steering shaft universal joint coupling – LHD shown (Sec 3)**

*Pinch bolt arrowed*

3.58C Removing radiator downwards

3.63A Unscrewing vibration damper centre bolt

3.63B Using a puller to withdraw the vibration damper

3.63C Removing the vibration damper

3.64A Typical engine support bar

3.64B Engine mounting top nut

3.66 Coolant distribution pipe bracket

3.67 Starter motor leads

3.68 Steering shaft coupling pinch bolt

74 Check that the crankshaft and camshaft sprocket timing marks are aligned at the nearest point to each other (photo). If not, turn the crankshaft as necessary.
75 Unbolt and remove the timing chain tensioner. Take care not to allow the spring-loaded tensioner plunger to eject (photo).
76 Lock the camshaft sprocket by passing a rod through one of its holes, and then unscrew the sprocket retaining bolt (photo).
77 Remove the camshaft sprocket, release the chain from the crankshaft sprocket and lift the chain and camshaft sprocket from the engine.
78 If required, the crankshaft sprocket, the Woodruff key and the chain guide can now be removed.
79 Clean away all old pieces of gasket from the cylinder block and timing cover flanges.

80 Remove and discard the sump pan gasket.
81 The gasket rear tabs may break off, so pick them out of the recesses in the rear main bearing cap using a sharp pointed knife.
82 If the crankshaft sprocket was removed, check that the key slots in the end of the crankshaft and camshaft are in alignment at the closest point to each other (photo).
83 Fit the crankshaft sprocket and chain guide.
84 Engage the chain around the teeth of the crankshaft sprocket.
85 Engage the camshaft sprocket in the upper loop of the chain in such a way that the camshaft sprocket will slip onto its key slot when its timing mark is aligned with that on the crankshaft sprocket (photo). Some trial and error may be involved in achieving this.
86 Lock the camshaft sprocket and tighten its retaining bolt to specified torque.

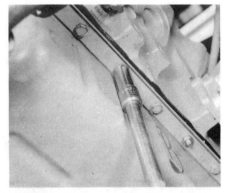
3.69 Unscrewing sump pan fixing bolts

3.71A Unscrewing crossmember side bracket fixing bolts

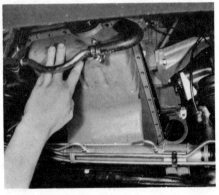
3.71B Removing sump pan

3.72 Unscrewing a timing cover bolt

3.74 Timing sprocket alignment marks (arrowed)

3.75 Timing chain tensioner

3.76 Unscrewing camshaft sprocket fixing bolt

3.82 Crankshaft and camshaft key and slot alignment

3.85 Fitting timing chain and camshaft sprocket

87 Retract the chain tensioner. To do this, insert the plunger (bevelled side entering), then release the pawl with a small screwdriver pushed into the hole in the tensioner body (photos).

88 Compress the plunger/slipper, and retain it in the retracted position using a cable strap or similar. New chain tensioners are supplied complete with a retainer (photo).

89 Bolt the tensioner in position, at the same time removing the plunger retainer. Tighten the bolts.

90 Locate a new gasket on the front face of the engine.

91 Renew the timing cover oil seal and apply grease to its lips.

92 Fit the timing cover, centre it and align it with the sump pan mounting flange.

93 Although a special tool (21-137) is available for centering the cover, a piece of plastic pipe or a socket of appropriate wall thickness will serve as a suitable substitute. Alternatively, measure the space between the crankshaft nose and the timing cover damper recess at several different points, and adjust the position of the timing cover until the measurements are equal. A strip of metal 14.0 mm wide will serve as a gauge if calipers are not available (photos).

94 Tighten the timing cover bolts and fit the Woodruff key, if removed, for the vibration damper (photo).

95 Apply jointing compound to the front and rear sump flange mating areas on the timing cover/cylinder block and rear main bearing cap. Make sure that the surfaces are perfectly clean. Checking that the rear tabs of the gasket enter the recesses in the main bearing cap, locate a new sump pan gasket on the crankcase (photos).

96 Fit the sump pan and screw on the nuts, then the bolts. Tighten progressively in two stages – see Chapter 1, Section 91.

97 Oil the lip of the timing cover oil seal, also the seal contact surface of the crankshaft damper.

3.87A Timing chain tensioner

3.87B Releasing tensioner pawl

3.88 Timing chain tensioner retracted with cable tie

3.93A Measuring crankshaft to timing cover gap

3.93B Using a socket to check crankshaft to timing cover gap

3.94 Timing cover fixing bolts (arrowed)

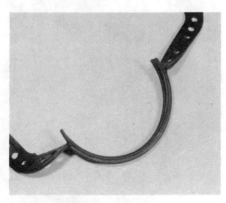

3.95A Sump gasket rear tabs

3.95B Sump gasket at rear main bearing cap

98 Fit the damper to the crankshaft, being careful not to dislodge the Woodruff key. Draw the damper into position using its bolt and washer.

99 Remove the bolt and apply sealant to the faces of the washer. Refit the bolt and washer, jam the starter ring gear and tighten the bolt to the specified torque.

100 Refit the crankshaft pulley – tighten the bolts to the specified torque.

101 Refit the crossmember side brackets and brake pipes.

102 Reconnect the engine mountings and remove the engine lift or jack.

103 Connect the steering shaft coupling with the steering wheel and front roadwheels in the straight-ahead position. Fit the pinch-bolt and tighten it to the specified torque.

104 Fit the starter motor and connect the leads.

105 Bolt the coolant distributor pipe to the timing cover.

106 Refit the alternator and steering pump drivebelts and tension them (photos).

107 Fit the fan and radiator, connect all coolant hoses, and fit the radiator upper shroud.

108 Fit the air cleaner cover with attachments.

109 Fill the engine with oil and coolant and connect the battery.

3.106A Alternator drivebelt tensioner strap bolt

### Timing chain – removal and refitting (engine on bench)

110 With the engine on the bench, first remove the sump pan, then set No 1 piston at its firing point, as described in paragraph 53 of this Section.

111 Carry out the operations described in paragraphs 72 to 100 of this Section.

112 Drain the engine oil, then remove the sump pan as described previously.

113 Unbolt the oil pump/intake pipe assembly and remove it, then extract the driveshaft, which is splined into the distributor shaft (photos).

114 Dismantling of the oil pump may be justified if there is evidence of low oil pressure, and it is known that the engine bearings are generally in good condition.

115 The operations are essentially as described in Chapter 1, Section 81, but note the design differences of the components (photos).

116 Refit the oil pump, tightening the bolts to specified torque.

117 Refit the sump pan as described previously.

118 Fill the engine with oil and coolant.

### Valve clearances – adjustment

119 The operations are essentially as described in Chapter 1, Section 93, but on 2.4 and 2.9 V6 engines the valve arrangement is changed (photos).

3.106B Power steering pump drivebelt tensioner bolt

### Crankshaft and bearings – examination and renovation

120 Refer to Chapter 1, Section 28. The crankshaft journals can be reground once (see Specifications). Undersize bearings may have been fitted in production – markings denoting this are as shown in Chapter 1, Figs. 1.10 and 1.11.

121 On the 2.4 V6 engine, separate thrust washers are used to control crankshaft endfloat; on the 2.9 V6 engine, No 3 bearing shells have integral thrust flanges.

---

## 4  Fuel and exhaust systems

---

### Fuel pressure regulator (2.4 and 2.9 V6) – removal and refitting

1  Disconnect the battery negative lead.

2  Place a suitable container below the engine and then remove the fuel return pipe and vacuum pipe from the fuel pressure regulator (photo).

3  Depressurise the fuel system using the vent valve (see photo 3.21). It may be necessary to depress this valve several times to fully depressurise the system.

4  Unbolt and remove the regulator.

5  Refitting is a reversal of removal but lubricate the sealing ring with silicone grease.

6  Once the regulator has been refitted and all items are connected, switch the ignition on and off five times without cranking the engine.

7  This will pressurise the fuel system, which should then be checked for leaks.

3.113A Oil pump and pick-up

3.113B Removing oil pump with driveshaft

3.115A Pick-up removed from oil pump

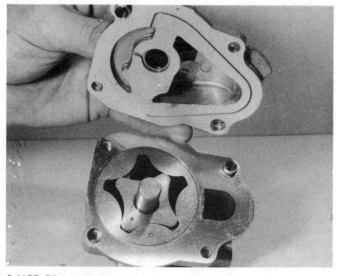

3.115B Oil pump cover removed

3.119A Valve arrangement (RH cylinder head) – arrow indicates front of car

3.119B Valve arrangement (LH cylinder head) – arrow indicates front of car

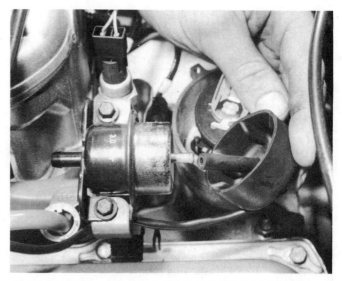

4.2 Disconnecting vacuum hose from fuel pressure regulator

*Fuel injectors (2.4 and 2.9 V6) – removal and refitting*

8   Disconnect the battery.

9   Remove the air intake pipes from the throttle housing.

10 Disconnect the link arm from the throttle housing and unscrew the two bolts which secure the throttle cable bracket.

11 Disconnect the vacuum pipes from the throttle housing, crankcase vent valve and the fuel pressure regulator.

12 Disconnect the throttle position sensor, engine temperature sensor unit, coolant temperature sensor and idle speed control valve electrical leads.

13 Extract the six Torx bolts which hold the air intake chamber in position.

14 Carefully withdraw the fuel injector multi-plugs (photo).

15 Depressurise the fuel system using the vent valve on the fuel rail.

16 Disconnect the fuel rail feed pipe and the fuel return pipe. This is best done at the wing valance and will require cutting the crimped type hose clips.

17 Use new worm drive type clips when reconnecting.

18 Unscrew the fuel rail retaining bolts and remove the fuel rail.

19 Extract the retaining clips and remove the injectors from the fuel rail.

20 Refitting is a reversal of removal, but observe the following points.

21 Renew all upper and lower injector seals, even if only one injector has been disturbed. Apply silicone grease to the seals.

22 If it is necessary to fit a new fuel inlet pipe to the fuel rail, the new connector is supplied with a captive 'tell-tale' ring, its purpose being to hold the connector teeth retracted. When the two halves of the connector are pressed together, the ring is ejected to show that the connection has been made successfully (photo). Fit the fuel pipe connector clip.

23 As soon as the injectors and fuel rail are installed and the fuel pipes connected, connect the battery and switch the ignition on and off twice without cranking the engine. Check for fuel leaks and then disconnect the battery.

24 Refit and reconnect all other removed and disconnected items.

25 Reconnect the battery.

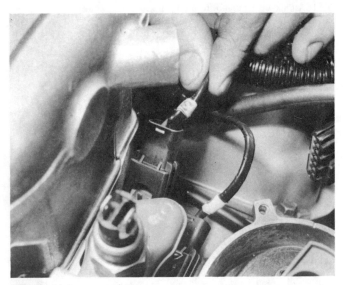

4.14 Fuel injector multi-plug

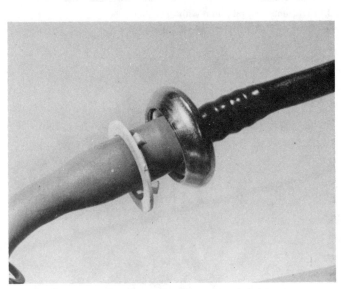

4.22 Fuel inlet pipe showing connector and captive ring

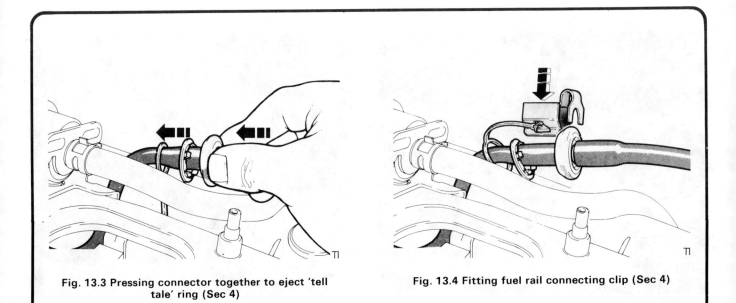

Fig. 13.3 Pressing connector together to eject 'tell tale' ring (Sec 4)

Fig. 13.4 Fitting fuel rail connecting clip (Sec 4)

### Fuel pump (2.4 and 2.9 V6) – removal and refitting

26 The operations are essentially as described in Chapter 3, Section 8 except that after refitting the pump, reconnect the battery and switch the ignition on and off five times without cranking the engine, then check for leaks at the pump unions.

### Fuel filter (2.4 and 2.9 V6) – removal and refitting

27 The operations are essentially as described in Chapter 3, Section 9 except that the system pressure should be reduced initially by slackening the fuel inlet pipe banjo bolt.

28 Once the new filter has been fitted, switch the ignition on and off five times without cranking the engine to pressurise the system, then check for leaks at the filter unions.

### Fuel rail temperature switch (2.4 and 2.9 V6) – removal and refitting

29 Disconnect the battery.
30 Disconnect the switch multi-plug.
31 Unscrew and remove the switch from the fuel rail (photo).
32 Refitting is a reversal of removal. Tighten the switch to specified torque.

### Fuel shut-off switch (2.4 and 2.9 V6) – removal and refitting

33 This device is designed to cut off pressurised fuel to the fuel injection system in the event of an accident. It does this by interrupting the fuel pump electrical circuit.

34 Disconnect the battery negative lead.
35 Open the tailgate and locate the switch, which is mounted near the tailgate lock.
36 Remove the trim panel (photo) and disconnect the switch multi-plug.

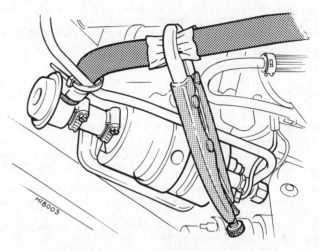

**Fig. 13.5 Fuel pump inlet hose clamped (Sec 4)**

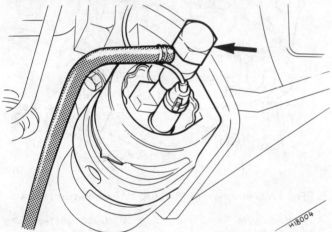

**Fig. 13.6 Fuel pump outlet hose banjo union – arrowed (Sec 4)**

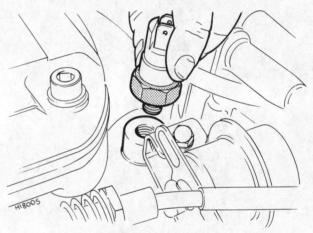

**Fig. 13.7 Fuel rail temperature switch (Sec 4)**

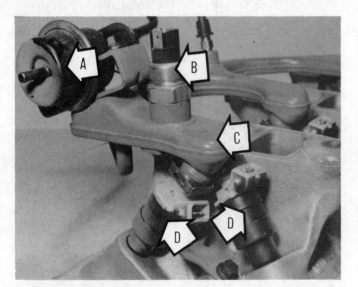

4.31 Fuel rail components
A  Fuel pressure regulator      B  Fuel temperature switch
C  Fuel rail                    D  Fuel injectors

4.36 Extracting luggage area rear trim cover screw

37 Extract the two fixing screws and remove the switch (photo).
38 Refit by reversing the removal operations, then depress the switch button to ensure that the switch has been reset (photo).

### Fuel injection system relays (2.4 and 2.9 V6)
39 Access to the relays is obtained by removing the facia top cover (crash pad) as described in Chapter 11, Section 39.
40 The relays are located on the passenger side as shown in Fig. 13.8.

### Idle adjustments (2.4 and 2.9 V6)
41 As with the 2.8 V6, idle speed is electronically controlled. For idle mixture adjustment see Chapter 3, Section 26. Basic idle speed adjustment can only be carried out by a Ford dealer using special equipment.

### Pierburg 2V carburettor (1.8 ohc, September 1986 on) – modification
42 As from the above date, a modified carburettor was fitted. It incorporates a secondary choke pulldown diaphragm which assists in reducing fuel consumption.
43 If such a replacement carburettor is to be fitted to earlier models, then always use a new mounting gasket and also carry out the following operations.
44 Obtain the special wiring loom and connect its multi-plug to the carburettor as shown in Fig. 13.10.

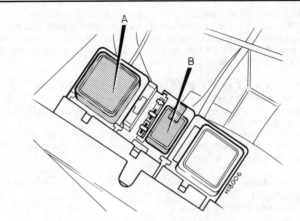

**Fig. 13.8 Fuel injection system relays (Sec 4)**

A   Power relay                                    B   Fuel pump relay

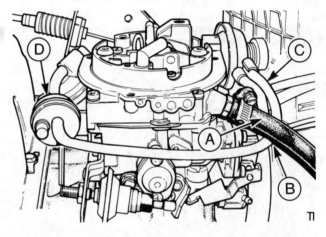

**Fig. 13.9 Later type of Pierburg 2V carburettor (Sec 4)**

A   Fuel inlet hose                        D   Diaphragm (secondary
B   Swivel clip location                        choke pulldown)
C   Diaphragm hose

4.37 Fuel shut-off valve

4.38 Depressing fuel shut-off valve button (trim cover in position)

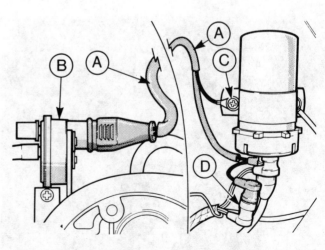

**Fig. 13.10 Wiring loom connections to the later type of Pierburg 2V carburettor (Sec 4)**

A   Loom                                 C   Earth
B   Secondary choke pulldown             D   Original coil connector
    diaphragm

45 Disconnect the positive feed wire from the ignition coil, and then connect the leads of the new loom to the positive terminal of the coil and the end of the disconnected positive feed wire.

46 Connect the loom earth eyelet to one of the ignition coil securing screws.

47 After fitting the air cleaner, check the carburettor adjustments – see Chapter 3, Specifications and Section 16.

### Unleaded fuel (2.4 and 2.9 V6) – general

48 In common with most other engines in the current Granada range, all 2.4 and 2.9 V6 engines can be run successfully on 95 octane unleaded fuel.

49 Some adjustment to the ignition timing may be necessary to achieve satisfactory running – consult your Ford dealer for details.

## 5 Ignition and engine management systems

### Distributor (2.4 and 2.9 V6) – removal and refitting

**Note:** *The distributor should not be removed without good cause, since the accuracy of timing achieved in production is unlikely to be regained. If difficulty is experienced in setting the timing after refitting, or if a new distributor has been fitted, the timing should be set by a Ford dealer using a STAR (Self Test Automatic Readout) tester.*

1 Disconnect the battery negative lead.

2 Disconnect the HT leads from the spark plugs, noting their locations.

3 Release the distributor cap and place it to one side, complete with leads (photo).

4 Turn the engine by means of the vibration damper centre bolt until No 1 piston is at its firing point (12° BTDC) (photo).

5 Mark the rim of the distributor body to indicate the point of alignment of the contact end of the rotor.

6 Mark the distributor mounting plinth in relation to the cylinder block.

7 Disconnect the distributor wiring multi-plug.

8 Scrape off the sealant from around the distributor clamp plate bolt. Unscrew the bolt and withdraw the distributor.

9 Before refitting the distributor, check that the pulley notch is still set to 12° BTDC.

10 Hold the distributor over its hole so that the mounting plinth and cylinder head marks are in alignment. Align the rotor (contact end) with the rim mark.

11 As the distributor is inserted, the rotor will turn due to the meshing of the drive gears. Anticipate this by offsetting the rotor a few degrees from its rim mark before pushing the distributor into place. A little trial and error may be required to obtain exact final alignment.

5.3 Distributor cap showing HT leads (numbered) and interference shield

5.4 Ignition timing marks (12° BTDC setting)

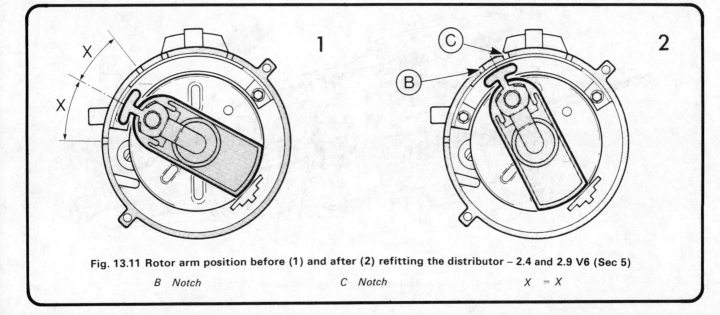

**Fig. 13.11 Rotor arm position before (1) and after (2) refitting the distributor – 2.4 and 2.9 V6 (Sec 5)**

B  Notch                    C  Notch                    X = X

12 Fit the clamp plate and tighten the bolt.
13 Refit the distributor cap, connect the spark plug leads, reconnect the vacuum pipe and the wiring plug. Reconnect the battery.
14 Run the engine to normal operating temperature and check the ignition timing as described in Chapter 4, Section 6.

### Engine management system module (1.8 ohc, January 1987 on)

15 A new type of module is fitted to these vehicles. It is smaller and located on the left-hand wing valance in the engine compartment.
16 The new module is known as the ESC Hybrid Module.

### Ignition timing adjustment (1.8 ohc, January 1987 on)

17 The effect of the octane adjustment leads (Chapter 4, Section 15) on models with the ESC Hybrid Module is as follows:

*Red lead earthed – 2° retard*
*Blue lead earthed – 4° retard*
*Red and blue leads earthed – 6° retard*

---

## 6  Manual gearbox and automatic transmission

### Manual gearbox – layshaft bearing modification (2.8 and 2.9 V6)

1 The layshaft gear front bearing has been modified on 2.8 and 2.9 V6 models built after June 1986. Instead of loose needle rollers and spacers, a caged roller bearing running on a spigot is used. The layshaft itself is no longer fitted.
2 Most of the overhaul procedures in Chapter 6 still apply. The important changes are as follows.
**Dismantling into major assemblies**
3 After removing 5th gear nut from the layshaft gear, remove the three bolts which secure the bearing spigot to the casing. Drive the spigot out of the casing.
**Bearing renewal**
4 Remove the front bearing from the layshaft gear by breaking the cage and recovering the rollers. Extract the bearing outer race with an internal puller.
5 Drive the new bearing into position with the lettering facing outwards.
**Reassembly**
6 Before fitting the layshaft gear rear bearing in the intermediate housing, temporarily fit the spigot and secure it with the three bolts.
7 When finally fitting the spigot, apply sealant to its mating face. Tighten the spigot bolts to the specified torque.

### Gearchange biasing mechanism – modification

8 From 1987 model year, the gearchange biasing mechanism (including the centralising spring and 5th gear locking components)

has been modified. The new mechanism is shown in Fig. 13.14.
9 Workshop procedures are largely unchanged. The locking pin and spring are no longer fitted beneath 5th gear locking plate. Old and new pattern components are not interchangeable.

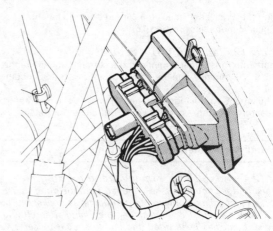

**Fig. 13.12 Later type of engine management module (Sec 5)**

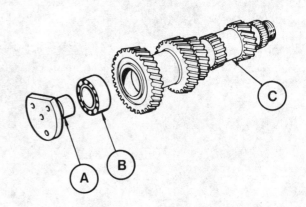

**Fig. 13.13 Later type of five-speed layshaft gear front bearing (Sec 6)**

A   Spigot                          C   Layshaft gear
B   Roller bearing

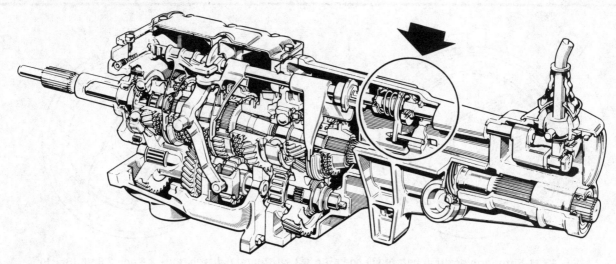

**Fig. 13.14 New gearchange biasing mechanism (Sec 6)**

*Automatic transmission fluid – contamination after component failure (all models)*

10 Failure of the torque converter, or of the automatic transmission itself, can result in the contamination of the transmission fluid with friction lining and/or metallic particles. If these particles enter new or previously undamaged components, further damage may occur.

11 If the torque converter is renewed, the transmission sump must be removed, the oil strainer renewed and the valve block cleared of debris. This work should be done by a Ford dealer or a transmission specialist. In severe cases of contamination the transmission will have to be dismantled for cleaning.

12 At the same time as the above work, or if the transmission itself is renewed, the fluid cooler lines must be flushed and the fluid cooler/radiator assembly be renewed.

## 7 Braking system

*Anti-lock braking system – modification*

1 From August 1986, certain modifications have been made to the anti-lock braking system.

2 The relays differ from earlier versions, the hydraulic pump is of iron construction instead of light alloy and a new pressure warning switch is used. The earlier rubber high pressure hose is replaced by a steel pipe.

## 8 Steering and suspension

*Tie-rod inboard balljoint – revised securing method*

1 The method of peening the balljoint to secure it described in Chapter 10, Section 5 can be disregarded if wished, and the following procedure adopted.

2 Apply Loctite 270 to clean threads and tighten the balljoint to the torque originally specified – see Chapter 10, Specifications. No staking or peening is required.

*Rear suspension alignment*

3 The toe setting and camber angle of the rear wheels are non-adjustable. For checking purposes however, the tolerances are given in the Specifications section of this Supplement. Any deviation found will be due to worn suspension components or to collision damage.

4 When measuring the ride height (necessary for camber angle checking) it should be measured extremely carefully between the centre of the wheel hub and the wheel arch according to the appropriate wing edge configuration.

*Rear suspension guide plate centre bolts (1987 on)*

5 From 1987 model year, the tab washer which secures the guide plate centre bolt on each side has been deleted. A self-locking bolt and plain washer are used instead.

6 The new bolt and washer should be fitted to earlier models if the old bolt has to be removed for any reason. The tab washer should be discarded.

7 The tightening torque for the new bolt is the same as the old one (see Chapter 10 Specifications).

## 9 Bodywork and fittings

*Heater coolant valve – removal and refitting*

1 Disconnect the radiator lower coolant hose and collect the coolant in a clean container.

2 Disconnect the coolant and vacuum hoses from the heater coolant valve.

3 Unclip the valve from the mounting bracket.

4 Refitting is a reversal of removal. Refill the cooling system on completion.

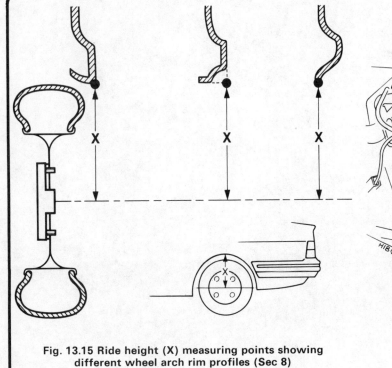

**Fig. 13.15 Ride height (X) measuring points showing different wheel arch rim profiles (Sec 8)**

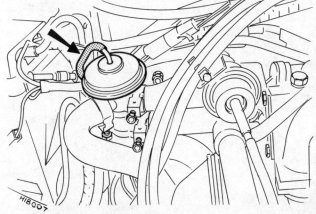

**Fig. 13.16 Heater coolant valve (Sec 9)**

*Vacuum hose arrowed*

## 10 Electrical system

### *Headlamp dim-dip lighting system*
1   1987 models are fitted with a headlamp dim-dip lighting system to comply with new regulations.
2   The system uses a relay-controlled resistor circuit. When the sidelights are switched on, with the ignition also on, the headlamps come on automatically at one-sixth of normal dipped beam power.
3   The idea of the system is to prevent driving with only the sidelights illuminated.

### *Low air temperature sensor (ice alert function)*
4   On later models, this device and its multi-plug connector are located under the top rail behind the radiator grille (photo).

10.4 Later location of low air temperature sensor

# Index